Peter Titelman, PhD
Editor

Triangles
Bowen Family Systems Theory Perspectives

Pre-publication
REVIEWS,
COMMENTARIES,
EVALUATIONS . . .

Triangles
Bowen Family Systems Theory Perspectives

Titles of Related Interest

Clinical Applications of Bowen Family Systems Theory edited by Peter Titelman

Emotional Cutoff: Bowen Family Systems Theory Perspectives edited by Peter Titelman

Triangles
Bowen Family Systems Theory Perspectives

Peter Titelman, PhD
Editor

Routledge
Taylor & Francis Group
New York   London

PUBLISHER'S NOTE
The development, preparation, and publication of this work has been undertaken with great care. However, the Publisher, employees, editors, and agents of The Haworth Press are not responsible for any errors contained herein or for consequences that may ensue from use of materials or information contained in this work. The Haworth Press is committed to the dissemination of ideas and information according to the highest standards of intellectual freedom and the free exchange of ideas. Statements made and opinions expressed in this publication do not necessarily reflect the views of the Publisher, Directors, management, or staff of The Haworth Press, or an endorsement by them.

Identities and circumstances of individuals discussed in this book have been changed to protect confidentiality.

Cover design by Marylouise E. Doyle.

Library of Congress Cataloging-in-Publication Data

Triangles : Bowen family systems theory perspectives / Peter Titelman, editor.
     p. ; cm.
   Includes bibliographical references.
   ISBN: 978-0-7890-2774-0 (hard : alk. paper)
   ISBN: 978-0-7890-2775-7 (soft : alk. paper)
   1. Family psychotherapy. 2. Bowen, Murray, 1913- 3. Triangles (Interpersonal relations) I. Titelman, Peter.
   [DNLM: 1. Bowen, Murray, 1913- 2. Emotions. 3. Family Relations. 4. Interpersonal Relations. 5. Psychological Theory. 6. Systems Theory. BF 531 T821 2007]
RC488.5.T75 2007
616.89'156—dc22

                                                                    2007039817

Dedicated to Murray Bowen, MD, for creating his unique systems theory of human functioning, and for the influence he had on the editor, the contributors, and his many students. His thinking and teaching has had a powerful impact on the personal and professional lives of the editor and many others who knew him.

CONTENTS

About the Editor   xv

Contributors   xvii

Preface   xxi

Acknowledgments   xxvii

PART I: TRIANGLES IN BOWEN THEORY AND NATURAL SYSTEMS

Chapter 1. The Concept of the Triangle in Bowen Theory: An Overview   3
Peter Titelman

Introduction   3
Bowen's Movement from Psychoanalytic to Systems Theory:
   From the Individual to the Dyad to the Triangle   3
The Concept of Triangles in the Context of Bowen Theory   16
The Relationship Between the Concept of the Triangle
   and Other Concepts in Bowen Theory   33
The Process and Application of Detriangling   41
Summary   60

Chapter 2. The Regulatory Function of the Triangle   63
Laurie L. Lassiter

Introduction   63
The Triangle in Other Species   66
The Undifferentiated   69
A Broader View of the Triangle's Function   71
The Triangle and Increasing Differentiation-of-Self   77
A Clinical Example   80
Conclusion   85
Summary   88

Chapter 3. Triadic Relationships in Nonhuman Primate Family Systems 91
Lynn A. Fairbanks

Introduction 91
Vervet Monkey Triadic Relationships 92
Conclusion 103

PART II: TRIANGLES AND DETRIANGLING IN THE THERAPIST'S OWN FAMILY

Chapter 4. Bowen's Effort to Differentiate a Self: Detriangling from Triangles and Interlocking Triangles 109
Peter Titelman

Introduction 109
A History of Triangles in the Luff-Bowen Family
  and Business 110
Bowen's Detriangling Efforts Over a Twelve-Year Period:
  1954-1966 119
Bowen's Breakthrough Experience, Detriangling
  from Interlocking Triangles: 1966-1967 120
Summary 128

Chapter 5. Exploring Emotional Triangles in Past Generations of a Family 129
James B. Smith

Introduction 129
Differentiating a Self 131
Father's Family of Origin 132
Mother's Family of Origin 139
Author's Family of Origin 144
Conclusion 153

Chapter 6. Triangles at the Time of a Chronic Illness and Death   **157**
Anthony J. Wilgus

Introduction   157
Family Data   158
Significant Triangles   160
Principles and Detriangling   163
Outcomes   169
Conclusion   171

Chapter 7. Efforts to Understand Early Triangles in the Therapist's Extended Family   **173**
James C. Maloni

Introduction   173
Background   174
The Malonis and the Pistillis   179
From Italian to American Triangles   180
Levels of Functioning and Triangles   182
Multigenerational Emotional Process and Triangles   184
Impact on the Therapist's Work   186

Chapter 8. Triangles Revisited   **189**
Jack LaForte

Introduction   189
Triangle One: Mother, Father, and Son   190
Triangle Two: Husband, Wife, and Child   198
The Emergence of Interlocking Triangles   201
Summary of the Early Family of Origin Work   204
The Follow-Up to the Effort   206
Nodal Event: Shifts in the Balance   208
An Effort to Bridge the Emotional Cutoff
   Between Son and Mother   216
Conclusion   218

Chapter 9. Observation of Triangles in a Human-Canine Pack　221
Linda M. Fleming

Introduction　221
Members of the Pack　222
Establishment of the Pack　226
Identifying the Triangle　231
Interlocking Triangles　233
Social Status Change and Symptom Formation　235
Stabilization　236
Summary　239

PART III: TRIANGLES IN CLINICAL PRACTICE

Chapter 10. Triangles in Marriage　243
Phillip Klever

Introduction　243
Factors Contributing to Triangling in Marriage　245
Common Marital Triangles　248
The Clinical Work with Marital Triangles　255
Clinical Example　259
Conclusion　263

Chapter 11. Child Focus: Triangles That Come and Stay　265
Eva Louise Rauseo

Introduction　265
Consultation with Bowen Theory　268
Clinical Reports　269
Summary　289

Chapter 12. Triangles in Stepfamilies　291
Kathleen Cotter Cauley

Introduction　291
The Therapist's Position As Stepdaughter and Stepmother:
Knowing the Blind Spots　292

Clinical Application: Does Differentiation Make
    a Difference?   299
Summary and Conclusion   309

**Chapter 13. Triangles in Families with Substance
Abusing Teenagers**   **311**
    Anne S. McKnight

Introduction   311
Triangles   312
Substance Abuse in Families   315
The Concept of the Triangle in Clinical Work   329
Summary   330

**Chapter 14. A Family Affair: Triangles in Extramarital
Relationships**   **331**
    Eileen B. Gottlieb

Introduction   331
Triangles   331
Extramarital Relationships   332
Family Affairs   335
Case Studies   339
Summary   353

PART IV: TRIANGLES IN ORGANIZATIONS

**Chapter 15. Sibling Triangles and Leadership
in a Family Business**   **357**
    Peter Titelman

Introduction   357
Leadership in Family Business   357
The Application of Bowen Theory Concepts
    for Understanding and Working with Family Business   360
The Family Business and Its Presenting Problems   364
History of the Family in Business   365
The Consultation Format and the Consultants' Functions   370

Course of the Consultation 373
Conclusions 380
Summary 385

Chapter 16. The Business of Triangles 387
Leslie Ann Fox

Introduction 387
The Company 388
Systems-Based Approach to Managing Business
    Relationships 391
A Systems-Based Consulting Approach 395
Conclusions 401

Chapter 17. Triangles in the Academy 403
Ona Cohn Bregman

Introduction 403
The Setting 404
Operationalizing the Triangles 405
Conclusion 415

**PART V: TRIANGLES AND EMOTIONAL PROCESS
IN SOCIETY**

**Chapter 18. Triangles in Societal Emotional Process
with an Example from the Russian Revolution** 421
Katharine Gratwick Baker

Introduction and Overview 421
Definitions and Theoretical Considerations 422
Triangles and Emotional Process in Society 423
A Historical Example 425
Emotional Triangles in Three Families 427
Triangles in the Realm of Ideas 440
Succession and the Consolidation of Power 441
Conclusion 448

**Chapter 19. The Triangle As the Cornerstone
of the Government of the United States of America**   **451**
Edward W. Beal

Introduction   451
Background   454
The Debate Over the War for Independence   455
Who Would Be Governed?   457
How the Government Would Run   458
Period of Anxiety   459
Development of the Constitution   460
The Relationship Between the Separation of Powers
    Triangle and the Three-Fifths Triangle   468
Conclusion   473

**Chapter 20. Triangles, Leadership, and the United States
Supreme Court**   **477**
Ann V. Nicholson

Introduction   477
Bowen Theory, the Emotional Process, and the Triangle   479
The Emotional Process on the Court, Triangles
    in Action, and the Impact of Leadership   483
Chief Justices of the U.S. Supreme Court   484
The Stone and Vinson Courts, 1941-1953   495
Conclusion   501

**Chapter 21. 9/11: Societal Emotional Process
and Interlocking Triangles**   **503**
Carol Moran

Societal Emotional Process   504
Interlocking Triangles   508
The Citizen Self   518

Appendix   **523**

Index   **525**

ABOUT THE EDITOR

Peter Titelman, PhD, maintains a private practice in clinical psychology, specializing in Bowen family systems therapy, consultation, professional education, and supervision in Northampton, Massachusetts. Dr. Titelman has been leading a consultation group on the professional's own family for more than twenty-five years, and is an American Association of Marriage and Family Therapy Approved Supervisor. Dr. Titelman is a principal in Baker and Titelman Associates, a consulting firm based in Northampton, Massachusetts. He is also a founding member of the New England Seminar on Bowen Theory in Worcester, Massachusetts. He is the editor of *The Therapist's Own Family: Toward the Differentiation of Self, Clinical Applications of Bowen Family Systems Theory,* and *Emotional Cutoff: Bowen Family Systems Theory Perspectives*. Dr. Titelman has taught and supervised graduate students as an adjunct faculty member at Antioch New England Graduate School, Keene, New Hampshire; Massachusetts School of Professional Psychology, Newton, Massachusetts; St. Joseph's College, West Hartford, Connecticut; and Smith College of Social Work, Northampton, Massachusetts. He has given presentations and training events nationally and internationally, including teaching Bowen family systems theory at the Society of Family Consultants and Psychotherapists in Moscow, Russia. Titelman has presented papers at the following Bowen centers: The Bowen Center for the Study of the Family, Washington, DC; Center for Family Consultation, Evanston, Illinois; New England Seminar on Bowen Theory, Worcester, Massachusetts; Princeton Family Center for Education, Princeton, New Jersey; The Vermont Family Center, Burlington, Vermont; and the Western Pennsylvania Family Center, Pittsburgh, Pennsylvania. His current research interests, in addition to the triangle concept in Bowen theory, include emotional cutoff and obesity.

CONTRIBUTORS

Katharine Gratwick Baker, PhD, is a family business consultant and executive coach with a private practice in Northampton, Massachusetts. She has taught Bowen family systems theory at the Society of Family Consultants and Psychologists in Moscow, Russia, and is the editor of *Teoriya Semeinykh Sistem Murraya Bowena* (Kogito-Tsentr, 2005), a collection of articles by Bowen and others, that has been translated into Russian. Her research interests include observation of societal process in the Soviet Union and Russia over time. She is a principal in Baker and Titelman Associates (www.bakerandtitelman.com).

Edward W. Beal, MD, is a clinical professor of psychiatry at Georgetown University Medical School, Washington, DC, and an adjunct faculty member, Bowen Center for the Study of the Family, Washington, DC. He is the co-author of *Adult Children of Divorce* (Dell Publishing, 1991) and co-editor of *A Failure of Nerve* (Church Publishing, Morehouse and Seabury Books, 2007). Dr. Beal is in private practice in psychiatry in Bethesda, Maryland.

Ona Cohn Bregman, MSS, is a clinical social worker. She retired from her position as associate professor of Social Work at Syracuse University where she chaired the Family Mental Health concentration from 1991 to 1998. Ms. Bregman continues to maintain a private practice in Bowen systems psychotherapy, consultation, and supervision.

Kathleen Cotter Cauley, MEd, works with individuals and couples at the Center for the Study of Human Systems in Falls Church, Virginia. She is on the faculty at the Center, which offers training in Bowen family systems theory for clergy in the Extraordinary Leadership Seminars. Ms. Cauley maintains contact with her private practice in Tampa, Florida, where she lived from 1985 to 2002. She is a founding member of the Florida Family Research Network.

Lynn A. Fairbanks, PhD, is a professor in the Department of Psychiatry and Biobehavioral Sciences at UCLA and Director of the Vervet Research Colony. She has been studying mother-infant behavior, social development, and family relationships of vervet monkeys for over thirty years.

Linda M. Fleming, PhD, is an associate professor and the director of training in the Counseling Psychology Program at Gannon University in Erie, Pennsylvania. She has research interests in family systems and gender issues as well as psychotherapy process and outcome.

Leslie Ann Fox, MA, RHIA, FAHIMA, is CEO and cofounder of Care Communications, Inc., Chicago, Illinois, a national health information management (HIM) consulting firm. Applying Bowen family systems theory to organizations, she has integrated the theory into her approach to leadership and consulting, and teaches seminars on a framework for leading transformational change in healthcare organizations for the American Health Information Management Association (AHIMA). She has presented papers at the Midwest Family Systems Symposium in Evanston, Illinois, and at the Georgetown Family Center's Conference on Organizations in Washington, DC, April, 1995.

Eileen B. Gottlieb, MED, LMFT, is the director of the Family Center in Delray Beach, Florida where she has practiced psychotherapy for twenty-five years. She also serves as education director for the Florida Family Research Network, a nonprofit organization that provides Bowen theory training conferences and seminars for Florida-licensed mental health professionals and nurses. Ms. Gottlieb has written and presented papers on aspects of Bowen theory at scientific meetings nationwide.

Phillip Klever, LCSW, LMFT, is in private practice in Kansas City, Missouri. He has written articles on Bowen family systems theory in professional journals: *Family Systems: A Journal of Natural Systems Thinking in Psychiatry and the Sciences; Families, Systems & Health; The American Journal of Family Therapy,* and *Contemporary Family Therapy,* as well as two chapters in two previous books on Bowen theory edited by Peter Titelman. He is also conducting a longitudinal study on marriage.

Jack LaForte, PhD, is a licensed psychologist in private practice in Northampton, Massachusetts where he maintains his clinical and consulting practice, specializing in family therapy. Dr. LaForte is an AAMFT Approved Supervisor. He is a principal in LaForte and Associates, consulting to family-owned businesses. LaForte has taught and supervised graduate students as an adjunct faculty member at Antioch New England Graduate School,

Keene, New Hampshire, and the Union Institute and University in Cincinnati, Ohio.

Laurie L. Lassiter, PhD, LICSW, has a private practice in the Northampton and Amherst, Massachusetts, area, and she is a consultant to parents at the Child Guidance Clinic in Springfield. Her triangle hypothesis is based on analysis of collections of audiotapes and notes of individuals' sessions with Bowen during the 1980s and on a study of social species, including microbial social and interspecies community life, with Lynn Margulis, PhD, at the University of Massachusetts.

James C. Maloni, PhD, is a retired clinical psychologist living in Pittsburgh, Pennsylvania, and Naples, Florida. He is a faculty member of the Western Pennsylvania Family Center in Pittsburgh, Pennsylvania. His current area of study is societal issues related to the Rwandan genocide and postcolonial leadership in Africa.

Anne S. McKnight, LCSW, EdD, is on the faculty of the Bowen Center for the Study of the Family, where she teaches, supervises, and runs the Intern Clinical Program. She worked for twenty-three years in a substance abuse program, during the last ten of which she saw families of teenagers. She is currently in private practice in Arlington, Virginia.

Carol Moran, MSW, is a faculty member of the Center for Family Consultation, Evanston, Illinois, and is in private practice in Wilmette, Illinois.

Ann V. Nicholson, RN, MS, CS, is in private practice in the Boston area. She has taught in various nursing programs at the undergraduate and graduate level. She is the current chair and a founding member of the New England Seminar on Bowen Theory in Worcester, Massachusetts. She has presented Bowen theory in both academic and community settings, but primarily at conferences sponsored by the Bowen Center for the Study of the Family, Washington, DC, and the New England Seminar on Bowen Theory. Her research interest is on leadership and societal process.

Eva Louise Rauseo, RN, MS, CS, is a faculty member, Bowen Center for the Study of the Family, Washington, DC; a board member, Center for the Study of Natural Systems and the Family, Houston, Texas; and program director, El Paso Education Programs in Bowen Theory, a part of the Center for the Study of Natural Systems and the Family, El Paso, Texas. Her clinical and research interests are clinical studies of emotional cutoff and the ongoing study of families in the midst of migration.

James B. Smith, MS, is a founding member of Western Pennsylvania Family Center in Pittsburgh, Pennsylvania, and is currently its faculty director. A licensed psychologist, he is clinical director of Family Connections, Inc., Wheeling, West Virginia, and maintains a private practice in Pittsburgh, Pennsylvania. He is interested in the clinical application of Bowen theory, its contribution to psychology, and the place of Bowen in the history of Western thought.

Anthony J. Wilgus, ACSW, is an associate professor of social work at the University of Findlay, Findlay, Ohio. He has presented papers at both the annual Georgetown Family Center Symposium, in Washington, DC, and the Midwest Family Systems Symposium in Evanston, Illinois.

Preface

This volume is a compilation of essays on the theoretical explication of Murray Bowen's concept of the emotional triangle and its applications. It is perhaps the most important of his concepts—after differentiation of self—in his seminal contribution, Bowen family systems theory. It can be said that the cornerstone of Bowen theory is the concept of differentiation of self and the other seven concepts refer to the way individuals, couples, and families express their differentiation/undifferentiation in the presence of anxiety or reactivity. Differentiation is that concept which describes the central process in an emotional system; the way the forces of individuality and togetherness are expressed and integrated. Triangles and interlocking triangles are the smallest basic unit of an emotional system, the central way through which emotional process is both transmitted and stabilized in the multigenerational emotional system, or any emotional system for that matter.

Although this book focuses on one concept in Bowen theory, emotional triangles, a full understanding of any of Bowen's concepts involves understanding each one of the eight major concepts in the theory, and other peripheral ones, in the context of the interrelationships among them. As I have done in the past, I refer the reader who is unfamiliar with Bowen theory to read the original writings of Bowen (1978), and the clearest and fullest expositions of the theory by Kerr and Bowen (1988) and Papero (1990). Readers are also referred to my edited volumes: *Clinical Applications of Bowen Family Systems Theory* (Haworth, 1998), *Emotional Cutoff: Bowen Family Systems Theory* (Haworth, 2003), and *The Therapist's Own Family: Toward the Differentiation of Self* (Aronson, 1987), for additional applications of Bowen theory.

In teaching Bowen theory it is commonly observed that the individual being taught or coached finds that the concept of the triangle makes quick sense and is intuitively grasped. The triangle and the other seven Bowen theory concepts were devised by Bowen to be macro-level concepts—a parsimonious attempt to understand all of human emotional functioning with the fewest concepts possible. It is also very clear that a real understanding of the triangle concept takes serious study that requires the learner to use a new lens to see how an emotional system operates and how one is part of that system. Bowen theory, and the triangle concept in particular, is both very simple and very complicated, especially when one is trying to see the triangles in which one is embedded.

Throughout the short history of psychiatry and psychology the unit of study and the locus of understanding of human functioning have generally been the individual, impacted on by nature or nurture. Then in the 1940s and 1950s a focus on the dyad, particularly the mother-offspring dyad, became important. Out of this movement came attachment theory. However, with the introduction of systems theories and the work of Bowen in particular, the unit of focus for understanding behavior and emotional functioning became the triangle, and the interlocking triangle. At this point, cause and effect thinking as an explanation for human behavior shifted to a view of the family as a multigenerational emotional unit. Bowen theory conceives of the triangle, the three-person system, as the smallest unit of an emotional system. Nevertheless, even today it is difficult for both laypeople and mental health professionals to truly grasp and integrate this systems concept into everyday life and clinical practice. The ability to move from the individual paradigm for conceptualizing human functioning to a systems paradigm remains elusive. This volume is a small effort to further present Murray Bowen's contribution of moving toward a natural systems view of the individual in the context of the family and society.

All but one of the contributors have had direct contact with Murray Bowen. The majority of the contributors have been involved in studying, applying, and teaching Bowen theory in their own lives and their various practices and training endeavors for more than twenty-five years. They share the same conceptual base: Bowen theory. Each contributor however has his or her own way of understanding, articulating, and applying the triangle concept.

The book is divided into five parts: theory, the therapist's own family, clinical applications, organizational applications, and societal applications. The organization of this volume represents an effort to present applications of Bowen's concept of the triangle in a wide variety of arenas: the family, the organization, and society. In addition, the triangle and efforts to detriangle are described in relation to the practitioner and his or her own family and to individuals in their nuclear families, their families of origin, and their extended families. Bowen's conception of interlocking triangles provides a bridge between the primary triangle of the parents and offspring, to secondary triangles within the wider family, the multigenerational family emotional system, associations with nonfamily members in a variety of organizational and institutional settings, and finally to the largest emotional systems, the arena of emotional process in society.

Bowen theory, and in this case the concept of the triangle, provides a theory of human functioning, not a theory of psychopathology. It describes how all emotional systems function. The triangle is a concept that applies not only to humans but also to nonhuman primates and a variety of other social species. Triangles and interlocking triangles are the web through which emotional process is transmitted and maintained.

Part I: Triangles in Bowen Theory and Natural Systems provides a theoretical context for understanding the triangle concept and its application. It also includes an example of the presence of triangles in nonhuman primates. The first chapter, which I have written, provides a historical and conceptual overview of the concept of the triangle in Bowen theory, and it presents the process and application of detriangling. In Chapter 2, Laurie L. Lassiter describes a particular view of the regulatory function of the triangle and how the triangle is central in the effort to increase differentiation of self. Chapter 3, written by primatologist Lynn A. Fairbanks, provides an example of the presence of triadic awareness and functioning in a particular species of nonhuman primate, the vervet monkey. She illustrates how the concept of the triangle is useful even in a species in which the family system does not revolve around the mother, father, and child triangle.

Part II: Triangles and Detriangling in the Therapist's Own Family presents six chapters that explore the therapist's effort to understand and apply the concept of the triangle, and interlocking triangles, in the context of differentiation of self. In Chapter 4, I describe Murray Bowen's differentiation of self effort in his own family with a focus on his detriangling efforts in interlocking triangles. I seek to further elucidate the underlying intentions, process, and goals that Bowen (1978) wrote about in his essay, "On the Differentiation of Self." A history of triangles in the Luff-Bowen family and business provides a context for Bowen's differentiation of self effort. In Chapter 5, James B. Smith describes the primary and central triangles in four generations of his family. He delineates these triangles and how they interlock to highlight the multigenerational process in the family. In Chapter 6, Anthony J. Wilgus describes with clarity and objectivity the presence and functioning of triangles at the time of a chronic illness and death, in this case the death of his wife. He provides some important principles that he relied on while living through this experience. In Chapter 7, James C. Maloni provides a description of his efforts to understand early triangles in his extended family. From a Bowen theory framework, this kind of in-depth family of origin research and understanding is an important part of the therapist's differentiation of self in his or her family of origin, which has many implications not only for the functioning of the therapist in his or her own family but also for his or her clinical work. In Chapter 8, Jack LaForte presents his own differentiation of self efforts with their trials and tribulations, in both his family of origin and nuclear family, with a particular focus on the relationship between triangles, nodal events, anxiety, and undifferentiation/differentiation. In Chapter 9, Linda M. Fleming presents her observations of triangles in a human-canine pack. Pets, such as dogs, as living responsive beings, can be a part of emotional triangles with humans. In this case, the author of this chapter describes how the introduction of one dog, and then a second, led to triangles involving herself and her future husband.

Part III: Triangles in Clinical Practice includes five chapters that apply the concept of triangles and interlocking triangles to a variety of clinical issues. In Chapter 10, Phillip Klever describes the place and function of triangles in the arena of marriage. He presents factors contributing to triangling in marriage and common marital triangles. He goes on to describe clinical work with marital triangles and a clinical example. In Chapter 11, Eva Louise Rauseo examines the presence of triangles in the child-focused family. Bowen theory holds that when a child is expressing the symptoms in the family—physical, emotional, or social—that child is a part of a child-focused family. She describes a number of triangles that present in families that are child-focused. She describes clinical interventions with them. In Chapter 12, Kathleen Cotter Cauley describes triangles in stepfamilies. She begins her chapter by discussing the therapist's position—that is her own position in triangles as a stepdaughter and a stepmother in her own family. In Chapter 13, Anne S. McKnight describes the presence and function of triangles in families with substance abusing teenagers. She presents a variety of vignettes and shows how the concept of the triangle can be used in clinical work with these families. In Chapter 14, Eileen B. Gottlieb writes about the particular type of triangle that involves extramarital relationships. She describes how extramarital relationships are a family affair in that they are generated by fusion within the marital relationship that in turn is embedded in the unresolved attachments of that couple to their respective parents.

Part IV: Triangles in Organizations includes three chapters that expand the application of the concept of the triangle beyond the family to triangles that create an interlock between the family and nonfamily relationships. In Chapter 15, I describe a case of sibling triangles and leadership in a family business. The description of the business, its history, and the consultation process is contextualized by an initial discussion of leadership in family business. A case is made for the possibility of leadership by a collection of individuals rather than hierarchical leadership, depending on the stage of the business and the level of differentiation of the individuals involved in the ownership and management of the business. In Chapter 16, Leslie Ann Fox describes her effort as owner and CEO of a business to lead and manage it through the principles and application of Bowen theory. She describes a systems-based approach to managing business relationships and a systems-based consulting approach. In Chapter 17, Ona Cohn Bregman describes the concept of the triangle in the context of a graduate department in a university and how the triangles are operationalized.

Part V: Triangles and Emotional Process in Society includes four chapters that apply the concept of the triangle and interlocking triangles beyond family and nonfamily organizations to the macrosystems level of emotional process in society. All of these levels of human emotional systems—and a variety of nonhuman living systems as well—are interlocked. It is part of the power of Bowen theory, and particularly the concept of the triangle, that it can provide a comprehensive blueprint for human functioning, and possibly for all emotional systems. In Chapter 18, Katharine Gratwick Baker describes how triangles function in the context of societal emotional process and how the levels of the family as a system and societal process are intertwined. Her view is that societal emotional process is an arena in which all of the concepts of Bowen theory apply. She draws upon the Russian revolution for examples, describing the relationships between Lenin, Stalin, and Trotsky, their families, and in the revolution of which they were a part. In Chapter 19, Edward W. Beal describes the triangle as the cornerstone of the government of the United States. He writes both of the tripartite structure of our government, the executive, legislative, and the judiciary branches, and the human interaction between the members of these branches that form triangles. In Chapter 20, Ann V. Nicholson writes about triangles, leadership, and the U.S. Supreme Court. She examines the functioning of a number of chief justices and looks at how their individual functioning is expressed within the process of each of their courts, in the context of their relationship to the political and historical times, and to the other branches of government. In Chapter 21, Carol Moran describes societal emotional process and interlocking triangles using as an example the relationship between the governments of the United States and Saudi Arabia, the resource of oil, and the populations of Saudi Arabia and the United States. She raises and answers, in the affirmative, this question: Can Bowen theory's concept of *differentiation of self* provide guidelines to the individual for defining the *citizen self* during confusing and dangerous times?

Materials drawn from clinical cases presented in this book have been modified in order to protect the confidentiality of these individuals and their families.

Though each contributor presents the concept of the triangle from his or her perspective on Bowen theory, it is my belief that the book as a whole provides a view that is consonant with Bowen's conception.

REFERENCES

Bowen, M. (1978). *Family therapy in clinical practice.* Northvale, NJ: Jason Aronson, Inc.

Kerr, M.E. and Bowen, M. (1988). *Family evaluation: An approach based on Bowen theory.* New York: W.W. Norton and Company.

Papero, D. (1990). *Bowen family systems theory.* Boston: Allyn and Bacon.

Titelman, P. (Ed.). (1987). *The therapist's own family: Toward the differentiation of self.* Northvale, NJ: Jason Aronson, Inc.

Titelman, P. (Ed.). (1998). *Clinical applications of Bowen family systems theory.* Binghamton, NY: The Haworth Press, Inc.

Titelman, P. (Ed.). (2003). *Emotional cutoff: Bowen family systems theory perspectives.* Binghamton, NY: The Haworth Press, Inc.

Acknowledgments

I offer my appreciation to all the contributors who provided their best thinking on a variety of significant topics. I have learned a great deal from all of them.

Thanks go to Michael Kerr, MD, Jim Smith, MS, Joanne Bowen, PhD, and Judy Bowen Kowalski, MD, for providing thoughtful comments and editorial suggestions regarding the introductory chapter on the concept of the triangle in Bowen theory, and the chapter on Bowen's effort to differentiate a self: detriangling from triangles and interlocking triangles.

Catherine Rakow, MSW, generously shared her research on Bowen's years at the Menninger Foundation.

Randall Frost, MDiv, deserves thanks for raising interesting questions both to this editor and to others in the Bowen theory community about what constitutes a triangle in Bowen theory.

I want to acknowledge the terrific graphic design work of Elizabeth Utschig, and Paulis Webber for her willingness to complete this work.

Grateful acknowledgment is extended to Vidhya Jayaprakash for her careful copyediting and patience and to Amy Rentner, senior production editor, and Patricia Brown, editorial production manager, for their support.

I want to thank my wife, Katharine Baker, PhD, for her abundant generosity in reading the manuscript (particularly my own chapters), and providing thoughtful comments, a keen editorial eye, and a willingness to talk about Bowen theory and triangles at the oddest time of day or night.

While credit must be given to the individuals acknowledged above, I take sole responsibility for any shortcomings or inaccuracies—factual or theoretical—that this book may contain.

PART I:
TRIANGLES IN BOWEN THEORY
AND NATURAL SYSTEMS

Chapter 1

The Concept of the Triangle in Bowen Theory: An Overview

Peter Titelman

INTRODUCTION

This chapter provides a historical and theoretical overview of the concept of the triangle in Bowen family systems theory. The chapter is divided into six sections. Following this introduction, the second section describes Bowen's movement from psychoanalytic to systems theory: from the individual, to the dyad, to the triangle. The third section defines and describes in detail the concept of the triangle in the context of Bowen theory. The fourth section describes the relationship between the concept of the triangle and other concepts in Bowen theory. The fifth section deals with the process and application of detriangling. The last section is the summary of the chapter.

BOWEN'S MOVEMENT FROM PSYCHOANALYTIC TO SYSTEMS THEORY: FROM THE INDIVIDUAL TO THE DYAD TO THE TRIANGLE

This section describes the origins of Bowen's thinking about triangles as he moved from psychoanalytic to systems thinking. His thinking evolved from an individual, psychoanalytic model, beginning in his early training at the Menninger Foundation, to a focus on the unresolved symbiotic relationship within the dyad of mother and child. Later during his research on schizophrenia and the family, at the National Institute of Mental Health (NIMH), Bowen broadened his focus to the mother-father-child emotional unit. First described as *the interdependent triad,* he later renamed it the *triangle* when further fleshing out the concept.

The Menninger Foundation, Topeka Kansas, 1946-1954

Following a six-year stint in World War II, serving as a physician stationed in England, Bowen was impressed with the impact of stress on human functioning. He changed his professional path from becoming a heart surgeon to becoming a psychiatrist.

Bowen completed his psychiatric residency at the Menninger Foundation in Topeka, Kansas, between 1946 and 1949, continuing his stay at Menninger's as a staff psychiatrist from 1949 to 1954. Bowen chose to do his training at the Menninger Foundation because it was the Mecca of psychoanalytic training at that time. Bowen undertook his own personal training analysis, while he was a candidate at the Topeka psychoanalytic institute.

Bowen made a point of meeting Karl Menninger, MD, when he arrived at the Menninger Foundation. Bowen's daughter (J. Bowen, 2006, personal communication) recalled he "always thought it important to have a relationship with the leader. I know one of his most important principles was to maintain solid relationships with Menninger's while he was there, during his exit, and afterwards." Bowen was well received both by the psychiatric leaders of the Menninger Foundation, the Menninger brothers, Karl and William, and by his fellow psychiatric residents.

A fellow resident, Gerald Aronson, MD (2002, personal communication), described Bowen as being somewhat older than most of the others, having spent several years in the army before entering Menninger's for training. His maturity and sense of responsibility were qualities for which his peers respected him, and he was viewed as a leader.

While at Menninger's, Bowen's first theoretical model was undoubtedly an individually based, intrapsychic, psychoanalytic one, and the core of his therapeutic method involved an intricate understanding of transference and countertransference. However, Bowen (1995) was not afraid to experiment with therapeutic technique. This included supporting emotional regression in schizophrenic patients and treating them in their premorbid infantile states.

Although intrigued with psychoanalytic theory and treatment, Bowen seems to have had a jaundiced view of it, believing from the beginning that it lacked an adequate theoretical base through which to connect it with the natural sciences. He was on the library committee at Menninger's and read voraciously in the area of natural science, searching for a scientific base for human behavior. His American pragmatism rooted in his childhood, in the small town of Waverly, Tennessee, may have made him leery of a theory based on literary myth and out of contact with the natural sciences, particularly those stemming from evolutionary, biological underpinnings.

By the end of Bowen's time at Menninger's his thinking was already moving from an individual to a dyadic model, focused on the symbiotic attachment between mother and child. At that time Bowen was aware of the work of Frieda Fromm-Reichman (1950) and her concept of the *schizophrenogenic mother* with its focus on the ambivalent symbiosis between the mother and the schizophrenic offspring.

While at Menninger's Bowen became interested in how the family played a part in the development of psychiatric disorders. However, as Bowen (Simon, 1979) described it, at that time it was unconventional for a psychiatrist to meet with the family members of their patients:

> If the therapist had contact with the family, it could contaminate the transference. The working plan for psychiatry back then was to hire social workers to keep families from interfering in the therapeutic relationships. . . . You were considered to be inept, even to the point of malpractice, if you saw relatives. That was the strength of the prohibition against seeing other members of a patient's family. . . . During this time I was working with families here and there, doing work mostly in the evenings and on weekends. . . . You could say what I did was sort of undercover, working out my ideas in my own head. (Simon, 1979, p. 3)

Bowen (1978) most likely received some support for his interest in the family from William C. Menninger, "who considered the family as an important area for study" (p. 185).

Bowen (1978) learned a great deal about emotional process, particularly the way emotional fusion and triangles operated, among the staff during his tenure at Menninger's. He began to observe how emotional triangles formed in the work system. Knowledge gained from this experience was a factor in his developing the concept of the triangle. Later he (Bowen, 1978) would write: "The patterns of all emotional systems are the same whether they be family systems, work systems, or social systems, the only difference being one of intensity" (p. 485).

When anxiety was present, he saw how triangles were expressed through gossiping and diagnosing absent colleagues. When he left the work system at Menninger's for a trip or vacation it became clear to Bowen that he could be more of a defined self, regarding his own developing thinking about family systems. As soon as he flew back to Topeka, and returned to the work system, he would feel the emotional forces of togetherness attempting to pull him back into conventional individual, psychoanalytic thinking.

Bowen (1978) described how his involvement in that work system was one of his great learning experiences about how emotional systems work, and particularly in regard to triangles.

> Gossip is one of the principle mechanisms for "triangling" another into the emotional field between two people. . . . In that work system much "triangling" took place at coffee breaks, social gatherings, and bull sessions in which the "understanding ones" would "analyze" and talk about those who were not present. This mechanism conveys, "we understand each other perfectly (the togetherness side of the triangle). We are in agreement about that pathological third person." At social gatherings people would clump, and each apparently unaware that all the clumps were doing the same "triangling" gossip about them. (p. 485)

Bowen's early presentations at Menninger's on the family were met with initial enthusiasm and support, followed by confusion, and criticism. However, he continued with his new thinking. Eventually, members of the work community became very critical, describing his focus on the family as coming out of his own personal psychopathology (Sykes-Wylie, 1991, p. 28). Bowen stayed on course, but realized that he would have to leave Menninger's and find another institution where a "different kind of thinking would not be a problem for the environment" (p. 3). His experience at Menninger's was part of the basis of Bowen's description of the three predictable stages in a family's, or any emotional organization's, reaction to an individual's effort to differentiate a self: (1) "You are wrong"; (2) "Change back"; and (3) "If you do not, these are the consequences" (Bowen, 1978, pp. 216, 495).

Bowen (1978) considered the experience of the intense emotionality during the years he spent at Menninger's as one of the fortunate experiences in his life. It made it easier for him to see the same phenomenon in all other work systems, as well as in the family.

Bowen's relationship with the Menninger Foundation came full circle when he returned there to be honored in June 1985. Bowen was presented with the Arthur Marshall Distinguished Alumnus Award, to honor an alumnus who has made an outstanding contribution to the field of psychiatry and mental health.

It is worth noting that Karl Menninger, MD (1991), in a letter written to Bowen on July 17, 1985, indicated, in retrospect, how much he admired and valued Bowen's efforts to be a self and to develop his own way of thinking and doing therapy, separate from the psychoanalytic mainstream:

> My dear boy:
>
> You are still a boy to me, one of my young boys grown up, who seemed wise enough to advise and help me in trying to marshal 100 other boys into learning how to help people. I don't think I made a success of it as it may seem to some. I get lots of praise, but I wish now I had talked more just *about helping* people not "treating" them, but listening to them in the gentle, kind way that you do. I didn't teach you that. You taught lots of other people that, which makes me happy. I am glad that they want to learn from you, Murray, I learned from you, too.
>
> You did a lot of good by coming here, showing yourself to these young people and telling them what you try to do and encouraging them in trying to (imitate it).
>
> I don't care so much about it being psychoanalytic, but I want them to follow you.
>
> Sincerely,
>
> Karl Menninger, MD, FAPA (p. 6)

National Institute of Mental Health, Bethesda, Maryland, 1954-1959

In 1954 Bowen was appointed to the position of Chief, Family Studies Section, Clinical Investigation, National Institute of Mental Health, National Institutes of Health, U.S. Public Health Service, Department of Health, Education, and Welfare.

At the onset of Bowen's NIMH research project on schizophrenia and the family, young individuals diagnosed as schizophrenic were hospitalized and their parents were invited to live in the ward with them. Initially it was only the mothers and their schizophrenic daughters that cohabited at the hospital. The initial hypothesis for the research involved only the dyad. In an interview Bowen stated: "The problem in the patient was a product of the symbiotic relationship with the mother. I interpreted symbiosis very broadly to mean both the positive and negative over attachment between child and mother" (Simon, 1979, p. 3). Bowen (1978) described this symbiosis, in 1957, "as a developmental arrest which at one time was a normal state in the mother-child relationship" (p. 4). Bowen called it "a state of two people living and being for each other; of one being sick for the other to be well" (Bowen, 1995, p. 38). In a project paper note found in the Bowen Archives, it was written:

> The attachments that are called "symbiotic" are present in a wider range of clinical problems. . . . In schizophrenia for instance, it seems to me to make sense to say that half of the problem is in the patient and the other complementing half is in the mother. (Bowen, 1954, pp. 3-4)

Bowen's research began with the admission of a young woman on November 1, 1954. Her mother arrived several days later. By 1954-1955, three mother-daughter pairs were living on the ward (see Rakow, 2004, p. 3). The observations in the first year led to extending the hypothesis to consider the symbiotic relationship between a parent and child as only a fragment of intense attachments in the larger family (Rakow, 2001). By August 1955, plans were being discussed for including the father in the study. At Christmas 1955, the first father joined the project with the mother and impaired child, and a sibling arrived soon after. An analysis of the project written by Bowen in December 1955, describes the change as follows: "From seeing schizophrenia as a process between mother and patient to an orientation of seeing schizophrenia as a manifestation of a distraught family that becomes focused in one individual. This reflected a shift in the hypothesis in the operating theory base . . ." (Rakow, 2004, p. 10). Beginning in December 1955, Bowen began working only with patients whose mothers and fathers were available and willing to participate with the patient in the treatment program (Bowen, 1958).

The observations of the mother-father-child triad as the key to the understanding of schizophrenia were the precursors of the concept of the emotional triangle. Bowen's incipient understanding of the parental-child triad as the pathway for the circuitry of emotional attraction and distancing, both the glue and mode of transmission of family emotional process, would become the basis for his conceptualizing of the triangle as the basic building block of the nuclear family.

In 1955, Bowen began working on what would eventually be called the concept of the triangle, and by 1956 the NIMH research group began thinking about and using the term triad (see Bowen, 1978, p. 373). In his first published article, "Treatment of Family Groups with a Schizophrenic Member," originally published in 1957, Bowen (1978) alluded to the triangle dimension of schizophrenia while describing the mother-child symbiosis: "The father passively permits himself to be excluded from the intense twosome and marries his business or other outside interests" (p. 4).

In Bowen's (1978) second published paper, "The Role of the Father in Families with a Schizophrenic Patient," published in 1959, and co-authored with Robert Dysinger, MD, and Betty Basmania, MSW, he wrote, "The patient's function is similar to that of an unsuccessful mediator of the emotional differences between the parents" (p. 22).

In Bowen's (1978) third paper, "Family Relationships in Schizophrenia," originally published in 1959, he further elucidates the pattern he saw in the interdependent triad and how it was interrelated with marital distance or emotional divorce and the over/underfunctioning reciprocity between the parents:

> There was an emotional distance between the parents that we called the emotional divorce. The family conflict seemed to remain pretty much in the father-mother-patient triad and to involve normal siblings less than was anticipated. The parents were separated from each other by the emotional divorce, but either one could have a close relationship with the patient if the other parent permitted it. The most common family configuration was one in which the overadequate mother was attached to the helpless patient and the father remained peripheral to the intense mother-patient twosome. (p. 43)

Bowen (1978), in his fourth paper, published in 1959, described the key role of the child in stabilizing the mother-father-child triad through the processes of projection[1] and over/underfunctioning reciprocity in the following way:

> As I currently see the mother-child equilibrium, the mother was securely in the over-adequate position to another human being, this human belonged to her, and it was realistically helpless. She could now control her own immaturity, by caring for the immaturity of another. With her emotional functioning more stabilized in the relationship with the child, the mother became a more stable figure for the father. He

---

[1]Bowen (1978) describes the projection process as follows: "The mother feels and thinks about the child as a baby and treats him as though he is a baby. When the child accepts the projection, he becomes more infantile. The projection is fed by the mother's anxiety. When the cause for her anxiety is located outside of the mother, the anxiety subsides. For the child accepting the projection as reality is a small price to pay for a calmer mother. Now the child is a little more [in]adequate. Each time he accepts another projection, he adds to his increasing state of functional inadequacy" (pp. 128-129).

could better control his relationship to her when her functioning did not fluctuate so rapidly. He tended to establish a more fixed position of aloof distance from the mother, similar to his relationship with his own mother. This new equilibrium came to be a fixed way of functioning for the father, mother, and child. I have referred to this as "the interdependent triad." The child was the keystone. Through the relationship with the child the mother was able to stabilize her own anxiety and to function on a less anxious level. With the mother's anxiety more stabilized, the father was able to establish a less anxious relationship with the mother. (p. 56)

The emotional immaturity of both of the parents, their incumbent anxiety, the emotional divorce between the parents, the projection process whereby anxiety is transferred from mother to child, and, the mother-offspring symbiosis as expressed in the overfunctioning/underfunctioning reciprocity are the features of the process that Bowen described as the interdependent triad, the precursor of the emotional triangle, as it would later be designated.

In an interview with Berenson in 1976, Bowen (1978) said:

The thinking about this [the concept of the triangle] started in 1956 with the use of the term "interdependent triad" to describe the emotional "stuck-togetherness" between father, mother, and the schizophrenic offspring. The term triad was well defined in the literature and was within bounds of an acceptable term for the research. We continued to use triad about two years. (p. 399)

In other words, Bowen seems to be saying that at one level, it was necessary to use terms that would communicate with the outside research world in order to continue to do the family research. In this case Bowen and his research group understood the three-person phenomenon as an emotional process, different from what is meant by the psychoanalytic term Oedipal triad. However, political considerations seemed to dictate that the term triangle not be used at that time.[2]

During the NIMH years Bowen moved further toward a natural systems theoretical model. In "A Psychological Formulation of Schizophrenia,"

---

[2]In the Bowen Archives, Bowen (1956) uses the term "triangle" in a short, unpublished paper, "Discussion of Dr. Harold Searles' paper, 'The Effort to Drive the Other Person Crazy.'" Searles' (1965) paper was published in a collection of papers on schizophrenia and related subjects.

written about 1956, and only published posthumously in 1995, Bowen (1995) wrote:

> The theoretical base for the research for the project is psychoana-lytic. . . . The specific effort is to "reach toward" the medical and bio-logical disciplines rather than toward the nonmedical disciplines. . . . The operating method for "reaching toward" the biological disciplines is to formulate medical and biological events in a psychological frame. A major effort is to keep the psychological conceptualization adap-tive to biological events. . . . Briefly, the biological is used as it refers to life processes such as birth, growth, reproduction, and death which are common to all protoplasmic life. (p. 22)

Observations that led to Bowen's being able to "see" and then conceptu-alize the emotional triangle during this period of his career involved the in vivo observation of triangles in the exaggerated version found in the hospi-talized families with schizophrenic offspring. This research experience led him to be able to see the same processes in all families, albeit in less dra-matic form. Bowen learned a great deal about the triangular emotional pro-cess by observing and managing the interaction between patient, family, and therapist; the therapist and other staff members, and individual or mul-tiple members of the family; and the relationships between the staff and multiple hospitalized families.

Bowen continued to be in his own analysis between 1954 and 1960 in Washington, DC, and continued to be a psychoanalytic candidate. Bowen (1978) describes his relationship to psychoanalysis and how he eventually left that movement to continue developing his own family systems theory:

> From 1948 to 1960 I was a candidate in psychoanalytic institutes, where certain phases of training were interrupted by a move and by research activities. Every small point in theory was debated at length even before the move to Washington in 1954. I learned more psycho-analytic theory from debating about the research than from taking courses in the institute. An occasional psychoanalytic theorist would see the point but have no ideas about how to proceed. The main prob-lem was not in the theory but in those who practiced the theory, who could not see beyond the dogma. The debates became cyclical and nonproductive and they used time needed for [family] research. My membership in the group became an issue between those who sup-ported me and those who opposed. Supporters wanted me to accept membership and then follow the research. One senior analyst said,

"I give up my concern about you and psychoanalysis. It now needs you more than you need it." Finally a supporter asked me to do one more round of debates. I agreed. The following day he called to release me from the promise. The following day I submitted my resignation. This phase took about six years. (p. 397)

During the period from 1954 to 1960, not only was Bowen in analysis, but he was also observing his own emotional functioning and that of his family members within his nuclear family and family of origin, particularly in the primary triangle of his parents and himself (see Bowen, 1978, p. 530). And he was making efforts to better define himself in the context of his nuclear family (Kerr and Bowen, 1988, p. 374).

Georgetown University Medical Center, Department of Psychiatry, Washington, DC, and Outpatient Private Practice, Bethesda, Maryland, 1959-1967

In 1959, after his research grant at NIMH was not renewed, Bowen searched for another setting to continue his theoretical and outpatient clinical work on schizophrenia and the full range of human functioning in the context of the family emotional system. Bowen had a number of possibilities but he decided to move to the department of psychiatry at the Georgetown University Medical Center. He believed the university's Jesuit orientation and the assurance that he could follow his own direction provided the most fruitful opportunity to develop his pioneer thinking. Bowen was moving toward a brand new theory of human functioning in the context of the family. His affiliation with Georgetown University continued throughout the rest of his career, ending only with his death in 1990.

About 1961, Bowen began using the term triangle instead of the term interdependent triad (see Bowen, 1978, p. 358). In a note in the Bowen Archives, in the National Library of Medicine, Bethesda, Maryland, Bowen wrote:

The connecting link came much closer for me in the period about 1961-2 when I began to perfect the concept of "triangles" so well that the concept could be used predictably in the clinical situation. Anyone who could manage himself in a triangle could modify relationship patterns in the threesome. People behave the same in a triangle whether they are in the family or outside the family. (Bowen, 1978, p. 9)

Between 1962 and 1964, Bowen was able to define the triangle clearly (Bowen, 1980b).

The first use of the term triangle did not appear in publication until 1966, in an article titled "The Use of Family Theory in Clinical Practice" (1978). On the one hand, Bowen describes the triangle as "one of the important concepts in this theoretical system . . . the basic building block of any emotional system" (p. 174). On the other hand, he states that while the triangle is one of the important systems concepts, he did not include it with the other concepts ". . . because it has more to do with therapy than the basic theory" (p. 174). It is unclear to this author why Bowen described the triangle as more of a clinical tool at that time, rather than as a basic theoretical concept, as he would do in later writing. However, it is possible that Bowen described it as he did at that time, because (1) the triangle was so important as a therapeutic/coaching principle; (2) Bowen was immersed in clinical work and in his own family work, where the triangle was emerging in his application of his theory; and (3) it may have been an inadvertent oversight in the way Bowen (Kerr and Bowen, 1988) organized his paper, for the *Comprehensive Journal of Psychiatry,* as he was rushing to complete it in order to meet the editor's deadline (see p. 379).

In his last published essay, Bowen (Kerr and Bowen, 1988) looked back and commented on the significance of his understanding of the triangle concept to the integration of his family systems theory in 1966:

> The idea of triangles was the cement that integrated the concepts into a single theory. I simply could not do a routine paper when my mind was so close to new facts about triangles. When the journal was published in October 1966, no one knew the effort that had gone into the integrated theory. . . . From the time that manuscript was mailed in August 1966, I became a different person. The change was so immediate and so profound that it influenced changes in the Georgetown program that have continued through the years. (p. 379)

The description in the following text, from the 1966 paper, includes Bowen's (1978) understanding of interlocking triangles, and defines triangles in what would become a standard way:

> When emotional tension in a two-person system exceeds a certain level, it "triangles" a third person, permitting the tension to shift within the triangle. . . . An emotional system is composed of a series of interlocking triangles. The emotional tension system can shift to any of the old preestablished circuits. (p. 174)

From 1959 through 1967, Bowen was broadening his theory from a focus on schizophrenia and the family, to accounting for all levels of human functioning in the context of the family, in the context of working with higher functioning outpatient families, and in his training of psychiatric residents, and other mental health professionals. In 1966, Bowen first put together his theory in an integrated form, including the first six concepts (differentiation of self, nuclear family emotional system, family projection process, multigenerational transmission process, sibling position, and triangles). It would not be until 1975 that Bowen (1978) formally added the seventh and eighth concepts of his family systems theory: societal regression (later referred to as emotional process in society) and emotional cutoff (see pp. 382, 385).

Bowen expanded his focus from the nuclear family emotional process and triangles to including the importance of the family of origin and extended family, and the interlocking triangles in the family as a multigenerational family emotional system or unit. By the late 1960s Bowen was beginning to develop his understanding of interlocking triangles.

Bowen's Work on His Own Family and the Development of the Concept of Interlocking Triangles

From 1955 to 1967, Bowen had been making trips home to visit his family of origin and his extended family with limited progress. Beginning in 1955, Bowen (Kerr and Bowen, 1988) started to apply the knowledge he was gaining in his research to his own nuclear and extended families:

> This included data from my extended families. Before that I knew very little about my extended families. In a matter of ten years I had collected essential life data on some 16 of my extended families, as far back as 200 to 300 years. (p. 374)

On February 11, 1967, he arrived home on another visit with a plan, based on his developing understanding of interlocking triangles. His goal was to have the triangles come to him rather than for him to pursue absent members of the triangles. Even his nuclear family did not know his plan. He wrote:

> The key triangles knew the time of my arrival. My arrival on February 11, 1967, was a hallmark in the history of the family. Every important triangle in the family met in one living room. For some 12 years I had been making regular trips home, with a little progress on each trip.

I expected February 1967 to be a little better. By the time this new meeting was 30 minutes old, *I knew that I was totally successful on the first try.* I was inwardly exhilarated, not because it had been helpful to me or my family, but simply because *I finally knew one way through the impenetrateable thicket which is the family emotional system.* (Kerr and Bowen, 1988; emphasis in the original, pp. 379-380)

Bowen was exhilarated by the fact that his understanding of interlocking triangles indicated that he had not only found the missing link for how emotional process is expressed in the family emotional system, but he also believed he had found a methodological approach to getting himself outside of the swirling emotional fusion process propelled by the force of togetherness, even if only for brief segments of time. This breakthrough led to a major change in therapeutic focus. Bowen now began focusing on coaching individuals seen alone or in the context of the couple to place their efforts on defining a self in the context of the family of origin and the extended family.

The concept of triangles and interlocking triangles, and Bowen's Herculean effort to apply his understanding of triangles and interlocking triangles in defining a self, through detriangling, will be described in detail in the following sections of this chapter and in Chapter 4.

Summary

In summary, the in vivo observation of triangles in the exaggerated version found in the NIMH research families with schizophrenic offspring, led Bowen to see the same processes in all families, including his own family, albeit in less dramatic form. Other observations that led to Bowen's being able to "see" and then conceptualize the triangle and interlocking triangles, included his clinical work and his efforts in his own family.

This part of the chapter described the origin of the triangle concept in the context of Bowen's evolution from psychoanalytic to systems thinking beginning gradually during the Menninger period, making a leap during the NIMH research period, and crystallizing in the initial years during the period at Georgetown University, in private practice, and through his efforts to applying his understanding of triangles and interlocking triangles in his differentiation of self efforts in his own family. The triangle concept, like all of Bowen's theory, developed through a circular inductive-deductive process involving his research and clinical observation, efforts to modify his functioning in his own family, and his development of a theory of human behavior that would be synchronous with evolutionary theory and other natural systems theory and research.

THE CONCEPT OF TRIANGLES IN THE CONTEXT OF BOWEN THEORY

This part of the chapter is divided into the following sections: (1) two perspectives: Bowen's family systems emotional triangle and Freud's psychoanalytic Oedipal triad; (2) triangles: the evolutionary biological foundation of emotional systems; (3) misunderstandings of Bowen's natural systems theoretical basis for the triangle concept; (4) the triangle and interlocking triangles in Bowen theory; and (5) primary and secondary triangles.

Two Perspectives: Bowen's Family Systems Triangle and Freud's Psychoanalytic Oedipal Triad

Bowen (1978) chose the term emotional triangle to convey that the concept had a meaning different from the meaning of the concept of the *Oedipal triad* in psychoanalytic theory: "As the concept evolved, it came to include much more than the meaning of the conventional term triad, and we therefore had a problem communicating with those who assumed they knew the meaning of triad" (p. 373). Bowen believed that the triangle concept proved "a far more exact way of understanding the father-mother-child triangle than do the traditional Oedipal complex explanations" (p. 374). Not only is the psychoanalytic theory of the Oedipal complex limited to the mother-father-child triad, fixed during a child's development at about the ages of four to six, but its theoretical focus is limited to the issue of the sexual instincts and their developmental instinctual unfolding emerging from within the intrapsychic life of the individual child. Only secondarily does it focus on the actual behavioral interaction in the parental-child triad. In contrast, Bowen's triangle concept focuses on the myriad expressions of fusion and distance that express the degree of integration of the emotional, instinctual forces of individuality and togetherness. In this regard, Bowen (1978) wrote the following: "Psychoanalytic theory, without specifically naming it, postulates the Oedipal triangle between both spouses and the child, but it is awkward and inaccurate to extend this narrow concept into a broad one" (p. 307). The triangle concept in Bowen can deal with relationships between all members of a family throughout their lives, within both the nuclear family and the extended family.

Freud and his psychoanalytic descendents have made the Oedipal triad central in their theories and modes of intervention. However, the Freudian conception of the triad is based on intrapsychic phenomena and their focus is on distortion in phantasy and dream of early parental imagos. When Freud rejected the *seduction hypothesis* as the basis of the etiology of hysteria, about the turn of the century, replacing it with a hypothesis of a developmental genetic, *intrapsychic phantasy* hypothesis, he made the actual ongoing interpersonal, interactional patterns between the child and parents secondary to the epigenetic unfolding of the Oedipal conflict as an intrapsychic process.

Freud's famous case of "Little Hans," the prototype for the theory of the Oedipal conflict of a neurotic type, is interesting as much for what familial dynamics Freud did not consider relevant, as for his formulation of the four-year-old Hans's phobia of horses as a symbol of castration anxiety. The latter was hypothesized as a reaction to unconscious fear of retaliation by his father for his unconscious erotic desire directed toward his mother and the unconscious wish to replace his father.

Interestingly, Freud's intervention with Little Hans was through consultation with the father. Was that a precursor of family therapy? Perhaps, but this author would suggest that had Freud been focusing on the marital conflict between Little Hans's parents he might have conceptualized the triadic, Oedipal situation as involving actual overcloseness between mother and son, and distance between husband and wife. In other words, Freud failed to deal with the interpersonal triangle in favor of dealing with the intrapsychic triad. Anecdotal reports about Little Hans's family indicate that Freud's intervention via the father led to symptom resolution for Little Hans, and the disappearance of his horse phobia, but his parents' conflict increased, ending in divorce. An understanding of triangles would have made comprehensible the increase of tension between the spouses following the abatement of the son's symptoms.

In psychoanalytic theory, the Oedipal complex, emerging within the parental-child triad, generates a range of anxiety in the child based on the unfolding of instinctual forces within the child. In Bowen theory, the triangle may generate anxiety in a child or either parent, or some other member of the family or nonfamily member, while two others experience a calmer, less anxious state. Or, two members may be anxious and the third may be calm.

The triangle concept in Bowen theory expresses how the emotional life of the multigenerational family is transmitted through multiple generations. In Bowen's theory the triangle stabilizes anxiety in a twosome, at the expense of increased anxiety in a third person.

Triangles: The Evolutionary Biological Foundation of Emotional Systems

Bowen theory asserts "that the triangle, a three-person emotional configuration, is the molecule or the basic building block of any emotional system, whether it is in the family or any other group" (Bowen, 1978, p. 373). The term emotional for Bowen refers to the instinctual forces man shares with other forms of life, particularly other primate species. It is taken for granted in Bowen theory that the emotional process that inhabits a triangle takes place in a relationship system. Therefore, when Bowen theory refers to the emotional triangle, it refers to a process that occurs in both the emotional and relationship systems. The triangle is a process that takes place in both human and nonhuman primate emotional systems. Whether emotional triangles exist in other species is a researchable question. Although the emotional system, with concomitant anxiety binders, may occur in other forms of life forms, the triangle as an anxiety binder and a means of regulation on the part of the emotional system is restricted, for the most part to human and nonhuman primates. Triangular functioning occurs in some other species, particularly social mammals. This author assumed that the emotional triangle and interlocking emotional triangles emerged in the evolutionary period when social mammal and bird species appeared, and two parents and/or an extended family were needed in order to successfully raise an offspring. Species that evolved to the dyadic level, where only one parent raises the offspring, are earlier evolutionary forms of life. Still earlier species, in which no parent is needed in the developmental process, do not appear to manifest emotional triangles or emotional interlocking triangles.

As de Waal and Embree (1997) have demonstrated in studying chimpanzees and other nonhuman primates:

> The evidence that is available currently is certainly sufficient to show that triadic awareness is by no means restricted to our own species. Rather, we share with other primates an evolutionary heritage as a basis for not just physical traits, but behavioral traits and predispositions toward social intelligence as well. (p. 16)

Misunderstandings of Bowen's Natural Systems Theoretical Basis for the Triangle Concept

Bowen's effort was to ground his family systems theory in natural systems thinking, and to create a theory of human functioning that was consonant with the facts of evolutionary biology. He expressed dissatisfaction with his choice of the term triangle, a term taken from mathematics, insofar as he sought to create a family systems theory congruent with emotional-instinctual processes present in the life sciences, specifically evolutionary biological theory. Bowen (1978) wrote:

> If I had to do it over again, I probably would have found another term, but I still do not know what it would be. The triangle concept came from watching people as they go through a dance or drill or fixed pattern of movement. It continues until the anxiety builds up or decreases. Suddenly, on an observable cue, they go into counter marching or another fixed pattern. This is all knowable, and predictable. (p. 400)

Some practitioners who have come in contact with Bowen theory, including some who purport to adhere to the theory, have misunderstood or chosen to deviate from Bowen's natural systems underpinnings. They have mixed Bowen theory ideas with psychological theories, including psychoanalytic theory, and other ideas from other branches of science. In Bowen's words (1978): "When I began thinking triangles, I was thinking emotional flow and counter-flow, I did not anticipate that many would hear it as geometry" (p. 400). Bowen may have been referring to, among others, Thomas Fogarty, MD, a student of his and a gifted clinician and creative systems thinker.

Fogarty's mixing of biological, natural systems thinking with the scientific disciplines of mathematics and physics led to an unfortunate confusion. Fogarty (1975) describes a variety of types of triangles such as equilateral, isosceles, and other mathematically named triangles. The notion of an equidistant triangle does not fit with Bowen's view that a triangle always consists of two close positions and one distant one. Fogarty (1975), in mixing the models of mathematics and physics with biology, drew inadvertently upon the general systems theory of Von Bertalanfy (1975). In contrast, Bowen used biological evolutionary theory as a consistent basis for his assumptions about human functioning.

The Triangle and Interlocking Triangles in Bowen Theory

In Bowen theory, triangles are the smallest stable building block of any emotional system. According to Bowen (1978), a two-person system is stable as long as anxiety is low, but when it rises it automatically draws in the most vulnerable third person and becomes a triangle. Although the triangular process in families is always shifting, it also involves patterns that repeat over time, in which people often come to have fixed positions in relation to each other. Predictably, triangles have two close individuals in the inside positions, and one that is in the outside position. In an anxious system the preferred position is on the outside. In Bowen's (1978) words:

> In periods of calm, the triangle is made up of a comfortably close two-some and a less comfortable outsider. The twosome works to preserve the togetherness, lest one become uncomfortable and form a better to-getherness elsewhere. The outsider seeks to form a togetherness with one of the twosome, and there are numerous moves to accomplish this. (p. 373)

Figure 1.1 illustrates the development of a triangle. In this figure the dia-gram on the left indicates a calm relationship, in which neither individual seeks to triangle in a third person. The diagram in the center illustrates ten-sion or conflict in the relationship, with the more uncomfortable individual, A, triangling in a third person, C. The diagram on the right shows the result of the triangling: the conflict has been covered over between A and B, and it has been shifted out of that original twosome, into the relationship between B and C. In this process the tension between A and B has been decreased, or covered over, at least for the time being.

Triangling is an ever-present process in the presence of microscopic changes in the comfort levels of dyadic relationships within the larger emo-tional unit (nuclear, extended, or a combination of both). It goes on all the time, below awareness and in awareness, in everyday life. Frequently trian-gles emerge, or crystallize, when the calm stability of a two-person system is unbalanced by anxiety in the wake of a nodal event such as marriage, the birth of a child, children leaving home, divorce, disease, death, or other

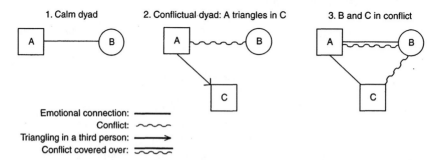

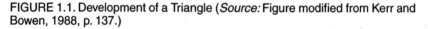

FIGURE 1.1. Development of a Triangle (*Source:* Figure modified from Kerr and Bowen, 1988, p. 137.)

transitions in the course of the family life cycle. The additions or losses of family members are the most significant factors in altering the stability of an emotional system, either negatively or positively. The emergence of a triangle can either stabilize or destabilize a two-person system, or even a larger system, for example, a nuclear or extended family.

From the perspective of Bowen theory, the family is an emotional unit and the emotional processes are the expressions of the hypothesized instinctual forces of togetherness and individuality. The introduction of acute or chronic anxiety[3] into a relationship system unbalances these forces. The calm stability of the two-person system is disrupted, decreasing, for example, a couple's ability to deal directly with each other. Anxiety in conjunction with the twosome's functional levels of differentiation can lead to the engagement of a vulnerable family or nonfamily member in a triangle. The *inside,* or *togetherness* positions are preferred when anxiety is low, and when anxiety is high the *outside* position is preferred. When the emotional process cannot be contained within a triangle, *interlocking triangles* are formed within and across the multiple nuclear families in the larger multigenerational family emotional system. Triangles and interlocking triangles express the predictable movement of emotional process in internal and physical, or geographic space. The focus in Bowen theory is on the emotional space— whether it be expressed internally or externally. The phrase, "old triangles, new players" (Moynihan-Bradt, 1984) describes certain functioning positions, patterns, and issues in triangles that are passed down in a family through the emotional process of interlocking triangles. Old triangles, new players also refers to the way new individuals enter new relationships that very frequently replicate the old relationship patterns they have tried to shed, and in turn they often become a part of interlocking triangles.

Bowen (1978) describes the process of interlocking triangles as follows:

> In a state of tension, when it is not possible for the triangle to conveniently shift the forces within the triangle, two members of the original twosome will find another convenient third person (triangle in

---

[3]Fleshing out Bowen's concept of anxiety, Kerr (Kerr and Bowen, 1988) defines and distinguishes acute and chronic anxiety in the following manner: "Acute anxiety generally occurs in response to real threats and is experienced as time-limited. Chronic anxiety generally occurs in response to imagined threats and is not experienced as time-limited. Chronic anxiety often strains or exceeds people's ability to adapt to it. Acute anxiety is fed by fear of what is; chronic anxiety is fed by fear of what might be. While specific events or issues are usually the principal generators of acute anxiety, the principal generators of chronic anxiety are people's reaction to a disturbance in the balance of a relationship system" (p. 113).

another person) and now the emotional forces will run the circuits in this new triangle. The circuits in the former triangle are then quiet but available for reuse at any time. In periods of very high tension, a system will triangle in more and more outsiders. A common example is a family in great stress that uses the triangle system to involve neighbors, schools, police, clinics, and a spectrum of outside people as participants in the family problem. The family thus reduces the tension within the inner family, and it can actually create the situation in which the family tension is being fought out by outside people. (p. 479)

Figure 1.2 is an illustration of how interlocking triangles emerge in a nuclear family. There are of course multigenerational interlocking triangles and interlocking triangles that involve members of the family in combination with individuals who are nonfamily members.

Interlocking triangles can shift anxiety far away from an original anxious dyad to the most vulnerable individual in an emotional system. However, the discomfort will not disappear in the system because anxiety in the original dyad, although covered over, has not been alleviated.

Bowen (1978) describes a three-person system as one triangle, a four-person system as four primary triangles, and a five-person system as nine primary triangles. The progression multiplies significantly as systems get

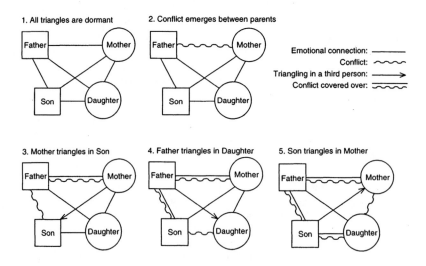

FIGURE 1.2. Development of Interlocking Triangles (*Source:* Figure Modified from Kerr and Bowen, 1988, p. 140.)

larger (p. 479). Interlocking triangles always exist when there are more than three members in the emotional system, the most important example for our consideration being the family, which is a complex multigenerational emotional system.

Primary and Secondary Triangles

This author (Titelman, 2003) has found it useful to employ the terms *primary* and *secondary* triangles in a way that seems consonant with the intent of Bowen theory. The terms primary and secondary triangle do not describe a new phenomenon, but they can be a useful way of observing and working with the different parts of the larger whole, interlocking triangles. A primary triangle refers to a triangle between parents and an offspring, and a secondary triangle involves any triangle in which at least one position, or more, is occupied by one person who is not part of the primary triangle.

A secondary triangle can involve siblings, grandparents, aunts, uncles, or cousins. Secondary triangles involve many configurations within and outside the family. Examples include in-law triangles; same generation, intergenerational, and multigenerational triangles; combination family and nonfamily triangles; triangles in family business and nonfamily business; and, a variety of triangles involving individuals or families with individuals or groups of people within nonfamily organizations, including small and large social or governmental groups.

The terms primary and secondary refer to the temporal origin of triangles. They do not necessarily indicate their level of significance in regard to a particular issue or clinical focus at any given time. For example, in a particular clinical case a triangle involving two siblings and a parent, or three siblings, is a secondary triangle, but it may be most significant at a given time, in a particular clinical situation. However, the primary triangle, that is the father-mother-child (or two parent figures and child), is the basic triangle, and all secondary triangles spin off from it, or interlock with it, both in the nuclear family and the extended family.

Characteristics of the Triangle

This section is divided into four parts: (1) what constitutes an emotional triangle; (2) process and structure in the triangle; (3) the triangle as an involuntary and voluntary process; and (4) the function of triangles.

What Constitutes an Emotional Triangle

Must an emotional triangle be made up of three persons? Must all three persons be alive? Can more than one person occupy one corner or position in the triangle? Can an organization or social institution or structure be part of a triangle? These questions are frequently raised by students of Bowen theory and are not simple to answer.

Bowen's (1978) own writing always refers to the triangle as involving three people (see pp. 174, 198, 306, 373, 398). This follows logically from the notion that the triangle is a living, biological system in which there is either reciprocal movement or potential reciprocal movement between the three. Bowen (1978) does acknowledge that many people can be part of one or more positions within the triangle. He spells this out in the following statement: "In a multiple person system, the emotional issues may be acted out between three people, with others relatively uninvolved, or multiple people clump themselves together on the poles of the emotional triangle" (p. 307). According to Bowen (1978), two or more people "may bond together for one corner of a triangle for one emotional issue, while the configuration shifts on another issue" (p. 479).

Some practitioners of Bowen theory, notably Fogarty (1975; see pp. 46-47) and Guerin, Fogarty, Fay, and Kauto (1997) theorize that a dead family member, or a long absent person, an idea, a fantasy, a process, or an institution, can occupy the third point of a triangle. Kerr (Kerr and Bowen, 1988), the current director of the Bowen Center for the Study of the Family, wrote: "A live third person is not required for a triangle. A fantasized relationship, objects, activities, and pets can all function as a corner of the triangle. For all the facets of a triangle to be played out, however, three live people are *usually* [emphasis added] required" (p. 136). In a personal communication, Kerr (2005) indicated a change in the way he would address this issue: "Someone suggested that alcohol could be the third point on a triangle involving a husband and wife. I asked when the last time was that Jack Daniel's said: 'We have got to stop doing this!'"

Kerr (2005) said further:

> I would write differently now. I think it is cleaner to restrict triangles to three active people. Alcohol would be a distancing mechanism. Dr. Bowen was often loose about this, such as when he talked about a triangle with the deity. Anyway, that is where I come out, but I realize others may be in a different place.

According to Kerr (2005, personal communication), the view most congruent with Bowen theory, and supported by the Bowen Center for the Study of the Family as of 2006, is as follows:

1. An emotional triangle is made up of three living people. It is a living, biological system (a pet, being a living being, may qualify as a potential third member of an emotional triangle). All three are emotional participants and are able to act and react to the other two members of the triangle.
2. A deceased person, idea, fantasy, institution, religion, or other nonliving concept or object is *not* considered part of an emotional triangle.

Smith (2003) makes a distinction between the multigenerational family system, which includes all living and dead members of a family, and the multigenerational family emotional system, consisting only of living members of the family. Part of the confusion about what constitutes a triangle stems from the difference between the theory of the triangle and the clinical use of the concept. Clinically, many Bowen trained professionals have utilized the idea that a dead family member is a part of the multigenerational family system. In that sense he or she is often experienced as being emotionally alive, and appears to function as if he or she is a part of triangles. Another way of thinking about the place a dead family member continues to hold in triangles is expressed in the idea of "new players, old triangles." In other words, the functioning position, for example, of a dead mother in relation to her son may be inhabited by a new player, the son's wife.

A dead person, a religious issue, ideology, or institution, among other issues, beliefs, and objects may be part of an individual's effort to detriangle in a family or nonfamily situation. This will be discussed further in a later section on clinical applications of triangles and detriangling.

Drawing in part upon Smith's (2003) distinction between the multigenerational family system and the multigenerational family emotional system, this author proposes making a distinction between two kinds of triangles: emotional triangles and two forms of *mental construct triangles*. Bowen's emotional triangle has been defined and described in previous text. It consists of living family members and/or nonfamily persons, as illustrated in Figure 1.3.

A partial mental construct triangle includes a mix of living and nonliving entities. The use of the term mental construct is meant to connote the fact that one point of the triangle is occupied by an entity that comes out of man's brain, rather than being a living, biological entity. This form of triangle consists of two or more living individuals, occupying two positions, with the third position occupied by a deceased person, idea, religion/philosophy, or fantasy, among other nonliving entities. These triangles might also be described as quasi-triangles. They are not emotional triangles. Partial mental construct triangles have an anxiety binding function, but the nonliving entity located at one point of the triangle is a mental construct. The presence of a partial mental construct triangle may also allow two individuals to avoid identifying and dealing with a living but absent, or unseen, third member of an emotional triangle. Figure 1.4 illustrates two examples of this type of triangle.

A mental construct triangle is based entirely on mental construction. It does not include any biological entities. Therefore it is not an emotional triangle. It is an organizational model. An example of this would be the tripartite structure of the U.S. government: the executive branch (the president and his appointees), the legislative branch (Congress), and the judiciary branch (the Supreme Court and other branches of the judicial system). Figure 1.5 illustrates this type of triangle.

Of course, there are other organizations or institutions that may be comprised of tripartite structures. There are, for example, at the societal level,

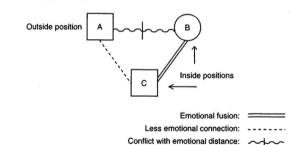

FIGURE 1.3. Emotional Triangle

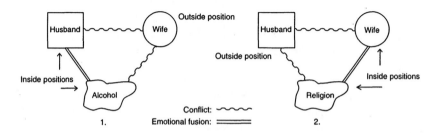

FIGURE 1.4. Partial Mental Construct Triangle

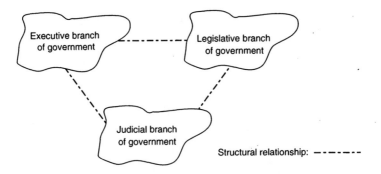

FIGURE 1.5. Mental Construct Triangle

triangular relationships between nation states that are codified in treaties as well as triangles that are less formal. These organizational triangles are not emotional systems in themselves, but they may modulate or control the emotional process that exists between the people who occupy positions within the tripartite structural divisions that make up the organizations or institutions. These nonbiological, societally created triangular entities are not emotionally driven relationship systems in and of themselves.

Kerr (2005, personal communication) reinforces this distinction when he wrote, in a personal communication, that the concept of the triangle can be

> cautiously extended to societal process. I do not consider the three branches of our government to be a triangle in the Bowen theory definition of the term. I consider the three branches a structure that is designed to minimize the impact of emotional process on decision-making. In other words, the three branches might be considered an administrative structure designed to prevent triangling. I do not know of course, if our founding fathers would agree.

The three branches of the U.S. government are triangular arenas in which emotionally driven relationship triangles, made up of humans and often inhabited by many individuals at one or more of the three points, unfold. They function on a continuum of differentiation from highly emotionally driven to more thoughtfully based, goal-directed functioning, in the context of the degree of acute and chronic anxiety that exists within and between the people who inhabit them. When, for example, the tripartite government is examined in terms of individuals, or the small and large groups of people who occupy the three positions of the triangle, then it is accurate to describe this phenomenon as an emotional triangle, or interlocking emotional triangles, consonant with the understanding of the emotional triangle offered by Bowen theory.

Process and Structure in the Triangle

Bowen (1978) described the triangle as a phenomenon characterized by an ever-moving emotional process consisting of instinctual emotional forces and counter forces:

> The emotional forces within the triangle are constantly in motion from moment to moment, even in periods of calm. Moderate tension states in the twosome are characteristically felt by one, while the other is oblivious. It is the uncomfortable one who initiates a new equilibrium toward more comfortable togetherness for self. (p. 373)

> The emotional forces within a triangle are in constant motion, from minute to minute and hour to hour, in a series of chain reaction moves as automatic as emotional reflexes. (p. 470)

In Bowen theory, the focus has been much more on the notion of the emotional process, and less on the part that structure plays in understanding a particular concept or the interlock of concepts. Nevertheless, emotional process takes place in the context of structure and structure always contains emotional process. The process focus asks the *How* question. It addresses how each part of the system, or each person, affects and is affected by the others in the family, or nonfamily, system. The focus on structure asks the *Who, What, When,* and *Where* questions. The *Who* question asks who the people are who make up the triangle. The *What* question addresses the issues around which the triangles typically form; and the *When* and *Where* questions address the time(s) and space(s) in which the triangle unfolds.

Bowen (1978) never refers directly to the place of structure in writing about triangles. Perhaps the reason is because he believed it led to seeing patterns and process in too static a way. He did allude to the idea of structure when he wrote: "Each of *the structured* [author's italics] patterns in triangles is available for predictable outcomes in families and social systems" (p. 374). It seems to this author that Bowen's description of two individuals occupying inside positions and one occupying an outside position is a description of the basic structural pattern that makes up a triangle. The constant oscillating movement of distancing or pursuing is the emotional process. When Bowen describes the fixed patterns and postures that each person maintains in triangles he is in effect describing the structured or structural dimension of the triangle:

> Over long periods of time, a triangle will come to have long-term postures and functioning positions to each other. A common pattern is one in which the mother and child form the close twosome and the father is the outsider. In this triangle, the minute to minute process of emotional forces shifts around the triangle, but when the forces come to rest, it is always with each in the same position. (p. 479)

Kerr (Kerr and Bowen, 1988) has described the functioning positions within a triangle as consisting of *an anxiety "generator," an anxiety "amplifier,"* and *an anxiety "dampener"* (p. 142). Kerr also refers to three functioning positions that make up a triangle: *the distancer, the projector,* and *the absorber.* The functioning positions represent the structured patterns of behavior that the three individuals in a triangle embody and around which the emotional process flows.

The Triangle As an Involuntary and Voluntary Process

The emergence of triangles is an automatic or involuntary process that is part of the nature of emotional systems. However, at times, the human, and other nonhuman primates (deWaal and Embree, 1997), intentionally and actively enter into, evoke, and promote the triangle process. In contrast, for the most part, detriangling is an intentional process that involves cognitive awareness and a thoughtful, goal-directed strategy. However, in the course of everyday life in the family, detriangling can occur automatically or unintentionally. For example, the conflict between a parent and a child can be automatically modified by the nonanxious contact with a second parent who is, at least for the time being, residing in the calmer, outside position of the triangle.

The Function of Triangles

Triangles can function to reduce the anxiety of one or more members of a family, or any other emotional system, when the stability of a comfortable closeness/distance between two individuals is thrown out of balance. The unbalanced emotional system can be stabilized through the transfer of anxiety by involving a third individual. Another function of the triangle—implicit in Bowen theory—is the binding of anxiety through control or regulation of one or more individuals in the original dyad, the nuclear family as a whole, and in the larger system, the multigenerational family emotional system. These functions of the triangle bind anxiety for one or more members of a family, the nuclear family, and the extended family as an emotional unit, at the expense of a third member.

The triangle can function to transfer anxiety in the emotional system by involving a third individual. The triangle transfers anxiety from within a two-person unit (A and B, for example) when A, the more uncomfortable of the two, engages a vulnerable and willing third person, C, who previously was in an uncomfortable outside position. In this new triangle A now has a sympathetically comfortable position in C, who now occupies the other inside position. B now moves into the uncomfortable outside position. A second variation of this triangle would involve A criticizing B to C with C and B becoming conflictual and occupying the uncomfortable inside positions, with A moving to the more comfortable outside position.

Triangles and interlocking triangles can function to regulate the equilibrium in the emotional system. The triangle exerts emotional control over the individual in order to maintain togetherness in the family. One of the ways the triangle functions for this to occur is when a child goes along with the parental view (often the mother's view). He or she does this in order to calm his or her mother, in the context of some emotional distance in the marital dyad. Having a calmer mother is calming to the child, even though he or she is giving up *self* in this reciprocal process. The process of regulation through triangles also occurs when two or more individuals explicitly, or implicitly, threaten the third person with punishment or expulsion from the family for not following "the party line." Bowen (1978) describes the three-stage verbal and nonverbal message that the family emotional system communicates to an individual making a differentiation of self step. It also applies when any individual's behavior or posture is such that it threatens the balance of togetherness or the emotional equilibrium of the family. The three-stage message is: "(1) You are wrong; (2) Change back; (3) If you do not, these are the consequences" (Bowen, 1978, p. 216). This message is imparted through a triangling process whereby, for example, the parents, in the inside positions of the triangle, try to exert pressure on their son or daughter, who resides in the outside position, not to marry a particular individual. The parents may invoke family values, rules, or family loyalty, among other pressures, to criticize their offspring's choice, in order to bring him or her back into the fold of family togetherness. Finally the family may threaten, or carry out, the expulsion of their offspring if he or she does not comply with the wishes of the parents. Their threats are expressed on behalf of the anxiety of the family emotional system as a whole.

The regulatory function of the triangle is not control for the sake of power. Rather the control of individuals in the system serves the purpose of maintaining the stability of the family unit. Ultimately, the triangling process lowers anxiety in the family system as a whole—the multigenerational family emotional system—through interlocking triangles, at the expense of one, or more, individuals. In so far as the family emotional system's anxiety is managed by triangles and interlocking triangles, one can say that the triangle can function as a mechanism of regulation or control. It lowers acute anxiety in the service of the family's current functioning, with mixed results in terms of the family's long-term survival. A regulatory function of the triangle is implicit in Bowen theory. Evolutionary biology distinguishes between proximate and ultimate explanations of behavior. According to Fairbanks (2007): "A proximate explanation describes the mechanisms that control how a system works, while an ultimate explanation is concerned with how such a system could have evolved" (p. 7). A proximate explanation for the triangle process is that it manages anxiety in the family unit. An ultimate explanation for the existence of the triangle process is that it maintains the coherence and survival of the multigenerational family. These functions of the triangle are also found in nonfamily emotional systems.

In regard to the function of triangles, Kerr (2005) wrote:

> triangles can function to do x, y, or z. A triangle can function to stabilize a two-person system. Interlocking triangles can function to shift anxiety around a system. A triangle can function such that two people can keep a third person (with the third person's complicity) in his or her place. Triangles can function this way in families and non-family groups. Triangles may function in other ways that we do not yet recognize. We can know how triangles function by sticking with how, what, when, and where questions, which are all provable.

The triangles can stabilize or destabilize a dyad by the addition or subtraction of a third person. Kerr (Bowen and Kerr, 1988; see pp. 138-139) describes these processes. The following is an example of the destabilization of a stable dyad by the addition of a third person: the addition of a child to a marriage can have the impact of modifying a nonconflictual marriage into one that is conflictual because the investment of time and energy in the child has a negative effect on the balance of togetherness of the couple. The following is an example of the destabilization of a stable dyad by the removal of a third person: conflict between the couple may increase following a child leaving home when the child is no longer available to be triangled into the parents' conflicts.

Here is an example of how an unstable dyad can be stabilized by the addition of a third: a marriage with conflict may become calmer with the birth of a child. The latter may allow the couple to shift its focus of anxiety away from each other and onto the child. The following is an example of how an unstable dyad can be stabilized by the removal of a third person: a problem child, adept at playing one parent off against the other, leaving home is no longer evolving conflict between the parental dyad.

Berenson (Bowen, 1978), in an interview with Bowen, raised a frequently asked question: Is the triangle a "natural way of being" or is it a failure of dyadic interaction? (p. 400). Bowen (1978) answered the question by describing the paradox of the triangle as both stabilizing and disruptive for the emotional system:

> A triangle is a "natural way of being" for people. It is not inaccurate to think of the triangle as a failure in a two-person relationship, but that is a narrow view of the larger relationship system. When anxiety is low and external conditions are ideal, the back and forth flow of emotion in a twosome can be calm and comfortable. The two-person relationship is unstable in that it has a low tolerance for anxiety and it is easily disturbed by emotional forces within the twosome and by relationship forces from outside the twosome. (p. 400)

> A two person relationship is emotionally unstable, with limited adaptability for dealing with anxiety and life stresses. It automatically becomes a triangular emotional system with a much higher level of flexibility and adaptability with which to tolerate anxiety. (p. 401)

An open family or nonfamily emotional system characteristically involves triangles that are not fixed, compared to a closed system that is characterized by rigid triangles. An open system is one that is characterized by open, direct one-to-one communication between its members in a considerable number of their dealings with each other. A higher level of differentiation characterizes its members; individuality is relatively high, and while the togetherness forces are in play, there is a respect for and encouragement of individuality. A closed family or nonfamily emotional system is characterized by rigid or fixed triangles in which communication is unclear, closed, and characterized by secrets between its members. It must be pointed out that there is a continuum between closed and open emotional systems, and there are no emotional systems that are either completely open or completely closed, just as there are no individuals or families that are fully differentiated or completely undifferentiated.

The distinction between the ever-changing open triangles in an open system and the static or rigid nature of the triangles in a closed system can be understood by viewing triangles as occurring along a continuum. Less rigid or less fixed triangles are found when differentiation is relatively high and chronic anxiety relatively low. They are relatively open and ever changing, and the functioning positions of the individuals involved are flexible and can vary. Triangles described as rigid or static occur when differentiation is relatively low, chronic anxiety is relatively high, and functioning positions among the participants are relatively fixed and rigid.

Summary

The first part of this section contrasted Bowen's family systems view of the triangle with Freud's psychoanalytic view of the Oedipal triad. The second section was the evolutionary basis of Bowen's view of the emotional system and the triangle, followed by commentary on the misunderstanding of Bowen's natural systems theoretical basis for his theory of understanding and intervening with families, and specifically in regard to the concept of the emotional triangle. The last part of this section presented a broad description of the concept of the triangle and interlocking triangles. This included an examination of the characteristics of the triangle: what constitutes a triangle, process and structure in the triangle, the triangle as an involuntary and voluntary process, and the function of triangles.

THE RELATIONSHIP BETWEEN THE CONCEPT OF THE TRIANGLE AND OTHER CONCEPTS IN BOWEN THEORY

In order to fully understand each of Bowen's concepts—in this case the emotional triangle—it must be considered in the context of Bowen theory as a whole. In this section the concept of the triangle is related to each of the other seven major concepts in the theory: differentiation of self, the nuclear family emotional system, the family projection process, emotional cutoff, sibling position, and societal emotional process. Relating the triangle concept to each of the other seven concepts is a somewhat artificial process. Each concept is fluidly connected to and impacts upon the functioning of the multigenerational family emotional system or unit. The process of triangles is closely linked to all the other concepts, and it also links them to each other. The reader is referred to the seminal works on Bowen theory (Bowen,

1978; Kerr and Bowen, 1988; Papero, 1990) for further explanation of how the concepts are interconnected.

Bowen's effort was to create a theory in harmony with the natural world, specifically the natural science of evolutionary biology. The emotional system is a product of several billion years of evolution. It is the driving force of the family and other relationship systems.

Bowen postulated that the family is an emotionally driven relationship system:

> Operationally I regard an emotional system as something deep that is in contact with cellular and somatic processes, and a feeling system as a bridge that is in contact with parts of the emotional system on one side and with the intellectual system on the other. (Bowen, 1978, pp. 158-159)

According to Bowen theory (Titelman, 2003):

> The concept of the relationship system is a description of what happens among family members, their communications and interactions, whereas the concept of the emotional system is an explanation of what happens. The emotional system refers to what "energizes" the family system, and includes those aspects that humans have in common with other forms of life. It includes automatic, instinctual mechansim such as finding food, fleeing from enemies, reproducing, rearing young, and other aspects of social relationships. (p. 19)

Bowen (Kerr and Bowen, 1988) postulated that the emotional system is governed by the interplay of two hypothetical, instinctual life forces: *togetherness and individuality* (see p. 59). Both forces are rooted in biology. The individuality force propels an organism to follow its own directives, to be an independent and distinct entity. The togetherness force propels an organism to follow directives of others, to be a dependent, connected, and indistinct entity.

From a Bowen theory perspective individual behavior takes place within the relationship system in the multigenerational family, connected to a variety of other relationship systems, driven by the emotional system.

Differentiation, Anxiety, and Triangles

The family is an instinctually, emotionally driven system that responds to the ebb and flow of stress with varying degrees of anxiety. The two most important variables in Bowen family systems theory involve the interaction between the level of differentiation of self and the degree of chronic anxiety.[4] Each of the other seven concepts that make up Bowen theory will be expressed differently depending upon an individual's level of differentiation and how that is integrated with his or her level of chronic anxiety. The triangle process is ubiquitous. Yet when differentiation is high and anxiety is low it is hard to observe, and it does not usually interfere with the functioning of the family.

Bowen described differentiation of self as the capacity to separate thoughtful goal-directed response from emotionally reactive response. The concept defines people according to the degree of differentiation or fusion (a synonym for undifferentiation) between intellectual and emotional functioning (see Bowen, 1978, p. 362). Bowen saw this capacity as lying along a continuum in human functioning. Pair bonding, or marital choice, takes place between couples that function at approximately the same basic level of differentiation of self.

Bowen differentiates basic self from functional self in the following ways. Basic self is made up of those principles, core beliefs, and positions that are not dependent on the relationship. Basic level of differentiation is usually fixed by the time an individual reaches adolescence or young adulthood and remains relatively fixed from then to the end of an individual's life. Unusual life experiences or a structured effort to raise one's level of differentiation can lead to some degree of change in level of basic differentiation.

Functional level of differentiation refers to the phenomenon in relationships whereby an individual "borrows" or "lends" self to the other, and in so doing is either overfunctioning or underfunctioning. Both sides of this relationship dance involve a compromise in functioning.

Differentiation of self is the core theoretical concept of Bowen's theory of the family as an evolution-based multigenerational emotional system. The other seven concepts describe how undifferentiation, or fusion, is managed through symptom patterns in an individual, a couple, a single nuclear family, and multiple nuclear families. Ultimately the multigenerational transmission process of the level of differentiation of the family leads to continuity

---

[4]While chronic anxiety is not considered to be one of the basic concepts in Bowen theory, it is a basic to understanding how the individual and the family as a whole function from a Bowen perspective. It refers to the responsiveness of the human organism to react to others around the issue of comfort/discomfort in the context of the balance of closeness and distance. The definitions of acute and chronic are provided in note 3.

or extinction of particular family branches. Even societies display emotional process and variation in the level of differentiation at a macro level of human functioning.

Bowen describes differentiation as being similar to the process of the differentiation of cells in embryology and biology (see Kerr and Bowen, 1988, p. 362). It is the floor plan or architectural design for guiding the development and life course of the individual and the family. Triangling and detriangling manage and guide the emotional process with its varying integration of the instinctual forces of individuality and togetherness that constitute the emotional system in the family, and possibly all of life.

The triangle is the ubiquitous process—but not the only process—that manages undifferentiation in conjunction with anxiety in the face of the inevitable nodal events, both positive and negative—such as births and deaths—that are part of the life of the human family. Insofar as all humans are not fully differentiated, they live with some degree of chronic anxiety. One-to-one or open, person-to-person relationships cannot be constantly maintained. The lower the levels of differentiation and the higher the levels of chronic anxiety, the greater the presence of triangling, and the more likely that rigid triangles develop in a family. Conversely, the higher the levels of differentiation and the lower the levels of chronic anxiety, less triangling occurs, and less rigid triangles develop. However, as noted in previous text, no family or other emotional system is ever free of the ubiquitous presence of the triangling process and triangles.

Differentiation is a naturally unfolding evolution-driven, automatic, emotional process that comes out of the emotional system. At the same time the intentional effort to work on the defining or differentiation of a self through a planned course of action, based on the thinking system, comes out of the neocortex. .

Triangles and interlocking triangles are natural evolution-based processes. The three-person unit, the triangle, is the basic building block of the family, both biologically and psychologically. Detriangling is a process that involves a carefully planned course of action based on a thoughtful understanding of the self of the differentiating—one in relation to his or her family and other significant relationships, usually under the guidance of a coach trained in Bowen theory.

The Nuclear Family Emotional System and the Triangle

Bowen's nuclear family emotional system concept is a description of the patterns of emotional functioning in a single generation. It consists of three basic patterns through which the family manages its fusion or undifferentiation in the face of anxiety: marital conflict or distance; dysfunction in one spouse, the over/underfunctioning reciprocity between the spouses, whereby one spouse lends self and the other borrows self, with the result that one spouse manifests emotional, physical, or social symptoms; and impairment of one or more children, in other words, the projection of the anxiety of the parent(s) to a child, so that that child expresses the family anxiety through emotional, physical, or social symptoms.

In the first pattern, distance or conflict between spouses, a third person is, inevitably, triangled into the process. For example, a couple in which one partner is distancing and the other partner is pursuing may eventually develop conflict or mutual distance and then become stabilized, at least temporarily, perhaps through an extramarital affair, a common form of triangle.

In the second pattern, the overfunctioning/underfunctioning reciprocity, characterized by emotional, physical, or social dysfunction in one spouse, a child may, for example, become allied with his or her overfunctioning parent with the underfunctioning parent residing in the outside position.

In the third pattern, impairment of one or more children, parents operate as a fused parental "we," that is, the inside positions of the triangle, and they project their fusion or undifferentiation onto one or more children.

The Family Projection Process and the Triangle

The concept of family projection process highlights the triangular emotional process that exists in all nuclear families. The chronic anxiety of the parents, in conjunction with their level of fusion or undifferentiation, is transmitted to one or more of their children, and is picked up and bound by that offspring(s) in the form of emotional, physical, or social symptoms. In the family projection process, a more detailed process of parental transmission of undifferentiation in the face of anxiety to one or more children may impair one or more children in the father-mother-child triangle. In other words, the family projection process is a special form of the triangle, and it is seen most profoundly in a child-focused family, but it is present to some degree in all families.

The Multigenerational Transmission Process and the Triangle

The multigenerational transmission process describes how the level of differentiation decreases in particular individuals, and increases in others, in all families over multiple generations. It accomplishes this through the mechanism of triangles and interlocking triangles. This process assumes that all members of every nuclear family, in each generation, have relatively equal levels of differentiation. However, the child(ren) who receives the greatest amount of the projection process ends up with a lower level of differentiation of self than the parents. He or she is the most triangled child in a family. Conversely, the child(ren) who receives the least amount of the projection process ends up with the same or a higher level of differentiation of self than his or her parents, and is the least triangled child in a family. The degrees of difference in differentiation of self are small but they are meaningful in terms of basic level of self. Over multiple generations this process leads to some members of the family having extremely low levels of differentiation, characterized by chronic emotional, social, and physical difficulties, and others functioning at relatively high levels of differentiation, with still others falling at points in between.

Emotional Cutoff and the Triangle

The concept of emotional cutoff deals with the way people separate themselves from the past in order to start their adult lives in the present generation. The mechanisms for this process are internal emotional distancing or a combination of internal and physical emotional distancing between the generations, and between individuals and nonparental or nonfamily significant others. A cutoff between an offspring and a parent(s) is always an expression of unresolved attachment between child and parent(s).

The editor of this book (Titelman, 2003) has previously described the relation between the triangle and emotional cutoff (see p. 33). In the context of the child growing away emotionally from the parent and the parent promoting that process, cutoff develops in response to the degree of intensity of fusion in the parental triangle. For example, cutoff as a response to fusion between the generations can involve a shift from the child being in the inside position with a parent (more often with the mother, with the father in the outside position) to the child moving into the outside position. At an intense level of emotional fusion, this occurs through a process of *tearing away,* and predictably engaging another individual to fuse with, often through marriage. In the new interlocking triangle the new couple occupies the inside positions, with one or both parents occupying the outside position.

Another possibility is that a cutoff between a parent and an offspring may not change the triangle, but rather it may change the form of the expression that emotional fusion takes. For example, mother and son may continue to occupy the inside positions of the triangle with the father in the outside position, but instead of the togetherness getting expressed by stuck-together-fusion between mother and child, it is now expressed by cutoff-fusion.

The less undifferentiation, or fusion, within the nuclear family, and the less fixed the parental-child triangle, the smoother the process of emotional separation between offspring and parents. It will be more of a process of growing away, rather than tearing away. And the triangling process will be less intense and less fixed.

Sibling Position and the Triangle

The concept of sibling position (Bowen theory) based on the research of Walter Toman (Toman, 1969), as presented in his book, *Family Constellation,* provides a personality profile of each sibling position and allows one to know the typical or expected characteristics of sibling functioning positions, with Bowen's (1978) caveat, "all things being equal" (p. 385). Bowen points out that in many families all things are not equal. For example, a first-born child, who is born with a severe physical disability, will not receive or fulfill the expectations for leadership that come with this functioning position under normal conditions. In this case the youngest born may not occupy the functioning position of follower or creative spirit, but he or she may step up to the position of leader.

Toman speaks about the complementarity of sibling position functioning much as Bowen speaks about the reciprocal functioning between family members. According to Toman (1969), in marriage the partners may have complementarity, partial complementarity, or noncomplementarity in their sibling positions. The degree of complementarity depends on the presence or absence of rank or sex conflict. An example of complementarity is an older brother with a younger sister married to a younger sister with an older brother. The husband who is the older brother with a younger sister will have neither sex nor rank conflict with a wife who is the younger sister of an older brother. The husband is used to relating to the opposite sex and to being the captain of the sibling team while the wife will also have no rank or sex conflict. She is used to relating to the opposite sex and is used to being a lower ranked member of the sibling team. An example of noncomplementarity in marriage is the reverse of the example in the previous text. A man who is an older brother with a younger brother married to a woman who is the older sister with a younger sister will have both rank and sex conflict.

How an individual functions in his or her sibling position depends on the following individual and family factors: (1) the level of differentiation and amount of chronic anxiety of the individuals who inhabit those sibling functioning positions; (2) the level of differentiation or flexibility of the family as a whole; (3) the unresolved issues of both parents in relation to their own sibling position; and (4) the unresolved issues related to sibling position interactions in the multigenerational family.

Sibling positions and triangles are interlocked insofar as in a family constellation one or more siblings is in the inside position with one or the other parent, while the other sibling(s) is invariably in the outside positions in those triangles. Typical triangles are the *good* child being in the inside position with one or both parents and the *bad* child in the outside position. Sibling triangles include triangles with other siblings, with siblings and parents, with parents and grandparents, with siblings and grandparents, and with uncles and aunts, among other combinations.

Emotional Process in Society and the Triangle

The final concept in Bowen theory, emotional process in society, is an overarching emotional arena in which the other seven concepts, in conjunction with the concept of anxiety, can be applied to larger social units found in society. Bowen (1978) believed that triangles exist in all relationships. His interest in emotional process in society included his desire to understand societal chronic anxiety. He postulated this was the product of the population explosion, diminishing supplies of food and natural resources necessary to maintain man's way of life on earth, and the pollution of the environment that is clearly threatening the balance of life upon which human survival depends (see p. 386).

Although it is acknowledged that this concept is more speculative than those grounded in the family, it was based on research in which interlocking triangles were observed involving delinquent adolescents and their parents, and the court system. In the 1960s Bowen (1978; see pp. 413-451) observed the way the nuclear family triangle interlocked with society in an emotionally regressive direction. His observations led him to believe that the postures of permissive, child-focused parents, and the overly lenient courts, social service agencies, and schools were resulting in an imbalance of adolescent rights over responsibilities. The parents were turning to the court system to manage and control their delinquent children, and societal systems in turn were triangled in by the families. For example, a delinquent child might be aligned with an overly permissive mother in the inside positions, with an overly strict, but ineffective, father residing in the outside position of the triangle. Over time, as the adolescent's behavior becomes difficult to control, the triangle often shifts to the parents joined in the inside positions, with the angry adolescent in the outside position in the triangle. Eventually, the parental-child triangle may shift to include the other siblings as appendages to the parents. As further breakdown in the parent-adolescent triangle unfolds, with more antisocial behavior occurring, the school, court, and other social service agencies are triangled in and become a part of the interlocking triangles. These social institutions are at a relatively low level of differentiation, and reflect the level of the society at large. They not only react to the family's anxiety, but they often increase it. The triangling process can and does move from the smallest microlevel, the nuclear family, all the way up to the largest and most complex societal structures—through a myriad of interlocking triangles.

Summary

This section briefly related the concept of the triangle to each of the other seven primary concepts in Bowen theory, and to the supporting concept of anxiety. The triangle was related to anxiety and differentiation; the nuclear family emotional system; the family projection process; the multigenerational transmission process; emotional cutoff; sibling position; and emotional process in society. Initially, it was pointed out that a full understanding of the triangle, or any of the other concepts, calls for an understanding and appreciation of how each concept is related to all the other concepts. All concepts in Bowen theory are interrelated and reciprocally intertwined.

THE PROCESS AND APPLICATION OF DETRIANGLING

The focus of this part of the chapter is on the theory and activity of detriangling in clinical and nonclinical arenas. Detriangling also occurs in nonclinical efforts with nonfamily triangles, or with triangles involving a mix of family and nonfamily members. This section provides a description of the process and application of detriangling, a significant part of the effort to define or differentiate a self in relation to one's family.

For a thorough understanding of the concepts of differentiation of self and the clinical process that goes into the effort to raise one's level of differentiation of self, the reader is referred to the work of Bowen (1978), Kerr and Bowen (1988), Papero (1990), and Titelman (1998).

This part will be divided into the following sections: (1) the attitude of neutrality and detriangling; (2) detriangling and the evolution of Bowen's clinical approaches; (3) principles and strategies in the process of differentiation of self; and (4) principles, processes, strategies, and clinical issues in detriangling in the context of differentiation of self.

The Attitude of Neutrality and Detriangling

The process of coaching someone in a differentiating effort, and that of the clinician working on his or her own differentiation of self, has many components. One of the most important steps involves the clinician becoming more neutral in relation to his or her own family and the clinical families with whom he or she is working.

Bowen was masterful in his capacity to be neutral and nonreactive toward his own family, and to the clinical families with whom he worked. His understanding of the value of neutrality, "the neutral hovering, non-judgmental attentiveness," the attitude he had learned from psychoanalytic theory and from his own personal analysis, was transformed as his focus shifted from the individual patient to the family as an emotional unit. This occurred when he began his research and therapy with families having schizophrenic offspring, at the National Institute of Mental Health in 1954. There he was confronted with tidal waves of emotions, not only between himself and the diagnosed schizophrenic patients, but between himself and the other family members, and between himself and the research and hospital staff with whom he was closely involved in day-to-day clinical research. For Bowen, neutrality had become a research-clinical attitude that involved learning, or increasing the practitioner's capacity to be less reactive toward, and more emotionally outside of the triangle, or detriangled from the family emotional system.

The concept of neutrality in psychoanalytic theory is tied to a therapist's management of his or her countertransference.[5] Psychoanalysts attempt to avoid contaminating their perception of the patient by avoiding direct contact with the patient's family. Instead they deal with the patients' memories, phantasies, *imagos,* and subjective descriptions of the patient's family. In this context, neutrality relates purely to the analyst or psychoanalytic therapist's effort to keep his or her own biases and immaturities from intruding on his or her own functioning, in order to keep from distorting the effort to be, more or less, a blank screen upon which the patient can project his or her transference.[6]

---

[5]Feelings and impulses the therapist has toward his or her patient that are derived from his or her experiences in relation to his or her own family members are ideally dealt with by the analyst or psychoanalytic therapist in his or her own analysis or therapy.

[6]Patterns of positive and negative feelings that originate from the patient's family relationships, particularly those involving the parents, emerge in this process.

As Bowen began to conceptualize the family, including the extended family, as the unit of treatment, whether there was one person, or two or more family members in the consultation room, his therapeutic effort was to stay in emotional contact with the identified patient and his or her real life family. For Bowen neutrality was being able to be in contact with the whole family, whether they were present or not, without taking sides—being able to see the issues from the perspective of each member of the family— even while he most often met with one family member or a couple. Neutrality, from a Bowen theory perspective, requires that the therapist not get polarized on one side of an issue or with one person in the family. Neutrality is the attitude, or stance, that allows the Bowen-oriented coach to stay detriangled, or at least make a continual, concerted effort to get himself or herself unstuck from the automatic, emotional triangling process of the clinical family or the therapist's own family.

Systems thinking is characterized by detachment from the polarizations of good, bad, passive, and active that include fusing with one family member and putting the other(s) in an outside, negative position. Therapy from a Bowen perspective seeks to develop a positive working relationship with the clients, but not one that is based on empathy for the individual as the victim of family trauma or misunderstanding. The Bowen-oriented coach does not seek to empathize by putting himself or herself in the shoes of the client(s). Rather, the effort is to stand beside the client, lending a hand to the client as he or she sees that his or her family members have foibles, weaknesses, and strengths like all human beings. When the coach perceives the mother, father, sister, brother, among others, as bad or good figures, he or she has lost his or her neutrality and is polarized. Polarization may take the form of being triangled with a client(s), or against a client, in relation to one or more of the client's family members or other individuals in the client's life.

Detriangling and the Evolution of Bowen's Clinical Approaches

Detriangling in the presence of an emotional issue is the most important activity through which an individual can become a more differentiated self, and less a part of the unthinking herd. The basic principle in Bowen's theoretical-therapeutic system is that an emotional issue between two people will automatically resolve if they are able to remain in contact with a third person who is free from the intensity of the emotional field between them, while at the same time actively engaging with each of them.

For the human, triangling is a natural, automatic process. For the most part it is out of the awareness of the individuals engaged in it. However, the effort to detriangle is, for the most part, a planned course of action based on the thinking system. It is an activity generated in the neocortex of the brain.

Initially, during his research at NIMH, Bowen met with the nuclear family: mother, father, and schizophrenic offspring. His focus was on modifying their emotional stuck-togetherness, in order to bring about some degree of differentiation within—what he called at that time—*the undifferentiated family ego mass.*

Bowen's basic clinical stance, detriangling, evolved in his practice as his understanding of triangles grew to include interlocking triangles. This led to modification of this original therapeutic approach. He shifted to working with the marital dyad, removing the schizophrenic member of the family, when he came to understand and formulate the concept of the triangle. At that point the therapist (as Bowen was still describing himself) replaced the schizophrenic patient with himself, while making an effort to avoid being emotionally caught or stuck in the triangle with the marital/parental couple.

Eventually Bowen understood that the basic parental-child triangle was embedded or interlocked in triangles involving each spouse/parent in their families of origin, and those triangles were interlocked in still other triangles in the larger extended family making up the multigenerational process. It was at this point that Bowen began describing his effort as being that of a *coach* rather than a therapist to one or more individuals in a family, undertaking the effort to define or differentiate a self in the family of origin and extended family.

Bowen chose the term coach because the focus was no longer mainly on the therapist's staying detriangled from the couple or family. At this time his focus was to coach an individual to go back to his or her family and make an effort to detriangle from various primary and secondary triangles, in the service of differentiating a self. In other words, the term therapist refers to the therapist's management of self in relation to the family members, and the term coach refers to teaching, supervising, and consulting with a family member in his or her detriangling efforts, and other aspects of differentiating a self. He or she implements this effort outside the consultation room, in the context of contact with his or her family. In this book the term therapist is sometimes used synonymously with the term coach. However, the term therapist is used more frequently when referring to work with more than one family member together in the consultation. The term coaching is most often used when referring to the consultation process with one family member.

The focus of coaching is on supervising the self-management of the most motivated family member. At the same time, self-management is still an important dimension in the coach's effort to be effective. The coach provides consultation to the differentiating-one, that individual who is motivated to take responsibility for making changes for self in the context of the family.

Bowen developed two ways of working with triangles in his effort to facilitate the process of differentiation of self. In the first, he worked with the couple, the two most important members of the family. This was based on his understanding of the triangle and his therapeutic effort to detriangle from the couples' effort to triangle him into the fusion of the emotional system. In the first approach, Bowen would replace the symptomatic child. When the couple would attempt to triangle him into the problem, to take sides with one or the other of them, he would listen to each of them, ask thoughtful questions, and stay out of the emotional system, remaining neutral, but in touch with both members of the couple. Bowen believed that if the therapist can relate meaningfully to both family members without getting emotionally caught up in the family system, progress can be made in reducing the emotional fusion between the spouses.

In the second approach, Bowen coached an individual with the idea of working on the differentiation of self in that individual's own family. This was based on Bowen's understanding that a primary triangle is always embedded in interlocking triangles. He would coach a motivated family member to develop a personal relationship with all important living relatives:

> This activates old family relationships grown latent with neglect. Then, with the advantage of objectivity and the knowledge of triangles, the task is to detriangle old family triangles as they come to life. . . . It is easier to "see" self and modify one's self in triangles a bit outside the immediate living situation in the nuclear family. (Bowen, 1978, pp. 317-318)

Principles and Strategies in the Process of Differentiation of Self

In coaching an individual in his or her differentiation of self-effort, there are three other principles, and their applications, besides detriangling self from emotional situations: developing person-to-person contact with all significant living relatives and becoming a better observer and controlling one's own emotional reactiveness. These three processes are interlinked. Each of them affects and is affected by the other two. However, some level of person-to-person contact and the capacity to observe with increased objectivity the part self and others play in the family is necessary in order to attain the capacity for successfully engaging in efforts to detriangle self from emotional situations with significant family members. A relatively differentiated person-to-person relationship with each parent, as opposed to relating to them as an emotional amalgam, will necessitate successful efforts to detriangle from one's parents during emotional situations in which one can be more objective and less reactive than they are. The same process holds true for developing one-to-one relationships with other significant family members.

Detriangling in relation to the clinical family, and coaching the differen-tiating-one, or more than one, to detriangle in his or her family of origin and extended family, is one of the four basic functions of the therapist or coach. The other three are (1) defining and clarifying the relationship between the spouses or between the differentiating-one and his or her family; (2) dem-onstrating differentiation of self or taking I-Positions and coaching one or more family members to take I-Positions; and (3) teaching one or more mem-bers of the family how family emotional systems operate. A short descrip-tion of these three processes will be presented here. For further elaboration of these coaching processes, as part of the larger effort in differentiation, or defining self, the reader should consult Bowen (1978) and Titelman (1998). The processes, principles, and techniques of detriangling in the context of defining a self, or differentiating a self, will be described in the following segment of this section.

Defining and Clarifying the Relationship Between the Spouses

Defining and clarifying the relationship between the spouses is aimed at lowering anxiety, thereby reducing symptoms. Its purpose is to assist the couple in maintaining a structure of communication in which the spouses speak to the therapist instead of directly to each other. The goal is to assist them in thinking about their behaviors and feelings, rather than expressing them. The couple is encouraged to identify the emotional triggers, the nega-tive stimuli, mannerisms, gestures, facial expressions, and tones that evoke negative reactions (see Bowen, 1978, p. 249).

The therapist or coach focuses on process rather than content. He or she elicits a comment from one spouse and then avoids possible triangling by getting the other to respond with his or her thoughts about the other's com-ments. This process sets the stage for differentiation of self. Both members of the couple begin to achieve an awareness of self and other, as well as the differences between them that their previous fusion would not allow. This permits both to be clearer about their own beliefs and principles and to be able to hear those of their spouse, two important aspects of defining self.

In coaching an individual, the differentiating-one, the coach's effort is to facilitate his or her capacity to observe his or her own participation in the family of origin and extended family, in order to understand the emotional process, patterns, and functioning of the family.

Defining an I-Position

The coach's *defining an I-Position* to individuals or families in clinical practice is expressed in terms of defining principle for action in regard to what he or she thinks or believes, and what he or she will or will not do in the therapeutic setting. This in turn stimulates one, or more, of the family members to begin to take I-Positions. The therapist's or coach's I-Positions serve both as a model for differentiated behavior and as a form of detriangling.

Teaching How Family Systems Operate

Teaching how family systems operate is another function of the systems coach or therapist. The goal is to teach clinical family members how emotional systems function and the part they play in the system. Family members can thus modify their reactivity through controlling the part self plays in their relationship problems. Having an intellectual roadmap through which to understand one's family system and one's participation in it is useful. When anxiety is high, teaching is done more indirectly—through I-Positions, parables, or stories that illustrate the successful management of clinical dilemmas undertaken by other families. When family anxiety is lower, teaching can be more didactic and direct.

Principles, Processes, Strategies, and Clinical Issues in Detriangling in the Context of Differentiation of Self

Detriangling is a significant part of the effort to define or differentiate a self in one's own family, the basic goal of Bowen family systems therapy. It is the central activity in the process of differentiation of self, both for the coach who is working with an individual, or couple, for increasing the level of differentiation, and for the client(s) who is making an effort to work on differentiation of self in relation to his or her nuclear family, family of origin, and extended family. The coach, guided by the Bowen theoretical-therapeutic system, seeks to modify the functioning of the central, most important triangle. If this triangle is modified, and the members of that triangle can stay in contact with other members of the family, the entire family system will automatically change (see Bowen, 1978, p. 470). However, in order to modify the central or primary triangle, it is necessary to detriangle from the interlocking triangles found in the nuclear family, family of origin, and extended family—in which the primary triangle is embedded.

The coach or therapist works to detriangle himself or herself in three arenas: (1) making efforts to get outside of the emotional system of his or her own family; (2) making efforts to get outside the client(s) family emotional system; and (3) making efforts to coach the client(s) in detriangling in their differentiation of self-efforts, within their families and nonfamily relationships.

The process of detriangling self from emotional situations in the service of differentiation is interrelated and includes three main components: The first is being in neutral, person-to-person contact with the emotional system by working toward having person-to-person relationships with those members of the family who are involved in the significant triangles in which the individual plays a part. The second process is becoming a better observer and controlling one's own emotional reactiveness. The third process is working to get outside the emotional pull of the family system, by putting the other together with the other and putting self outside of the emotional system. The three processes are circularly interrelated. Without them, detriangling and differentiation of self cannot take place.

An individual cannot detriangle from the significant triangles in his or her family until he or she has become less emotionally reactive to, and a better observer of, self in his or her family, and has developed a modicum of person-to-person contact with significant family members. If one puts the other together with the other and puts self outside the emotional system without being in person-to-person contact, the outcome will be emotional distance, rather than detriangling. In other words, one cannot be distant or cutoff from the emotional system if one is seeking to detriangle from the primary triangle and the interlocking triangles in which the primary triangle is embedded. Person-to-person contact is the ground upon which detriangling can occur. When detriangling is successful, or at least headway is made with it, then a solid, differentiated person-to-person-relationship can begin to form. This is the process of differentiation. Being detriangled means being in an emotional relationship with others, without being emotionally fused with them, or distant or cutoff from them. It means taking an I-Position and maintaining it against the pressure of the others to join or ally with one or the other of their sides, or both sides, yet keeping a relationship with all members of the interlocking triangles of which one is related.

In addition to coaching one or more family members to be in a neutral position, emotional contact with other family members of the significant interlocking triangles while seeking to get outside of the emotional system, Bowen developed strategies to detriangle self from clinical families and the therapist's own family. These included introducing reversal, humor or seriousness, adopting a research attitude, utilizing systems questioning, and utilizing partial mental construct triangles.

It is important to note that Bowen (1980a) did not believe that clinical application of the theory should involve the rigid adoption of techniques. He believed:

> The therapist who has done a reasonable job of differentiating a self in his family of origin can . . . remain emotionally contained, and automatically devise his own techniques for effective reversals [or other clinical strategies]. The poorly differentiated therapist becomes emotionally involved in the family problem, is unable to contain his own emotionality, and he has to rely on "techniques" to get himself out of the situation. (p. 3)

The Use of Reversal and the Use of Humor or Seriousness

If an individual, or more than one family member, is emotionally polarized or stuck on one side of an issue or debate, a reversal is a comment that frees the coach, or the family member who seeks to be in a neutral, detriangled position. It is an attempt to be outside the polarizing, overly close, or distant positions within the reactive, emotional process that generates triangles. Bowen (1980a) describes the reversal in the following way:

> The term "reversal" came from the effort to find an opposite or different posture from that dictated by the family system. The reversal was an effective way for the therapist to defuse the intensity of emotionality in the family, and stay in contact with the family while staying outside the emotionality. (p. 3)

The following is an example of the use of a reversal in a session with a couple. A husband complains about his wife's "bitchy behavior," after work in the evening. The coach's response might be: "What other ways can your wife be effective in bringing you out of your depression?" In asking this question, the coach indicates that he is not allying, or triangling, with the husband. He implies that the wife's behavior has a function in this emotional system. The question also aims to have the husband focus less on his wife's problems, and more on his own responsibility for how he functions individually, and in the marital relationship. The coach's comment reverses the expectation that the family member has that the coach will join them against another family member.

When the individual or family members are being overly serious, the coach may use humor to detriangle. The following is an example of the use of humor to detriangle. A wife says that her mother-in-law is always giving her housekeeping tips and she feels unfairly criticized. The coach responds: "Is it hard for you to appreciate how much your mother-in-law wants you to succeed in providing the perfect home your husband deserves?" Or if the individual or family members being coached are avoiding being serious— in both cases being unable to get perspective—the coach may utilize a comment of a serious nature to stay detriangled, and both reduce the level of anxiety in the family and get outside the anxiety field expressed by the family. An example of such a comment is a coach who hears the family making fun of a distraught family member and says: "Your brother's dilemma, in my view, is not a laughing matter. He is facing a serious challenge, not to be dismissed lightly."

Adopting a Research Attitude

From the time Bowen started his research on schizophrenia and the family at NIMH, he observed that he did better therapy when he could view each clinical family as a research project from which he and the family could learn. The focus of his therapy from that time on was not on fixing the family, but on encouraging each family member, or at least one member of a family, to take a research stance—to become a research observer exploring how his or her family functioned as an emotional system and what part he or she played in that functioning. The clinical effort when both the coach and the client(s) adopt a research stance involves an attitude of always wanting to learn something new about oneself and about the family. It is an attitude that is neutral about what is, rather than what should be. In this attitude one suspends judgment in order to learn about how self and the family function as an emotional unit without getting emotionally drawn into taking sides with one or more family members, or having a stake in a particular outcome of the coaching.

The Use of Systems Questions

Systems questioning avoids cause and effect questions (questions that imply blame, polarization, and value judgments regarding right or wrong behavior—individual rather than systems understanding). Systems questioning keeps the focus on emotional process rather than content.

A detriangling systems question, on the issue of a husband's emotional distancing in response to his wife's request for more closeness might be: "What emotional trigger precedes your moving farther away from your wife?" Or, another example: A wife begins to cry and the coach asks the husband: "When your wife cries, what response does that generate in you?" Through this question the coach avoids being drawn in to supporting or taking sides with either spouse.

Systems questions in clinical work can increase objectivity on the part of both the clinician and the family member(s) by putting the focus on understanding the who, what, when, where, and how in relation to the present situation and the history of the family's functioning. This form of questioning has a detriangling benefit as it avoids attacking, defending, or withdrawing on the part of the coach who asks the question.

Teaching How Emotional Systems Operate: The Use of Partial Mental Construct Triangles

A clinician may use a partial mental construct triangle as a device in detriangling from one or more family members. The coach often teaches one or more family members how family emotional systems operate. Also, teaching about the emotional system serves the function of helping the coach to detriangle from the family. When anxiety is high in the family, Bowen would teach indirectly through the use of parables and stories. An example of this could be, for example, a story about how another couple had dealt with an issue in their marriage. When anxiety is lower and differentiation a bit higher, the teaching may be more direct. The partial construct triangle in this example involves the therapist, the individual or couple being coached, and the teaching process and content as the third leg of the triangle. The coach seeks to stay in the outside position and separate himself or herself from the teaching material. In this way the individual or couple deals more directly with what is being taught without being emotionally overly involved with the coach.

The use of evolutionary biological theory, for example, using vignettes from nonhuman primate behavior, is one way a coach, working from a Bowen theory perspective, seeks to stay detriangled from the family being coached.

The use of Bowen theory as part of a partial mental construct triangle facilitates the coach's effort to stay detriangled from the content that obscures his or her ability to see the family emotional process swirling around him or her. In this process, the coach and the theory occupy the outside position together, and two or more family members occupy the inside positions of the triangle.

The introduction of ideas from Bowen theory with a couple or an individual can facilitate an increase in objective observation and neutral thinking about one's own family process as the ideas are less emotionally loaded than the issues with which the family is dealing. Yet, it clarifies emotional principles that can be extrapolated to apply to the human dance in which the client is involved. In this way, the introduction of systems theory into the coaching can provide another way to facilitate a detriangling effort on the part of an individual being coached.

Clinical Issues and Detriangling

This section presents: (1) detriangling within triangles when one member is absent; (2) detriangling in marital triangles; and (3) detriangling in the primary triangle by accessing secondary triangles through the use of multigenerational triangles.

Detriangling in Triangles with Absent Members

There are a variety of situations in which individuals in the triangle are absent. In these circumstances it is hard for the other two individuals to grasp how the absent member is still an active member of the triangle. In these situations this is another obstacle in the effort to detriangle self from both the other individual who is present, and the one who is not present. The following are examples of triangles with an absent member that the coach or therapist encounters in clinical practice: (1) a single parent or divorced family triangle; (2) the remarried family triangle; (3) the extramarital affair; and (4) a dead person in the context of triangles.

The first example to be presented involves *detriangling in divorced families.* A divorce ends a marriage, but it does not end a family emotional unit. The emotional triangles continue through the children and become interlocking triangles that transmit the multigenerational emotional process of the families in which they occur.

It is not unusual in a divorced family that children are caught in the triangle between their parents. Many clinicians are familiar with scenarios in which one or both parents talk negatively about the other parent to the child. The child may then ally with the parent who is complaining about the other parent or the child may defend the parent who is being attacked by the other parent. The inside positions will vary depending upon the present and historical circumstances, and the history of the child's relationship with both of his or her parents. These shifts in the triangle, with the child and one parent in the inside positions, and the other parent in the outside position, can be difficult, and take their toll. However, an important and more covert triangle is the one in which the two divorced parents have little or no contact with each other, often for long periods of time. There may be an extensive cutoff between the parents with the child being caught up in this process. For example, the child and one parent may become very fused, and the child may also cut off from the parent in the outside position. If a child is seeing both parents, he or she may have split loyalties. In some situations the parents do not speak with or about each other, and the child does not tell either parent about his or her experience of the other parent. This may occur in part because he or she is trying not to get caught in the negativity between the parents, and out of loyalty does not express his or her conflict with either parent to the other. This is not differentiated behavior, but rather emotional distance. If, for example, a child is having difficulty with one parent who has an alcohol problem, the child out of loyalty to that parent may not mention it to the other parent, even if he or she is the custodial parent. However, the child keeping this secret may become more conflictual with the custodial parent, and it will be very difficult for that parent to recognize how alive the mother-father-child triangle is because the parents are cutoff from each other. The basic effort the coach makes in working with one divorced or single parent is to provide a helping hand to the client to see the invisible triangle—to understand how triangles operate, and to work on bridging the cutoff with the divorced spouse. It is a rule of thumb that, in order for the divorced parent to have a less conflictual or distant relation with the child, it will be necessary for the client to deal with the emotional cutoff from his or her former spouse.

Often the divorced parent thinks that by divorcing, he or she is "home free," with the possibility of better relations with his or her children, and perhaps providing better relationships in a remarried family constellation. This leads to disillusionment when the opposite takes place. The parental triangle never disappears, although it may become hidden. A parent may experience the problem either in self or in the child, or within their dyadic relationship. It may be felt to be outside of the impact of the divorced parent who has "disappeared." Of course this turns out to be untrue. When the clinician can coach one divorced spouse to begin to move toward contact with the other, taking responsibility for his or her part of the problem in their communication and relationship, positive things can happen in his or her relationship with the child who is perceived, and may really be, difficult.

The child may temporarily become angry that his or her parents are in better contact and may be talking together about him or her as a parental dyad, putting the child in the outside position. The child may feel deprived of temporary gains achieved by playing the parents off against each other for certain strategic reasons. Or the child may feel that the parents have forfeited their rights to be a parental unit because of their history of bad behavior toward each other. However, if the effort to detriangle in the divorced family through bridging the cutoff with one's former spouse is sustained—often in the face of roadblocks put up by both the ex-spouse and the child—it will most likely bear fruit in both the relationships between each parent and the child, and between the divorced spouses, and in future generations.

The second example is *detriangling in remarried families.* Triangles abound in remarried families, but the one discussed here involves the relationship between the divorced spouses and the new spouses. In many cases when there is a remarriage the divorced spouse and the new spouse are at odds. The remarried ex-spouse is in an inside position with his or her new spouse occupying the other inside position, and they are both in conflict with the ex-spouse who is in the outside position. One example of a fruitful way to modify this triangle, to detriangle within it, is for the clinician to coach the client to utilize the "back-door" triangle (Moynihan-Bradt, 1984). This phrase refers to the divorced wife, for example, developing a working relationship with the new wife regarding the issues involving the children. This can be a bridge to beginning better communication between the two ex-spouses.

The third example is *detriangling in the context of the invisible member in extramarital affair triangles.* The triangle in an extramarital affair involves a nonmarried individual occupying an inside position with one spouse occupying the other inside position, and the other spouse occupying the outside position. Although the nonmarried individual occupies an inside position in the triangle, he or she is often *unseen* or *invisible* to the spouse occupying the outside position. When this occurs, the outsider may suspect the existence of an affair, but may have no acknowledgement or concrete evidence of its existence. However, its presence impacts the balance of closeness/distance in the marriage. It goes without saying that the secrecy, or denial, that takes place within an extramarital affair often makes the triangle very rigid, and provides a severe obstruction to modifying it, particularly if the spouse in the outside position is the one seeking to modify his or her position. The clinician may coach the client who is the outsider to work on being less reactive to his or her spouse, and to observe and work on the part she or he plays in creating an imbalance in the marital relationship: too much distance (response to fusion) or too much closeness (fusion).

One difficult but useful move the spouse in the outside position of an affair can seek, with coaching from a clinician—if he or she can control emotional reactivity—is to seek out the individual who is having an affair with his or her spouse, and develop nonreactive, nonconflictual contact. Contact by the spouse in the outside position with the outside party, will automatically shift the triangle in the direction of less closeness between the spouse and third party having the affair. The caveat for this intervention is that the coach should not propose it if the client's level of differentiation is relatively low and the levels of acute and/or chronic anxiety are high. This detriangling effort is more likely to be useful when the individual initiating it can be neutral about whether his or her marriage can be resuscitated.

Another variation on the absent member theme that occurs in an extramarital affair triangle is the presence of a partial mental construct triangle. The reader will remember that an emotional triangle consists of three living individuals. A partial mental construct triangle consists of two living individuals and a fantasy, idea, religion, alcohol, or a dead person, among other nonliving entities. The partial mental construct triangle in this context would involve one spouse experiencing fantasies involving being emotionally close, sexually or otherwise, with another person. In this type of triangle the spouse having the fantasies is in the inside position with the fantasized other, and the other spouse is in the outside position. However, whether this partial mental construct triangle stabilizes or destabilizes the marital relationship, depends on the specificity of the closeness/distance balance of the particular couple involved. In some cases this triangle might continue to increase distance in the marital couple and increase marital difficulties, particularly if the spouse who is fantasizing about a nonspouse becomes extremely distant from his or her spouse and the other spouse is feeling too distant and lacking in adequate closeness with his or her spouse. In another couple the presence of a fantasized other may stabilize the marital relationship insofar as it may energize, in the short run, the spouse who is having the fantasized affair, who then brings that increased sexual arousal back into his or her relationship with his or her spouse, thereby enhancing the satisfaction of the marital pair.

The clinician, while meeting with the couple together, may suspect that the distance between two spouses comes from anxiety in one or both spouses but cannot get a handle on what it is about. The coach may decide to meet individually with each spouse to get a clearer view of the unseen factors that are impeding the marital relationship and creating unseen triangles. Such individual meetings may lead to the discovery of a triangle in which the third member is a fantasy-other. Most likely that fantasy-other is both generated and sustained by anxiety related to the imbalance of closeness/distance found in both the spouse who is experiencing fantasies about another person, and the spouse who is not. The clinician has many options including exploring the link between the current fantasies and those that the spouse may have experienced in previous relationships, as well as the characteristics of the primary triangle and possible extramarital triangles that may have existed in the families of origin. Other issues involving anxiety related to sexual identity, work, and physical health may be important factors for the clinician to explore. Other partial, mental construct triangles, seen or unseen, may involve work, hobbies, and religion. They too may be serving to stabilize or destabilize marital relationships.

The fourth example is *the place of a dead family member in the context of triangle and detriangling*. Earlier in the section on what constitutes a triangle (see pp. 24-28), a dead member was described as not being part of an emotional triangle, insofar as an emotional triangle involves three living individuals with each one able to, at least potentially, react and act in response to the other two individuals. A dead person can be part of a partial mental construct triangle as described earlier in the chapter (see pp. 25-26). Detriangling may involve a dead person through a process whereby the coach directs a family member to work on *old triangles, new players,* by working on the interlock between a partial mental construct triangle and a current, emotional secondary triangle.

For example, a woman had a distant and conflictual relationship with her father, a warm and fused relationship with her mother, and her parents had a distant and conflictual relationship with each other. In that triangle the woman and her mother occupied the inside positions and the father occupied the outside position. Then the father died, the woman married, and a secondary, interlocking triangle emerged consisting of a conflictual, distant relationship between the woman and her husband, a warm, close relationship between the woman and her mother, and a conflictual relationship between the woman's husband and her mother. A coach could help the client, the woman, to explore the primary triangle that existed when her father was alive, and to see how her current position in the current triangle with her husband and her mother repeats the same pattern as that which existed in the primary triangle. Her husband is in a similar functioning position in the current triangle as her father had been in the primary triangle when he was alive. The opportunity to compare the historical triangle with the living one leads to a clearer view of both the original triangle and the current one. The client becomes less emotionally reactive and less polarized about the primary triangle, and the positions she, her mother, and father took in maintaining it. This newly gained objectivity about past emotional process can help the woman to detriangle in the present triangle of self-husband-mother.

Detriangling in Marital Triangles

As discussed in the section on the basic principles of detriangling, Bowen moved from working with parents and children together, to meeting with the two parents/spouses. He removed the triangled child and substituted himself as the third member of the triangle. The difference of course was that he was neutral and objective, and acting from a differentiated outside position. This effort was guided by the idea that the couple would be encouraged to work on differentiation of self without having recourse to triangling in one or more of their offspring.

The following is an example of detriangling through the substitution of the therapist/coach for the triangled child or other individual. The therapist's effort is directed at modifying the marital fusion that goes through cycles with the balance of closeness and distance becoming uncomfortable for one or both of the partners, expressed as distance or conflict, or a cycling of both distance and conflict. After a period of conflict, at some point one spouse may distance from the other by triangling in another individual: a friend or lover. Now the individual in the affair and his or her partner are in the comfortable inside positions and the other spouse is in the uncomfortable outside position. This triangle does not involve a "bad guy" who has an affair, and a "good guy" who is the victim. In order to coach the detriangling effort in this situation, the clinician must be able to see that a reciprocal process is in place that leads to a level of discomfort in the balance of closeness/distance in the marital relationship. The therapist/coach, if he or she is detriangled from the couple, sees that their dilemma unfolded in the context of certain nodal events or stressors, a certain degree of acute and chronic anxiety, and a certain degree of undifferentiation. These factors can destabilize or stabilize this emotional system. Of course the extramarital affair is not a triangle unto itself, but rather it is interlocked with triangles involving each spouse's relationships in their nuclear family, their families of origin, and their extended families. Likewise the outside party in the affair is also involved in a myriad of triangles in his or her nuclear family, family of origin, and extended family. All of these triangles interlock and meet in the situation of the affair.

The clinician has many options based on his or her multigenerational assessment of the family, as presented either by one spouse or the couple. Detriangling, in the context of differentiation of self, in this case an extramarital affair, can involve providing a neutral setting in which the couple can explore the issues that have unbalanced the closeness/distance balance. If the coach does not have an allergic reaction to the spouse who is having an affair, and is not overly sympathetic toward the spouse who has been "cheated on," then the possibilities for detriangling are vastly improved. At least the clinician will not get triangled by the issue of the affair, through being pulled into an inside position with the "betrayed" spouse. The latter scenario could be a factor in driving the spouse in the outside position even closer to his or her lover. Or he or she might be overtly, or covertly, wanting to "drop off" his or her spouse with the therapist, hoping that he or she may thus feel less guilt in continuing the affair or leaving the marriage through divorce. The reactivity in the family and in the clinician are both significant factors that can undermine the success of a detriangling effort.

Detriangling in the Primary Triangle by Accessing Secondary Triangles: The Use of Multigenerational Triangles

In this chapter primary and secondary triangles have been described as follows: a primary triangle involves the child and parents. A secondary triangle is a triangle in which at least one position is occupied by an individual who is not a member of the primary triangle, in other words it could be a sibling, grandparent, uncle, aunt, or nonfamily member.

The following is an example of accessing the primary triangle through a secondary triangle. A coach may suggest that an individual, an older son with a younger brother, who is having difficulty getting closer and less conflictual with his father, and less fused in his relationship to his mother, seeks to develop a relationship with one of the father's siblings, for example his older brother. The latter may either have an easy or more difficult relationship with the individual's father, but in either case he is part of a secondary triangle with the individual and the father by virtue of the fact that he is both the uncle to the individual and a brother to the individual's father. In the course of getting to know the uncle better and getting to understand more about his father as a younger brother to an older brother, the client may become less reactive to his father. He will get a better picture of some of the key issues and relationship patterns that occurred in the father's family of origin, including his relationship with his parents (the individual's grandparents). A more objective view of the father usually leads to a decrease in emotional reactivity. This will predictably make the client's access to his father easier, and thus enhance his efforts to develop a one-to-one relationship with him within the context of the interlocking triangles of mother-father-self, uncle-father-self, father-grandfather-grandmother, as well as the interlocking triangles of father, uncle, grandmother, and grandfather. Undoubtedly, this individual working on differentiation of self in part through detriangling, will benefit from working in the same way with members of his or her maternal extended family. This is so because the primary triangle is always embedded in interlocking triangles through which the emotional process, the lifeblood of the family, flows and is transmitted in a multigenerational process.

The following is a second example of detriangling using a multigenerational triangle. A mother is involved in a conflictually fused relationship with a ten-year-old daughter who is expressing defiance, and other behavior problems. The coach may suggest that the mother explore her relationship with her own mother. (Of course the mother-daughter dyad is part of the primary triangle of mother-father-child, but for purposes of this vignette that triangle and its interlock with the grandmother-mother-daughter will not be discussed. However, the coach undoubtedly will also be interested in that interlocking triangle.) The relationship between the client and her mother may have been quite similar to that of the present mother-daughter relationship. In this effort, the multigenerational triangle of grandmother-mother-child is engaged. It can be valuable for the mother to revisit her relationship with her mother with its positives and negatives. At this point the mother may be less reactive to her mother than she is to her daughter. By engaging with her mother she may, with the use of coaching, be open to input as to how to deal with the problems she is having with her daughter. The grandmother can become a resource for her daughter regarding mothering, based on the degree to which the mother is able to manage her reactivity with her mother, and gain a more balanced view of her—a view of her mother as having tried to provide the best mothering of which she was capable, with both her weaknesses and strengths. This effort with her own mother, which is part of the secondary triangle—grandmother, mother, and daughter—can play an important part in the modification of the mother-daughter relationship. How that impacts the primary triangle of mother-daughter-father is important, but is not discussed here.

The applications of detriangling in the arenas of the therapist's own family, clinical practice, organizations, and society are elaborated in other chapters of this book.

Summary

This section examined the following factors in the process and application of detriangling: (1) the attitude of neutrality that allows an individual to undertake detriangling efforts; (2) the evolution of Bowen's clinical approach, from detriangling in the nuclear family and the couple to detriangling in the family of origin and extended family, with the additional understanding of interlocking triangles; (3) principles and strategies in the process of differentiation, and the context for detriangling; and (4) principles, processes, strategies (the use of reversal, humor or seriousness, systems questions, adopting a research attitude, teaching how emotional systems operate; the use of partial mental construct triangles) and clinical issues in detriangling (including examples of detriangling in triangles when one member is absent;

detriangling in the marital triangle; and detriangling in the primary triangle by accessing multigenerational triangles).

SUMMARY

In this chapter the author has provided a historical and theoretical overview of the concept of the emotional triangle in Bowen family systems theory. The chapter began by tracing Bowen's movement from psychoanalytic to systems theory: from the individual, to the dyad, to the triangle. This was followed by an examination of the concept of triangles in the context of Bowen theory. Then the relationship between the concept of the triangle and other concepts in Bowen theory was presented. Finally, the process and application of detriangling was explored.

REFERENCES

Aronson, G. (2002). Personal communicaiton. E-mail. December 1, 2002.

Bertalanfy, L. V. (1975). *Perspectives on general systems theory: Scientific-philosophical studies.* New York: G. Brailler.

Bowen, M. (1954). Project paper. Murray Bowen Papers, History of Medicine Division, National Library of Medicine, Bethesda, MD.

Bowen, M. (1956). "Discussion of Dr. Harold Searles' paper, 'The Effort to Drive the Other Person Crazy,'" Murray Bowen Papers, History of Medicine Division, National Library of Medicine, Bethesda, MD.

Bowen, M. (1958). Personal Correspondence Letter to Gerald Aronson, MD, Murray Bowen Papers, History of Medicine Division, National Library of Medicine, Bethesda, MD.

Bowen, M. (1978). *Family therapy in clinical practice.* Lanham, Maryland: Jason Aronson, Inc.

Bowen, M. (1978). File, family psychotherapy in families with a schizophrenic member, p. 9. Murray Bowen Papers, History of Medicine Division, National Library of Medicine, Bethesda, MD. Excerpts reprinted by permission.

Bowen, M. (1980a). Clinical Addendum. Department of Psychiatry, Georgetown University School of Medicine. *The Family Center Report,* 2(2), 1-3.

Bowen, M. (1980b). *Defining a self in one's family of origin—Part I.* Videotape Produced by the Georgetown Family Center, Washington, DC.

Bowen, M. (1995). A psychological formulation of schizophrenia. *Family Systems: A Journal of Natural Systems Thinking in Psychiatry and the Sciences,* 4(1), 5-18. Permission to quote granted by the Georgetown Family Center, Washington, DC.

Bown, J. (2006). Personal communication. E-mail. Reprinted by permission.

de Waal, F. and Embree, M. (1997). The triadic nature of primate social relationships. *Family Systems: A Journal of Natural Systems Thinking in Psychiatry and the Sciences, 4*(1), 5-18.

Fogarty, T. (1975). Triangles. *The Family, 2,* 11-20.

Fromm-Reichman, F. (1950). *Principles of intensive psychotherapy.* Chicago: Chicago University Press.

Guerin, P., Fogarty, T.F., Fay, L.F., and Kautto, J.G. (1997). *Working with relationship triangles: The one-two-three of psychotherapy.* New York: The Guilford Press.

Kerr, M.E. (2005). Personal communication. E-mail. February 15, 2005. Reprinted by permission.

Kerr, M. and Bowen, M. (1988). *Family evaluation: An approach based on Bowen theory.* New York: W.W. Norton & Company.

Menninger, K. (1991). Letter from Karl Menninger. *AFTA (American Family Therapy Association) Newsletter, 44,* Summer. Excerpt reprinted by permission.

Moynihan-Bradt, C. (1984). *Old triangles, new players.* Linda Bates Memorial Lecture, Leeds Veterans Administration Hospital. Leeds, MA.

Papero, D. (1990). *Bowen family systems theory.* Boston: Allyn and Bacon.

Rakow, C. (2001). Oral introduction. Seminar on Dr. Murray Bowen's NIMH research with visiting guest, Warren Brodey, MD, and Betty Basmania, MSW. Western Pennsylvania Family Center, Pittsburgh, PA, August 28, 2001.

Rakow, C. (2004). *Contributions to Bowen family systems theory from the NIMH project.* The Importance of Research for Family Theory and Therapy, Conference Sponsored by the North Shore Counseling Centre, Vancouver, Canada, March 5, 2004, 1-16. Excerpts reprinted by permission.

Searles, H. (1965). The effort to drive the other person crazy: An element in the aetiology and psychotherapy of schizophrenia. In H. Searles (Ed.), *Collected papers on schizophrenia and related subjects* (pp. 254-283). New York: International Universities Press.

Simon, R. (1979). Part II—Adventures in "The Great Democracy": An interview with Murray Bowen. *The Family Networker, III*(5), November-December, 1-7. Excerpts reprinted by permission.

Smith, W. (2003). Emotional cutoff and family stability: Child abuse in family emotional process. In P. Titelman (Ed.), *Emotional cutoff: Bowen family systems theory perspectives.* Binghamton, NY: The Haworth Press.

Sykes-Wylie, M. (1991). Family therapy's neglected prophet. *The Family Therapy Networker,* March/April, 25-37, 77.

Titelman, P. (Ed.). (1998). *Clinical applications of Bowen family systems theory.* Binghamton, NY: The Haworth Press.

Titelman, P. (Ed.). (2003). *Emotional cutoff: Bowen family systems perspectives.* Binghamton, NY: The Haworth Press.

Toman, W. (1969). *Family constellation* (2nd ed.). New York: Springer Publishing Company, Inc.

Chapter 2

The Regulatory Function of the Triangle

Laurie L. Lassiter

INTRODUCTION

This chapter describes the regulatory function of the triangle at the level of the emotional system. Complex regulatory mechanisms are being discovered at the most basic levels of life. What was once known as *junk* DNA, for example, has been found to perform essential regulatory functions for the genome (Siepel et al., 2005). Are there unknown regulatory mechanisms involved in the guidance of individual organisms by their reproductive/social systems? Is it possible that people have little or no awareness of systematic processes that guide their behavior? If, as Bowen (1978) believed, there are orderly processes at the family and social group level to guide individuals, what are those processes?

The *regulatory-function-of-the-triangle hypothesis* proposes that the triangle is a *systematic, hidden* means by which the emotional system controls individuals. Although the hypothesis offers an explanation for how individuals within an emotional system are governed by the system, it examines only one means of this control, the two-against-one triangle, and does not dispute that there may be other ways the emotional system maintains governance over its members. Based on observations of behavior in human beings and other social species, the hypothesis is a step toward further observations and future scientific experiments that may support it, refine it, or refute it.

The term *triangle*, retained in the name of the hypothesis for its accuracy in describing the two-against-one process that this hypothesis describes, also serves as an acknowledgment that the root of the hypothesis is in Bowen theory, without which none of this further thinking about the triangle would be possible. Indeed, each return to Bowen's writings and taped talks has been accompanied by a sense that he has already covered the territory and is waiting there for others to catch up. Bowen was adept at holding a large amount of complex detail in his mind at any time, and seems to have maintained and promoted a posture of open questioning throughout his life, knowing more than he said.

Bowen's view of the triangle as coercive shows up, implicitly, in an early article, "Treatment of Family Groups with a Schizophrenic Member," originally published in 1957 (see Bowen, 1978, pp. 3-15). Though he does not use the term *triangle,* he had been thinking toward the concept of the triangle theoretically since 1956, a year before the article was written. Presented in March 1957 in a paper at the Annual Meeting of the American Orthopsychiatric Association, this first chapter is an early description of two-against-one. He describes a daughter with schizophrenia whose mother attempts to force her to give in to the emotional system by urging other family members to view the daughter as "sick," and then urging the staff on the psychiatric unit at Bowen's National Institute of Mental Health (NIMH) research study to do the same. This early description shows how the triangle functions to control, and that though two-against-one may be its minimal configuration, the triangle is not limited to that; but, through a system of interlocking triangles, may become many-against-one, as in Bowen's example.

The regulatory-function-of-the-triangle hypothesis explores this one aspect of the triangle—as a means of control, or regulation—and develops it as a complete idea in itself. It explains how individuals in social species may be forced to function in ways that threaten their own well-being in order to contribute to the survival and reproductive success of the emotional system. In fostering the greatest likelihood of overall survival and reproductive success, social species have evolved through an emotional system that exerts pressure on its members, especially on some members, to be something other than what they are as individual organisms, especially during times of threat. Each is under pressure, though to different degrees, from the emotional system, and, at the same time, each individual contributes to the pressure on others to function as components of the system.

The triangle, as a two-or-more-against-one process, is the bottom line of emotional pressure. Though an individual may or may not be able to stand her ground with her mother, for instance, she faces a different level of challenge when her mother complains about her to father, siblings, aunts and uncles, grandparents, and perhaps to her husband, children, and even her employer! In Bowen's example, the mother of the daughter with schizophrenia attempts to enlist her daughter's psychiatrist and nurses—to surround her with people who agree with each other about her. The automatic reaction of the daughter, of course, is to retaliate by going to people with complaints about her mother.

Although the continually shifting configurations of two-against-one can be viewed at the level of the people involved, as each individual seeks a comfortable position in relation to the others and uses the triangle to exert pressure on others, on a broader level it is a regulatory process that insures the survival of the emotional system by regulating its component entities, whether cells or organisms.

Evidence for the regulatory-function-of-the-triangle hypothesis includes (1) a study of the biology literature describing social species; and (2) documentation of the progress and difficulties encountered when individuals are coached to raise differentiation-of-self levels in the family of origin, that is, to increase self-regulation versus regulation by the emotional system. Hidden triangle threats become active in what Bowen referred to as *change-back messages* when a person takes steps to self-direct. As the emotional system reacts to regain control of the individual making the attempt, the triangle threat of others taking sides against the individual—and *invitations* to the individual to join the emotional process—become exaggerated, and therefore visible.

Throughout this paper, the triangle is described as an automatic, instinctive process based on *coercion, deception,* and *exploitation.* The use of these terms has been carefully considered over time. Taken from animal behavior literature, they in no way imply moral judgment; they are used entirely descriptively. In addition, the triangle is a systems concept that does not include individual culpability. At the same time, those willing to observe and take responsibility for their part in these automatic behaviors can reduce their participation in them and increase their emotional flexibility, as well as contribute to conditions that make it possible for others to observe and change. That these covert behaviors can be brought into awareness to a degree makes it possible to use knowledge of the triangle to increase *differentiation-of-self* through a process that will be described later in the chapter.

The triangle is distinguished here from the person-to-person, or *one-to-one* relationship. Connection to others without emotional dependency, emotional pressure, or using others as allies in triangle activity is held as possible, within limits. Bowen introduced the person-to-person, *one-to-one,* relationship as that relationship of one person to another person that is not governed by the automatic reactions of the triangle. The one-to-one relationship— as opposed to two-to-one, or two-or-more-to-one—in its essence is hypothetical, in that it is unlikely that any person has entirely achieved it.

Though one may argue that no relationship is free from the pressures of the triangle—pressures that would be difficult to rule out entirely because they occur largely outside of awareness—the theoretical distinction is worth making. Bowen (1978) maintained the idea of the one-to-one relationship as that relationship theoretically not governed by the triangle.

THE TRIANGLE IN OTHER SPECIES

Bowen's (1978) study of human reproductive units in the 1950s was made up of parents and grown offspring living together on a psychiatric ward for up to a year or more at a time. Equivalent to a biological field study, the twenty-four-hour daily documented research led to observations that can generalize to the conclusion that social/reproductive systems regulate the individuals that make them up, through a network of interlocking triangles. Bringing to light the phenomenon called the *triangle* made it possible to see a previously unknown world of interactions, based on the coercion and deception characteristic of emotional pressure. As these processes are hidden from view and automatic—occurring for the most part without the awareness of those involved in them—a theory that can describe them was necessary in order to begin to see them.

No comprehensive theory describing the regulation of the individual by the social group has come out of biology, though eclectic reports from the life sciences suggest parallels of regulation of the individual by the social group in other social species, from bacteria to baboons (Ben-Jacob, 2004; Sapolsky, Alberts, and Altmann, 1997). The life sciences lack a theoretical approach to integrating these facts. Bowen adds something new to the study of life: the idea of an *emotional system (emotional* in the sense that Darwin used it, meaning *instinctual)* that regulates individual organisms; and a singular use of a term borrowed from embryology, *differentiation*.

In biology, the term *differentiation* refers to developmental processes by which simple, apparently homogeneous cells, tissues, or structures may specialize into complex, mature form and function. Identical cells within a multicellular organism may differentiate or specialize into cells involved in vision, or into cells involved in breathing, though the cells start out genetically the same. Some biologists would see a related process in animal development whereby individual social insects, such as ants or bees, differentiate, or specialize—structurally as well as functionally—into adult form and function, organized at the level of the group (Gordon, 1999).

Bowen introduced a new idea to biological concepts of differentiation: individual organisms or individual cells can be *more* or *less* differentiated.

Differentiation, or *differentiation-of-self,* in Bowen theory is the degree to which an individual in a social species is free to function effectively for survival and reproduction as an integrated individual and a part of the whole, managing its relationship to the larger unit, neither isolated from it, nor merged with it as an undifferentiated component. *Undifferentiated* has to do with the degree to which an individual functions—and is produced by the system to function—as a component of the system, and is therefore impaired as an individual. Biologists have not adequately explained variations in functioning based on something different from genetic differences or random developmental accidents in the individual. When one can observe how a reproductive/social group functions as a unit, systematically regulating the individuals that comprise it, with more constraints on some than on others, Bowen's idea of more or less differentiated individuals begins to make sense.

A *reproductive unit,* defined here as a social system of genetically related as well as unrelated members, which produces organisms that mature and can reproduce, may also produce a percentage of immature, undifferentiated organisms that function for the reproductive unit as a whole. A *social system* is defined as a unit made up of interacting organisms that are capable of regulating self to a degree, as well as capable of being regulated to a degree by the larger unit of which they are a part. In the biological literature, an individual's reproductive group may overlap with his or her social group, as in Homo sapiens during most of its evolutionary history. The terms *unit, system, emotional system,* or *group* are interchangeable here; the assumption is that any cohesive, interdependent group functions as a system, having the same fundamental characteristics as other living systems.

Bowen (1978) suggested that the triangle is so basic that it probably exists in the reproductive/social units of other species as well. Can the emotional system, with the triangle as its basic building block, and *differentiation-of-self* be understood as one unified phenomenon that occurs across species? Can the concepts be modified to be broad enough to be applied to the reproductive/social group regulation of individuals in social species in general? Applying Bowen theory to other species boils it down to a theory of how reproductive and other social groups regulate the individuals that comprise them in order to maximize the likelihood of survival and reproductive success of the group. Social groups regulate individuals that live, to differing degrees, as parts of those larger units.

If the emotional system guides, or regulates, the individual, "how" does it do so? The triangle is understood here to be a specific mechanism, in the sense of a *means* or a *method,* for the regulation of an individual within, in this case, the *human* emotional system—a "how" of that emotional guidance system. Biologists have used the term *mechanism* to refer to a fundamental process involved in or responsible for an action, reaction, or other natural phenomenon—the "how" of a life process. The use of the term *mechanism* here is meant to emphasize the specificity and consistency of the function of the triangle and does not imply living things are like machines, that life processes are mechanically determined, or that life processes can be fully explained by laws of physics and chemistry. It refers to the "how" of a life process—how the organized system exerts control over the individual.

Every emotional system, regardless of the particular life form, is assumed to have regulatory mechanisms. What is equivalent to the triangle in other species would be that mechanism, or those mechanisms, that form the "how" of the guidance function of the emotional system. The triangle as a specific and identifiable mechanism in human reproductive and social systems has *three* positions: *two*-against-*one* (often *two-or-more*-against-*one*). As a broadly identifiable phenomenon across species, however, it is not necessarily a three-position process. While two-against-one processes can be identified in other species, notably in dolphins (Connor et al., 2000) and in at least some nonhuman primates (De Waal, 1982), regulatory mechanisms that may not be made up of threes but are equivalent in function to the triangle are assumed to occur in all social species.

The question in looking at the cellular slime mold, for instance, is not: Where are three cells, or three organisms, in association? The question is instead: What guides the individual by the social and reproductive unit? What is the mechanism that makes it possible for independently living organisms to stream together to form a single, unified structure, guided in positions and behavior defined by the larger unit rather than by the individual organisms?

In the cellular slime mold, the reactivity of the individual amoebae to the pheromone, or social hormone, cyclic adenosine monophosphate (cAMP), excreted by each individual, makes it possible for the system to control the individual. Even when genetically identical, individuals develop with varying degrees of reactivity to the pheromone. Those with the greatest reactivity to the pheromone are the same individuals who excrete the largest amount of it into the system. The greater the intensity of reactivity to the pheromone, the more likely the individual is to move into position to become part of the dead stalk that will support others that move into position to become the reproductive body of the multicellular structure, forming future generations. The individuals in the pre-spore position of the structure move in a deliberate, orderly manner, while the movement of those in the pre-stalk position is characterized as chaotic and hyperactive, with a greater number of the pheromone receptors on their surface. Once the individuals are in the pre-stalk region, they are stimulated to release more cAMP into their surroundings (Bonner, 1998).

Individual amoebae that develop the greatest reactivity to the social hormone resemble human beings who develop the greatest reactivity to social cues, in that their fate is to function as components of the system in ways that may undermine their own well-being and successful reproduction. Is there a common principle at work? Can the triangle be identified in the cellular slime mold?

Whatever mechanisms in the cellular slime mold determine that some individuals will become the dead stalk, while others will become the living spores, they do not seem to involve a three-position process that regulates the functioning of individuals. For this reason, although the word triangle contributes some precision in describing the specific human mechanism, it is an inadequate word for the concept of mechanisms across species that regulate the individual to function as a part of the emotional system. The triangle is rather one example of a broad category of regulatory mechanisms. The assumption that all social species have such regulatory mechanisms, accompanied by a search for them, may open a door to biological research into the nature of the individual organism in its life within a system, and how a system exerts control over individuals—especially some individuals.

THE UNDIFFERENTIATED

Reproductive units across species, from bacteria (Ben-Jacob and Cohen, 1997), to cellular slime molds (Bonner, 1998), to human beings, appear to function in fundamentally similar ways. They produce some relatively mature, differentiated organisms. However, there is evidence that they also produce some immature, relatively undifferentiated organisms that may fulfill a function for the reproductive unit as a whole. In general, the less differentiated organisms have the genetic resources to become differentiated adults, but through development, during periods of particular vulnerability to the constraints imposed by the system, their lives take a different course, based on the needs of the reproductive/social unit. In the cellular slime mold, although the individuals may be genetically identical, some will form the dead stalk supporting other individuals that develop into the new spores that continue into the future generation. Undifferentiated *Escherichia coli* bacterial cells, produced by the colony to function for it, form the edges of the colony to protect the more centrally located reproducing bacteria (Shapiro, 1997). In animals, plants, and other multicellular organisms, many individual cells die in programmed cell death as part of a predictable process of development that leads to the survival of the organism. How individual organisms can also function like cells in multicellular units is being studied in bacteria (Shapiro and Martin, 1997).

One implication of Bowen theory is that human beings, governed by the same basic forces of reproduction and development as other organisms, may also produce immature, less differentiated individuals to function for the system. Why does one child develop greater sensitivity to emotional pressure, drawing emotional reactivity from family members? Does *coordinated* anxiety about a child's illness, or *coordinated* anger at a child's rebelliousness, lead to an increase in the illness or misbehavior? Do family members unknowingly participate in automatic emotional processes that harm one or more of their members? If the lack of differentiation in the family is focused systematically on one child, does that free other children in the sibling group to grow and develop? Are the undifferentiated unknowingly produced and exploited by the family, making increased differentiation in others possible, securing for those others a greater likelihood of survival and reproduction?

Everyone is vulnerable to function as a component of the emotional system, depending on (1) level of differentiation-of-self, and (2) degree of perceived threat to the system. To the degree that living as a component of the system takes precedence in a life history, individual functioning tends to be impaired. The undifferentiated, as components of the system, are available to absorb a disproportionate share of the effects of stress on the system. While freeing others to develop into mature, integrated individuals, the undifferentiated are left behind, immature and impaired.

The least differentiated are more likely, all things being equal, to develop the most severe symptoms, including violence to others, violence to self, drug and alcohol addiction, mental or emotional illness, and physical illness. The development of symptoms may generally be a side effect of the organism's impairment as an individual, as it functions as an element in the larger system. Functioning to promote the greater likelihood of survival and reproduction of the group may be accompanied by a lesser likelihood of individual survival and successful reproduction. In some cases, the development of symptoms may facilitate the system more fully making use of that individual, as the symptoms impair the individual's ability to function independently, leaving her vulnerable to increased exploitation by the system.

Individuals at lower differentiation-of-self levels are programmed to take things personally, to be preoccupied with how others feel about them, to be more sensitive to rejection, and to be more emotionally reactive. It is the individual's sensitivity to emotional pressure that allows for greater control of the individual by the system. The lower the differentiation-of-self, the more the individual life course is determined by pressures from the family or social environment. These individuals are not only the recipients of more than their share of emotional pressure from others but also exert more emotional pressure. They are disproportionately involved in carrying out the regulatory triangle processes that may contribute to survival for the system as a whole but also lead to the relatively impaired functioning of self and some others.

At low differentiation-of-self levels, individuals, vulnerable to emotional pressure (having been produced in part to be governed by emotional pressure), also use emotional pressure to get what they want. Though largely unaware of it, they are pressured with regard to what to think, what to feel, and how to act, and they pressure others with regard to what to think, what to feel, and how to act. Some restrict their family and social interactions and may live almost like hermits to get away from the intense emotional pressure that surrounds them whenever they are around others, especially significant others. Yet, when they cut off from the emotional system, they tend to have increased difficulty, as they have been programmed to function as part of the emotional system and are unable to guide themselves independently. Dependent on the emotional system to guide self, if they cut off from one social system, they predictably become involved in an intense new relationship, seeking a new social system for guidance in order to be able to function.

While the interpersonal characteristics of the extremely undifferentiated make the phenomenon more obvious, Bowen's differentiation-of-self scale suggests that a lack of differentiation, lying on a broad continuum of variation, is characteristic of the human condition; the difference between people is one only of degree. Variation in level of differentiation-of-self—the degree to which an individual lives as a component of the emotional system— explains the observable extreme variation in human functioning.

A BROADER VIEW OF THE TRIANGLE'S FUNCTION

The regulatory-function-of-the-triangle hypothesis, while based on Bowen's theory of automatic behavior, sets itself apart by examining more fully how the triangle is involved in the development and ongoing exploitation of the undifferentiated, which to a degree describes all of us. The function of the triangle to control the individual—the use of force to pressure the individual to give in to *functioning for* and *being exploited by* the emotional system—is a secondary theme implicit rather than explicit in Bowen's explanation. Bowen (1978) observes how a parent "covertly does things to block the child's development" (p. 4), or can be observed "to force the anxiety or psychosis onto a resisting, fighting, victimized, reluctant patient" (p. 7). Yet in his descriptions of the triangle, he did not develop the idea that the triangle functions to force the individual to be used by the system. He devoted his time instead to describing the minute shifts in what he referred to as the two inside positions and one outside position of the triangle.

First, note that Bowen used the term *outside position* in two different ways, and it is important to distinguish between them. Bowen's description of individuals seeking an inside position of the triangle during periods of relative calm, as well as seeking the outside position during periods of stress, was of a constantly shifting process of emotionally reactive position-taking. Yet Bowen also referred to taking the *outside position* as acting outside of the control of the automatic pressures of the emotional system. For the sake of clarity in this discussion of Bowen's description of the triangle, the outside position is understood to be a reactive position. Taking a position outside of the automatic reactivity of the triangle will be discussed later in the chapter. This section is devoted to summarizing Bowen's detailed view of the inside and outside positions of the triangle, and clarifying the different perspective offered by the triangle hypothesis.

Under periods of relative calm, or periods of only moderate tension, Bowen held that the desirable position is one of the two inside positions, characterized by agreement and approval. The individual in the outside position, a position of rejection, will seek to be part of the twosome, and push one of the individuals in the established twosome into the outside position. The individuals in the inside positions will attempt to maintain their positions, or either may seek to form a twosome with the outsider and push their former partner into the outside position; hence the threat of rejection, as I would see it, can pressure an individual to cave in, in order to maintain an inside position.

Triangles inevitably shift, with new configurations of insiders and outsider. Though a triangle may rest in a characteristic position, for instance, with mother and daughter on the inside, and father on the outside, the threat that either mother or daughter may take an inside position with father, rejecting the former partner, is always present as a threat that constrains individuals.

Bowen described how, under periods of increased tension, the outside position is the desired position, in a stance of "You two fight it out, while I sit back, outside of the range of the attack and counter-attack of conflict." Both inside positions, and the single outside position, are based on individuals seeking increased comfort: to be in a warm and close connection with another, or to be outside the range of attack going on between two others.

In summary, Bowen explained the continual movement of the triangle as a result of individuals seeking an inside position during periods of relative calm—and the outside position during periods of increased tension.

Bowen's description of the triangle as made up of people constantly seeking a more comfortable position or seeking to keep an already captured position, and shifting the anxiety associated with rejection or attack away from themselves, is accurate within one frame of reference. The view presented here, however, offers a broader frame of reference: that the triangle is a two-against-one mechanism that regulates the individuals within a system. Although the terminology of *two* and *one* is awkward, and may lack the vividness of *inside* and *outside,* the emphasis on *one,* the individual, pressured to be a component of the system, contributes to this broader perspective of the function of the triangle. This hypothesis looks at the same phenomenon Bowen observed, but from the—so to speak—*point of view* of the system itself, rather than from the perspective of the individual people involved in the process.

When two individuals are in conflict, with a third backing out to avoid attack (what Bowen referred to as taking the outside position under periods of increased tension), that third individual is also poised to take sides with one or the other in the conflict. The two in conflict, each trying to force the other to give in, will tend to appeal to the third to join them in a two-against-one process. In this case, both individuals in conflict seek a twosome with the temporarily unengaged third. The third may side with one, go back and forth siding with one and then the other depending on the emotional pull of the others' arguments, or, assuming a pretended or temporary position of neutrality, wait for a later opportune moment to take sides. In the absence of obvious side-taking, the threat of two taking sides against the individual remains present. Generally, the mere threat is enough to constrain the individual.

Although in Bowen's model the two who are in conflict are in the inside positions, in the view presented here, the two who are in conflict *do not* make up a twosome in the sense of the two-against-one phenomenon. Rather, the twosome in the sense of two-against-one will be the two who eventually team up against the third; it is likely to occur when the one hanging back takes sides with one of the two in conflict, but it may also occur when the two fighting join together to turn on the one hanging back. As stated above, the individual in the outside position is in an emotionally reactive position. At each position, individuals are seeking to avoid the hot seat and to force someone else into it—ideally all the while *appearing* to care about another.

A mother and daughter taking sides to pressure brother to stop smoking may *appear* to care about him while the effect of their pressure may be to undermine his free functioning, making it more difficult for the brother to succeed in taking initiative, whether to stop smoking or to take some other action for himself. A mother taking sides with her son in order to protect him from his father whom she perceives as too strict a disciplinarian may appear to be caring for her son, all the while increasing the tension and estrangement between him and his father, and increasing his dependence on her. In order to remain in the inside position of the triangle with his mother, the son is not free to accept overtures by his father. In both these examples, the stated intention is to have a positive effect on another, while the actual function, or effect, of the two-against-one process is to undermine individual freedom to function as a responsible person. Rather, the individual ends up functioning more as a component of the emotional system.

By focusing on the differentiation-of-self scale of values and each value's assumed corresponding degree of sensitivity to the two-against-one threat of the triangle, the relationship of the triangle to variation in differentiation-of-self comes into view. The lower the level of differentiation-of-self, the greater the sensitivity to the threat of being pushed into the "outside," or "one," position; and the more the individual is regulated, or controlled, by the triangle.

Based on his observations, Bowen often spoke about the individuals in a triangle shifting anxiety in the system. When two people have tension in their relationship, he held that they tend to involve a third and shift the anxiety to that third person. He described parents who regain a feeling of closeness with each other and reduce tension in their relationship by focusing on a problem in one of their children. The child ends up with increased tension, or anxiety, while the parents have less. This triangle hypothesis looks at the same set of interactions from the perspective of regulation of the individual.

For example, the individual child, depending on the degree of sensitivity to the triangle, gives in to functioning as a component in the system in order to avoid the "one" position—or, if already in the "one" position, in order to regain an inside position with one parent. One child in every sibling group is programmed to be more sensitive to the threat of two-or-more-against-one. The more the parents exert emotional pressure on the child, using offers of praise as well as threats of rejection inherent in the triangle (the praise and approval of an inside position; and the threat that if the child does not cave in emotionally, the parents will team up in rejecting and criticizing him), the more the child will grow up to react to emotional pressure and to exert it on others, that is, to have a lower differentiation-of-self level. That child grows up more as a component of the system, relative to the other siblings, who are freer to grow into relatively mature, integrated individuals.

The intensity of the cues—both invitations and threats—inherent in the triangle correlate with the degree of inability of the individual to guide self confidently without reliance on those cues. The inability to guide self, accompanied by vulnerability to seek praise and to avoid rejection, is a source of chronic anxiety, or stress reactivity. The lower the differentiation-of-self level, the greater the sensitivity to the triangle. The greater the need to be in one of the *inside* positions, accompanied by reactivity to expulsion from an *inside* position, the higher the level of chronic anxiety and stress reactivity.

The highly developed stress response in the human to social relationships makes possible the control of the individual by the emotional system—through the sensitivity of an individual to other individuals, and especially to the threat that others may join together against the individual. The triangle, as the bottom-line control mechanism, predictably used as a last resort of emotional pressure, alternately triggers anxiety, or stress reactivity, when one does not give in to the emotional system, and relieves it when one does give in. This trigger of anxiety, and the alternating relief of it, resides in the following process: the threat of being pushed to the outside, or *one* position, of the two-or-more-against-one process triggers stress; and the invitation into the comfort and approval of one of the two-or-more inside positions relieves it.

The emotional system exists as a unit, which responds to the environment to bring about the greatest likelihood of survival of the group by maintaining a degree of control over the individuals that make it up. To be most effective, it relies on a coordinated response from its members, especially during periods of threat. The lower the differentiation-of-self level, the more the emotional system exerts control—as those individuals with lower differentiation-of-self levels cannot guide themselves effectively independently of the system. The triangle exerts the needed control, depending upon differentiation-of-self level, to guarantee a coordinated response. Under times of perceived threat to the survival of the unit, the synchronicity of response is automatically increased, and the triangle activity is intensified to bring about a more coordinated response to a crisis. This explains the increase of automatic triangle activity when anxiety is increased. The greater the threat, the more individuals are pressured to function as elements of the system, forming a coordinated response in order to guarantee the greatest likelihood of the overall survival and successful reproduction of the reproductive/social unit.

Bowen (1978) wrote that there was a nongenetic, but genetic-like differentiation-of-self transmission in the multigenerational family. He considered whether there was a central nucleus in the family, analogous to the nucleus in the cell that houses the genetic instructions. Rather than a nucleus, it seems that it is the network of interlocking triangles that provides the instructions for the overall directions of the emotional system. Although there are constant shifts in who is in an inside position and who is outside, the emotional programming that is sustained over time through the emotional pressure of the interlocking triangles is surprisingly rigid and enduring. As generations pass, people are born and die, but the basic emotional programming is sustained. What holds that emotional programming in place is the complex, nuanced network of systematic threat, rejection, approval, and praise of interlocking triangles.

The regulatory-function-of-the-triangle hypothesis is not inconsistent with Bowen's statements about the triangle and does not dispute the several possible functions of the triangle that he implied: (1) to stabilize a two-person relationship, (2) to shift anxiety, (3) to increase balance or equilibrium within a system, or (4) to deal with the problem of anxiety in a system. Bowen did not identify the triangle as a specific mechanism at the level of the emotional system that functions to regulate the individual. This hypothesis provides that broader view of the triangle's function—as though from the point of view of the emotional system. By doing so, it connects the dots, so to speak, of Bowen's concepts of emotional system, triangle, and differentiation-of-self. Here are some of the assumptions in the hypothesis that point out the interrelatedness of these concepts:

1. The emotional system has been an effective partial guidance system in social species. It is a partial guidance system, in that no social group relies entirely on emotional pressure for guidance; there is always a degree of direct perception and judgment of reality—differentiation-of-self. The greater the reliance on the emotional system for guidance, the more members of a social group will rely on cues from each other, rather than on direct perception of the environment.

2. The triangle as a mechanism in *Homo sapiens* produces on a graduated continuum both relatively differentiated individuals *and* relatively undifferentiated individuals—those that function more as elements of the emotional system and less as persons in their own right.

3. The triangle pressures every individual to some degree throughout the life span to function for the emotional system, but there is wide variation in differentiation-of-self levels, which have corresponding degrees of sensitivity to the triangle.

4. The triangle is deceptive and coercive in nature. It uses emotional pressure to coerce individuals to think, feel, and act for the emotional system, and to maintain the emotional programming from the past through future generations. Deception is an essential ingredient in nudging an individual to function for the system in ways that may be detrimental to that individual.

5. The triangle not only transfers stress; it triggers the stress response in people as a way to control them. It relieves stress to a degree temporarily when the individual gives in to emotional pressure.

6. Anxiety is triggered when the emotional system is not adequately controlling the individuals that comprise it. Under perceived threat, triangles become more active to create a coordinated response to crisis. Another way to understand the phenomenon that appears to be the spread of anxiety in an anxious system is that the system is reacting to not having adequate control of the individuals that make it up for a coordinated response in a crisis. All human beings are sensitive to a degree to the anxiety triggered by lack of control in an emotional system, and will react to it automatically, which explains the way reaction to a crisis in an individual family can spread into the community.

7. The triangle hypothesis accounts for the "change-back" messages Bowen described, as the emotional system seeks to regain control of the individual.

8. Knowledge of the triangle offers motivated individuals a degree of freedom from automatic reliance on the emotional system as a guidance system. Within the context of a broad understanding of how the emotional system functions, the triangle can be utilized as a predictable technique to increase differentiation-of-self levels.

THE TRIANGLE AND INCREASING DIFFERENTIATION-OF-SELF

How one thinks about the relationship of the triangle to differentiation-of-self determines what one does about the problem. If shift of anxiety is the basic issue, that is one thing. If control of the individual by the triangle is the basic issue, one may take a different action. From the viewpoint of this triangle hypothesis, "putting the others together and self out" (Bowen's idea stated in his last years) *allows* oneself to be put in the hot seat by the emotional system. Not participating in the automatic fancy footwork of the universal dance to avoid the "one" position allows oneself to be pushed into the "outside" or "one" position of the two-against-one mechanism. One does not place oneself in the outside position; the emotional system does that automatically when an individual steps out of the ongoing stream of triangle activity and is not controlled by the threat of being pushed into the outside/one position.

Consider the earlier scenario of two in conflict with one seeking what Bowen referred to as a more comfortable, "outside" position in order to avoid the conflict. If that individual, watching the two in conflict, does not seek to avoid the hot seat, but rather "puts the others together and self out" as Bowen has hinted, the others will tend automatically to form a twosome and seek to put that individual in the hot seat—the outside or one position. It is as if the emotional system, which works to regulate its members through the mechanism of the triangle, reacts to reengage a member who seems to have dropped out of the game—a game that from the emotional system's point of view is the only game in town, leading to the conditions that perpetuate the survival of the system.

Although there is a wide range of variation in sensitivity to the triangle, all people seem to be controlled to a degree by the emotional pressures of the triangle. In cases when an individual does not give in to a significant degree to the emotional pressures of the triangle, within his or her particular differentiation-of-self level, the system reacts as though something is dreadfully wrong. The lack of emotional coordination sends a signal throughout the system, which will intensify its efforts to control that individual. In almost every case, the individual will then comply. If the individual still does not comply, the system will threaten to push the individual out, reacting as though a "loose cannon" must be changed back or rejected. In nature, outside of the planned effort guided by the theory that Bowen pioneered, an individual who systematically does not give in to the emotional pressures of the unit of which he or she is a part, is unheard of, and generally would be a loose cannon that poses a danger to the survival of the unit.

If an individual can consistently "put the others together and self out," without being controlled by the emotional pressure of the threat of the outside, or one, position, this process leads gradually, predictably, to increased independence from the guidance of the emotional system. From the viewpoint of this triangle hypothesis, which sees the basic issue as control of the individual by the triangle, systematically being willing to endure the outside/one position is a way to work toward self-regulation—and to dependably raise the differentiation-of-self level.

Bowen stated that the effort to increase differentiation-of-self level is made around an emotionally charged issue. The family reacts to a gradual revealing of the hidden, denied emotional process in the family by teaming up against an individual who reveals it. To bring the emotional process calmly out into the open is to no longer be controlled by it. The one issue that is more charged than any other is: who is in the driver's seat—the individual or the emotional system? This is the basis of "change-back" messages. It is only when the individual has become more differentiated, and has demonstrated this to the emotional system of the family, that the emotional system relaxes the intensity of its control over the individual, as the differentiation-of-self level increases in the individual and the family as a whole.

The effort to utilize the triangle to increase differentiation-of-self involves these steps, which are familiar to students of Bowen:

1. First, the individual becomes an observer of the emotional process and contains his or her own reactivity to the family-of-origin. The capacity to observe and to contain reactivity also increases as a result of the successful effort, as reactivity lessens.

2. The individual puts two significant other family members together and self out, while gradually revealing the emotional process in the family. For example, identifying the emotional process that goes on between one's parents, one might say to mother, "Do you think you are worrying enough about father?" and to father, "What do you do to get mother to worry about you?" A unique aspect of the effort is giving up emotional investment in the outcome. The effort is to be more responsible for communicating to the family based on one's perceptions rather than going along with pressure from others; the effort is not to change the family, that is, it is not to stop mother from worrying about and monitoring father.

3. Gradually, the individual puts all of the interlocking triangles together, and self out. For example, to sister, "Are you giving mother enough help in monitoring dad?" A successful effort requires having no allies and gradually being able to accept being pushed into the outside/one position in all triangles—an inevitable, short-term product of standing alone.

4. When the family reacts by engaging the two-against-one triangle process, "*We* don't like what you are doing," putting the individual in the outside, or one position, of two-against-one, the individual does not react back, and does not stop the effort of putting all the interlocking triangles together and self out.

This is, of course, a simplified schema. Such an effort, though probably the most direct way to raise the differentiation-of-self level, involves an effort sustained at least over a period of several years or more, guided through a complex web of details to avoid the inevitable pitfalls and potential dead-ends that arise. The end result: objective knowledge of how the family functions and humility in understanding more accurately what one's place in it is.

Documentation of the process of increasing differentiation-of-self by putting the others together and self out provides evidence that the triangle functions to control. When one thinks and acts outside of the control of the emotional programming of the system, the triangle, as the basic building block of the emotional system, will predictably become active to trigger a stress response in the individual making the effort. To raise differentiation-of-self, the individual endures the stress response without withdrawing the effort—in other words, without stopping putting the others together and self out in order to avoid stress.

When an individual does not change course in order to avoid being pushed into the outside/one position, and turns down the invitation to join with two-or-more, the emotional system's efforts to control the individual through the triangle become exaggerated and visible. Especially at lower levels of differentiation, faced with an individual family member's successful effort toward differentiation-of-self, the emotional system, with the other *family members acting as one,* may openly criticize, threaten, and attempt to involve one's children or spouse, or even contact one's employer (in an action like the one in the earlier example provided by Bowen of the daughter with schizophrenia and her mother, who enlisted both family members and psychiatric staff to side with her against her daughter), if the effort is not given up; and alternately praise and compliment, and promise future praise and approval if the effort to increase differentiation-of-self *is* given up. Finally, the emotional system may try to push an individual out of his or her family as the effort to be a more integrated individual becomes more successful. The actual risk of being permanently rejected, however, is extremely small or nonexistent, as long as the individual does not give in to being guided by emotional reactivity to the family's actions. For instance, even if the family becomes reactive enough to disown the individual, the individual is likely to be successful in regaining contact by calling family members within a few months. The family is eager to involve the individual again. The threat of rejection functions as a means to control the individual: the family emotional system does not actually want to get rid of its family member; it merely wants to be in control of him or her. The point here is that it is the concerted reaction of family members, in response to calm and politely worded statements—that step outside the emotional programming by putting the others together and self out—which reveals the function of the triangle.

A CLINICAL EXAMPLE

The following clinical example of coaching a woman in an effort to increase differentiation-of-self covers an initial four-month period from September through January, a kind of snapshot of the first months of a coached effort that continued for several years. The purpose here is briefly (1) to demonstrate the use of the triangle in an effort to increase differentiation-of-self, and (2) to provide evidence of the triangle function to control, as the family reacts to the individual effort. The example is offered for its research value, as it demonstrates the reactivity to triangles of an individual, along with her effort to use the theory and coaching in order to act outside of the reactivity.

Limited to a demonstration of how the emotional system functions during an effort toward differentiation-of-self, this example, presented here for research purposes only, does not include a discussion of the complex role of the coach or the responsibility of the individual being coached. Needless to say, the freedom of an individual to accept or reject coaching and to integrate the coaching into an increasingly objective view of the family, as well as the ability of the coach to remain outside of the emotional programming of the family in such an effort are complex and important areas; but they will not be addressed in this chapter. Unfortunately there is not enough space to address the predictable misunderstandings that may arise from presenting brief clinical material. No claim is made for the quality of the coaching or that the same decisions would be made again by either coach or client.

The client, Jane, a clinical social worker, sought coaching after a decade or more of previous exposure to Bowen theory. Coaching occurred by phone as well as in person, due to both geographical distance from the coach and the helpfulness of a few ten-minute phone conversations with the coach at points of high anxiety in the family.

The family included the client, Jane, her husband, and their two children, including Jim, their ten-year-old son; Jane's older sister, Sue, Sue's three children from a previous marriage, and Sue's husband, Ben; Jane's younger brother, Dave, his wife, Nell, and their two young children; and Jane's mother. Figure 2.1 provides a simple family diagram.

There had been an incident at a family get-together over the summer. Ben was playing in the lake with the kids while the other adults were observing the play from the shore. During the horseplay, Ben made a game of pulling down the swim trunks of the younger kids. Although none of the adults on shore spoke about it at that time, there was a lot of discussion about it later over the summer. The family split between those who accused Ben behind his back of child sexual abuse, including Nell and, to some degree, Jane and her mother, and those who said it was nothing, including Dave and Sue, who remarked that it was "just playing around," and that the other side was making a mountain out of a molehill. Ben was not involved in the discussions and knew nothing of them.

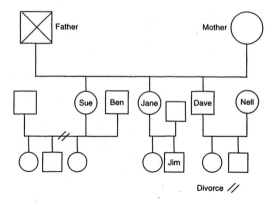

FIGURE 2.1. Family Diagram

JANE: In September, Jane, based on coaching, sent letters out to the family, including Ben, stating that she had heard a lot of things from the family about Ben pulling down the kids' swimsuits at the lake, and that she had decided to take a middle ground on the issue *(putting the others together and self out alone)*. Based on the coaching, she carefully left her husband out of the loop, telling him nothing about her effort in the family *(self alone)*.

BEN TO JANE: He wrote back saying that she had ruined his marriage and that he would never speak to her again *(threat to Jane of two-against-one triangle, as Ben is married to Jane's older sister)*.

JANE TO BEN: [Jane's reported automatic reaction was to defend herself and to involve her child, by saying that if it weren't for Jim, vulnerable at ten, she would not have said anything about what had happened at the lake.] Based on the coaching, she did not defend herself or mention her son. She wrote to the whole family: "Why is my taking a middle ground upsetting the family?" *(putting the others together and self out alone)*.

JANE'S MOTHER TO JANE: "What was the purpose of what you did if it wasn't to cause problems between Ben and Sue, and to alienate Ben? Was Jim upset about what Ben did? I'm upset to see bad things happen between my children. Have a heart-to-heart with Sue" *(threat to Jane of two-or-more against-one, i.e., Sue, Ben, mother, etc.)*.

JANE TO SUE: [Jane's reported automatic reaction was to begin to question whether she was trying to break up Sue and Ben *(the pressure of the triangle to control individual perception and thinking)*]. Based on the coaching, she didn't defend herself. She said to Sue: "I don't know why mother wants me to have a heart-to-heart talk with you. If she thinks there's something important to say to you, why doesn't she tell you herself?" *(putting Sue and Mother together, self out alone).*

BEN: [Jane reported that Ben refused to have Thanksgiving with the family, that the family is upset about not having the holiday together; Jane had an automatic reaction that she is to blame for there not being the traditional family holiday together *(threat of two-or-more-against-one).*

SUE TO JANE: *(crying)* "Is Jim upset about what Ben did?" [Jane reported an automatic reaction to use her son as a way to manage her family relationships *(to give up the "one" position, by making her son responsible for her actions in place of herself).*] She refrained from using her son in this way.

JANE: [Jane reported her ongoing automatic reaction was to apologize to everyone, and that perhaps by apologizing to all she could make the Thanksgiving dinner happen. She reported she continued to blame herself for the family not having Thanksgiving together. She refrained from apologizing.]

JANE TO BEN: With coaching: "I would like to see you on the holidays. I look forward to more opportunities to take the middle ground with you, Sue, Mother, Dave, and Nell" *(putting the others together and self out alone).*

MOTHER TO JANE: "How can you make light of something like this?" [Jane's mother was referring, reported Jane, to both the "sexual abuse" and the "breakup of the family." Jane reported feeling that she was to blame for the breakup of the family.]

JANE TO MOTHER: With coaching: "I hope your sons and daughters are taking things seriously for your sake" *(putting the others together and self out alone).*

MOTHER TO JANE: "I think Sue really loves Ben." [Jane reported this was the first time her mother ever spoke in this positive way about Ben.] "Why are you causing a breakup of their marriage?" *(threat of two-or-more-against-one).*

JANE TO BEN: [Jane reported feeling that she believed she was causing the breakup of Sue and Ben's marriage. Her automatic reaction was again to apologize to everyone and to urge everyone to get together for the holiday.] With coaching: "Mother said Sue really loves you" *(putting Mother, Sue, and Ben together, and self out alone).*

BEN TO JANE: He thanked her for her letter and apologized for the "nasty tone" of his previous letter.

SUE TO JANE: "Ben said you are an amazing person. 'Haven't I told you that all along?' I said to him."

JANE: [Jane reported experiencing a sudden relief.] "It was like I did this great thing." [Her automatic reaction was to accept being "an amazing person" *(to give up the "one" position and to accept the approval of an inside position).*]

JANE TO SUE: With coaching: "People who are called amazing don't impress me as much as they impress all of you" *(putting the others together and self out alone).*

Everyone attended the family Christmas holiday.

DAVE TO JANE: "Do you really think it's wise to put these issues out on the table and say them to people?" [Jane reported her automatic reaction was to stop bringing up issues, for fear it would alienate people *(threat of the two-or-more-against-one).*]

MOTHER TO JANE: Jane's mother said she agreed with Dave that it isn't wise to put the issues out on the table. Her mother then cancelled a dinner date with Jane to go to dinner with Dave instead *(two-against-one).* [Jane reported being shocked by her mother's action and feeling rejected, and feeling that she would probably never be close to her mother again.]

JANE: [Jane reported an automatic reaction to stop bringing up issues and to gain her mother's approval.] With coaching: she wished Mother and Dave good luck in the New Year in their efforts to keep the family quiet on issues *(putting Dave and Mother together and self out alone).*

MOTHER TO JANE: Jane's mother demanded to know why Jane was wishing them good luck in keeping the family quiet on issues.

JANE TO MOTHER: [Jane reported an automatic reaction to blame her mother for denying issues in the family and to convince her that Dave was wrong on this, and that she, Jane, was right.] With coaching: "I think you and Dave must have a good reason to do it" *(putting Dave and Mother together and self out alone).*

MOTHER TO JANE: "No one's telling anyone to be quiet."

JANE TO MOTHER: "Don't you and Dave think you should?" *(putting Dave and Mother together and self out alone).*

NELL TO JANE: Jane reported that Nell had assumed that Jane was rejecting Ben completely. When she observed Jane at Christmas, she said: "I'm disappointed in you" for getting along with Ben *(threat of rejection to Jane from inside position with Nell).*

JANE: [Jane reported that she wanted to explain herself, to explain why she's talking to Ben, and to try to convince Nell to see it her way.] With coaching: "I hate it when I disappoint any of you" *(putting Nell together with other family members, and self out alone).*

MOTHER AND DAVE: They made plans to get together without Jane, plans that would usually include her *(two-against-one).* "Now they're not even making a pretense of including me."

JANE TO MOTHER AND DAVE: With coaching: Jane told Dave and her mother that she is so glad Dave and Mother are close and agree on things *(putting Dave and Mother together and self out alone).*

MOTHER TO JANE: "You ask why the family is taking it seriously. Well, you did practically call Ben a pervert. You can't joke around about that" *(threat to Jane of two-or-more-against-one).*

JANE TO SUE: With coaching: "Why does Mother keep bringing up that Ben is a pervert?" *(putting Mother and Ben together and self out alone).*

JANE: In January, Jane reported: "Things are loosening up. People are talking to each other more openly."

Documentation of systematic, sustained individual efforts to raise differentiation-of-self in the family of origin, using the triangle as the basis of the effort, has led to surprising observations. These observations contribute evidence for a view of the regulatory function of the triangle in the human. The triangle seems to be a mechanism for the human social system's control of the individual throughout its life history, as well as a mechanism that determines variation in the degree of differentiation-of-self in each generation within the relationship system. Strictly speaking, differentiation-of-self refers to the degree of freedom from governance by, and automatic use by, the larger whole. It is characterized by the degree of an individual's capacity to manage, or regulate, its relationship to the larger unit of which it is a part.

CONCLUSION

After Bowen's 1967 breakthrough, using the triangle in his effort in his family of origin, documented in what became known as the Anonymous

Paper (Bowen, 1978), his medical students and residents in psychiatry spontaneously began to apply what they learned from Bowen in their own families. By the middle 1970s, Bowen's concepts of the triangle and differentiation-of-self had become popular; hundreds of people attended his conferences. This popularity gave a false impression that the theory was successful. In fact, concepts were borrowed from the theory and combined with different approaches in the burgeoning family therapy movement. These other approaches emphasized technique over understanding the essential problem. People began to apply Bowen theory before they had more than a superficial understanding of it, and often without a skilled coach. It is possible that no one besides Bowen himself had mastered (to the degree to which he had mastered it at that time—he continued experimentation and development of the theory to the end of his life) an understanding of the use of the triangle as a technique in working toward differentiation-of-self. Bowen himself may likely have been still in a stage of trial and error after his initial breakthrough. Many people had gotten the impression that it was effective to increase anxiety in the family in an effort to raise differentiation-of-self. For all these reasons, the results were at times disastrous, as untrained, enthusiastic people tried things out on their families that sometimes led to explosive reactions.

By the early 1980s, Bowen was moving away from a public emphasis on the triangle as a technique. In the videotaped interview with Bowen by Michael Kerr, MD, "Defining a Self in One's Family of Origin, Part 2,"* Bowen's opening statements reflect the importance he placed on the triangle:

> It's terribly difficult for one to proceed with something like this without an awareness of theory and triangles, because this governs everything. . . . To me the most important thing of all in this is that systems theory and triangles knows [sic] the way through an emotional block. The problem is not in the theory. The problem is in the person and the implementation of it. (Bowen, 1980)

Later in the tape, Bowen introduces the error of "confrontation" in the family and the problems created by people dealing with reactive, explosive families:

BOWEN: For the average person with a family that . . . you know, acts out and reacts all over the place, the task there is to calm self down so self can go on board and be present in the family and not react too much.

KERR: . . . So would you probably—do you think less about triangles now with your own family than you used to, or is it, still . . .

BOWEN: Triangles are very important for understanding it theoretically. I mean there's the blueprint. But people tend to get too involved in look- · ing for the triangle and trying to detriangle a self. And I tend now to not bother that much with the triangles. I just like to go sit alongside the family and not react.

Made for public viewing during a climate of reactivity, this videotape has led many to suppose that Bowen did not view the triangle as essential in the effort to bring about differentiation-of-self. However, Bowen's next point on the videotape is, "For the average person who is going to put time and energy into this, they need a coach, who is someone who has already covered the ground. . . . That's a very important one. . . ." Bowen the private coach was, understandably, different from Bowen the public speaker, especially during periods of increased reactivity to his theory. Though Bowen moved away from much public discussion of the triangle, it is unlikely that he stopped his own clinical research of the concept. In the late 1980s, in the last years before he died in 1990, he returned to public statements that successful increase of differentiation-of-self scale levels occurs only in the context of the triangle.

The use of the triangle as a technique in the effort to increase differentiation-of-self remains an area of research rather than widely disseminated information. Although it may be the most effective technique to increase differentiation-of-self, it is generally poorly understood. Bowen identified the triangle as the "blueprint" for an effort to raise differentiation-of-self. Did Bowen engage in ongoing research and experimentation that contributed to the continued development of the theory, including the triangle?

In the 1980s, Bowen turned away from public descriptions of therapy and the effort to increase differentiation-of-self and toward an explicit discussion of the family as a product of evolution and a view of the human in terms of what the human has in common with all of life. It is through the examination of the triangle from the perspective of evolution that it can be studied most effectively—not as an expression of Bowen's personality as some have viewed the use of the triangle in the Anonymous Paper—but as a factually-based concept, applicable broadly to all social species. From a broader understanding of the function of the triangle—to regulate the individuals that make up an emotional system—the concept can be studied scientifically and applied predictably in an effort to raise differentiation-of-self.

SUMMARY

The triangle is a hidden mechanism responsible, at least to some degree, for the development of variation in human beings in differentiation-of-self levels. The triangle governs all individuals, to the degree that they lack differentiation-of-self, throughout the life history. The triangle, once its functioning is well understood, can be utilized in a carefully designed effort to raise differentiation-of-self.

The regulatory-function-of-the-triangle hypothesis offers a basis for further research in two interrelated areas: (1) the effort to increase differentiation-of-self, and (2) the effort to move the theory toward the life sciences so that it may be applied to observations of other social species. The effort to increase differentiation-of-self leads to a predictable exaggeration of triangle processes within the emotional system to reengage the individual, so that these processes may be more easily studied and applied to an increased understanding of regulatory mechanisms in other social species as well. Reciprocally, knowledge from the life sciences, contributing to a basic understanding of the phenomenon described by Bowen theory, informs the effort to increase differentiation-of-self.

A regulatory mechanism that guides an individual organism, to a degree determining its life course, may be consistent with observations in the life sciences. If the concept of the triangle includes an understanding not only of the transfer of anxiety, but also of the *triggering* of anxiety in the complex, subtle exertion of pressure on the individual, it may apply broadly to chemical processes triggered by social relationships, such as the pheromones that govern the cellular slime mold, and the chemical signals in the brain that orchestrate automatic behavior in *Homo sapiens.*

Do regulatory processes occur in life on various levels, from genes to cellular function, to reproductive and social systems? Consider the cellular slime mold: individual amoebae forming dead stalk for the preservation of the social group is not possible without mechanisms for control of the individuals by the larger social group. The broader view presented here of the function of the triangle as a mechanism for the control of individual behavior accounts for how individuals may behave against their own best interests as members of a reproductive or other social group. They may behave in ways that do not further their own survival and reproduction, but that instead contribute indirectly to others being relatively free to develop and reproduce successfully.

What is the function of the paradoxically high level of social anxiety that has been documented in human beings? Social anxiety seems in many instances to work against the survival and successful reproduction of the individual, yet it may promote survival on the level of the group by insuring a coordinated response from individuals, even in some cases against individuals' best interests. Do the implications of the regulation of individuals by an emotional system contribute to a discussion of units of selection, including group selection? What is the relationship of these epigenetic developmental processes to genetic processes and evolution? These questions remain to be answered by further research.

REFERENCES

Ben-Jacob, E. (2004). Bacteria harnessing complexity. *Biofilms,* 1, 239-263.

Ben-Jacob, E. and Cohen, I. (1997). Cooperative formation of bacterial patterns. In J. Shapiro and D. Martin (Eds.), *Bacteria as Multicellular Organisms* (pp. 394-416). Oxford: Oxford University Press.

Bonner, J. T. (1998, August 4). A way of following individual cells in the migrating slugs of Dicyostelium discoideum. *Proceedings of the National Academy of Sciences, USA, 95*(16), 9355-9359.

Bowen, M. (1978). *Family therapy in clinical practice.* Northvale, NJ, and London: Jason Aronson.

Bowen, M. (1980). Defining a Self in One's Family of Origin—Part 2. *Videotape produced by the Georgetown University Family Center,* Washington, DC.

Connor, R. C., Read, A. J., and Wrangham, R. (2000). The bottlenose dolphin: Social relationships in a fission-fusion society. In J. Mann, R. C. Connor, P. L. Tyak, and W. W. Hal (Eds.), *Cetacean Societies: Field Studies of Dolphins and Whales* (pp. 91-126). Chicago: The University of Chicago Press.

De Waal, F. (1982). *Chimpanzee politics: Power and sex among apes.* New York: Harper & Row, Publishers, Inc.

Gordon, D. M. (1999). *Ants at work: How an insect society is organized.* New York: The Free Press, of Simon and Schuster Inc.

Sapolsky, R. M., Alberts, S. C., and Altmann, J. (1997, December). Hypercortisolism associated with social subordinance or social isolation among wild baboons. *Archives of General Psychiatry, 54*(12), 1137-1143.

Shapiro, J. A. (1997). Multicellularity: The rule, not the exception. Lessons from *Escherichia coli* colonies. J. Shapiro and D. Martin (Eds.), *Bacteria as Multicellular Organisms* (pp. 14-49). Oxford: Oxford University Press.

Shapiro, J. and Martin, D. (Eds.). (1997). *Bacteria as multicellular organisms.* Oxford: Oxford University Press.

Siepel, A., Bejerano, G., Pedersen, J. S., Hinrichs, A. S., Hou, M., Rosenbloom, K. et al. (2005). Evolutionarily conserved elements in vertebrate, insect, worm, and yeast genomes. *Genome Research, 15*(8), 1034-1050.

Chapter 3

Triadic Relationships in Nonhuman Primate Family Systems

Lynn A. Fairbanks

INTRODUCTION

Murray Bowen saw human behavior as a part of evolution, governed by natural forces that are evident in other biological systems. He recognized the value of looking at animal social systems to gain insights into the functioning of human families. This chapter follows that tradition by exploring triadic relationships in nonhuman primate families, with specific examples from vervet monkeys.

The vervet is an Old World monkey that is widespread in riverine forests and savanna woodlands throughout sub-Saharan Africa. Vervets live in extended family groups that contain multiple generations of females and a number of unrelated adult males (Cheney and Seyfarth, 1990). Vervet life begins with a strong and exclusive mother-infant bond that lasts for the first year. Juveniles continue to live with their mothers throughout the four to five year period of immaturity, and females remain in their mother's group for life. Vervet family relationships include affiliative bonds and social support, but they also include conflict and competition between family members. Mothers and infants go through periods of conflict over weaning, carrying, and other aspects of maternal care. Siblings compete for their mother's attention, and later for dominance position within the family. The family as a unit cooperates with other families in protection from outside threats and defense of the group territory, but also competes with other families for dominance and access to resources within the group. This type of extended family grouping, which is typical of the majority of primate species, creates many opportunities for triadic relationships.

This chapter focuses on triadic relationships involving mothers and infants, and demonstrates how relationships with babysitters, adult males, and grandmothers influence the nature of the mother-infant bond. The descriptions presented here are based on data on vervet family relationships observed over the last twenty-five years at the UCLA-VA Vervet Research Colony. In each of these cases, we can see incipient elements of the triangles that are part of emotional regulation in human family systems.

VERVET MONKEY TRIADIC RELATIONSHIPS

Mothers, Infants, and Babysitters

When a vervet infant is born, everyone in the group comes over to check it out. Juvenile females show a particular fascination with young infants and will compete with one another for a chance to hold and carry them (Fairbanks, 1990; Lancaster, 1971). Mothers differ in how comfortable they are with all this attention. Some mothers increase their hold on the infant and try to avoid the caretakers. Others willingly let young caretakers have their infants, and take advantage of the time off.

This variation is illustrated in the experiences of Pansy and Winnie, two female infants who were born to very different mothers. When Pansy was born, she was the center of attention of the group. Her mother, Poinsettia, was one of the founding females of the colony and alpha female of her social group. Although not a pretty female, Poinsettia was a relaxed and confident leader. She was frequently seen intervening in disputes among other group members, and was very effective at keeping peace among the females. Poinsettia showed little maternal anxiety or concern when Pansy was born. As a new mother, she freely allowed the juvenile females to carry Pansy, even in the first few days after birth. One of the juvenile females, Fran, became her regular companion and was the most frequent babysitter for Pansy. During the first few months of life, infant Pansy spent almost one quarter of her time being carried around by Fran, while Poinsettia relaxed or foraged on her own. Pansy appeared to be comfortable being played with and introduced to other group members. Later she became a socially successful and well-adjusted juvenile female with a wide network of friends.

Pansy's early life contrasted sharply with the early experience of Winnie. Winnie was the daughter of Wanda, a low-ranking female from another social group at the Vervet Research Colony. Wanda was a tense and anxious mother. She could usually be seen in a rigid upright posture, alert and ready to respond to potential danger, with her arms wrapped tightly around Winnie. Penny was a juvenile female who was eager to "babysit" Winnie, but Wanda rebuffed her efforts. When Penny came over to touch or inspect Winnie, Wanda would turn away and hold Winnie even closer. Winnie hardly ever left her mother's side during those early months. She did not spend much time relating with other females in the group, and when she did, she would get signals of fear and anxiety from her mother.

The mother-infant-"babysitter" triad has a number of potential tension points. Juvenile females are eager caretakers and, for the most part, their intentions are benign. Nevertheless, a newborn infant is at greater risk of harm from injury or dehydration with a young caretaker than with its mother. This risk is greater for a low-ranking mother, who may have trouble retrieving her infant, than it is for a high-ranking mother, who can always get her infant back when she is ready (Fairbanks, 2003; Hrdy, 1976; Silk, 1999). The difference between the maternal styles of Poinsettia and Wanda, described earlier, can partly be explained by their social status in the group. A high-ranking mother like Poinsettia can safely leave her infant with her babysitter, while a low-ranking mother like Wanda has a harder time controlling the babysitter's behavior and has to worry more about her infant's safety. Thus, the addition of the babysitter had very different consequences for the mother-infant relationship in these two different situations.

In captivity, vervet infants spend an average of 10 percent of their time being carried by caretakers in the first few months of life, but this period varies considerably across infants (Fairbanks, 1990). Restrictive mothers, like Wanda, may never allow their infants to be taken by babysitters, while a tolerant mother, like Poinsettia, may allow her infant to spend 10 to 30 percent of its daytime hours with caretakers. This provides a considerable relief for the mother, and it also influences the mother-infant relationship. Figure 3.1 shows the percentage of time that vervet infants spend more than 1 meter away from their mothers in the first three months of life for high-caretaking and low-caretaking triads. All infants gradually increase their time away from the mother as they grow and develop, but this process is accelerated for infants in high-caretaking triads.

Time away from the mother is important in several aspects. Infants, like Pansy, who spend more time away are introduced to other group members sooner and develop independence from the mother at an earlier age (Fairbanks, 1996). From the mothers' point of view, extended time off the nipple frees the mother to rest or forage unencumbered. In the wild, mothers have to spend more time foraging to meet the extra caloric demands of lactation and infant carrying (Altmann, 1980; Altmann and Samuels, 1992).

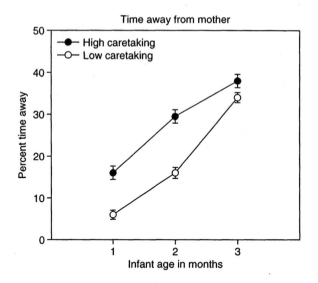

FIGURE 3.1. Mean percentage time infant vervet monkeys spend more than 1 meter away from their mothers, by amount of caretaking by babysitters. Error bars are the standard error of the mean. *Source:* Redrawn from Fairbanks, 1990.

Even in captivity, more time off the mother leads to earlier conception and shorter interbirth intervals, compared with mothers who have their infants with them most of the time (Fairbanks, 1990; Hauser and Fairbanks, 1988). As long as the risk to the infant is low, mothers like Poinsettia can benefit from using babysitters by an increase in fertility and reproductive success.

Juvenile babysitters can also benefit from the time spent caretaking other females' infants. Numerous researchers have speculated that juvenile females learn mothering skills by caring for others' infants (Hrdy, 1976; Silk, 1999). A longitudinal analysis at the Vervet Research Colony supported this idea. Females who spent more time carrying and caretaking infants when they were juveniles were more likely to successfully rear their own first infant (Fairbanks, 1990). Fran, Pansy's regular babysitter, is an example of a female who turned out to be a capable and comfortable mother when she gave birth for the first time two years later.

The evolutionary biological explanation for the mother-infant-babysitter triad involves balancing costs, risks, and opportunities for both mothers and caretakers. As the risks to infants of high-ranking mothers are low, they can take advantage of the benefits of having a babysitter and increase their reproductive success. Low-ranking mothers are more protective to balance the higher risk to their infants, and they are not able to gain the same reproductive advantages from using babysitters (Fairbanks, 2003). The cost-benefit trade-offs for a juvenile female will depend on her own time and energy balance. A large infant can be 25 percent of the weight of a yearling female, and carrying it for any distance can be quite a chore. Infant carrying and caretaking can also be time consuming and cut into the amount of time a young female has available for other types of play (Fairbanks, 1990). These factors need to be weighed against the long-term benefits of increased competence later in life.

Fitness Models: Proximate and Ultimate Explanations

The type of explanation used above to understand the mother-infant-babysitter interactions is based on evolutionary biological cost-benefit analyses. In these types of models, it often sounds as if the monkey mothers are expected to read actuarial tables and perform complicated calculations based on energy allocation, projection of risk, estimates of gene frequencies in the next generation, and so on. Measuring the cognitive capacity of nonhuman primate species is a hot area in primatology today. Current research suggests that monkeys do have some concept of numbers and are able to recognize triadic social relationships (Cheney and Seyfarth, 1990; de Waal and Embree, 1997; Tomasello and McCall, 1997), but even the most enthusiastic advocate of nonhuman primate intelligence does not believe that the evolutionary biological models reflect what is going on in the minds of the monkeys. Instead, the models predict the evolutionary outcome of different courses of action in response to specific circumstances. They assume that organisms will evolve the ability to recognize and respond to cues in a way that will usually produce the predicted outcome.

Evolutionary biology distinguishes between proximate and ultimate explanations of traits. A proximate explanation describes the mechanisms that control how a system works, while an ultimate explanation is concerned with how such a system could have evolved. Ultimate explanations focus on the consequences of a particular trait for individual survival and reproductive success, or fitness. Evolutionary biological models use knowledge about population genetics and ecology to develop mathematical predictions that explain why some traits are favored over others, in some species and not in others. These models are all anchored to the basic principles of natural selection and population genetics.

Knowing that a characteristic or a trait should evolve says little about the proximate mechanisms that explain how it works. For example, detecting danger can rely on visual, auditory or chemical communication, or on some combination of these. The advantage of having a good danger detection system is provided by natural selection. The proximate mechanics of the system are usually based on sensory, physiological, and emotional systems that are already well developed in the species.

Emotional systems are likely to be important proximate mediators of the triadic relationships being considered here. Emotional reactions can effectively change the priority and likelihood of different behavioral responses because they contain important information about the state of the organism and its environment. The expression of emotions like fatigue are a good gauge of energy expenditure and the amount of energy reserve that an individual has left. Anxiety reflects uncertainty and potential risk in the environment, and fear is a potent indicator of true danger. Expressions of comfort or of attachment create positive feedback for behavioral reactions. As emotional reactions are graded, they can allow for fine-tuning of responses to varying social and environmental conditions. Combinations of different emotions, such as fatigue and anxiety, can lead to complex outcomes that weigh both the costs and benefits of behavioral choices.

Biologists who study animal social systems often use ultimate, evolutionary explanations for behavioral traits. Psychologists tend to focus on proximate physiological and emotional causes of behavior. These are two different aspects of the same problem that are complementary, not contradictory. For each ultimate explanation, there has to be a proximate mechanism, and for each proximate mechanism there has to be a reason why it evolved.

In the discussion of the mother-infant-babysitter triadic system, the explanations given above were based on the fitness consequences of the actions of the parties involved. Writing this chapter has led me to also consider the emotional mechanisms that are likely to be mediating these actions. Murray Bowen saw the benefits of viewing human relationships in terms of our knowledge of natural social systems, but the reverse is also true. A deep understanding of human triadic relationships can inform our understanding of primate social relationships.

The emotional system is the proximate mediator that leads monkeys to make adaptive choices in the mother-infant-babysitter triad. Mothers, like Wanda, who are besieged by caretakers they cannot control, become anxious. Mothers who are anxious about their infants increase the intensity of the mother-infant relationship and try to exclude the source of tension, the caretaker. Mothers, like Poinsettia, who are more in command of their social environment, are more relaxed about caretaker attention. They loosen the mother-infant bond and include the caretaker in infant care.

The nature of the mother-infant-babysitter triad would be expected to influence the infant's emotional state and ability to relate to others. In the case of the anxious mother, the infant may become overly dependent and relatively isolated from other group members. In the case of the more relaxed mother who lets her infant be carried off by caretakers, the infant would develop independence sooner and become more integrated into the social group, but it may have a less secure relationship with its mother. In these two scenarios, the personality and social circumstances of the mother dictate the emotional dynamics of the triadic system, and the effects on infant development.

The evolutionary biologist believes that these types of emotional responses have evolved because they generally serve the best interests of the individual, within the constraints of the current environment. In three person systems, there are compromises and adjustments as each individual tries to adapt as best as they can, and what appears to be painful or dysfunctional may be the best solution available under the circumstances.

Mothers, Infants, and New Adult Males

In vervet monkey societies, females spend their entire lives in the group where they were born, but males lead a more itinerant life. Most males leave the natal group when they reach puberty, and travel alone or with another emigrating male to a neighboring group (Cheney and Seyfarth, 1990). Immigration into a new group is a stressful process. The males must not only compete with the resident males for dominance, but they must also gain the trust and acceptance of the females in the group. Immigrant adult males can pose a serious threat to young infants, and in some primate species, infanticide is common when a new male joins the group (Hausfater and Hrdy, 1984). Owing to this threat, females are extremely wary of adult male strangers and they typically form coalitions to chase them away. It can take months before new males are comfortably integrated in a group.

Examination of the mother-infant-adult male triad at the Vervet Research Colony reveals an interesting shift in the mother's behavior toward her infant when new males are present in the group. This is illustrated in the case of Olivia and Oscar. Olivia was a successful vervet female who raised a new infant every year. She was usually a relatively laissez-faire mother who would allow her infants to come and go at their own pace. A few months before Oscar was born, the previous breeding males had left and two new adult males were moved into the group. This created a lot of excitement in the group. At first, Olivia joined with the other females to chase the new males. When her infant Oscar was born, she kept a close watch and would not allow either of the new males to get close. When Oscar wanted to climb down and explore the world, Olivia kept a hand firmly attached to his arm or tail. At the slightest sign, she would grab Oscar and pull him back. Oscar would struggle to get away, but to no avail. Gradually, as Oscar grew older, Olivia began to relax and let him go. The new males, who had initially been frightening, now became interesting to Olivia. She came into estrus when Oscar was about five months old. At this time, she started sitting near and grooming one of the new males. Now, when Oscar would approach her to cuddle and nurse, she would often push him away. Oscar would try again, and she would cover her nipples and sometimes even threaten him.

The presence of the new males caused Oscar's early experience to be very different from that of his siblings. His mother restricted his early attempts to explore the environment when he was young, and rejected his desire to be held and fed when he was older. While his siblings had the opportunity to regulate their own needs for stimulation and comfort, Oscar learned to accommodate to the restrictions imposed on him by his mother. Two years later, Oscar was relatively cautious and fearful when confronted with new and potentially threatening situations.

The presence of new males is a factor that influences maternal restrictiveness for all females in a social group (Fairbanks and McGuire, 1987). Most infants begin to explore the area around the mother during the second and third month of life, using her as a secure base for exploration. As Figure 3.2 indicates, the tendency for mothers to restrain their infants during this time is significantly higher with new males in the group than with long-term resident males. (In this sample, most of the new males had been in the group for three to seven months when the infant was born.)

Our interpretation of this finding is that mothers increase their investment in maternal care in response to the greater risk to the infant. In this case, a moderate increase in maternal protectiveness can result in a large benefit in terms of infant survival. Looked at from the perspective of the emotional system, mothers, like Olivia, experience an increase in anxiety because of the presence of the new adult male in the group. As a mother with a young infant, she is particularly sensitive to the potential threat posed by the stranger, and she will be more tense and wary when he is in the vicinity. In the mother-infant-new adult male triad, the tension between the two adults leads to an increase in closeness between the mother and infant and a distancing of the adult male. The mother enforces these changes by restricting her infant's movement and by keeping the infant away from the adult male.

As the infant grows and develops more independence, and as the mother approaches the time when she becomes sexually receptive again, the dynamics of the mother-infant-new adult male triad changes. The new male

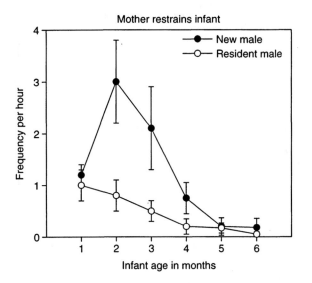

FIGURE 3.2. Mean frequency per hour that vervet mother restrains infant by infant's month of life, with new males versus resident males in the group. *Source:* Redrawn from Fairbanks and McGuire, 1987.

poses less of a risk to the older infant's safety, and the infant is better able to survive on its own without extra maternal care. To the evolutionary biologist, the mother's cost-benefit analysis shifts away from continued investment in her current infant toward preparation for investment in the next infant. The emotional and physiological mediators of this shift are a reduction in anxiety in the relationship with the new adult male and hormonal changes that make the mother more interested in sexual activity. Behaviorally, the mother responds by being more rejecting toward her infant. Figure 3.3 shows the rate of maternal rejection (preventing the infant from gaining contact and access to the nipple) for mothers in groups with new males versus resident males, by the infant's month of life. The rate of rejection increases for all mothers as they approach the time they are ready to conceive again, but the increase is more dramatic for mothers in groups with new adult males (Fairbanks and McGuire, 1987). New males are more attractive as sexual partners than males who have been resident in the same group for years, and females are more likely to get pregnant in years with new males in the group.

The outcome of this process is a reduction in the intensity of the mother-infant bond and an increase in interactions between the mother and the new

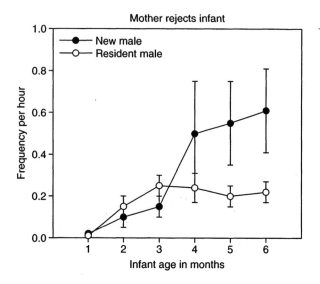

FIGURE 3.3. Mean frequency per hour that vervet mother rejects infant by infant's month of life, with new males versus resident males in the group. *Source:* Redrawn from Fairbanks, 1988a.

adult male in the mother-infant-male triad when the infant reaches five to six months of age. This shift causes anxiety for infants like Oscar, and the increase in maternal rejection is accompanied by an increase in infant distress cries. For the captive vervets at the Vervet Research Colony this transition is relatively benign, but under different circumstances, isolation of the infant while the mother consorts with adult males can be a very stressful experience. Among rhesus monkeys living in large free-ranging groups, most infants become agitated and some show signs of acute depression in response to rejection by the mother at this time (Berman, Rasmussen, and Suomi, 1994).

Mothers, Infants, and Grandmothers

Vervets live in multigenerational family groups and many infants have mothers, grandmothers, and even great-grandmothers living in the group. Motherhood is a challenge for young adult female vervet monkeys. Many are still establishing their position in the female dominance hierarchy, at the same time as they are bearing their first infant. Evidence from the Vervet

Research Colony has shown that a young adult mother does better when the infant's grandmother is still in the group (Fairbanks and McGuire, 1986).

The importance of the mother-infant-grandmother triad is illustrated in the differences between Dawn and Allie, two young mothers who had their first infants in the colony. As a young adult female, Dawn still had a close relationship with her mother Dot. The two spent a lot of time sitting together and were frequent grooming partners. This was a period of stability in the female dominance hierarchy, but if there were any conflicts, Dawn could depend on support from her mother. When Dawn's first infant, Derek, was born, Dawn increased the amount of time she spent sitting near her mother. When Derek was two to three months of age, he would frequently go back and forth between his mother and his grandmother. As she had the security of her mother's presence, Dawn was a relatively relaxed mother and she permitted Derek to come and go at his own pace.

Allie's experience as a first time mother was quite different. Allie had lost her mother the year before, and she had to actively defend her position in the middle of the female hierarchy with only her younger sister for support. When her infant, Ari, was born, she was a relatively anxious mother. Allie tried to avoid other females who were interested in holding and carrying her infant, so she was always on the move. When Ari tried to get away to explore the area around his mother or to play with other infants, his mother would hold him back. Allie would sit with her arms folded closely around Ari, trying to protect him from the world.

These two examples illustrate how the presence of the infant's grandmother influences the mother-infant relationship. First, the older matriarchs have a stabilizing influence on adult female social relationships. They maintain their position at the head of the family, and female affiliative and dominance relationships tend to be stable and predictable. When an older matriarch dies or is removed from the group, females from other families may take advantage of the opportunity to challenge the existing dominance hierarchy and rise in rank. Rank challenges affect the stability and social relationships of all group members.

The grandmother also acts as a "safe place" for a young adult mother to sit when she is worried about too much attention from caretakers. This is particularly true for first time mothers (Fairbanks, 1988a). Finally, the grandmother acts as a sitting and grooming partner for both mother and infant, and spends time carrying and caring for her grandoffspring (Figure 3.4a). When the infants are a little older and coming and going on their own, they approach their grandmother more than any other adult female except for the mother (Figure 3.4b).

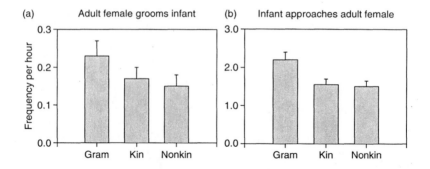

FIGURE 3.4. Mean frequency per hour of behavioral interactions between vervet infants and their maternal grandmother (Gram), other adult female kin (Kin), and nonkin adult females (Nonkin). *Source:* Redrawn from Fairbanks, 1988a.

Young mothers and infants who do not have a grandmother in the group have to manage without any of these advantages. The mothers are more anxious and protective toward their infants (Fairbanks, 1988b). The infants are restricted in their attempts to explore the world around them, and they take longer to develop independence from the mother compared with infants with grandmothers (Fairbanks, 1988a).

The evolutionary biologist looks at the mother-infant-grandmother triad in terms of life history strategies and reproductive success. Females that live a long time are able to provide benefits that promote the reproductive success of their adult daughters and the survival of their grandoffspring (Fairbanks, 2000). This system selects for longevity and the maintenance of affiliative bonds between mother and daughters that persist into adulthood.

The proximate mechanisms that lead to the above outcomes involve regulation of emotional systems. In mother-infant-grandmother triads, the grandmother creates a safer and more predictable social environment that reduces maternal anxiety and allows the mother to be more relaxed in her interactions with her infant. As the infant gains independence from the mother, it forms its own relationship with the grandmother. This scenario underscores the value of having a third individual to balance and buffer an intense dyadic relationship like the mother-infant bond. Mothers and infants who do not have this outlet are more likely to form overly dependent bonds that may have long lasting effects on the emotional development of the infant (Fairbanks and McGuire, 1988).

CONCLUSION

In Bowen family systems theory, triangles emerge as social strategies to transfer anxiety. When a two-person system becomes unstable because of stress, a triangle forms to shift some of the stress away, and protect the two-person system from disintegrating. The level of differentiation, or independence, between the participants also influences the functioning of the triangle system. Triangles involving poorly differentiated relationships tend to become rigid and dysfunctional, while those between well-differentiated individuals are more likely to function as open and adaptive three person systems.

The vervet monkey triads described here share many features with the triangles defined by Bowen theory. For the mother-infant-new adult male triad, tension with an outsider increases closeness in the two-member mother-infant system. Anxiety and tension are shifted around the triangle when the mother later becomes attracted to the new adult male. The outsider is brought into the triangle and the preferential position of the infant is jeopardized. As in Bowen family systems, this dynamic influences, and is influenced by, the level of differentiation among the members. High anxiety mothers form overly restrictive relationships with their infants that retard emotional separation of the infant from the mother. Overly rejecting mothers may also increase anxiety and this leads to difficulties in the emotional regulation of the infant. Vervet monkeys do not have language and they are not as smart as people, but their family relationships can be remarkably similar to those found in human families.

The vervet monkey mother-infant-grandmother is typically a benign and positive triangle. The grandmother is the group member who is most likely to form a supportive and noncompetitive relationship with the mother. Grandmothers can reduce external tensions that increase anxiety for the mother, and can reduce her burden by sharing some of the responsibilities of infant care. This is more similar to an open triangle in a well-differentiated family system. Triangles involving babysitters are more problematic because the help offered by the babysitter is risky to the infant and involves more conflict for the mother. In the vervet triads involving babysitters, the social status and anxiety level of the mother were important factors influencing her ability to use this relationship in a positive way.

The vervet family relationships described here are typical of those that have been reported in other nonhuman primate social systems. They show that there is evolutionary continuity between the family systems of monkeys and people, and that the concept of the triangle can be used to understand nonhuman as well as human family relationships.

REFERENCES

Altmann, J. (1980). *Baboon mothers and infants.* Cambridge, MA: Harvard University Press.

Altmann, J. and Samuels, A. (1992). Costs of maternal care: Infant-carrying in baboons. *Behavioral Ecology and Sociobiology, 29,* 391-398.

Berman, C. M., Rasmussen, K. L., and Suomi, S. J. (1994). Responses of free-ranging rhesus monkeys in a natural form of social separation. I. Parallels with mother-infant separation in captivity. *Child Development, 65,* 1028-1041.

Cheney, D. L. and Seyfarth, R. M. (1990). *How monkeys see the world: Inside the mind of another species.* Chicago: University of Chicago Press.

De Waal, F. and Embree, M. (1997). The triadic nature of primate social relationships. *Family Systems, 4,* 5-18.

Fairbanks, L. A. (1988a). Vervet monkey grandmothers: Interactions with infant grandoffspring. *International Journal of Primatology, 9,* 425-441.

Fairbanks, L. A. (1988b). Vervet monkey grandmothers: Effects on mother-infant relationships. *Behaviour, 104,* 176-188.

Fairbanks, L. A. (1990). Reciprocal benefits of allomothering for female vervet monkeys. *Animal Behaviour, 40,* 553-562.

Fairbanks, L. A. (1996). Individual differences in maternal style of old world monkeys. *Advances in the Study of Behavior, 25,* 579-611.

Fairbanks, L. A. (2000). Maternal investment throughout the life span. In P. F. Whitehead and C. J. Jolly (Eds.), *Old world monkeys* (pp. 341-367). Cambridge, MA: Cambridge University Press.

Fairbanks, L. A. (2003). Primate parenting. In D. Maestripierin (Ed.), *Primate psychology. The mind and behavior of human and nonhuman primates* (pp. 144-170). Cambridge, MA: Harvard University Press.

Fairbanks, L. A. and McGuire, M. T. (1986). Age, reproductive value, and dominance-related behavior in vervet monkey females: Cross-generational influences on social relationships and reproduction. *Animal Behaviour, 34,* 1710-1721.

Fairbanks, L. A. and McGuire, M. T. (1987). Mother-infant relationships in vervet monkeys: Response to new adult males. *International Journal of Primatology, 8,* 351-366.

Fairbanks, L. A. and McGuire, M. T. (1988). Long-term effects of early mothering behavior on responsiveness to the environment in vervet monkeys. *Developmental Psychobiology, 21,* 711-724.

Hauser, M. D. and Fairbanks, L. A. (1988). Mother-offspring conflict in vervet monkeys: Variation in response to ecological conditions. *Animal Behavior, 36,* 802-813.

Hausfater, G. and Hrdy, S. B. (1984). *Infanticide: Comparative and evolutionary perspectives.* New York: Aldine.

Hrdy, S. B. (1976). Care and exploitation of nonhuman primate infants by conspecifics other than the mother. *Advances in the Study of Behavior, 6,* 101-158.

Lancaster, J. (1971). Play-mothering: The relations between juvenile females and young infants among free-ranging vervet monkeys (*Cercopithecus aethiops*). *Folia Primatologica, 15,* 161-182.

Silk, J. B. (1999). Why are infants so attractive to others? The form and function of infant handling in bonnet macaques. *Animal Behaviour, 57,* 1021-1032.

Tomasello, M. and Call, J. (1997). *Primate cognition.* New York: Oxford University Press.

PART II:
TRIANGLES AND DETRIANGLING
IN THE THERAPIST'S OWN FAMILY

Chapter 4

Bowen's Effort to Differentiate a Self: Detriangling from Triangles and Interlocking Triangles

Peter Titelman

INTRODUCTION

This chapter illustrates how Murray Bowen, MD, applied detriangling in his differentiation of self efforts. Bowen not only created a new systems theory of human behavior, but he was the first to apply the clinical application to himself, an effort that would later be described as *the therapist's own family work*. It was as Herculean an effort as Freud's own self-analysis through his interpretation of dreams more than 100 years ago. While Bowen often spoke of having dreamed his systems theory—at least the integration of the concepts into a whole theory—he certainly did not use dream interpretation to understand himself in the context of his family. Rather, he applied his own theory of differentiation of self, with a focus on understanding triangles and interlocking triangles, and then developed a plan to detriangle from the significant interlocking triangles in his own family of origin.

This chapter describes Bowen's effort to extract himself from the middle of the emotional process in his family of origin, in 1966-1967, during a time of some family anxiety that was focused on the way family members were functioning within the family business. The family business with presenting anxiety became a vehicle for Bowen to apply his understanding of the triangle, interlocking triangles, and the process of detriangling in order to understand the process that was maintaining the undifferentiation, or fusion, in a family—in this case his own—and to seek a way through the thicket of the family emotional process. Part of Bowen's effort to differentiate or define a self in relation to his family involved applying his newly discovered knowledge of interlocking triangles. This led to a breakthrough in Bowen theory and clinical practice. The importance of Bowen's effort to test his newly integrated concept of interlocking triangles and detriangling was described briefly in the first chapter of this book. His effort culminated in a planned family experience on February 11, 1967. That effort is described and analyzed as a vehicle for understanding detriangling, and specifically what it means to get outside of an emotional system, through the process of detriangling from interlocking triangles. Examples of Bowen's action plan will be used to illustrate how he went about implementing his plan to detriangle from the interlocking triangles in his family, but the reader is encouraged to seek out Bowen's (1978) full account, "On the Differentiation of Self" (see pp. 467-528).

A HISTORY OF TRIANGLES
IN THE LUFF-BOWEN FAMILY AND BUSINESS

This segment traces the history of the major triangles in Bowen's family that played out around issues in the Luff-Bowen family business, over the course of eighty-eight years. The process described here involves three generations and eighty-eight years.

The business, Luff-Bowen, Inc., a five-generation business that existed for 119 years (1879-1998), consisted of a number of retail stores and services, including a funeral home, located in a small town in Tennessee. Figure 4.1 provides a five-generation family diagram of the Luff-Bowen family.

Bowen's maternal great-grandfather founded the family business in 1879. His maternal grandfather was the second head of the business. At his death in 1916, Bowen's father became the head of the business and shared the ownership with Bowen's mother and maternal uncle. The latter sold his share of the business in 1959 to Bowen's second brother, the thirdborn sibling.

Bowen was the oldest son of five siblings. He was a psychiatrist living in Washington, DC, married, with four children. He described himself as the emotional leader living away from home. His first brother, the secondborn, was an energetic businessman living in another state. He was married and had one child. Bowen's second brother, the thirdborn, named after their father, became the head of the family business at the end of the 1960s. Bowen (1978) described him as functioning as "the head of the clan at home" (p. 486). He was married and had three children. Bowen's first sister, the

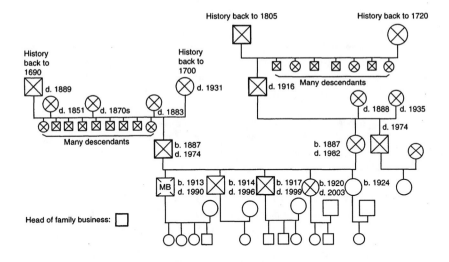

FIGURE 4.1. Bowen Family Diagram

fourth child, was the child most triangled in the family. She was married to an employee of the family business with two children. The second sister, the fifthborn, married a man who owned his own business. He eventually sold his business and came to work for the Luff-Bowen family business. She had one child.

The material for this chapter is drawn mainly from Bowen's (1978) paper, "On the Differentiation of Self," describing his efforts at differentiating a self in his own family through the application of his recently gained understanding of the significance of interlocking triangles. The triangles described by Bowen reflect the anxiety generated by nodal events and the balance of differentiation/undifferentiation in the intertwining emotional process of the family and the business.

Bowen (1978) is careful to describe how triangles in his family, and in all families, are a universal phenomenon and are not pathological. He noted that problems cannot be located in one person, rather they are always situated within triangles:

> Family theory would say that the negative side of the triangle is merely a symptomatic expression of a total family problem, and to focus on issues in one relationship is to misidentify the problem, to convey the impression that the problem is in this one relationship, and to make the triangle more fixed and less reversible. (p. 489)

Triangle One

The first major triangle in the combination of home and business included Bowen's father, mother, and maternal half uncle, the three owners of the business following the death of Bowen's maternal grandfather in 1916. Bowen (1978) pointed out that

> in calm periods a triangle functions as a comfortable twosome and an outsider: My uncle was the outside one, which caused no problems for him since he had a close relationship with his mother who was relatively uninvolved in business issues. (p. 489)

The first triangle is illustrated in Figure 4.2. In stressful periods a triangle has two positive sides and a negative side. Bowen (1978) describes this family triangle during stressful periods in the following terms:

> Any member of a relatively fixed triangle perceives himself as "caught." My father was caught between his wife and her brother, my uncle between his sister and her husband, and my mother between her husband and her brother. My father was the one most active in business and also in civic and community activity. In the business he represented expansion and "progress." My uncle represented caution, and he functioned as the loyal opposition. (p. 489)

In times of stress the negative side of the triangle was between Bowen's father and his uncle. The conflict was generally indirectly expressed as discontent between the two men communicated through Bowen's mother (see Bowen, 1978, p. 489). Figure 4.3 illustrates the first triangle when stress was present.

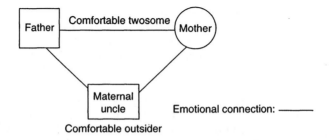

FIGURE 4.2. Triangle One: Under Low Stress

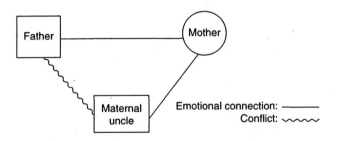

FIGURE 4.3. Triangle One: Under Stress

A second version of the first triangle developed during the period after Bowen and his siblings had left home for college and World War II. Bowen's uncle and aunt constituted one corner of the triangle, with the negative sides being between them and Bowen's parents. Bowen's mother was working in the business full-time due to difficulty finding employees during the war. The third point consisted of members outside the family, including employees. Bowen (1978) states that generally the negativity between his parents and his uncle and aunt tended to be expressed by his aunt through verbalizing her discontent outside of the family. Several years later, according to Bowen (Wiseman, 1996),

> the family went into a hell of an uproar in 1959, which was about eighty years out. And that's when Uncle was influenced by his wife. He was sort of a passive fellow. But his wife got into a spat about running the business. And, well, when he got into the thing with Uncle's wife they got into a big fight. I remember one big fight, when Dad bought a new ambulance, which was fairly expensive, and she didn't like it. And she slapped Dad one day and knocked his glasses off. (p. 58)

Figure 4.4 illustrates the second version of the first triangle described in previous text. As the negative side of a triangle is merely the expression of a total family problem, one wonders if Bowen's aunt was also expressing emotional reactivity for her husband, Bowen's uncle, related to issues of financial and business control. It is often easier to see the problem as being initiated, or even caused, by an outside member of the family, rather than seeing the *outsider,* in this case Bowen's aunt, as being the one who is merely expressing the total family problem.

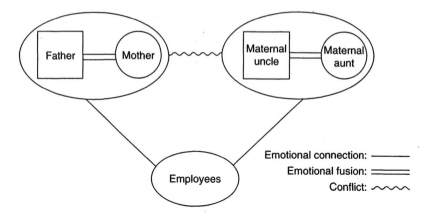

FIGURE 4.4. Second Version of Triangle One

Triangle Two

When Bowen's younger brother and sisters and their husbands became active in the business after World War II, there were, according to Bowen (1978), "shifting alignments on lesser issues" (p. 490), but the basic triangle involving the family and the business now consisted of Bowen's father and brother at one corner, his mother and younger sister at another, and his uncle and aunt at the third. Figure 4.5 illustrates the second triangle.

Bowen (1978) wrote:

> Stress occurred around the issue of expansion of the business and when my brother pressed for his share of the business. With each period of stress there would be discussion about dividing the business, some new recognition of my brother's contribution, and a new period of calm. This sequence continued until the time came when, in a new period of stress, my uncle sold his half to my second brother and retired. (p. 490)

At this point the business was reorganized with the brother holding 50 percent of the stock and Bowen's parents holding 25 percent each. Bowen (1978) alluded to the problem when he wrote:

> The family tended to see the new arrangement as the final solution. This is another predictable characteristic of emotional systems. When

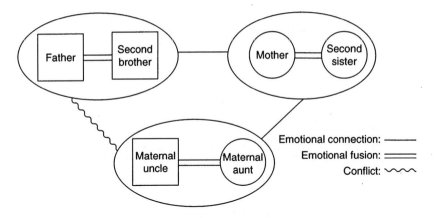

FIGURE 4.5. Triangle Two

the focus of the symptom is removed from the system, the system acts as if the problem is solved. If the system could think instead of react, it would know that it would be only a matter of time until the symptom surfaced elsewhere. (p. 490)

Bowen knew that the exiting of the problematic aunt and uncle would not be a final solution. The second triangle suggests that when the negative side was removed, conflict between the two previously calm sides would flare up under stress. It seems predictable that the issues of financial control and leadership of the business would rise again involving conflict between Bowen's siblings, his parents, and himself.

Triangle Three

Until stress emerged about eight years later, in 1966, the central triangle involved father and son on the inside of the business, and Bowen's mother and younger sister in the outside corner. During calm periods, there was no emotional pressure for the outside members to move in or the insiders to move outside. Figure 4.6 illustrates the third triangle when the emotional system was calm.

Bowen's (1978) original hypothesis, after the reorganization of the business, was that in the significant triangle in the family and business consisting of his father, mother, and second brother, the negative side of the conflict would be between his brother and his mother. He again elaborated

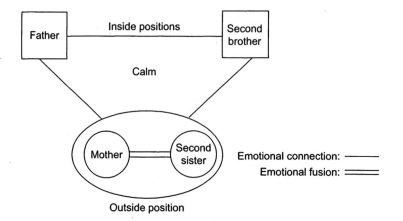

FIGURE 4.6. Triangle Three

on the importance of the business to the family emotional process when he wrote that

> the prevailing stress in my total family was connected with the busi-
> ness. Early in this period, my second brother developed a brief symp-
> tom slightly suggestive of a malignancy. Since the "go power" for the
> family rested with him, anxiety went very high for a week until the
> possibility of malignancy was ruled out. Thereafter, the stress was re-
> lated more to health issues in my parents and disposition of the busi-
> ness in case of their deaths. My parents were getting quite old and
> each serious-appearing illness in either sent out some kind of an alarm,
> and precipitated some kind of family reaction. (p. 504)

Triangle Four

The central triangle now consisted of Bowen's father in one corner; his mother, youngest sister, and youngest sister's husband in another corner; and Bowen's second brother and his nuclear family in the third corner. The conflictual side of the triangle existed between the mother and youngest sister and her husband on one side and the second brother and his nuclear family on the other side. Figure 4.7 illustrates the transformation of the fourth triangle when stress arose.

The presenting stress involved the death of Bowen's second brother's wife's brother in November 1966. He had been a vigorous businessman liv-

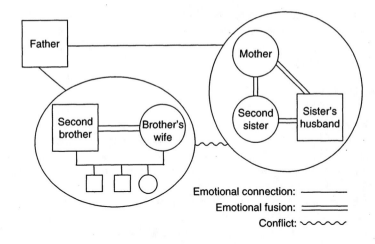

FIGURE 4.7. Triangle Four

ing in another state, he was a "head of the clan" like Bowen's second brother, and Bowen predicted that his death would send emotional shock waves through his family of origin. This prediction was based on Bowen's developing understanding of interlocking triangles. His prediction was correct. He noted that anxiety moved from his sister-in-law to his brother to his youngest sister. About two weeks later an overt disagreement in the central family triangle became an "alive" issue for discussion throughout the family. This issue involved, once again, the issue of control of the family business. According to Bowen (1978):

> My second brother was pressing my parents for a small block of stock, which would give him control of the family business. My father, in the togetherness side of the triangle with my second brother, was agreeable, but my mother was opposed. (p. 507)

Interlocking Triangles: Five

Another factor that led to Bowen's understanding of interlocking triangles was his ability to see the relationships within and between a set of triangles: the primary triangle of himself and his parents, and the significant triangle involving himself, his second brother, and his mother. While Bowen believed that several years of effort had helped him get a fairly clear operating position in relation to both of his parents, he recognized that the growing distance between himself and his second brother was interlocked with his relation to his parents, particularly his mother. Figure 4.8 illustrates these interlocking triangles.

Triangle Six

Bowen (1978) wrote that he and his second brother had always been close. However, in retrospect he realized that after the reorganization of the business there was an increasing pattern of his pursuing and his brother distancing from him. Bowen would make efforts to get together with his second brother when he came to visit his family of origin, but each time his brother would leave for a vacation or a business trip. The distance between Bowen and his second brother increased, and the family stories about the brothers increased. Each of them was hearing stories about the other from the family network, but they were not seeing each other face to face. As the brother rarely wrote letters, there was a cutoff of communication. Bowen (1978) described how the interlocking triangling led to a new triangle:

> An important triangle . . . at this time was the one between my mother, my second brother, and me. I had worked very hard on the triangle with my parents and me, assuming that my problem would be solved. Now a new version of the problem had been displaced onto the new triangle. (p. 505)

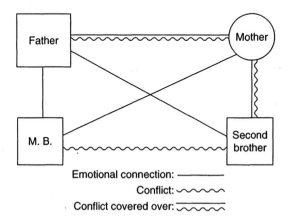

FIGURE 4.8. Interlocking Triangles: Five

Figure 4.9 illustrates the triangle involving Bowen, his mother, and his second brother. This triangle became active when conflict arose in the business. At that time Bowen (1978) describes his mother communicating, directly or indirectly, to his second brother, that Bowen was on her side, and his brother would react as if this were a reality (see p. 505). Bowen began to realize how this triangling process operated during some of his trips back to Tennessee. His mother would gossip to him, telling stories implying that she and he were in agreement about the second brother.

BOWEN'S DETRIANGLING EFFORTS OVER
A TWELVE-YEAR PERIOD: 1954-1966

Bowen (1978) wrote that one of the useful ways of detriangling from secret communication is to go directly to the third person and report the message in a neutral fashion. Bowen was unable to do this as he was out of effective contact with his second brother, who was avoiding him. Telling his mother he was neutral was not a sufficient method of detriangling. He (Bowen, 1978) tried several other ways of detriangling: for example, just listening to his mother's stories and eventually commenting: "That's one of the better stories" (p. 505). However, this was also not effective.

Bowen had believed that differentiating a self was a two-step process: (1) developing person-to-person relationships with one's parents, and (2) detriangling self from one's parents. His assumption was that if one differentiates a self from one's parents that is sufficient. However, from years of not achieving his hoped for goal of not getting fused into the family system when

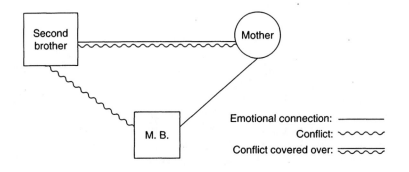

FIGURE 4.9. Triangle Six

he visited them, he realized that something was missing in order to achieve this goal. This led him to search for a new direction.

During the previous twelve years of working on differentiating himself in relation to his family, Bowen (1978) was looking for a way "to be able to have an entire visit with the family without becoming fused into the emotional system. I still had not significantly found a way to extricate myself before the visit had ended" (p. 503).

Bowen had had some notion of interlocking triangles for ten years, but had not fully integrated it into his theory or clinical work. In his paper (Bowen, 1978), "The Use of Family Theory in Clinical Practice," written in August, 1966 (originally published in 1967), he expressed his fuller understanding of the importance of interlocking triangles in the functioning of the family. The concept of interlocking triangles provided a blueprint to overcome his previous obstacles in his effort to be in contact with his family of origin without being caught in the interlocking triangles of the family emotional system.

BOWEN'S BREAKTHROUGH EXPERIENCE, DETRIANGLING FROM INTERLOCKING TRIANGLES: 1966-1967

Bowen realized, in retrospect, that he was not neutral and that detriangling would take a more action-oriented way of defining himself. His goal was to focus on the triangle that consisted of his mother, second brother, and himself, and ideally he wanted to include his father as well. This would involve his primary triangle in which he had done most of his work, and the *interlocking* new triangle in which conflict had emerged: that is to say, the second brother, mother, and himself.

Achieving an outcome in which he would *get outside* of the family emotional system, and at the same time *be in contact* with it, involved a highly complex plan of action. He developed the plan over two months prior to a visit with his family of origin, all of whom, but one brother, lived in a small town in Tennessee. Bowen brought together all the significant triangles and interlocking triangles in his family in one room on February 11, 1967. By being able to observe and diagram the predictable triangles and interlocking triangles, being an objective observer of the emotional process in the family, and controlling his own emotional reactivity, he was able to carry out his plan. However, it is important to note that this plan was preceded by a twelve-year effort to understand and modify his own position in his family. Prior to this effort his focus was on developing person-to-person relationships with all members of his family of origin, particularly his parents, and important members of his extended family, gathering a multigenerational family history, and making efforts to differentiate a self in the primary triangle of himself and his parents.

In the past Bowen had been fairly successful at detriangling from one triangle, only to have the tension move into another triangle. In order to break through the communication of "secrets," he prepared for all the peripheral triangles that might surface in response to his detriangling effort. He developed a plan that would create a "tempest in a teapot" by evoking the interlocking triangling process in his family by bringing all members of the significant interlocking triangles together. It was necessary for Bowen to raise the emotional temperature in his family, creating a "tempest in a teapot," because anxiety in his family was for the most part relatively contained. If the family was an emotionally explosive or highly anxious one, then he would not have sought to raise the anxiety level. In that case he would have tried to decrease the anxiety as part of his intervention.

In raising the temperature in his relatively quiet family Bowen (1978) devised a way to put himself outside of the emotional process, in order to stay detriangled from each and every family member. His effort was to avoid having any "allies" with other family members, putting all of his family members in an emotional clump. As Bowen's second brother had been avoiding him, he wanted to devise a plan by which his brother would seek him out (see pp. 505–508).

In spite of the recent issue of ownership of the family business, Bowen (1978) decided to resurrect old emotional issues:

> The recent conflict over the business would still be sufficiently alive during the visit, but to focus on that would make the issue into a reality issue. So, I devised the plan to stir up the family emotional system, using old issues from the past around which to work. (p. 508)

Another part of the plan was to include the first brother who was an important part of the family, but lived in a different state and tended to distance himself from the family emotional process.

Bowen's action plan called for a series of letters, phone calls, and discussion with family members utilizing a number of different positions and strategies while maintaining a neutral position: reversal, not holding gossipy secrets by telling stories, humor, and putting the other together with the other and self outside. All of these moves could only be effective because of his extensive prior efforts to *develop* and maintain considerable emotional contact over time with the significant members of his family. Bowen's strategy was to have an emotional issue for each of the key members of the family.

Initially, Bowen called his first brother and told him about the "awful conflict" in the family, telling him his help was needed, and the date Bowen was going to be home. Here Bowen was using exaggeration to try and engage this brother in the family gathering.

Bowen's greatest effort went into writing a long letter to his second brother in which the focus was on their own relationship with each other and their relationship within their nuclear family. Bowen related stories he had heard about his second brother, told him everyone knew about these stories, and that the family had warned him not to tell the brother lest he get upset. He asked his brother why he had not found out what the family was saying about him, particularly about him and the business. Bowen (1978) said he did not care who controlled the business, but he "recognized his second brother's contribution to the business and to the entire family" (p. 509). This approach allowed Bowen to separate himself from the stories and insure that his brother would want to meet and deal with him when he came for the visit, rather than avoid him. It would bring him to the family table. Bowen also employed reversals, imploring his second brother, who he knew to be an overfunctioning, overresponsible individual in the business and the family, to be more responsible for the business, their parents, his wife and children, and his despondent sister. Bowen (1978) wrote: "I would be home on a specific date, but since I had already said all that was necessary in the letter, it would not be necessary to see him unless he had something to say to me" (p. 510). He signed his letter, "Your Meddlesome Brother." Bowen wrote that letter exactly two weeks before his trip home.

At the same time he wrote to his first brother to tell him the exact date he would be home, and he told him that if he cared about the family he would come home to help clear up this terrible situation. At the same time, Bowen also wrote to the first of his younger sisters saying that he had heard about her distress and had written to her brother to help her out until he got there. He signed that letter, "Your Worrisome Brother." These letters were designed to stir up a "tempest in a teapot," in order to put Bowen outside the emotional system, without allies, to detriangle himself from the family group by putting each of them together with the others and putting himself out of the emotional anxiety wave that washed over the family emotional system.

A week later Bowen called his parents with the excuse of finding out who would meet him at the airport. He really called to get a reading of the results of the letter to his second brother. His mother reported that his brother was furious about the letter Bowen wrote to him. Bowen pretended that he did not know what letter that could be, indicating he had not received or sent a letter to that brother in a long while. Bowen's mother said his second brother had a signed letter from him, was showing it around, and would take care of Bowen when he arrived. Bowen now knew that his second brother would meet with him. The plan was working. Why was Bowen not admitting to his mother that he wrote the letter? The answer is that he did not want to share his strategy for getting his brother to meet with him and the family. He did not want her on his side. He did not want to be in the inside position of the triangle consisting of his mother, second brother and himself. He wanted to be in the outside position.

Within a few hours of his phone call with his mother, Bowen (1978) wrote several additional letters. One letter was to his youngest sister, the one who functioned as the responsible woman in the second generation. He told her that he had just found out that he had upset his second brother by writing some things to him, but he could not imagine what they could possibly be. He wrote her: "I was deeply grieved because that could upset the whole family, and as 'Big Mother' she had a responsibility to do whatever was necessary to soothe him with whatever Big Mothers do to calm people" (p. 511).

Bowen went on to ask his sister to keep his thoughts confidential as he did not also want to upset their mother. He asked her to immediately advise him as to what he could do to make amends to "Little Brother." He added that if his thoughts were upsetting his second brother maybe he could think different or "right" thoughts. Bowen signed this letter, "Your Anxious Brother." The strategy behind this letter seems to have been to move his second brother and first sister together, and continue to put himself in the outside of yet another triangle.

In the same mail, Bowen sent an exactly opposite letter to his mother in which he admitted sending the letter to his second brother, saying he did not tell her because he was afraid she would ruin his plan to make Little Brother angry with him, and draw his brother's anger away from the family. Then he told her that this was to be kept confidential and any leak would ruin the entire strategy. He signed his letter, "Your Strategic Son." Bowen later found out that his mother's reaction to his letter was to describe it as a crazy letter and not knowing what to do with it, she burned it. Therefore, Bowen's letter to his mother served to back her away from being his ally in the triangle consisting of his second brother, mother, and himself. It may have even moved her in the direction of his second brother.

The day before Bowen's trip, he received a letter from his youngest sister saying that his second brother and their parents had spent a couple of hours together, discussing the horrible letter he had received from Big Brother, and his second brother had apparently won them over to his side. Bowen knew that his mother and brother were now in the inside positions, and Bowen was where he wanted to be, in the outside position of the mother-second brother-self triangle. The father, who never apparently was in conflict with the second brother, appears to have been appended to the mother's inside position in this situation. This already might have broken the logjam in regard to the second brother's seeking the extra block in order to gain a controlling interest in the family business. Therefore, in the midst of setting up a "tempest in a teapot" centered around rather small emotional issues in the family, Bowen created a situation in which the current larger issue of the family business ownership took a back seat and began to dissolve as a live issue. At the end of the second sister's letter she wrote, "I am back of you if I can be of help. I am really looking forward to your visit this time. It should be very interesting" (Bowen, 1978, p. 512).

The high level of positive feeling coming from youngest sister toward Bowen sent a warning to him that her approach represented the kind of togetherness he was seeking to avoid. His response was to tell her that he was going to tell the family she had invited him home to help her with her "Big Mother" position. In response, his youngest sister stopped taking sides with Bowen by indicating that she took seriously the issues Bowen had raised.

Again, the purpose of Bowen's efforts—the conflicting messages—was to prevent any one family segment or person from getting on his side. He wanted to be in the outside position in every triangle that made up the interlocking triangles. In this way he would not be caught in the triangles, and the peripheral benefit of this differentiation effort would be that the others would be more likely to deal directly, person-to-person with each other. They could thus deal with their conflicts without being able to triangle Bowen, actively or passively, into the family fixer position. The only letter that was not circulated between family members was the "Strategic Son" letter to his mother, which she had burned.

The trip was planned so that Bowen would stay two days with his family, then go to a medical meeting with his wife for three days, and then return to spend two days with his family. Bowen's wife had no knowledge of what he had been planning to do with his family. He had not told her because in order to be effective when differentiating a self, each planned move must come solely from the person who makes the effort. The decisions and actions, for better or worse, are the responsibility of the individual taking the action. To share the plan with another person who is a part of the system raises the level of anxiety and inevitably brings failure.

Bowen and his wife arrived late Saturday evening at his parents' house. There was no word from any segment of the family on Sunday morning. Bowen, his wife, and his parents were invited to an early afternoon meal at his youngest sister's and her husband's house. After the meal the second brother telephoned to say he was checking around town to find out where his older brother was, and he would be there in a few minutes. Now his second brother was seeking Bowen, instead of Bowen pursuing him, and the presence of the second brother and his wife made up the perfect group for the meeting Bowen had long rehearsed. All the important triangles in the family system were represented. Bowen's (1978) immediate goal was to "avoid defending anything, or attacking any issues, to avoid getting angry even with provocation, and to have an instant casual response to any comment" (p. 513).

After Bowen's second brother arrived and exchanged greetings, he quickly took out "the letter" and said he wanted to discuss the letter Bowen wrote when he was drunk. Bowen parried the comment lightly by saying that was the advantage of living where booze was cheap. The meeting went on for two hours and Bowen reports that it was all personal space. The second brother, his wife, and Bowen were the principals in the center, with Bowen's mother just behind them. The conversation was centered between the second brother, Bowen, and his mother. The brother reacted most strongly to a story about himself and threatened to sue Bowen over it. Bowen's response was to tell his second brother that he should find out who started the story and prosecute that person. There was more talk about stories and Bowen told his brother he was surprised that he did not know what others were saying about him. He hoped his brother would pay more attention to these stories as he lived there all the time, and Bowen only heard them when he came to visit. Then the second brother and his wife began to tell negative stories about Bowen. His response was to be amused and he told them he was surprised they had not heard some really good ones about him. They would if they had just paid attention and listened better.

Toward the end of the meeting, Bowen's brother accused him of being in league with their mother, starting during a trip that Bowen and she took to explore some of her family history. At that point Bowen (1978) said:

> "You are intuitive about some things! How did you know about that? You're right. That's when she and I planned the whole thing." Mother responded vigorously with, "That's the biggest lie I ever heard! I will never tell you anything else again." I turned to my brother and said, "Now you see how she tries to wangle out of things, when she is caught with the truth." (p. 513)

From the family meeting just described, it is clear that Bowen was not reactive to the anger of his brother and sister-in-law. He used reversals and humor to detoxify the anger of his brother. Then, when the brother put Bowen and their mother in the togetherness of the inside positions, the reader can see how Bowen deftly detriangled himself by exaggerating his connection with his mother, with the result that she denied her efforts to get Bowen to side with her against his second brother. She indicated she will no longer be telling Bowen stories about others. When the brother and his wife were leaving the family meeting, his wife indicated that she understood the problem triangling had wrought in the family, when she said: "I never saw such a family in all my life. I think we should do more talking *to* each other and less talking *about* each other" (Bowen, 1978, p. 513).

By the time the Sunday meeting was over, Bowen knew that he had accomplished what he had set out to do: (1) he went through an entire family visit without being triangled, or without being fused into the family emotional system; (2) he had interrupted the anxiety wave in the family; and (3) he "also knew that my postulations about interlocking triangles were accurate by the time the family meeting started" (Bowen, 1978, p. 514).

The following day after the family meeting, Bowen knew that there was follow-up work he needed to do. He needed to continue being in relationship with the family system, even though there was an inclination for the feeling system to withdraw and seek comfortable distance, resulting in the system "tightening up." Although he did not want to go see him, Bowen knew he had to make the effort to seek out his second brother, who he knew was still angry and reactive. He found him alone and willing to talk. After a little small talk, and assurance that the issue of the family business would not come up, Bowen asked him if he was still mad. The second brother responded with a detached, "Hell, no!" After offering to tell him some more stories Bowen had heard about him, with the brother declining to listen to them, or receive them by mail, Bowen accepted his brother's position, and then passed on a compliment he had heard about his brother. This lightened his brother up, and Bowen and his brother proceeded to have their first person-to-person talk in many years.

Later in the day, Bowen made person-to-person contact with his first sister. In the course of telling her about his second brother's effort to take care of her and her not wanting to listen to him, Bowen experienced his detriangling efforts as coming naturally. He also had a good phone contact with his first brother, with whom he brought up his delinquency for not coming home for the weekend and told him as he had failed to solve the family's problems, it was up to him to come home and deal with the family's emergency situation.

Bowen and his wife left for the three-day meeting. When they returned to visit the family for two more days, he found his family calmer than they had been in a long time. His second sister and her husband were even more casual and detached than before. He had his first person-to-person talk with her in many years. His second brother's son stopped by to say goodbye to Bowen, which he usually did not do, and he thanked Bowen for coming home for the week. A later telephone conversation with the first brother went well and Bowen did much detriangling with him. His wife tried to ask about Bowen's "plan and strategy" but he avoided getting triangled with a new ally. Bowen's mother wrote to him saying: "With all of its ups and downs, your last trip was the greatest ever" (Bowen, 1978, p. 516). After returning to his own home, Bowen had an exchange with his first sister in which he told her how he was continuing to try to get other family members to take care of her. She responded by kidding about how Bowen himself did nothing to take care of her. She went on to say she was perfectly capable of taking care of herself at this point.

The family was calmer over the next three years than it had ever been before. According to Bowen (1978), "the family has been on the best overall level of adaptation in many years. There have been anxieties and small crises, but they have been less intense than formerly" (p. 516).

After that differentiating effort, Bowen found that he was able to draw upon his experience of detriangling from interlocking triangles to get himself outside the family emotional process, in order to define an I-Position, apart from the family anxiety.

In regard to the impact of the "family experience" on the family business, Bowen (1978) wrote: "The issue between my parents and brother about stock and control of the family business completely faded after that 'family experience' weekend" (p. 516). In a telephone interview with Bowen's second brother (May 1998), almost thirty years after Bowen's differentiating efforts, the second brother told this author, in essence, that the issue was no longer significant. He reported that he "paid his parents and got control of the business in 1969." Therefore, the transfer of control from the parents to the second brother took place approximately two years after Bowen's "family experience" (his planned differentiating effort). Bowen's report of his experience confirmed his idea that by focusing on the anxiety in the family, in the context of interlocking triangles, family business issues were dealt with more constructively. Also the family could deal more directly with each other in regard to family emotional relationship issues in general, and when these issues were addressed there was less emotional reactivity in the family.

Bowen indicated that the emotional issues underlying the triangles and interlocking triangles that formed around relationships in the family business ultimately related to anxiety regarding potential loss of significant members of the family, that is to say the parents, who were getting older. Their impending deaths and the potential dissolution of the family, through the loss of key members, most likely was the bedrock issue underlying the anxiety in this family.

SUMMARY

Bowen's efforts to get outside of the family system, and at the same time be in contact with it, involved a variety of planned actions through which he brought the significant triangles and interlocking triangles in his family together. He did this through the use of humor, reversals, and putting the other together with the other and putting himself outside the emotional system; remaining objective, neutral, and maintaining and developing solid person-to-person relationships with the significant members of his family.

It is clear that Bowen's intention and success in his differentiation of self effort in relation to his family of origin, through his effort to detriangle from interlocking triangles, was done in order to get outside of the emotional system of his family, while at the same time being a responsible member of the family. This effort was in part successful because it was not an effort to change or fix the family. Bowen's primary goal was to change his way of being in relation to his family. Nevertheless, the effort to work on self may lead to a byproduct whereby the family as a whole may change its basic level of functioning.

Bowen's expansion of the triangle concept to include interlocking triangles and his efforts to detriangle from them led to a major breakthrough, both in the development of Bowen's family systems theory and in its application to differentiation of self. Under the direction of a coach, detriangling of triangles and interlocking triangles became a significant part of the theoretical-therapeutic blueprint for other Bowen trained coaches in their efforts to increase their differentiation of self levels, and for utilization in their clinical work.

REFERENCES

Bowen Jr., J. (1998, May 15). Telephone conversation with the author.

Bowen, J. (2006, June 12). E-mail to this author.

Bowen, M. (1978). *Family therapy in clinical practice.* Northvale, NJ: Jason Aronson, Inc.

Wiseman, K. K. (1996). Human social systems: Introduction. In P. A. Comella, J. Bader, J. S. Ball, K. K. Wiseman, and R. R. Sagar (Eds.), *The emotional side of organizations: Applications of Bowen Theory* (pp. 57-59). Washington, DC: Georgetown Family Center.

Chapter 5

Exploring Emotional Triangles in Past Generations of a Family

James B. Smith

INTRODUCTION

Psychiatrist Murray Bowen (1978) discovered from clinical practice and clinical research that the family is the basic unit for understanding human functioning. Family is broadly defined by the author to include every person emotionally attached to one individual. Bowen viewed the family as an emotional and relationship system. Emotional is synonymous with instinctual, specifying that the family is a biological unit. System denotes the interdependence of the family unit, distinguishing it from a collection of unconnected individuals. Bowen saw the emotional system as the force that motivates and the relationship system as the way the emotional system is expressed.

Bowen found that emotional, social, and physical symptoms in individuals develop in the interplay of automatic, emotional forces in the family. For example, unregulated use of alcohol—or depression or cancer—in an individual is symptomatic of a stressed family system. Conceptually, this is night and day from viewing symptoms as indicators of flaws in individuals. Bowen also found that the family is the unit in which symptoms ameliorate. Change comes when one family member relates more maturely to others in

---

Author's note: An early draft of this chapter was distributed to the author's extended family for comments, corrections, and additions. What he has learned from their generous responses and from subsequent conversations with them in the editing and rewriting of the chapter cannot be overestimated.

the family at times of higher family stress about the uncomfortable issues between them. Conceptually, this is light years away from viewing symptoms as individual flaws to be fixed with psychotherapy and/or medication.

Bowen also discovered predictable relationship patterns in this interplay of automatic emotional forces in human families. When the threshold for *anxiety, tension,* or *discomfort* in any twosome (A + B) is exceeded, a third person (C) is automatically included. *Comfort* for A + C (or B + C) is then restored in their *togetherness.* The excluded third person (B or A) is then in a less comfortable outside position. When the threshold for anxiety in the original threesome is exceeded, other persons are automatically incorporated (D + E + F + G and so forth) in order to absorb anxiety and reestablish equilibrium in the system. Bowen called these automatic relationship patterns *emotional triangles* and *interlocking emotional triangles,* indicating that they are biological rather than mathematical in nature, and specifying that they are the most stable human emotional and relationship unit.

There is evidence of similar if not identical processes occurring elsewhere in the natural world, such as in the social systems of higher primates (de Waal, 1989). It is assumed that emotional triangles have evolved over tens of thousands of years as the human has evolved, functioning to regulate both anxiety and individual functioning in human social systems. They are adaptive mechanisms that have evolved along with other adaptive mechanisms such as swallowing, the knee-jerk, and fight-or-flight reactions. As with other involuntary responses that can be controlled voluntarily, the human can also *voluntarily* manage the *involuntary* functioning of triangles, as well as intentionally create triangles.

With his highly evolved prefrontal cortex, the human has the capacity to regulate self as a separate organism within the emotional-instinctual forces of triangles. This involves a variable involuntary and voluntary capacity to observe the flow of anxiety in triangles and to take deliberate and thought-out positions, separating self from others in the triangles about the issues driving the triangles, while remaining in the relationships. Bowen identified this process as differentiating a self or defining a self. It is assumed that emotional triangles involuntarily regulate individual functioning much more often than individuals regulate their own functioning as separately defined individuals in relationships.

Emotional triangles occur involuntarily in all human relationships all of the time. This is observed even in the most casual of relationships with persons meeting for the first time. This can be tested by watching self and others at a social event where one is a stranger. Triangles are highly evident in relationships of long duration and extended history, in which more rigid *functioning positions* develop, for instance in a mother, father, and child triangle in a nuclear family, with two fixed on the inside and one outside. These less flexible triangles can be observed over generations in a family in response to specific issues at times of higher family stress, the players changing, but reciprocal functioning positions—for example, overresponsible and underresponsible, comfortable and uncomfortable, and inside and outside— remaining relatively unchanged. Issues that emotionally glue families together over generations vary from family to family and from generation to generation in the same family. These issues include choice of marriage partner, child-raising, political, moral, and religious beliefs, irresponsible behavior, and educational and vocational choices, among many others. An individual less able to involuntarily or voluntarily differentiate a self in a family is more vulnerable for all physical, emotional, and social problems. In contrast to a structural view of problems, the author understands all life problems to be *functional dysfunctions* that develop in individuals in order to maintain equilibrium in emotional systems.

DIFFERENTIATING A SELF

The author has been a student of Bowen theory for thirty years. He has made a continuing effort to differentiate a self in his extended family. Based on Bowen theory (Bowen, 1978, pp. 539-543), this effort has taken the following form:

- Working toward person-to-person relationships with all *living* family members
- Working toward knowing *dead* family members by gathering factual information, separating what is known from what is unknown, testing hypotheses, evaluating actions taken, and raising questions for future research about them
- Becoming a more detached observer of self and manager of reactivity in self
- Detriangling self from emotional situations
- Learning from the triangles in current and past generations

In this chapter the author focuses on understanding emotional triangles in his parents' generation, how they connect to his grandparents' and great-grandparents' generations and to the family in which he grew up. Hypotheses are formed and questions posed, based on his observations of past and current emotional triangles and from other ideas and concepts in Bowen systems theory (Bowen, 1978). What is known is distinguished from what is unknown, with the source(s) of evidence indicated. Family research, the investigation of public documents and of private documents that came to him following the deaths of his parents in 1976, has been ongoing during these thirty years. This research has occurred at a variable rate.

This thirty-year effort at defining a self in his family has resulted in a gradually more objective view of the past and the present. The opacity between objective or *public fact, functional facts,* and *guesswork, opinion,* or *family lore* has become more transparent. The author assumes that there is a direct connection between understanding emotional triangles in past generations and understanding triangles and defining a self in the current generation. He believes that how past generations of families have functioned has the most influence on and is the best predictor of current and future family functioning. Understanding current triangles allows one to predict future and past triangles; understanding past triangles permits one to predict current and future triangles. This understanding is both voluntary and involuntary, as is the process of becoming aware of connections between relationship patterns in the past and current generations of a family. Coming to better understand any *particular* family results in a better understanding of *all* families.

FATHER'S FAMILY OF ORIGIN

The author's father, Clyde James Smith Jr., was the only child of Clyde James Smith and Maude Carrie Little (see Figure 5.1). Clyde James Smith Jr. was born in Los Angeles, California, in January 1907 and died in Carmel, California, in November 1976. Whether or not his parents had any other pregnancies, Junior, as he was called by his parents and extended family, did not know. It is speculated that his mother wanted more children, perhaps a girl, but his father did not, after experiencing the intense attachment between his wife and son. It could well be that his mother was unwilling or unable to have more children.

It is known from the author's conversations with his father, and from surviving pictures of Junior's family of origin that his father was raised a "Little Lord Fauntleroy," with long golden curls that the author's mother said were cut only after Junior began school, a practice apparently not uncommon at the turn of the twentieth century. A lasting impression is that he was the "apple of his mother's eye," and that as he grew into adulthood, the relationship with his father became increasingly conflictual and distant to the point of cutoff in later adulthood.

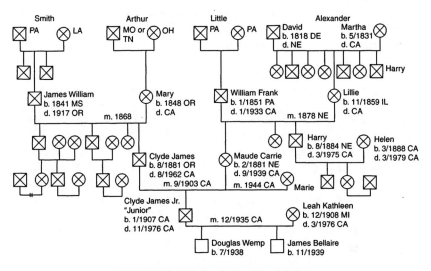

FIGURE 5.1. Father's Family of Origin

There is no evidence as to his parents' courtship, how they met or how their families viewed their courtship and subsequent marriage. It is known from public and private records that they were married in 1903 in Los Angeles. During the courtship their relationship was probably comfortable. This idea comes from the idea in Bowen theory that the most comfortable period in any mating relationship is during courtship when both desire to make a good impression on the other. Their wedding pictures depict two handsome individuals. Tension and distance between them probably increased before and perhaps during the pregnancy, as evidenced by the intensity of the reported attachment between mother and son during their lives. A more inflexible triangle in his family of origin seems to have been Junior and his mother on the comfortable inside, his father on the uncomfortable outside.

Junior was raised in Los Angeles, in a strict Methodist household that did not condone the use of alcoholic beverages. It was never asked whether the Methodism and the prohibition against alcohol were joint decisions by his parents or if it came more from one or the other parent to whom the other submitted. The fact that his father was said to have been active in the temperance movement in California, that he was politically very conservative and reportedly a member of the John Birch Society in later years, and that he probably had the last word in the family suggests that it came from him.

It is conjectured that his mother went along with her husband, buffering her son from his father. This would have functioned to secure their comfortable inside positions and his father's uncomfortable outside position in this emotional unit.

Junior graduated from Los Angeles High School in June 1923 and went to Stanford University, presumably beginning that September, even though he would have been only age sixteen at the time. To what degree was it his decision that he should go to college? How much was it his decision to go to Stanford University? How much were these decisions influenced by others? Who influenced the decisions? Knowing how much a decision is made for self or made for others is important in evaluating the ability to define a self. It is speculated that both going to college and going to Stanford may have been more his mother's idea, her younger brother's idea, or that Junior prevailed upon his mother to win his father's approval if indeed it was mostly his idea. Junior told the author that he went to Stanford because his mother's younger brother had attended there. This has not been documented.

It is believed that Junior initially majored in electrical engineering, which as the author's older brother suggested, was not so trivial an achievement for the social chairman of Theta Xi fraternity who had access to the best sources of bootleg alcohol in San Francisco (D. Smith, 2005, personal communication). The guess is that it was his father's decision as to his major. Surviving documents suggest that he was a serious student. When Junior later switched majors to general engineering, he said that his father had not approved.

Junior said he "totaled" many cars during his college years. It is assumed that at least a few of these accidents were alcohol related. It is not known for sure how much his father, who reportedly promoted the prohibition movement in California, knew about this. It is guessed that his father knew a lot and imagined more, and that he was critical of it. It seems likely that Junior "let loose" when he left home. It is suspected that Junior was very different from his father, and was an enigma to him. He probably took after his mother in many ways. It is also possible that Junior was like his paternal grandfather, to whom his father may have been reactive.

There are documented times of unregulated alcohol use throughout Junior's life, probably beginning in his university days. Using Bowen theory, it is hypothesized that these were times of higher family stress, originating in intense reactivity to his father's strongly professed beliefs about alcohol when growing up. It is conjectured that his father's beliefs may have been in turn a *reaction* to the unregulated use of alcohol in his family of origin. This has not been documented. It is assumed that if his father had held views on monogamy in marriage that were as intensely held as his views on alcohol use, Junior might well have been as reactive to that, and promiscuous at times of higher family stress. The author understands from Bowen theory that such use of alcohol and the reciprocal reactivity of others is symptomatic of a stressed family system rather than of a flaw in an individual, an individual *functional dysfunction* that maintains system balance. The author's effort at developing an individual relationship with his father when he began the study of his family in 1975 focused on becoming less reactive to his father's unregulated use of alcohol. This was crucial to his then embryonic understanding of differences between individual theories of human functioning and Bowen theory.

Junior graduated from Stanford in general engineering in June 1928. He was given a trip to Europe as a graduation present, probably by his maternal uncle and aunt. He pursued graduate work in architecture at the Yale University School of Architecture, probably between 1928 and 1931. He said this was paid for by this uncle and aunt. Reportedly, Junior went to Chicago to work for the first time in architecture, designing World's Fair buildings in 1931.

Junior's professional goal for himself was architecture. It is not known when this goal began to develop, and who, if anyone, was influential in this. Architecture may have been his goal in his teenage years and was dormant in college as he perhaps went along with his father's wishes. It may have been stimulated by the European trip. It is not known whether his father and other family members were for or against architecture as his career, or how much this may have influenced Junior's decision. It is hypothesized that the best indicator of when Junior was on course in his life was when he was actively pursuing architecture.

Paternal Grandfather's Family of Origin

Junior's father, Clyde James Smith, who was known in his family as Clyde, was the youngest of three brothers and a sister born to James William Smith and Mary Arthur. It is known from census records that Clyde's two older brothers and his older sister were born in what was then Washington territory, and that Clyde was born in August 1881, in Arlington, Oregon, a small town on the Columbia River in western Oregon. Factual knowledge about the sibling positions of one's progenitors, as well as knowledge of sibling position theory, allows the student of family systems to make hypotheses about family relationships, both with one's siblings and with one's parents (Toman, 1976). For example, the youngest son of a youngest son relates differently to a youngest son than with an oldest son, all things being equal. Sibling position theory also indicates that an only child takes the sibling position of the same sex parent. In fact, Junior related to his son, the author, much as his father, Clyde, related to him, with concern and criticism. It is guessed that Clyde's father, J. W. Smith, related to him in a similar way. It is hypothesized that this youngest son of a youngest son of a youngest son *interlocking triangle* functioned to put each of these three individuals more at risk for dysfunction in their lives.

Junior recalled that his paternal grandfather was one of three brothers born in Mississippi and had traveled to the Oregon Territory "at the age of nineteen on horseback." Junior also recalled that he had two brothers, one involved in building the New York City subway and the other a Florida orange grower who went to Princeton University. This has not been documented. It is known from census records that Junior's grandfather was born in Mississippi about 1841, but it is not known when, with whom, and for what reasons he set out on this trek, if indeed this is what happened.

It is presumed that this happened about 1860. The major social issue in Mississippi at that time, with the United States at the brink of civil war, was slavery. A decisive question was whether the northern or southern view of this issue would take root in the West, whose development would determine the nation's destiny (D. H. Wood, 2005, personal communication). It is conjectured that how James William Smith and his family related to this issue might have been significant in his decision to leave Mississippi for Oregon Territory. To what extent was his decision to leave Mississippi for Oregon a *reaction* to what others in his family thought, for example, his father? How emotionally loaded was the issue of slavery in his family? To what extent did J. W. Smith come to his own view on slavery, based on his own careful consideration of the issues? How much was his view influenced by the views of his parents or other family members? How able was he to hold a view that might be different from them and still maintain viable relationships with them? How much subsequent contact was there between him and the past generation of his family in later life? How these questions are answered would provide some evidence about his ability to differentiate a self in his family. The distinction is made in Bowen theory between migration to accomplish self-directed goals and migration to get emotional distance, the latter eventually resulting in emotional cutoff between those and subsequent generations of a family.

Junior believed that his paternal grandfather, J. W. Smith, met and married his paternal grandmother, Mary Arthur, in Arlington, Oregon, where it has been documented that his grandfather was a merchant and farmer. It is known that they were married about 1868 in Wahkiakum County in what was then Washington territory. It has also been documented that she was born about 1848, in the Oregon Territory, which then included the states of

Oregon and Washington. Her mother was born in Ohio, her father was from Missouri or Tennessee, and her maternal grandparents were from England. Further facts about them, their relationships and how decisions were made about their migration would provide further evidence of her ability to define a self in her family.

There is no factual family history of the years in which Clyde and his siblings grew up. Junior recalled that his paternal grandparents and their young children moved from Oregon to Los Angeles when his father was one year old. This would have been about 1882. This has not been documented. It is known from census records that the family was living in Los Angeles in 1900. It is not known how far in school Clyde went. He was not listed as being in school in the 1900 census at age eighteen. It has been documented that both brothers married, that both of them had children, and that his sister never married, living in later years with her mother. Nothing is known about their relationships growing up and in adulthood.

From private records, as well as census records, it is known that his paternal and maternal families lived geographically close to each other when Junior was growing up. It seems that once Junior left for college, however, ties between his father and his older siblings loosened or perhaps were cut, as were his ties with his wife's family. It is possible these latter ties were never strong. The author does not recall having any direct contact with either of these extended families growing up. Research of private documents indicates that many of his father's and mother's extended families were living when the author was growing up and that Junior and his wife had some contact with them over many years into later life. The author also remembers his father talking about these people. There is no evidence that there were any lasting relationships between Junior and his maternal and paternal cousins and their children as adults.

What led to the distance and apparent cutoff between Clyde and his brothers and their families and his wife's family that extended into the author's generation? It is hypothesized that there may have been emotional cutoff between his father, James William Smith and his family of origin, and between Mary Arthur Smith and her family of origin. It is speculated that Clyde's decision to marry whom he did and when he did was to some degree fueled by his parent's opposition to this decision, and that Clyde felt and functioned as an outsider in his family. From emotional triangles in subsequent generations—including Junior and the author—from surviving letters, and from the author's observations it is known that Junior had difficulty living up to his father's expectations and was the focus of his criticism. Other supporting evidence for this is Clyde's distance and cutoff from his siblings and their families as an adult, and the intensity of relationships in the family he started.

Paternal Grandmother's Family of Origin

Junior recalled that his mother, Maude Carrie Little, the oldest of three children, with a younger sister and brother, was born in Omaha, Nebraska, in February 1881. Census records indicate that the younger sister died at an early age. Surviving pictures and the recollections of Junior and his wife suggest that Maude was an outgoing and social person. It is guessed that Junior and his mother were kindred spirits, "two peas in a pod," both something of a puzzle to Clyde. Nothing is known about Maude's ambitions for herself. Junior recalled that his mother and her younger brother, Harry, were close as children and adults.

Maude's father, William Frank Little, was born in Pennsylvania in 1851, and her mother, Lillie Alexander, was born in Illinois in 1859. It is guessed that they met in Illinois. The fact that Lillie Alexander was one of eight children, born to a person who appears from census records to be a prosperous hardware merchant in Effingham, Illinois, shows up in the 1860 and 1870 census records. Mr. Little shows up in the 1870 census as a farm worker in a not too distant Illinois town. A census record from Seward, Nebraska, indicates that they were married there in 1878. Census records of 1880 further indicate that Lillie Alexander's parents and her three younger siblings were then living in Lincoln, Nebraska, her father then employed as a tin-maker. From this, it seems likely that this couple, her parents, and her three younger siblings traveled from Illinois to Nebraska sometime in the mid-1870s. How this decision was made and by whom is not known.

Junior's maternal grandparents subsequently traveled to Los Angeles prior to 1900. It is not known exactly when the move occurred. Census records of 1900, 1910, 1920, and 1930 document their residence in Los Angeles, and that Mr. Little was a lemon grower in 1900, who had retired by 1910. Census records from 1910 to 1920 also indicate that Junior's maternal great-grandmother, Martha Alexander, and a maternal great-uncle, Harry Alexander, the youngest of the eight children, were part of this move, the great-grandmother being the "head" of the household. It is guessed that her husband died in Lincoln, Nebraska. Additional facts about them, their relationships, and their immigration would further evidence the ability of Junior's mother to differentiate a self in her family.

Junior and his wife both told the author that his mother died in September 1939, of cancer, six weeks before the author was born, and in the same hospital. The author's older brother reported that Junior had told him that she had died just prior to his birth in July 1938 (D. Smith, 2005, personal communication). That she died after Douglas was born has been documented. This is an example of functional facts. What each was told functioned as facts for them.

Clyde remarried in the Los Angeles area in 1944. The author remembers an audiotape in which his paternal grandfather's second wife, Marie, was introduced to Junior and his family who were then living in Detroit, Michigan. Nothing factual is known about her. The author remembers in later years her talking for her husband, both in correspondence and in person, and that he went along with this. From the author's observations it seems that, with his second wife, Clyde found a *comfortable togetherness* with a more kindred spirit that perhaps had eluded him in the past. It fits the facts that this togetherness fueled the emotional distance and eventual cutoff between father and son. Surviving letters between Junior and his father and stepmother evidence the intensity of the distance and conflict between father and son at the end of Clyde's life.

Junior's wife and their children—the author and his brother—were included in the outside position of this triangle. They seem to have gone along with it. Happy childhood memories as a toddler and a teenager on family vacations notwithstanding, the author recalls having little contact on his own with his paternal grandfather in young adulthood. He recalls mostly criticism from his paternal grandfather about how he was living his life. The author did not attend his grandfather's funeral and has no recollection of being aware of his death until many years later. Research to date has been unsuccessful in tracing the whereabouts of Clyde's second wife. It is assumed that she is dead. It is hoped that she "left some tracks." Knowledge about her and her family would make possible further hypotheses about the functioning of the author's extended family.

MOTHER'S FAMILY OF ORIGIN

The author's mother, Leah Kathleen Wemp, was the older of the two girls of Ernest Edgar Wemp and Alvira Myrtle Bellaire (see Figure 5.2). It is not known whether or not there were any other pregnancies. Kathleen was born in Oxford, Michigan, in December 1908 and died in Carmel, California, in March 1976. Few facts are known about her preteen and teenage years. It is known that Kathleen's family of origin moved to nearby Detroit, Michigan, where her father, an entrepreneurial automotive engineer, was a successful, self-employed designer of clutches and transmissions and who held many patents. It is known that Kathleen graduated in June 1928, from

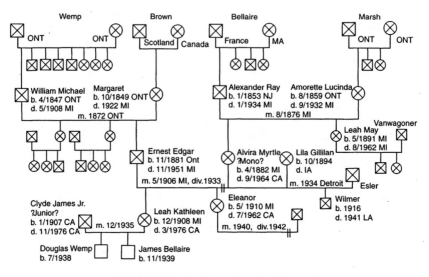

FIGURE 5.2. Mother's Family of Origin

Northwestern High School in Detroit, was a member of that school's "Hall of Fame," and worked on the art staff of the newspaper.

Kathleen said she aspired to a career in medicine when she was young. Her father did not approve. Kathleen said that she gave in to his wishes, saying that this was a bittersweet decision. In doing this, she said she kept his approval, but at the price of giving up a cherished dream. It is the author's impression that his mother had difficulty taking a position for self that differed from her father while being able to maintain a viable relationship with him. In lighter moments near the end of her life, she agreed with the author's view that she did the next best thing to becoming a doctor—she became a patient. Included in surviving private documents is a plethora of detailed observations of her physical health as an adult.

Shortly before or after graduating from high school, Kathleen came down with a serious physical illness. Several other major illnesses followed throughout her life. She said later she believed that this illness had physically and emotionally weakened her, and that it had affected all of her subsequent life functioning. Using Bowen theory it is hypothesized that the intensity of the illness mirrored her intense togetherness with her father and that it served as a functional dysfunction in her family of origin and in the family she and her husband started. The author wonders what his mother would make of the idea of functional dysfunctions.

It is hypothesized further that recurring serious physical health problems throughout her life were related to Kathleen's fixed position on the inside of a triangle with her father. Although there may have been times of reactive distance between them, for example, after he divorced and remarried, it is the author's opinion that it was difficult for either to differentiate a self in the face of this lifelong togetherness. The outside position of this triangle consisted of many people over the years, including her mother, her sister, her suitors, her husband, and her children. Using Bowen theory it is assumed that this inside position was at times comfortable and at times uncomfortable, depending on the level of family stress. The higher the level of family stress there was, the more uncomfortable it was to be on the inside. It is guessed that the most significant event—stressor—in her extended family was the death of her father.

With the amelioration of the serious physical illness, and apparently with her father's blessing, she began a career in art, another love of her life, enrolling at the School of the Art Institute in Chicago in October 1928. A transcript of her work there indicates she was in school for the 1928-1929 academic year. It is guessed that recurring health issues may have played a part in her not continuing this course of study through to completion. Another piece of the puzzle may be that art was not her first love. The stock market crash in 1929 may also be related to this, as well as the timing of other family events in the early 1930s. It is guessed that Kathleen remained in the Chicago area after that. It has been documented that she dated extensively at this time. A strikingly handsome and social woman, as evidenced by surviving pictures and personal observation, Kathleen was pursued by and had many male relationships, which is also confirmed by surviving pictures.

Maternal Grandfather's Family of Origin

Kathleen's father, Ernest E. Wemp, was the youngest of three children and only son to William Michael Wemp and Margaret Brown. Ernie, as he was known, was born in Dover Township, Ontario, Canada, in November 1881, and died in Detroit, Michigan, in November 1951. The genealogy of his family, later used by this author, originated with the author's older brother when he was in high school in Detroit, Michigan, in the early 1950s. His systematic research of his mother's family traced Ernie's family to the Netherlands in the sixteenth century. This effort occurred long before the conveniences of online research. Ernie's paternal family originally had migrated to Ontario, having left upstate New York for Canada because they were loyal to Britain at the time of the Revolutionary War. The "tracks" of this branch of the family can be followed from Amherst Island, Ontario, to Chatham, Ontario, and then to the Detroit, Michigan, area, before arriving in Oxford.

Ernie's father, a physician who was born in April 1847, in Amherst Island, Ontario, Canada, was the oldest of eight children. From census records it is known that his parents and siblings moved to Dover Township, Ontario, apparently just after he and Margaret Brown were married about 1872. "Maggie" Brown Wemp was also born and had grown up in Amherst Island, where it seems likely she knew Dr. Wemp. It was in Dover Township that their children were born. According to census records, the Wemps immigrated to the United States, to Detroit, Michigan, in 1883, and later to Oxford, Michigan, then a farm town northwest of Detroit, where he lived the rest of his life, dying in May 1908. The 1900 census indicates that Dr. and Mrs. Wemp and Ernie also lived in Royal Oak, Michigan, in the Detroit area. It is known that "Maggie" Brown Wemp's father was from Scotland and that her mother was Canadian. She reportedly died in Oxford in 1922.

Kathleen's goal of a career in medicine may be related to the fact that her paternal grandfather was a doctor. Kathleen was born seven months before he died. It is not unknown for one who is born at the same time as one who dies to be emotionally programmed to carry on for them. Ernie's disapproval of his older daughter going into medicine may have been related to a hypothesized prickly relationship with his father, with distance/conflict between them, perhaps driven by Ernie's reactivity to growing up in a small town, the demands made on a small town doctor, the limited income, and the risks, among other issues. This speculation is supported by the "good life" that his entrepreneurial efforts subsequently allowed Ernie and his extended family, including the author, to have. Ernie may also have been against women working outside of the home. It is not known what ambitions his wife had for herself personally and professionally, or if this was a source of tension in their marriage and subsequent divorce.

Maternal Grandmother's Family of Origin

Kathleen's mother, Alvira Myrtle Bellaire, known as Mono, was the older of two girls born to Alexander Ray Bellaire and Amorette Lucinda Marsh. She was born in May 1882, in Cadillac, Michigan, a small town in the central part of the lower peninsula of Michigan and died in Carmel, California, in 1964. It is known that her mother's family had immigrated to Michigan from Canada and before that, England. Her mother was the oldest of three. Surviving pictures and documents indicate a comfortable togetherness in the family in which Mono grew up. There is no clear indicator of Mono's relationships with her parents. Whom she married and how she lived her adult life suggests her *reactivity* to the simple life of a Michigan small town.

Mono's father, A. R. Bellaire, was born in January 1853 in New Jersey, the oldest of four children. He migrated to Michigan from New Jersey at the age of twenty-one, where he remained all his life. It is not known why he went to Michigan, although a document regarding another branch of the family describes Michigan in 1830 as being the "Eldorado of the West" (Gass, 1918). This suggests that he was pursuing a defined goal for self rather than cutting off from the past. It is known that he and his wife married in August 1876, there being public and private documentation of their fiftieth wedding anniversary (*Oxford Leader,* 1934). Census reports document that Mr. Bellaire's father, Frederick Bellaire, was born in France, had immigrated to New Jersey from Germany, and later lived with his oldest daughter and her family in New Jersey after his wife's death. There is no indication of what contact, if any, there was between Mono's father and his father and sisters later in life.

It is not known for sure when or how Mono and Ernie met, although it is guessed they knew each other growing up, if not in high school, perhaps in church. There are many surviving pictures of Ernie and Mono, alone and with their two girls, and with his and her parents and grandparents. Kathleen said that in Ernie's travels in pursuit of professional interests, her father had extra marital relationships. The guess is, that if this was true, it may have been triggered by a growing distance and conflict in his marriage that was reciprocally related to the degree of time and energy he put into his work, and/or hypothesized distance, and perhaps emotional cutoff from his parents and past generations of his family. Extra marital affairs are viewed here as functional dysfunctions rather than as character flaws.

Ernie and Mono were married in 1906, and divorced in 1933. According to sibling position theory their marriage should have been a relatively good fit in that Ernie was a younger brother of sisters and Mono was an older sister. However, there was a five-year gap between his birth and the birth of his next older sister, indicating that he probably functioned more as an only child, taking on more of the position of his father, the oldest of eight. The guess is that Ernie may have had the last word in his marriage, but his wife did not back down from him and there may well have been times of significant heat and light. It is also possible she had the last word, which may have been a precipitate for his leaving the marriage. She was a small woman in stature, but functioned as an older sister, one who stood her ground with anyone. Their divorce occurred while Kathleen was in Chicago and had already met and begun to live with Junior, her husband to be, whom she later married in 1935. It is hypothesized that the loss of the physical closeness with his daughter, Kathleen, followed by her plans to marry, or at least her "getting serious," is what finally triggered the divorce.

In 1934 Ernie married Lila Gillilan, a successful businesswoman whom he had apparently known for some time. It is guessed that this occurred in Chicago. There is no documentation of this wedding. The marriage met with Kathleen's approval. Ernie remained in this second marriage until his death in 1951. It is hypothesized that his second marriage provided a comfortable togetherness for Ernie that was lost in the physical and emotional distance of his daughter, and perhaps had eluded him in his first marriage. It is noted that the remarriages of both of the author's grandfathers were to women who seemed to "appreciate" them more than their first wives.

The divorce apparently suited Mono. She never remarried. The author has the impression that the relationship between Ernie and Mono remained prickly for the remainder of their lives. There is some correspondence from Ernie to Mono in the private documents in regard to issues regarding their children and to the financial arrangements between them, but no references about their postdivorce relationship are found. The author has no memory of ever seeing them together or talking about one another.

Mono and Kathleen's younger sister, Eleanor, lived with each other the remainder of their lives, except for a brief period when Eleanor married. It is noted that the author mostly thought of and related to these two as one emotional unit, a functional *we-self,* "Monnie and Auntie Eleanor," rather than as two individuals, just as he thought about and related to his grandfather and his second wife as a *we-self,* "Hoo-Hoo and Little Grandma." The *we-self* phenomenon became most obvious to the author in the way he thought of and related to his parents, "Mother and Dad," until the last years of their lives, when he began an effort to relate to them as individuals in the first year of his effort to define a self in his family.

Eleanor was married in 1940, and divorced two years later with no children. Kathleen seemed to have good relationships with her mother, sister, and stepmother throughout their lives, as evidenced by the author's recollections and surviving correspondence. He guesses that there was a prickly relationship between Mono and Lila from how they talked about each other. He does not recall ever seeing them together.

AUTHOR'S FAMILY OF ORIGIN

Junior and Kathleen—Kay and Clyde as their friends and children knew them—met in Chicago, reportedly on October 31, 1931, friends having arranged their meeting (R. K. Smith, 1994, unpublished notes). They both told the author that after meeting each other they were monogamous. Shortly after meeting they began living together in Chicago. Though not uncommon in the latter part of the twentieth century, the author assumes that this was not the norm in the 1930s. It is not known definitively what their families thought of this and the question was never asked. It seems likely that neither family approved, that Junior's family, particularly his father, would have been vocal in his disapproval, and that probably his mother defended him—and Kathleen—which would have further reinforced the inside and outside positions in this triangle.

Her father and mother probably disapproved of Kathleen and Junior living together before marriage, which may have insinuated some distance into the relationship between Kathleen and her father and mother. This would be an example of fluidity of functioning positions in triangles, even in relatively fixed triangles. One can be on the inside one moment and on the outside the next moment, depending on the issue and the level of family stress at the time. However, it was probably less an issue for them than it was for Junior's father and mother. It probably would have been less of an issue for Junior's mother than his father, given her relationship with both her son and future daughter-in-law. It probably was less of an issue for Kathleen's father than her mother, as well. The point is that there may well be differences in marriages about such things, depending on the triangles. How marriage partners manage such differences is an indicator of the ability to define a self in a family.

Evidence for differences between her parents on the issue of Kathleen living with someone before marriage can be found in the fact that Kathleen said that her father confided to her about his private life as an adult. She reported to the author that her father had introduced her to Lila—his future second wife—and confided in her about his intention to divorce her mother and marry Lila long before the events transpired. It seems possible that in their respective dealings with the opposite sex, Mono would have thought that Kathleen was her father's daughter, another variation of the same triangle about a different issue, father and daughter on the inside and mother on the outside. Further, Kathleen later voiced her concern to the author that he would take after her father in his dealings with the opposite sex—another interlocking triangle.

It is also known that Ernie did not approve of Kathleen's marrying when she did, and perhaps whom she did. In a letter dated October 3, 1938, to his then ex-wife, three years after Kathleen's marriage, in regard to a letter he had received from their younger daughter, Eleanor, he writes:

> I don't believe she (Eleanor) and Cliff should rush things too much. . . .
> You know how it worked out with Clyde (Junior) and Kay (Kathleen)
> . . . this will probably be a repeat of their experience and we will be the
> ones who are called upon to keep things going.

The clear implication is that they were not prepared financially to marry. Would they have ever been prepared? Was the issue really that Junior was not prepared? This issue was present throughout their married lives. It is the central issue observed by the author in later years that divided Junior and Kathleen. Did Ernie really mean "we" or was he referring to himself? When would it have been a good time for Ernie's daughter to marry Junior? Would any prospective mate have met with his approval at any time?

They were married in December 1935, in Beverly Hills, California, a year after her father remarried. Why were they married then and why in California? It seems likely that for Kathleen, the decision to be married then was less a self-defined decision than it was an involuntary togetherness response to her parent's divorce and her father's remarriage. Perhaps it was also a response to her father's message that she was rushing into a marriage. Consistent with how future decisions were made in their marriage, it is guessed that Junior went along with her decision, even if he thought differently. However, it also fits the facts that Junior would want to be married in California where he had grown up.

Kathleen said she had a close relationship with her mother-in-law, Maude, whom she later described to the author as "an angel on earth." Evidence supporting this closeness was discovered in the form of letters between these two in which Kathleen is arranging to live with Junior's parents in Los Angeles prior to the marriage. Was moving there Kathleen's idea? Was it her mother-in-law's idea? Was it someone else's idea? Was Kathleen the daughter that Maude always wanted but never had? Was Maude the mother that Kathleen wanted but never had? To what extent was Kathleen's decision self-defined? The outside position of one triangle with Kathleen and her mother-in-law on the inside is seen as her mother, in response to a hypothesized loss of her approval and/or the issue of which of the two was the better mother. The outside position of another triangle with Kathleen and her mother-in-law on the inside is seen as her father, in reaction to the issue of his remarrying and/or the loss of his approval. It is the author's opinion that all of these triangles occurred involuntarily, largely, if not entirely, out of awareness.

Although there probably was some reactivity to what her parents wanted or approved of involved in the decision to be married in California, and in Beverly Hills, it probably reflected more the "taste for the good life" that both Kathleen and Junior shared. This "taste for the good life" directed many subsequent decisions affecting the family that Junior and Kathleen started. The author's opinion is, that, to a considerable degree, if not always, this contrasted with, and was in reaction to, the lifestyle of her grandfathers, and her mother's younger sister and her family, who all lived in "small town" Oxford. The author recalls that he thought of the "Oxford folks" and his family respectively as the "country mice" and the "city mice."

Junior and Kathleen remained in Los Angeles following their marriage. Junior pursued what he said was a promising architectural career, in the ranks of an up and coming architectural firm. It is not known how Kathleen occupied her time during these years before her children were born, and how, if at all, these first married years changed their relationship. It is guessed she pursued professional interests using her artistic talents.

It seems clear that having children was not high on the list of priorities for Kathleen. In a surviving letter to her father in Detroit during her pregnancy with her oldest son who was born in July 1938, in California, Kathleen voices strong concerns about whether she can be an adequate mother. Was this something that she also discussed with her mother? Was the adequacy of her mother to be a mother an issue for her at this time? Consistent with the hypothesis that Kathleen and her mother-in-law made up the comfortable inside positions of a triangle with her mother on the outside about the issue of being a good mother, it is plausible that she discussed her concerns more with Maude than with Mono.

Surviving pictures and correspondence, and the author's recollection, indicate that, from the time Douglas was born, through the birth of the author, until the time "the boys" were teenagers, caretaking of them was done primarily by housekeepers. These facts suggest that the author and his brother were relatively out of the emotional spotlight in their family of origin. In Bowen theory there is the idea that offspring who are out of the emotional process will have a long-term functioning advantage over offspring in reproductive units in which they are at the center of the emotional focus.

Kathleen told the author that following the birth of Douglas she was advised by her physician that for health reasons it was not advisable for her to have any other children. Douglas reported to the author that his mother told him that she was advised not to have any children prior to her pregnancy with him (D. Smith, 2005, personal communication). Further, Kathleen told Jim B., the author, as she called him, that she had almost died in the process of giving birth to him. Douglas reported that he was also told this by his mother (D. Smith, 2005, personal communication). The objective facts are not known. What was she told by her physician? Did she almost die in either or both cases? Being advised not to have children and almost dying in childbirth with either or both children were functional facts. Both the author and his brother lived their lives as if they were facts.

The author is confused by, but grateful for, his mother's decision to have had children. It is guessed that at any time in her life having children would have been a threatening prospect. Complicating the matter for her was the fact that at this time the country was beginning to become increasingly more involved in the events of World War II. From surviving correspondence, it is known that Kathleen was afraid of being left alone to fend for two young sons. It is hard for the author to imagine his mother being left alone to raise her children. It is a fact that she felt that way. It is speculated that Kathleen's decision to have children was triggered more by the onset of her mother-in-law's cancer and the anticipated loss of this important relationship. It is guessed that the decision gained Kathleen further comfort and approval from her mother-in-law.

It is not known what Junior thought about having one, let alone two children. It is hypothesized, that, in this decision, as in most major decisions, he would have gone along with whatever decision his wife made about having children, no matter his opinion. The significance of this, as the author understands it, is that with each such decision Junior is giving up more self, useful to the system in the short term and detrimental to him and the system in the long run. Shortly before his death Junior told the author that he thought he had not been much of a father. The principal focus of his life had always been his wife, which he thought was abundantly clear in how he had lived his life. The fact that he died eight months after she did supports this viewpoint. The author has described the death of the *we-self* of his parents elsewhere (Smith, 1978).

James Bellaire Smith, the author, was born in November 1939, in Los Angeles, California. Junior had become involved professionally in the architecture of armed service training camps at this time. As the entrance of the United States into World War II became increasingly imminent, Kathleen was said by Junior to have prevailed upon her father, Ernie, who had begun to design clutches and transmissions for army vehicles in Detroit, to take Junior into his employ, thereby guaranteeing that Junior would not be drafted into combat duty. Her father reportedly agreed. There is no documentation of this. Kathleen's fear that her husband would be drafted was certainly a piece of this puzzle. However, it seems clear that the larger puzzle piece was the togetherness pull on Kathleen to be closer to her father again, to reconnect with him and to regain his approval following the death of her mother-in-law. There was a reciprocal pull for Ernie to have his daughter closer to him again. Thus, daughter and father are again in the inside positions of this triangle, both giving up self to the system in the process.

Although he said he disagreed with his wife, Junior also said that he gave in to her decision. It is not clear whether Kathleen gave him an ultimatum or not. In later years, Junior said that she did. He said that he had to give up his life course in architecture "or else." It is not clear whether the "or else" meant that he would lose his marriage, his children, his marriage and his children, or what. It is also believed that he was not eager to give up the good life and pursue combat duty.

It is not known what Junior's father thought about the decision. The fact is that moving to Detroit from Los Angeles further fueled the emotional distance between Junior and his father. Following his first wife's death Clyde had been more present in the life of his son and his young family. Did the death of his wife, Maude, make that possible? Had her death made it possible for him to be on the comfortable inside of a triangle with his son, at least for a change? Did this comfort then slip away just as fast when his son and his family left? Douglas and Jim B. have childhood memories of their paternal grandfather's regular visits at the back door, calling out "Hoo-Hoo"—a term of endearment that stuck—to his two delighted grandsons. Surviving pictures document this presence.

Junior and Kathleen moved to Detroit, Michigan, probably in 1943. It fits the facts that the separation from his son and his grandsons fueled Clyde's decision to remarry. It is not known if he had thought about remarriage prior to this. Early letters from Clyde and his second wife seem hopeful about the future. Later letters strongly suggest that "they" felt rejected by Junior, Kathleen and "the boys." Junior and Kathleen, and sometimes their sons, had returned to California periodically for vacation visits in subsequent years with his father and stepmother. The author was always aware at these times and in later years how strained the relationship was between Clyde and Junior, as well as between his grandfather and himself.

Junior was never able to successfully maneuver in the emotional pulls between the *we-self* of his father and stepmother and Kathleen and her family. The most comfortable position for Junior was on the *outside* of this triangle. His episodic unregulated alcohol use worked for the system, while it was dysfunctional for him. It is hypothesized that his father, Clyde, functioned in a similar position in the family in which he grew up, but to a lesser degree, and with a different symptom; that is, Clyde was more of a self in his family, was less cutoff from his family, and was less symptomatic than Junior. How the author's grandfather was symptomatic, if he was, is unclear. It is further guessed that, being the youngest of a youngest of a youngest, the author emotionally inherited this functioning position from his father and grandfather. In this position he was at risk for giving up even more self to the system, being even more emotionally cutoff from his family, and being even more symptomatic than his father and grandfather before him, the unresolved issues of the past continuing into the future.

A functional dysfunction in one person works to maintain equilibrium and comfort in the triangle for others in the short term. What is more viable for the system in the long run is the effort on the part of any one person in the system to differentiate a self within the system. This is typically uncomfortable for that person and for the system in the short term. If that person is able to maintain his position for self with others in the system and to continue to relate to them about the issues between them over the long haul, each person in the system will become less glued to the system and freer to be a self. The author subscribes to the idea, from Bowen theory, that the best legacy anyone can leave his children is for *him* to "grow up" more in his family, that is, to work on his own differentiation of self.

Although any person can make this effort at any time, the author also understands from Bowen theory that some persons are better situated to make this effort than others by virtue of their functioning positions in their families. With both of his parents being the focus of the emotional process in their families of origin, neither of them was well situated to do this. As emotional process in his family of origin was contained largely within the marital relationship, the author and his brother were *not* in the emotional spotlight. It is argued that, consequently, he and his brother were each in a better position to involuntarily and voluntarily differentiate a self in his family than either parent.

Another view of this addresses how players change in the functioning positions of interlocking triangles over generations while the positions remain relatively fixed. After her mother-in-law's death, Kathleen seemingly took her place in a more comfortable inside position with Junior, continuing to fix Clyde in an uncomfortable outside position. In turn, his discomfort was relieved in the togetherness of his remarriage to Marie. In this case what worked for the system also worked for the individuals, at least in the short term, given the comfortable relationship togetherness for everyone. There is nothing inherently good or bad, or right or wrong, about being on the inside or outside of triangles, or in being comfortable or uncomfortable. The more one is fixed involuntarily in either position by family emotional process, unable to differentiate a self in the relationships, the more at risk one is to be off course in one's own individual life course and for the full range of life's problems.

After World War II was over, Junior and Kathleen remained in Detroit, although there was no further risk of Junior being drafted, her mother and sister were in California as were his father and stepmother, and Junior's first choice professionally was to return to California. Junior began to collaborate with Ernie who had resumed his entrepreneurial work with automatic transmissions and clutches. The working hypothesis is that the reciprocal comfort in the togetherness with her father remained an irresistible force for both Kathleen and Ernie. It is guessed that it was her decision to remain, and that Junior went along with it, unable and/or unwilling to risk the consequences of the former "or else," for example, his marriage, his children, and the "good life," among other issues. There were undeniable potential financial rewards as well. It is known that Junior also received considerable pressure from Ernie's second wife, Lila, to remain doing this, citing potential financial outcomes and loyalty to Ernie. Kathleen's mother and sister also strongly encouraged this. It is not clear whether Ernie also pressured his son-in-law to remain. If it enhanced the likelihood that his daughter would remain, it seems likely that Ernie also would have supported Junior staying. For Junior to have decided to pursue his own personal goals, to define a self in opposition to these seemingly overwhelming consensual emotional and relationship forces, seems Herculean at best.

Junior's decision to go along with his wife and to continue to work with her father in the resumption of his automotive engineering projects continued to reduce discomfort and maintain equilibrium in the triangles, and to put both Junior *and* Kathleen in continuing jeopardy for symptoms, in the form of Junior's periodic unregulated use of alcohol, and Kathleen's chronic physical problems. The decision to place Douglas and Jim B. away from home at a boarding farm for a six-year period at this time also served to maintain equilibrium in the triangles, "the boys" being in what was then an outside position in this interlocking triangle with their parents and extended family. The facts indicate that this outside position was less comfortable for Douglas than it was for the author. Again, the thesis here is that this position outside the emotional spotlight of the family emotional process left both boys freer, relatively speaking, to move ahead with their lives as adults.

Ernie died unexpectedly in 1951. Kathleen and Junior continued to remain in Detroit, with Junior "carrying on Ernie's work," initially full-time and then part-time, eventually working part-time and then full-time in architecture. Consistent with the author's earlier hypothesis that Junior was most on track in his life when he was in architecture is that arguably his best work in architecture was accomplished during these last few years in Detroit when he was doing full-time architecture. Here too, it is assumed that Kathleen made the decision to remain, with other family members, particularly Lila, also urging Junior to "carry on Ernie's work," with Junior initially continuing to go along with the decision, before returning to architecture. It is not known how the decision was made to close down "Ernie's work." How much did Junior take the lead in this, if at all? How much did he wait for others to make that decision?

Junior, Kathleen, and their sons returned to Los Angeles in July 1956. Douglas would begin Stanford that fall. The author had one year of high school remaining. He remembers being against the decision to leave Detroit, saying to his parents that his life was there. He cannot remember if he came up with a plan to accomplish staying. Although Junior was unable to find the kind of architectural work he had hoped for in Los Angeles, he worked steadily in architecture during the last two decades of his life with many productive years.

Kathleen's physical health continued on a downhill slide. Before leaving Detroit she had contracted a serious physical illness that devastated her physically and emotionally following the death of her father. This decline in physical health is viewed as a functional dysfunction. The degree of emotional strength she had borrowed in the comfortable togetherness with her father seems clear. She said later that she hoped that the return to California would signal an improvement in her health and in Junior's professional fortunes. The author views this as less of a goal directed decision of either of his parents than an involuntary effort to borrow as much emotional strength as they could from the togetherness of their families in California. It is hypothesized that it was this togetherness force that drew them back to California, just as it had drawn them to Detroit earlier. It was also the same force to which their sons—the author and his older brother—responded in their own ways in the natural process of their growing away from their parents and establishing their own lives.

Kathleen and Junior decided to move to Carmel in 1958, an area in central California that they both loved, and to which they were drawn at an earlier and happier time in their lives. The author's view is that this was a more voluntary, goal-directed decision. He does not know how this decision was made, or by whom. This move took his parents geographically away from the togetherness of surviving family members in southern California, with a plan that Junior would establish his own practice, a long, quietly held dream. A house and property were purchased. Junior was initially able to find adequate work for income. He subsequently put great effort into developing a private architectural practice that was marginally successful, but difficult for him to sustain. Eventually he began doing any kind of work he could get in his field. His subsequent desperation is evidenced by copies of surviving letters to prospective employers. These letters also document his unwillingness to succumb to life's pressures. At such times of higher family stress Kathleen berated Junior for his inability to better provide for her. He reciprocally complained angrily and bitterly that he had always been Ernie's "junior" and was never needed, loved, or appreciated.

Kathleen's mother and sister subsequently bought property in the Carmel area with the goal of moving closer to Kathleen and Junior. That move never came. Kathleen's sister died a week after Douglas's wedding in late June 1962. Junior's father died within weeks after that, as did Kathleen's aunt in Oxford, Michigan. Kathleen's health and individual functioning took a brief but decided upswing as she cared for her mother who was hospitalized in the Carmel area shortly after this. After Mono died in 1964, Kathleen's physical health began deteriorating again. The author views these events as a delayed emotional shockwave, dating to the death of her father a decade earlier.

In the following years, Kathleen and Junior became increasingly reclusive, the focus of their lives together being on her physical functioning. Neither Douglas nor Jim B. remained in good emotional contact with their parents after leaving home for college. There was periodic contact, typically with Kathleen or Junior pursuing their sons for more contact. Douglas had told his brother that when he left for college he would only make "duty visits" home. Likewise, Jim B. said that the only way he could maintain a viable life course for himself was to remain distant from them. He began studying Bowen theory in 1972, on his own, and then began a coached effort at differentiating a self in his family in January 1975. A planned visit to see his parents shortly after this work began was subsequently described by the author in the following way:

> I stayed away, fearing I wouldn't be able to get out of the house once I got in. The few visits I did make there were with my heart in my hand, ending usually by my pulling out in the middle of the night when they were asleep. My brother stayed away, furious that he couldn't get into the house. The few visits he made ended in shouting matches and bruised feelings. One of the strategies considered . . . was to take my brother with me on my visit home. I would get us *into* the house and he would get us *out*. (Smith, 1979)

Kathleen was diagnosed with cancer in October 1975 and died six months after it's onset in March 1976. Junior was diagnosed with cancer within a month of his wife's death. He chose not to have any treatment, saying that his whole life had been for his wife, and that when she died, he said he had nothing to live for. He died eight months later.

CONCLUSION

This chapter has described emotional triangles over several generations of the author's family. Researching these triangles has been part of an ongoing thirty-year effort to differentiate a self in his family. In this chapter, emotional triangles are understood to be involuntary and voluntary regulators of anxiety and individual functioning in human families, adaptive mechanisms that have evolved in the human over many tens of thousands of years. Differentiating a self, the capacity for involuntary and voluntary prefrontal cortex thinking that permits self-regulation in triangles at times of higher stress, has also evolved humans. Knowing current triangles in a family allows one to predict and identify future and past triangles. Knowing past triangles in a family permits one to predict current and future triangles.

The author has known many of the facts presented here for many years, some long before he began researching his family. It has been in a continuing effort to "connect the dots" within the fabric of ongoing life events and study, using Bowen theory as the theoretical road map, that he has come to know the facts in a far richer way. The author has become clearer about what is factual and what is not factual. He has come to find that some of what he assumed was factual was not. He has also become clearer about the importance of distinguishing between what is objective or public fact, what are functional facts, and what is guesswork, opinion, or family "lore." He has become clearer about how his father's episodic unregulated alcohol use and his mother's periodic serious physical illnesses worked to stabilize triangles in their families of origin and the family they began. He has come to see for the first time how his functioning position on the outside of the emotional process of his family of origin better situated him to voluntarily differentiate a self.

It should be clear to the reader that, although this has been a thirty-year effort, the author has only begun to scratch the surface. What is known is far outweighed by what is unknown. What is transparent is far outweighed by what is opaque. Each objective and functional fact that is gathered raises more questions and challenges presumed understanding. Triangles in which positions have been more fixed over time have been described in this chapter. Other triangles are alluded to in passing. A chapter could be written about every triangle in the multiple generations of this family, those mentioned and those not mentioned, describing the subtle shifts and nuances in response to changes in level of family stress on the family over time, and related shifts in individual functioning.

Differentiating a self is a lifetime process. The process of writing this chapter, a nodal event in itself, has coincided with many other nodal events in the author's extended family, including the marriages of his children, the birth of his first grandchild, the marriages of nieces and the births of their children, more connection with his brother, his sister-in-law, and his nephew and nieces and their families, a restructuring of his workplace life, the anticipated move from a house in which his children have grown up, as well as a renewed family research effort in which he is coming to identify and know dead family members, and to connect or reconnect with living family members and old friends, and a beginning effort to learn neurofeedback.

The author believes that differentiating a self is an organic process. Just as one cannot make grass grow faster by pulling on it, one cannot hurry this process. One can only hear what one can hear, see what one can see, know what one can know and do what one can do.

REFERENCES

Bowen, M. (1978). *Family therapy in clinical practice.* New York: Jason Aronson.

de Waal, F. (1989). *Peacemaking among primates.* Cambridge, MA: Harvard Press.

Gass, H. R. (1918). *Genealogy of John and Rebecca Gass.* Mobile, AL: Author.

Oxford Leader. (1934). Vol. LII, No. 42, January 12, p. 1.

Smith, D. (2005). Personal communication.

Smith, J. (1978, November). Towards a descriptive empirical understanding of family systems theory: Some work in progress. Presented at the *Second Pittsburgh Family Systems Symposium,* Pittsburgh, PA.

Smith, J. (1979, April). Personal and family reactions to my parents' deaths. Presented at the *Third Pittsburgh Family Systems Symposium,* Pittsburgh, PA.

Smith, R. K. (1994). Unpublished notes.

Toman, W. (1976). *Family constellations* (4th ed.). New York: Springer.

Wood, D. H. (2005). Personal communication.

Chapter 6

Triangles at the Time of a Chronic Illness and Death

Anthony J. Wilgus

INTRODUCTION

During times of relative calm within a family, triangles may be dormant or at least difficult to detect (see Kerr and Bowen, 1988, p. 135). However, major events and transitions offer an opportunity to observe the triangular process in much greater detail. A long-term, serious illness in a younger family member and a subsequent death provide an excellent research laboratory for examining many triangles in bold relief. This chapter explores the ebbs and flows of these relationship networks during the chronic illness, subsequent death, and funeral of a woman in midlife. A detailed description of the husband's efforts to identify the pertinent triangles as well as his attempts to negotiate a self in the midst of these powerful forces follows.

The introductory section offers an overview of the cast of characters and a brief discussion of the nature of the illness and the shifts precipitated within the immediate and extended families. Murray Bowen's seminal article, "The Family Reaction to Death" (Bowen, 1978), provided the author with a framework for identifying significant triangles that functioned within and around the medical system as well as the key triangles operating within the immediate and extended families. Of note here is the fact that triangles have a content base that can obfuscate the process. How that content is illustrative of an underlying family process is an area for some discussion within this segment.

The husband's attempts to negotiate these key triangles is the focus of the next portion of the chapter. Some basic principles that the husband defined for himself provide the framework in which to view the attempts to establish a more solid person-to-person relationship in the major triangles in which he was involved. Detriangling from the illness and his wife, dealing directly with key parties in the medical system, stating positions clearly to key family members during the dying and funeral process are some of the approaches employed in addressing the relationship process.

Finally, a description of the outcomes of these efforts in both the short-term and long-term completes this study. From traversing the emotional climate during the dying process to reporting on the functioning of key family members more than two and a half years after the death, this chapter suggests an optimal outcome for those paying attention to the triangular process and addressing issues clearly and thoughtfully.

FAMILY DATA

Figure 6.1 presents the family diagram. This nuclear family consisted of the spouses who were married in 1977, the husband twenty-nine and the wife twenty-three; this was the first marriage for the wife and the second marriage for the husband, who had a daughter born in 1973 from his first marriage which lasted five years. In 1980, the couple had their eldest daughter and in 1983 a second daughter was born. The husband was the eldest brother of a brother and two sisters in his family of origin, and his parents are still living. The wife was the third child and only daughter, having two older brothers and two younger brothers. The second brother died in 1972 after an accident in Ireland, and her father died in 1999 from prostate cancer while the wife was quite ill. Her mother still survives.

The nuclear family process within the wife's family of origin involved her in the most intense triangle with her parents. Erupting in a more full-blown fashion during adolescence, the more common pattern was one of overt conflict and distance between the daughter and the mother and an alliance with the father. Symptom manifestation in the daughter encompassed depression for which she received treatment in both high school and college. Upon the daughter's marriage, this primary triangle would become prominent during longer visits and vacations with her parents, characterized by a continual tension with her mother surfacing in both brief verbal arguments and some emotional distance.

During the courtship and early years of the couple's marriage, there were patterns of intense conflict followed by periods of some emotional distance. Over time, the predominant mode of interaction became one in which the wife would typically defer to the husband, mirroring to some extent their

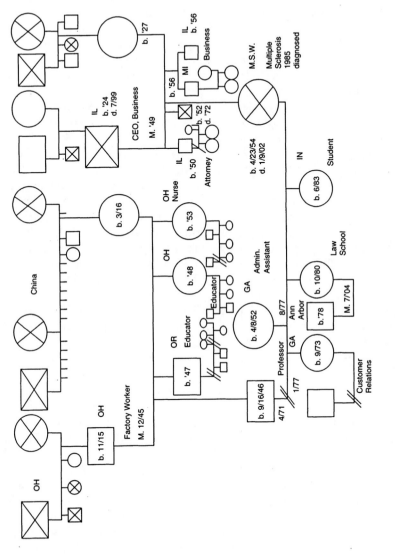

FIGURE 6.1. Family Diagram

159

respective sibling positions (he as an oldest brother of a brother and sisters and she as primarily a younger sister of brothers). With the birth of the first daughter, some tension in the marital relationship shifted as the mother was somewhat anxious about this birth. Calm prevailed with the advent of the second daughter. By this time, the principal mechanisms for managing anxiety included a mixture of emotional distance, a peace/agree position in the marriage with the wife in the less dominant position, and a lesser degree of focus on the eldest child.

Shortly after the birth of the second daughter, the wife developed symptoms of fatigue and bladder problems which she attributed to the pregnancy. Following an episode with double vision around 1985, she received a tentative diagnosis of multiple sclerosis from her family physician which was definitively confirmed in 1988 by magnetic resonance imaging (MRI). The disease itself remained rather tranquil for a period of four years before more rapid deterioration occurred. At this time, the clinic from which she received medical treatment diagnosed the multiple sclerosis as primary, chronic, and progressive, the most virulent manifestation of this illness. Over a nine-year period, the wife gradually lost gross and fine motor functioning, in addition to enduring severe insults to her cognitive functioning. In the last year of her life, she remained confined to a hospital bed and was nourished through tube feeding. She was unable to verbalize, but she did communicate in a variety of nonverbal ways. Total care for the wife occurred in her household and was given by the husband and a privately hired nurse who developed a highly positive relationship with the family.

SIGNIFICANT TRIANGLES

When a family member has a serious health condition, or any type of symptom for that matter, there exist many triangles, with the illness being at one point of all of them. In the relationship between the husband, the wife, and the multiple sclerosis, the tendency would be for the husband to relate to the wife "through the lens of the disease." The wife described this succinctly when she admonished her spouse, "Please don't treat me like a patient." This type of interaction can be quite subtle and quite pronounced. Voice tones can change when verbally interacting with the person with the disease, and they are not dissimilar to the intonations that a parent has with a younger child, or adults have in their conversations with the elderly. Infantilization of the person with the illness and relating to "the others" around her are ways in which these types of triangles may function.

A commonplace triangle exists between the patient, the illness, and the medical establishment. As the wife's situation worsened, communications with the wife diminished and the physicians, nurses, social workers, and other therapists were inclined to address the husband. Despite her halting speech at one point, the wife was keenly aware of this process. After a visit to the clinic, she indicated that she always felt worse after these visits. At a later point, a growing number of communications would take place "behind her back" under the guise of being helpful and rationalized by her apparent declining cognitive state. Another way of thinking of this process is to view the acceleration of this interaction as connected to the anxiety in the medical system relative to its inability to stem the tide of the illness.

On another level, the triangling would operate from a fix-it orientation embedded in the nurse, doctor, or social worker. For example, if the wife communicated to the social worker that she "hated her disease," the social worker would be quick to diagnose this condition as depression, suggesting psychotherapy along with medication. After all, her insurance would cover it. Similarly, when the wife was clearly unable to engage in much motor activity, the nurse suggested a rigorous program of physical therapy without consultation with either the husband or the wife. Tension would then shift so that the husband would engage the medical establishment in defense of his spouse.

For the wife's family of origin (parents and siblings), the periodic visits during which they witnessed the increasing decline of their daughter and sister took its toll. Triangles in this case would involve an intense focus on the illness, vividly portraying what the woman could *not* do. Particularly challenging for this family was witnessing the cognitive decline of a woman who had had a great intellect. Hence, quite understandably on an emotional level, the "tragedy" of the situation would result in "talking about" her rather than "talking to" her. When the tension in the triangle involving the woman, her illness, and her parents would reach a high, anxiety would seep into the relationship between the husband and his in-laws. It would go like this: The wife's family would see the helplessness and hopelessness of the daughter's situation; the husband would attempt to focus on the upside of the wife's functioning, for example, her grace under extremely difficult circumstances. Consequently, the tension in the original triangle now involved the husband.

Of particular import here is the history of the woman and her role in the triangle with her parents. As the only female offspring, and for a variety of other reasons, she was the object of the projection process in her family of origin. Locked in a symbiotic attachment with her mother which would play out negatively, especially during adolescence, she would align with her father, who would vacillate between his daughter and his spouse. Never quite developing "her voice" within this primary triangle, her "done in" position became more pronounced with the onset of the illness. In one striking example, the woman's mother had planned an outing on a day when the symptoms of the illness contributed to greater fatigue. The woman did *not* want to go on this trip. As she walked out the door, she grimaced to the husband, "I *really* do *not* want to go." However, her ability to be a self with her mother was highly compromised. The onset of the multiple sclerosis further intensified some aspects of this long-standing process.

Another set of triangles operated around the husband and wife, the wife's illness, and the husband's family of origin. A deeply religious family, some members engaged the wife in various prayers and other practices, including the use of holy water, holy cards placed in strategic locations throughout her bed and household, and even visits to places where miracles purportedly occurred. These family members related to the illness via religious artifacts and rituals, seeing the wife as a "patient in need of a cure." The tension in this triangle involved the husband who took up the issue with his father or his sisters around the imposition of their religious beliefs on his hapless wife.

Upon further review, however, the historical triangle between the husband and his two parents sheds some light on what was transpiring in the current situation. Being involved himself in a symbiotic attachment with his own mother, the husband had managed the intensity in that relationship by emotional and/or physical distance, with a good dose of open rebellion and counterattacking when in close quarters. His difficulty in defining himself more clearly as a person in the original parental triangle played itself out in battles around "religion" in the health care of his wife. This exploded in the months preceding her death when his father incessantly pressed him on whether the wife had been "baptized." It also involved the wife's mother when she received a call from the husband's father inquiring whether her daughter had been duly immersed. Unresolved issues in the husband's primary triangle within his family of origin, then, appeared related to the illness and religion, but really had more to do with the husband's undifferentiation.

Within the nuclear family, the illness played a role in the relationship between the parents and the two daughters. One variation on this theme included the elder daughter attempting to step into a parental role with the younger daughter because of the mother's failing health. Of course this effort was vigorously repelled by the vociferous younger daughter who maintained, "You're not my mother. I already have a mother." The father also played a part in this by asking the eldest daughter to do things he would not have ordinarily asked, had the mother been healthy. Not surprisingly, the elder daughter was a bit more involved in the parental triangle than the younger daughter. Some of the mother's focus, however, was muted as the illness progressed. At times the triangle involving the daughters, their parents, and the larger family would spill over into the extended network. Upon one occasion, as the husband spoke to his father about the challenges of caring for the wife, his father remarked, "Your daughters should not be so involved in their high school activities and should help more at home." Tension then erupted between the husband and his father.

During the period when the wife's condition was rapidly declining and the daughters were at their respective universities and preparing to return home, they would ask their father: "Will Mom be alive when we return?" At the same time, they would ask for direction from the father relative to the timing of their return home, invoking, quite naturally, concern for their mother. Although seemingly innocuous and logical queries, an analysis from a relationship perspective might view their queries about the mother as fueled by the anxiety of the impending death, thereby asking the father to speak for their mother.

Of course, there were triangles of every shade and hue not mentioned in this brief overview. Continually in motion, the anxiety surrounding the worsening of the wife's health was active in *all* systems surrounding the woman, for example, the medical system, the extended family network, and friends, giving rise to whispers and communiqués "about the patient" without direct communication with either the husband or wife (see Bowen, 1978, pp. 322-323). Exacerbation and proliferation of triangles were quite predictable as a family member progresses toward death. Does Bowen theory offer clues that will suggest some avenues for managing oneself in the midst of high anxiety and the accompanying explosion of triangles? One person's attempts, utilizing a rudimentary knowledge of the relationship process, is the topic of the subsequent section.

PRINCIPLES AND DETRIANGLING

Having a set of clearly defined, nonnegotiable principles was of immeasurable value to the husband in finding his way through the plethora of triangles (Wilgus, 2004). Coming largely from within himself and rooted in some awareness of the complexities of triangling, the principles articulated by the husband served as a blueprint for examining himself in relationship to all those connected with him and his wife. The major principles and how they functioned in the process of defining a self, or detriangling, follow.

Principle: There is a human being behind every symptom, and that person is *not* defined by an illness. Every effort will be made to connect with the thinking, feelings, and fantasies of that individual.

Given the fact that the way out of a triangle is the establishment of a person-to-person relationship with each and every individual/family with whom one is connected, the husband found that relating to the *person behind the symptom* was the "way out" of being drawn into a triangle by the multiple sclerosis (MS). He could relate to his wife as an invalid or as a "patient," thereby failing to encounter the person who was his wife. While her physical and cognitive functioning shifted, he could still interact with her as a person while acknowledging the realities of her condition. Talking to her as a grown-up, continuing their playful interaction, and sharing with her the things that only occur in a marriage were some of the ways in which he detriangled from the illness. When she would tell him that she "hated her MS" he would respond by saying that he would be quite worried if she told him that she "loved her MS." This never failed to elicit laughter from her, the levity that comes from being recognized as a person.

Principle: The spouse with the chronic illness, however severe, is responsible for self. She is a thinking person, capable of making decisions about her own body, psyche, and spirit.

While the husband may have been somewhat successful in interacting with his wife on a person-to-person basis, there were members of the medical establishment and the wider extended family who found this difficult to do. For instance, as the wife's tremors increased dramatically, the neurosurgeon directed his commentary to the husband indicating that *he* would be the one having to make some difficult decisions. Although the wife was in the examination room, the communication about her went on with the spouse. At this point, the recommendation was for experimental brain surgery. Upon leaving the hospital on the long drive home, the husband simply explained to the wife what the physician had recommended, seeking her opinion on this option. "That's the stupidest thing that I've ever heard," replied the wife, and no further mention of this alternative was made again. The physician's attempt to involve the husband as the "expert on his wife" failed, due to a knowledge of triangles and the nonnegotiable principle.

From another angle, the husband's sister, a devout Catholic, would ask her brother if she could either say some prayers over the wife or sprinkle holy water around the bed. Despite his own set of beliefs on the lack of efficacy of such practices, the husband told his sister: "Ask her." Even though the wife was barely monosyllabic in the final months of her life, the husband would direct all such inquiries to his spouse. From his understanding of triangles, he believed that this was a matter of the relationship between the two sisters-in-law.

In the weeks prior to her death, a complicating medical condition contributed to a couple of challenging alternatives: surgery to remediate the problem (a short-term solution that could result in increased pain and possibly death) or the cessation of the use of the feeding tube which would inevitably lead to her death. After getting as many facts as possible from the surgeon, the husband went directly to the spouse even though she was unable to speak. Although her living will provided some guidance, it was her utterance in the affirmative when asked, "Honey, do you want to die?" that illuminated the way through a series of potentially loaded triangles. Adhering to the principle defined earlier, the husband acceded to her wishes and she died peacefully at home after five days, surrounded by her daughters, mother, husband, and college friends.

> *Principle:* Issues between the wife and her parents were present long before the chronic illness manifested itself. While the husband cannot manage that triangle *for* his wife, he *can* stay thoughtfully connected to all parties without trying to "shape up" any person or relationship.

As the wife's illness progressed, the husband felt the pull toward "speaking for her," particularly in relationship to her parents. As they related, quite naturally, to the horribleness of the disease, the husband wanted to change their way of thinking so that they could see the beauty of their daughter's courage, from his perspective. From a triangular process, then, the tension in the primary triangle of the wife and her two parents had now shifted to that between the husband and particularly the wife's mother. At some point, he was aware that he was engaged in battles for which he was ill-equipped. After some attempts to gain greater objectivity about the workings of this triangle, he understood that he could neither "shape up" his wife, in other words, have her be more of a self with her mother nor "shape up" the mother to get off her daughter's back. What he *could* do, however, was formulate a relationship with the mother-in-law that did *not* involve his wife. Although quite challenging for him, he was successful in maintaining open and viable contact with her so that his thinking could be as clear as possible about the things that mattered to him. For instance, he could view his wife's functioning in a very different manner from that of her parents. At the same time, he could back off from them, giving them the respect to view their daughter in their own way.

> *Principle:* The conflict that emerged in the husband's family of origin around the issue of religion directly related to his unresolved attachment in the primary triangle in which he was embedded. Efforts, then, were directed at defining a self in this triangle instead of battling over religious matters.

During the last year of the wife's life, the interaction between the husband and his father became more conflictual, particularly around the religion of the wife. In regard to content, the father relayed his concern for the soul of the wife in the afterlife; relating only to the content, the husband engaged his father in bitter disputes about religion, either by defending himself or attacking the father. It was difficult for the husband to see the part that he played in the maintenance of the triangle (his father, himself, and his wife). At some point, however, he caught a glimpse of the fact that this tension was simply a reworking of his own undifferentiation in the primary triangle with both of his parents. He had been symbiotic with his mother in an over-positive manner and highly conflictual with his father throughout his developing years. The conflict now shifted around a new issue—that of the ill spouse's eternal salvation. Clearly, this was a smokescreen for the unresolved process at work.

In a lengthy letter to his father, the husband decided to address the relationship between himself and his father along with the role that the mother played—over the duration of their lives as father and son. Conciliatory in nature, the son's letter explained that before either of them died, he hoped they could find some peace in their relationship even though they were quite different people. He maintained: "You are the only father I will ever have, and I am the only eldest son you will ever have." A thoughtful chronology of emotional events was part of the correspondence. Again, the effort was to shift the focus from the interlocking issues of religion and the wife to the heart of the matter—the difficulty in the original parental triangle.

Subsequent to this letter, which the husband asked to be kept only between the two of them, there was a palpable loosening of the intensity in the relationship. The battles around religion diminished. On the day the wife died, the father and mother visited the home and said good-bye to their daughter-in-law, respecting the son's wishes that they keep their prayers silently to themselves. And the son and the father, who never acknowledged the letter, came to a new understanding manifested in greater humor and playfulness that had long been lacking in their relationship. Of pertinence to the husband was the fact that he suddenly had an awareness of the role that *he* had played in maintaining this triangle. Once he shifted his stance, the entire relationship shifted. There was a subtle, concomitant shift between the husband and his mother, manifested by greater distance. This became more apparent in the following year when the husband made some strides in moving toward his mother. As he engaged her in a more intimate conversation that only involved the two of them, the mother commented, "We haven't talked like this in a long time." At the time of the shift with his father, however, this distance was less observable. Again, this was a powerful illustration of how triangles operate and what can be done when one person significantly shifts a position.

> *Principle:* Chronic illness is a condition that resides in the marital relationship. The spouses are responsible for managing that situation. Children can be concerned but they are *not* responsible for the well-being of either parent.

When the functioning of a significant family member, in this case, the mother, deteriorates, it is not surprising that the family will attempt to occupy that vacuum. It was no accident that the eldest daughter (an oldest sister of sisters) would try to take over some of her mother's functioning. Aware that this triangle could be potentially harmful over the long term for not only the oldest daughter, but for the youngest as well, the father would communicate both verbally and in actions the following message: your mother's health is something that is between us parents. While the children were naturally concerned, they heard the message that they needed to be involved in the tasks and responsibilities of children at their stages of development. Although both daughters were only too willing to assist the father or the caregiver at varying times, they both heard the fact that the grown-ups were in charge on this matter. Consequently, they maintained an adolescence replete with many school activities, both curricular, and extracurricular. When the eldest daughter would attempt to usurp her mother's role vis-à-vis the youngest daughter, both parents would communicate to her that they were fully capable of handling her little sister. This detriangling of the illness from the children and placing it in the marital relationship freed them up to do the things they needed to do at that point in their lives.

> *Principle:* Open communication and action during the dying process and funeral in the presence of the family and friendship networks are paramount.

Throughout the active dying process, which lasted five days, the husband maintained direct communication with all the significant family members. When there were issues that related to others, he endeavored to remove himself from that dyad. For example, both daughters were at the very beginning of their academic semesters at some distance from the family home when they heard their mother was in the process of dying. Conflicted as to what they should do, they asked their father if their mother was going to live until they returned home. Sticking to the facts, he simply replied that he did not know. When looking for direction relative to the timing of their trip home (for it was quite likely the mother would die while they were en route as they were both out of state and at some distance from the family home), the father placed the issue between them and their mother by saying, "If your mother could speak, what might she tell you to do?" Upon hearing this question and forced back into the relationship with their mother, the answer became apparent. They decided to handle the collegiate issues even though it would entail a delay of a couple of days. At the same time, the husband had carefully told the wife exactly what was occurring with the children in as calm a way as possible. He softly told her what day it was, what the daughters were doing, and when they would return home. He did not want to exert any undue pressure on the wife nor interfere with the dying process. As it transpired, the daughters arrived on a Tuesday, and their mother died on Wednesday. Clearly, the mother had some unfinished business that needed to occur with her daughters. Staying out of the triangles perhaps allowed that to occur.

As the wife was dying, the husband also contacted the wife's mother and siblings along with her best friends. He described exactly what was occurring—both what was known and what was unknown. When the wife's mother who lived at some distance and her three brothers asked to be present during the process of her dying, the husband welcomed them. When her two best friends from college asked to fly across the country to say good-bye to the wife, he also welcomed them.

At the time of the death, the husband took the lead in informing the key members on both sides of the family by phone and in person. The daughters informed their own set of friends directly and there were many visitors to the home. Rather than leaving the funeral details to others, the husband again set the tone. Despite a tradition in the wife's family of not having an open casket, he honored his wife's wishes and orchestrated an open viewing with plenty of time for family and friends who were traveling from across the country. Rather than leaving the details of the funeral service to a minister, he again led the way with his daughters and brother, putting together the entire celebration of his wife's life. The youngest daughter asked to sing; he agreed. The older daughter asked to deliver a tribute to her mother; he again agreed. He delivered the eulogy.

If triangles are suggestive of a closed system (see Bowen, 1978, p. 324), then a more open communication system would result in fewer triangles. The period of the active dying process, the visitation, and the funeral service was characterized by candor and openness within the nuclear family, the extended family network, and the friendship network. People spoke openly about their varying relationships with the dead spouse; there was laughter, storytelling, and tears. The husband's father, with whom there had been such intense conflict, warmly embraced his son. The Catholics in the family joined together in the Unitarian Universalist service, being moved by the actions of the husband and the daughters. Getting through triangles allowed, for a moment, at least, a thoughtful and calm relationship system that was free to do what it needed to do in a time of great loss.

OUTCOMES

The value of a knowledge of triangling and its impact upon the immediate and extended families are apparent. Despite the pressures that typically come with having a chronically ill family member, an awareness of triangles and what to do with one's own position in a particular triangle, leads to a significant reduction in the tension within the entire family unit. Pressures accompanying such situations can lead to a fragmentation of the family unit. Through one person's understanding of the relationship process, along with a motivation and ability to do something about his own part in the process, the unit can remain intact, as it did in this particular case. Of course, triangles were constantly present and would flare up periodically. Unresolved attachments with both spouses' families of origin played a prominent part in the family. Nonetheless, the clear definition of principle along with the ability to work on being a separate self, that is, detriangling from other relationships, permitted this family to negotiate this terrain with lower anxiety than might be predicted for this degree of trauma.

At the same time, during the apparently darkest moments of the active dying process and all the funeral proceedings, a sense of calm dominated the landscape. People were able to express their thoughts and feelings freely about the illness and their relationship with the dying spouse. With Bowen theory offering a beacon of light in what would typically be quite daunting circumstances, the husband's leadership seemed to pervade the entire group. In this atmosphere, people felt free to do what they needed to do. For instance, the wife's mother had some difficulty with the fact of the open casket, and she chose to remain by a doorway in the funeral home. The daughters welcomed their many friends in their own unique ways. Three former spouses of family members braved the potential intensity of not just the death process but the presence of their ex-spouses to pay their respects to the family. Indeed, one divorced couple later rekindled their relationship and remarried, their first joint venture in years being the attendance at the wife's funeral. And the sense of calm led to moments of humor as well. When the husband's ex-wife entered the funeral home, she embraced him weeping and saying, "I am so sorry about her death." After she cried for a few moments, he whispered in her ear, "Death is a hell of a lot easier than divorce," whereupon she pulled back from him and laughed. It is possible to detriangle from death itself!

Adhering to principle and attempting to maintain as many one-to-one relationships as humanly possible also gave the family the ability to function as a team, doing what they needed to do during the illness, the death process, and its aftermath. One of the husband's nieces described her view of how this played out in the family:

> No "poor me" here. You and the girls accepted Aunt Carol's condition and integrated it into your everyday lives. Yes, she had MS, but that's the way things were. Amanda kept singing, Taryn kept studying and you kept teaching. When faced with adversity, we must keep the ball rolling. (H. St. Hilaire, 2002, personal communication)

This orientation contributed to the higher functioning of the spouse with the illness as well, from this niece's perspective, as she continued:

> Fine. How can one word convey so much meaning? "Fine" means Aunt Carol hung in there when the going got tough and lived her life with courage and tenacity. "Fine" means she was proud of her girls. "Fine" means there's so much more to Aunt Carol than a disease. Aunt Carol taught us how to be brave and how to live a "fine" life. (H. St. Hilaire, 2002, personal communication)

Implicit in these comments are the translation of the principles articulated earlier by the husband, in other words, that the wife was much more than the sum of her symptoms. Detriangling and the clarity of principles, then, enhanced both her physical and emotional well-being.

Focusing on the person-to-person relationship process, thus, contributes to an atmosphere of openness maintained throughout the period of sickness and in the major transition of the death process. Rather than whispers or behind the back comments about the ill person, the facts were dealt with openly and calmly. When the wife's situation deteriorated, the husband spoke directly to her, and she was able to respond to him in a way that was absolutely clear about her wishes. In other words, she was ready to die. This knowledge, without relying on the input of experts or other family members, contributed to a sense of purpose and direction that was evident to all. The husband's sister indicated that her indelible image of the death and funeral proceedings was that of the strength of the family, including the wife, the husband, and the two daughters. People were dealt with directly. Death was dealt with directly, and the family did not blink. Almost immediately, significant family members were speaking about the dead woman in the past tense. Free to recount stories about her, without elevating her to sainthood, family and friends laughed and cried in the reminiscing.

At the time this chapter was written, it had been two and a half years since the death of the wife. The eldest daughter graduated from college, worked in Washington, DC, for two years, and then began law school. She was married to a fine young man in the summer of 2004. The youngest daughter was then in the final year of college majoring in psychology and preparing for graduate school in social work. Incidentally, both daughters returned to their respective universities subsequent to their mother's death, completing highly successful years, much to the amazement of family and friends. The husband returned to his teaching responsibilities, taking some time for himself during the summers to visit family and friends. At that time he began seeing a woman, the minister at his daughter's wedding and a dear friend of both his daughters and his wife. The wife's mother had continued to be present in the many family events such as graduations, weddings, and holidays. Symptoms were mild in all of the members, despite the untimely death of the wife, mother, and daughter.

CONCLUSION

Bowen theory provides a way of thinking about the human condition. Moreover, it provides a road map for behavior in the midst of the challenges encountered as part of human condition. The triangle is a concept from Bowen theory that contributes to both an understanding of the human phenomenon and a framework for managing the self in the midst of life's many challenges, even those fraught with high emotionality such as the chronic illness and death of a family member outside of the typical life cycle. This way of thinking which leads to a way of acting and being can lead to a thoughtful resolution of one of life's major events, in other words, the death of a family member. It *is* possible to think more clearly when the emotions run deep. It *is* possible to adhere to principle armed with the knowledge of how one functions in the human relationship system. It *is* possible to act in ways that allow self and others to be who they need to be and do what they need to do without getting on their backs or involving others in their dilemma.

REFERENCES

Bowen, M. (1978). *Family therapy in clinical practice.* New York: Jason Aronson.
Kerr, M. E. and Bowen, M. (1988). *Family evaluation.* New York: W.W. Norton.
St. Hilaire, H. (2002). Personal communication. Reprinted by permission.
Wilgus, A. J. (2004). Peace follows principle: Theory comes alive in the face of death. *Family Systems Forum, 6*(2): 1-15.

Chapter 7

Efforts to Understand Early Triangles in the Therapist's Extended Family

James C. Maloni

INTRODUCTION

The major focus of this chapter is the centrality of understanding and monitoring one's relationship with parents and the triangular components involved. This is the imprint which composes the pattern of all other important relationships. The more one learns about this central triangle, the more curious one becomes about the emotional programming and triangles of previous generations. One's parental relationship patterns were also imprinted by certain emotional triangles.

This chapter will cover the author's father and his emigrating from Italy with his mother to the United States. The triangular relationship with his parents, the early death of his father, and subsequent relationship patterns with his siblings and mother will be discussed. The earlier years in Italy will be described. They highlight the difficult circumstances surrounding the marriage of the father's parents. Triangular patterns in Italy evolving into parallel configurations in the United States will be depicted. The father's levels of functioning throughout his lifetime will be explored in conjunction with various triangular relationships. The transmission of the family triangles via the multigenerational emotional process will be briefly described. How learning about triangles in one's own family impacts the clinical work of the therapist will also be discussed.

The author began systematic work on his extended paternal family system over thirty years ago. For the first sixteen years of his life, the author grew up within the emotional environment of his paternal grandmother who had immigrated to this country from Italy along with her firstborn son, John, the author's father. She loved to describe the small village and its people that she had reluctantly left to join her husband who was living in the United States. This couple and their son John represented and transmitted numerous interlocking emotional triangles, many of which originated in Italy. This work is an attempt to further the understanding of several of these triangles.

BACKGROUND

John died on January 31, 2001, after celebrating his eighty-eighth birthday in December. He lived twice as long as his father, Paul, who died in 1927, as depicted in Figure 7.1.

John lived the first five years of his life with his mother and her parents in Italy. In 1918, John and his mother Rose came to the United States to join his father who had been living in this country. Owing to his father's early

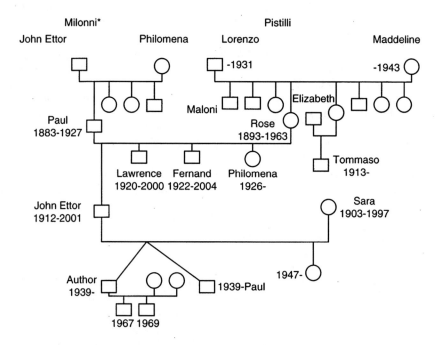

FIGURE 7.1. Paternal Family Diagram (*Changed to Maloni in the United States; referred to only as "Maloni" in the text.)

death, John lived less than ten years of his long life with him. As with John, Paul's father also died young.

Even though he lived within a block of his father's extended family in Italy, John apparently had no contact with them. His mother Rose also had little or no contact with her husband's extended family. As the story has been told, Paul had no contact with his mother once he married Rose.

John was closely aligned with his mother and her extended family. The first five years of his life were imprinted solely with his maternal family system. This was the same network of people who opposed the wedding of his mother, Rose, to his father, Paul, and apparently shielded him from exposure to his paternal family. Rose's parents had chosen a different suitor for their daughter to marry. This suitor apparently came from a family more similar to Rose's family in status and socioeconomic accomplishments. In addition, there had been some form of feud between Rose and Paul's families. It is unknown whether this feud occurred prior to or during Rose and Paul's courtship.

The Early Years in the United States

John reported that when he and his mother came to the United States, seeing his father was like meeting a stranger. Apparently they were unable to reverse this early imprinting for the next nine years before Paul died. The early pattern, coupled with the absence of continuity in the parental relationship, contributed to a rather inflexible triangle among son, mother, and father. This was the prevailing climate a few years later when John's younger brother, Lawrence was born.

Lawrence was Paul's first born in an emotional and perhaps functional sense. According to John's report, his father showed little restraint in openly expressing his special affection for the first son born in this country. He called him "papa's boy." Even though Lawrence preceded him in death, John went to his grave with moderately intense reactions to these circumstances in his early life. The overt nature of these reactions was fixed on his father. Owing to Paul's premature death, the animosity which obviously evolved between father and son was not mediated by time and other factors. Paul's death occurred when John was entering adolescence, which may have helped to further fuel the intensity of the son's reactions.

In the triangle with his father and brother Lawrence, John manifested little animosity toward the latter, at least when discussing these relationships as an adult. Some of this was probably related to the interlocking triangles with both parents, and with mother and brother. Rose modeled ongoing animosity and faultfinding toward her husband, which also lingered throughout her lifetime. As John was always a good student and Rose an effective teacher, this dance between them regarding Paul was exquisitely tuned. Rose's emotional distance from her husband, and geographical distance from extended family, reinforced her intense focus on her offspring. This perhaps contributed to John's positive attitude toward his brother Lawrence.

After his father's death, John became "the man of the house," which probably increased Lawrence's dependence on his older brother. In later years, John, five foot four in stature, spoke unabashedly about cherishing being perceived as "the big man." Lawrence's adaptive personality style was able to fit nicely with John's aspirations for special status. This younger brother's compliance allowed John to convert the status issue into a positive caretaking relationship with his brother.

Within a couple years of his father's death, John's leadership status was tested when his mother informed her family that she was taking them back to live in Italy. Having become thoroughly acclimated to this country by this time, John resolutely resisted his mother's wishes and refused to cooperate with her plans, as mother, son, and his siblings have told the story to their children and grandchildren, Rose prepared to return to her motherland with the three younger offspring, leaving John in this country as he wished. Apparently Lawrence and the next younger brother, Fernand were swayed by John's influence and sided with their older brother against their mother. According to all the reports, Rose relented and decided to keep her family in the United States. It appears that it became easier for her to think about this decision in terms of her offspring's wishes rather than maintain her plan. In the triangle with John, his siblings, and his mother, this family had evolved into the firstborn offspring, who happened to be male, gaining the dominant position. Some of this would have been a natural progression as John was more fully exposed to the English language and American culture than the other family members. The mother and family had learned to rely on him for everyday practical matters prior to this triangular showdown regarding where they would establish permanent residence.

John also repeatedly told the story about numerous suitors who wanted to marry his mother. Once again, during his reporting of this, John showed little hesitancy in admitting how he would strategically manipulate his younger siblings to influence their mother against accepting the marriage proposals. John was also successful in this venture as his mother never remarried. Similar to the triangular pattern in the residence issue, Rose apparently made her decision according to the togetherness climate in the nuclear family. It is possible that she used other criteria to decide in one or both cases and found it more convenient to report her decision as if it were based on the recent family poll. When discussing his mother's marriage proposals with the author not long before his death, John reflectively commented on his desire to maintain the leadership position in his family of origin. He consistently chose to describe this in terms of "the big man role" in the family. As an old man, he seemed to enjoy the fact that he had been so persistent, strategic, and even cunning in successfully achieving his goals as an adolescent.

As alluded to earlier, the absence of geographically available family members in Rose's life was probably a major factor in her giving in to her firstborn and other offspring. This is a good illustration of how specific circumstances at various times in a family's life are influential in the way triangles are played out and decisions are made. This then forms a pattern and imprint for later generations. The intensity of the triangular issues activated at the time in her life when she married Paul suggests immaturity having an impact on decision making. Immaturity and reactivity in the context of major life decisions often go hand in hand with difficult life circumstances, and this appears to be what Rose was confronted with.

The Early Years in Italy

Rose and Paul married in Italy in 1912, probably during one of his periodic trips back to Italy from the United States. Twenty-nine years of age at the time of the marriage, Paul was ten years older than his wife. He had emigrated to America at the age of eighteen, ostensibly for work. Little is known about the wedding, but the family emphasized Rose's rebellion against her parents, especially her mother, and marrying Paul rather than the young man chosen by her parents. In spite of apparent socioeconomic and class differences, Paul's family (the Malonis) and Rose's family (the Pistillis) lived less than a block away from each other. Little or no contact occurred between these families at the time of the wedding.

His father had died several years prior to Paul's emigrating to the United States. He was sending much of his money to support his mother and younger siblings. Once he married, Paul no longer gave financial support to his family of origin. This was given as the major reason that his mother disowned him, which began the permanent physical and emotional cutoff between mother and son.

For several years Rose resisted Paul's urging her to join him in the United States as their permanent place of residence. While Paul had sacrificed his relationship with his mother and siblings for this marriage, the intensity of Rose's previous reactivity to her parents had apparently decreased once she became a mother. It appears that she was enjoying her life in Italy with her son and extended family, even though her relationship with her mother, Maddeline, remained tense. With the birth of the son, the triangle with her family of origin and husband apparently shifted. It appears that she was less emotionally connected with her husband. Her connection with her father, Lorenzo, was strong and this was also the case with certain siblings, especially the sister immediately following her, whose name was Elizabeth.

Rose was the fourth of the eight offspring of her parents. She was the secondborn female child immediately preceding Elizabeth. Elizabeth's son Tommaso was born one month after John. As Rose and Elizabeth had been close while growing up, John and Tommaso were playmates as young children. This intergenerational connection left a strong imprint. Almost a half century later when John first revisited Italy as an older adult, he and Tommaso resumed an engaging relationship. During John's last trip to Italy in 2000, three months prior to his death, parallels were drawn between early and later behaviors in relation to John and Tommaso. A prime example was Tommaso's good appetite for food, in marked contrast to John who was an inconsistent eater. This difference was quite apparent during their last meal together. When John was a young boy in Italy, Rose would take her son over to her sister's home at mealtimes in the hope that Tommaso's eagerness for food would have a positive impact on John's eating habits. This illustrates the high degree of close daily contact between Rose and her sister and their offspring during the early years in Italy.

In some families, the birth of offspring reduces the degree of the female's togetherness drive toward her mate. For some females the function of the mate has been fulfilled at least for the time being. Total commitment toward raising and enjoying the offspring becomes central to her daily life. Being able to do this within familiar surroundings and with the support and assistance of extended family is intrinsically satisfying to this endeavor. Such was Rose's situation at the time Paul was first pursuing her to join him. It was reported to the author that after several years of this, Paul gave Rose the ultimatum of joining him or sacrificing the marriage. It is unknown whether the financial aspect of the ultimatum was a primary factor for Rose when she finally complied with her husband's request. It could have been that as John was of school age, she saw this as an opportunity to give her son a better education. In Rose's view, education was always a high priority in spite of her only finishing eighth grade. Another factor could have been that after five years of full-time mothering with her first born, Rose's reproductive drive was now directing her toward additional children. Her strong Catholic background would influence her to fulfill this goal within the context of an already existing marriage in spite of diminishing attraction.

After more than twenty-five years of discussion directed toward family of origin issues, within a year of his death, John spoke about the day he and his mother left their birthplace to come to America. In his usual terse and verbally efficient style, John discussed how he had never forgotten the look on his grandfather Lorenzo's face. This had occurred some eighty years earlier. Implied in this was the intense attachment of father, daughter, and grandson, and the realization that probable permanent separation was suddenly replacing years of daily contact. This high degree of togetherness involved specific family dynamics. As alluded to earlier, it appears that Rose and her mother, Maddeline, never satisfactorily resolved their differences. Maddeline would forever be portrayed as emotionally unavailable in contrast to the totally positive view of Lorenzo. It can only be surmised as to how these interlocking triangular dynamics were played out on a daily basis in those early years in Italy.

THE MALONIS AND THE PISTILLIS

Little factual information is available regarding the relationship between Rose and Paul's families of origin. What is known is that during the second decade of the twentieth century, they were geographical neighbors in the small village town of Cori in the province of Latina, fifty kilometers southeast of Rome. Rose's family, the Pistillis, owned considerable land, which represented a moderately high level of socioeconomic security and generations of residence in this village town. Paul's family, the Malonis, was more nomadic and had never established roots in this town where the norm was that families had known each other for several generations. It was reported by family members that Cori was founded earlier than Rome. It is not known when the Malonis arrived in Cori or whether they came before or after the premature death of Paul's father, who reportedly died during surgery in Rome. The prevalent view is that they were renters rather than owners of the land and home in Cori.

Paul's physical and emotional cutoff from his family of origin was probably related to numerous factors, including the earlier feud between the two families. What seems probable to the author is that Paul's display of exploration, initiative, and energy in finding profitable work in America probably afforded his mother and siblings a more comfortable level of physical survival than they had experienced for some time, if ever. This would suggest that the issue of family responsibility and perhaps loyalty would be quite intense, given such basic circumstances.

This cutoff between Paul and his mother and siblings perhaps served the function of reducing the level of responsibility for this firstborn Italian male. Although it is common in families for the firstborn offspring to replace the same-sex deceased parent in fulfilling family responsibilities, the Italian

custom and expectations appear to increase the intensity of this goal sometimes. Although the practical aspect of earning more money in America
would have been desirous for young immigrants such as Paul, it is also possible that the geographical distance from his family gave him some relief
from the daily reminder of his responsibilities toward his family of origin in
Italy. The absence of the watchful and expectant eyes of mother and younger siblings perhaps allowed Paul to actively persuade his Italian bride to
come to America. After numerous pleadings over several years, Paul was finally successful in having his nuclear family leave the homeland and come
to his new world. At this point, he had become more fully liberated from the
expectations of the traditional world to become a full-time citizen of his
new country and leader of his new family.

FROM ITALIAN TO AMERICAN TRIANGLES

John's description of separating from his maternal grandfather at an early
age was in sharp contrast to his account of joining his father in America. In
describing this first meeting, John emphasized the disappointment related
to his father not being physically present when wife and son first arrived at
their new place of residence in America after weeks of arduous travel. This
imprint would be the foundation of disapproval and provided fuel in the triangular dynamics of this newly activated nuclear family.

In an equally absolute and finalized manner, Paul would replace his
mother-in-law, Maddeline, as the person whose position would remain on
the outside. The inflexible triangular interactions in the family of origin
would continue in this newly operating family of procreation as shown in
Figure 7.2.

As it was similar to the former pattern involving the grandmother, this
pattern became fixed and permanent long after Paul's death and throughout
the lifetimes of Rose and John. Mother and son appeared to be thoroughly
and irreversibly fused in their joint perception of the two outsiders. In both
cases the outsider was the same-sex parent of mother and son. As Rose separated from her parents in her midtwenties and would never see them again,
there was never any opportunity to update information and/or to view the
less extreme aspects of the positively and negatively perceived parents. Thus
in her case, the absoluteness of the negative view of the same-sex parent was
forever matched by the totally indiscriminate positive view of the opposite-
sex parent.

In the case of John and his parents, the premature death of his father also
allowed no opportunity for son and father to modify their relationship in

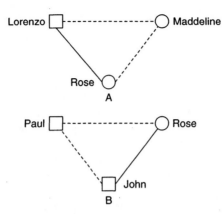

FIGURE 7.2. Triangles in the Family of Origin (*A:* Triangle with Rose and Father [Lorenzo] inside, Mother [Maddeline] outside. *B:* Triangle with Rose and Son [John] inside and Husband [Paul] outside.)

later life. There was one period of time when John utilized his good thinking abilities and was able to present a somewhat more balanced view of his father. Included in this description was that his father had musical skills and utilized this to contribute to some recreational activities for the family, which John portrayed as enjoyable and noteworthy. For the most part, however, including during the last year of his life, the view of his father was driven by the early imprint and long-term emotional programming.

In terms of how John perceived his mother, there was ample opportunity to gain a more balanced and discriminating picture. This was aided by the close proximity of John's nuclear family to his mother. John's wife, Sara, and Rose developed a positive and mutually respectful relationship over many years of living next door to each other. John was able to learn from and accept Sara's thoughtful and usually restrained description of his mother. Perhaps since he had ample practice in opposing his mother when he was a young man, John was more prepared as a husband to deal with the complex triangular interactions in the family involving wife and mother. Also, prior to coming to live with his mother, John and Sara had lived with Sara's mother when they were newly married. According to all accounts, John was effective and apparently comfortable in this triangle. The physical vulnerability of his mother-in-law at that time in her life, and the generally dependent nature of Sara, appeared to fit with John's well-developed caretaking abilities.

LEVELS OF FUNCTIONING AND TRIANGLES

John's effectiveness in dealing with the triangles between his mother and siblings when he was an adolescent and later in life with his wife and mother-in-law, and wife and mother probably illustrate his well-learned pragmatic adaptiveness and instinctive strategic skills. When this author was growing up, John often spoke about the early battles he encountered with peers who physically and verbally accosted and tested him regarding his Italian heritage. From his stories, it appears that he gained considerable early experience in counteracting such overt prejudice and bigotry. Utilizing a broad assortment of physical and social strategies, John eventually developed popularity in his peer group.

To what extent learning how to deal with adversity and successfully managing various triangular situations both inside and outside the home represents a basic level of functioning or involves more of a relationship-oriented reciprocity of functioning is an important issue in understanding the basic foundation of behaviors. The compelling life story of John as an Italian immigrant who, in spite of hardship, utilized the American system to gain a quality education and an upper middle class socioeconomic level of living is a good case study.

John was clearly above average and probably functioned at the superior level of intelligence, particularly throughout more than twenty years of formal education. Although he never completed his dissertation, he had completed the other requirements for a doctoral degree in education. This level of intelligence was also probably manifested in his early career as an administrative employee for the state of Pennsylvania, military service during World War II, and later as a teacher of mathematics for junior high school students. John also manifested a wide variety of abilities and skills. In addition to an aptitude for mathematics and science, John was also a handyman, skilled at building and repairing. As a boy and young man John probably exhibited above average skills in sizing up social situations and learning how to effectively negotiate and manage his way through relatively complex predicaments.

Such an array of abilities and skills probably represents a fairly high level of basic functioning. Also, a fairly high level of basic functioning is exhibited by John's relative consistent use of careful thinking in making major decisions throughout most of his life; much of the same could be said about his three children and nine grandchildren.

On the other hand, reciprocal functioning, related to dominant position in triangular interactional patterns, is also apparent in the earlier described family situations. Fusion and togetherness were paramount in the early years in Italy as his existence was given special status by the extended family. This status was apparent during his later visits to Italy, especially the last one just three months prior to his death. The Italian name of "Titarella," signifying specialness, was always reserved for him by these relatives. In his early years in the United States, he enjoyed privileged status with his mother in relation to his father, and later with his siblings in relation to his mother.

For the most part John was able to maintain his special status position in his family of origin, largely due to the willing compliance of his siblings and with the cooperation of their nuclear families. There was one temporary exception to this pattern leading to a partial cutoff with a brother-in-law, which was reversed at a later date. It was observable that "being the big man" remained a sensitive issue for John throughout his life. Circumstances were generally favorable for maintaining the usual triangular configurations in the large extended family. Health and finances were largely positive, which helped to keep anxiety at a manageable level. John's wife Sara and their three offspring as adults were quite cooperative in respecting the tradition of showing respect to the husband and father and allowing him to have his way in most major areas.

For several years prior to his death, John and his adult twin sons discussed a particular period of time when the triangles had shifted, placing him in the outside position. During this time, he had moved his nuclear family from a small town in central Pennsylvania where his father had initially immigrated, to the suburbs of Washington, DC. This was against the wishes of his mother and twin sons, but with the full support of his wife, Sara. In retrospect, his decision was a good one, and he was able to maintain his course in spite of some strong pressures to change direction. During the discussion in later years with his sons, the latter gave John considerable verbal accolades for making and staying with this decision. It was also acknowledged, however, that a significant price accompanied this decision. His mother possibly never forgave him for this decision. Rose lived a little over seven years after this move, having developed cancer a couple of years later. For Rose, a decision of this nature could only trigger the memories of those early years after her husband had died and she was attempting to decide whether the family should go back to Italy or stay in the United States. At that time, as previously discussed, John's strong position was to stay, in spite of her preference to return to Italy. In both situations, John had gotten his way.

In the waning years of his life, John seemed preoccupied with the dilemma his mother had had when he moved his family. At that time she had refused to join him. Perhaps the emotional significance of moving outside the home area, which had replaced the Italian home, was penetrating John at deeper levels toward the end of his life. His wife had preceded him in death by three and a half years. Perhaps, the long-term togetherness with Sara had cushioned and covered the earlier attachment to his mother. John and Sara were married for sixty years. Approaching his own death, particularly without his wife, perhaps gave him new understanding of his mother's last years. Also, the early attachment to his mother may have been reactivated at some level. This would illustrate a more subtle form of the shifting of triangles based upon the current relationship structure and life circumstances. When Sara was alive, John was responsive to her wishes and preferences. This included that period of time when John moved his nuclear family away from the area where his mother was living. He was able to manage his responsiveness to his mother's wishes via the relationship process with his wife. At the end of his life and without his wife, John's fusion with his mother and maternal grandfather during his early years at the time he was leaving Italy for America was possibly reawakened.

As alluded to earlier, John's decision to move his nuclear family, in spite of opposing pressures, illustrates a higher level of basic functioning in his life. Long-term planning, considerable preparation and careful research went into this major decision. Support and encouragement from Sara were crucial during this process. This was a central factor in his resisting negative pressure from his mother, twin sons, colleagues, and friends. The clarity of his long-term goals for himself and his family appeared to be an intrinsic factor, which aided him in offsetting his unfamiliarity with the outside position in major triangles operating in his immediate relationship system.

The complexity of the interlocking emotional triangles, which impacted the relationship with his mother, probably requires a more systematic focus and careful attention. This was a major event in the family's life, which triggered long-term anxiety and reactivity dating back to John's early years with his mother. This involved the central triangles operating in Rose's life when she was a young adult and new mother and was confronted with the dilemma of how to make a radical separation from extended family and homeland to solidify a marital union that was made during a time of considerable reactivity.

MULTIGENERATIONAL EMOTIONAL PROCESS
AND TRIANGLES

At the time the author and his fraternal twin brother were born, the former was named after the maternal grandfather while the latter was given the name of John's father, Paul. This was similar to John being named after his paternal grandfather and his brother Lawrence being given the name of the maternal grandfather. A moderate level of emotional conflict evolved, with John and the new Paul being aligned. The author was more connected with Sara. This reflected a milder version of John's fusion with his mother and distance from his father. Although the author was involved in fusion with both parents and twin brother, with each being more pronounced at various times, one prevalent triangle was Sara and the author on the inside and John on the outside. During the author's first marriage, the earlier tension between father and son was acted out between father and daughter-in-law. This process is diagrammed in Figure 7.3.

In the author's nuclear family, a version of his triangular relationship with parents was acted out. Each of the author's sons had particular times in their growing up when the predominant triangle was mother and son on the inside and father on the outside.

The intense and irreversibly inflexible triangle between Paul and Rose and their families of origin contributed to a set of circumstances which evolved into a rigid triangle among Paul, Rose, and John. The more severe version of this triangle, in the next generation, was played out in Lawrence and Fernand's families. In each of their cases, the tension between their spouse and their mother prevented consistency and continuity in relationships. Unlike their older brother, Lawrence and Fernand were unable to take on their mother, in defense of their wives, which further reinforced the tension among the family members.

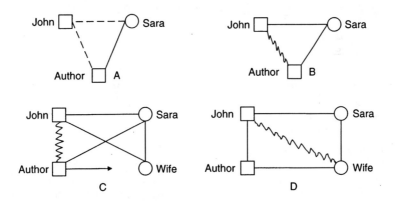

FIGURE 7.3. Multigenerational Triangles (*A:* Triangle with Author and Mother inside and Father outside. *B:* Tension develops between Author and Father. *C:* Author's wife becomes triangled into the tension between Author and Father. *D:* Tension shifts to Father and Daughter-in-Law.)

Legal divorce can be considered a form of cultural variation on how the emotional process is manifested in recent generations. Emotional divorce apparently pervaded Rose and Paul's marriage. All four of their offspring experienced long-term singular marriages. In the following two generations eight divorces have occurred in the lives of the seventeen family members who married. This percentage is average for this period of time in our culture. However, it probably reflects a level of basic functioning that has difficulty responding to the increased complexity of modern living with a commensurate degree of flexibility.

IMPACT ON THE THERAPIST'S WORK

Much emphasis in Bowen theory has been given to the study of one's family of origin (Bowen, 1978; Kerr and Bowen, 1988). The relevance of the family therapist's pursuit of such an endeavor, as an intrinsic feature of training and preparation, has also been given considerable attention (Titelman, 1987). Understanding and managing key triangles in one's family of origin is both challenging and rewarding. The rewards include early detection of the existence of specific triangles and a better sense of how they are influencing behaviors. Opportunities to apply carefully thought responses in such situations can be useful in gaining flexibility in important relationships.

As mentioned earlier, the author has devoted much time and energy throughout his career to this work. In addition to personal gains, this pursuit has facilitated his effectiveness in helping individuals and families better understand what they are dealing with. This effectiveness includes providing a climate of normalcy when communicating observations about an individual family. Becoming acquainted with the underbelly of his own family triangles has made it possible for the author to avoid the common trap of reducing clinical observations to abnormalities or dysfunctional behaviors.

Over time, the author has become clearer about the ongoing nature and multiple levels of understanding involved in this study of triangles. In the case of the author's family, gaining access to a variety of resources occurred over many years. This included repeated visits to the small village town in Italy. The author benefited from his father having lived a long life of relatively sound physical and mental health. The repetition of the central triangles across generations in the Maloni family speaks to the fundamental nature of emotional programming. Individuals changed but the same basic patterns continued. They are imprinted in earlier generations, driven by a combination of functioning levels and anxiety, and situated in a context of particular circumstances.

Perhaps the major advantage of understanding and monitoring the central triangles related to one's parents and earlier generations is that it provides a framework to increase one's neutrality in clinical work with other families. It is a natural reaction to side with one family member over another, whether this be your own family or a clinical family. The strenuous emotional work-out, aided by an intellectual plan, to become more neutral in one's own family has significant impact on becoming less invested when working with other families.

Writing this chapter has helped the author to observe how the transmission of emotional triangles becomes operative at various times in the individual's life and in the family's life. For example, the author was surprised to discover that his father's and grandmother's view that she had married beneath herself was becoming increasingly attractive as this chapter was unfolding. When his father was alive and advocating this point of view, the author utilized the goal of neutrality to provide a counterpoint position. Now that his father was no longer available to articulate this aspect of the family emotional program, the process toward neutrality became more difficult. The reflexive tendency to adopt the consensual family perception was visible.

Even though the Pistilli family was more successful than the Maloni family in terms of socioeconomic success, they were probably functioning at a similar level of emotional maturity. One could argue that circumstances were primary in bringing Rose and Paul together, as they lived in the same neighborhood. This was an important factor especially since Rose was relatively young at the time of her initial emotional connection with Paul, and probably was not permitted to move about the village to meet young men. Not only were these two young people equally smitten in their early attraction, but both families apparently manifested similar levels of emotional reactivity toward the situation. Each had their own concerns pertaining to family circumstances, but the similarity was that both families were equally caught in an instinctive response to their offspring and to each other. Each family had their own set of expectations, neither of which fit with this marriage. Even though they indirectly agreed on not approving of the marriage, their reactivity toward each other seemed to dominate their behaviors.

This experience suggests that becoming a paragon of neutrality is probably not realistic or even useful. The ongoing process of monitoring emotional triangling in self is important. The expectation that one reaches a point where this is no longer necessary is to be monitored in and of itself. This is one important lesson, among others, that the author has learned from this exercise.

REFERENCES

Bowen, M. (1978). *Family therapy in clinical practice.* New York: Jason Aronson.

Kerr, M. E. and Bowen, M. (1988). *Family evaluation.* New York: W.W. Norton and Company.

Titelman, P. (Ed.) (1987). *The therapist's own family: Toward the differentiation of self.* Northvale, NJ: Jason Aronson, Inc.

Chapter 8

Triangles Revisited

Jack LaForte

INTRODUCTION

Over twenty years have passed since my early efforts to rework the central interlocking triangles in my life that included my parents and myself, and my son, my first wife, and myself. At that time, I was able to trace the *projection process* from my maternal grandmother to my mother, from my mother to myself, and from myself to my son (LaForte, 1987). In twenty years a lot of life can be lived and a lot of changes can take place. My life is no exception. My parents died, I was divorced, moved three times, remarried, and I became a grandfather.

In this chapter, I analyze the genesis of the two most significant triangles in my life. I reexamine my family of origin work, assessing the impact it has had over the past twenty years, and describe and analyze the consequential shifts and realignments which occurred subsequently in my family system. Also, the impact of nodal events like births, deaths, divorce, a child leaving home, marriage, and remarriage will be assessed and discussed. Finally, I present my analysis and understanding of how triangles have impacted my family system during the course of my life.

In 1987, I identified the major triangles in my family, described the persons involved and how the triangles functioned. At the time (LaForte, 1987) this was very useful information as it enabled me to gain a better understanding of my family and myself. The genesis of such a significant phenomenon as the primary triangles in one's life is surely worthy of serious thought, especially since the implications are great and long lasting.

With a metaphorical magnifying glass in hand, I decided to look back in time and examine those early periods of my life. What were the precipitating events that altered the course of fused relationships? What were the conditions that altered what appeared to be a stable balance in a fused relationship? How do fused dyads reconfigure into rigid triangles?

TRIANGLE ONE: MOTHER, FATHER, AND SON

The first pivotal event took place in the common space on the first floor of the brick elementary school in Bensonhurst, Brooklyn. It was in the mid-1950s and the school was P.S. 121. I was seven years old. It was my first day of school. My mother brought me to school as the other parents brought their children. The teacher in charge asked the children their names shortly after they entered the building and directed them to the line forming for their new classes. This gathering of children and parents seemed like quite an event. Parents were bringing their children to school for the first time. Teachers and school administrators were busy bringing order to the crowd of parents and children. Once I was told what line to go to, my mother and I said good-bye. I proceeded to join in line with my new classmates. I felt a little nervous but proud at the same time. In line I looked around, sizing up my new classmates. I saw some children with whom I would want to play. I smiled and made eye contact with one of the kids in the line in front of me. I was feeling comfortable and excited about my new status. I was now a school-aged kid. When adults would now ask me what school I went to I could proudly say, "I go to P.S. 121." I looked forward to actually talking to some of the other boys once the situation became more causal. Then I heard a voice behind me saying, "Jackie, are you all right?" I turned to see my mother again. I felt embarrassed and annoyed with my mother for coming back and asking me that question. I said, "I am fine, I am fine. You can go home!" The expression on my face was more powerful than the words. The look of annoyance on my face became riveted in my mother's memory. This I would find out later. I felt boxed in, protected when I felt I did not need to be protected. I was happy to be on my own. Why was my mother treating me like a such a young child? My "Please let me be on my own!" reaction to my mother's intrusion surprised even me.

Before that first day of school experience my mother and I were a close happy dyad. As a preschooler, I enjoyed years at home with my mother. I liked helping her water the indoor plants, talking to her as she did house work, and watching her use the sewing machine. I loved sculpting clay animals at my play table and showing them to her. She often sang the song "You Are My Sunshine" with a melancholy tone. The lunches together in the kitchen were special because it was just the two of us together. Dad and my older sister were at work and school.

Our experience during that first day of school changed the relationship. We experienced a conflict as never before. It was hard to put a finger on it at that time, but the memory of the event remained. Now, in retrospect, it is clear that it was the beginning of the pattern of pursuer and distancer between mother and son. The dynamics in the primary triangle consisted of a distancing son, a mother pursuing closeness with her son, and a father who was distant from the son and fused with his wife.

The pattern which became activated during the first day of school continued through college and beyond. When it came up, my mother would be angry with me and complain to my father about me, "What an uncaring, unfeeling son we have." On the other hand, I did not think badly of my parents. Rather, I was usually preoccupied with the activities in which I was involved. It was not that I did not want contact with them, I just did not have the same need to call, write, or visit as often as they wished after I left home for college. When the issue of not having more frequent contact came up, my father always took my mother's side. He chimed in on her criticism and told me how much I hurt my mother instead of expressing his own view. In a frustrated, emotionally reactive mode, I would get angry and want to distance myself even more. This pattern continued for over thirty years until I embarked on my earlier family of origin work (LaForte, 1987).

Figure 8.1 is a diagram of my family of origin, my parents, sister, and self. The following set of diagrams in Figure 8.2 illustrates my conceptualization of the primary triangle in my family of origin showing the activation of the triangle as anxiety increases on the Family Anxiety Scale (FAS)[1] below the family diagrams. *A:* The triangle is inactive and the level of chronic anxiety (cf. Kerr and Bowen, 1988, pp. 112-117) is at the baseline low level for

---

[1]The Family Anxiety Scale (FAS) is developed to illustrate the dynamic interrelationship between anxiety in the family system and simultaneous shifts which occur in the family emotional system over time. The x axis of the FAS indicates the level of anxiety in the family system on a scale ranging from 0 to 100 with "0" showing no anxiety and "100" the highest level of anxiety. Clinicians or family researchers assess the level of anxiety at a given time in the family system and assign a level (number). The y axis on the FAS shows the movement of time while shifts are occurring in the family. Preestablished intervals are assigned that are congruent with the time period studied. For example, to study rapid shifts in the family, a very short time frame, such as seconds or minutes, is established. Conversely, when studying slowly coalescing shifts in the family system, an extended time frame, such as weeks, months, or even years, will be utilized.

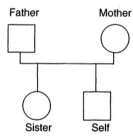

FIGURE 8.1. My Family of Origin

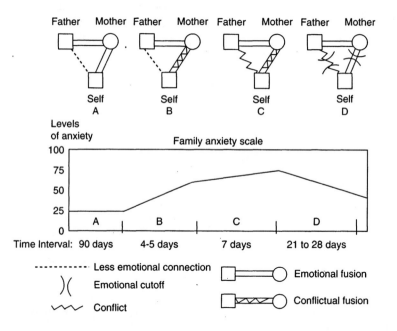

FIGURE 8.2. Anxiety and the Activation of the Primary Triangle

the family. *B:* Tension develops between my mother and myself and the level of acute anxiety (cf. Kerr and Bowen, 1988, pp. 113-117) increases sharply into the high range on the FAS. *C:* Father becomes triangled into the tension between my mother and myself, and acute anxiety continues to increase. *D:* A temporary emotional cutoff occurs and the anxiety begins to abate.

My Father's Position in Triangle One

Recently, I thought more about the role my father played in the primary triangle (triangle one). Most of my efforts to understand the primary triangle had focused on my mother and me. This was largely because we were the ones most reactive to each other. During the summer of 2004, I visited in Vermont with two of my paternal aunts; Connie aged eighty-nine, and Sadie aged seventy-six years old. They are two of my father's three sisters. Their positions in the birth order are the second child and the youngest child, respectively. The visit with my aunts gave me the opportunity to ask them questions which helped me go beyond the surface and form a better understanding of my father's role in my primary triangle, and develop more neutrality by stepping further back and looking at additional aspects of the family system.

My father and his siblings were the second generation of an Italian immigrant family. Figure 8.3 shows his nuclear family. My father was the oldest. His father, although gainfully employed in Italy, had trouble finding and keeping a regular job in the United States. This was due to his health and acculturation issues. My father as the oldest son took on the role of provider at a young age to help his family survive.

During our lunch in Vermont, my aunts shared stories about my father as a youngster, when they were all young adults, and in the early days of their marriages. According to my Aunt Connie, my father was very strict with her when she was a single woman. She recalled an incident in which she got a ride home in a car with a young man. When my father learned of this he slapped her face and told her never to do that again. The signs of her hurt and anger showed on her face even after all the years that had gone by. She said he was very protective of his family. What puzzled me was the fact that my father never showed that behavior in our family. He never hit his children or raised a hand to my mother. This story made more obvious my father's functional parent position in his family of origin. He acted not only in

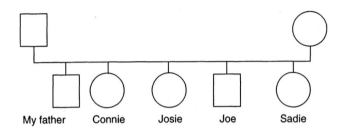

FIGURE 8.3. My Father's Family of Origin

the position of the older Italian brother, but as a stern parent protecting his family's reputation.

My other aunt, Aunt Sadie, the youngest of the sisters, quoted what she said was my mother's favorite saying, "Cleanliness is next to Godliness," delivering the statement in my mother's sometime self-righteous tone. I remembered my mother being focused on cleanliness, but she never preached to me about it. Both stories presented my parents as older siblings. My mother was in the functional oldest position in her family of origin, even though she was the younger sister of two older brothers, and the oldest of three sisters in her family of origin. My mother was older than my father's sisters. During the conversation, my aunts implied that my mother tried to position herself as the older sister with them, but my father's sisters did not accept this.

Sadie told another story which evoked childhood memories of an early situation in which my parents were in conflict. I must have been seven or eight years old at the time. They argued about whether or not to go to his sister Sadie's wedding. My paternal grandfather was deceased by the time of the wedding. The custom in this case is for the oldest brother to give the bride away. Sadie asked my father and he agreed to give her away. However, Sadie and her fiancé Sal never discussed this with my mother. My mother felt that something so important should be discussed with them as a couple. Sadie, who is the youngest sister and not much for protocol, disregarded my mother's concerns and went ahead with the wedding arrangements without including my mother in the discussion. This was a great source of conflict between my parents.

At issue was the question of my father's loyalty. According to my mother, who was insulted and angry, his position should be to stand with her. She threatened to not go to the wedding if this discussion did not take place. My father, who had been close to his family, especially his mother, was in a bind. He did not want to choose between his wife and his family of origin. He hoped my mother would give in, but she held her position, so they argued for weeks. They were two oldest siblings (one actual and the other functional) each insisting that the other reverse his or her position.

As it turned out, Sadie never did call the meeting my mother asked for; my father gave away the bride; and my sister, mother and I attended the wedding. Along with my mother's concession was the understanding that her involvement with my father's family of origin would change; she would distance herself from participating in the relationship. My father would have to handle his family on his own. As a result of this change, my father became less involved with his own family, and as a family we saw them less frequently. Eventually, my father visited only my grandmother on Sunday mornings and often by himself.

The series of family diagrams in Figure 8.4 shows the activations of the triangle with my father, my mother, and my father's youngest sister Sadie, and the increasing and decreasing levels of anxiety from the low to high and then to moderate: in *A* anxiety is low and relationships are calm; in *B* conflict erupts between my mother and my father's sister Sadie and anxiety becomes acute; in *C* conflict erupts between my father and my mother regarding the handling of the wedding and anxiety increases; in *D* the level of anxiety begins to decrease as emotional cutoff is established between my mother and Aunt Sadie, along with distance between my father and his family of origin, and a calm fusion is reestablished between my parents.

Another way that chronic anxiety manifested in the nuclear family was in the fusion of mother and son. When my parents were in conflict they tended to argue and then distance themselves from each other. During the distancing phase my mother tended to draw closer to me. If it fit with my needs at the time, we would enjoy mutual closeness. If, however, I was unavailable,

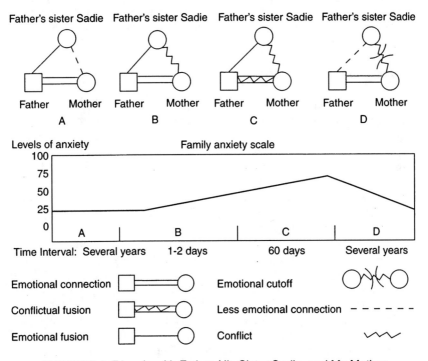

FIGURE 8.4. Triangle with Father, His Sister Sadie, and My Mother

then the focus of the conflict turned to me. As a consequence of my not being available, my mother would complain to my father about me, and he would join her in the inside position in the triangle. My father always took her side and told me to go along with my mother regardless of what his position was on the matter. His objective was to calm my mother's acute anxiety and bring peace. I felt that he and I did not have a one-to-one relationship because of this until after my mother's death.

In a conversation a couple of years before my father's death in 1994, while sitting at the beach at Cape May, New Jersey, my father told me out of the blue about the night I was conceived. He said he was in a romantic mood and had a good feeling that they would conceive that night if they made love, so he convinced my mother to be intimate. Generally she was not too interested in sex, but agreed, and sure enough that night I was conceived. It felt awkward hearing about my parents' sex life, but at this time in my father's life he became more open and real when talking about his life, and at this juncture we were both adults in a relatively open, one-to-one relationship. The story raises another factor, the limited degree of intimacy in my parents' relationship and to what degree this issue was a factor in the emotional triangle. Perhaps it was less threatening to have closeness with a son than with the husband.

My Position in the Primary Triangle

The central source of conflict for me in my family of origin was balancing the force of fusion between my mother and me, and asserting my own autonomy. I am the only one in my family of origin to hold the position of youngest sibling. As was mentioned earlier, my father was the oldest sibling in his family of origin; my mother was in a functional oldest position in her family of origin; and my older sister is the older of the two of us. All three of them were competent doers. Between my parents and sister all the important functioning in the family was carried out. This was both a blessing and a curse for me. I did not have any important daily tasks to perform or responsible decisions to make. As a child I could play without being disturbed, and as a teenager I was free to pursue my interests, like playing drums, pondering the meaning of life, and participating in team sports. As a youth I had the luxury of exploring my interests and developing my creativity. My parents and sister, on the other hand, lived life with their noses to the grindstone. At the same time, they decided what we ate, how we spent time together, the house's decor, which relatives visited, when and where we vacationed, and so on. In those areas I had little or no power. They decided all the important and unimportant matters, and I was expected to go along. As the youngest

I was conflicted. I wanted more of a voice in decision-making, but my opinion was not heard. I remember saying to myself, "Forget it, let them do it their way," and "When I have a chance I will do it my way." Much of the time I spent imagining how I would do things when I had the chance. I looked at furniture in the stores and asked myself, "If you were furnishing this living room, what would you choose?" "If you were . . ."

As the youngest my voice was the smallest. As a child going out with my family, I remember always expecting my parents to speak for me. This is an example of the passive position I was in with them. At times, as a younger child, I felt I was there as the observer. In a restaurant, for example, my parents would speak to me and then to the waiter. Later it was hard for me to speak up for myself.

Outside the home I found I was taken more seriously. I found I did have a voice and others were often open to my ideas. A majority of my efforts were focused on extracurricular activities and school. Outside the home I felt I had the opportunity to develop a self, but inside the home it was more a question of protecting a self.

My position in the triangle was either trying to be a self or trying to protect a self. I was trying to move a self to the outside position in the primary triangle. Being a self meant taking as much responsibility for organizing my life in the manner I felt was meaningful and not being bound by family convention. The positions I sometimes took were disrupting of the status quo and disturbing to the family. These positions which departed from my family's way increased the level of acute anxiety in the family at times. For example, in high school my desire was to go to an out-of-town four-year college when I graduated. My family expected me to go to a local college like my older sister, live at home, and commute. In my family, the notion of a child leaving home before he married was unthinkable. It troubled my parents to entertain the thought. For me however, I believed that attending a four-year out-of-town college would be the best way to further my learning and growth. I also knew if I really wanted to realize this goal, I would have to take full responsibility to make it happen. As a teenager it was frightening to feel the weight of the task ahead, without support from family, or the know-how to achieve the goal. As I continued in high school, I eventually found a way to realize this goal so that my parents could accept it.

My Sister's Position in the Family

My sister's position in the family was the compliant oldest who shared and supported the status quo in the family. She was close to both parents. She helped my mother with housework, studied hard to be a good student, socially limited her extracurricular school activities to the honor society meetings, and attended church with the family on Sundays. Her manner was pleasant and soft-spoken. When conflict arose in the family she tended to stay neutral and smooth conflict by being empathic to each person without getting triangled. For example, I may have been critical of a decision my parents made that affected both my sister and me. I complained to my sister about my parents' decision with the intention that she would agree with me and together we would protest the decision. My sister would hear my argument but not agree with me, consequently not joining me in a triangle with my parents. At times, my mother complained to her children about something my father did. My sister took the same approach with my mother. She heard her out, but did not agree to join my mother in a triangle with my father.

Where Did My Mother's Anxiety Come From?

My mother was overprotected by her family. She was the oldest of three sisters, but she had two older brothers and an overprotective mother. Her mother told her at a young age that boys were not good and that she was always to stay away from them. My mother had a warm relationship with her father, but her mother was the more dominant one in that household, and more influential with my mother. Although my mother was quite intelligent, neither of her parents encouraged her to pursue an education or a career. If she wanted to do that she had to do it on her own. This was very unlikely for her as a second generation Italian-American girl. She had hoped they would support her in continuing her education, but at age fourteen, my mother gave up her schooling to work and help her family. When she was at home she helped her mother with the cooking and cleaning. My mother adapted herself to her family at the expense of her own education and career development. Her potential as a person in her own right was never realized outside the family. My mother wanted what was best for her children, but at the same time we were expected to adapt to the family system as she did. This created a conflict for her because what was sometimes "best" for the children departed from the family's status quo. My mother's anxiety developed in relation to men, with the world outside of family, and the fear of being abandoned by her loved ones, including me.

TRIANGLE TWO: HUSBAND, WIFE, AND CHILD

The genesis of the second major triangle, which consisted of me, my wife, and my son, emerged several months before the birth of our son. We had only been married a little over a month when we found out that she was pregnant. It was a great surprise to both of us. At that time, our future was uncertain. I had started a new job five months earlier as a college administrator. I had applied for conscientious objector status and was waiting for a date for a hearing with my draft board. After completing her first semester of college in Boston, my wife had left college and moved to Connecticut to marry me. When we learned that she was pregnant, she and I responded differently to the news. I accepted the news and hoped it would be special for both of us. Although the pregnancy was not planned, I was willing to make the best of the situation, thinking, "This happened for a reason, and it must have a great purpose." My spouse on the other hand was quite frightened and became anxious about the whole process over which she felt she had no control. The news of the pregnancy disturbed the emotional balance in the relationship that took a few years to realign.

I may have underreacted to the news. I was already on emotional overload with my pending conscientious objector hearing ahead of me, beginning my first professional job, a new marriage, a puppy, and a house of our own. I was acutely anxious about the outcome of my draft board decision. In one instant my life could change significantly. My approach to life at that time was impulsive. I took on all that I could because I did not know what tomorrow might bring. I was involved in a lot of significant things all at once. It was difficult for me to be fully emotionally present to my wife at that time.

The ingredients for a triangle began to brew which was manifested as acute anxiety about the pregnancy on my wife's part. My anxiety was related to my wife's reaction to the pregnancy. Her anxiety about the pregnancy dovetailed with my anxiety about the draft and my success at my new job. My wife's anxiety took the form of physical concerns about bodily changes, the pain of birth, and with her changing status from a student, to a wife, and now to becoming a mother. Her reaction was to emotionally withdraw from me while I continued to submerge myself in my work. She was adamantly against having her husband join in the preparation or the planning of the method of delivery. She said it was her body and she would have the delivery the way she wanted, discarding my suggestion for natural childbirth.

My reaction to my wife was great disappointment. I felt trapped with her in a situation over which I had no control. I tried to contain my disappointment, but it must have come through. I tried to placate her and tolerate the situation by taking an aloof position. I minimized the actual impact of the pregnancy on her.

From being a happily fused, young couple that lived in a cottage on an idyllic country road, we suddenly became an acutely anxious, emotionally overburdened, distant young couple. Attempts to discuss the problem failed to bring understanding or changes in the situation. The course was set and the process was underway. The triangle that emerged was my wife with an anxious focus on our unborn child, and me on the outside, or peripheral position, preoccupied with my new job, and my draft situation.

Figure 8.5 shows the development and the activation of the primary triangle in my nuclear family: in *A* a stable dyad; in *B* a fused dyad with an acutely anxious husband and wife in conflict; in *C* continued conflict and distancing in the couple, with an emotional wife overloaded by the forthcoming responsibility of caring for the unborn child, and husband critical of the way in which the wife was handling the situation; in *D* once the child was born, the primary triangle is established, with the mother and child fused and occupying the inside positions and the husband in the outside position. In the new configuration the husband is overinvolved with his work, and the wife becomes the exclusive caregiver, with conflict between husband and wife, and husband and son in a connected, but somewhat distant position.

Looking at the triangle from the wife's perspective, what were the factors that led to her part in the nuclear family triangle? As a child she experienced a great loss in the sudden death of her father, followed by an "emotional shock wave," as described by Bowen (1978; see pp. 324-328). Her grief-stricken

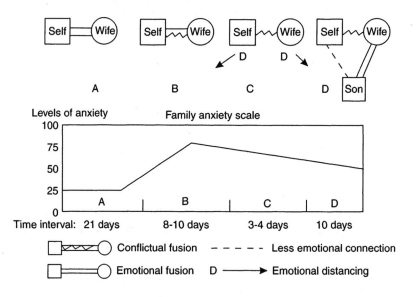

FIGURE 8.5. Nuclear Family Triangle

mother had to take on the full responsibility of providing for herself and her two young daughters, my wife being the older of the two sisters. The death of the father created an imbalance in the organization of the family emotional system.

Prior to his death two interlocking triangles existed in the nuclear family which consisted of my wife and her father in the close inside positions with her mother and sister in the outside position, and her mother and sister in the inside position with my wife and her father in the outside position.

After her father's death, the second interlocking triangle dissolved leaving a primary triangle which consisted of the mother and her younger sister in the inside positions and my wife in the outside position.

When my wife's and my emotional systems combined, I joined her in the inside position reestablishing the configuration of two interlocking triangles in her family of origin. I occupied the close inside position (as her father had earlier) with her, and her mother and sister were in the outside positions. Once we were married and conflict emerged in our marriage, my wife could not rejoin her family of origin in an inside position. Consequently, she shifted her emotional connectedness to the child. Figure 8.6 shows the triangles in my wife's family of origin, the reestablishment of interlocking triangles with my inclusion in the family, and later her fusion with our son.

THE EMERGENCE OF INTERLOCKING TRIANGLES

When looking at the first triangle, one can see conflict between my mother and me, my father joined with his wife against their son. As a teenager, I applied myself to outside activities and friends as my way of counterbalancing the primary triangle with my parents. After my marriage, my wife became a

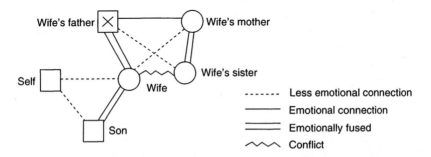

FIGURE 8.6. Interlocking Triangles: Wife's Family of Origin and Family of Procreation

part of the triangle as conflict arose between my mother and wife. My wife and I were in the inside positions and my parents remained in the outside position.

The conflict came about between my wife and my mother during my parents' early visits to our home. When they visited my parents had a habit of bringing a lot of food with them without telling us in advance that they were planning to do this. This disrupted the plan my wife and I had for the menu. There was one incident in particular that was pivotal. During a visit, my parents brought a roast to cook. My wife was not expecting to cook a roast, and the oven was not cleaned well enough to show a guest, let alone a mother-in-law. My wife was quite embarrassed when my mother opened the oven door and said, "Oh, my dear, this oven isn't clean." My mother was in the functional oldest sibling position in her Italian family of origin and positioned herself as the matriarch in relation to my young wife. I tried to explain to my wife that this is the custom in Italian families. At the same time, I too was annoyed at the way in which my parents came to visit and took over the kitchen disregarding our wishes. I was reactive to my parents on this issue during their visit. The conflict with my parents brought my wife and myself closer. We joined together in the inside positions of the triangle, with my parents together in the outside. Now there were two interlocking triangles.

The second major triangle, which consisted of me, my wife, and our son, in the family of procreation, started during the pregnancy, as was noted earlier (see Figure 8.5). After the birth of the child, the mother-son-father triangle shifted from the wife, the unborn fetus, and the husband, to the wife, the child, and the husband. In this triangle the mother and the son were in the inside positions and I was in the outside position. My wife became the primary caretaker and I played a peripheral role. My wife positioned herself as the authority on the care of the child. Everything had to be done a certain way or it was considered wrong. She was not open to alternative methods or different approaches. My wife used childcare issues as a way to control and dominate the relationships in our nuclear family. She took on a protective, overnurturing mother role with the child. I, on the other hand, was more distant and rigid as far as boundaries were concerned with the child, and more demanding as far as expectations for the child were concerned. At times, I wanted more couple time and less family time. When differences between my wife and me came up, we argued without resolution and then dropped it. As our child got older, he participated more actively in the triangle. He knew that if he made a fuss, or complained, his mother would always take his side. Sometimes when differences came up between myself and my son, we turned to my wife for resolution. My wife was unsure how to handle the situation and consequently became stuck. An example of this occurred one Sunday when we went to visit a local park. Upon arriving at the park we parked the car and got out. My son immediately went to the right and I to the left. My wife literally stood in the middle and said, "What should I do?" I said, "I think we should go this way." My son said, "I want to go that way."

Before my son went to school the patterns were well established in the nuclear family. When anxiety arose in any member, conflict frequently followed which activated the triangle. Any member of the nuclear family could activate the triangle. As an example, I might find something my son did annoying and confront him about it. My wife would intervene by telling me to leave him alone. I resented her intrusion and would be upset with her. At other times, I would intrude when she and my son were in an argument usually by taking her side against him. This of course was inappropriate, but it was my attempt to join with her. My intrusion into their one-to-one usually resulted in both of them getting angry with me. There were also times when my son intruded between my wife and myself. She and I would be getting emotionally close, and my son would become disruptive, triggering a shift from being a relaxed couple into being anxious parents having to correct their son. In yet another example, my wife would be overindulging our son and I would point this out and get a negative reaction from both of them.

My need to assert control over my son was the manifestation of my reactivity, which grew out of my mother's attempts to control me. My level of differentiation of self was being transmitted in my nuclear family to my son through the family projection process. My anxiety would be transmitted to my son, just as my mother's anxiety was transmitted to me. Figure 8.7 shows this process. When I felt anxious I tended to need order in my environment. If I felt things were out of order, my level of anxiety increased, as did my urge to control the things and people around me. My tendency was to focus on my son's activities, criticizing him for not doing his chores, or for watching too much television.

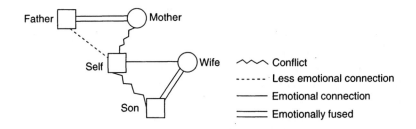

FIGURE 8.7. Interlocking Triangles: My Family of Origin and Family of Procreation

On the intergenerational level, when anxiety arose between my mother and myself, it usually had to do with our differing needs for togetherness and separateness. My mother wanted a close connection and I was satisfied with a more distant connection. After a lack of contact on my part, my father contacted me to complain that I had not been in touch with them for a while which hurt my mother. My mother would then join in and criticize me for not caring about my family. I would listen and then at some point disagree with her. Eventually, I became frustrated and reactive. Typically, my frustration led to cutoff (this process is illustrated in Figure 8.2). With my anxiety high I turned to my wife to complain about my mother in an effort to lower my anxiety by triangling her to my side. In this triangle I enjoyed the inside position with my wife while my parents were in the outside position. The two triangles merged together to form interlocking triangles.

Within the framework of the two major triangles there were also a series of minor interlocking triangles. When low levels of anxiety were present between two or more family members small shifts occurred within the interlocking triangles. As an example, on occasion my son joined with his parents in being critical of his grandparents, particularly if they were being overprotective during a visit. On other occasions, I joined my mother in being critical of my father around his unwillingness to be more active. Other times my wife and I joined together and were critical of the way our son spent too much time lying on the couch.

SUMMARY OF THE EARLY FAMILY OF ORIGIN WORK

The thrust of my family of origin work came in my effort to detriangle myself from the triangle with my parents (see Figure 8.2). I focused my effort on increasing the amount of contact with each parent and lowering my reactivity, especially in relation to my mother. Over the years my father and I had little one-to-one contact. The goal of the effort with my father was to bridge the gap by interacting more with him. The typical pattern with telephone calls to my parents was for my father to answer the telephone and then quickly turn the phone over to my mother. One of my strategies was to not let my father pass the telephone off so quickly. So, I purposely said, "Hey, Dad, wait a minute. There is something I want to ask you." I had a question prepared that was designed to hold him on the phone for a few moments. During the brief conversation it felt as though my anxious father was holding a hot potato that he had to toss to my mother as quickly as possible. However the discomfort eased over time, and the conversations got a little longer. Controlling my reactivity to my mother was challenging. I tried to be positive, patient, and control my anxiety as I felt it rise.

A second aspect of the strategy was to attempt to shorten the cooling off period if conflict occurred. I made a concerted effort to contact my parents with a written communication or call them on the telephone within the period of a week. I found that it was unnecessary to discuss the content of the previous conflict, but to focus on something of mutual interest.

Having a goal and a plan for my family of origin work helped a great deal. It enabled me to think about what was occurring and this helped to lower the level of my emotional reactivity. I came to the realization that what my mother really wanted was basic: to feel her son cared about her and that he wanted to include her to a greater extent in his life. The working hypothesis was that the conflict was set off by my mother feeling a lack of sufficient caring and wanting assurance from her son in the form of more contact. With this hypothesis in mind I began to make more of an effort to show my parents that family was important to me. This started when I asked my parents to send me pictures of the family for a project that I planned while I was doing my family therapy training. I decided to organize a little booklet that contained a series of significant photos that revealed family relationships and patterns. As there were several hundred family photos to sort through, I asked my parents if they could select approximately one hundred photos. This would not only narrow the number of photos to be sent, but also gave us a project to work together on. They appeared to be surprised at my request, but happily embraced the project with me. I believe this marked the beginning of a major shift in my relationship with my parents.

The plan to detriangle myself from the second interlocking triangle focused on trying to establish more of a one-to-one relationship with my son. In essence, I moved from a distant position to a closer position. This included making an effort to control my own anxiety, and in general be less reactive to my son. I tried spending more time with him, throwing the football in the back yard, driving him to soccer practice, and watching guy movies together. I also tried not to intervene when a disagreement came up between my wife and son. The object was to try to be more accepting of my son's behavior, develop some positive connections with him, and be neutral instead of critical. The objective of this planned effort was not only to establish a more positive relationship with my son, but also to decrease the tension between my wife and myself regarding our son.

It was theorized that by going to the source of my anxiety, the primary triangle with my parents, and in particular, the conflict with my mother, the level of my anxiety would diminish over time. From my perspective, this in turn would decrease the emotional charge that was underlying my reactivity to my son. This effort was relatively successful. I found that my effort on each of these two different levels brought a benefit to the other level. When I came to experience lower levels of anxiety in dealing with my parents it transferred to lower levels of anxiety with my son. Less tension in the nuclear family resulted in less anxiety in dealing with my parents.

THE FOLLOW-UP TO THE EFFORT

The time from the early 1980s to my mother's death in 1990, can generally be characterized as a period of comfortable contact in the family system. More opportunities emerged for closeness between my parents and myself. There was an increase in the number of annual visits to New Jersey from the usual two to five or six. The Sunday afternoon telephone calls to and from my parents were warm and genuine, as compared with the former obligatory and reactive calls of the past. A greater sense of mutual support and appreciation was experienced, and, occasionally, close late-night conversations took place between my mother and myself. Overall, I found that more choices were possible for my actions and reactions. I experienced a new sense of increased space between myself and others which afforded me ample time to respond to whatever I was dealing with. Figure 8.8 illustrates the primary triangle during this period.

I took on a grown-up position, which included a leadership role at times. As I felt more accepted and the level of conflict diminished significantly, I became more involved as a trusted family member in family affairs. I played an active role and was consulted on medical and other important issues by my parents. I was privy to private family information like their wills and financial matters. During the time I spent away from the family, I was exposed to a greater gamut of experiences than within the extended family. I called upon these experiences in my role as an advisor, which became very important toward the end of my parents' lives. For instance, when it was de-

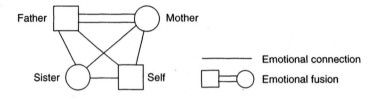

FIGURE 8.8. Triangle in My Family of Origin in a Calm State

cided that my father needed to be in a partial care facility, as he no longer was able to care for himself alone in the family home, I was the one who was responsible for selling the family home.

When my mother was hospitalized for a series of minor strokes, I led the discussion on medical treatment and was the one who signed the health proxy. When my mother passed away, I was the one who received the call from the doctor informing the family of her death. I was the one who told my sister and father of the death. I led the effort with my sister to make funeral and burial arrangements including the painstaking task of selecting the pink dress and casket in which she would be buried.

In the period after the earlier family of origin work, the nuclear family became subdued and less problematic. The marital relationship also became less conflicted and more enjoyable. During this period a kitchen renovation project got underway which had been pending for a few years. A new recreational activity of canoeing was added to outdoor weekend activities. This added activity was very enjoyable for us as a couple, and sometimes our son joined in.

The relationship between my son and me lightened up. The emotional temperature in the house was generally cooler. The triggers that ignited our reactivity in the past were dormant.

Peace and agree was the primary mode of interaction between husband and wife. Large differences were put at a safe distance for the sake of not provoking conflict. I was less reactive to my son and my wife, but still did not feel emotionally compatible on a deep level with my wife. I struggled with two ways of thinking about my marital unhappiness. Did it represent my own low level of differentiation of self or was my unhappiness a result of not being honest with myself and not accepting responsibility for my personal discontent? These questions were often followed by the questions: Should I work harder on my effort to differentiate myself from my family of origin, or am I ignoring my marital problem? Sensing the enormous consequences of the latter, I chose to go with the former. Then there was the question, whether I was avoiding working on the marriage, or really working on differentiation.

A significant factor that influenced my marriage was the stabilizing role my mother played in promoting and reinforcing a stable marriage. My parents celebrated over fifty years of marriage. The Italian Catholic cultural and religious influences were strong in their view of marriage and family. My mother is quoted in an interview I had with my parents in 1980: "You only have one chance with marriage, so you better make it good." Her advice to following generations was: "Family is most important, remember that. . . . There is nothing like your own blood." I disagreed to some extent with my parents' dictums, yet at the same time, was influenced by them. The conflict for me included my own independent thinking versus loyalty to family values with which I did not agree, connection versus cutoff, and stability versus chaos. I resented what I believed to be the simplistic and oppressive nature of their view. I, however, as the son, felt the power of the force of family loyalty and was unwilling to deal with the consequences of disrupting my life and the family system.

A good deal of my emotional and physical energy was directed to career development, while what remained was absorbed by home and artistic projects. I achieved professional success by obtaining licensure as a psychologist during this period. I was elected and served as president of the statewide marriage and family therapy organization. Together with a close colleague, I purchased a commercial building that was converted to offices.

This period can also be characterized as a period of worldly attainment. With some help from my parents, my wife and I bought a larger house in a lovely neighborhood in town. I was recognized in the professional community. I was asked to teach in a graduate program, and had a number of agency and family business consultations, and I was successful in the eyes of my parents. My parents enjoyed my success and frequently said that they were very proud of me.

As the primary triangle in the nuclear family became inactive a new benign triangle developed. The new triangle, which is illustrated in Figure 8.9, consisted of my wife and our cat named "Little Guy," fused and in inside positions, with my son and myself sharing the outside positions. This was a "meta-level" triangle as it was a triangle that we could joke about. The object of the projection process in the nuclear family was now the cat.

NODAL EVENT: SHIFTS IN THE BALANCE

The nodal event that shifted the balance in the emotional system came with the unexpected death of my mother on August 19, 1990, an example of

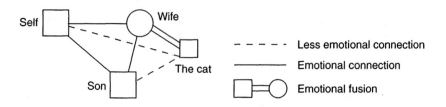

FIGURE 8.9. Triangle in the Nuclear Family Calms, but the Cat Gets Triangled

an "emotional shock wave" that reverberated long after death. She became ill a week before the first family reunion, which I had spearheaded a year earlier. Ironically, the inspiration for the reunion came during a conversation with a cousin when we agreed it would be wonderful to celebrate the family on a happy occasion and not a funeral.

An uncle, who lived in the area where the reunion was to take place, and I organized the reunion. Excitement built as the date drew closer. My mother looked forward to this special event with great relish. In preparation for the reunion she overexerted herself, even though the reunion was intentionally planned to be held at a restaurant so relatives would not be coming to my parents' house. My mother was intent on cleaning the house nevertheless. Her obsessive desire to have an extra clean house, even though it was unnecessary, got her in trouble. A week before the family reunion my mother felt sick, as though she had the flu. She went to see her doctor who cautiously decided to hospitalize her, as he needed more time to diagnose her condition. She was diagnosed with a series of minor stokes. The strokes continued for a couple of weeks, until the big one came and it was over.

My mother was in the hospital in a semiconscious state when the family members got together for the reunion. It was a bittersweet gathering. The joy of the event was taken away as the guest of honor lay in the hospital. It was sad that my mother, for whom family was so important, could not be there to experience this special family event. The most meaningful aspect of the event was sharing contact with the adult cousins who had not been seen since childhood, and meeting their wives and children.

The most moving experience for me occurred the night before my mother's death. My sister, father, and I fed her what turned out to be her last meal. Sitting at her bedside, my sister and I took turns feeding our mother the courses of her dinner. She lay there in semiconsciousness, nodding and occasionally smiling with each mouthful. It was a very intimate connection slowly bringing the spoon to her mouth, placing it at her lips and waiting as she took the spoon with the soft food into her mouth and then swallowed it. She had fed me and now I finally fed her. The feeding had a rhythm of its own. Then when she was finished, we wiped her mouth and hands and gently brushed her teeth. With a smile on her face she contentedly fell asleep and died.

The death of my mother came to represent the end of a long era in my life. Whether I would admit it or not, I strove throughout my life to meet the expectations she had of me. I wanted to prove to her she could be proud of me even if I did it my way. My life until her death was driven by this. In the end I felt that she was proud of me. A few years later, it was time for my father to give up his home due to his age and mental condition. My sister made arrangements for him to stay at a special care facility in her community and I took responsibly for selling my parents' house. With the sale of the house and my father's relocating to Texas to be near my sister, another chapter in my family's life together was closed.

Pandora's Box Is Opened

A turning point in my marital relationship can be traced back to an argument that occurred between my wife and myself shortly after my mother's funeral which reactivated the conflict in the relationship. Approximately two years later the fallout from my mother's death was fully felt. Bowen (1978) predicts after a nodal event such as the death of a significant family member, frequently another member of the family will become symptomatic (see pp. 325-328).

The funeral was in the morning. Afterward, my wife and son, and my sister and her nuclear family members went back to my parents' house with my father. My sister and I had been in New Jersey for several days to be with our mother before she died. It was emotionally draining. Our spouses and our children joined us for the wake and funeral during the last couple of days. It was mid-afternoon and I was emotionally exhausted. I began to get anxious about returning home. I approached my wife to tell her it was time to leave. She put me off, so a little later I went back to her and restated my desire to leave. She said, "I'll leave when I'm ready." This raised my anxiety even more. An argument ensued in front of my sister, brother-in-law, nephews, and father that was very embarrassing to me. My wife, who had brought the cat along, said she did not feel the cat was ready to be cooped up in a cage again for several hours for the ride home. I went to get the cat who was wedged behind a large wardrobe in the garage. Eventually he came out. I remember thinking in my reactivity, "That's it. It is perfectly clear that we are not on the same emotional wavelength. She seems to care more about the cat than me, and what I have gone through. If she is so bonded to the cat, she can have the cat. I'm out of here." What I referred to earlier as the benign triangle of the cat, and my wife in the inside position, and my son and myself on the outside position was not so benign. The triangle was no longer able to bind the reactivity that came up. We finally left and returned home. However, in my mind that was the turning point in the marriage.

I have wondered if my reactivity was a result of grief, or whether the death of my mother meant that I was no longer bound to the marriage. In retrospect, I realize I was unhappy in the marriage. The grief from the loss of my mother took the form of agitation, anxiety, and reactivity which was directed at the marital relationship. As a result of the loss I felt less interested in just getting along with my wife and less motivated to continue in the *peace and agree* approach. Perhaps for my wife the loss of her mother-in-law rekindled the feelings of the loss of her father as a child. We became reactive to each other. I was vocal in expressing my disagreement and my wife too held to her contrary position. Our level of undifferentiation of self, that had manifested itself in the nuclear family predominately in the form of projection onto a child, now took the form of overt marital conflict.

On occasion, the topic of a marital separation came up. Included in the conversations would be statements like: "We married at a young age . . ." "We have been together longer than most of our friends." "We are like a plant that has become pot bound." "Maybe if we separate we have a better chance to grow individually."

As our reactivity continued, we became less tolerant of each other. Those aspects of my self that I wanted to develop most were the same aspects that my wife seemed to find most annoying. The times when I was feeling most expansive were typically the times when my wife was most critical of me. In turn, those activities that she found most interesting, I found boring.

A nagging issue that resurfaced after my mother's death and contributed to my frustration and reactivity at home was the fact that my son decided not to leave home to go to college. He wound up attending a local college and continued to live at home into his midtwenties. I was disappointed that he did not seek more independence, as I had when I was his age. I also felt that my wife had colluded with him to keep him at home and emotionally dependent.

Those times when I was able to physically separate myself from my nuclear family triangle on a get away adventure sea kayaking in the Florida Everglades, I felt I could leave my present life behind and not return. I even found my career as a psychologist had become too constricting. Even though I had struggled to become a psychologist, I felt that I had ironically become one-dimensional as a person who acted like a psychologist all the time. Everything in my life was predictable. I had lost my spontaneity. I decided I needed change. I did not know what change, but change meant the survival of the vitality I had left for life. During this period I fantasized about change, and opened myself up to the possibility of change, and I looked for opportunities for change. I thought, "Someday, I will not be in my present situation." However, the future was unknown to me.

The fall of 1992 was the turning point. After I returned from a weeklong professional conference, my wife and I talked more concretely about a separation. We were weary of the continued marital conflict. We went about the business of planning my move out of the family home. My wife helped by looking at newspaper ads for an apartment for me.

While the wheels were in motion to separate I met a woman to whom I was attracted and who was interested in pursuing me. After I met this woman for lunch I brought up the topic of dating others to my wife while we were separated. My wife agreed. I admit I was not completely honest with her about my new interest in the woman with whom I had lunch. My excitement in this new love interest fueled my effort to actually find an apartment and to move out of the family home, which I did in a month's time.

New Triangles Develop

Not too long after our conversation about dating, my wife learned of my new relationship. At first she did not seemed bothered, but eventually she became angry and a new triangle became activated. This triangle consisted of me and my new friend in the inside positions, and my wife in the outside position. Soon this triangle interlocked with the fixed triangle in my nuclear family that consisted of my wife and my son in the inside position and with me on the outside position.

The level of anxiety in the nuclear family went from chronic to acute. The newly established interlocking triangles were not able to bind the intensity of the acute level of anxiety. Consequently, additional triangles formed with some family members and with many of our friends. Later other triangles developed with each spouse and our lawyers.

My new partner and I isolated ourselves. Our relationship was emotionally fused. Preoccupied with this consuming new relationship I had less contact with some friends, and other friends reactively cut off from me. Before long it was evident that the woman with whom I became so involved had an alcohol abuse problem. The problem had been contained during the early stages of the relationship, but once we lived together it became apparent. My position in the relationship became that of the overfunctioner.

Now the dynamic in my primary relationship consisted of an underfunctioner and an overfunctioner in a fused relationship. The reality for me now was that I went from a relationship in which my undifferentiation manifested in projection to a child and marital conflict to dysfunction in a spouse (significant other). This situation raises the question of whether the earlier work with my family of origin and nuclear family changed in any way the basic level of my differentiation of self or whether I experienced a temporary increase in my functional level of differentiation due to a period of calm?

Over time a shift took place in the nuclear family in the relationship between my wife and son. Without my being physically present in the home, my wife came to rely more on her young adult son for emotional support and to help maintain the house. This intensified the fusion in the relationship.

My son, age twenty-three years old, was attending the local university and living at home. What had been a fused dyad for more than twenty years erupted into conflict as our son began to get seriously involved with a young woman who was attending college in the area.

During this time, my son and I were getting together on occasion. The opportunities to get together were usually initiated by me and held at a neutral site like a restaurant for breakfast or lunch in an effort to stay in touch. I tried to cultivate a one-to-one relationship with my son. He used physical and emotional distance to avoid dealing with his anxiety. During the separation I continued to support the household and my son while he lived in the family home and attended college. Neither my wife nor my girlfriend were discussed on these occasions. The topics of discussion were aimed at learning about my son's college experience, and how things were going at home. My son typically presented as if everything was fine, appearing to keep his feelings and thoughts to himself.

Finally my son initiated contact with me when he decided he wanted to start his own business. He had received an inheritance from my paternal grandparents. The account for the inheritance funds was set up so that two signatures were required: my son's and mine. I insisted on this stipulation since my son was entitled to receive the money at eighteen years old. The amount exceeded ten thousand dollars, was invested, and was growing in value. I wanted to ensure that the money would be used for the purpose for which it was intended by his grandparents: as a nest egg for his future, such as for further education or for a down payment on a house, but not to purchase a car or fancy stereo equipment, among other things. The two signatures would be required until my son matured to the level that he could responsibly manage the inheritance himself.

My son wanted to use the money in his inheritance to start a dance club. The idea was to open a dance club in an unused theater in the neighboring town. A friend of his claimed to have knowledge of house clubs, but no funds to invest. My response to his request was "no." I suggested that my son wait until he finished college, which was less than a year away. If he still thought it was a good idea, then I would reconsider the possibility. This response was not acceptable to him. He continued to pursue me and insist that he should have access to the money. Then my wife got involved. She contacted me and insisted that I release the funds to our son. My wife had already loaned him several thousand dollars to help start the club, but now he needed more money to purchase a sound system for the club. The sound system was expensive to rent, but even more expensive buy. I thought the whole thing through and finally decided to release the money. This decision was based on my desire to step back from the reenergized triangle with him, his mother and me, and to neutralize my position in my effort to detriangle. If my son and his mother thought that it was a wise use of the money, let it be up to them to take responsibility for it. The consequences or benefits would be theirs. I went to the club to support my son. The club stayed open for about six weeks and then closed due to a lack of a significant response from the public and further lack of funds.

Postscript to the Dance Club Project

My son closed the business owing his mother about eight thousand dollars. He agreed to pay her back by working at the house and giving her a monthly payment. Both performing the work and paying back the money became a source of conflict between mother and son. He eventually left home owing his mother money.

After the closing of the dance club, my son and his girlfriend spent more time together. At times he practically lived in her college dorm. Meanwhile my wife's demands on our son at home went unmet. Eventually he got an apartment near his girlfriend's campus and they spent most of their time together at his apartment.

Tension increased between mother and son. A new triangle became activated. My son's mother and his girlfriend became embroiled in conflict, and my son found himself in the middle. He tried to distance from his mother and appease his girlfriend, but this would last only for a short while, and then tension would increase. Eventually, my son felt he had to choose between closeness with his mother and his girlfriend. This was similar to my father's situation discussed earlier in this chapter when his youngest sister planned to wed and my mother felt slighted. My son chose his girlfriend, much to his mother's chagrin. The new triangle consisted of my son and his girlfriend in the inside positions, with his mother in the outside position.

After a year and a half I extricated myself from the fused relationship with the woman with whom I had been involved in the overfunctioning position. After the breakup I found I was left with a great sense of loss and acute anxiety. I hypothesize that my acute anxiety was a reaction to the accumulation of all the losses I had experienced during the previous few years, beginning with the death of my mother, and including the loss of an intact nuclear family, loss of my rootedness to family, loss of home, and the loss of hope for a happy future in the new relationship.

During the autumn of 1996, approximately four years after the initial separation, my ex-wife and I were divorced. After the divorce we have maintained contact although it is minimal. The emotional intensity of the relationship has subsided and we are civil with each other.

In the spring of 1998 my son and his girlfriend married in a quaint town on the coast of Maine. The wedding was limited to immediate family and their partners. I attended with my new significant other (whom I later married), and my ex-wife came unaccompanied. The relationship between my son and his mother continued to be strained as the triangle with my son's wife, my son, and his mother continued to be active. In June 2001, a daughter was born to my son and his wife. This nodal event brought the opportunity to resolve the conflict between my son, and his wife, and my ex-wife. My son's mother made an attempt to become more involved with her granddaughter and son's wife. The birth of the granddaughter intensified the emotional system. With the level of anxiety high, reactivity and conflict erupted. The triangle rigidified and then emotional cutoff followed. By the time the granddaughter was four, the emotional cutoff was rigidified. Figure 8.10 shows the emotional cutoff between my son, his mother, and his nuclear family.

Life's Next Phase

After a series of short unpromising relationships, I found a partner with whom I was emotionally compatible and I remarried. We had been in a relationship for six years before becoming engaged, and eight years before getting married. My new wife is the mother of two sons ages sixteen and twenty-five. The elder son is presently living in Spain where his paternal roots are, and the younger son divides his time between living with his father and us. As a stepparent, I found my level of anxiety lower than during my earlier life experience raising my biological son and married to my previous wife.

My new wife was well accepted by my son and daughter-in-law, and she also got along with her new stepson and her daughter-in-law. She is happy to have a step granddaughter and eager to help them by volunteering to babysit and provide other parenting support.

I have maintained regular contact with my son. The relationship has developed and become close. He and I offer each other mutual support and

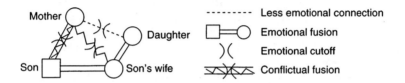

FIGURE 8.10. Interlocking Triangles: My Son, His Wife, Mother, and Daughter

respect. The new family configuration now consists of my son, and his wife in close relationship; emotional cutoff with his mother; my son and myself in a close relationship with me and my new wife; and my ex-wife and myself in a distant relationship.

AN EFFORT TO BRIDGE THE EMOTIONAL CUTOFF BETWEEN SON AND MOTHER

While I was steeped in the process of the writing of this chapter and thinking about my family, I was concerned that my son and his mother had not been speaking to each other for more than four years. I felt sad that my ex-wife does not know her granddaughter. Nor does my granddaughter know her paternal grandmother. I believe everyone is missing out. Even though both my son and his mother had told me separately that they had been trying to get together to resolve their differences it was not happening. I thought perhaps I could help, as I am in touch with each of them and feeling fairly neutral toward my ex-wife. She and I maintain a pleasant, but distant relationship and my son and I have become closer especially since he became a father and is more mature, and our father-son relationship is relatively separate from the primary triangle of myself, my son, and his mother, my ex-wife. With this inspiration I contacted each of them to volunteer my help. They both readily agreed to meet with me at a neutral site. My son requested my office.

In June 2005 the process began. We met five times. My goal during this process was to maintain neutrality, keep my anxiety low and stay detriangled. The focus of the meetings was on the one-to-one relationship between son and mother. They decided to start by going back to the period when the conflict began, which was after the dance club closed with each describing their experience. A series of concerns were raised, such as feeling a lack of respect, not being heard, being closed out by the other person, not being emotionally available, being used to do things around the house, being used for financial reasons, left to deal with the problem of broken possessions, feeling closed out, not accepting our son's wife, and feeling the other does not know them.

At each meeting they picked up where they left off previously continuing to describe their experiences. The theme of my son's position was, "We have to learn to compromise." The theme to his mother's position was, "There is a lot that has to be fixed."

During the fifth meeting my ex-wife questioned my motivation for encouraging this process. The same issue had been raised at the first meeting and my response was accepted, so we had proceeded with the meetings. Now she suggested that we all meet with a therapist and discontinue these meetings. As we discussed the matter I felt frustrated and my neutrality became compromised. My son said he thought I did not need to be a part of the therapy, but he agreed to participate himself. I was frustrated because I thought we were making very good progress toward a normalized relationship in the not too distant future. Starting a new venue would mean going back to the beginning again. I asked my ex-wife what she thought we would do in therapy that we were not doing now. She said, "Express strong feelings." I responded by saying, "I thought we already did that. What good do you think that does if more feelings are expressed?" We reached an impasse. I bowed out wishing them good luck. They both thanked me for my help in getting the process started. We concluded the joint meetings.

As I reflected after the last meeting it occurred to me that my neutrality was compromised as the intensity in the system increased and the force for change back emerged. I realize I am still part of the triangle, and I could not be truly neutral. I felt neutral because of the counterbalancing force of my current marriage. I fooled myself and that led to the overfunctioning of being *therapist* rather than father and ex-husband. I was taken aback by my ex-wife's wish to end the meetings. Perhaps she was feeling pressure from the system to change. Instead, the pressure shifted to me and I felt a pressure to take the outside position. This would mean reverting to an old position and a possible shift toward the old triangle. What was different this time, however, was the fact that I was able to manage my anxiety and regain some neutrality in the meeting. I came around to supporting the new venue, and my son took a clear position on the issue stating, "The work is between you and me, Mom."

A few months went by during which time my son and my ex-wife exchanged telephone calls. Eventually the calls resulted in their agreeing to a face-to-face meeting not at a therapist's office, but at the home of my ex-wife. At that visit my son reiterated his position with his mother, "If you want to have a relationship with me you must have a relationship with my whole family, including my wife." He suggested that my ex-wife call his wife and that they try to resolve their conflict. Within a few days a call was made and later returned. At the time of the call both my ex-wife and son's wife were ready to forgive and move forward. My son's wife invited my ex-wife to visit their home and meet our granddaughter. My ex-wife was cordially welcomed by my son and his wife to their home. The visit went well according to everybody involved.

During the months prior to the resolution of the conflict, and the cutoff, my son and his wife discussed the possibility of having a second child. He being the more reticent of the two agreed to try for another child on the basis that this time they approach the process differently than they had with their first child. "We are not going to be isolated as we were before; we are going to have a life." His wife agreed and so the effort commenced. She is now pregnant.

My daughter-in-law reported that in earlier discussions with my son he stated, "It is about time we all move on. I do not want to have a second child having this cutoff continue, and it is time our daughter got to know her grandmother." This statement according to my daughter-in-law made it clear to her that any ambivalence my son had in the past about reconciliation with his mother was resolved. His readiness to move forward was now clear. This signal from him helped her in her decision to work things out with her mother-in-law.

I hypothesize these factors led to the deactivation of the triangle with my son, his wife, and my ex-wife: my son's *I-Positions* with his mother and his wife; the willingness of my ex-wife and daughter-in-law to let go of past conflict, and begin to deal with each other in a direct and positive manner; the decision of my son and his wife to expand their family by planning for a second child; and the nodal event of the actual pregnancy.

The day following the reconciliation my son, his wife, and our granddaughter were invited to dinner at our house. At the house, my granddaughter told me she has another Nana. I asked her how that was for her, and she replied, "Good."

Figure 8.11 illustrates the shift from emotional cutoff to connection between my son, his mother, wife, and daughter.

CONCLUSION

If the triangle is the stitch, then interlocking triangles are the weave of the fabric of our emotional life. By identifying, understanding, and making some gains in repositioning myself in the most significant triangles in my life I was able to increase my level of differentiation of self. This was possible through the guidance of a coach, making a plan, and taking action to which others

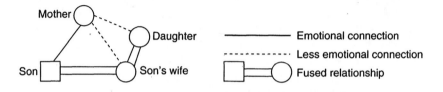

FIGURE 8.11. The Detriangling Between My Son, His Wife, Daughter, and Mother

responded. The period immediately following my initial family work was characterized by professional success, calm stable family relationships, and lower levels of acute anxiety.

Nodal events in conjunction with undifferentiation and oscillating levels of anxiety played a significant part in triggering the unbalancing and rebalancing of my family system and were pivotal in ushering change. With change there were losses and gains. Within two years of the death of my mother my functional level of differentiation of self gave way to the lower level of my basic level of differentiation of self. Marital conflict erupted, acting-out occurred on my part, a separation, and finally a divorce. The level of acute anxiety for me after the separation was high, and remained high for about four years. Finally, my functional level of differentiation of self increased again and has remained steady for approximately ten years. This is evidenced in a stable and rewarding relationship with my significant other/wife and her family, a lower level of acute anxiety, a close meaningful relationship with my son and his family, continued success in my professional career, and a budding career in fine art photography.

An interesting question is, how much of my increased functional level of self is based on the compatible relationship with my new wife, as opposed to an increase in basic level of differentiation? This should be determined over time when my level of functioning is examined over my lifetime with consideration given to the functioning of other significant people in my life from the past, present, and future generations (Kerr and Bowen, 1988).

REFERENCES

Bowen, M. (1978). *Family therapy in clinical practice.* New York: Jason Aronson Press.

Kerr, M. and Bowen, M. (1988). *Family evaluation.* New York: W.W. Norton and Company, Inc.

LaForte, J. (1987). Efforts to modify one's position in interlocking triangles. In Titelman, P. (Ed.), *The therapist's own family: Towards the differentiation of self* (pp. 115-152). Northvale, NJ: Jason Aronson Press.

Chapter 9

Observation of Triangles
in a Human-Canine Pack

Linda M. Fleming

INTRODUCTION

This chapter explores the question, "How do a changing environment and the triangles that develop within it affect pack behavior and physical health in canines and people?" To answer this question, I will use observations of my two dogs, my husband, and myself over a four-year period during which there were significant environmental changes. Research on the social behavior of wolves *(Canis lupus),* domestic dogs (*Canis familiaris;* Thomas, 1993), and other species (Candleland, Bryan, Nazar, Kopf, and Sendor, 1970) helped to predict which member(s) of the pack became symptomatic during particular conditions. Change in residence was not related to behavioral or physiological symptoms in the dogs; however, change in pack membership was followed by increased symptoms in the dogs and humans. Drawing from Bowen family systems theory as a conceptual guide, these findings will be discussed in terms of triangles and how they function in the family emotional system. Observable changes in physical health and behavior followed environmental changes that modified the member's position in the triangle. Observations suggested that when one member of the triangle managed his or her own anxiety and provided a more consistent role within the triangle, stability and decreased symptoms in its members followed. The ability of the leader to see the pack as an emotional unit was essential to help pack members function more effectively.

MEMBERS OF THE PACK

Linda

When the pack was formed in July 1995, I was a thirty-two-year-old, white female in the process of buying an old house. I was a doctoral student at the University of Pittsburgh in the counseling psychology program, beginning my fourth year of studies, which included coursework, field placement, and beginning my dissertation. I had no children, and was prone to winter colds, seasonal allergies, and occasional bouts of irritable bowel. I had separated from, and subsequently divorced, my first husband in 1992. My father had died of cancer eleven months previously. My older sister, who was married with two children, and my now-widowed mother, lived in Arizona, where I had grown up and gone to high school.

In my family of origin (see Figure 9.1), my mother was an overfunctioner who worked tirelessly to maintain calmness in the family (a position in which I have found myself). My father was an underfunctioner at home, devoting much time and energy to his work as an electrical engineer. My sister's relationship with my mother was more conflictual than mine; I was the child who was able to calm my mother. My mother worried about my older sister much more than she worried about me. On the other hand, my relationship with my father was more conflictual than his relationship with my sister. My sister and I got along well. We were very close in age (only eleven months apart), and often played together. We rarely fought, and, as adults, we maintain a close relationship. Although my family had three cats while I was growing up, I had never lived with a dog.

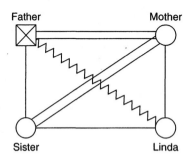

FIGURE 9.1. Linda's Family of Origin

Gryphon

Gryphon was a twenty-pound West Highland white terrier who came to live with me in July 1995, when he was about six years old. He had been placed for adoption at a local animal shelter after living the first six years of his life with a family in a middle-class, suburban neighborhood. They had two young children, one aged three years and an infant. When they gave him up for adoption, they told the shelter workers they did not have enough time to care for the dog. Their report of Gryphon at the time of placement at the animal shelter stated that Gryphon would urinate and defecate in the basement on paper provided by the owners, he did not bark excessively, urinate when excited, bite, chew, get carsick, or jump on people. He came when called, and knew the commands "Sit," "No," and "Down."

When I first saw Gryphon, he looked as if he had not been groomed in over a year. Although he was a white dog, he looked more like a cairn terrier, which is a brown terrier. His hair was long, and severely matted. Underneath the mats, his skin was bright red and appeared irritated. A visit to the veterinarian revealed he had a staphylococcus infection in his skin. Both ears were infected. Within a few days of taking him home, he developed a bladder infection. During the first week he lived with me, we were going for a walk when we could hear the sounds of young children. Gryphon's ears perked up, he appeared to be more alert, and he ran toward the sounds. When he got closer, his ears and tail drooped and the added energy disappeared. I suspect he thought he had heard the children from his previous family, but I have no evidence to support that opinion. He was returned to the animal shelter for the weekend as I was scheduled to be out of town, and over the weekend, he began repeatedly throwing up. He remained at the shelter for an additional month until his health stabilized. He underwent several tests, none of which could explain his digestive problems. I visited him several times each week, taking him for walks and playing with him in the shelter.

His original name was Beamer; however, I did not like the name so I changed it soon after adopting him. For the first several months Gryphon lived with me, he never wagged his tail, although he greeted me at the door each evening. He continued to throw up frequently and often had dreams that appeared to be nightmares. While sleeping, Gryphon would bark, become restless, and appear very agitated. When I would wake him, he often appeared disoriented and would want to be held and petted.

He often flinched when I would reach down to pet him; I learned that if I called him by his new name prior to petting him, he did not shrink from my touch. When outside, if I called him to come to me, he would stand still and tremble. If I then walked over to him, he would flinch. Gryphon frequently urinated and defecated in the basement (the previous family had stated he was trained to do this; however, it was not a behavior that I was pleased with), and he had problems with colitis.

He had recurrent ear infections and repeated vomiting for the next three months. I took him to the veterinarian in November 1995 to request an anti-anxiety medication as he appeared to be so anxious he was unable to learn new commands (such as "Come" and "Sit"). The veterinarian prescribed a sedating medication, but I never gave Gryphon any of it as the behaviors suddenly disappeared. He became more attentive to me and began to learn new behaviors. For several weeks prior to the visit to the vet, I had been trying to teach him to come to me by using food treats and rewarding him. My attempts had been completely unsuccessful, but within days of the visit to the vet, he was happily running across the yard to me. He began to wag his tail at me, and with the neighbors, whom he came to know. Vomiting became less frequent, and he no longer had bouts of colitis. He slept more calmly, and urinating in the basement became an infrequent event. It was such a dramatic change I was astounded. I began to think that the trip to the veterinarian had been a pivotal event. I have often wondered if taking him in the car somewhere and then bringing him home had somehow solidified his relationship with me, abating his fears of abandonment. Whatever the explanation, he became healthier, calmer, and less fearful of being touched. In fact, he became affectionate, sitting on my lap, asking to be petted, and approaching the neighbors to be petted. By December 1995, we had developed into a close dyad. In canine terms, a stable pack of two.

Shayne

Shayne joined the pack in March 1996. I was enjoying having a dog so much, I decided that two dogs would be even better. Shayne was a mixed breed dog with some sheltie in his parentage. At a healthy weight, he was about thirty-five pounds. Shayne had spent the first six years of his life living in a home with about thirty other dogs. He had a great deal of contact with the other dogs in the home, but much less contact with humans. He was brought to the shelter in September 1995, following a humane society rescue. In his crate at the shelter, Shayne displayed many signs of anxiety. He required a large ten-gallon bucket for water as he would tip over anything smaller. When people would walk past his cage, he would sit on his hind legs and paw at the air.

Shayne had been placed with a family for five days in October 1995. It is unknown why he was returned to the shelter after such a short period of time. He stayed at the shelter until January 1996, when a family consisting of a mother and two boys adopted him. He lived with that family for five days. One day the boys were not home as they were visiting their father. The mother was working two jobs and was gone from the house for over twelve hours. Shayne had been tied to the kitchen table and he chewed one of the kitchen chairs into splinters. They returned him to the shelter after that incident.

A report on Shayne's behavior from his second owners stated that he had a limited vocabulary of commands (coming less than 50 percent of the time, not understanding the words "stay" or "sit"). It was reported that he would urinate if he became excited; he jumped on people, urinated and defecated in the house, and had become destructive in the house. He was not aggressive, did not bark excessively, traveled well in the car without getting carsick, and got along with male and female humans of all ages. When I first met Shayne at the shelter, the staff were considering euthanizing him, as they were concerned that, after two failed placements, he would be unable to adjust to living with a family. In a last ditch attempt, they were training Shayne to walk on a leash, to "sit," "stay," and "walk" in a very ritualized manner. I returned after a week with Gryphon to see how the two dogs would get along. After spending a few minutes sniffing one another, they ignored each other. On March 3, 1996, Shayne came home with Gryphon and me.

On his leash, Shayne would walk when directed; pulling so hard that my hands would become numb from the tightness of the leash. When something in the environment startled him, such as a person walking down the street or a dog barking, he would sit on his hind legs, wrap his front legs over the leash, and spin in circles, wrapping himself up in the leash. If I intervened and loudly said to Shayne, "No!" he would stop and sit. Shayne also had significant medical problems. He had arthritis in his hind legs, often to the point where it was difficult for him to get up after having slept for a period of time. He had frequent bouts of colitis.

The question that begs to be answered at this point is why I would choose to adopt an animal with such obvious problems. As a doctoral student in counseling psychology, I was learning about interventions with people. I thought I could help Shayne adapt to human family living and I could learn something about change processes and nonverbal communication at the same time. I had no idea what I was really going to learn.

Gryphon was accustomed to a dog-human culture, and was knowledgeable about human social custom; therefore the Gryphon-Linda dyad worked well because he could adapt to me. However, being an only dog since puppyhood, he was unfamiliar with dog-dog culture, and had difficulty adapting to Shayne's presence. In contrast, Shayne was very knowledgeable about canine social customs and knew very well how to interact with Gryphon, but he was a novice when it came to a human-dog culture, so he did not know how to adapt to me. When Shayne joined the pack, he was in the outside position in the triangle, and experienced conflict with both Gryphon and myself. In effect, Gryphon knew what the rules should be with me, but had no idea how to interact with Shayne. Shayne knew how to act with Gryphon, but had no idea how to act with me. Being familiar with only human culture, I did not know how to act with either of them. I was also unfamiliar with dog-dog culture so I didn't know how they should act with one another. This was a disaster in the making to which I was completely oblivious.

ESTABLISHMENT OF THE PACK

Once at home, the dogs and I became an emotional triangle. Shayne jumped on the couch and sat there, growling at Gryphon if Gryphon attempted to get on the couch. Gryphon sat on the floor looking up at the couch, obviously confused by Shayne's behavior. I told Shayne, "No," but he persisted and a friend who was visiting slapped Shayne's nose. He stopped for the moment, but our troubles were just beginning. Shayne and Gryphon constantly competed over food, toys, and my attention and affection. Viewing the triangle in action, Shayne, who occupied the outside position in the triangle, wanted an insider position. He would become aggressive with Gryphon, who would then turn to me for protection and comfort. I would provide that comfort, thus preserving Gryphon's and my positions as insiders in the triangle. After nine months of unsuccessfully trying to negotiate three different sets of expectations, and failing to see the triangle in action, I went for help.

In December 1996, I took Shayne to my veterinarian who diagnosed Shayne with "separation anxiety" and prescribed an antidepressant, amitriptyline. It helped some behaviors, but made others worse. In March 1997, I took Shayne to a veterinarian who specialized in animal behavior. A copy of her report from that first visit reads as follows:

> Behavioral consult—very nervous and anxious at home. . . . Very insistent for attention and proximity to owner. Shakes and trembles if his couch is occupied. Very anxious, controlling. Was on Amitriptyline 25 mg BID + 2 months. Has been off two weeks. While on Amitriptyline gradually increasing shows of aggression to other dog over food, toys, "his" couch, spot on bed. Urinates in house when left alone. Dining room usually—only if owner doesn't come home by dark. Is destructive in crate. Is not destructive when free in house, only urinates if owner left after dark. Suspect dominant and anxious. When anxiety

reduced by Amitriptyline, leads to increased dominance. Work on dominance behavior modification, drug therapy for anxiety. Wants to sleep at head of bed, other dog also sleeps on bed—other dog was there first. Will sleep under bed if owner insists. Will growl at other dog if in his spot. Remove all toys and sources of aggression. Provide bed for him not shared with other pets.

While her evaluation was focused on Shayne and his behavior, I began to realize that I needed to become the consistent leader of the pack. This was quite a wake-up call for me, and the beginning of my awareness that this problem we were all having did not just reside with Shayne. Following my discussion with the veterinarian and reading the information she provided on dogs, I realized that my egalitarian, democratic ways were not useful for the dogs, and were in fact, a large part of the problem we were all having. While I was attempting to impose my human thinking on the canine brain, I did not realize I was asking them to do something they were not capable of doing. My feminist ideals of shared power did not fit with the canine mind.

A canine pack is an emotional system in which a hierarchy, with clear boundaries and expectations that determine their behaviors, is created. A hierarchy is established and maintained in a pack using ritual behaviors that demonstrate dominance, subdominance, or submission. The most dominant male and female are the alpha dogs; subdominant dogs have less status, while the lowest ranking dogs are the omegas. Thomas (1993) suggested that dogs in a pack are at their most comfortable and stable when everyone knows his or her rank and has accepted it. The alpha male and female are secure in their positions, while the lowest ranking dogs are secure in theirs as well. This creates a stable pack with low anxiety. When stress is low, the members of a triangle are better able to function as emotionally separate individuals. By creating a hierarchy in which everyone knows how to behave, dogs effectively create a lower-stress environment that ultimately provides greater autonomy for its members.

In their dog minds, Gryphon and Shayne knew there needed to be a leader of the pack, and I was not meeting their expectations. If I was not going to be responsible for the leadership of the pack, one of them had to be the alpha dog, and both Gryphon and Shayne were vying for that role. In short, it was a highly anxious pack with no clearly defined leader. Kerr and Bowen (1988) wrote that "an unstable twosome can be stabilized by the addition of a third person" (p. 139). This was certainly the case for us. There was significant conflict between the two dogs. When their squabbles were less intense, I would stay removed from it (see Figure 9.2). When they became more intense, I would become particularly irritated and distressed (see Figure 9.3).

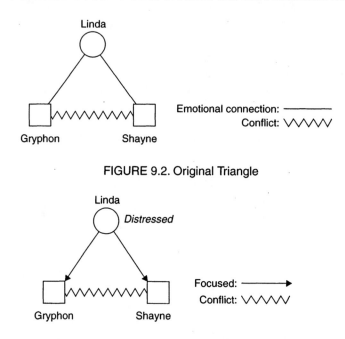

FIGURE 9.2. Original Triangle

FIGURE 9.3. Linda Asserting Herself

I would then intervene, tell both dogs what to do (in dog terms, take an alpha position) and they would calm down temporarily (see Figure 9.4). When they calmed down, I calmed down, but then would renege on my leadership responsibilities and no longer tell them what to do. This left the leadership role again unfilled and open for dispute.

At the time, however, I perceived the problem to reside in Shayne. I believed that if he could only learn how to get along with Gryphon, things would be fine; this is why the conflict in Figure 9.4 involves me with Shayne. I did not see the triangle in operation, nor did I understand the canine mind. Thus, with my inconsistent leadership, their anxiety increased until their behavior became an irritant to me, and I would rise back to the alpha position. We needed to establish a clear hierarchy, with me as alpha, and Gryphon as beta. As he was the last dog to arrive at the house, Shayne was designated as omega.

After the visit with the veterinarian in March 1997, I removed all the dog toys from the house to eliminate competition opportunities for the dogs. I learned how to be a dog. When Shayne jumped on the bed in the evening,

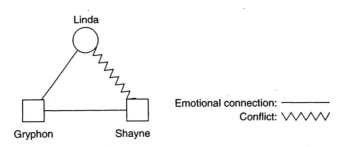

FIGURE 9.4. Viewing Shayne As the Problem

I growled at him, bared my teeth, and pushed him off the bed. Another strategy I employed for telling Shayne he was doing something that I did not find appropriate was to grab his throat. I learned quickly to either growl or grab his throat with my hand. If I grabbed his throat and growled simultaneously, Shayne would urinate in abject submission. While it certainly reinforced my position as alpha dog, it also created quite a mess, so I chose to use a less intensive dominance move. From growling and neck-grabbing strategies, we moved into a more human response—just saying "no."

We also established ritualized ways in which Shayne could receive the affection he wanted. When Shayne was calm and lying on the couch doing nothing, I would occasionally reach over, pet him on the head, and tell him he was a good dog. In my physical affection with Shayne, I was careful to touch him only on the head and shoulders. The veterinarian had made this suggestion to me with the explanation that Shayne might become over stimulated and sexually aroused with more overall body touching. If Shayne perceived affection from me as sexual in nature, this might diminish my status as alpha.

When Shayne came to me and asked to be petted, I would not reach down and pet him. That would have told him that I did what *he* wanted me to do, thereby allowing him to be dominant over me. Instead, when he would come to me, I would tell him to "sit." When he sat down, I would then pet him and tell him he was a good dog. In this way, he was responding to my command, and then was rewarded for his obedience to me. Being an intelligent dog, Shayne learned this sequence of behaviors very quickly and would come to me and sit down without being told. I was initially concerned that if I provided attention, I would be allowing him to be dominant over me. After more thought, I decided I could provide affection toward him since he was being proactively compliant.

As Gryphon already knew how to live with humans and his behaviors were less problematic for me, I modified my training with him. I did not growl at him or grab him by the neck; Gryphon already knew what the word "no" meant. I employed the strategy of telling Gryphon to sit prior to being petted. Five years later, Gryphon still needed to be told. For example, there were times when Gryphon would get so excited about going outside that he literally could not sit to have his leash attached. He would sit for approximately one second, and then he would jump back up, wiggling, and wagging his tail energetically. During the initial six-month training period, I would take at least five minutes before walks trying to get Gryphon to sit without success. After that six-month period, I modified my command from "sit" to "stand very quietly," a behavior Gryphon could successfully achieve.

Perhaps it was my inconsistency or an intellectual limitation on Gryphon's part that created this shortcoming. It was equally possible that Gryphon's failure to learn to sit was a function of the Linda-Gryphon-Shayne triangle. As I consider my relationships with each dog, I always felt more affectionate toward Gryphon and calmer in his presence compared to the way I felt toward Shayne. I did not discipline Gryphon as severely as I did Shayne, frequently allowing his behavioral infractions to go unaddressed, and quite probably, unnoticed. This was not the case with Shayne. His behaviors were duly noted and closely controlled. With triangles, anxiety in one relationship is reduced by focusing on a third party who is unconsciously pulled into the situation to lower the emotional intensity of the original pair. The greater the unresolved tension, the more likely the triangling will lead to an overly intense attachment with the third person by one of the original pair. It is likely that my difficulties with Gryphon were never truly resolved, but instead, as Shayne was triangled into the relationship, my anxious focus shifted toward him, and my relationship with Gryphon became closer. Another fact of triangles is that as they become more rigid and entrenched, they not only prohibit us from identifying the actual sources of conflict, they also limit the growth of individuals in them. My inability to effectively discipline Gryphon is an indication of the triangle in action and may have limited his ability to learn.

On the way home from the veterinarian after that visit in March 1997, I stopped at a Goodwill store and purchased an upholstered love seat just for Shayne. With two couches now in the living room, I discovered that Shayne still became agitated when Gryphon lay on the couch with me, leaving no room for him. Shayne would pace back and forth and growl at Gryphon (who would ignore him, or at the most, open one eye). I began telling Shayne to lie on the other couch, and after a very brief period of time, he began to do this more on his own without the threatening behaviors toward Gryphon. Over time, this couch became "Shayne's couch," a place where Shayne could always go. However, it was less preferential than the other couch, which I would sit on with Gryphon. This strategy not only eliminated the competition between the dogs, but also reinforced Gryphon's position of dominance over Shayne.

During this time, Shayne would become very anxious when I would leave the house, and while I was gone he was destructive. On several occasions, he destroyed the bathroom, shredding the shower curtain, clearing all objects on the counter, on the shelves, and destroying bottles of shampoo. Less destructive days were marked by the shredding of paper, or urinating and defecating in the dining room. I attempted to crate Shayne only to have him break out of the crate in a matter of minutes. When I locked the crate, he worked so hard to break out, that he bent the bars, bruised his nose, and broke many of his teeth. Crating was clearly not an option, so I barricaded both dogs together in the living room to limit the destruction to a single room.

During that March visit to the veterinarian, Shayne's amitriptyline was increased to 50 mg per day and an antianxiety medication, acepromazine (Xanax), was added to the mix. It was to be administered one hour prior to my leaving the house. The acepromazine seemed to have little effect on Shayne's behavior once I left the house, so I discontinued it. One day, when Shayne was having a bout of colitis, I realized I had run out of Imodium, an over-the-counter antidiarrheal medication. In desperation, I gave him ½ mg of acepromazine, thinking if the colitis was stress-related, the acepromazine might alleviate the colitis. It worked beautifully.

I continued to use the Xanax for colitis, as I viewed the colitis as an indicator of a high level of anxiety for Shayne. We also continued with the behavioral training (or I should say, more accurately, *my* behavioral training). I worked on being a more consistent alpha dog and consistently reinforced Gryphon's dominance over Shayne. With the hierarchy established, Shayne's behavior improved considerably. He no longer defecated or urinated in the house. He began to ask to go outdoors when he needed to. His colitis became less frequent, and his destructiveness in the house diminished to paper shredding.

IDENTIFYING THE TRIANGLE

Things went well briefly until I experienced a host of stressors. My grandmother died; I was having significant financial problems as a graduate student with limited income; I had hit a deer on the way home from work one evening and smashed up the side of my car. Two weeks later, the car caught on fire and was totaled so I needed another car (fortunately, I had not bothered to fix the car after the deer incident). I was trying to work on my dissertation, which was exceedingly frustrating, and in the midst of all this, I traveled to Arizona to visit my mother to help her sort through some of my father's things (he had died about a year earlier). During this time Shayne regressed. He again began defecating in the house, had several episodes of colitis, and, once again, he demolished my bathroom. I was at my wit's end. I met with the veterinarian again, requesting an increase in medication (the amitriptyline was increased to 75 mg). I recall telling her that he had been doing better, but I had noticed he was terribly reactive to my moods. Even when I did not believe that I behaved differently, Shayne picked up on my mood and reacted physically and behaviorally. When I was the individual who was highly anxious, Shayne was the one who acted it out. Given this high degree of emotional fusion between us, I believe that if I had taken the Xanax, Shayne would have been less symptomatic. I might have felt better too!

Now that I was beginning to see how my emotions and behavior affected Shayne, I began to more carefully observe both dogs' behavior in relation to my own. This was the beginning of my thinking of the group as an interrelated system. One of the identifying features of triangles is the automatic shifting of anxiety from one individual to another. Not all individuals are affected in the same way—some are more vulnerable to anxiety than others. Kerr and Bowen (1988) noted there are triangles in which some individuals could be

> characterized as the anxiety "generator," a second person as the anxiety "amplifier," and the third as the anxiety "dampener." The "generator" is typically accused of setting the emotional tone for the triangle or (family). . . . While the "generator" may be the first person to get nervous about potential problems, he [*sic*] is not the cause of the anxiety that circulates in the triangle. The "amplifier" adds to the problem by his inability to stay calm when the generator is anxious. . . . The "dampener" uses emotional distance to control his reactivity to the others, but at a certain level of tension he can be relied on to become overly responsible for others in order to calm things down. (p. 142)

I observed that when I, as the "anxiety generator," became distressed, Shayne would become symptomatic, either through physical symptoms or behaviors. Shayne, in this case, was the "anxiety amplifier." On the other hand, Gryphon often acted as the "anxiety dampener" by hanging back or attempting to provide some consolation to me. At those times he would insist that he sit on my lap and push his nose into my hand so I would pet him. This example of canine empathy was calming to me.

I noticed that Shayne was much more sensitive and reactive to my mood than Gryphon. While Gryphon always greeted me at the door with a wagging tail, I realized that if I came home grumpy from my day, Shayne would look at me and begin shaking. I began experimenting with changing my behavior when I returned home, trying to be more cheerful. Shayne, however, was a very astute observer of my emotions and behavior. When I thought I was doing a pretty good job of pretending to be happy even though I was grumpy, he could see right through me. After a stressful day, I might put a smile on my face and have a cheerful sound to my voice, and he would still tremble on his couch. If I returned home and was indeed in a good mood, smiling and cheerful, Shayne would look at me for a few seconds, and then he would jump off the couch to greet me. There were times when I thought I was cheerful, and Shayne would still tremble on the couch. At those times, I decided to evaluate my emotional state. I discovered that I had not been attending to my own distress at those times. Shayne was never wrong. He was often more aware of my moods than I was myself; in other words, he felt my anxiety more acutely than I did. Once I realized that, I began to use Shayne as a barometer of my own emotional functioning. When Shayne would begin to exhibit symptoms, I would take that opportunity to evaluate myself. That process ultimately taught me to become more aware of more subtle emotional reactions in myself.

With the hierarchy established in the pack, it had to be continually reinforced with ritual behaviors. Gryphon began to show his submission to me in the evenings when he would jump on the bed and roll over on his back so I could rub his belly. Shayne would demonstrate his submission after his meal, when he would come over to me, sit without being told and look at me. I would pat him on the head for a couple of seconds and then he would go lie down. Gryphon would show his dominant status to Shayne by taking his rawhide bones and eating them, and occasionally eating out of Shayne's dog bowl. Shayne would show his submission to Gryphon by not protesting. I would show my ritual dominance by making them sit for food and affection, and reinforce Shayne's position relative to Gryphon's by always petting and feeding Gryphon first and allowing Gryphon to sleep on the bed with me while Shayne was required to sleep on the floor under the bed.

INTERLOCKING TRIANGLES

Sometimes it is not possible for anxiety to be managed within a single triangle. When this happens, the anxiety spreads to other triangles in an interlocking fashion. Anxiety that is not managed within a three-person group often spills over to involve a fourth person. With the addition of a new member to a system, or the loss of a member, the system must readjust to accommodate the change. This change in the system creates stress in its members. Furthermore, when a new member is incorporated into a three-member group, the possible number of triangles increases to four. The anxiety that was originally managed within a single triangle may now be spread over multiple triangles. These multiple triangles have the potential to provide greater flexibility to the system to manage anxiety. This was the case for us.

Jim: The Fourth Member of the Pack

Our pack of three, our triangle, had stabilized until it was disrupted when I began dating Jim. Jim was thirty-three years old when we met. He worked in computer sales, and had recently completed his bachelor's degree in math education. He was generally healthy, although prone to irritable bowel, and had difficulty falling asleep during times of stress. With his irritable bowel symptoms, he was a perfect fit for our family pack, since he had gastrointestinal symptoms just like the dogs and I had.

For few months, there was not much change in the pack. Jim would appear on weekends, and he and I would leave the dogs at home while we went off on our dating adventure. When the four of us would go on walks, Jim occasionally gave commands to the dogs, which they would consistently ignore. I would say the same words, for example, "Come here" or "Stay," and the dogs would respond appropriately. It was clear at this time, the dogs did not consider Jim to be a member of the pack.

During the summer of 1998, things changed dramatically. I left on a trip to Europe for a month, leaving Jim as house and dogsitter. When I returned, I discovered that Jim had usurped my alpha position. My first day back from Europe, I went to take the dogs for a walk. I took the leashes from their peg and asked the dogs, "Wanna go for a walk?" In the past, this question would have been met with much leaping and excitement. That day, the dogs looked at me, then at Jim. When he said, "Go ahead," they began leaping and jumping. For the next two weeks we were a pack of four, with Jim as the alpha. I was the subdominant, followed by Gryphon, with Shayne as omega.

Then Jim moved to Warren, Pennsylvania, a small town three hours north of Pittsburgh, and for the next ten months, the pack became one that fluctuated between a three-member pack during the week and a four-member pack on the weekends. As the primary caretaker, I regained my position as alpha dog within the first month, with Jim moving to a subdominant position.

Gryphon appeared to have the most difficulty coping with the constantly fluctuating pack. For the first couple of months, Gryphon would inevitably vomit on the Sunday evening or Monday morning following a visit from Jim.

He became quite clingy with me, begging to be held and petted frequently. When I would work at the computer, Gryphon would scratch his front paws against my legs, asking to be picked up and placed on my lap. When Jim visited, Gryphon would follow him around so much that Jim nicknamed him "My Shadow." When Jim and I sat on the couch, Gryphon got into the habit of squeezing himself in between us, preferably sitting on both of our laps simultaneously. Shayne would lie on the other couch or on the floor at our feet, which was typical for him.

A notable change during those several months was the change in sleeping arrangements. I had a queen-sized bed and always slept on the right side of the bed. Gryphon had always slept at my feet, with Shayne sleeping underneath the bed, usually directly below my head. When Jim would visit, he would sleep on the left side of the bed. Gryphon began jumping on the bed in the evening and positioning himself on the left side of the bed. Either Jim or I would have to pick him up to move him to his designated place at the foot of the bed. Inevitably, at some point during the night, Gryphon would creep up to the far-left side of the bed and curl up next to Jim. I would often wake up to find Jim next to me with Gryphon sleeping underneath Jim's arm. When we first began the weekends only-four-member pack, Shayne continued sleeping underneath the bed. After the first few months, there was a week when Shayne attempted to sleep in Jim's place after Jim had returned to his apartment for the workweek. One night, Shayne jumped up, only to find Gryphon already there, snarling and snapping at him. I wondered if Shayne thought that since the top three dogs slept on the bed, he could become one of the top three; with Jim gone, he felt he now deserved a place on the bed. I was firm in my insistence that Shayne sleep underneath the bed, and this behavior stopped.

SOCIAL STATUS CHANGE AND SYMPTOM FORMATION

Studies of other species suggest that changes in social status are associated with change in physiological activity. Candleland et al. (1970) studied groups of chickens and squirrel monkeys. They found changes in social relationships were associated with a corresponding change in heart rate. The relationship between heart rate and social rank was curvilinear, with the highest and lowest ranking members having the highest heart rate, and the middle ranking members having a lower heart rate. They also found that when animals changed social rank, their heart rate changed accordingly. As their study used unrelated animals from a variety of sources, it is unclear if a global statement about change in social rank determining heart rate can be made.

Understanding the relationship between social rank and physiological change helps to predict which dog will become symptomatic. With a three-member pack during the week and a four-member pack on the weekend, Gryphon's social rank in the pack fluctuated from being the second highest ranking dog, to the third highest. Gryphon's vomiting, clinging, and apparent anxiety suggest that he may have experienced physiological changes in relation to his changing rank. Jim experienced greater difficulty sleeping on weekdays than on weekends; I had greater difficulty sleeping on weekends. Shayne did not appear to have difficulty adapting (no obvious increased physiological reactivity) to the weekly pack fluctuations. This might have been related to his status as omega. Despite changes in the pack membership, Shayne's position never fluctuated; he was always the omega.

When applying these observations to triangles, the stress of the physical distance in Jim's and my relationship created a higher level of anxiety in our dyad. As Jim's moods and mine were generally positive (being in a new love relationship is invigorating and exciting), our symptoms were minimal. However, the anxiety was sufficient enough to include a third member. In our emotional system of four members, this time it was Gryphon who was the most vulnerable to the stress and became symptomatic.

During that school year, we adapted to the routine of a pack of four on the weekends and a pack of three during the week. Gryphon's colitis decreased and eventually stopped altogether by the last few months. Shayne had only two episodes of colitis during that time (both occurring the week I returned to work after I had been home ill with the flu for a week). Shayne's arthritis was in remission (if there is such a thing for arthritis). He did not appear stiff or sore and did not need any aspirin toward the end of the school year. Gryphon's vomiting reduced to his more normal levels. They both appeared to pout when I left the house in the morning (lying on the couch with their heads resting on the cushions, their eyes looking up at me, ears down), which was typical for them. However, there was no destruction, even when I forgot to put the gates up and they had free access to the house. In fact, I watched both dogs crawl underneath the gate at the top of the stairs. However, the ritual of putting up the gate appeared to have a calming effect on Shayne. He respected that boundary, even though it was ineffective as a physical barrier.

STABILIZATION

Jim and I were married in July 1999, and he moved into the house permanently. The following summer we moved from Pittsburgh to Erie, Pennsylvania. Since my marriage to Jim, the interlocking triangles became very clear (see Figure 9.5). Jim and I were clearly fused; Gryphon and Jim were fused, while Shayne and I continued to be fused together. For Gryphon, Jim was the alpha and I was the beta. Gryphon was more responsive to Jim's commands, often ignoring me, while responding to Jim. He would frequently follow Jim around the house, and often sleep at his feet. He assumed a consistent sleeping position at the bottom of the bed or even on the floor, and did not challenge either Jim or me for our positions on the bed. When he was frightened, hurt, or not feeling well, he tended to come to me for comfort.

Shayne continued to be primarily attached to me, more responsive to my commands, following me around the house, and sleeping at my feet. He was taken off all medication in December 2000, and his positive behavior maintained. There were no more episodes of destruction. He did not have any bouts of colitis for several years, even when we moved to Erie or when Jim and I went on vacation for a week or two and left the dogs at a kennel. His arthritis returned at times, but I was unable to connect times of limping with any changes in the household. It appeared to be more related to cold weather or when his activity level was limited (such as when he was kenneled for a period of time) and may have been also a function of the aging process. He retained his nighttime sleeping position under the bed.

My symptoms decreased as well. I had some symptoms of irritable bowel when I began a new job, but that stopped after the first two months, and I had no other symptoms after that. Jim had symptoms of irritable bowel at the time we moved, but those symptoms remitted within a month. These changes in the dogs, Jim, and me suggest that the hierarchy had stabilized and the level of acute anxiety had subsequently decreased. I believe this calming was due to three major factors:

1. My attempts to provide more of a leadership role in the pack. For me, knowing what to do with the dogs calmed me down (a little education was a great help). With my behaviors demonstrating clear dominance, the dogs calmed down.
2. Consistency of pack membership. For both Jim and myself, having a reliable relationship was calming for both of us, and I believe that calmness was reflected in the dogs. As I see it, Shayne was (and still is) the barometer of my emotional reactivity. His ability to maintain his behavior without any medication as well as his overall improvement in physical health is an indicator of the relative calmness.
3. Seeing the system as a system and the triangle as a triangle. As long as I was focused on Shayne as the problem, we made no progress in changing behaviors. When I began to see the problem as residing in

the system rather than in Shayne, we began to make progress. Shayne was able to make significant improvement, and I did as well. I believe that if Shayne had not been such a highly sensitive dog, I may not have increased my own self awareness to the degree that I did.

With a hierarchy, those individuals at the top of the hierarchy have the greater power to make changes in the emotional system. In human families, changes in one or more of the adults have a greater impact on how the family functions as a system than any changes that a child may make. In that sense, there is a natural hierarchy in families in which adults (parents) wield more power than children. With a cross-species emotional system, change in the system is more likely if it comes from the dominant animal. In this case, the human brain is more capable of complex thought and problem-solving than the canine brain. Change in a human-canine emotional system would need to come from one or more humans, given their greater brain capacity and dominance in the hierarchy. As was discussed earlier in this chapter, the Linda-Gryphon-Shayne triangle, that formed within our human-canine emotional system remained unchanged until the human (Linda) took a dominant role. Viewing my own behavior as part of the problem (i.e., beginning to see the problem not as residing in Shayne, but residing in all of us) and taking responsibility for it was essential to a more stable pack. Finally, having a fourth member added to the emotional system provided the system with greater flexibility to manage stress and conflict, through the subsequent development of interlocking triangles. Instead of Shayne being the most vulnerable member of the three-person pack, and the sole symptom bearer, in the four-member pack that role was shared with Gryphon.

Therefore, one can consider the dogs to be the recipients of the humans' emotional projection process, analogous to the functioning position occu-

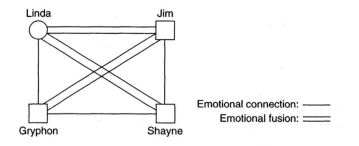

FIGURE 9.5. The Interlocking Triangles

pied by children in a family. This triangling helped decrease the anxiety between Jim and me, just as the triangling of my sister and me functioned in my own family of origin. The continuing effort for me to work on my own reactivity in my relationship with Jim helped to decrease the cross-species, canine-human triangling that is inevitable in a blended family pack.

SUMMARY

Bowen family systems theory provided a framework for understanding the functioning of members of a human-canine pack. Developing an understanding of how the problem resided in the system was essential to developing a solution to the problems of the family pack. When the problem was initially viewed as residing in a single individual, this individualistic thinking impeded the ability to understand the complexity of the triangles in the larger system. Furthermore, individualistic thinking did not require the humans in the canine-human pack to consider their participation in the problem. When the principles of Bowen family systems theory were applied, it required the author to consider her role in the problem and take responsibility for the problem. This change allowed for more thoughtful flexibility in developing solutions to the problem.

REFERENCES

Candleland, D. K., Bryan, D. C., Nazar, B. L., Kopf, K. J., and Sendor, M. (1970). Squirrel monkey heart rate during formation of status orders. *Journal of Comprehensive Physiological Psychology, 70,* 417-423.
Kerr, M. E. and Bowen, M. (1988). *Family evaluation.* New York: W.W. Norton.
Thomas, E. M. (1993). *The hidden life of dogs.* New York: Houghton Mifflin.

PART III:
TRIANGLES IN CLINICAL PRACTICE

Chapter 10

Triangles in Marriage

Phillip Klever

INTRODUCTION

Adults often experience their greatest immaturity within marriage. The immaturity expresses itself in efforts to change the spouse, criticism, put-downs, belligerence, defensiveness, withdrawal, passivity, over helpfulness, and/or irresponsibility. These patterns of reactivity are driven by lack of a well-defined self, an oversensitivity to the spouse, and dependence on the spouse for one's well-being. These patterns generate discomfort ranging from mild frustration to rage or despair. One instinctual response for managing these inevitable emotional states within a marriage is triangling—moving toward a third party to reduce the discomfort in self (Bowen, 1978; Kerr and Bowen, 1988; Papero, 1990). Triangling manifests in thoughts or fantasies about others, feelings for others, or behavior toward others. Common third parties in marriages are children, families of origin, affairs, friends, and community helpers.

Differentiation and Marital Triangles

At the highest levels of differentiation, an individual has a high degree of emotional self-regulation. At this level a couple talks openly with each other about most of their anxieties and tensions and has little need to spill it out into other relationships. However, a highly differentiated couple does not operate in a cocoon. On the contrary, each has active one-to-one relationships with appropriate boundaries with family, friends, co-workers, neighbors, and community members. A mature network of relationships provides a supportive context for the individuals and the marriage relationship.

At the lowest levels of differentiation, an individual has a low level of emotional self-regulation and is more highly dependent on relationships to help manage emotionality. In addition, the couple has little ability to address emotionally laden issues. One or both spouses may be cut off from their families of origin and community. Or they may be putting their unresolved anxieties into intense relationships with others—children, family, affairs, friends, and/or the community. This is less a result of a character flaw, and more a result of the natural processes of a poorly differentiated system.

Stabilizing and Destabilizing Marital Triangles

The undifferentiation in a marriage is a steady challenge to a couple. The ebb and flow of anxiety adds to that challenge. The pressures of undifferentiation and anxiety in the marital relationship are managed through distance, conflict, projection, overaccommodation, and triangling. The triangle tends to relieve discomfort for at least one of the spouses and in the short term keeps the marriage from exploding or dissolving. A triangle stabilizes a marriage when it helps to absorb the marital anxiety, and the spouses can accept the marital distance that is a part of the triangle. For example, a wife may have a more personal relationship with a woman friend, sister, or mother, than she has with her husband who does not like to talk much about personal matters. She may find comfort in complaining about her husband to her sister. He may be glad that his wife does not bother him with all of her complaints or worries. She may be more satisfied with the responses of her mother than her husband, and she may be more relaxed with her husband after a conversation with her sister. However, the stability a triangle offers to a marriage is not as solid as the stability that comes from applying the principles of differentiation.

A triangle destabilizes a marriage when one of the spouses perceives the third party as a threat to marital togetherness. This perception can happen with an increase of anxiety or with a change in the marital relationship. At higher levels of anxiety, less thinking is available to realistically evaluate the degree of threat related to shifts in the marital relationship. When one or both spouses perceive an increased threat, sensitivity to marital togetherness is intensified. One example of a destabilizing triangle is a husband who is thinking of leaving his marriage to be with his new girlfriend. Another example is the couple mentioned in previous text. The wife's involvement with her sister may be more destabilizing when the husband becomes more stressed in his work, and he wants more attention from his wife than she is willing to give. He then starts to complain to his wife about her always being with her sister. Another way the triangle may be destabilizing occurs when the wife's sister begins to encourage the wife to get out of her marriage, and the wife becomes more irritable or distant with her husband.

FACTORS CONTRIBUTING TO TRIANGLING IN MARRIAGE

Instinctual Inheritance

Triangles are a part of the natural world. The pair bond's primary function in nature is to create a triangle—to produce viable offspring. In some species the pair bond is the most adaptive unit for reproduction. This is two coming together to produce a third. The pair bond is also an adaptation to face threat in the environment. One example is the klipspringer, a small antelope-like animal in Africa. The male and female are seldom more than five meters from each other in order to protect themselves and their offspring from potential predators (Dunbar, 1984). The two are brought together against a third. Polygamous animals form triangles for the same purposes— reproducing, promoting viability of the young, protecting each other from threat, and acquiring food and shelter. The programming for triangles has a deep evolutionary history.

The Multigenerational Family

Each multigenerational family has a history of marital triangling. That history influences the patterns of triangling for each individual. The grandparents, aunts, uncles, cousins, parents, siblings, and stepfamily members have enacted various types of triangling—problems with families of origin or stepfamilies; over focus on children and child problems; affairs; or over involvement with religious institutions, politics, or community activities or helpers. Each pattern contributes to a predisposed mind-set about how to relate to the children, family of origin, outside relationships and sexuality, and religious and community involvement. For instance, a multigenerational family with a pronounced involvement in politics may create a mind-set that over emphasizes community service and sleights the marital relationship or the self. A research example of the multigenerational influence on patterns of triangles comes from the first five years of a research study of newly developing nuclear families (Klever, 2004). Child dysfunction in the newly developing nuclear families was associated with the level of child dysfunction in the multigenerational family. The level of child dysfunction in these multigenerational and nuclear family triangles reflected the degree of immaturity or undifferentiation that was expressed in child focus or child triangling. Couples from multigenerational families with high levels of child problems tended to have children with a greater number of problems or more severe problems, as compared with couples from multigenerational families with low levels of child problems. Those couples tended to have children with fewer problems.

Lack of Self-Regulation and Need for Other-Regulation

Emotional self-regulation is more possible when one's thinking and emotional processes are integrated, or when one has access to cognitive resources in the midst of emotionally intense situations. This integration of thinking and emotion reflects a high level of differentiation. A lack of self-regulation occurs when emotional process takes over and cognitive functioning is inhibited or flooded. Some examples are impulsiveness, compulsiveness, distancing, obsessing, rigidity, indecisiveness, freezing, depression, aggressiveness, or hyperactivity. With less self-regulation, people are more dependent on relationships to manage their discomfort or emotionality. Spouses with less self-regulation demonstrate more mutual regulation. With mutual regulation the spouse's emotional state is more dependent on his or her perception of the partner's facial expression, tone of voice, mood, appearance, approval, accommodation, sameness, directiveness, financial success, health, or physical presence. For dissatisfied couples in conflict, a husband's and wife's physiological reactivity is regulated more by the partner's behavior than by the self (Gottman, 1994). The paradox of mutual regulation in marriage is that the more a spouse depends on the partner to manage internal emotional states, the less reliable the partner is over time in effectively regulating the spouse. This pattern leads to seeking a third party to help handle one's internal state. This process often is not in the individual's conscious awareness.

Marital Distance

The more fused a husband and wife are with each other, the more difficult it is for the couple to openly discuss differences and emotional issues. Although all marriages manage their fusion with some combination of distance, overaccommodation, conflict, blame, and defensiveness, marriages with more emotional fusion demonstrate these patterns with more intensity. These patterns make it more difficult to discuss or do problem solving with personal or marital concerns. Marital distance promotes triangling, and triangling promotes marital distance. With marital distance usually one or both spouses turn to a third party for involvement. This may range from going out drinking with the guys five nights a week to complaining about one's spouse to one's mother.

Spouse Focus

Almost all couples come into therapy with a focus on their partner's problems. A spouse knows clearly what his or her partner does that he or she finds aggravating, but is usually less clear what the partner is up against in being married to himself or herself. Seeing the problem primarily in the partner, and not in the relationship, or in self promotes triangling. When the partner is seen as the problem and difficult to be with, a spouse often searches for someone who is relaxed, fun, and comfortable. The following are common comments in clinical sessions: "I don't have problems in any of my other relationships." "The children and I enjoy each other. My spouse is no fun." "My parents and sister talk openly with me just fine, but he never opens up to me." The implication is that the problem is with the spouse and not in self or the marriage.

Unclear Principles or Standards for Outside Relationships

People have clearly defined principles and standards for self, marriage, and other relationships at high levels of differentiation. Standards are less clear with less differentiation of self. Having a set of well-reasoned standards is an aid to directing the self with relationship pressures and internal turmoil. For example, when a parent is overinvolved with a child, he or she is usually under-responsible for self and to the marriage. When a spouse has attending to one's own well-being and to the health of the marriage as his or her standard, child-focus is reduced. Another example is being clear about the boundaries in work relationships, friendships, community involvement, and family of origin relationships. In a clinical session, the author asked a man who had been unfaithful, "What is your standard for fidelity? And how did you come to that value?" He responded, "I've always been taught that infidelity is wrong, but I've never thought about why it's wrong. I guess I thought as long as my wife never found out, it didn't hurt anybody." His comments reflected the lack of a reasoned standard for fidelity in his marriage.

Stress

Increased stress increases the vulnerability of a marriage to having more intense triangling. A relatively stable marriage can be destabilized with an increase in stress. For example, Mr. and Mrs. Borne had been married for ten years when she had an affair. They reported that during most of the ten years the marriage was open and positive with occasional tension about parenting. In the ninth year of marriage, Mrs. Borne's father was diagnosed with cancer. Mrs. Borne's role with her parents was to mediate their conflict, which increased after the cancer diagnosis. Mrs. Borne felt overwhelmed with her parents' problems and more irritated with her husband. She reported being flirtatious at work as an escape from her problems and feeling less in control of her attractions now that she was overwhelmed. This emotional pattern, driven in part by the increased stress, contributed to her acting on her sexual impulses with a co-worker.

COMMON MARITAL TRIANGLES

The Family of Origin

Marriage begins as a triangle. Every new spouse has some degree of unresolved attachment with his or her parents (Bowen, 1978). The unresolved attachment is the inability to be a separate individual while being involved with one's parents. This is expressed in various ways—an "independent" distance, cutoff, accommodation to keep the peace, concern about the parent's approval, rebellion or polarization with the parent, efforts to change the parent, contempt, idealization, inability to see weaknesses, worry, anger, financial support, unnecessary caretaking, or sympathy (Klever, 2003). The parent and adult child often involve the adult child's spouse in managing the unresolved attachment. In turn, the emotional intensity of a marriage makes the husband and wife vulnerable to triangling in the parents as a third party in their marriage.

The spouse gets drawn into a triangle with the partner's parents in several ways. First, the marriage itself may be a way the adult child attempts to take a more outside position with his or her parents. Although marriage contributes to a shift in the primary triangle, at lower levels of differentiation the individual clings to the new spouse to attempt to pull out of the stuck togetherness with the parents, or the new spouse is adopted into the family fusion. Second, the spouse may unwittingly step in to deal with the in-laws, while the partner relates passively or ineffectively with his or her parents.

This often creates conflict between the spouse and the partner's parents and between the couple. The partner and his or her parents may stay relatively calm. The level of fusion in the parent-adult child relationship sets the blue print for the level of fusion in the marriage.

How the spouse becomes a third party of the partner-parent relationship and how the parents become a third party for the marital relationship varies. The following are some configurations of the triangle with a couple and their parents.

The Bad Parents and the "Stuck Together" Couple

One way for handling the unresolved attachment between the parents and adult children is to overtly cut off. The adult child and his or her spouse initially hold on to each other to get away from the "bad, evil, sick, dysfunctional, crazy, or toxic" parents. The following is an example of such a triangle.

Mr. and Mrs. Wilson reported that they fell in love with each other because they had so much in common and really understood each other. They both came from "dysfunctional families" with mental illness, divorces, instability, and an inability to have any personal relationship. They believed that they had finally found someone who would love them and help them escape from their "sick" families. This marriage was formed with the parents rigidly on the outside and the couple in an intense fusion. As Bowen theory predicts, this "positive" fusion was difficult to sustain. Their tight togetherness began to unravel within the first year of marriage with the stress of his work travel and their heavy dependence on each other. They became more and more distant with increasingly critical thoughts of the other, which was the same way they handled their emotional sensitivity with their original families. Three years into their marriage, Mr. and Mrs. Wilson initiated consultation for marital tension related to another marital triangle. Mr. Wilson had a "one night stand" and Mrs. Wilson consequently contracted a sexually transmitted disease. In clinical consultation they had an aversion to examining the triangle with their parents and saw little hope in dealing with the distrust and distance that had developed in the marriage. The couple terminated the consultation after six sessions and filed for divorce.

The Good Parents and the Distant, Tense Marriage

Mr. and Mrs. Denner, who had been married for one year, initiated clinical consultation due to marital tension. Mr. Denner saw his wife as more loving and attentive to her parents, sisters, nieces, and nephews than to him.

In addition, he was upset that she was not warmer to his family. The couple had sex once every three months, and she pulled away whenever he initiated a discussion about a tense issue. Mrs. Denner saw her husband and his family as confrontational. She wished that her husband would not be so sensitive to her moods and relationships with her family. She said, "I have to be nice to my family, and with you I can be myself and show my true moods."

Mr. Denner and his parents had a fairly high degree of fusion. He had daily contact with his mother and father. Whenever he had a stressor during his day, he would call his mother to talk with her and ask her to help him with his feelings. When the clinician asked him, "What thoughts do you use yourself to help you with your stresses?" He looked wide-eyed at the clinician and said, "I don't have any thoughts I use to handle my stress. I've always relied on my conversations with my mother or a friend to help me." He went on to say that his wife was not as receptive as his mother to his need to discuss problems. His family often argued and resolved hurt feelings within minutes.

Mrs. Denner felt very close to her family. They never argued or discussed anything that might upset the other person. They understood her and gave support to her in a way her husband could not. She had daily contact with her father and mother. She said she was a "daddy's girl" and would do almost anything to please him.

This couple's unresolved attachment to their families of origin sustained the spouses' outside position in the triangle. The degree of Mr. and Mrs. Denner's dependence on the family of origin made it difficult to emotionally self-regulate or to contain emotional issues within the marriage. They each doubted that the other could help with each one's anxiety. Distancing from the families of origin was not the solution. Such a move would have placed more demands on the marriage than either spouse knew how to handle. A more productive direction developed through clinical consultation was for the spouses to develop more abilities to emotionally self-regulate, to begin to reduce their emotional dependencies on their families, and to be more self-defined and less reactive with each other.

The In-Law Problem

From the beginning of the marriage Mr. and Mrs. Moore went weekly for Sunday dinner at Mr. Moore's parents' home. Mrs. Moore soon tired of the weekly obligation and her father-in-law's regular critical comments and racial slurs. She occasionally confronted her father-in-law about his comments, which triggered his indignation and her husband's anger at Mrs. Moore for "rocking the boat." When she tried to talk about it with her husband, he defended his parents and said he did not want to hurt their feelings by not going to the weekly dinners. Mrs. Moore saw her husband putting his parents ahead of her. Mr. Moore saw his wife as being hard to get along with and uncooperative. They fought about this regularly, followed by distance. Mr. Moore saw Mrs. Moore as mean in these interactions which quickly overwhelmed him.

Mr. Moore's unresolved attachment with his parents manifested in a duty-bound, superficial relationship. The thought of talking personally with his parents made him anxious. He anticipated his father's anger and defensiveness and his mother's hurt and withdrawal. This anticipation stirred his feelings of guilt and immobilized him. He tended to silently feel sorry for and sympathetic to his mother and intimidated by his father, while Mr. Moore's sister affiliated with her father and was distant with her mother.

Mrs. Moore, in spite of the tension with her in-laws, communicated more with them than her husband did. After several years of marriage, she saw that her husband was not going to do anything about her concern, so she began occasionally to cancel their Sunday obligation. Although Mrs. Moore characterized her relationships with her parents as more open than Mr. Moore with his parents, there were limitations. For instance, ten years into Mrs. Moore's marriage, her mother stated that she could not handle Mrs. Moore's emotional upset about problems in her life. So Mrs. Moore stopped talking about her struggles with her mother. This was a key loss of support for Mrs. Moore.

In contrast to the three previously described couples, triangles in highly differentiated families show flexibility and the unresolved attachment is hardly noticeable. The husband and wife have achieved a relatively mature separation with each of their parents before the marriage, and the new spouse is not caught in the partner's relationship with his or her parents. In addition, the husband and wife contain most of their emotional reactivity within the marriage, and do not bring the parents into their emotional issues unless the anxiety is unusually high. This does not mean that the parents or husband and wife never talk about their marriages or their relationships with each other. Instead they are open with the third party listening and responding more neutrally to the issues between the twosome. Sides are not taken and the third party puts the issue back to the appropriate twosome.

Children

When a couple is less open and/or unable to address differences effectively, the husband or wife often diverts extra energy and involvement to the children. The emotional connection may be stronger with a child than with the spouse. Sometimes the couple comes together in their focus on the children. This may stabilize the marriage as long as they can cooperatively focus on the children. More often, a parent and one child are together with the other parent on the outside. Mothers tend to be on the inside position with the children, while fathers are prone to be on the outside. However, the father may develop a togetherness with one child while the mother develops a special relationship with another child. The inside position of the parent-child may be calm and cozy or intensely conflictual. The triangle with the wife and child on the inside and the husband on the outside can be a fairly stable triangle as long as the husband and wife are content with their marital distance. The marriage becomes more threatened when the husband or wife is dissatisfied with his or her lack of connection, the child starts to separate from the mother, or the child moves closer to the father.

Marital Togetherness Destabilized with the Addition of a Child

Mr. and Mrs. Peel described their first five years of marriage as being "joined at the hip." They did everything together when they could, and they thoroughly enjoyed each other. When they had a child in the fifth year of their marriage, this marital togetherness changed. Mrs. Peel put most of her emotional energy into her child. Mr. Peel felt resentful of all the attention the child received and missed the good times with his wife. When he complained about this, his wife dismissed him as being immature. Mrs. Peel thought he would grow out of this and eventually adjust. This was the first time in their marriage that they had conflict. Their marriage grew increasingly distant. When the child was two years old, Mr. Peel started an affair with a woman at work. The couple came for consultation when the child was three years old, and they were in the eighth year of their marriage. Mr. Peel had moved out and proceeded to divorce his wife.

Marital Togetherness Stabilized with Children

Mr. and Mrs. Phillips married with the goal of having children. They spent the first twenty-five years of their marriage devoted to their children and not each other. Parenting was the primary topic of conversation. The couple had no activities they shared with each other except their children's activities. When the couple went to the theater, the husband fell asleep. When they played golf together, the wife was bored. Their conversations about the children were engaged, energized, and connected. However, if Mr. Phillips discussed problems he was having in his work, his wife was opinionated and he withdrew. If Mrs. Phillips talked about a book she was reading or a feeling she had about a friend, Mr. Phillips acted disinterested. When the children left home, the marital distance was more apparent, and Mr. Phillips developed cancer. Hopeless about connecting with his wife, Mr. Phillips had an affair and separated from his wife during his cancer treatment. Unable to address their emotional distance, several years later Mr. and Mrs. Phillips divorced.

The Wife and Child on the Inside and the Husband on the Outside

Mr. and Mrs. Moore, who were described in an earlier section, struggled with five years of infertility. During that time Mrs. Moore said that Mr. Moore was unsupportive. He was ambivalent about having children, while she was driven to be a parent. She had always imagined herself as a mother. She was elated when she finally had her first child. At that time Mr. Moore was absorbed in significant work problems and continued to experience chronic episodes of depression. Dissatisfied with her marriage, Mrs. Moore threw herself into raising her new daughter. Within the first several years she began to suspect something was wrong with her daughter. Mrs. Moore was outgoing and emotionally expressive, and her daughter was withdrawn and extremely shy. Though the daughter was bright in school, she was isolated from her peer group, which caused great worry for Mrs. Moore. With great intensity Mrs. Moore would talk about this worry with her husband. He would polarize with positive comments about his daughter Cathy, tell his wife that she was overreacting, say that his daughter was shy just like him, and implored her "not to worry." This infuriated Mrs. Moore, and they would erupt into a verbal battle, followed by their retreat. Later Mrs. Moore tried to bring her husband out of his withdrawal, but to no avail. This pattern repeated several times a week through most of the daughter's growing up.

Affairs and Outside Relationships

Personal relationships outside the marriage can be the sign of a strong marriage, especially if the couple has an open, personal relationship with each other. When the couple is distant or estranged, personal relationships outside the marriage can be stabilizing or destabilizing. Some couples maintain a comfortable distance with each other by having separate friends with whom they play or talk personally and openly. This type of triangle becomes more reactive when one of the spouses desires more marital connection, the friend is of the opposite sex, or the spouse and friend have a sexual attraction.

Several factors contribute to a couple being vulnerable to an affair. Affairs are rooted in an individual's and couple's undifferentiation, or their need for another to provide fulfillment, and the inability to moderate yearnings for an emotional or sexual connection. A perception of marital distance or a shift in the marital togetherness is another key variable. One is more susceptible to an affair the more one manages anxiety and uncertainty through a sexual or emotional connection with a partner. One step in this susceptibility is regularly turning to sexual fantasy about a particular person to manage anxiety. Another step in setting up this triangle is regularly flirting with others in person or over the Internet. A multigenerational history of infidelity and an unclear value system about marital faithfulness may also contribute to this type of marital triangle. The author found in a clinical sample of seventy couples with infidelity as the presenting problem that 40 percent had a parent who had also had an affair. Affairs also seem to be more prevalent during times of higher stress.

Mr. and Mrs. Houser and the Other Woman

Mr. and Mrs. Houser "fell in love" immediately with each other, courted for three months, and then married. This was their second marriage, and they believed that this marriage was very different from their first dysfunctional marriages. After two years of marriage, Mrs. Houser was depressed from stress at work. She became more irritable, withdrawn, and sexually unavailable to her husband. Mr. Houser felt frantic about the loss of attention from his wife. He started to confide in a woman at work and soon developed a sexual relationship with her. In the first consultation session with the couple, Mr. Houser said, "I'm an attention hound. I cannot live without attention from a woman. When I saw that my wife couldn't give me attention, I knew I had to get it from somewhere." The high degree of fusion in this couple helps to illustrate the basic factors in an affair—the underlying marital fusion, the shift in togetherness with the wife's depression, the need for the other, the lack of clear values or self-definition about fidelity, and the increase in stress. Although the degree of fusion in this couple was quite high, these variables are applicable as well to couples with less fusion.

Triangling with the Community

Couples sometimes involve the community in their marital turmoil. This may be neighbors, religious institutions, clergy, political organizations, service groups, mental health providers, or the legal system. These third parties vary in their ability to see the systemic nature of marital problems and to respond neutrally. Community helpers are especially vulnerable to marital triangling. Clergy, faith communities, mental health professionals, and the legal system can easily get caught taking sides, especially when moral issues such as infidelity are involved, or when one of the spouses has a diagnosable problem, such as depression, alcoholism, compulsive spending, or criminal behavior.

When Helpers Take Sides

Mrs. Elder asked Mr. Elder to separate after he relapsed back to drinking, viewing Internet pornography, and engaging in dominating behavior. Mrs. Elder had a concentrated focus on Mr. Elder as the problem. This had been her perspective for many years. Her individual therapist and minister both focused on Mr. Elder's psychopathology or "brokenness" and offered her support in dealing with her troubled, lost, and destructive husband. Her minister prayed with her for her husband's healing and recovery. Although the helpers' support to Mrs. Elder was helpful in relieving her anxiety about the marriage, it promoted a one-sided view of the interplay in the marriage. The missing systems perspective was that Mrs. Elder was indecisive and passive in dealing with her husband, which encouraged Mr. Elder's take charge position in the marriage. She was then usually critical of whatever direction he set. She regularly made efforts to block Mr. Elder's relationship with the children and turned to her family of origin for her primary support. In the outside position, Mr. Elder handled his frustration with his wife with angry outbursts and withdrawal into compulsive behavior.

THE CLINICAL WORK WITH MARITAL TRIANGLES

Assessing Marital Triangles

The assessment of marital triangles is an assessment of the couple's involvement with each other and with outside relationships. The first step is assessing the marital patterns of emotional reactivity—distance, conflict, over/underfunctioning, and triangling. Components examined are the degree of openness and self-awareness, time spent together, ability to discuss differences and emotional issues, degree of defensiveness, intensity of conflict, ability to listen, physical affection and sex, and the mind-set about self and the partner (Klever, 1998). The history of the marriage and its emotional patterns are also part of the assessment.

The next step is assessing involvement in outside relationships—family of origin, friends, children, affairs, and community resources. During an

initial session often one of the spouses highlights a problematic triangle—
an affair, a husband who is uninvolved with the children, or a meddling
mother-in-law. Although couples do not complain about triangles that tend
to stabilize the marriage, they are also useful to assess. Some questions that
probe the triangle are these: "How does the amount and quality of time with
your spouse compare to your time with your children, friends, family, syna-
gogue, or your affair?" "Do you have a more personal relationship with
someone other than your spouse? Who?" "Generally, who do you think
most about—yourself, your spouse, your mother, your children, your affair? When you think about each person, what is the nature of your
thoughts?" From these and other assessment questions, an assessment of inside and outside positions in the triangle can be established.

Developing Understanding About Triangling As Emotional Process

Triangling is one of the ways threat is managed in the human and other
animals. In the human this automatic process may be modified or moderated
through self-awareness and cognitive understanding of the process. Consistent detriangling requires a new way of thinking. Clinical work based on
differentiation of self promotes the employment of thinking in the face of
real or perceived threat. Understanding of triangling is developed through
the couple's observations and heightened self-awareness. The couple's observations of their thoughts, feelings, and behaviors are the data from which
the clinician and couple learn about the couple's process. When the initial assessment is sufficiently complete, and when the couple's anxiety is reduced
so they can hear; the clinician can then begin to teach the theoretical concept of the triangle. As the triangle is a part of life, most people easily understand the concept, but integrating the understanding into one's behavior is
a more difficult task. The clinician also models detriangling by developing a
one-to-one relationship with each spouse, maintaining neutrality about the
content, and acting from a systems understanding about the couple.

Managing Emotionality Within Self and Within the Marriage

The triangle forms to handle the perceived threat in self and in a relationship. Learning to manage individual and couple emotionality is the work of
differentiating a self—maintaining the ability to think objectively in the
midst of emotional processes and sustaining a separate self in the midst of
relationship pressures. Increased differentiation of self reduces the need to
involve others in managing individual and relationship anxieties. This is not

pretending to not need others or managing emotionality through distance. Some examples of clinical questions are these: "How could you guide yourself through your upset?" "What internal resources can help you?" "What are the plusses and minuses in complaining about your husband to your sister?" "What would be ways to handle your marital frustrations other than to get more involved with your girlfriend, son, priest, mother, sibling, or another significant person?" With increased differentiation, the self and the couple can work through, contain, and deal with the emotionality of life through mature living, clear thinking, and open discussions that are not overridden with emotional reactivity. As the self and couple take responsibility for their emotional process, they can and do talk openly with others about themselves with less dependence and without putting their anxiety into other relationships. No couple is without dependencies on others, but at higher levels of differentiation the dependence is less and is dealt with more maturely.

Relating to Third Parties Responsibly

Marriages do not function in isolation. The spouses each have a relationship history and usually function in a network of family and/or community relationships. These relationships, past and present, influence the marriage; and the marriage influences how each spouse relates to the family and community. When the marriage is cut off from outside relationships, the marriage is more intense and emotionally reactive. When one or both spouses are over involved with others, one of the spouses is put in an outside position. When the marriage is more dysfunctional, the spouses distribute the anxiety into relationships with the larger family, friends, and/or community. The clinical work with marital problems usually includes the husband and wife developing more responsible relationships with third parties. After one understands his or her position in the interlocking triangles, he or she works to develop mature one-to-one relationships with others instead of relationships driven by the emotional forces of the triangle. For spouses who get overinvolved with someone outside the marriage, the clinical work may be focused on developing clearer boundaries in such areas as flirting, engaging in sexual contact, talking about one's spouse's personal information, and turning to one's children for primary emotional support.

Clinical Management of the Marital Triangle

One of the clinician's challenges with couple problems is managing the marital triangle. Couples are usually sensitive to the clinician's relationships with each partner. Each is monitoring whose side the clinician is taking. The couple watches with whom the clinician talks more, makes more eye contact, smiles or laughs with more. In addition, attention is paid to whose side the clinician takes on content issues—excessive spending, sexual distance, a verbally abusive mother-in-law, or yelling at children. The couple is assessing, "Does the clinician agree with me or my partner?" During a wife's description of a fight with her husband, she referred to a zucchini fritatta she had made that her husband rejected. The clinician gave a slight chuckle because of a huge sack of zucchini in his own refrigerator that needed to be dealt with. When the husband presented his view of the fight he said, "My rejecting the zucchini fritatta wasn't so unreasonable because even you [the clinician] chuckled when she talked about it. Obviously, you wouldn't have eaten it either." The following are some examples of subtle or direct invitations for the clinician to take sides (Klever, 1998):

- a wink of the eye, a look, a smile or frown, as if to say, "We know what's really going on here";
- a funny story of the "incompetent" spouse that draws the therapist into laughing with the "competent" spouse;
- flattery for the therapist or being a "good" patient who is motivated to apply theory, while the spouse could not care less; and
- directly saying or asking, "Obviously, our marriage was doing fine until she had an affair. You do not think it's okay for a wife to be unfaithful, do you?" or "I have thought more about what you said last time about the distance in the marriage. I would agree that my husband's inability to communicate has been the main problem" or "I am wondering how you and I can help my husband with his problem with anger."

Managing the triangle effectively, means maintaining contact with both spouses if both are involved in a session, staying focused on process rather than content, and maintaining a keen awareness of the dynamic of the triangle throughout therapy. When the clinician is thinking systemically and monitoring his or her emotional reactivity, neutrality and detriangling are automatic, and the course of therapy takes a more thoughtful direction.

The Clinician's Fusion with the Couple

Every clinician has a life experience with marriage or partner relationships and a legacy about marriage from his or her multigenerational family.

This emotional programming affects the clinician's inclination to take sides with a couple. It is useful for the clinician to know and understand his or her internal mind-set about marital relationships and his or her position with the parents' marriage(s). A clinician brings to the clinical couple those patterns of emotional reactivity, unless the clinician has worked on a more differentiated understanding and response to his or her parents' marriage, marriages in his or her family, and his or her own marriage. For instance, if a clinician is especially close to her kind, nonconfrontational father, and conflictual and distant with her dominating mother, then she might tend to feel more positively about husbands and negatively toward wives, especially with "peace-agree" husbands and confrontational wives. Another example is a clinician whose wife is having an affair. He might find it hard to sustain a neutral position toward unfaithful spouses in his clinical practice. A clinician is more likely to manage his or her emotional reactivity when he is applying a systems framework to his or her own personal relationships, working on his or her one-to-one family relationships and staying as detriangled as possible with his or her family. For example, the clinician with the kind father and dominating mother can get more neutral about her parents' marriage, when she sees how each of her parents contribute to the marital tension. Her father's kindness avoids conflict and influences her mother's irritability. Her mother's irritability contributes to the father's distance.

CLINICAL EXAMPLE

The Moore Family

The two problematic triangles for the Moore family were described in earlier sections. One was Mr. Moore, Mrs. Moore, and their daughter Cathy. The second one was Mr. Moore, Mrs. Moore, and Mr. Moore's parents. This section describes the process of detriangling in each triangle. Figure 10.1 is the Moore family diagram.

The Triangle with the Daughter

Three general directions guided the couple in addressing this triangle. One was for Mrs. Moore to slow down her focus on and anxiety about her daughter. She believed something was very wrong with her daughter, and that helping the daughter was up to Mrs. Moore because her husband was "out of touch" with the daughter. Mrs. Moore blamed her teenage daughter's depres-

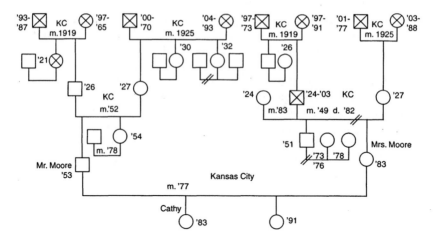

FIGURE 10.1. The Moore Family Diagram

sion and shyness on Mr. Moore's distant relationship with Cathy. One step in slowing down her overinvolvement was seeing her daughter's depression and social isolation as being related in part to Mrs. Moore's anxious focus on her daughter. She understood this intellectually within the first three months of consultation. However, to begin to apply this knowledge took nine more months. During those months she observed herself continuing to obsessively worry and to automatically pursue her daughter with suggestions and questions to ensure the daughter's happiness and day-to-day success with friends. Mrs. Moore also observed her daughter continuing to isolate from her peer group, withdraw from Mrs. Moore, and act sad and irritable. In consultation she discussed these "failures" and alternative ways of thinking about and responding to her daughter's struggles. One day Mrs. Moore "got it." She saw what to do and how to think differently in the "emotional moment" when her daughter expressed dejection. Instead of rushing in to help her daughter, she made a brief, neutral comment. After that shift, Mrs. Moore's anxiety about her daughter was somewhat reduced and her flexibility in response increased.

A second direction for the triangle was Mr. Moore developing his one-to-one relationship with his daughter. He seldom, if ever, had a personal conversation with her. She likewise rebuffed his ineffective efforts to interact with her. Cathy had many of the same critical views of her father that Mrs. Moore had of her husband. Mr. Moore began to make a more consistent effort to talk with and listen to Cathy. As she would continue to frequently give him one-word answers or roll her eyes, he worked to slow his usual distancing reaction.

The third and most pivotal relationship in the triangle was the marriage. The goal was for Mr. and Mrs. Moore to establish a more personal relationship, slow their reactivity with each other, and reduce their polarity about their daughter. Their reactivity limited their level of openness. When Mrs. Moore was worried, upset, or frustrated, she would express herself with an edgy intensity. Mr. Moore immediately felt flooded with anxiety and anger. He pulled away or responded with defensiveness and critical comments such as, "Why do you have to get so upset?" "Stop being so negative about Cathy!" Mrs. Moore would then say, "I'm trying to tell you what I'm feeling. Why can't you listen to me!" The interaction would often escalate into mutual put-downs and name calling with Mr. Moore withdrawing into a depressed state for several days of not talking, which infuriated Mrs. Moore. Occasionally at the peak of her anger, Mrs. Moore would hit her husband. She was tired of spending years trying to bring Mr. Moore out of his shell and saying things so he would not get upset, which felt like being a mother to her husband.

Several shifts occurred after months of repeating their cycle. First, Mr. and Mrs. Moore started to curb the put-downs and name calling. Second, the thinking each had about the other was challenged in the clinical consultation. Each saw the other as being the primary contributor to Cathy's problems. Over time they began to see that the problem was not only in the other, but also in their individual and marital reactivity. They also saw that efforts to criticize or change the spouse's parenting were futile, disrespectful, and a significant contribution to the family reactivity. This new way of thinking eventually helped to decrease their reactivity with each other. A third element was Mr. and Mrs. Moore developing an understanding of how anxiety was expressed in themselves and in their relationships. This understanding of triangles helped to reduce blaming and to improve one-to-one relationships. Another part of the shift was each developing more acceptance and understanding of the other. Mrs. Moore developed more acceptance of her husband's withdrawal and lack of initiative, and Mr. Moore grew to understand that his distancing and his wife's overt intensity were both forms of emotional reactivity.

The Triangle with Mr. Moore's Parents

Mr. and Mrs. Moore developed three directions for dealing with this triangle. One was for Mrs. Moore to step out of being the primary link between

Mr. Moore and his parents. When Mrs. Moore saw how she was involved in the unresolved attachment between her husband and his parents, she more easily relinquished her "connector" position. She reduced the frequency of telling her husband and his parents about each other. She saw how much of a burden she had taken on for her husband's relationship with his parents.

A second direction was for Mr. Moore to address his unresolved attachment with his parents. He developed a clearer understanding of his pattern of accommodation and avoidance of conflictual and emotional issues. He also understood how he saw his parent's marriage through his mother's eyes and not from his father's perspective. He began to see how both his parents contributed to their marital tension. He did several things to cope with the overwhelmingly anxious feeling he had with his father and mother. Mr. Moore and his father had weekly superficial luncheons with each other, which had the potential to be a forum for more personal one-to-one interactions. Mr. Moore first practiced in clinical consultation what he might say to his father during these luncheons to define more of a self and examined how to handle his anxiety. When he began to be more open with his father, he made note cards to remember what he wanted to say, because without them he knew he would lose his thoughts.

Two issues in particular provided fodder for Mr. Moore's openness with his father. One issue was Mrs. Moore, and the other was Cathy's problems. Mr. Moore's father felt sorry for Mr. Moore in having to deal with such a difficult wife, and his father blamed Mrs. Moore for the strained relationships in the family. Before Mr. Moore began clinical consultation, he had never responded to his father when he made critical comments about Mrs. Moore. Internally Mr. Moore tended to agree with his father's position that Mrs. Moore was a difficult person and had caused much family tension. When Mr. Moore understood that a key part of the tension was the unresolved attachment between his parents and himself, as well as his marital distance, he could see a new way of addressing his father's criticalness. He started to make comments to his father about strengths in his marriage and his shortcomings as a husband. Mr. Moore also talked with his father about how he had been afraid to disagree with his father due to his strong opinions and Mr. Moore's desire to not upset the relationship.

A second issue that Mr. Moore addressed with his father was his daughter Cathy. Mr. Moore's father was critical of their parenting of Cathy, which caused Mr. Moore to doubt his parenting decisions and especially to doubt his wife's leadership in parenting. Mr. Moore had seldom defined his position about parenting with his father, so Mr. Moore began to define his view of parenting to his father. To reduce Mr. Moore's anxiety with this step meant reducing his need for his father's approval and accepting their differences of opinion. Mr. Moore also broadened the lens by discussing aunts, grand-parents, and cousins who were shy and eccentric, who had committed suicide, and who had been diagnosed with schizophrenia, bipolar disorder, and depression.

The third direction was for Mr. and Mrs. Moore to continue to address their marital reactivity. Mr. Moore reduced his criticism of Mrs. Moore's relationship with his family, and Mrs. Moore reduced her criticism of Mr. Moore's family and his relationship with them. This was again based on a new way of thinking about the triangle—that each party made a contri-bution to the progression or regression in each of the relationships, and that taking responsible action for self was more mature than trying to change or criticize the other. These changes were mixed with old patterns. With emo-tional triggers related to Mr. Moore's parents, Mr. and Mrs. Moore's critical thoughts and comments about each other and his parents resurfaced.

The work that Mr. and Mrs. Moore did on themselves in each relation-ship had a ripple effect throughout the family. As Mr. Moore took on more responsibility for his relationship with his parents and daughter, his wife re-laxed somewhat and the marriage improved. As Mrs. Moore became less the connector between Mr. Moore and his parents, they began to connect more with each other. As Mrs. Moore developed some emotional separation from her daughter, Mr. Moore was less critical of his wife. As the couple became less reactive with each other and other family members, Mr. and Mrs. Moore began to discuss and pursue their personal goals. This couple observed themselves in these interlocking, intergenerational triangles. This approach broadened their scope for understanding the problem and for de-veloping a plan to make a difference.

CONCLUSION

All marriages develop in a web of family and community relationships. The clinical goal is to promote mature one-to-one relationships that do not undermine the marriage, but help promote a more differentiated marriage and self. This requires spouses to think systemically, to be responsible in managing their emotional reactivity through integration of their thinking and emotion, and to sustain a self in the midst of relationship pressures. This clinical process also requires the clinician to think systemically and to apply this understanding in his or her own family relationships.

REFERENCES

Bowen, M. (1978). *Family therapy in clinical practice*. New York: Jason Aronson.

Dunbar, R. (1984). The ecology of monogamy. *New Scientist, 103,* 12-15.

Gottman, J. M. (1994). *What predicts divorce?* Hillsdale, NJ: Lawrence Erlbaum Associates.

Kerr, M. E. and Bowen, M. (1988). *Family evaluation.* New York: W.W. Norton and Company.

Klever, P. (1998). Marital fusion and differentiation. In P. Titelman (Ed.), *Clinical applications of Bowen family systems theory* (pp. 119-145). Binghamton, NY: The Haworth Press.

Klever, P. (2003). Marital functioning and multigenerational fusion and cutoff. In P. Titelman (Ed.), *Emotional cutoff: Bowen family systems theory perspectives* (pp. 219-243). Binghamton, NY: The Haworth Press.

Klever, P. (2004). The multigenerational transmission of nuclear family processes and symptoms. *The American Journal of Family Therapy, 32*(4), 337-352.

Papero, D. V. (1990). *Bowen family systems theory.* Boston, MA: Allyn and Bacon.

Chapter 11

Child Focus: Triangles That Come and Stay

Eva Louise Rauseo

INTRODUCTION

Anxiety is contagious. Humans generally know this. The subtle and not-so-subtle process of passing anxiety among closely related family members is basic to every family. In *child focus* some special conditions appear to narrow that process to a more regular shift of anxiety to one or more offspring in the ever-present triangles. In Bowen theory, this process is described in detail as *the family projection process* (see Kerr and Bowen, 1988, p. 210).

Dr. Bowen described the family projection process in many ways. The importance Dr. Bowen (1978) placed on this process is highlighted with this description of the child-focused family:

> The child-focused family is one in which sufficient family anxiety is focused on one or more children to result in serious impairment in a child. The child-focused energy is deeply imbedded, and it includes the full range of emotional involvements from the most positive to the most negative. (p. 297)

The family projection process takes place in a triangle. A family dealing with chronic anxiety has a number of automatic mechanisms that can reduce anxiety for the moment. Usually, the triangle is the basic mechanism to shift anxiety in an emotional system. It does not rid the system of anxiety but rather shifts it around from one person to the other. This is, for the most part, an automatic process outside of awareness. In the triangle, two who are close and one outsider provide the basic structure in which the dance of anxiety takes place. The jockeying for a place of comfort changes with different levels of anxiety within the triangle.

Focus on a child's life events with worry, praise, or blame often temporarily relieves the anxiety that is chronic for parents dealing with their own poorly defined relationship in the marriage and the original family. Families in which this projection process is most intense and rigid are often described as *child-focused families* (see Donley, 2003). The underlying emotional process is often hidden from the view of family and professionals. Although the parents often present a picture of a loving couple, the process of child focus is commonly inherited from the past and resides in a certain distance in the marriage that eliminates dealing effectively with the real issues that arise in the couple's relationship.

There may be thousands of variations on the themes that families with children encounter in this process of shifting anxiety. In a couple where the intensity of living together is accompanied by sufficient chronic anxiety, the shifting anxiety in the triangle often works to keep the adults' anxiety at a tolerable level. When effective, it allows the couple to continue to live and function in the world, provide necessary resources and care for activities of daily life. If the anxiety exceeds a tolerable level, the family unit becomes disorganized, ordinary tasks are left undone to be taken up by others, and some individuals can become symptomatic.

A natural spot for anxiety in a family unit with adults and children is the worry or preoccupation with a child or children. As described above, this can leave the adults more or less free to handle life's tasks. There are obviously times when the anxiety in the family exceeds a level that can be handled by the triangle(s) in the unit, and many times the symptoms in the child actually add to the overall anxiety in the family. However, the symptoms in the child generally keep the couple focused on the child without the requirement of addressing other issues in the chronic anxiety of their lives.[1]

Back to the Beginning

When two people are married, the unresolved relationships with their parents and their families generally transfer into the new relationship.[2] The

---

[1]Chronic anxiety is higher in families with lower levels of *differentiation of self*. Differentiation of self is a key concept in Bowen theory that defines an individual's ability to be sure of "self" in dealing with the emotional pressure of the most important relationships. It also defines the ability of an individual to integrate both thinking and feeling in response to the challenges of life. Higher levels of differentiation have more flexibility in dealing with anxiety.

[2]The level of differentiation in the new couple will be similar to the level of differentiation achieved by both individuals in their own families. Unresolved relationships represent the amount of undifferentiation to be absorbed in the new family unit.

initial harmony in the marriage often represents the comfort both find in leaving behind the tense and unresolved part of the past. The magic of romance makes it unlikely that either can see the way those relationship processes will be repeated in the marriage. Sooner or later, those unresolved tensions generate sufficient chronic anxiety in the couple, and they use previously learned automatic responses to manage that anxiety on a daily basis. Emotional distance functions as one of the possible automatic mechanisms for dealing with higher anxiety. During a time of distance in the marriage, a child's needs may become an attractive focus for a parent. When the distance becomes chronic, the child's importance to a parent grows greater and greater. The triangle often results with a mother and child in an unusually close relationship and a father distantly critical of the way things are going.

The triangle may shift dramatically when the relationship between mother and child becomes too intense, sometimes manifested by symptoms in the child. Frequently, the mother turns to the father to help relieve the tension. Then the parents are momentarily united in their concern and/or criticism regarding the child. Commonly, the father acts with the mother to try to change the offspring with some version of pleading, threatening, punishing, or directing the change. With this change in the triangle, the child's issue that arose in the intensity of the mother-child relationship is now in focus while the parents unite to solve the *problem*. Then, as the tension is relieved, the triangle will again shift back to its usual spot with mother and child occupying the close/united part of the triangle and the father once again distant.

There is great variation in this process in families where child focus is a major way of responding to both chronic and acute anxiety. The way a child becomes a major participant in the unresolved relationship of the couple can come about in a number of ways:

1. The pregnancy and birth appear to solidify an uncertain bond between husband and wife at a particular time in the marriage making the child especially important to the stability of the marriage.
2. The child is perceived as especially important to one of the spouse's parents.
3. The child comes into the world with (imagined or real) qualities of a parent causing the family to view the child as an extension of one parent.
4. The child is different in any number of ways: features, skin color, handicaps, among other ways, and this often results in overprotection or worry on the part of one or both parents.
5. The child is born around the death of a significant person in the family system with more anxiety evident in relationships with this child.

6. Infertility issues that result in extended treatment or adoption can make the child more important or the parents altogether more anxious to have the perfect child.

There are a number of background processes that influence the intensity of family triangles that result in child focus and symptoms in children. The emotional process in the parental families provides emotional learning that continues into the present and the future. At the same time, a family that is cut off from the emotional connections with the parental family is likely to find the triangles within the nuclear family more intense and rigid. The anxiety in the family then is contained as if in a *pressure cooker* rather than being able to disperse to a larger group. Finally, the level of differentiation and maturity of the parents is a critical factor in the potential for projection of anxiety within the family unit.

An extreme example of the rigid triangle is found when the father is in such an outside position that he does not play a significant role in raising the child. This can intensify and prolong the emotional symbiosis of mother and child.[3] One example is the single parent who is overinvolved with her child during the early years and then is horrified to discover that she has an acting-out adolescent. The parent then often looks for others in the community in place of the father to help her deal with the problems which are *the fault* of the offspring or the distant father. She tries to distance herself from this relationship with her no-longer close child and looks for a close relationship, distancing for the moment from the difficult offspring. This does not resolve the relationship but gives temporary relief to the intensity.

CONSULTATION WITH BOWEN THEORY

Consultation using Bowen theory offers families an opportunity to see themselves as a part of a larger system that has a number of influences on their current functioning. From the larger perspective, a certain percentage of people with significant symptoms in their children may be able to focus on their own process of differentiation in all significant relationships, including the triangles with a difficult, focused child.

---

[3]Emotional symbiosis refers to a relationship in which the functioning of both mother and child are dramatically tied to the relationship. This is a normal condition of infancy and early childhood, but the extent to which it continues through the life of the child is important in determining the level of differentiation and life course of the offspring.

Clearly, the role of the consultant is not to impose a formula from theory but to offer the parent as many tools toward objectivity as possible. To suggest that a mother can stop her worry or focus on a child is a useless exercise. However, a parent who can gradually observe the way his automatic functioning influences the family and note his own vulnerability to the reactivity of others can gradually find a more solid place to stand for *self.*

CLINICAL REPORTS

Three detailed clinical reports will demonstrate more clearly the issues that can be observed in the triangles of child-focused families. The patterns observed can provide a more subtle and complex view of child focus than abstract concepts alone. Figure 11.1 is a key for the process diagrams.

Family A—Divided Loyalties

This clinical example emphasizes a number of different challenges, but the evidence of triangles in managing chronic anxiety is clear in the marriage and in the larger family. The flow of the anxiety from *family of origin* to marriage and to a *focused* child is documented in many instances.

The mother, Mrs. A., describes herself as having grown up with divided loyalties. She describes triangles that existed from the beginning of her life in which she was aware of the competition for her loyalty that existed between her grandmother and her mother. As the youngest of three girls, she

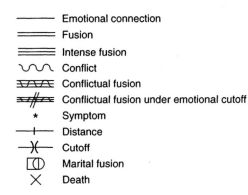

FIGURE 11.1. Key for Process Diagrams

spent a great deal more time with her grandmother, even referring to her as "Mama." Mrs. A.'s mother had been primarily invested in her first child, and by the birth of her third daughter, she had reached a point of giving up on some parts of her role as a mother. Raising children appeared to be less interesting and more difficult than spending time in an active social life with friends. At the same time, her husband's drinking had become a major issue in the life of the family. Although he functioned well in the world, the family life revolved around protecting his reputation and keeping his drinking secret from the world outside. As the youngest child, Mrs. A. was slightly less involved in her mother's anxiety and was free to spend some relaxed time with her father who was a real resource to her. However, the emotional distance from her mother was always a mixed blessing for Mrs. A.

Mrs. A. was always aware of the family anxiety about her older sister with whom she had a very special relationship. This sister was her mentor and probably her idol. This relationship was among the most important in her childhood, and the family anxiety about her sister colored her life. She saw herself generally staying in the shadow of both older sisters in many ways. Figure 11.2 illustrates Mrs. A.'s primary triangles.

When Mrs. A. finished college and chose a mate, her marriage did not fit the social expectations of the family in terms of her husband's education and profession. She was aware that the marriage would create a certain amount of conflict and emotional distance in some parts of the family. In a short time it was also clear that her husband did not get along with her mother, and she was again living with *divided loyalties,* this time between mother and husband. However, the reactivity of her husband to her mother generally permitted Mrs. A. to have a closer relationship with her husband who always took her side in this triangle. Figure 11.3 illustrates Mrs. A.'s in-law triangle.

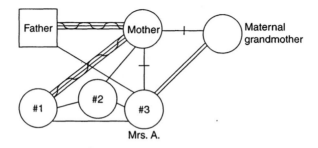

FIGURE 11.2. Mrs. A.: Primary Triangles

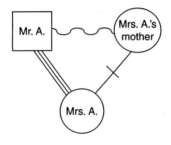

FIGURE 11.3. Mrs. A.: In-Law Triangles

In the early years of marriage, Mrs. A. was happy to pursue her own career goals and enjoyed working before her first pregnancy. About four years after the marriage, Mrs. A. gave birth to their first child, a girl. She recalls feeling very incompetent and overwhelmed with a colicky infant. She quit her job to be more available to the family, but found little relief from this change.

Mr. A. was not much of a caregiver or helper but was anxious for his wife to get beyond the anxiety about her role as mother. Primarily, as his daughter grew into the preschool years, he tried to get this child to do whatever his wife wanted in order to keep his wife calm. In other words, he took sides with his wife in the struggles she had with this difficult child. The wife, on the other hand, was devoted to helping her daughter—in spite of being anxious and overwhelmed much of the time. This tense, energetic daughter could get into a scene with her contemporaries and teachers, fighting her way through preschool and beyond. She could pick a fight almost anywhere and was always seen as an outsider with friends. Her mother naturally wanted to help, but seldom had any idea what to do.

The second child, a son, was born when the daughter was four-years-old. Mr. A. was more attentive to their son. When Mr. A. started traveling more in his work, Mrs. A. was home with more family responsibility. Her anxiety continued to focus primarily on her daughter and she was relatively relaxed with her son. At the same time, she was involved with her husband in his business and was subject to catching the anxiety about the business. Her husband's anxiety generally took the form of criticism of his wife which she recalls as a big factor in her increasing chronic anxiety as a young mother. This anxiety usually took the form of tension and worry about her daughter and about her own ability to be a good mother. Figure 11.4 illustrates Mrs. A.'s child focus.

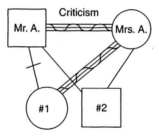

FIGURE 11.4. Mrs. A.: Child Focus

During the early childhood of these offspring, the A. family experienced greatly increased anxiety when Mrs. A.'s father suffered a cerebral vascular accident (CVA) and was somewhat limited for the rest of his life. He was an extremely competent person and the most involved parent for Mrs. A., so his illness was especially difficult for her. During this time, Mrs. A. recalls more problems for her daughter with friends and school. It was also a time of financial uncertainty and that was accompanied by her husband's frequent travels.

Mrs. A.'s father died about ten years after his initial CVA. In the same year, her older sister died in an accident. In that year, Mrs. A. lost two of the most emotionally important people in her original family. Her daughter was fifteen years old. Mrs. A. went through depression, and some of her attention to her daughter was diverted to her own grief. Her daughter continued to have some acting-out issues in school and took refuge in a relationship with a boyfriend who later was discovered to be deeply involved in drugs.

Mr. A. continued to be distant from his daughter except when he felt required to help with his wife's anxiety. Mrs. A. turned to her religious faith to help her deal with the symptoms in the family and her anxiety. It was obvious that her daughter continued to have more serious acting-out symptoms in her first years in college.

One final incident was important in calling attention to the situation. Mrs. A.'s mother had a heart attack and at the same time her daughter went to the hospital emergency room after taking an overdose of aspirin. Both recovered. The chronic and acute anxiety in the family appeared to be bound in the symptoms of mother and daughter, with Mrs. A. clearly involved in the chronic tension in both relationships. Mr. A. continued in his posture of reactivity to his mother-in-law and his partial cutoff from his daughter. Figure 11.5 illustrates the A. family with increasing symptoms.

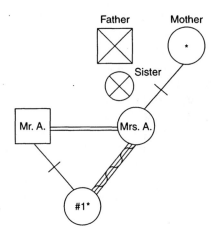

FIGURE 11.5. A. Family: Increasing Symptoms

Clinical Consultation Based on Bowen Theory

Following this incident, the daughter decided to return to study in a local college. Mrs. A. was aware that the symptoms in her daughter were fairly serious. She sought therapy that was based on the study of the family emotional system. Mrs. A. was already aware that she had some part in the tension in the family. She quickly took on the project of studying herself in the relationships. She began to observe the way in which her husband's anxiety over economic issues could transfer directly to her, and then how quickly the anxiety could shift to their daughter. Mrs. A. began to notice that her automatic reactions were often as intense as when her daughter was an infant. At that time, Mrs. A. started to study Bowen theory and found some aspects that were helpful to her in observing her own functioning.

Recognizing that she was not going to directly change her daughter, Mrs. A. became a very good student of her own anxiety and the relationships where it was most deeply embedded. Early in the study, she made an observation that was key to changing the projection process in the family.

Mrs. A. observed that her husband's distance from his daughter left both her daughter and herself more vulnerable to the tension that was alive between them. During a rather calm time in the family, she observed that her young adult daughter made somewhat successful overtures to her father for a more personal relationship. When Mr. A. was able to be available to his daughter, Mrs. A. was more relaxed and their daughter was less reactive in all her relationships in the family and in the world. With this observation, Mrs. A. began to find ways to remove herself from her usual position in the triangle and let the natural relationship between Mr. A. and his daughter develop. Contrary to her usual posture, this position required her to have some confidence that this relationship actually existed and that it was actually good for the family. As she became more and more confident in this position, she saw dramatic changes in her daughter's behavior. The serious acting-out symptoms essentially subsided.

The changes in Mrs. A. were not universally accepted in the family, but Mrs. A. was sure enough of her observations that she continued to make space for the growing relationship between her husband and daughter. Much later, when her husband was bothered by a chronic physical problem, he was less available to both his wife and his daughter. The old tensions resurfaced. Although this incident was uncomfortable, it confirmed to Mrs. A. that her observation was accurate and helped guide her through another difficult time.

As in all families, the old processes tend to repeat many times in the triangle of Mr. and Mrs. A. with their daughter. If Mrs. A. becomes overwhelmed by her daughter's behavior, Mr. A. can be counted on to enter the process on Mrs. A.'s side, trying to *shape up* his daughter. However, when Mrs. A. is less reactive to her daughter's plight, the extreme reactivity in Mr. A. to his daughter appears to change. He is able to be a resource to her again. Also, when Mrs. A. can think about her daughter as capable of solving a number of adult problems, Mrs. A. finds ways to communicate her new posture in action that is a benefit to the entire family. Figure 11.6 illustrates decreasing tension in the A. family.

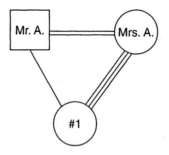

FIGURE 11.6. A. Family: Decreasing Tension

In another key relationship, Mrs. A. started to find a way to think about her less than personal relationship to her mother and the emotional cutoff that had existed from childhood. The cutoff was consistently reinforced in the marriage, and the new thought of a personal relationship with her mother was almost unthinkable. However, simply calming her reactivity to her own mother allowed her to be more thoughtful about ways to be different in this important relationship and later gave her more flexibility with her daughter. For practice on a regular basis, she was able to take on the project of defining herself more clearly in the triangle with her mother and her next older sister. She found that thoughtful efforts in this challenging triangle helped her gain confidence in her ability to stand up for herself and she also gained some new objectivity in all her relationships.

When Mrs. A. discovered the way her husband's anxiety could reinforce her own reactivity to her mother, she found a way to separate herself from her husband's extremely negative view of her mother. He was still taking his wife's side in a relationship where his negativity about her mother partially reassured him of a connection to his wife. When Mrs. A. no longer responded to this connection in the same way, it began to moderate the level of reactivity between Mr. and Mrs. A. about her mother.

Mr. and Mrs. A. have had many opportunities to practice the changed postures in their relationship. With a variety of symptoms in the family, the chronic anxiety remained fairly high for many months. The difference for Mrs. A., however, has been her ability to step back from the intense anxiety, often after the patterns of reactivity are already in place. Using Bowen theory as a way of thinking through some of the issues in the reactivity has allowed Mrs. A. to be present in many more difficult family situations and to gain some clarity for her own functioning. These events have included providing care for her mother after a serious CVA and managing her sister's pressure to take on more and more responsibility for her mother; her daughter's miscarriage and successive pregnancy; the later birth of a granddaughter that was particularly difficult. In many of these situations, Mrs. A. experienced the anxious demand to choose between mother and daughter or to be in two places (with mother and daughter) at the same time. The automatic tendency to focus on her daughter's problems to the exclusion of others in the family has changed dramatically. However, the *divided loyalties* and the automatic anxious reactivity in the triangles continue, but Mrs. A. has a growing ability to make decisions about her own posture in the triangles that are less about *loyalties* fueled by anxiety and more about realistic requirements for each of the people in the family, including herself. Figure 11.7 illustrates increasing connections for Mrs. A.

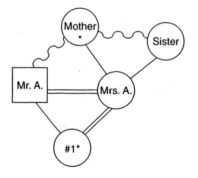

FIGURE 11.7. Mrs. A.: Increasing Connections

Family B—A Fatherless Child

Family B. illustrates a dramatic closeness evolving between a mother and an only child with acting-out symptoms showing up in adolescence. This close attachment was probably complicated by factors related to divorce, emigration, and emotional cutoff. The history of problems with this child may be understood best in the multigenerational history of anxiety about distant or absent fathers starting with the mother's maternal grandmother. The maternal grandmother was part of a group of youngsters who emigrated together after the death of the oldest male child, apparently in the face of hunger and relationship problems. The myth was that both parents had died, along with the son, from the flu epidemic in 1910, but archival research does not substantiate this. The fact is that five siblings, from age seventeen to six, emigrated together in search of a home. The maternal grandmother, as a youngest, found a substitute mother in her oldest sister, but no father figure was available. She considered herself a *fatherless child.* She married a man sixteen years her senior who died when her oldest child was four years old. Mrs. B.'s mother saw herself as another fatherless child. Figure 11.8 illustrates Mrs. B.'s position in a fatherless family.

Mrs. B.'s mother married a man who was very dependable as a provider, but he was very distant from family in the early years. He learned to use work to stay distant from family anxiety. He worked long hours and left his wife to deal with his mother and all the extended family issues.

Mrs. B.'s parents had a familiar characteristic of child focus. The parents' relationship was outwardly very loving but never one in which they could handle difficult or personal issues in dealing with family tensions.

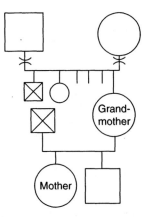

FIGURE 11.8. B. Family: Fatherless Child

The mother assumed the roles of nurturer, connecter, supporter, disciplinarian, and communicator for four children. Each of the first three had a special version of focus from their mother as follows.

#1, Male—overprotect with high expectations
#2, Female—worry, overprotect, and diagnose
#3, Female—overvalue as helper and problem-solver (Mrs. B.)

Mrs. B. (#3) observed her father's role in dealing with her mother. Her mother was anxious about her only son's health, school, eyesight, and numerous daily challenges. She was anxious about her first daughter's poor development and nervous ways. When the intensity of the problems with either of these got too great, the father was notified to hurry home from work and deal with the problems. He did as he was bid, and the offspring responded well for the moment. Then he returned to his distant position and the mother took over as the central figure. This cycle kept on repeating itself. In the midst of the mother's anxiety, her third child (Mrs. B.) found a way to soothe her mother's anxiety and was always valued as an extraordinary helper. In spite of this, she was cautioned not to *outshine* her somewhat handicapped sister. She learned to keep herself very close to her mother and monitor her behavior to help keep family tension manageable. Figure 11.9 illustrates the emotional process in Mrs. B.'s family of origin.

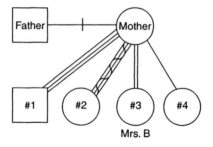

FIGURE 11.9. Mrs. B.: Family of Origin

When Mrs. B. married the first time, she continued to stay close to her family as her mother's helper. She did not consider having children in this marriage and sensed that the marriage (highly approved by parents) might not be the right relationship for her—considering the idea that her mate needed as much care as a child.

In her second marriage, Mrs. B. went back to the man she had loved before, one clearly disapproved of by the whole family. She lived with him for three years until they decided to have a baby. Mrs. B. had been hesitant to have a baby in this relationship due to Mr. B.'s social drinking. However, he promised to give up the drinking if they had a baby. They were married in the early weeks of the pregnancy, but Mrs. B.'s anxiety about the drinking increased. The day the baby came home from the hospital, Mrs. B. was clearly an anxious new mother and Mr. B. was simply ready to celebrate. He went out drinking and thus began the cycle in which Mrs. B. inserted herself between the infant and her father—to protect her baby. The cycle was in place with increased drinking, more focus on drinking, distance in the marriage, and an extreme closeness between mother and infant. The triangle was clear from the beginning. Mrs. B. inserted herself between her daughter and husband, leaving a large distance between the daughter and her father and substantially increasing her intense connection to her only child. When the baby was four years old, a tense divorce was in place and the distance between father and child was complete. Figure 11.10 illustrates emotional cutoff in the B. family.

During this time, Mrs. B.'s parents emigrated from Mexico to the United States and Mrs. B. took over her father's small business. She enjoyed the independence, worried about being a single mother, but found her life quite complete. However, there was much pressure from family and from within her to restore the family closeness. She had started to observe something

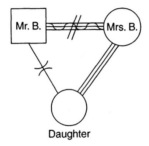

FIGURE 11.10. B. Family: Cutoff

about her intense connection to her mother in individual therapy, but the pressure from the family to be together again was great. When her daughter was eight years old, she emigrated with her older sister to join the rest of the family in the United States.

When Mrs. B. arrived in the United States, she discovered that, although her older sister had legal papers, her own status was not so easily settled. She was, in fact, undocumented and unable to work. A number of factors increased the anxiety of the family group living together. The group included Mrs. B., her daughter, her older sister, and her parents. They lived in a very small home, with decreased economic resources. Her aging parents were required to work, but with her uncertain immigration status, Mrs. B. was unable to work and pursue her own separate life course. In this situation, the family life was like a pressure cooker, cut off from family connections in Mexico, and extremely dependent on each other both realistically and emotionally.

The triangles took shape in a fairly rigid way, with Mrs. B.'s father in his usual distant position, always vigilant to observe the posture of his wife. The primary focus of the group soon settled on Mrs. B.'s young daughter. Sometimes other family members joined Mrs. B.'s mother, in being critical of the child, while Mrs. B. tried to be a *shield* for her daughter in the process. (The process was not unlike the process that had evolved in the marriage with the alcoholic spouse cutting the daughter off from the larger family.) This process continued over several years. Figure 11.11 illustrates a rigid triangle in the B. family.

Not surprisingly, the daughter developed a variety of acting-out symptoms. As a young teenager, the child's symptoms took the form of running away, trouble with truancy and police, then a marriage at age fifteen.

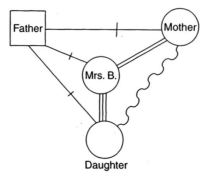

FIGURE 11.11. B. Family: Rigid Triangle

Clinical Consultation Based on Bowen Theory

Mrs. B. sought consultation and studied Bowen theory as she encountered her own and her daughter's symptoms. Mrs. B. initiated consultation for her depression when her daughter was age nine. She indicated that she was overwhelmed by the extremely capable position of her advice-giving mother, feeling less and less capable as a mother. Her depression was evident as she tried to find a solid place to stand between her mother and her growing daughter.

She also recognized the intense triangle with her sister and her mother where she was encouraged to take pity on her symptomatic sister. She was often asked by mother to help resolve her sister's many social and emotional problems. Her automatic pattern was to take on the task of fixing her sister to calm her mother.

Mrs. B.'s first real change came as she was able to separate herself from her mother in dealing with her sister. She established a separate relationship with her older sister and soon found a way to resist her mother's appeals to help in this relationship. Needless to say, her mother was upset by the change in her daughter. Soon, however, her sister was able to make real changes in her functioning, beginning to drive, and eventually to have social relationships. Mrs. B. was also able to use the idea of the triangle and the projection process in sorting out some of her dating relationships.

Mrs. B. took on the challenge of building a personal relationship with many family members both in the United States and in Mexico by phone and e-mail. She negotiated a relationship with her sister-in-law in the midst of her brother's divorce. She studied Bowen theory through this time and applied the ideas more consistently in all her relationships.

The most stubborn relationship existed in the triangle with Mrs. B.'s mother and daughter. As other family relationships became more flexible, the rigidity of this triangle was more evident. The intensity existed in the context of the distance from the extended family and from Mrs. B.'s ex-spouse who remained in Mexico. For several years, Mrs. B. tried to resume contact with her ex-spouse to provide an outside resource to her daughter, but that was unsuccessful. The distance between the daughter and her father appears to leave the anxious impression in the family of another fatherless daughter. How much this contributes to the chronic anxiety in Mrs. B. and her parents is not clear, but it is in their awareness.

The acting-out behavior of the daughter continued and grew. At age fifteen, the daughter entered into a brief marriage. After a few months, the daughter was ready to return home and was able to obtain an annulment. After the failed marriage, Mrs. B. decided not to rescue her acting-out daughter again by welcoming her back into the three generation home in the old posture. As one step in the changed posture, Mrs. B. decided to move out of her parents' home to live with friends. At that time Mrs. B. tried to find a way to be a more independent adult in relationship to her parents and her original family. This left her daughter to work out an arrangement to live with her grandparents if she chose to do so. Finally, based on the young daughter's pursuit of a new, calmer relationship with her grandparents, the grandparents decided to offer their granddaughter legal adoption. This gave her the advantage of legal residency status and the potential for activities beyond the very tight confines imposed by an undocumented status while waiting for papers.

The old triangle then shifted to greater distance between Mrs. B. and her daughter, with her parents in a position of still being critical of Mrs. B. as a mother. In her posture as a mother she continued to allow her daughter to work out her family relationships without advice or interference. In the family, it appeared as if the projection process moved temporarily from Mrs. B.'s young daughter to focus more on Mrs. B. herself. In this configuration, the daughter's functioning improved dramatically. The daughter soon dedicated herself to being a very good student and finally finding a part-time job, made possible by her adoption and her new immigration status. Figure 11.12 illustrates decreasing symptoms in the B. family.

Mrs. B. worked to manage her new posture with less reactivity, keeping the door open for a new relationship with her daughter. However, she did not try to step into the old overhelpful posture with her parents that had gained her so much approval. During this move out of her parent's home, Mrs. B.

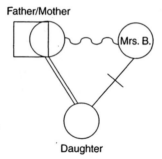

FIGURE 11.12. B. Family: Decreasing Symptoms

met her future spouse and was married. She tried to manage the critical posture of her parents with regular contact while pursuing more of an adult life for herself. The functioning of her daughter remains vulnerable to anxiety in the family, but the extreme symptoms are gone.

Mrs. B.'s importance to her parents continues, along with criticism of her posture as a mother, but she is more relaxed in her response. She is now able to put energy into the new marriage, studies, and work. The triangle with her mother and daughter is not as rigid as in the past and all appear, at the moment, to have more flexible functioning. Mrs. B. is aware that there will be a lifetime of challenges in these relationships, but the progress is visible.

Family C—Distance in the Marriage

This clinical example shows a common pattern in child focus of distance in the marriage. Distance in the marriage is part of all the clinical examples, but it is more visible in the ongoing history of this family. Mr. and Mrs. C. were married at age twenty-six and twenty-one respectively after dating for three years. Both were in college, and Mr. C. was working at low paying jobs while in college. Both were emotionally distant from their families with a fair amount of superficial contact with their extended families. The first pregnancy took place within two months of marriage and was welcome if somewhat overwhelming to both. Months into the pregnancy, Mrs. C. graduated from college and began her first professional job. Mr. C. temporarily stopped his studies to take on additional work. Mrs. C.'s family lived nearby and was available with small gifts and regular advice. The couple lived in a period of

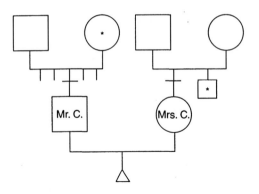

FIGURE 11.13. C. Family: Families of Origin

romance that was punctuated by short conflicts and distance around different ways of managing life's demands.

Mrs. C.'s family had additional stressors at the time of the pregnancy and birth. Her maternal grandparents had just moved into her parents' home and her grandmother was showing signs of dementia. Mrs. C.'s brother, a senior in high school, was also exhibiting some symptoms of emotional distress.

Mr. C.'s family lived over 2,000 miles away and was not in close contact at that time. Mr. C.'s mother was diagnosed with diabetes and had gall bladder surgery sometime during the wife's pregnancy, but did well. The couple's pregnancy represented the first grandchild on both sides of the family. Figure 11.13 illustrates the families of origin of family C.

Child #1

The tension in the extended families brought about more closeness between the newlyweds, with some underlying tension. The birth of their first child, a daughter, was followed by serious symptoms in Mrs. C.'s brother, a *nervous breakdown* and diagnosis of *fugue state,* at the time of his high school graduation. There was also increasing dysfunction in her maternal grandmother.

Mrs. C. had difficulty establishing breast feeding which she continued stubbornly for about four months until she went back to work and Mr. C. renewed his studies. This first child was an alert child who did not sleep well, and cried a bit more than most. At age four she was hospitalized with a severe case of asthmatic bronchitis at the same time that her great-grandmother was

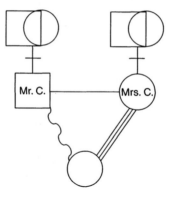

FIGURE 11.14. Mrs. C.: Initial Child Focus

placed in a nursing home. Over her life as a child and adolescent she was very bright, timid, and socially reserved. This daughter had a somewhat tense relationship with both parents growing up, with mother overly worried and father overly critical. Figure 11.14 illustrates Mrs. C.'s initial child focus.

Child #2

The second child, a son, was born sixteen months after his sister. His conception took place in a period of disillusionment in the marriage. The anxious mother and critical father developed increased conflict and distance that in some families might have gone toward separation and divorce. Instead, their second child was conceived and the marriage more firmly sealed. During the pregnancy, economic problems continued with Mrs. C. working and Mr. C. studying and working.

This child's birth coincided with the father's decision to take a job in his career field, even before completing his courses. Economically, life was easier; extended families were less anxious, and this birth was calming to the system. Breast feeding went well, this son was a happy, bright child and welcomed by Mrs. C.'s family as an almost perfect version of their not so perfect son. Mrs. C. was usually relaxed with this child who had an easy childhood, almost idyllic by his own description. Mr. C., by contrast, was critical of his son's absent-mindedness and reactive to the closeness between mother and son. Child #1 reacted to Child #2's favored position with some of her own complaints, but she and he were very close. In adolescence Child #2 had some mild asthma, and like his sister, was a very good student.

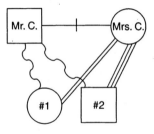

FIGURE 11.15. Mrs. C.: Shifting Child Focus

However, when he left home as a college sophomore, he developed a life-threatening illness. He was able to continue his college career and move toward his life goals in spite of the anxiety the illness brought to him and the system. Figure 11.15 illustrates Mrs. C.'s shifting child focus to Child #2.

Child #3

The third child, a son, was adopted when Child #2 was four years old. Relative infertility and the ease of adoption for certain ethnic/racial groups of children made this an easy option. However, Child #3's adoption took place much more quickly than expected after application. He was six weeks old and a wiry, thin infant who began to thrive on all the attention and activity of two siblings and two consistent parents. He had lived in an orphanage since birth and had some feeding problems before his adoption.

The parents' marriage was still in a period of relative distance, with ongoing differences about dealing with children. The marriage had limited intimacy, but Mr. and Mrs. C. took advantage of church activities and programs to build common interests. This was particularly effective when anxiety was low. When anxiety was high, Mrs. C. attempted to push for more intimacy in the marriage. When that failed she turned to children and outside activities.

The extended families were not positive about the adoption, but Child #3 found a special place in the lives of his mother's parents. He arrived in the family a few months after Mrs. C.'s maternal grandmother's death and a few months before the death of her maternal grandfather. He was less important to Mr. C.'s family and had less connection with them in his childhood.

Child #3 was more difficult for Mrs. C. to understand. He had problems in school and that became a special concern to his mother. He also had a tendency to fight when the tension was high. His childhood was described as

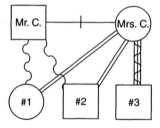

FIGURE 11.16. Mrs. C.: Shifting Child Focus

a mix between fun and struggle, and he became the primary focus of his mother's concern. As Mrs. C. struggled with the serious illness of Child #2, even more intense problems surfaced in Child #3. He became seriously rebellious and took up alcohol and drugs in his adolescence. At age eighteen he was asked to leave home until his behavior was more acceptable. Figure 11.16 illustrates Mrs. C.'s shift of child focus to Child #3.

Child #4

The fourth child, a daughter, was adopted when Child #3 was eighteen months old. She was four months old and had been cared for lovingly in a hospital extended care nursery by nuns who found her a delight. Shortly before adoption, she was moved to the orphanage to search for adoptive parents. A rapid placement of this child was encouraged due to her screaming and obvious unhappiness in the orphanage. She was a charming child who fit easily into the family but was frequently the object of Child #3's anger or negative attention. She was close to her mother in her early years but seldom had the negative or critical focus from her father.

The parents' relationship was calmer when she was a baby, and both extended families received her easily. Her mother's family had no serious events at that time, and the only major life change took place when she was one year old. Mr. C. was laid off from his career position during his company's restructuring and this was followed by a major move. This was apparently a good time for Mr. and Mrs. C. who saw it as a new adventure that allowed some geographic distance from Mrs. C.'s family. Other moves followed that removed the family from extended family contact and support, but Child #4 never received the worry or overconcern that the other three children had received. Her relative freedom may reflect the fact that the family was calmer at the time of her adoption and the parents' anxiety was

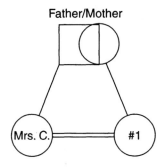

FIGURE 11.17. Mrs. C.: Connecting with Parents

already directed to the older siblings. Her growing up was less eventful than that of her brothers, although she had some difficulty making transitions from *the known* to *the unknown* as she moved from different levels of education, college, and even the move out of the home. Each time, though, she managed these transitions well. Figure 11.17 illustrates Mrs. C. connecting with her parents.

Clinical Consultation Based on Bowen Theory

Mrs. C. was introduced to Bowen theory in graduate school when the older children were adolescents. She was interested in the theory, and eventually sought consultation. She was aware of the emotional cutoff with her parental family, and made her first efforts to decrease that cutoff. In the cutoff, it appeared that most of the tension between Mrs. C. and her mother went directly to her first daughter. As Mrs. C. made genuine contact with her own mother, Child #1 was much freer of the projection process in this triangle.

Child #1's most dramatic symptoms in the beginning of consultation took place after Mrs. C.'s parents had visited the area for several months. As Mrs. C.'s mother left the area, her daughter (Child #1) had to be hospitalized with asthma for the first time in ten years. Fortunately, Mrs. C. could see the way her anxiety about her relationship to her mother was passed on to her daughter. Mrs. C. spent many years developing a person-to-person relationship with her mother and less aligned to her father. In the process, this daughter was able to move with more confidence into her college and adult years, free of major symptoms. Figure 11.18 illustrates Mrs. C. opening family contacts.

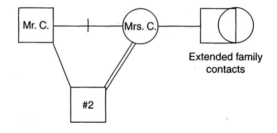

FIGURE 11.18. Mrs. C.: Opening the Family Contacts

Mrs. C.'s renewed interest in consultation came when Child #2 was diagnosed with a serious illness. Although he was successful in his efforts to establish his life direction during and after his illness, the serious illness was a wake-up call for Mrs. C. She made major efforts to reduce her overattachment to this child, primarily by making greater efforts in her connections to extended family. As she defined herself in relationship to her mother, her mother became a resource that she had never been for Mrs. C. As she was less attached to Child #2, she saw changes in this son's relationship to his father. It was clear to the whole family that the father's critical posture had changed.

The illness, however, created high anxiety that both parents handled quite differently. Mrs. C. was overtly emotional, tearful, and Mr. C. was stoic and silent. Mrs. C. was seeking communication and Mr. C. was seeking distance. The overall distance between the parents increased, and they managed the distance and anxiety partly by work and family business. As Child #2 moved on with life, Mrs. C. noted that the tension in the marriage had not changed dramatically. Figure 11.19 illustrates increased marital conflict and decreased child focus.

Child #3 was caught in the family tension that continued and this was aggravated during his brother's health problems. His acting-out behavior was a challenge for Mrs. C. During her consultation she slowly discovered the ways in which her disappointment in her husband and their emotional distance could trigger a big upset in this son. This often erupted into acting-out behavior on the son's part. Mrs. C.'s awareness of the connection to the marriage gave her a clue that was finally useful in changing her position in the family. Although neither parent was successful in getting this son to be accountable during many of his adolescent years, the small steps that Mrs. C. was taking to be surer of herself with her husband eventually allowed her to take a substantial stand with both her husband and this son. When she was

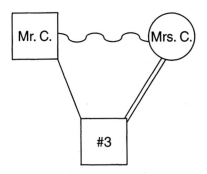

FIGURE 11.19. C. Family: Increased Martial Conflict and Decreased Child Focus

finally sure enough of herself, Child #3 was able to return home and resume his efforts to grow up. He continued to face some major challenges. Mrs. C. was consistently clearer in her ability to deal with the challenges and this son's life course began to change.

Child #4 continued her relatively calm movement through adolescence, into college, and into adulthood. She was seldom the subject of consultation.

SUMMARY

Clinical families provide valuable ways to observe the challenges of child focus in a family. The families demonstrate the long, hard work required to shift some part of the projection process in a family with a significant child focus and lower level of differentiation. The primary effort required to be a *self* in the marriage is often the most difficult place for most parents with significant child focus. The ebb and flow of anxiety in a family is reflected in the increase in symptoms in the most vulnerable individuals in the most rigid triangles. More quiet periods are often facilitated by increased contact with extended family and the availability of more flexible triangles in the larger unit.

Each family in this chapter shows some of the impact of the unresolved relationships from the past while also demonstrating different aspects of child focus in the nuclear family unit. The efforts of each family show both the value and the limitations encountered by a parent willing to examine his or her own functioning and to use Bowen theory as a lens through which to see *self* more accurately.

REFERENCES

Bowen, M. (1978). *Family therapy in clinical practice*. New York: Jason Aaronson.

Donley, M. (2003). Unraveling the complexity of child-focus. *Family Systems: A Journal of Natural Systems Thinking in Psychiatry and the Sciences, 6*(2), 147-161.

Kerr, M. and Bowen, M. (1988). *Family evaluation: The role of the family as an emotional unit that governs individual behavior and development*. New York: W.W. Norton and Company.

Chapter 12

Triangles in Stepfamilies

Kathleen Cotter Cauley

INTRODUCTION

For nearly three decades in working with stepfamilies, it has become apparent to me that self-management on the part of the therapist is of utmost importance. During this time I have also been involved in my own effort to manage myself as a stepmother and stepdaughter in my nuclear and extended families. The interlocking triangles in the therapist's family and the clinical family, viewed through a Bowen family systems theory lens, are the focus of this chapter.

The first section covers a detailed description of my efforts at differentiation in my position as a stepmother and a stepdaughter. This will address triangles around death, divorce, and remarriage; levels of chronic anxiety; and conditions under which the triangles are activated.

The effect of this personal effort on my clinical work is described. This includes consideration of shifts over the years in my ability to manage myself in the complex triangles of life in stepfamilies. Such shifts include an increased ability to observe with a broader view, to develop a respectful attitude about the complexity of these families, and to manage myself in a highly charged emotional climate. There is also a mind-set of maintaining curiosity and interest as the clients manage their position in the triangles, and of seeing clients' dilemmas as opportunities for differentiation as they attempt to think amidst the myriad relationships and connections in which they live.

I have been able to observe markers in my ability to be patient and tolerant in systems with swirling alliances shifting beneath the surface, often out of direct view. I describe how to resist pressure for a quick solution and how to avoid an advice-giving stance. In working with stepfamilies and through knowledge of Bowen family systems theory, there is an increased ability to observe what is universal to the triangles in all families and what might be unique to stepfamilies. Often only one member of the stepfamily is the motivated person, and Bowen theory provides a way of thinking for that family member that can make a difference.

The second section includes clinical case examples that highlight the ideas set forth in section one, and covers various types of triangles in stepfamilies. In describing these clinical examples, I demonstrate that an ongoing effort at differentiation can make a difference in the therapist's ability to be a resource to stepfamilies.

THE THERAPIST'S POSITION
AS STEPDAUGHTER AND STEPMOTHER:
KNOWING THE BLIND SPOTS

I became a stepdaughter in 1976 at age twenty-six, when my father remarried seven years after the death of my mother. An appendix, included at the end of the book, explains the symbols used in the figures in this chapter. Figure 12.1 is the family diagram.

With a narrow mind-set, I stepped naively into a situation that was full of emotional land mines. I discovered these over and over again every time I made a misstep. Nothing had prepared me for the intensity involved in this transition, and for the emotional impact that it would have on my life. Having heard it described by clients, I had only an intellectual understanding of the process. The visceral reality was something altogether different. I believed that a stepparent "stepped into" the place of another person who was absent from the family via death or divorce—a nice, altruistic thought that emerged out of my overly positive mind-set. Now I think about it as a process of "step by step . . . step in . . . step back . . . always observing the triangles."

I had read a very helpful book by Emily B. Visher, PhD, and John S. Visher, MD, called *Old Loyalties, New Ties: Therapeutic Strategies with Stepfamilies* (1988). This book provided an anchor for me in the early years. They spoke of the complexity of these families and of the importance of gathering information about the relationships that precede a stepfamily. They referred to the three "Ls" of loss, loyalty, and lack of control (see p. 216). It was that last "L" that captured my attention. After all I was a reasonably calm person, or so I thought until I became a stepdaughter. My immature behavior was a shock to me. I have now come to understand this as my reactivity to the shifting triangles.

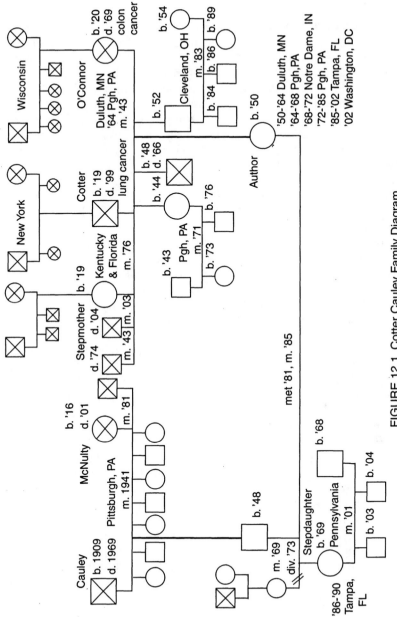

FIGURE 12.1. Cotter Cauley Family Diagram

293

I stumbled upon Bowen theory in 1977. The ideas were interesting to me, but I was convinced that stepfamilies were somehow different, more complex, and requiring a larger piece of paper for the family diagram. I was, in fact, one of Bowen theory's greatest critics. I had never seen any reference to Bowen stepfamily systems theory. However, by 1980, I was desperate and asked a supervisor on the staff at the agency where I worked to be my first coach. I set out on a journey into the ideas of Bowen theory that continues to this day. The journey began as an effort to convince myself that Bowen theory is helpful to stepfamilies, and I had only myself to take along on this project. My anger, disappointment, and general angst would have to be left behind. Not only was I reactive to my stepmother, but I was acting with immaturity by spreading my emotional upset on a regular basis to others in the family. Interlocking triangles were available and just a conversation away.

In 1985, I married and became a stepmother to my husband's fifteen-year-old daughter. My coach had been very useful during the four years of dating. Whenever my romantic ideas emerged, she would say "Do you understand what it means to marry someone who has a child?" She talked about the impact of triangles and the depth of attachment between parent and child. I naively thought that the emotional impact would be minor. As it turned out, she was providing important groundwork for the future.

My husband and I had complementary sibling positions. Long before we met, each of us had lost a parent in 1969, and had lived with the surviving parent during a period of young adulthood. I lived with my father after college from 1972 to 1976. My husband lived with his mother after his divorce from 1973 to 1981. These periods allowed us to know our parents well as adults, and to send them off to their second marriages after the deaths of their first spouses.

Shortly after our marriage in 1985 we moved from Pittsburgh, Pennsylvania, to Tampa, Florida. This put me in closer proximity to my father and stepmother, who lived in Naples, Florida, in the winter, and were less than a three-hour drive from Tampa. This proximity provided frequent opportunities for visits until my father's death in 1999.

My stepdaughter, at age sixteen, moved from Connecticut to our home in Florida and stayed from 1986 until 1990. It was during this time that I was able to observe my functioning as a stepmother and to attain a different and more objective view of my stepmother. The effort that I have put into these relationships has been extremely difficult and perhaps the most rewarding in terms of my own maturity and my functioning as a coach to others in the clinical setting. There were many years of focusing on my stepmother as "the problem." I would tell endless stories about her lack of depth, socialite interests, attention to perfect order, and material possessions (in other words, I took a blaming stance). A similar pattern emerged with a focus on my stepdaughter, as we all lived through her very intense two-year eating disorder as a teenager. I knew that Bowen theory directed me to observe the interlocking triangles with her mother, her grandparents, my husband, and myself. However, I learned for myself just how blinding child focus can become.

In this chapter, I focus on how triangles and knowledge of Bowen theory were essential in my efforts at differentiation. This shift in my thinking and functioning stretched over many years. Currently, I have a very good relationship with both my stepmother and stepdaughter. There is always the management of ambivalence, a struggle to stay with Bowen theory and an effort to avoid the tempting distraction of the latest gossip in any relationship. I now see the gossip and blame and diagnosing of the other as anxiety binders, using them as signals that I am off course and have some work to accomplish.

Return to the Original Triangles

The triangles in my original family continue to provide the roadmap to my dilemmas in stepfamily life. My functioning position was a comfortable niche and I felt included. I was the third of four children, with a sister six years older, a brother seventeen months older, and a brother two years younger. We lived in northern Minnesota until 1964, when my father was transferred to Pittsburgh, PA, with his work in the steel industry. The chapter following the death of my older brother in 1966 is important history. His sudden death in a car accident occurred just ten days before he had planned to leave home for college. The shifts in the family relationships included some depression in my father and unspoken distance that permeated my parents' marriage. This emotional distance was an effort to manage pain by avoiding open discussion about my brother's death. Another shift was my older sister's decision to stay home instead of moving away to a midwestern city, as she had planned after college. Additional events included the emergence of my mother's medical symptoms in 1968, as I departed for college, her colon cancer diagnosis in November 1968, and her death in October 1969. The anxiety from these cascading events was high, and a family theme emerged that worked against differentiation: "Don't upset Dad, he has been through enough." The following seven years were a time of closeness for the family. My younger brother and I were single and remained so until our thirties. We spent time together, traveled with our father, and attended events in the extended family. There was reciprocity in this that worked for everyone, as the loss of two family members in three years was managed with increased togetherness.

In 1973, my younger brother was diagnosed with juvenile diabetes, a symptom that I now have come to see as part of the shock wave of shifting triangles during those years (cf. Bowen, 1978, p. 324). As described, the seven years between my mother's death and my father's remarriage had been full of family contact and increased togetherness. These were years of getting to know my father as an adult. In 1976, when he married someone who was very interested in him and less interested in personal family relationships, the togetherness of our family as I knew it was threatened. It was at this time that I decided that stepfamilies were "different." I had no way to conceptualize how the shifts in relationships following my brother's and mother's deaths allowed for entry of a member who wanted to join the family. We were unprepared for a new member who would focus on the marriage and, with my father's participation, leave the rest of us in the outside position.

In 1978, my father and stepmother moved away from Pittsburgh, Pennsylvania, to Lexington, Kentucky, where he worked until his retirement in 1985. After that time they spent summers in Kentucky and winters in Florida. My reactivity to their relocation was pronounced, but it was not until I stumbled in my functioning that I took a serious look at the triangles that were swirling through our family and the extended family. My father was in a very important position in the extended family with his sisters and their children, and with my mother's siblings and their children. During his seven years as a widower these relatives had enjoyed increased time with him, and they were surprised and confused as this contact decreased when he remarried. This reactivity in the extended family was part of the interlocking triangles.

My efforts to "plug into" my stepmother in familiar ways were not met with openness. In coaching I came to understand the original triangle with my parents and myself, but could not see my intensity in this new stepfamily as playing a part. In the triangle with my mother and father I had easy access to each of them without the other feeling threatened. As a stepdaughter in the absence of that niche of feeling included, I was very reactive. Only when I became a stepmother and tried to attach to my stepdaughter in ways that she could not manage did I begin to see triangles and my part in them. Then, I began to observe the activation of my primary triangle when I was in contact with my father and stepmother. My place had been a special one with my parents, and I began to notice my father's efforts to balance this new triangle in a similar way. I observed how his efforts to avoid conflict in all of the triangles added to increased family tension over the years to follow. I started to see how quickly my stepmother could react to any memory of my mother and how alive my mother's ghost was in the triangles. My work at differentiation included seeing my reactivity as part of the equation, and making efforts to be more cognizant of this when I was with them.

In dealing with my stepdaughter, I now had the triangles with her mother and grandparents constantly in my head as a data point for understanding my own reactivity to being in the outside position. There had been geographical distance between my husband and his daughter since her mother moved away when their daughter was three. He had regular holiday and summer visits but his daughter's primary involvement was with her mother and maternal grandparents. My husband and I had unrealistic expectations about the intensity of these connections and I quickly found myself joining him in his outside position. This togetherness focus was an automatic response to the system. Despite my knowledge of interlocking triangles I learned about the obstacles that can affect an effort at differentiation.

Knowledge of triangles enabled me to let go of the intensity which took the form of hurt, anger, and disappointment. It was difficult to think that my stepmother and stepdaughter were not interested in attaching to me with the intensity that I desired. I began to focus on self without the eye on the other, to maintain relationships in my family of origin, to utilize prayer to calm myself in the midst of internal turmoil, and to move forward in a very different way.

Michael E. Kerr (2001) describes triangles in the following manner:

> Triangles reflect the emotional fusion or lack of differentiation that exists between the people involved. It is difficult to see triangles because it depends on recognizing how each relationship affects every other relationship in the triangle. . . . Patterns in triangles emerge from three basic patterns: Forces of emotional attachment between people; chronic anxiety generated by disturbances in emotional attachments; and mechanisms people use to cope with anxiety. . . . The most fundamental process that accounts for what people say and do in triangles is each person trying to get comfortable . . . each person trying to get into a position in relationship to the others that reduces his anxiety and enhances his emotional well being.

Lessons Learned

My ongoing effort has been to learn as much as possible about the facts of functioning in my family of origin and about my position in that broader system. I have continued the use of coaching in this endeavor.

Some of the beliefs that I try to remember are as follows:

- People often depend on their environment to calm down, and two people can get together with rapid speed and focus on a third as the problem.
- The effects of increased chronic anxiety and the activation of interlocking triangles can result in this anxiety coming to rest in one person, and the sensitivities of that person can add to the reciprocal nature of the process.
- Having one's "eye on the other" contributes to the inability to be a self.
- Triangles can be visible or invisible (through the telephone, in town or across the United States, dead or alive!).
- Stepfamilies and the nature of the attachments can be tenuous, and high anxiety is a hallmark of the early years, depending on the level of differentiation of the people involved. This heightened anxiety can cause even a well-trained person to forget the importance of gathering facts of functioning in the extended families and "former families" of people involved.
- Working on relationships has great value, when based on the principle that "it is important even if I don't feel like it." Taking this work on directly reaps many benefits to self and to the system. The ability to stop one's part in the immediate infectious nature of blame, gossip, and rapid spreading of anxiety through the use of triangles is all part of ongoing self-management. It is possible for stepparents and adult stepchildren to observe and to clarify the expectations that they have of one another. A stepfamily based on factual knowledge will move into the future in a different way than a family that is built on fantasy.

Markers of change in my own work included fewer moments of feeling "stunned" or "frozen in place." I have had an increased ability to be curious and to seek out rather than run from opportunities for contact in difficult situations. Ongoing opportunities abound to practice toleration of differentness and to increase my flexibility. Ambiguity and uncertainty are part of life, and membership in a stepfamily has provided the necessary training in managing the impulsive emotional surges that can be triggered on a regular basis. This practice has in turn increased my ability in all areas of my life to be still and to wait before jumping in where I do not belong.

An important juncture was when I decided in the mid-1990s that I probably would not have much of a relationship with my stepmother or stepdaughter. It was only in this giving up on what I had wished for and working at differentiation that I developed more realistic expectations. Differentiation is not just an effort to make contact with important others. It is about managing oneself in these relationships without running away or getting overinvolved. It includes a process of staying in contact and continually working toward emotional clarity for oneself. I have come to think of it in the following manner: step by step, the anxiety is around every corner. The triangles activate, interlock, and lock. The emotional landmines are many, and the terrain can be tough, depending on the attachments, of course, and on the intensity and on differentiation, that elusive concept. I must never stop thinking about it, never take my eye off it, or I risk plunging back into disappointment when I least expect it, stunned again, frozen in place in the triangles.

As I keep stepping up, stepping back, and tracking the motion, I watch the shifting alliances and loyalties. My effort is to trust theory, manage myself, and act in a mature manner. The intensity in self is amazing when another wants a different level of attachment. However, life goes forward, and these relationships become what they are, despite the longing for what might have been. Then, many years later, my stepmother who is now in her eighties, has been attaching to me! When this shift occurred, I was not interested, but Bowen theory told me that I had the ability. In June 2003, four years after my father's death, she married again. The whole family was in attendance. Her husband died only eight months later, and we have all maintained regular contact with her during these years.

As for my stepdaughter, she is now married and has two sons. She wants them to be my grandsons, not my step grandsons, because she says that I have been like a mother to her. Now what?!

Step in, but how far? It took me years to stop going in with my heart and to manage my disappointment. I had built my protective mechanisms with great care. Over time and with Bowen theory as a guide, I now go in differently and with more self, but not too fast. I keep thinking while attaching. It is humbling to realize that overfunctioning is difficult on others, and to pull away, and then to look behind and see that sometimes, after many steps, over many years, a gift appears. It is called a relationship. Welcome it!

CLINICAL APPLICATION:
DOES DIFFERENTIATION MAKE A DIFFERENCE?

The effects of this differentiating effort on clinical work are considered in this section. As I have improved my ability to manage myself in the complex triangles of my family, I have observed shifts in my clinical work. Such shifts include the ability to observe with a broader view and to bring a respectful attitude to this complexity. The ability to manage myself in a highly charged emotional climate is increased, as is the ability to maintain curiosity and interest as to how the clients manage their positions in the triangles. I have been able to describe clients' dilemmas as opportunities for differentiation as they attempt to think amidst their many attachments and interlocking triangles. I have observed markers in my ability to be patient and be tolerant in the face of conflict when I sit with stepfamilies as they find their way through the complexity. There is much less jumping in to help or rescue, and there is more waiting for ideas and solutions to emerge from the families. I am no longer overwhelmed by the number of people on the family diagrams of stepfamilies. Instead, I am now interested in watching the action of the triangles.

It is now possible to resist pressure for a quick solution, to avoid simplistic explanations, and in general to feel less stuck. The discovery of my own blind spots in the intensity of the interlocking triangles has assisted me in sitting in a complicated family system with a presence and knowledge that will not allow for any implication that the process is simple. This stance in the clinical work allows families to reorganize themselves in a fashion that is suitable for them. It is a position of deep respect for people who are able to endure the anxiety over a long period of time and not run away or distance themselves from it. The objective is to assist the family to become an organism that works.

Most of all, this therapeutic stance holds an appreciation of how embedded we all are in the triangles of our families, and the wisdom to know that it can be a long process of observation and effort between moments of "seeing" the part one plays and the part that others play in the relationship patterns.

Case Examples

Stepfamilies and Interlocking Triangles: Keeping a Broad View

Triangles with a father, stepmother, stepdaughter, and extended families are described in this example. Figure 12.2 presents the C. family diagram.

Mrs. C., the eldest sister of five siblings, was a physician who came for consultation. She included her husband at some of the meetings. They were a tall, striking couple, with an intellectually and emotionally charged relationship. This was a second marriage for Mr. C. and a first for Mrs. C. She had no children and he had three. The active triangle was Mrs. C., Mr. C., and his daughter, who was physically handicapped. Mrs. C. thought that this young teenager was capable of far more than she had been challenged to accomplish. A familiar pattern was that Mr. C. would alternately wel-

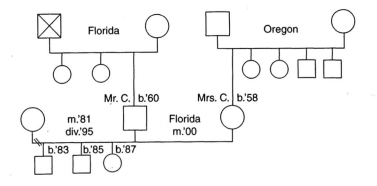

FIGURE 12.2. C. Family Diagram

come Mrs. C.'s advice and participation, and then criticize and diagnose Mrs. C. as "neurotic and obsessive." This was followed by Mrs. C.'s increased yelling that all of this was at the expense of the girl's potential.

Mr. and Mrs. C. were interested in a more objective way of managing their behavior with his daughter. Although Mr. C. hated to relinquish the idea that his wife acted crazy and therefore was crazy, he began to do so. He also was able to stop triangling in Mrs. C.'s sister to verify that Mrs. C. was the problem. He was interested in the concept of the triangle as a mechanism to manage himself. Mr. C. had not previously thought about his functioning position in his family of origin. His oldest sister had serious behavioral problems as a teenager and Mr. C. spent many years being angry with her, and trying to calm his mother's distress. He saw that in his own position as the youngest brother of sisters he was rarely criticized by his older sister or mother. The oldest sister absorbed most of the intensity. He could see that when his wife and daughter were in conflict he immediately rescued his daughter. This put his wife in the outside position and undermined any progress on his daughter's part. He also learned that his own heightened sensitivity to criticism did not allow for direct exchange with Mrs. C. He valued her opinions and outspokenness, except when it came to criticism of himself or his daughter.

Mrs. C., also interested in the concept of the triangle, saw that she was repeating the functioning position that she held in her family of origin. As the eldest, everyone turned to her for advice and solutions, particularly with regard to their aging parents. The siblings would then be critical if things went wrong and criticize Mrs. C. for being bossy. When, in her marriage, Mr. C. would pull in her sister to agree with him that Mrs. C. was crazy, this would infuriate her. She then would get loud and reactive, giving Mr. C. reason to think that he was perfect after all and that she carried the problem.

Understanding the concept of triangles gave Mr. and Mrs. C. a road map to see that the reciprocal functioning in their marriage had a much larger backdrop in the emotional field of their families of origin. They now were able to take things less personally, and to think their way through dilemmas. They learned to monitor signals in themselves when the intensity was high and the triangles were activated. Mr. C. liked to use a horse racing analogy to say, "Before I knew about Bowen theory the gate would go up and we were off to the races!"

Look for the Ghosts: Triangles After Death

This example covers triangles after death and remarriage with father, stepmother, and adult children. Figure 12.3 illustrates the J. family diagram.

Mrs. J. called for a consultation after being referred by a member of the clergy. She was the mother of four adult children and had been divorced for ten years. She was in a second marriage of three years with Mr. J., who was a widower with eight children. The mother of these eight adult children had died suddenly, and there was a high level of intensity and unsettled emotional business in the family. Mr. J. was seventy-eight years old and Mrs. J. was sixty-nine.

Mr. J.'s first wife was an older sister of four siblings and she overfunctioned in the family, with Mr. J. in the underfunctioning position. The four youngest adult children were left helpless and dependent upon her death. Mr. J. constantly bailed them out of emotional and financial trouble. Mr. J. met Mrs. J. two years after his wife's death, and they were married within that

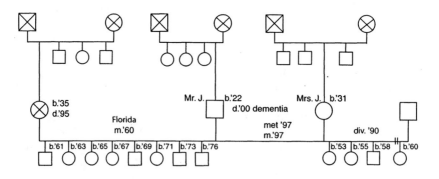

FIGURE 12.3. J. Family Diagram

same year. Mrs. J. was looking forward to becoming a member of this large family, yet as time proceeded, it appeared that although Mr. J. had eight grown children, none of them were particularly interested in a relationship with her.

Mrs. J. was a younger sister of brothers and her functioning position included looking to older men for guidance and leadership. She was baffled at Mr. J.'s inability to lead. She was also the daughter of an alcoholic mother, and was highly attuned to her environment and to the moods of others. She knew that this vigilance kept her on guard, and that she could appear emotionally distant.

Three years into the marriage, Mr. J. developed dementia. With the onset of symptoms, Mrs. J. hoped that his children would move to a more cooperative position, yet this did not occur. She was overwhelmed and angry when she came to the first meeting. Mr. J. was more and more reliant upon her and this led to a loss of flexibility in her ability to see her own children. That contact had kept her in balance.

In her description of this stepfamily, it became clear that Mr. J. had been in a passive, distant position in all of his relationships. He was a youngest brother of three sisters. Frequently he would say, "This is just too much to manage. I wish someone would tell me what to do." In this helpless position, he would turn to Mrs. J. for a solution, and she would step into relationships with his children. He had been hoping that Mrs. J. would fit right into the family, but he had done little to make a place for her. He would express disappointment to her that his children were not very polite or friendly to her, yet never took a position with them. This created an emotional field where criticism of Mrs. J. was rampant.

I encouraged Mrs. J. to bring Mr. J. to a meeting. She was highly motivated to get herself back on course and explained her dilemma to him directly in the meeting. This was the first time that she had been able to explain herself that clearly, and she realized that she had been protecting him from the details. I asked Mr. J. if he was able to address his beliefs and principles and to take a stand with his children. He thought that he could do so and made an effort in this direction. Mrs. J. was able to speak to him and not to his dementia. She now understood that he was the emotional leader of his children as long as he was alive, and if he couldn't take a stand then her outside position would remain. Although his symptoms progressed, her stance toward him shifted from anger to an awareness that she was not going to change the emotional system. She could, however, begin to manage her part in a different way.

Mrs. J. was more direct about what she needed. She made frequent contact with Mr. J.'s oldest son who was the leader of the siblings. She tried to ignore gossip, blame, and immature behavior. Her own functioning improved markedly as she connected more frequently with her own children. She became more assertive with Mr. J.'s children in explaining that she needed their help with Mr. J. Her efforts were not always met with assistance on their part, but at least she was more of a self in the family system.

Mrs. J. worked in a community where Mr. J.'s first wife was well known for her tireless volunteer activities. Mrs. J. had an "inside view of the family" yet was surrounded by others who idealized the first wife and had made her into a saint. Mrs. J. knew that it took a crisis before her eight stepchildren would come forward to help her out, but that she could not compete with the ghost of her stepchildren's mother. Her own pride had deprived her of acknowledging how isolated she had become in this multitude of admirers of Mr. J.'s first wife. When she began to learn about triangles she took things less personally and was able to function with less intensity in the family system and in the larger community. She learned to track her tendency to distance herself emotionally as she had done in her family of origin, to see how this behavior became part of the emotional field, and to recognize when people were becoming allergic to her.

The therapist's awareness of triangles is essential in a system where a stepparent is up against a family's active memories of a deceased parent. The silent expectations and judgments can be manifested in behaviors too numerous to list. It is extremely useful if the spouse of the deceased person can relate directly to the children and articulate expectations and guiding principles. If this does not occur, the new spouse can always step up and take on the difficult road toward differentiation.

Triangles That Tip the Balance

This example covers triangles with children after divorce and remarriage, and triangles after the death of an important leader. Figure 12.4 presents the B. family diagram.

Mr. and Mrs. B. were married for two years when they came in for consultation. They met at work and had a secret affair for two years previous to their marriage. Both Mr. and Mrs. B. were separated but not divorced when they met. Mrs. B.'s first husband was very hurt by her affair prior to the ending of the marriage. Intellectually, Mr. and Mrs. B. knew that each had unresolved attachments from their marriages. Mrs. B. had one son and Mr. B. had a daughter and a son. Mrs. B. came alone to sessions at times and with Mr. B. as well. She was trying to manage her position as mother and stepmother, and was pressing her husband to be more involved with his children who lived out of town. She could see that Mr. B. was close to her son who

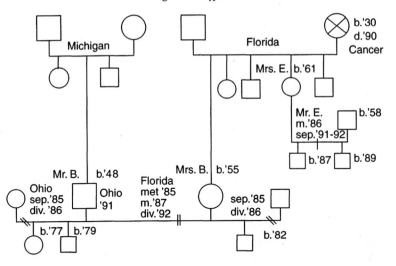

FIGURE 12.4. B. Family Diagram

lived with them, but that there was increasing distance and animosity with his ex-wife. Significant behavioral and emotional symptoms were emerging in his two children.

Mrs. B. also struggled with some feelings about her first marriage, and she had doubt about whether she should have divorced. Her belief was that her impulsiveness at the time did not allow any opportunity to make the marriage work. This triangle with herself, her first husband, and Mr. B. was active in her mind. She knew that it put her in an emotionally distant position in terms of fully attaching in her marriage, and that Mr. B.'s reactivity was related to her unspoken dilemma. She had seen this as the invisible triangle with her ex-husband, but soon realized that it was not so invisible after all.

Mr. B.'s geographical distance and his ex-wife's animosity about his affair with Mrs. B. spilled over to the children on a regular basis. Finally, he decided to take this on and be more responsible in managing conflict. He began to make regular trips to see his children, became involved with their teachers, went to therapy with them in their city, and dealt more directly with his ex-wife. He learned that emotional and geographical distance were mechanisms that he had used to manage himself for many years in his family of origin.

During this time, Mrs. B.'s mother was diagnosed with a terminal illness. Mrs. B. is the oldest female of five siblings. She was intimately involved in her mother's care. Everyone saw the mother as the emotional center and stability in their lives. Sons-in-law were very close to her as were her daughters, and all used her as a steadying resource in their marriages. She died seven months after her diagnosis.

In the year after her death, Mr. and Mrs. B. were trying to conceive a child. However, Mr. B. would waver in his thinking about whether this was a good idea. He was making more and more progress with his ex-wife and children, and his certainty about the importance of his involvement in their lives led to a decision to move near to them for at least a year or possibly longer.

Although Mrs. B. had encouraged this contact, a move away was not something she wanted for herself and her son, nor was she willing to leave her extended family in the aftermath of her mother's death. Mr. B. was willing to commute to see her regularly, but now Mrs. B.'s former conviction about the importance of his connection with his children became uncertain. Although she had encouraged him to become more responsible, she did not want a commuting marriage. She believed that this kind of distance led to the breakup of her first marriage when her husband was gone for extensive amounts of time for work.

Mr. B. was angry that she would not support this effort with his children, and both Mr. and Mrs. B. knew that it was her idea in the beginning. She saw this irony play out in numerous ways.

It was clear that Mrs. B.'s mother's absence was a noticeable void in their dilemma. Without that triangle their marriage had lost its rudder. Mr. and Mrs. B. stopped consultation and months later Mrs. B. came in to report that they had divorced. They saw this as the only solution they could manage. They knew that if they had continued to utilize Bowen theory, divorce would not have been their decision. However, the intensity was too great and cutoff was their relief valve.

By contrast, Mrs. B.'s younger sister Mrs. E. came for consultation during the year after their mother's death. Mrs. E.'s husband had been very close to her mother, and he announced that he wanted a separation shortly after her death. Mrs. E. was clear that this was out of character and somehow related to the attachment that he had had with her mother. She decided that her mother was no longer there to lean on and that she had to find her own strength. She was able to manage high levels of anxiety to give her husband room and he returned home in five months. Both Mr. and Mrs. E. reported a step up in functioning as a result of this effort.

As described in this case example, if a therapist is knowledgeable in Bowen theory, he or she is aware of triangles and the emotional shock wave that can occur after the death or threatened death of an important family leader (see Bowen, 1978, p. 324). If symptoms emerge in the emotional system, these marital difficulties or physical symptoms or accidents can be a reflection of the deep interdependency of family members on one another, and on the shifting relationships in the aftermath. These ideas can give people hope and endurance to ride this out as a natural storm. However, as in this family, there is variability in people's motivation to do so. The pre-death challenges can now become overwhelming efforts without the important triangle that helped them to manage life. Relief from this intensity can be far more alluring than the energy it takes to ride out the storm.

Staying in Contact: Triangles After Divorce

When stepfamilies are deciding how to handle situations that include family members from a previous marriage, it is important for the therapist to be able to remain a resource to them. Assisting these families to think clearly about their expectations and beliefs without telling them what to do is useful when they are going through a highly charged emotional time. Figure 12.5 presents the K. family diagram.

Mr. and Mrs. K. were divorced after ten years of marriage. They had three children. When Mrs. K. came for consultation, she reported that the triangle that absorbed the energy of the divorce related to an affair that she was involved in during the marriage. Mr. K.'s bitterness and hurt ran deep. Mrs. K. decided that if her children were to do well, she had to take this on directly and not run from her ex-husband. Mrs. K. ended the affair and worked directly on being a self with her ex-husband after the divorce. She had not been able to do this in the marriage, wilting easily at Mr. K.'s criticism. Mrs. K. learned to see that this was related to the triangle she had been in with her father, a highly critical man, and her mother, who was unable to take a stand in her own marriage. Mrs. K.'s position as the older child was to

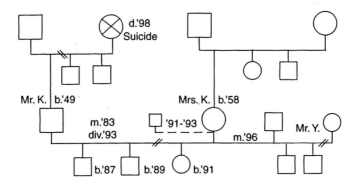

FIGURE 12.5. K. Family Diagram

rescue her mother and to protect her younger siblings from the father's anger. She had repeated this relationship pattern in her own marriage, rescuing her children at the slightest perception of her husband's anger.

Mr. K. was the eldest brother of three brothers, and his primary triangle had been an alignment with his father in a divorce from his mother. He had learned intense patterns of blaming women.

Mrs. K., no matter how caustic his response, became more and more of a self with her ex-husband. Three years after the divorce, she entered a second marriage to a man (Mr. Y.) who had two children, while continuing to work on the issues with her ex-husband. Mr. K. calmed down considerably over time, and he and Mrs. K. were able to be civil and cooperative with regard to the children. He did not see her new husband as a threat.

This is an example of one highly motivated individual who decided to make an ongoing effort at differentiation. She was motivated by her view of her involvement in her parent's marriage, and she did not want her children to live in similar distress. Mrs. K. obtained more objectivity about the reciprocity in her parents' marriage and her position in the triangle.

A marker of her success came when Mr. K. called one morning to report that his mother had committed suicide the previous evening. Mr. K.'s first call was to her. He wanted to tell the children exactly what had happened, but wanted to respect Mrs. K.'s opinion. She called for consultation. This is where a clinician's objectivity and knowledge of the system is important. Of particular importance is the idea that the family knows what it needs to do, and the therapist must not succumb to internal pressure to tell them what to do. I told Mrs. K. that Mr. K. seemed to know his course of action. As he was the eldest, and a leader in his family, it was important that his judgment be respected. Mrs. K. told Mr. K. that she would support his decision as it was his family. She really wanted to protect their two sons (ages eleven and nine) and their daughter (age seven) from the details of their grandmother's death, but she decided to let Bowen theory guide her decision.

Mr. K. gave the eulogy at his mother's funeral. His daughter asked to stand with him at the podium. Just as he was about to finish, he felt a tug on his shirt sleeve. His daughter wanted to speak. She stepped up and said to the congregation, "I just want all of you to know that my grandmother was a very nice person and I am going to miss her very much."

Mr. and Mrs. K. were well prepared for life in a stepfamily. This post-divorce and pre-stepfamily chapter is very important. Yet after divorce, when people are often looking for less contact with one another, the suggestion of more contact can seem like asking them to swim against a very strong current. Those who take up this challenge prepare themselves with the emotional courage necessary for optimal functioning in a stepfamily.

SUMMARY AND CONCLUSION

Although there can be numerous divorces, deaths, and remarriages on a family diagram, with knowledge of Bowen family systems theory, there is an increased ability to see what is universal to the triangles in all families and what might be unique to stepfamilies. Often, only one member of the stepfamily is the motivated person, and Bowen theory provides a way of thinking for that family member to make a difference. As described in this chapter, this ongoing effort at differentiation in one's own family and as a therapist in the clinical setting can have an impact on the therapist's ability to be a resource to stepfamilies. Rather than seeing a multitude of people coming together with many different agendas, one is able to see the family as an emotional unit. After many years I have come to believe that stepfamilies are more alike than they are different from all families.

REFERENCES

Bowen, M. (1978). *Family therapy in clinical practice.* New York: Jason Aronson.

Kerr, M. E. (2001). *Lecture series: Bowen family systems theory and its applications. Lecture #3: Individuality, togetherness, and triangles.* Video. Washington, DC: Bowen Center for the Study of the Family. Excerpts reprinted by permission.

Visher, E. and Visher, J. (1988). *Old loyalties, new ties: Therapeutic strategies with stepfamilies.* New York: Brunner/Mazel, Inc.

Chapter 13

Triangles in Families
with Substance Abusing Teenagers

Anne S. McKnight

INTRODUCTION

In developing the eight concepts of Bowen family systems theory, Dr. Murray Bowen (1978) concluded that the basic task of adult life is to differentiate a self in relation to the important relationships in one's life. He defined differentiation as the effort to become a mature human with the capacity to thoughtfully direct one's life in the face of the anxiety and emotion that permeate human relationships. The formation of that self begins in infancy in the cradle of the family and is forged in adolescence in the tension between the child's developing identity and the intensity of the parents' expectations and emotional investment in the offspring. The turbulence generated in teenage life is fueled by hormonal excesses, a developing brain, and an awakened perception of the complexity of the world. Its outcome is the preparation of the young adult to negotiate the tasks that face them—in life work, relationships, and independence.

What is not always evident is how the adolescent's position in the nuclear and extended family has a profound effect on this trajectory to adulthood. The teenager may look rebellious, compliant, passive, achieving, or depressed. This demeanor is the surface of an underlying complex of emotional patterns and coping mechanisms that has been formed in the child through the relationships of the family. The concept of the triangle is one way to understand how these relationships work, how anxiety is transferred in a family, and how patterns develop and are replicated to handle it.

TRIANGLES

Relationships between two people, when under tension, are unstable. That is, when two people experience tension, one or the other will turn to a third for connection. Triangles are a way to manage tension in families and social groups and often operate in patterned ways. The triangles are the basic building block of human relationships. They are difficult to identify until tension arises, but when one can observe the patterns, the triangles can be predictable.

In the nuclear family, every child is part of a primary triangle with the mother and father. A child's relationship with his or her mother exists in the context of the child's relationship with the father and the father's with the mother. For example, when a mother is having a difficult day with her daughter, she will communicate her frustration to the father when he comes home. The father will then discipline the child, transferring the tension from mother and child to father and child. Figure 13.1 diagrams the tension shifts from mother-daughter to father-daughter.

Every child in a family is in a primary triangle with the mother and father and with each one of their siblings and the mother and the father. So a family becomes a web of triangles which interweave, called interlocking triangles.

Triangles that cross generations exist in every family. They transmit a family's patterned ways of handling tension from one generation to the next. Each person exists in a web of triangles in his or her own family, in the primary triangle with his or her parents and with each sibling. However, the complexity goes on, with triangles between the spouses and their respective families, usually identified as in-law difficulties. For example, when ten-

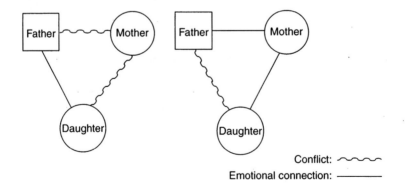

FIGURE 13.1. Tension Shifts from Mother-Daughter to Father-Daughter

sion arises between two spouses, the husband turns for comfort to his mother who the wife then resents as interfering. Figure 13.2 diagrams this process.

Triangles also extend across generations, between a child, a parent, and a grandparent. The tension between a mother and her mother may spill over into the grandmother criticizing and the mother defending her child. Figure 13.3 illustrates this process.

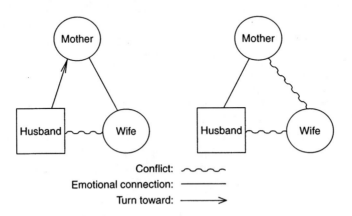

FIGURE 13.2. Husband Turns to Mother, Creating Tension Between His Wife and Mother

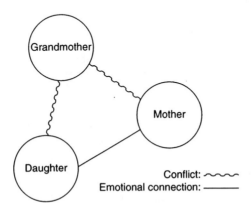

FIGURE 13.3. Grandmother Is Critical of Mother's Discipline of Daughter

Important in understanding triangles is that each person plays a role in how the triangle works. When one turns to another for comfort or support, this creates an "inside position" in a triangle, with the third in the "outside position." The inside is often viewed as a desirable, close-in position, with the outside uncomfortable and isolated. However, when tension escalates, the outside position can be more comfortable, sheltered from the intensity of the close twosome. An example of the inside-outside positions is illustrated in the single parent family: the relationship between the parents has an impact on how each parent relates to the child. When tension, conflict, or distance arises between the mother and father, one backs away, typically the father. The mother is then on the inside position with the child, and the father is on the outside.

When conflict arises between the mother and child as it often does in teenage years, the child is sent to the father, with the mother in the outside position. Even when the child has never known the father, the reactions of the mother to the father can have an intense impact on the functioning of the family. Figure 13.4 illustrates the previous process.

Another way the triangle functions is that two individuals agree that the third is a problem, a process of projection. The best example of projection is parents who focus on a problem child. In this scenario, the parents are in conflict with one another, but agree that the child is a problem. The child reacts to the worry and focus, and becomes less capable and independent. Important in any process of projection is the cooperation of the third, usually the child, who continues to give the other two reasons for labeling him as the problem. Figure 13.5 presents a diagram of the projection process involving a child.

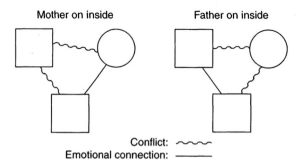

FIGURE 13.4. Mother on Inside and Father on Inside

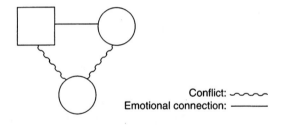

FIGURE 13.5. Projection on a Child

SUBSTANCE ABUSE IN FAMILIES

Substance use is a coping mechanism, a way of altering the human brain to feel lighthearted, gregarious, or relaxed. Alcohol, marijuana, cocaine, or prescription drugs are used to alleviate emotion, usually painful, despite negative outcomes which create more problems or pain. Patterns of substance abuse exist in families. Members may repeat the substance abuse, marry others with substance abuse, or take a position of abstinence from substances, often within the structure of a religious organization.

The use and abuse of substances can serve to regulate the emotional life of a family. A person's use of a substance can create a sense of space or separateness in a relationship, while in fact making the person more dependent and less capable. It is a buffer to closeness, a barrier to communication, and a means to fuel both conflict and passivity. Substances serve a function in the way people relate to one another, often creating an imbalance in families in which some individuals are viewed as strong and caretaking, while others are seen as dependent and needy.

The chronic use of a substance, such as alcohol, has some of the same characteristics as a relationship with a person. The individual turns to the substance for comfort, while turning away from intimate communication with important others. Although triangles are considered to operate among people, substance use plays a role in a triangling process. When tension arises between two people, one uses a chemical for comfort and support in managing the tension. Some people describe their use of alcohol or drugs similar to a relationship, so some professionals view the substance as the third side of the triangle.

The use of alcohol and drugs in teenagers has specific features that are consistent with their stage of development. In establishing identity, often teenagers look for experiences that are different from, or even forbidden by, their parents. They test the limits to see what makes sense to them. The use of drugs and alcohol by teenagers can be extreme to the extent that in adults it would be viewed as addiction. They drink to get drunk; they are poly drug users; they use risky drugs. Most go on to live responsible adult lives.

However, for some teenagers, the use of drugs and alcohol becomes a primary means of defining their identity, through use, friends, music, and lifestyle. The dependence on drugs is a reflection of the dependency in a relationship, an intensity which is both mediated and promoted by drug use. They believe they are defining themselves to their parents and society, yet the drug use leaves them dependent and incapable of taking the necessary steps to prepare for self-sufficiency. They drop out of school, live at home, drift into menial jobs. In this respect, the substance takes on a function in the triangle of mediating the relationships with the parents. The excessive use of alcohol and drugs appears to arrest the emotional development of the teenager while they are using them, leaving them less capable of navigating adult life.

With these ideas in mind, three families will be discussed to illustrate how the understanding of triangles can be used in addressing themes and issues relating to a teenager with a substance abuse problem.

The T. Family

Johnnie, the Teenage Rebel

When Johnnie first entered the room, he had "tough guy" written all over him. He was wearing his sweatshirt hood up and had on sunglasses. He bore no trace of the prep school that he had attended since grade school. At fifteen, he was a surly, angry mass of emotion. Although bright, his grades had plummeted; he got into screaming matches with his father at home; he had dropped his old friends and was associating with alarmingly, for his parents, street type people. Johnnie, according to his mother, had been a charming child until age nine when his angry outbursts started. He was sent to therapists, but when adolescence set in the problems escalated.

Johnnie is the oldest son of three children of an engineer and his wife who is a teacher. The parents, both forty-two, married in their early twenties. Mr. T. was in the military when Johnnie was conceived, and Mrs. T. went to live with her parents when he was born and until he was about two. Mrs. T. reports that her husband had a tense relationship with Johnnie almost from birth. In addition, the introduction of a child into her parents' household was a mixed blessing. Although Johnnie was adored by her parents, she ran into advice from her mother and admonitions from her father about the child's rambunctious behavior. Figure 13.6 presents the T. family diagram.

In this short history, the basic triangles that shaped this child's life begin to emerge. Johnnie, born in a somewhat anxious time in the couple's life, spent his first years with his mother. The pattern of reactivity about Johnnie was similar to that toward her older brother, Sam, when she was growing up. As a child, Sam had difficulties in school, was in conflict with their parents, and could be violent toward her. She hesitated to complain, as her mother always defended him, so she learned to be compliant, a good student, and a peacemaker. Her father, an only child of a poor family in which his father died early, had, through discipline and hard work, become a CEO of a small corporation. Sam never seemed to meet his father's expectations, did not complete college, and spent much of his life in rebellion.

Consider the triangles in this family. In Mrs. T.'s original family, the parents disagreed over handling the behavior of her brother, Sam. His learning disability resulted in hyperactive behavior and poor grades in school, and he became argumentative and combative in the family. In reaction, her father was often harsh, while her mother both worried and protected Sam from his father's discipline. Sam was on the inside position with his mother, with the

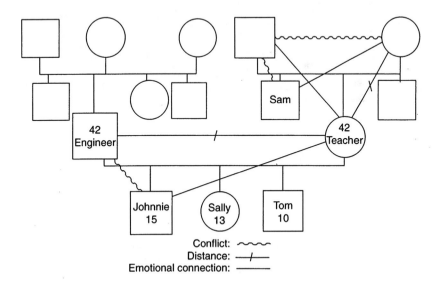

FIGURE 13.6. T. Family Diagram

father on the outside. Mrs. T. was on the inside position with her father, working for his approval and agreeing with him that Sam was a problem. She, like her father, agreed that her mother was weak and ineffective, leaving her mother on the outside. An interlocking triangle is formed among Sam, Mrs. T., and her mother. In this she was on the outside, never feeling her mother was hearing her observations about Sam's outrageous behavior. In the interlocking triangle with Sam and her father, Sam was on the outside, always the "problem child." Figure 13.7 illustrates this interlocking triangle process.

What is intriguing in families is the process through which an "emotional pattern" is transmitted from one generation to the next. Medical and emotional symptoms, such as heart disease, diabetes, depression, and substance abuse, are often observed to cascade from one generation to the next. However, these problems are also interwoven into a larger emotional process in which interlocking triangles are a regulating force. In her nuclear family, Mrs. T. had a role in a repeating pattern in which the oldest son absorbed the family anxiety, with the mother protecting and the father being critical of the child. Although she thought her mother "weak" in not disciplining her brother, she found herself overwhelmed by her own son.

Johnnie's father, Mr. T., an engineer like his father, is the younger of two brothers. Their mother, according to Mr. T., was a prescription "drug addict" and left the family when he was four. Their father, extremely busy with his work, kept the boys and eventually remarried a woman with several children. Charlie, Mr. T.'s brother, had a problematic growing up, but without the outrageous and violent overtones of Mrs. T.'s brother, Sam. Although Mr. T. had drifted a bit as a young man, when he married, he returned to graduate school to train as an engineer.

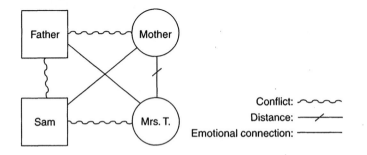

FIGURE 13.7. Interlocking Triangles

Mr. T.'s family poses some of the interesting questions about the repeating patterns of substance abuse in families. His is a family in which his mother, whom he barely knew and did not see after the age of four, was a substance abuser. The pattern of a child repeating the problem of a parent or grandparent they hardly know is not unique to this family. One important triangle for Mr. T. was formed through his reactivity to his mother, her addiction, and departure from his life and from Johnnie. In describing his fears about Johnnie, Mr. T. stated that his son's future was hopeless and that he would become a street person. He was convinced that no mode of intervention could be useful. The anxiety and fear from the relationship with his substance abusing mother, who left him at age four, flooded his relationship with Johnnie. Emotional reactivity is imprinted in each person in a way that is consistent with their experiences and important relationships and can be replayed, in spite of the death, departure, or distance of members of the original family. Conceptually this reactivity is transmitted through triangles. Figure 13.8 illustrates the transmission of anxiety from one generation to the next generation through a triangle.

Clinical Course with the T. Family

Mr. and Mrs. T. were seen to gather the history of the family and to understand their attempts to help their son. Johnnie had been seeing therapists since the age of nine and was presently seeing a psychiatrist for medication. An assessment was made of Johnnie, who was both depressed and angry with his parents. Johnnie had a history of substance abuse, starting with marijuana at about twelve, then progressing through a variety of drugs to using crack. He was associating with drug sellers in a dark world of nighttime dealing.

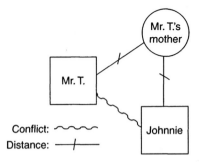

FIGURE 13.8. Transmission of Anxiety from One Generation to the Next Through a Triangle

The parents saw Johnnie as having a psychiatric problem that needed to be treated, rather than as an outcome of the emotional process in their family. They were overwhelmed and their reactive responses tended to fuel the family anxiety, without clearly addressing his behavior.

Mr. T. participated for a few sessions, but viewed his son's behavior as hopeless. Mrs. T. seemed more able to think in the midst of the emotionality, and she began to sort out her part of the problem. She saw that when her husband became emotional and critical of Johnnie, she stepped in to defend and protect him. She tried to mediate the tension between her husband and son, only leaving them more angry.

When she became less focused on calming their relationship and more thoughtful about her decisions and choices, she began to formulate some plans. This shift, not to either defend Johnnie or see him as sick as her husband did, created new possibilities for plans of action. She researched treatment options and made plans for him to enter a substance abuse program, followed by a year in a structured school environment.

While her son was away, Mrs. T. worked to understand functioning in her family, to not always be the peacemaker, to sort through her beliefs as a parent, and to take action on those beliefs. After a period of time in the school, Johnnie discussed his desire to return home and finish high school. After thought and discussion with her husband, she made the decision for him to come home, despite the opposition of the school. In that year, Johnnie returned to his school and successfully reintegrated himself in the family, managing to talk through his problems rather than turning to drugs or exploding in anger. He recently graduated from college and is in good contact with his family. For the T. family this is a different outcome than for either of the brothers of Mr. and Mrs. T., who continue to occupy the emotional positions as adults which they held in their families as children.

In this family, one member, Mrs. T., was interested in working on long-term change for herself. Her actions with her son and husband are one part of her effort.

The C. Family

Sadie, a Child of Divorce and Domestic Violence

The second clinical example reflects the work of a mother to think through her part in a triangle with her daughter and ex-husband over a period of about six months.

Sadie, a fourteen-year-old, was referred after an overdose with an over-the-counter drug for which she was treated at a local hospital. In coming to the first interview, she came dressed in black, with torn clothing, dark makeup, and dyed black hair. She reported a history of cutting herself, using drugs, and having uncontrollable angry outbursts since her parents' divorce two years earlier.

Sadie grew up abroad, living in France for much of her young life, as her father Mr. C. worked for an international corporation. She is the younger of two siblings, with her brother, Jake, five years older. The father was rigid and exacting in his discipline, with angry outbursts and physical punishment in response to noncompliance. During his teenage years, Jake increasingly became the recipient of his father's violence, including an incident in which the father choked him. After Jake attempted suicide and was diagnosed with depression, the father's violence began to be discussed by the family with professionals. The parents eventually separated. Figure 13.9 presents the C. family diagram.

Sadie was never the recipient of physical abuse, but she witnessed the events in her family. Her family dissolved about the time she entered adolescence and she was attending a loosely organized school in France. Her mother Mrs. C. was preoccupied and distraught over the separation. Without

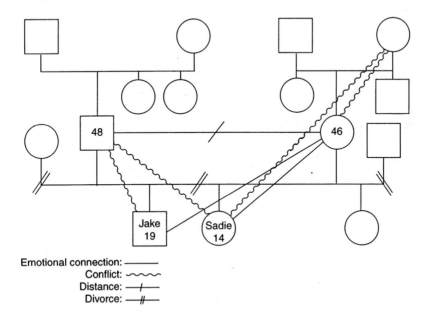

Emotional connection: ————
Conflict: 〜〜〜
Distance: —/—
Divorce: —//—

FIGURE 13.9. C. Family Diagram

her father's rigidity to constrain her, Sadie began to make her own decisions about drugs, class attendance, and friendships.

These events led to her difficulties when she first came to counseling. The primary triangle between her mother, her father, and herself changed when her parents separated. Her mother's alliance with her against her father shifted when he was not in the home to provide discipline. Although the mother and daughter had a delightful bantering relationship, Mrs. C. did not give Sadie much structure.

Mrs. C.'s marriage to Sadie's father was her second. She has a daughter from a previous marriage, who had similar difficulties to Sadie's and had dropped out of high school. Mrs. C. stated her husband pursued her in a whirlwind courtship. She was swept off her feet by his attentiveness and persistence. Only after they married, did she become aware of his temper and violence. She hesitated to intervene in his disciplining of the children, so as not to provoke him further. She tried to keep the peace with her husband, as she had with her mother as she was growing up.

Mrs. C. grew up with a mother she describes as being anxious and critical. She described herself as the problem child, as was her mother, Mrs. S., in her original family. Each was in the outside position with their older sister and their mother. Mrs. C. has a married older sister, with whom her mother had lived after the death of her father four years previously. She also has a younger brother, who has been married and divorced three times. Mrs. S., who had worn out her older daughter, came to live with the C. family when they returned to the United States. Mrs. S. criticized Sadie and Mrs. C.'s handling of Sadie's behavior. So the triangle was played out once again, with Mrs. C. protecting Sadie from her grandmother, and Sadie resenting her grandmother's intrusion.

Mr. C., Sadie's father, had no contact with his children since the divorce. He is the oldest, adopted by his family, before they had twin daughters. According to Mrs. C., her husband had been in conflict with his father and and had not been in touch with his parents over the period of years that he had been stationed abroad. Mr. C. had previously been married for six years, but had no children.

Two triangles exist in this family, with an intersecting point. Mrs. C. grew up in the primary triangle with her mother and father in which she worked to appease the critical reaction of her mother. This emotional patterning was replicated in the triangle with her husband and daughter, in which she sought to appease her husband. Figure 13.10 illustrates how these patterns of interactions are transmitted through triangles.

In reflecting on her inability to intervene with her husband when he was striking their son, she stated: "I thought if I got in the middle of that, it

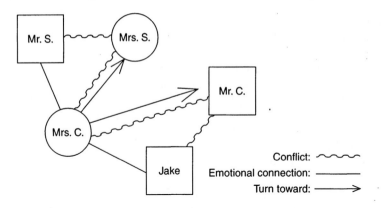

FIGURE 13.10. Patterns of Interactions Are Transmitted Through Triangles

would become worse, but I now feel guilty that I did not do more." These interlocking triangles between the generations become the vehicle for transmitting emotional patterns from one generation to the next. The reactions which Mrs. C. developed in childhood were played out with her husband and children.

Clinical Course with C. Family

Sadie went through a series of difficulties during the time she was in counseling. She skipped classes, refused to come to sessions, distributed drugs, and associated with friends who used drugs. However, her mother came to sessions on her own—to think through her reactions and contribution to the problems in the family and what she could do differently. Her understanding of her position in the triangle between her ex-husband and Sadie was useful in coming to some decisions about how to parent her daughter differently.

Mrs. C. realized she needed to define what she thought were reasonable limits and appropriate discipline that was neither rigid nor critical. She set up a contract for Sadie that delineated the requirements for Sadie's behavior and the consequences for not complying. Mrs. C. constructed this contract with Sadie's input, but she made the final decisions about it. The contract included no drug use, attending school regularly, and expecting Sadie to be in touch with her after school and on weekends. The contract was constructed as a means for Mrs. C. to define her thinking about her daughter's behavior and her own decision making, rather than a prescription for Sadie's behavior. Her attempt was to be clear, consistent, and calm by defining in advance with Sadie what behaviors were important to her and what actions she would take. A contract like this presupposes that the adolescent will test it, and the parent will have to take some action.

Mrs. C.'s change in behavior was based on her understanding of the triangle between herself, her ex-husband, and her daughter. She realized that she had developed a friendship type of relationship with her daughter as a counterbalance to her husband's rigidity and violence. When Sadie's father left the family, Mrs. C.'s laissez-faire approach offered her daughter no guidance to the world around her. Sadie believed that experience, rather than adult guidance, would teach her what choices she should make in life. She and her mother were in an alliance against her father. When one side of the triangle shifted by his leaving, their relationship was affected. What began as a protective, supportive effort by Mrs. C. became an ineffective, angry reactivity to her daughter. By defining her own beliefs and actions, Mrs. C. pulled back from the inside position in the triangle with her daughter.

The results of Mrs. C.'s efforts were dramatic. Sadie, as the months went by, began going to class regularly. She stopped using drugs and found that her old friends no longer appealed to her. She found her friend's drug use, skipping classes, and upsets as "too much drama." She generally let her mother know where she was, although this limit was tested several times and she was grounded for a week. Sadie began to dress in jeans and a shirt, with her hair its natural color. She began to look fourteen. Coming to sessions at this point, she talked about the guilt she felt about being the favored child in her family, who was not physically punished like her brother. She began to examine her angry outbursts, which were a teenage version of her father's anger. Finally, she concluded that she had not made good use of her first year in high school and decided to repeat the ninth grade, despite her dislike of school.

Theoretically, a triangle consists of the interactive relationships of three people. A change in one person affects the other two. In the primary triangle, Mrs. C. was in a less protective position with Sadie in reaction to her husband. Setting limits and enforcing them with Sadie was hard work for Mrs. C., but she was determined to be clear with her daughter. Although their relationship was filled with humor, she dreaded Sadie's outbursts when she did not get her way. However, Mrs. C. stuck to her plan. Her efforts triggered change in Sadie, even when her daughter refused to come to sessions.

Another outcome was Mrs. C.'s ability to take a stand in the triangle with her mother about her daughter. She took a position with her mother that Sadie was her responsibility. Her mother was angry about that decision, and moved

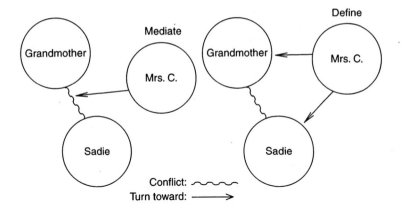

FIGURE 13.11. Shift in Triangle As Mrs. C. Took a Position

in with her brother within several months. This was a shift in the triangle with her mother and Sadie. The shift in the triangle is illustrated in Figure 13.11.

This single parent family is a powerful example of the custodial parent and a child united in the inside position in a triangle, with the noncustodial parent on the outside. Society and the family perceive the child as abandoned by the absent parent, who is more often the father. A family systems view is that the child and the mother are fused in an intense togetherness with the father in the outside position. This can serve to extrude him and to give little room for the mother to define herself to the child. Often the relationship between the mother and child explodes in adolescence, with the mother demanding that the father take the child. Then the most comfortable position for the mother is on the outside position in the triangle.

The J. Family

Carmina, in a Triangle of Three Generations

Carmina is a sixteen-year-old young woman of Puerto Rican descent. She was referred for counseling by a high school counselor after marijuana was found in her back pack at high school. She had been skipping school, her grades had declined in the last year, and she was hanging around a boy reputed to be in a gang.

Carmina was born in New York when her mother, Sylvia, was eighteen, unmarried, and living with Carmina's father, Enrique. Sylvia is one of the five children of Mr. and Mrs. J., a couple who had emigrated from Puerto Rico to New Jersey in 1975, when Sylvia was four. She was the third child, with two older brothers and a younger sister and brother. Her father, who worked in construction, left the family when Sylvia was fourteen. He went to live with his girlfriend whom he subsequently married after the birth of their daughter, Gina. Sylvia had been close to her father and was devastated by his departure. She had a scratchy relationship with her mother, which blossomed into full scale rebellion when she entered adolescence. She began using drugs and staying out all night with boys. Her older brother, José, tried to intervene, but had many responsibilities for his wife and young child. Finally at age seventeen, Sylvia was smitten with Enrique and followed him to New York where Carmina was born. Sylvia cut off contact with her family as her mother did not approve of her lifestyle. However, when Enrique left, Sylvia sank deeper into her drug use, and agreed that Carmina live with her grandmother, rather than be placed in foster care by the authorities. Figure 13.12 presents the J. family diagram.

Enrique is the fourth of seven children of a Puerto Rican family who lived in the Bronx when he was growing up. His mother was a housekeeper for a large hotel; his father worked in a kitchen. His mother was very religious and hoped Enrique would become a priest. He was attracted to the life of the streets and began as a lookout for a gang when he was twelve. He dropped out of school at sixteen, and did not find full-time work. He was the

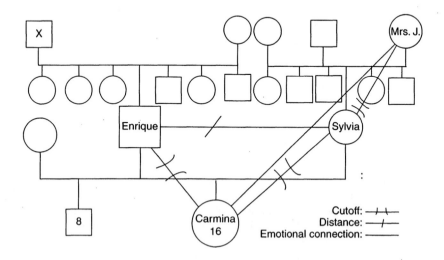

FIGURE 13.12. J. Family Diagram

object of much concern in his home, as his three older sisters had married and were beginning respectable lives, according to his mother. She did not want him to be a bad influence on his younger brothers and sister, so at eighteen he left home, sleeping in friends' apartments. He met Sylvia when he was visiting in DC. Sylvia and Enrique had a rocky, conflictual relationship for four years, which ended when Enrique left to live with another woman.

At age four Carmina came to live with Sylvia's mother, Mrs. J. Carmina, and was raised by her grandmother, as her mother's drug addiction deepened. Carmina saw Enrique twice after she came to live with her grandmother, but he had started another family which absorbed his attention. Sylvia was a phantom, calling sporadically and occasionally sending presents, but rarely visiting her daughter.

When Carmina was fourteen, her mother entered a drug treatment program in New York. During the period of her treatment, she began to assess her life and decided to make contact with Carmina. She wrote to her daughter and asked to visit her. At first Mrs. J. was hesitant to allow the visit, as Sylvia had been unreliable in the past. However, after several discussions, she came to visit. She told Carmina she wanted to change her life and become more involved with her. After that visit, Sylvia relapsed. About a year later, Sylvia contacted her again, began to visit, and made the decision to move to Washington, DC, to be closer to her daughter. She became employed and moved into a stable lifestyle.

Carmina, her mother, and grandmother are in a multigenerational triangle in a similar way to two parents with a child. Mrs. J. and Carmina are intensely attached to one another, with Sylvia on the outside position of this triangle. The grandmother protected Carmina from her mother's erratic behavior. With her drug addiction and distance, Sylvia's behavior put herself on the outside position in the triangle with her mother and her daughter. However, in contacting the family, she attempted to get out of that outside position and play a role in Carmina's life. This effort to be responsible upset the stability of the triangle and created tension between Carmina and her grandmother. Mrs. J. felt threatened by her daughter's wish to be involved, and Carmina was bewildered by the conflicting opinions of the two women. Figure 13.13 illustrates how Sylvia's moving toward her daughter, Carmina, upset the balance of the triangle.

The first signs of Carmina's problematic behavior began when her mother arrived to live near her. She found disagreements between her mother and grandmother over the rules she was to follow confusing as she was entering high school. The original tension that existed between Mrs. J. and her daughter when she was a teenager was retriggered when she returned to Washington, DC. Sylvia had handled that tension by using drugs as a teen-

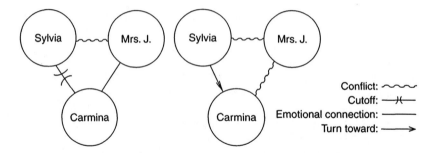

FIGURE 13.13. By Moving Closer, Sylvia Upset the Balance of the Triangle

ager, leaving home at seventeen, moving in with her boyfriend, and cutting off from her family. When she reentered the family circle, these unresolved issues and emotions reappeared, but were focused on Carmina. Sylvia believed Mrs. J. was too protective and strict with Carmina, a similar reaction to her own adolescence.

Clinical Course with the J. Family

After a family interview with Mrs. J., Sylvia, and Carmina, which became heated and volatile, the family members were seen individually and together, often with two members, such as Carmina and her mother. The focus of discussion with Sylvia was sorting out her relationship with her mother, and understanding how to build a relationship with Carmina. Carmina's effort was to get her own life back on track, without becoming too focused on the conflict between her grandmother and mother. Mrs. J. tried to step back and listen to her daughter, rather than react defensively. She began to acknowledge that her daughter had made real steps to put her life back together and the move closer to the family was an opportunity to rebuild her relationships in the family.

Mrs. J. and Sylvia had an experience common to two parents making decisions about a child. They did not agree. Sylvia saw her mother as being rigid with Carmina; Mrs. J. thought her daughter permissive, leading to a path of drug addiction. Using the triangle as a frame of reference, each parent or parental figure is important to the child and can offer a different experience. Their different opinions are not the source of the difficulty. The problem arises when one parent steps between the other parent and the child. The parents or parental figures live out their disagreements through the child, rather than resolving them between themselves.

Most of the time, each parent does have useful input to the raising of a child. Mrs. J. came to realize that she could not protect Carmina from experiencing difficulties and choices in her life. Sylvia became more appreciative that structure, limits, and supervision, as well as building a relationship with her mother, were useful for her daughter. Both came to understand that using Carmina as a focus for their own unresolved tensions only created more difficulties for her.

The family continued in their consultations for a year. Sylvia continued to stabilize her life, entering a computer training program. She had more personal interchanges with her mother, with both beginning to gain some insight into the other's life. They attempted to define what they could agree upon as some basic guidelines for Carmina. This young woman became appreciative of her mother's efforts to change and to play a part in her life. Her grades improved, she attended school regularly, she tried out for cheerleading, and her friendships slowly shifted to other teenagers who were involved and interested in school and school activities.

THE CONCEPT OF THE TRIANGLE IN CLINICAL WORK

The triangle is one of nine concepts in Bowen Theory. As a concept, it is a lens through which to see interactions in a family, particularly between two parents and a child.

How are triangles useful for families to change?

1. Triangles are a tool to observe the interactions in a relationship system. Observation allows more room for perspective, rather than reactivity. Triangles can operate across generations, as well as in the nuclear family.
2. Triangles are based on the premise that dyadic relationships are unstable. Three people create the basic unit of interaction. To observe and understand the patterns of tension in a family allows choices about how to operate in it. When tension rises, two people are on the inside position, with the third on the outside.
3. The primary triangle between the parents and each child is the most formative emotional experience in an individual's life. This triangle is operative even when one parent is absent, creating an intense bond between the custodial parent and the child.
4. Understanding one's position in a triangle allows a person more clarity on how to define herself in each relationship. This particularly relates to two parents sorting through their ideas on how to raise a child,

without drawing the child into their differences. Parents do not have to agree on every aspect of raising a child. However, when one parent interferes with the decisions of the other, the child is drawn into an alliance with that parent.

5. Substances play a role in triangling in a family. A substance can intensify both distance and dependency in relationships. The adolescent can turn to substances for a lifestyle, set of relationships, and a means to mediate the relationship with his or her parents. The use of alcohol and drugs also plays a role in blocking the acquisition of life skills and emotional maturity that help the teenager make the transition to adulthood.

SUMMARY

The concept of the triangle illustrates the emotional process in families with a problematic child, such as a substance abusing teenager. In the primary triangle between the parents and the child, the child is often the focus of a projection process. In this triangle, the parents handle tension in their relationship by automatically focusing on the problems of the teenager. The teenager reacts to the focus through anger, rebellion, or depression, emotions which are often self-medicated through drugs and alcohol. Alliances are also formed in the primary triangle between one parent, who is protective or sympathetic, and the teenager leaving the other parent, perceived as harsh or unloving, on the outside. In each of these triangles, teenagers who are reacting to family life can turn to substances as a means to feel more separate or adult. However, the use of substances often interferes with their ability to fulfill the tasks of their lives, such as succeeding in school, friendships, or work, leaving them more dependent on their parents. Triangles also operate across generations, with a parent repeating patterns of interaction with a child similar to those in his or her original family. Three case examples were discussed to highlight how triangles are a concept that helps clinicians and family members observe, and ultimately work to change, the emotional process which fuels the problematic behavior of teenagers who are abusing substances.

REFERENCE

Bowen, M. (1978). *Family therapy in clinical practice*. New York: Jason Aronson.

Chapter 14

A Family Affair:
Triangles in Extramarital Relationships

Eileen B. Gottlieb

INTRODUCTION

This chapter describes and discusses extramarital behavior as an expression of the family emotional process. Offering a broader, factual, and more objective view of this phenomenon helps to explain the function of this behavior within the family in which it occurs. Extramarital relationships represent one version of the formation of a triangle whose function is to bind anxiety and stabilize the family emotional system.

This chapter will describe the facts about the relationship process in a family that is susceptible to the expression of this behavior. It will focus on the facts about how triangles originate, operate, and occur throughout the natural world. It will discuss the role of triangles in the development of extramarital relationships.

This chapter will examine three principal questions:

1. What are the facts about a family that develops an extramarital affair?
2. What are the facts about an affair that results in a divorce?
3. What can Bowen theory lend to a greater understanding of these processes?

TRIANGLES

The Nature of Triangles in the Living World

Life is governed by relationships between interdependent organisms. Symbiotic relationships that mutually benefit living things operate throughout nature. Inherent in these symbioses is an underlying tension related to the struggle to survive and reproduce. Darwin referred to this as the process of natural selection. One mechanism observable in living systems for managing the symbiotic relationships is the triangle. When the tension between two beings cannot be managed between them, another party is drawn into the process to help stabilize one of the original twosome. This two against one alliance temporarily stabilizes the tension by strengthening the insiders at the expense of the outsider. When a relationship between two insiders is calm the outsider is tense and uncomfortable in the outside position.

When tension develops between the insiders, as it inevitably does, the outsider is calm and more comfortable in the outside position. Due to the unstable nature of the relationship process among living things, triangles are always present and shift with changes in emotional states.

The extent to which a triangle stabilizes the emotional system depends on the capacity of the people involved to manage their relationships responsibly. The less able families are to manage emotional attachment and the anxiety it creates, the more susceptible the marriage becomes to symptoms. An affair is a symptom of the underlying emotional attachment and the anxiety associated with it present in the family. The same forces that are responsible for other physical, emotional, and social symptoms contribute to the development of extramarital affairs. They are one version of an intense, interdependent emotional process.

The Function of Triangles in Relationship Systems

Emotional attachment, interdependency, and reciprocity characterize social networks. Chronic anxiety and patterns for managing it evolve over generations and are observable in these natural systems. One way in which threats to the survival and well-being of the individual are managed is through the formation of relationships. One pattern of relationship management is the triangle. This pattern involves the projection of the anxiety in a relationship between two parties onto a third. The third party absorbs some of the problem and stabilizes the relationship between the original two. Once the new relationship becomes tense, the process shifts again to include either the original or another third party which, again, temporarily stabilizes these relationships. This process repeats itself over and over again until the tension is resolved or one party is eventually excluded.

EXTRAMARITAL RELATIONSHIPS

Extramarital relationships are one example of how triangles operate in the human family. Where there is significant emotional investment, heightened sensitivity, and extreme emotional reactivity between partners, triangles are more likely to be active. Extramarital affairs are one version of this process. When an emotional system is undergoing significant change and transition extramarital affairs may be more likely to occur.

Extramarital relationships can stabilize or destabilize a marriage. The more intense and prolonged the affair the more likely it is to create changes in the marriage. Marriages vary in their capacity to deal with the development of an affair. How the affair is addressed is an expression of the level of differentiation, degree of chronic anxiety, and the family emotional process that has evolved over the generations.

Families manage extramarital affairs in the same manner that they manage all other parts of the relationship system. Depending upon the degree of emotional attachment, the level of chronic anxiety, and the multigenerational patterns, families vary in the degree of symptom development. The more unresolved the emotional attachment between the spouses and their families of origin, the greater the degree of unresolved emotional attachment to one another. The more unresolved the emotional attachment between spouses, the greater the degree of unresolved attachment between parents and their children. Unresolved emotional attachment breeds chronic anxiety that is related to the underlying interdependence in a relationship. The more interdependence there is between family members, the greater the reaction to potential or real threats to the existing emotional balance in the relationships. Sensitivity to disturbances in key relationships is managed by patterns that develop across generations. This process can be observed in all families to some degree.

Variations in Extramarital Behavior

How the emotional system manages the intensity of the relationships and the chronic anxiety associated with the shifts in key triangles will determine whether an extramarital affair develops and to what extent it becomes a serious problem.

The function of infidelity is to maintain emotional equilibrium in a disturbed relationship system through inclusion of a third party resulting in a two against one and two in, one out situation. Affairs represent the inability to objectively adapt to changes in an interdependent emotional network. Affairs are not created equal. They occur along a continuum, more reactive and chronic to less so, with varying consequences.

The manner in which an extramarital relationship is handled within a family is a function of the family emotional process. The same forces that play a part in the expression of this problem also play a part in the solution.

Emotional interdependency, chronic anxiety, and the multigenerational process determine the impact of this situation on the family.

The objective capacity of people to assess the process in the relationships and focus on the part each one plays in the problem is the goal of Bowen theory. Learning to manage self in the triangle is a critical factor in the development of an affair. The ability to stay focused on managing self in relationship to the other parts of the triangle has significant consequences for the parties involved. When people are able to take responsibility for their functioning and allow others to do likewise, there is less anxiety and emotional reactivity, resulting in more stability in the relationships. More stable relationships are less vulnerable to symptoms such as extramarital affairs.

Marriage has been characterized in some instances by relationships where one party or the other develops an outside, intimate, emotional, and physical attachment. This phenomenon transcends all historical, cultural, chronological, sexual, political, economic, and religious considerations. It is observable throughout the human world as well as in other species. To the extent these liaisons, the existing marital relationship, or pair bond, and the surrounding emotional field, mutually influence one another, there is variation from situation to situation.

In *Family Evaluation,* Kerr (Kerr and Bowen, 1988) states that similar processes have been observed in the nonhuman world, albeit, to lesser degrees. He says that depending upon the organism's intellectual development and capacity for memory and recognition, some birds, mammals, and primates exhibit degrees of association, including social and mating relationships with partners outside the mating pair.

Jane Goodall (1986) describes that at some point during the early stage of full estrus, some males start to show possessive behavior toward the female. The higher the rank of the male in the hierarchy, the more he is able to monopolize the female to some extent. If his close proximity to her and his aggressive threats do not deter sexual advances, he may attack the female.

Frans de Waal (1989) also observes that at the Arnhem chimpanzee colony, the alpha male has clear control of mating rights and is "incredibly intolerant" when lower ranking males try to mate with any female in the colony. If he notices a clandestine copulation, it is the female who bares the brunt of his displeasure. As he is very likely to attack her, for the most part, the females refuse to comply with the courtship demands of lower ranking suitors. However, they do so eagerly, even through bars, when the alpha male is shut outside or in a different cage.

Goodall suggests that when the dominance hierarchy is relatively stable and most particularly when there is a clear cut alpha, there is not likely to be much fighting over the female, even when she is most fertile and surrounded by many adult males.

Stephen Emlen (1989) describes the adaptive significance of polygynous behavior among birds. Polygyny, the pairing of one male with more than one female, occurs when resource distributions are sufficiently uneven that the female can maximize her chance of leaving offspring by mating bigamously with an already mated male in high quality territory rather than monogamously with an unmated male occupying a lower quality territory.

T. Burke (1989) observes that female birds benefit from copulating with two males because their chicks are fed more and survive more with the help of two males rather than one. According to Bowen theory, triangular processes exist in all relationships. They represent automatic, instinctual reactions to discomfort and function to manage anxiety in living relationships. This process is presumed to be the relationship system struggling to restore harmony. The emotionally based nature of this process emphasizes short-term, immediate solutions aimed at restoring emotional comfort to the system. The most recent findings in neuroscience, including those of Gerald Huether (1996), emphasize the role of the stress response with its activation of the hypothalamus, pituitary, adrenal axis, and the release of corticoid hormones. This process occurs automatically in the face of a perceived or real threat. It continues until the organism finds a way to manage the fear and acts to restore its sense of well-being. Triangles are activated in this process.

FAMILY AFFAIRS

Most research in human behavior focuses on cause and effect thinking as opposed to a broader, more factual, systems view of functioning. Cause and effect paradigms limit investigations to a small number of variables that often do not account for variations in human behavior.

Extramarital relationships are treated in the literature as an individual process whose reasons for existence are limited to examining the dynamics of the marital dyad. At its worst, this examination involves a subjective assignment of blame, an identification of perpetrator and victim, and a polarized position as to detriment or value to the human family and society. At its best, conclusions about extramarital behavior are based on specific causes such as marital dissatisfaction and desire for change.

Bowen theory provides a way of thinking about extramarital behavior as a variation of the family emotional process. A broader, clearer, more neutral view of this process may permit families, clinicians, and society to understand better the facts about this phenomenon.

Bowen theory postulates that functioning is the outcome of emotional attachment and interdependent processes that operate in all relationship systems. These processes occur on both an instinctual and automatic basis, originating in the emotional brain as well as a more thoughtful level associated with the intellectual brain and its capacity to acquire, analyze, and act upon objective information.

According to Bowen, behavior is a broad multigenerational process that evolves through relationships over time. Depending upon the degree of emotional togetherness, the level of concern about mutual well-being and the mechanisms for managing these, each family displays its behavioral repertoire. Bowen (1978) wrote:

> In any one generation the family projection process involves each child with a different level of intensity. The maximally involved child emerges with a lower level of self than the parents. Minimally involved children may emerge with about the same level as the parents. Children relatively out of the process may emerge with higher levels of self. When each child marries at about the level from which he emerges from the nuclear family, some descendants in the family do better with life than their parents did, and others do less well. The multigenerational process provides a base from which to make predictions in the present generation and gives an overview of what to expect in coming generations. (p. 206)

Bowen observed that triangles are the product of the degree of emotional attachment, the level of chronic anxiety, and the multigenerational process. This includes the variation in anxiety management represented by extramarital relationships. Like all behavior, these relationships serve the system in some way. They function to maintain the emotional equilibrium associated with the individual and collective nature of life. An affair is the behavioral expression of emotional attachment, chronic anxiety, and relationship intensity. It is one version of triangular mechanisms for managing these relationships. Affairs are the system's emotional reaction to a disturbance in the balance of important relationships. They represent an inability to adapt effectively to changes in an interdependent emotional network. Extramarital affairs are one variation of emotional reactivity in the behavioral repertoire of a relationship system.

All extramarital relationships are not equal. Some are short-lived and appear to create little change in the relationship process. Others temporarily disrupt the relationship equilibrium. Still others spread to many interlocking triangles and eventually contribute to more permanent, widespread relationship difficulties. Whatever the level of intensity and reactivity that are observable, functional facts provide insight into the nature of this process.

Extramarital affairs develop in families where there is a high degree of emotional togetherness between spouses and between spouses and others in the extended family. Family members spend most of their time outside of work and other important responsibilities focused on each other's actions. This includes thinking about, reacting to, spending time with, fantasizing, or complaining about the other. There is an ongoing, sustained, high level of concern about meeting the requirements and expectations of others as well as those meeting the requirements and expectations of self. The issues that are the most highly charged emotionally are related to triangles continuing from each spouse's family of origin and the multigenerational past which include physical concerns, emotional or relationship issues, economics, intellectual, entertainment, and spiritual interests.

Families that are more susceptible to extramarital affairs show prolonged, repetitive attempts to take care of others and prolonged patterns of soliciting from others. They also present consistently strong reactions when one is unable to satisfy the requirements of others or self. A cycle of blame and guilt is part of this process. Likewise, there is a limited ability to observe and think about the process in the relationships. Problems are viewed as occurring in a person rather than in the relationship between people. Cause and effect views of relationship interaction result in polarized positions and stalemates. Functioning positions in the existing triangles are fairly fixed, polarized, and show limited flexibility between taking a stand for self and standing with the others. People in these families are either over- or underinvolved with one another. There is a multigenerational pattern of anxiety management through relationship togetherness or distance.

Extramarital affairs are more likely to occur in families where spouses are part of an emotional system undergoing change such as birth, death, departure, illness, career or financial changes, or relocation. When there is sufficient disturbance in the emotional equilibrium of principal triangles across the generations, existing constellations may be inadequate to manage the current level of anxiety and reactivity. The family is unable to contain anxiety effectively within the two-person relationship. In this case, an outside party is invited in, or volunteers, or both. This temporarily stabilizes the reactivity until the outsider takes sides and one of the original insiders is pushed out. Kerr (Kerr and Bowen, 1988) describes the new triangle as temporarily shifting the focus from spouses to the outsider, eventually increasing the focus on each other. Where no one in the system is able to be in contact with all other parties without taking sides and participating in it, symptoms are more likely to develop. One possible symptom is an affair. The greater the degree of emotional attachment, the higher the level of anxiety associated with it, and the stronger the blueprint for relationship focus, the more likely a family will polarize in the face of an extramarital relationship.

Extramarital affairs are one example of how triangles operate in the service of an anxious, undifferentiated emotional system. They can stabilize an unstable twosome or destabilize a stable twosome. A tense marriage becomes less tense when one partner has another relationship that absorbs some of his anxiety. A stable marriage becomes more tense when one partner shifts attention to another relationship. According to Kerr (Kerr and Bowen, 1988), a conflictual marriage can become more harmonious after an extramarital relationship when the couple shifts the focus of anxiety to the outsider. He describes how the loss of the outsider increases conflict, as the third party is unavailable for inclusion in the marital problem.

Kerr (Kerr and Bowen, 1988) indicates that understanding the facts about extramarital behavior depends on seeing each corner of the triangle as a functioning position that participates in the process. He describes that when it is conceptualized as a relationship.process, each individual's functioning and behavior represents his position in that process. The greater the inflexibility of functioning positions, the more predictable the behavior. As pressure shifts, no one in the extramarital triangle or other interlocking triangles assumes responsibility for self. The focus becomes management of the other. Partners emphasize their rights, not their responsibilities.

This is the point at which an extramarital affair has the potential to evolve into a divorce. The difference between the emotional process of an affair and that of a divorce is based on the degree of relationship intensity and emotional reactivity. The same processes operate in both situations, the only difference being the degree and extent to which they occur. The more reactive the family is to the togetherness, the more subjective the perceptions, the more automatic the responses, the more extreme the behavior, the more limited the options for managing itself, the greater the probability that a divorce will take place. Divorce results from the same process that creates an affair but it involves a broader range of triangles, more anxiety, polarization, and cutoff.

Mental health professionals working with families and their difficulties, have the potential to assist people in their ability to increase or decrease anxiety. They have the opportunity to expand knowledge and to lend a hand in the effort to work on differentiation of self, the capacity to know the facts about one's own functioning to better integrate the intellectual and emotional systems. Looking at extramarital behavior through the broader lens of Bowen theory brings into focus the interplay of emotional and relationship processes. Triangles, anxiety, and differentiation of self are otherwise missed in a more narrow, dyadic view. Assuming Bowen accurately observed the way relationship systems operate, can we use this knowledge to achieve greater flexibility in dealing with the interdependent emotional process that characterizes the family? Can we be objective in our effort to create more viable alternatives for living together?

CASE STUDIES

Bowen theory proposes that an individual's capacity to cope with the circumstances of life, including his or her most significant relationships, is the result of the family emotional process and his or her position in it. The family relationship system automatically determines, to some extent, how one thinks about self and others. The ability to be knowledgeable and thoughtful about this process makes a difference in family functioning. This process is projected from one generation to the next and influences functioning depending upon how much objectivity an individual is able to develop in a lifetime (Bowen, 1978).

The following case studies illustrate the presence of the family emotional process in the development of extramarital relationships. In each of the families this behavior represents a triangle that develops to manage the emotional attachment and chronic anxiety in the relationship system. These families vary in the impact of the triangle on the system and demonstrate the part that objectivity plays in this process. The more objective one is about the relationship process in the family, the greater the likelihood he or she will be able to stay connected to the past and manage the present effectively. Effectively managing the present has important implications for the future. The capacity of the present generation to manage shifts in key relationships influences how the future generation will stand up to similar challenges.

Family Number One

Mr. A. is sixty-three and his wife is forty-nine. They married in 1991, following the death of his former wife from breast cancer at the age of forty-one in 1987. They had been married for twenty-one years. That marriage produced two sons, one now thirty-seven and the other thirty-five. Both sons are college educated, employed in their father's business, and married. The eldest son has one child, aged ten, and the younger son has two children, aged eight and five. Mrs. A.'s son, aged twenty-nine, was born to a very brief first marriage. In 1978 she married her second husband who adopted her son. They divorced in 1989.

Mr. A. is the youngest of six children. His parents were married forty years until his father died at age seventy in 1967. His mother lived to age ninety-seven and died in 2003. His eldest brother died of cancer at age seventy-two in 2003. Although he has always had regular contact with his parents and siblings, until recently they did not know much about his personal life. He describes his role in the family as that of the beloved baby boy, adored by all except his immediate older brother with whom he had a difficult time. He has also maintained contact with his deceased wife's family over the years. Figure 14.1 presents the A. family diagram.

Mr. A. describes growing up in a close knit family circle where there was contact between the generations. He has a strong recollection of his maternal grandfather as being a "womanizer" and someone who always had a girlfriend. He also recalls that this was true of other uncles and friends in that generation. He does not believe this to be true of his own father.

Mrs. A. is also the youngest of four children. Her parents were married in 1944 and lived together until her mother died at seventy-eight in 2002. Mrs. A.'s mother had a stroke in 1989, broke her hip and was bedridden from 1999 until her death. Her older siblings are all living. She has had difficulties with her family relationships throughout her life. She has gone for years without contact with her sister. Most recently, she has not spoken to her son for two years. She has never maintained contact with her son's father or his family and has minimal contact with his adoptive father and family.

Mrs. A. refers to her father as a reformed alcoholic and sex abuser. She did not speak to him once she left home for college until the birth of her son. The relationship remained strained until her mother's stroke. They speak more often now, but still seldom see each other. She recalls her mother as a weak person whose life was controlled by her husband.

Mr. A. is a successful, affluent businessman who is financially helpful to his children and grandchildren. Mrs. A. is a college graduate who had a career in advertising and marketing prior to their marriage. She has not worked in twenty-three years. In 1998, during the recession, Mr. A. experienced his first financial reversals. At this time the marriage became conflicted and distant. They drank more heavily. Mrs. A. developed back problems and was prescribed medication for anxiety. Mr. A. experienced angina and was also prescribed medication.

In 1998, Mr. A. met a thirty-seven-year-old woman with whom he became emotionally and sexually involved. She had been married and divorced twice, with two children. He saw her frequently, especially when his wife

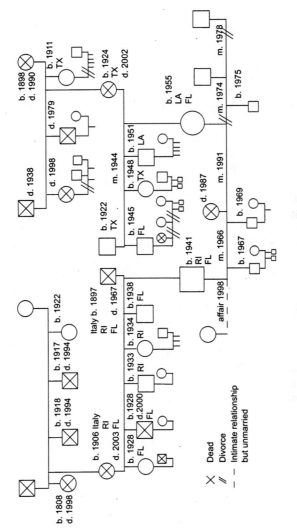

FIGURE 14.1. A Family Diagram

X Dead

// Divorce

– – Intimate relationship
     but unmarried

went out of town to their second home on the West Coast. As he developed new business ventures and his finances improved, he began to help support the new woman financially. He also introduced her to his sons, but not to their families, his mother, or siblings. He hid the relationship from all but his closest friends.

Eventually, Mrs. A. discovered the affair. The conflict and distance further increased. She threatened to leave. He promised to end the relationship. They consulted a professional on and off for several years. Mrs. A. stayed and became increasingly anxious and depressed. Mr. A. continued the other relationship in secret. Eventually, Mrs. A spent more time at their home on the West Coast. She bought a horse and began training and competing. They spent less and less time together. In 2002, her mother died and Mr. A.'s mother died in 2003. At the same time Mrs. A stopped speaking to her son. Mr. A.'s oldest son separated from his wife and began living with another woman.

In the spring of 2004, Mrs. A. hired a private detective. She discovered that the relationship between her husband and the other woman was continuing. She filed for divorce. After three months they decided to negotiate a financial settlement and again seek counseling. They are currently spending more time together than a year ago, while still residing on separate coasts.

Mr. A.'s older son has been involved with another woman for two years. He moves back and forth between his wife and daughter and the other woman. His younger son is concerned that the divorce will destroy the family financially. He has asked his father to make a decision regarding his marriage and stick to it.

This family illustrates the part that unresolved emotional fusion, chronic anxiety, and the multigenerational process play in the development of an extramarital affair. Emotional fusion refers to the symbiotic relationship observable in all human relationships. This symbiosis is characterized by interdependence, reciprocity, and emotional reactivity, and functions for the mutual benefit of both people in the relationship. Symbiotic relationships can be observed everywhere in the natural world from bacteria to social insects to mammals and primates. Human symbiosis involves the constant struggle to balance the need for togetherness or fusion with the need for individuality.

The more people are dependent on one another to meet emotional needs the greater the degree of chronic anxiety in the relationship. Chronic anxiety refers to the sensitivity to real or perceived shifts in the emotional involvement between people. The multigenerational process involves the patterns that have developed across the generations for managing emotional attachment and chronic anxiety. In marriage, these patterns include conflict, distance, physical, emotional, and social symptoms in a spouse, and projection of the anxiety onto a child. Extramarital affairs are one version of a triangle that evolves to manage interdependency. The role of the clinician is to assist the family in addressing the nature of the relationships between the past, present, and future generations. By focusing on the facts of functioning, maintaining emotional neutrality, and allowing the family members to take responsibility for their actions, the clinician offers them an opportunity to work on resolving some of the emotional attachment. When family members can be more emotionally separate yet not cut off from one another, chronic anxiety is lowered, and the automatic patterns for managing it, including the expression of triangles, are replaced by more objective, thoughtful choices.

Specific areas to be addressed in working with this family are the relationships between each spouse and members of each one's own family, children, and one another's families. The ability to make more contact with other important family members provides each spouse with the opportunity to become more clear about who he or she is, what he or she stands for, and what it takes to represent it to the others in his or her life. Being more present in these key relationships enables people to better manage the intensity and sensitivities associated with deep emotional attachments. This capacity for more open and real family relationships lowers the anxiety in the spouses. Lower anxiety fosters more objective expectations of self and the other leading to a more comfortable, satisfying, and stable marital relationship. Stable emotional units are better able to contain and manage anxiety without the expression of symptoms.

Family Number Two

Mr. G. is fifty-nine and his wife is fifty-five. They were married in 1983. Mr. G was previously married in 1972 and divorced in 1982. He has two children from the first marriage, a daughter and son aged thirty and twenty-seven, respectively. Mrs. G. was previously married and divorced twice. The first marriage lasted six months and the second from 1968 to 1976. She has two daughters from her second marriage, age thirty-five and thirty-two. All the children are college educated and working professionals. They are all married. Mr. G. has one grandchild and Mrs. G. has three.

Mr. G.'s father died in 2000 at the age of eighty-three. His eighty-three-year-old mother died in 2005. He has one younger brother who is fifty-seven. Mr. G. has always lived near his parents. Although he has been helpful to them financially, he does not consider himself close to them. He says they do not know him well. He describes his relationship with his brother as difficult. They have not spoken since their parent's deaths. Figure 14.2 presents the G. family diagram.

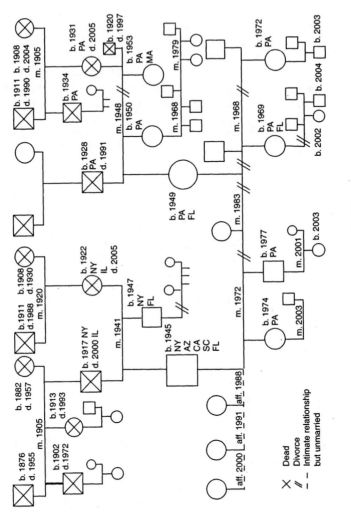

FIGURE 14.2. G. Family Diagram

X   Dead
// Divorce
– – Intimate relationship
    but unmarried

344

Mr. G. also has a distant relationship with his son. There were many years that they did not speak. He has always had contact with his daughter as well as his ex-wife. He helped raise his stepdaughters and has regular contact with them and their families.

He describes his parents as very intense. His mother focused most of her attention on her sons, especially Mr. G. She worried more about him than his brother. His father was extremely sensitive to his wife's concerns for Mr. G. They pushed both sons to succeed financially. Both did. Mr. G. is currently a successful businessman. His brother is a physician. Mr. G. has had problems with drug addiction and spent six months in a minimum-security prison in 1983. He has undergone drug rehabilitation and participates in a twelve-step program.

Mrs. G. is the oldest of three daughters. Her parents married in 1948 and divorced in 1964. Her father died at the age of sixty-three in 1991 of lung cancer. He had a history of emotional and physical disorders including suicide attempts and electric shock therapy. He had a long-term extramarital relationship. Mrs. G. did not speak to her father for fifteen years prior to his death. Her mother died at the age of seventy-three. She had lived alone since her second husband died in 1990. Mrs. G. and her mother always had a close relationship, although Mrs. G believes her mother made many mistakes in her life. Mrs. G. is also very involved with her daughters and their children. She is also in close contact with both her sisters and their families. She considers the family the most important part of her life. Mrs. G. helped create her husband's company and has worked as the administrator and bookkeeper for twenty years.

Five years into his first marriage, Mr. G. began to have extramarital relationships. In 1988 he began an affair that lasted eighteen months. Another extramarital relationship began in 1991, and continued until his wife discovered it in 1993. They agreed to seek professional help and decided to stay together if he ended the affair. He did. In 2000 he began another relationship with an employee in his company. After four years his wife informed him that she was suing for divorce. They again sought professional help. They continued to live together, but in separate parts of their home. They continued to work together in their business. He fired his employee. Mrs. G. was unsure that she wanted to continue the marriage. Mr. G. did not want a divorce. He believed he would solve his problem based on his previous ability to quit his drug habit.

After Mr. G.'s mother died in April 2005 and Mrs. G.'s mother died one month later, they divorced in July 2005. They live apart and continue to work in their family business together. They speak frequently outside of work and spend some time together with their children on special occasions.

This family illustrates the part that intense emotional interdependency, chronic anxiety, and the multigenerational process play in the development of multiple extramarital affairs. The clinician assists family members toward awareness of the degree of unresolved emotional attachment and cutoff that exists between the generations. Efforts to work on the part one plays in this process can lead to more effective relationships. With a better ability to manage self in relationship to important others, chronic anxiety is reduced. The lower the chronic anxiety the more family members can stay in good contact and resolve their issues without the inclusion of an outsider.

The death of both mothers may be a major factor in the decision to divorce. Neither partner has made much progress toward resolving his or her emotional attachment to the past, present, or future generations sufficiently to permit more objective expectations of self and each other. They continue to be incapable of managing the intense interdependence that operates in their marriage without living apart. It is the role of the clinician to assist any effort toward greater emotional autonomy and sustained emotional contact so that they may work toward managing their relationship without emotional cutoff.

Family Number Three

Mr. B. is fifty-five and his wife of twenty-two years is forty-six. Mr. and Mrs. B. met when she took a position in his company. They knew each other for several years before they dated. They married in 1982 and have three children. Their oldest child was born in 1986, the middle child in 1988, and the youngest in 1994.

Mr. B. is the youngest of three children. His parents were married for thirteen years when his father died at the age of thirty-nine in 1949. Mr. B. was seven days old. His sister was eighteen months old, and his older brother was four. His mother lived to age eighty-nine and died in 2004. Mr. B. has not spoken to his brother in forty years. His brother left home at the age of twenty. He had many childhood problems and at age eleven was sent to a school for emotionally disturbed adolescents. Mr. B. blames him for the family's problems during his childhood.

Mr. B.'s mother remarried in 1972 and moved to another part of the country. He always remained close to his mother and for five years before her death, he made six to eight trips yearly to visit her, sometimes with his family and sometimes alone. He has always been in good contact with his sister and her family.

Mrs. B. is the fourth of five children. Her parents are seventy-eight and eighty-five and have been married for fifty-three years. She has two older sisters, an older brother, and a younger brother. All her siblings are married with children. Her eldest sister has four grandchildren. She has always lived within a two-hour drive of her entire family. They maintain close contact, speaking every week and visiting frequently. Figure 14.3 presents the B. family diagram.

During the recession of 1989-1990 Mr. B. suffered business reversals. As the family had always enjoyed an affluent lifestyle, anxiety escalated. Mrs. B. became pregnant in 1990 and miscarried six weeks later. When she became pregnant in 1995 with their third daughter, Mrs. B. was elated. Mr. B. was not. Tension developed and the couple distanced. Mrs. B. began spending the entire summer at the family beach house leaving her husband in the city during the week to run his business.

In the summer of 1996, Mr. B. began an extramarital relationship with a young woman who worked for him. The relationship lasted eighteen months. It ended when his wife learned about it from another employee. Mr. B. spent two years consulting with a professional about his functioning, his relationships, and his life. Mrs. B. blamed him for their problems and did not seek help for herself.

Mr. B. has two male cousins who each had an extramarital affair with an employee of their companies. As a young college graduate he worked with both of them in the older cousin's company. Ten years later the younger cousin established his own company. He confided in Mr. B. that he was having a sexual relationship with a young woman who worked for him.

Mr. and Mrs. B. stayed together despite the increasing conflict and distance that characterized their marriage. They focused most of their attention on the children. Each of the three children developed behavioral problems over the next eight years. Their oldest daughter changed schools when she found it difficult to make friends. The middle daughter experienced phobias and was treated by a child psychologist for several years. The youngest has been in therapy for two years to deal with her temper tantrums and separating from her mother. At age ten she is still struggling to sleep alone.

In 2003, Mr. B. was diagnosed with high blood pressure. He has been on medication since then. His mother died in 2004. She had been close to his wife and children. He began having severe headaches and nightmares. He returned to therapy for a brief period. The marriage continues to be a challenge for him. He struggles to stay connected. He spends most of his free time with his children. He has developed closer ties to his sister and her family and one first cousin and her family. He invests heavily in his male friendships. He insists that he will never become involved in an extramarital relationship again.

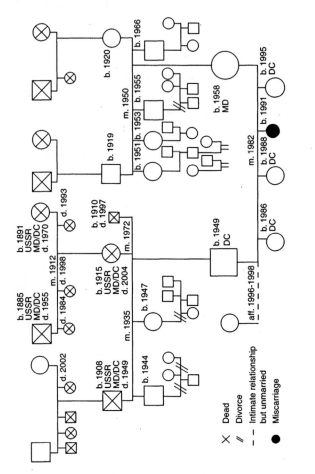

FIGURE 14.3. B. Family Diagram

348

Mrs. B. has increased her drinking. She has chronic neck and upper back pains. She has lost her libido and is uninterested in a sexual relationship with her husband. She has not worked since the birth of her third daughter. She spends most of her time involved in her children's school and athletic activities.

This family illustrates the role that unresolved emotional attachment, defined as a symbiotic relationship that mutually benefits the parties involved, chronic anxiety, and the multigenerational process play in the development of an extramarital affair. The role of the clinician is to assess the facts of functioning, to maintain objectivity and neutrality related to the family emotional process, and to assist family members in an effort to work on differentiation of self. The ability to gain more objectivity about the family emotional process and focus on one's part in it reduces anxiety in the relationships. Less anxious relationships create more stability and fewer symptoms. With greater stability and fewer symptoms, family members are better able to manage their own needs and they are more available to lend a hand to the other when it is necessary and possible.

Specific to this family is the ability to understand the triangles involving each spouse's unresolved attachment to his or her family of origin as well as the emotional process that involves their youngest child. The role of the clinician is to assist any effort to work on self while maintaining emotional contact with each other. Coaching to increase awareness of one's part in the family emotional process provides the opportunity to lower anxiety over time. Lowered anxiety permits more objective and responsible alternatives for managing the marital relationship.

Family Number Four

Mr. C. is fifty-five and his wife is fifty-four. They met in 1975 and have been married for twenty-eight years. He is a college graduate and a businessman. He was steadily employed for twenty-five years. In 1998 he started his own company which he closed in 2002. He is currently employed out-of-state, residing where he works five days a week and returning home for the weekends. Mrs. C. graduated from college. She is an artist and teaches dance. Since the birth of their son in 1984 and their daughter in 1988, she has devoted most of her time to raising them. Their son is currently a sophomore in a college out of town and their daughter is in high school and living at home.

Mr. C. was born in another country and with the exception of his mother is the only member of his extended family to ever live in the United States. He is the oldest of three. His younger sister lives with her family in their native country. His brother had been living there with his second wife and child until he died of cancer at the age of forty-eight in December 2004. The cancer was diagnosed in January of that year. Mr. C. has always remained in contact with his family. They have visited him yearly and he has traveled to see them several times a year. When he took his new job out of town, he moved in with his mother who had been living in the city where he is working for twenty years. She has recently returned to her native country after the diagnosis of her son's cancer and has remained there since his death. Figure 14.4 presents the C. family diagram.

Mr. C.'s parents were married in 1946 and divorced in 1974. His mother's two succeeding marriages also ended in divorce. His father lived with his second wife and their two children until his death in July 2000. Mr. C. recently learned that his biological father was his paternal uncle. He also died in July 2000. Mr. C. is currently suing his uncle's estate for his inheritance.

Mr. C. describes his role in the family as that of a leader. He attended an Ivy League college and was expected to succeed in the tradition of his paternal grandfather, father, and uncle. Most of his energy has been directed toward providing well for his family and trying to accomplish his career goals. Whatever time remained after these pursuits has always been devoted to his family. He says he never imagined himself without them.

Mrs. C. is the youngest and only daughter in her family. Her parents were married in 1946 and lived together until her father's death at age fifty-two in 1963. Her mother remarried in 1965 and divorced in 1972. Her eldest brother has been married twice and has no children. Her middle brother has never married. She describes her relationship with her family as difficult through the years. She believes her role in the family is that of caregiver and helper. Mrs. C. did not speak to her mother for two years. By the time her mother was diagnosed with cancer in 2002 they had reconnected. She spent six months caring for her prior to her death in May 2002.

The C.s' son had been using marijuana since he was sixteen years old. After much conflict between father and son, the son was treated for depression with psychotherapy and medication in 2000. At the same time, Mr. and Mrs. C. sought professional help for the conflict in their relationship. Their son's functioning improved and their relationship calmed down.

Mr. C. describes his health as good with the exception of chronic stomach problems that had been treated with ulcer medication from 1989 to 1993. As a child he received blood transfusions, and contracted hepatitis C. He has been in and out of psychotherapy for years. Mrs. C. has enjoyed exceptionally good health.

In July 2004, Mr. C. met a woman at his athletic club in the town where his wife and daughter reside. Although he had never before had an interest in anyone but his wife, he was immediately drawn to her and decided to

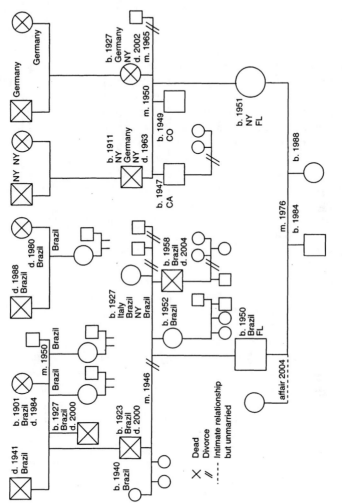

FIGURE 14.4. C. Family Diagram

351

pursue an extramarital relationship. He saw her every weekend for four months until his wife discovered the affair.

Mr. and Mrs. C. decided to seek professional help. They have determined that since the deaths of his father and uncle, the diagnosis of his brother's cancer, the death of her mother, the departure of their son to college, his relocation for work, and his mother's return to her native country, anxiety increased and distance mounted between them. She admitted thinking about whether they would remain together and preparing herself to live without him. He believes he feared the breakup and sought an outside relationship to stabilize the real and imagined changes in his life. He continued to see the other woman until recently when his wife again confronted him with ending their marriage. Since the affair he is experiencing headaches, has had two accidents with minor injuries, and sustained a thirty pound weight loss for close to a year. He has recently decided to end the affair and concentrate on his marriage. They are each working on understanding their own functioning better, defining themselves more clearly in their relationship, and staying better connected to their extended families. They are anxious and uncertain about whether they will stay together.

This family illustrates the role of unresolved emotional fusion, chronic anxiety, and the family emotional process in the development of an extramarital relationship. The ability of the clinician to focus family emotional process across the generations and help to identify markers of anxiety and patterns for managing it, can provide a more objective understanding of functioning. Objectivity reduces anxiety. Less anxiety permits people to live more thoughtful, less problematic lives.

Specific to this family is the difficulty each spouse has had in establishing and maintaining close contact with each other and with other important family members. Until recently they have been emotionally isolated from everyone in their lives except their children. One child has left the home and is in college. The other is preparing to begin college next fall. Addressing the emotional process in the most important triangles is key to managing the emotional intensity in the marriage. Managing the emotional process in these triangles can bring greater objectivity about self and others. With greater objectivity comes less anxiety. Less anxious people resolve differences with less inclusion of others.

Comments

These cases illustrate the role of unresolved emotional fusion, defined here as intense emotional interdependency, chronic anxiety, and the multigenerational process in the development of extramarital relationships. Extramarital behavior represents one version of the formation of a triangle whose function is to bind anxiety and stabilize the emotional system. An affair is a symptom of the underlying emotional attachment and the anxiety that is associated with it. The same forces that are responsible for other physical, emotional, and social symptoms contribute to the development of extramarital affairs. They are one version of an intense, interdependent emotional process and the patterns that evolve over generations for managing it.

Triangles are endemic to relationships in the living world. They are ever present and provide a way of stabilizing disturbed relationship systems. The more intense the emotional process in the family, the greater the chronic anxiety, the deeper the relationship patterns, the more susceptible the family is to symptoms. Families create triangles and families resolve them. Efforts toward differentiation of self are a factor in correcting problems that threaten the survival and well-being of the family. Knowledge of the emotional process in a family and the capacity to manage one's part in it contribute to outcome.

The role of the clinician in this process is to manage his or her anxiety in relationship to the parties involved in the problem. To the extent that a clinician understands the process in the family, is able to maintain objectivity about it, and pursues the goal of differentiation of self, families have a greater chance to resolve their issues more effectively.

Knowledge of theory and the ability to apply it to one's own life is the essence of differentiation of self. Training in Bowen theory emphasizes the responsibility for managing self in key relationships. The goal is to define an objective and viable position in relationship to the family and other important relationship systems. Differentiation of self involves the ability to take responsibility for one's own needs and requirements as well as lend a hand to others when necessary and possible.

The role of the coach in working with families trying to cope with extramarital affairs is to focus on differentiation of self. Assisting people toward an objective understanding of the facts about the emotional process across generations, and the impact it has on the system, helps to increase objectivity and reduce anxiety. Once this occurs the capacity of people to manage with less dependence on others develops. The freer people are to concentrate on life goals, the more likely they are to accomplish them, and to free others to do likewise.

SUMMARY

The concept of the triangle as described in Bowen theory offers a broader, factual, and more objective view of extramarital behavior and helps to explain the function it performs within the family in which it occurs. Extramarital relationships represent one version of a triangle whose function is to manage unresolved emotional attachment, bind anxiety, and stabilize the family emotional system. The extent to which a family is susceptible to extramarital behavior depends on the capacity of people to manage their relationships less emotionally and more responsibly.

Families with higher degrees of emotional interdependency will exhibit more chronic anxiety. These families display greater emotional reactivity to shifts in key relationships. The more anxious the emotional system, the more automatic and predictable the reactions to these shifts. The less able families are to manage intense emotional interdependency and the anxiety it creates, the more susceptible the marriage becomes to symptoms. An extramarital affair is a symptom of the underlying emotional fusion and the attempt to manage the anxiety associated with it. The same forces that are responsible for the expression of triangles elsewhere in the family contribute to the development of this phenomenon.

When families come to understand the facts about the nature of their relationships, the anxiety they generate and the multigenerational patterns that operate to manage them, the possibility exists for more effective lives. Clinicians with a working knowledge of Bowen theory and the concept of the triangle can assist people toward this effort.

REFERENCES

Bowen, M. (1978). *Family therapy in clinical practice*. New York: Jason Aronson.

Burke, T. (1989). "Parental care and behaviour of polyandrous dunnocks *Prunella modularis* related to paternity by DNA and fingerprinting." *Nature,* 338, 249-251.

de Waal, F. (1989). *Peacemaking among primates.* Cambridge, MA: Harvard University Press.

Emlen, S. (1989). "Contributions of bird studies to biology," *Science,* 246, 465.

Goodall, J. (1986). *The chimpanzees of Gombe.* Cambridge, MA: The Belknap Press of Harvard University.

Kerr, M. and Bowen, M. (1988). *Family evaluation.* New York: W.W. Norton and Company.

PART IV:
TRIANGLES IN ORGANIZATIONS

Chapter 15

Sibling Triangles and Leadership in a Family Business

Peter Titelman

INTRODUCTION

This chapter describes the presence and process of triangles and interlocking triangles in response to anxiety and their impact on the functioning of a family business. Efforts to modify this process using Bowen theory (Bowen, 1978) are presented. The problems and possibilities of collective leadership in a family business are illustrated through a case study in which three brothers share ownership and management of a business. In the case presented here, during the course of the consultation, the two younger brothers came to collectively lead the family business with their older brother. That outcome was possible because the three sibling partners worked to be responsible individuals, each providing leadership as part of a team.

LEADERSHIP IN FAMILY BUSINESS

This section will cover the following topics: (1) forms of leadership—a continuum from hierarchical to a collection of individuals; (2) stages of development in family business leadership; (3) functioning position in family business; and (4) the concepts of triangles, anxiety, and differentiation.

Forms of Leadership—A Continuum from Hierarchical to a Collection of Individuals

Many family consultants tend to view leadership as residing in one family member who typically operates the business in a more or less hierarchical manner. This author takes exception to this view, believing that collective leadership is not only possible, but may, in some instances, be optimal.

Bowen theory (Ferrera, 1996) views social hierarchies as emotional systems based on the interplay of the variables of anxiety and differentiation. Gilbert (1992) describes the calm social hierarchy in the following way:

> In a high level relationship, equality does not have to be worked at, it is just there. That equality is not based on tallying up individual assets; rather, it is a relationship stance, a posture assumed by individuals. Each accepts the other as no more and no less talented, responsible, or free than himself or herself. Respect for the other, so often pointed to as essential for relationship success, is based on the equal posture. (p. 103)

According to Ferrera (1996), Bowen believed that an organization would do best when it functioned *as a collection of individuals*. He distinguished between a collection of individuals and a group. Bowen distinguished between *a group*, as driven more by the togetherness force and a collection of individuals as driven more by the force of individuality. The interaction of a collection of individuals works to support individual functions, to spur each person to go further than he or she could go alone (see Ferrera, 1996, p. 207).

Stages of Development in Family Business Leadership

In the first stage of a family business, the first generation, an owner-managed, entrepreneurial structure is in place (Gersick, Davis, McCollom-Hampton, and Lansberg, 1997), frequently with a dominant, controlling leader. There is reciprocity between the structure of the family business and the form of leadership. Thus it is not surprising that the functioning of leadership in the transition to a sibling partnership invokes tension.

A second-generation family business often makes too many demands on a sole decision maker (Gersick et al., 1997). Survival of the family business at this stage of its existence, calls for a more shared form of management and ownership. It calls for the family business as an emotionally based system to evolve toward a new form of leadership in which the functioning positions of the leaders are based less on dominance and submission, and emotionally reactive, intuitive decision making, and more on objective, rationally based decision making. When this form of leadership is functioning it is characterized by the individuals in the leadership group taking responsibility for themselves by planning and executing their designated functions. However, a shift to a collective form of leadership is only possible when the second-generation (or any subsequent generation) participating family members operate at levels of differentiation that are relatively high and are willing to share the management of the business with their siblings. Sharing management and ownership takes place frequently in the second and subsequent generations of a family business, but successful family businesses and other organizations are more likely to last and continue to be successful into the future if the leadership involves a collection of individuals who each take responsibility for doing his or her part in maintaining the business.

Another way of describing the evolution of leadership in this family business, and one that many businesses led by siblings go through, is as follows: The first phase, the "alpha" phase, is hierarchical. It is characterized by *a sole entrepreneur owner/leader.* Chronic anxiety is high and functional differentiation is variable. The second phase is one of *shared ownership.* This is a more democratic phase that involves spheres of influence. Chronic anxiety is somewhat lower, and emotional reactivity is lessened. The third phase, which takes longer to emerge and evolve, if it takes place at all, is one of *leadership by a collection of individuals.* Achieving this requires a high degree of individual responsibility. It utilizes consensus decision making on major issues and majority rule decision making on lesser issues. Acute anxiety and emotional reactivity are decreased and the level of differentiation of the leadership is higher. This level of leadership can delegate responsibility or use more hierarchical structures to its advantage when appropriate. The designated and assumed positions of the sibling partners are more defined—less blurred—in a family business that is able to function as a collection of individuals as opposed to functioning as a rigidly hierarchical organization.

Functioning Position in the Family Business

From the perspective of this author, functioning positions in the leadership of a family business are determined by a number of factors:

1. *sibling position* (Toman, 1961);
2. the *functional needs of the system,* both organizational and emotional;
3. *nodal events,* including losses and additions of family members to the business, change in stage of family business leadership (such as from founder—as sole-leader—to collective leadership among siblings, or from sibling leaders to a consortium of cousins who share management and whose leadership may extend beyond one family line), and internally or externally generated crises;

4. the family and/or business *emotional projection process;* and
5. the levels of *differentiation* of the family members in leadership positions in the family business.

Functioning positions evolve or remain static (leading to the potential extinction of the family business) depending on the interplay among these factors within the time and space a particular family business occupies.

THE APPLICATION OF BOWEN THEORY CONCEPTS FOR UNDERSTANDING AND WORKING WITH FAMILY BUSINESS

Bowen theory lends itself easily to being applied to understanding the functioning of family businesses and providing consultation to them. A family business, unlike any other type of business or organization, is constituted by the overlap of the family and business emotional systems. The family business often involves a multigenerational emotional process in which the family emotional process that is transmitted over multiple generations, is also naturally transmitted over multiple generations within the context of the family business. The eight concepts of Bowen theory (differentiation of self, triangle, nuclear family emotional system, family projection process, multigenerational transmission process, emotional cutoff, sibling position, and emotional process in society) are all applicable in the arena of family business. The reader can refer back to Chapter 1 for an in-depth presentation of the concept of the triangle and interlocking triangles, and a description of the relationship between the concept of the triangle and each of the other seven concepts, in the context of Bowen theory as a whole.

The *emotional system,* a product of several billion years, is the force that drives the family business, as well as the family itself. The *relationship system* is a description of what happens among the members of the family business, family members, and nonfamily members. The emotional system refers to what energizes the family business and the family. Bowen (1978) postulated that the interplay of two counterbalancing life forces govern the emotional system: *togetherness and individuality.* The togetherness force propels an organism to the needs of the group and to follow the directives of others, to be dependent, connected, and indistinct from others or the group as a whole. The force for individuality propels an organism to follow its own directives, to be an independent and distinct entity from others and the group as a whole.

For the purpose of this chapter on siblings and leadership in a family business, the rest of this section will briefly discuss the concepts of differentiation, anxiety, and triangles.

According to Bowen theory there are two main variables in human functioning: *anxiety* and *differentiation*. Being alive, humans react to their environment along a continuum from underreactivity, to optimal reactivity, to overreactivity or anxiety. Kerr (2006) stated in a lecture that "An optimal level of emotional reactivity maintains an individual or family organism's psychological and physiological balance."

Kerr wrote that Bowen theory distinguishes between *acute* and *chronic* anxiety: "Acute anxiety occurs in response to real threats and is time limited. Chronic anxiety generally occurs in response to imagined threats and is not time limited" (Kerr and Bowen, 1988, p. 113). Kerr (2006) views "chronic anxiety as being related to threats generated by family and social process . . . and [it] maintains a heightened state of emotional reactivity in the individual and family organism."

Stressors in the environment and relationships trigger both acute and chronic anxiety. The relationship process in the business is affected by the acute anxiety caused by the ups and downs of the business's functioning in relation to the market, competitors, and other factors. Also, the family business is highly affected by the chronic anxiety of the family members that involves their long-term relationships and the relationship functioning of the multigenerational family emotional system. Stressors in the environment and relationships trigger both acute and chronic anxiety.

Differentiation is a natural, automatic process through which the human individual develops from being highly attached to the mother, in the context of the parental unit, to being a relatively emotionally separate self in relation to family and others. Bowen's differentiation of self scale illustrates how people reside along a universal continuum that describes the varying degrees of emotional separation that people achieve from their families of origin. The central characteristic that "best describes the difference between people at various points on the scale is the degree to which they are able to distinguish between the feeling process and the intellectual process" (Kerr and Bowen, 1988, p. 97) and the degree of separation, or lack thereof, between emotionally reactive and thoughtful, goal-directed functioning.

In a family, or in a family business, differentiation of self can be described as the ability of an individual to manage the interplay of the individuality and togetherness forces in a relationship process (cf. Kerr and Bowen, 1988, p. 95). Another way of describing differentiation of self that is very applicable to the relationships between family members in a family business is as follows: it is the ability to act for oneself, without being selfish, and the ability to act for others, without being selfless. Differentiation involves the capacity to be an individual while at the same time functioning as part of a team (cf. Kerr and Bowen, 1988, p. 63).

In Bowen theory an important distinction is made between basic level of differentiation and functional level of differentiation. Basic level and functional level of differentiation both involve an individual's capacity to separate the thinking from the feeling process and act on that understanding. The difference is that functioning at a basic level of differentiation is not dependent on the relationship process whereas functional differentiation is dependent on the relationship process. Basic level is considered to be relatively fixed by the time of young adulthood, and as it was described above, it is based on the degree of emotional separation an individual achieves from his or her family of origin. Basic level of differentiation is made up of those principles, core-beliefs, and positions that are not dependent on the relationship process. In addition, basic level of differentiation is determined by a multigenerational process that takes into account the parents' and the grandparents' (and even farther back) achievement of emotional separation from their respective parents.

Functional level of differentiation refers to the phenomenon in relationships whereby an individual "borrows" or "lends" self to the other, and in so doing is either overfunctioning or underfunctioning. Both sides of this relationship dance involve a compromise in functioning. The functional level of differentiation can only involve those beliefs, principles, or positions that are not part of an individual's basic level of differentiation.

An important question in the context of family business consulting is whether modification of basic level of differentiation can occur, or whether change in this context is limited to the functional level of differentiation of self. It is a generally held view by Bowen theorists and practitioners that basic level of differentiation only occurs when an individual, under the guidance of a Bowen-trained coach, works systematically on becoming more emotionally separated from his or her parents, in the context of working on emotional triangles and interlocking triangles in the family of origin and the extended family. It is commonly believed that increase in basic level of differentiation of self, as opposed to functional level of differentiation, cannot occur in efforts made solely in the work system, family business, or nonfamily business. From that perspective efforts to modify one's functioning in a nonfamily setting or by working on family relationships that do not include work on one's relationship with one's emotional attachment to one's parents, only lead to change in functional level of differentiation.

This author thinks that basic level of differentiation occurs when a higher level of functioning is sustained over a long period of time, does not revert to a lower level under the pressure of anxiety inducing stressors, and occurs in the context of relationships with family and significant others in which the individual is maintaining and defining himself or herself. It seems possible that coaching consultation involving members of a family business—a unique interplay of family and business—that is, oriented to raising the level of functioning, may result in an increase in the basic functioning of one or more of those family members.

This author would suggest that a rise in basic level of differentiation occurs when an individual's functioning improves and is maintained over a long period. To know if this rise in differentiation is basic would only be verifiable by observing and assessing the functioning of an individual's children and grandchildren. The point being made here is that it is theoretically possible that the level of basic differentiation might be modified in the context of family business consultation informed by Bowen theory, depending on the motivation of family business members, and the focus and quality of the consultation. However, for the most part, family business consultation, like family systems coaching, promotes change at the functional level, rather than change at the basic level of differentiation.

Turning to the concept of *the triangle and interlocking triangles,* triangular emotional process is a phenomenon that exists in both human and nonhuman systems. As de Waal and Embree (1997) have demonstrated in studying chimpanzees and other primates:

> The evidence that is available currently is certainly sufficient to show that triadic awareness is by no means restricted to our own species. Rather, we share with other primates an evolutionary heritage as a basis for not just physical traits, but behavioral traits and predispositions toward social intelligence as well. (p. 16)

Triangles are the smallest stable building block of a relationship system. They consist of three-person emotional systems involving patterns that repeat over time, in which people often come to have fixed positions in relation to each other. Predictably, triangles have two close individuals and one that is distant. The introduction of acute or chronic anxiety into a relationship unbalances the forces of togetherness and individuality. The calm stability of the two-person system is disrupted, decreasing the twosome's ability to deal directly with each other. Anxiety in conjunction with the twosome's functional levels of differentiation can lead to the engagement of a vulnerable family (or nonfamily) member in a triangle. In this way, the unbalanced emotional system is stabilized, even if temporarily, through the transfer of anxiety by involving a third individual.

Triangling is an ever-present process. It goes on all the time, below awareness, in everyday life. Frequently, triangles emerge or crystallize when the stability of a two-person system is unbalanced by anxiety in the wake of a nodal event such as the birth of a child, the leaving home of a child, illness, death, divorce, or other transitions in the course of the life of a family.

The function of the triangle is to manage anxiety in a twosome when the stability of a comfortable closeness/distance is thrown out of balance by involving the most vulnerable other person. Like a family, a family-owned business can respond to threats of dissolution, real or imagined, with increased anxiety. As anxiety and emotional reactivity increase, people's ability to think objectively is compromised, setting in motion a climate ripe for triangles to operate. A family business is often emotionally experienced as being equivalent to the lifeblood of a family. This response most often emerges automatically, from the founder of the business. This expression of emotional fusion can be shared by other members of the family business as well.

Anxiety, with ensuing triangling, moves downward from the top of a system, family, or other group. Those at the lower end of the hierarchy can become the focus of the projection process and conflict, sometimes to the extent of being excommunicated or "fired" by the system. However, as the removal from the emotional system of a triangled individual who is at the bottom of the hierarchy does not alleviate the conflict higher in the system, conflict will continue to erupt in a subsequent twosome (cf. Bowen, 1978, p. 374).

THE FAMILY BUSINESS AND ITS PRESENTING PROBLEMS

Rothstein Books, a wholesale distributor of textbooks to small and mid-sized high school and college bookstores nationally, is owned and managed by three brothers. When the sibling partners came to the author and his partner for consultation, the presenting problems were as follows: (1) conflict and distrust in family and business relationships (the oldest and youngest brothers had barely spoken to each other for eight months prior to initiating consultation); (2) cutoff between the youngest brother's family and the other brothers' families and their parents; (3) mutual distrust regarding time and productivity put into the business by the three brothers; and (4) lack of organization and a need for an office manager.

When the consultation began in 1994, the business was somewhat loosely organized. Figure 15.1 depicts the organizational chart for the busi-

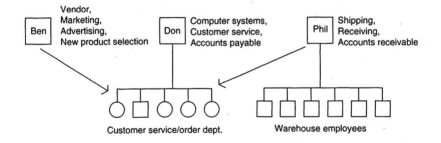

| Ben | Vendor, Marketing, Advertising, New product selection | | Don | Computer systems, Customer service, Accounts payable | | Phil | Shipping, Receiving, Accounts receivable |

Customer service/order dept.   Warehouse employees

FIGURE 15.1. First Organizational Chart

ness. Ben, the oldest brother, was in charge of communications, purchasing and marketing, and advertising. Don, the middle brother, managed the computer systems, handled accounts payable, and was ostensibly in charge of the five office employees. However, Ben and Phil, the youngest brother, often interfered with Don's management of the office staff. The boundaries in regard to this position were blurred. The youngest brother, Phil, managed the six employee shipping department, which handled accounts receivable.

HISTORY OF THE FAMILY IN BUSINESS

A brief multigenerational view of the family provides a context for understanding the roots of distrust, disappointment, and triangling in the family's history with a previous family business. It includes the history of the triangles in the family business. Figure 15.2 is a family diagram.

The Rothstein brothers' paternal grandfather, Sam, had worked in a business that was owned by his brother-in-law (their great-uncle John). The family story is that their grandfather was mistreated in that business, evoking mistrust and distress. Their maternal grandfather, Al, had a clothing business and pawnshop in which his three children (including their mother, Sarah) worked. Family lore has it that this grandfather and his oldest son were in an alliance that resulted in the youngest son feeling unappreciated and cheated. He quit the business and moved to the West Coast where he started his own business. Stan (the Rothstein brothers' father) attempted to mediate the dispute in his wife's family's business, but his efforts failed and left him with a "bad taste" in his mouth, wary of the pitfalls of family businesses. His negative experience with family businesses in his and his wife's families of origin undoubtedly had an impact on his view and functioning in a family business.

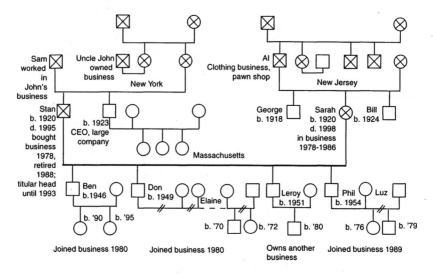

FIGURE 15.2. Rothstein Family Diagram

Nevertheless, Stan Rothstein bought the present family business, a text-book wholesaler, in 1978, and renamed it Rothstein's Books. Under his leadership and assisted by his wife, Sarah, the customer base grew from 30 to 500, over twenty years. Ben and Don, their two eldest sons, joined the business in 1980 and later became partners with their father. In 1988, their father reduced his involvement in the business to part-time and their mother retired. Phil, the youngest of the four sons, joined the business a year later and also became a partner. (Leroy, the third son, was never in the family business but owns one of his own.)

Stan remained the titular owner until 1993, when he sold the business to his three sons. At that time, Ben held 47 percent, Don held 25 percent, and Phil held 28 percent ownership. Don was given a lesser share in the business because his parents had already given him considerable help when he faced financial problems relating to two divorces. Phil was given less ownership because he had entered the business later than his older brothers. Thus the father instituted a business structure in which Ben, the eldest son, was "first among equals." At Phil's urging, the brothers later agreed to an investment schedule for Don and Phil that would lead to the three brothers achieving equal ownership, approximately five years after the consultation began.

Nodal events or stressors in the family that have impacted this family business include the following: in 1993, the mother was diagnosed with ovarian cancer; in 1995, the father died from a cerebral hemorrhage; in 1996, the mother had a recurrence of cancer that resulted in further surgery. The Rothstein brothers initiated consultation in April 1994, within a few months of their mother's initial cancer diagnosis, as conflict between the partners increased.

History of Triangles in the Family Business

A number of triangles, and interlocking triangles, characterized the Rothstein family business in the years before the brothers initiated consultation. This material was gathered during the assessment and the course of the consultation. Anxiety and conflict led over time to the activation and re-emergence of a number of intense triangles. A basic assumption of this author is that the emotional systems and the relationship systems of a family and their family-owned business overlap and are intertwined.

Early in the history of the Rothstein family business, when Stan (the father of the three sibling partners who came to the author for consultation) and his wife conflicted over various business matters, he usually emerged as the dominant decision maker. When the Rothsteins' oldest son, Ben, joined the business in 1980, he mediated conflicts and managed to keep calmly connected with both parents even when they were in conflict with each other. This calm triangle stabilized the conflict and lowered the acute parental anxiety without resolving it. Figure 15.3 illustrates this triangle.

As the younger brothers, Don and Phil, joined the business, triangles were activated with new players. Figure 15.4 illustrates this triangle.

Sometimes two of the brothers joined their father in the inside positions of a triangle, with the mother in the outside position. Figure 15.5 illustrates this triangle.

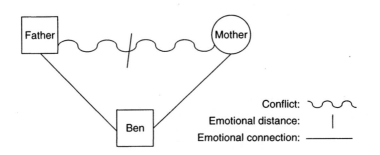

FIGURE 15.3. Father, Mother, and Oldest Son Triangle

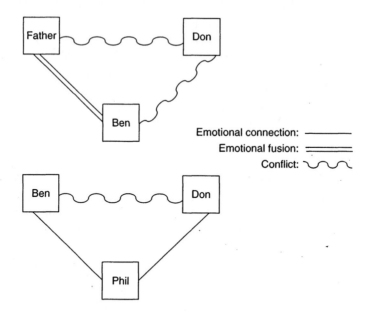

FIGURE 15.4. Triangles When Additional Brothers Joined the Family Business

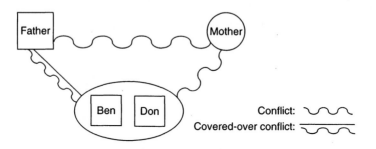

FIGURE 15.5. Father, Mother, and Sons Triangle

Alliances between family members would briefly stabilize the anxiety in the business, but new conflicts would emerge as an expression of the unresolved chronic anxiety in the family and the business.

At various points of especially high anxiety female family members left the business under duress. First the mother was pushed out of the day-to-day operations of the business, and later both Don's wife, Elaine, and Phil's wife, Luz, each of whom worked in a supervisory capacity with the office staff, became the focus of negativity and were excluded from the business. These females were less attached to the nucleus of the interlocking family and business systems as they were appendages through marriage to a family in a business consisting of a dominant father, a less involved mother, and three male siblings.

In summary, the original conflict between the parents at the top of the family business system moved downward into the sibling group through the activation of a series of interlocking triangles: (1) the father criticized each son to the other sons; (2) Don, who was the recipient of the greatest amount of the emotional projection in the family triangles, often became "it"; and (3) the negative projection of anxiety in the family business system shifted to the females of the family, first the mother and then two daughters-in-law or "outside females," all of whom left the business under duress. Figure 15.6 illustrates the interlocking triangle.

Inevitably, the anxiety in the family business system reemerged because the original issues within the partnership were not resolved. It was predictable that, following the exodus of both parents and two wives from the business, the three brothers would develop a conflictual triangling process among themselves, because they were now forced to deal with each other without these buffers. Figure 15.7 illustrates the triangle between the three brothers at the time of the initial consultation.

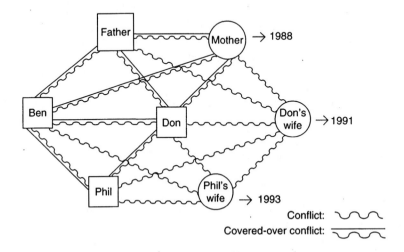

FIGURE 15.6. Interlocking Triangles

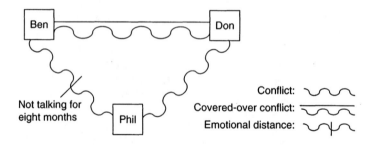

FIGURE 15.7. Triangle at the Initial Consultation

THE CONSULTATION FORMAT
AND THE CONSULTANTS' FUNCTIONS

This author and his co-consultant met with the three sibling partners for ninety-six sessions between April 1994 and June 2000. Each consultation session was one and a half hours in length. A session began with about five minutes of observations from each partner regarding his own functioning, the functioning of the partnership, and the issues he wanted to focus on in that session. The brothers then agreed on two or three issues they would focus on in that session. The session ended with a discussion of their intentions to follow up, individually or together, on decisions reached during the consultation. The consultants wrapped up the session with a short summary.

The use of co-consultants* was a part of this consultation from the beginning. The consultants had four significant functions during these sessions: (1) to assess and clarify the relationship processes between the family business partners and other family employees; (2) to maintain neutrality by working to stay detriangled from the partners; (3) to teach the partners how systems operate; and (4) to encourage the partners to develop business structures and procedures that would decrease reactivity when

---

*The author's co-consultant was Jack LaForte, PhD. Having worked together for twenty years, the author and his partner have learned to manage their emotional relationship with each other, allowing them to gain the benefit of having four eyes and four ears to observe the complex processes that family businesses embody. For a time one consultant may be more active, while the other listens and observes. Then the first may need a break and the other will take the lead. This usually is a fairly seamless process in which each consultant provides feedback and offers his ideas and questions. The author is neither recommending nor discouraging the use of co-consultants in the practice of family business consulting.

stress, from within the business or within the family, impacted on business productivity.

Assessing and Clarifying Relationship Processes

Assessing and clarifying the relationship processes among family business partners, other family members, and other nonfamily employees based on Bowen theory principles (Bowen, 1978) involves asking assessment questions as well as describing and delineating emotional process. It entails looking at the balance of the forces of individuality and togetherness and the capacity to be an individual while being a team player. It also involves looking at the multigenerational family/business history and functioning for patterns and processes of leadership, fusion, cutoff, over/underfunctioning reciprocity, pursuing and distancing, the projection of problems to someone in the next generation (or to an individual who is not a part of the biological family), functioning positions, triangles and interlocking triangles, and sibling positions.

Maintaining Neutrality and Detriangling

There is no more important function for the consultant than remaining neutral. The capacity for neutrality translates into not taking sides, not giving emotionally loaded advice, and not over identifying with any one partner—either the one viewed as the underdog or the one viewed as the dominant partner. Being neutral involves constant self-monitoring in order not to distance from the partners or to fuse with them. The consultants also seek to keep their focus simultaneously on *the family business as the client* and on each of its constituent partners. Neutrality is not a technique or a strategy, but a state of being that reflects the consultants' capacity to be separate individuals in the presence of the clients' emotionally driven family business system. It takes a certain amount of neutrality to implement detriangling efforts. Successful efforts to stay detriangled in turn increase the consultants' level of neutrality or objectivity, allowing them to think clearly about the emotional system of the family business without "getting stuck in it" or "running away from it."

Bowen (1978) described detriangling as the resolution of a tension system between two people in the presence of a third person who can avoid emotional participation with either while still relating actively to both (see p. 190). Bowen (1978) further elucidated the process of detriangling in this statement:

> When there is finally one who can control his emotional intensity and not take sides with either of the other two, and stay constantly in contact with the other two, the emotional intensity within the twosome will decrease and both will move to a higher level of differentiation. Unless the triangled person can remain in emotional contact, the twosome will triangle in someone else. (p. 480)

Whether working alone or with a colleague, all family business consultants are vulnerable to being triangled by their clients. The capacity to work at detriangling is determined by the level of differentiation of the individual or multiple consultants involved in the process. Co-consultants add a complexity to the potential triangling process, which necessitates their understanding and processing their consulting relationship in order to minimize this possibility. The value of working together as co-consultants depends on the capacity of each to maintain his individuality in the context of working as a team. Consultants cannot expect their clients to achieve what they themselves have not made a reasonable effort to attain.

Teaching How Systems Operate

Another function of consultants is to teach their clients how systems operate. When anxiety is high, consultants may prefer to teach indirectly by taking *I-Positions* regarding what they will or will not do. They may use parables, or *displacement stories,* that illustrate how other clients have achieved solutions to similar problems. Later, when anxiety is lower, the consultants may present materials that illustrate triangles or triadic awareness among members of other species. This may help clients understand the universality of their organizational and family problems. At other times, when anxiety is low the consultants may teach concepts, such as emotional triangles and multigenerational emotional process, directly from Bowen theory. In working with family businesses, it is particularly important for the consultant to help each partner define his or her own personal goals. Although the goals of the business and each individual interlock, they are not synonymous. This calls for constructive clarification of the different goals and needs of the family members within the business.

Coaching the Partners to Develop Business Structures and Procedures

A final function of family business consultants is to work with the family members to develop structures and procedures in the business that will decrease, or at least contain emotional reactivity, when stress, arising from acute or chronic anxiety, affects business productivity. A family business that either lacks structure or is structurally too rigid may function smoothly when stress is low. However, when the stress level rises, flexible structures and procedures allow the organization to maintain its equilibrium, whether this entails riding the turbulent waves of a business cycle or managing relationship conflicts within the family business.

COURSE OF THE CONSULTATION

The course of this consultation, ninety-six sessions, is divided into four phases, each with a different theme:

- First phase, April 1994-June 1995: *Lowering anxiety* (twenty-one sessions)
- Second phase, October 1995-June 1997: *Having the emotional space to work together* (twenty-four sessions)
- Third phase, September 1997-September 1998: *Developing a more optimal balance between individuality and togetherness* (twenty-three sessions)
- Fourth phase, October 1998-June 2000: *Expanding the business beyond kinship* (twenty-eight sessions)

The three Rothstein brothers had the ability to describe and elucidate their experience of sharing leadership in a family business with colorful, colloquial language. The author here seeks to describe the clients' emotional process in terms of Bowen theory, but through the lens of the clients' own experience and language.

First Phase: Lowering Anxiety

The consultants' initial assessment consisted of individual interviews with the three Rothstein brothers who owned the business, followed by a group interview. The consultants then presented their written assessment in a session with the group. They described what they saw as the problems and strengths, the family themes and processes including triangles, fusion, and underlying issues involving the multigenerational transmission process, and their recommendations. The consultants initially proposed ten meetings with the brothers over a fifteen-week period. The first five were to be weekly and the next five every other week.

In the assessment session, Ben referred to the fusion among the brothers as "being in each other's pots." By this cooking metaphor he meant that they interfered with one another's work activity, failed to respect work-related boundaries, and did not permit one another to define themselves functionally.

In the first phase of the consultation, the sibling partners began to communicate more openly and with less conflict. Ben began to accept his younger brothers in leadership functions. Ben noted, "We can all be together in the space I used to occupy alone." The brothers began to move from communicating through e-mail and informal chats to meeting on a regular basis to set up tasks. Although they sought to be less confrontational than their father had been, they had difficulty dealing with conflict and reaching consensus. Don and Phil began to work on a joint project and started consulting with each other when they grew anxious about their functioning in their own operating spheres.

Following the death of their father, in January 1995, stress in the family business system increased. Their father had continued to play a limited role until his death. Now distrust increased as the sibling partners again debated what constituted equal work. Feelings of helplessness led to increased triangling. Don and Phil were in conflict, but Ben was able to avoid taking sides.

At the end of the first phase of the consultation, the three brothers had begun talking about expanding the business. In June 1995, after a little more than a year, the sibling partners were beginning to make plans to update the computer system and hire an office manager. Confident that they had made some progress in lowering anxiety and decreasing conflict among themselves, the brothers decided to take a break from the consultation, knowing that they could return at a future time if other issues arose.

Second Phase: Having the Emotional Space to Work Together

Following the recurrence of their mother's cancer, in October 1995, the brothers decided to return for further consultation. Besides their mother's illness, other stressors on the family business and on their relationships with each other were easily identified. Phil's marriage was in crisis, and Don's significant other had decided to leave the area to go to graduate school. There was predictable leakage of anxiety between the family and the business systems. Because of the stress and renewed conflict, the siblings had failed to move forward on updating the computer system or hiring an office manager.

The triangle intensified as Don and Phil alternated in "victim" and "bully" positions, while Ben slipped into a nonproductive "mediator" position. Although Ben did not openly take sides, Phil felt that his older brother covertly agreed with him.

The issues identified at that time included fairness of workloads, the need to bring in new employees, boundaries in jobs, and lack of trust among the partners. Reciprocally, thoughtful functioning was down, and emotional reactivity and anxiety were up. Distrust emerged as each one felt that his brothers were taking advantage of him.

When the conflict heightened to the point where Phil threatened to withdraw from the consultation, the consultants decided to meet individually with each brother and then give feedback to the group. The consultants wanted to focus on each brother's sense of autonomy and separate functioning, hear each brother's point of view, stay outside the intensity of the triangle, and lower anxiety so that the brothers' thinking would be clearer, and so they would not lose the gains they had made during the previous phase of consultation.

Following the individual meetings, the consultants brought the brothers back together the following week to give them written and verbal feedback describing the family and business issues they had observed to be intruding on the business working relationship, with particular focus on the triangles. The brothers were now able to acknowledge and take responsibility for their own part in the conflict and its antecedents in the way emotional process had played out in their family of origin.

At this point the business issues facing the sibling partners were much the same as they had been in June 1995. They still needed to professionalize the office and overhaul the computer system. Phil wanted to explore new areas in the business where he could play a larger role.

Don noted that "the business exists to take care of the partners." Don and Phil's ultimate goal was "cashing out," whereas Ben wanted to stay in. They began exploring various options. Don began upgrading the computer system, and all three participated in the search for an outside computer consultant. When faced with some marketing difficulties, Ben sought help from his brothers, something he had been unable to do in the past. Don and Phil began working together on a business problem that Don had not been able to solve by himself. All in all, the relationship among the three sibling partners was more peaceful and more engaged.

During this period, the sibling partners reorganized the office and began delegating more tasks to the newly hired supervisor of the office staff. Don also got help in backing up the computer and hired someone to take over the accounts payable. Facilitated by Ben, Phil began to work more closely with the vendors, which he found more interesting than running the warehouse. This also represented taking more leadership on Phil's part. By the spring of 1997, as the partnership forged ahead, Ben described himself as having formerly been in the "driver's seat," whereas now he was sharing the driving.

The brothers began focusing more on issues with their employees and competitors and less with each other. They devoted more of their time to strategic planning. The consultants were now coaching the sibling partners in their efforts to detriangle in their relationship with the supervisor and the office staff. Phil began coaching a foreman in the warehouse on how to deal with the inevitable triangles between workers and foremen that develop as a business becomes more complex and hierarchical.

More formal organization led to a decrease in emotional complexity. The partnership was increasingly characterized by open, one-to-one relationships rather than by triangles. When the emotional temperature was down, the sibling partners could talk calmly about possible exit plans or issues that were previously hot. The partnership stayed on an even keel even when sales fluctuated.

Changes effected during the second phase of the consultation included increased delegation of responsibility to nonfamily employees and the adoption of professional office practices and customer relations procedures. As Phil put it: "We can work alone or together." Ben cited "a movement toward the integration of our personal visions." One of the sibling partners noted that the working process was like "looking at the same page with different lenses."

During this period, the sibling partners came to understand that they all tried to control each other in the same way that their father had controlled them; they accepted that each had differing personal goals and plans for achieving them.

Third Phase: Developing Individuality

After a three-month break, in September 1997, the Rothsteins returned for additional consultation. Although the current stressor in the family was their mother's cancer surgery, the sibling partners did not let the anxiety related to her illness slip into the business emotional process.

This phase of the consultation focused on each brother's developing individuality in the context of the partnership group rather than conflict among the sibling partners and the various anxiety-driven triangles. In particular, the brothers sought consultation on management issues involving emotional relationships and conflict in the office. They identified a triangle in which the three sibling partners occupied one leg, the customers occupied a second leg, and the office staff a third leg.

Phil described the higher functioning of the partnership during this period in terms of a jazz metaphor: "It's like trading fours, it's nonhierarchical, you all get to solo." In a jazz combo the group plays the theme or the chorus together, and each player also gets the chance to solo.

In December 1997, the sibling partners reorganized the company's customer service function. Don was relieved of this responsibility, for which he was grateful. He had felt that Ben and Phil were constantly usurping his customer service duties, a function for which he did not feel well suited. Ben and Phil took over the supervisory function, with Ben being on duty in the mornings and Phil in the afternoons. Figure 15.8 portrays the modification of the organizational structure of the Rothstein family business.

The sibling partners also implemented a two-thirds majority decision-making process for resolving small and midlevel business decisions. This represented a move away from the need for unanimity, which often resulted in stalemates and inefficiency in making decisions.

The sibling partners held fruitful weekly meetings with a more structured agenda organized by Phil. Ben continued to include Phil in shared management functions and new activities. The brothers avoided making Don "it." Ben noted that they were making progress in moving away from a patriarchal model, or what he referred to as the "big Daddy model." He described the functioning within the family as being less anxious, which led to improved functioning in the business. Phil found he was happy to be supervising the office staff and felt more creative in the business. Don reported being less anxious, functioning better in a crisis, and being better able to plan for the future while working more productively.

The brothers' lives outside the business were increasingly active. Ben became involved in tai chi and piano, Phil began playing jazz saxophone in a local band, and Don joined the board of directors of a local art center. Each brother was also involved in structured physical exercise. They found they were each doing more of what they wanted to do and at the same time being responsible to the business.

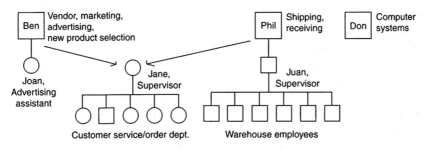

FIGURE 15.8. First Modification of the Organization

Ben continued to make an effort to move toward a collective management model, including Phil and Don in the development of a strategy for dealing with one of their largest vendors. All three brothers met with key members of the other company, relieving Ben of the responsibility for making a solo marketing effort. Although this joint presentation did not culminate in the result they hoped for, the sibling partners resisted the temptation to blame each other, and continued to collaborate together and provide new options for each other.

Fourth Phase: Expanding the Business Beyond Kinship

In the fall of 1998, with the business growing, the central issue was how the sibling partners could go beyond family members in continuing to expand or sell the business. The brothers were considering expanding, merging, selling, or some combination thereof. They talked with a possible buyer, which predictably provoked anxiety and reactivity among themselves. Phil and Don felt anxious that Ben might not agree to a deal because he wanted more money or wanted to continue to work for the business. The issue was raised that Phil and Don might miss working in the family business if they cashed out. Mistrust between the brothers was, however, a "minor blip" on the screen, and this triangle proved transient.

During the winter of 1998-1999, as an alternative to selling the business, the three sibling partners also seriously considered the idea of adding two new partners who might buy them out in a couple of years. One brother questioned whether they would be bringing in two outside partners or "adopting" two sons (since the potential partners were quite a few years younger than any of the brothers). They talked of adding new partners and described this possibility as becoming a "stepfamily."

In the end, in the spring of 1999, the sibling partners decided not to merge, but to expand the business with the hope of selling it a few years down the road. They borrowed considerable capital in order to develop Internet capacities and build a new addition to the physical plant in preparation for adding key new employees.

They also began thinking about forming an advisory board of directors, which represented a further step in reaching beyond themselves in order to gain wisdom from others (both kin and nonkin). The board would consist of an attorney, a banker, the head of another family business, their highly successful paternal uncle (with whom their father had been quite competitive), and their fourth brother (a successful entrepreneur who owned his own business).

The brothers worked together to hire a chief operating officer (COO) and a computer programmer, as well as other new employees. As these employees began to make important contributions to the business, new triangles emerged. Predictably the new COO became involved in a triangle involving two supervisory employees who were anxious about his presence. Phil coached the COO in detriangling from these relationships. Another triangle involved Ben, a marketing assistant, and the Internet consultant. The sibling partners had become adept at not getting caught in triangles, or at least were better able to recognize when they were participating in a problematic triangle. They could also coach their co-workers in detriangling when triangles involving employees developed. Figure 15.9 portrays the third evolution of the organizational structure of the Rothstein family business.

The brothers celebrated an important milestone in the expansion of the business in the summer of 1999, when the database was hooked up to a Web site. The company's catalog was now accessible to customers via the Internet. As Phil put it, they had moved from running "a lemonade stand to Lemonade, Inc." The brothers also entered into a joint venture with an Internet company (which was owned by the two principals with whom they had previously been negotiating a merger) and a large retail chain of 500 bookstores.

Phil's functioning as a leader and negotiator in the joint venture, contract development, and as overseer of the COO signaled an important rebalancing

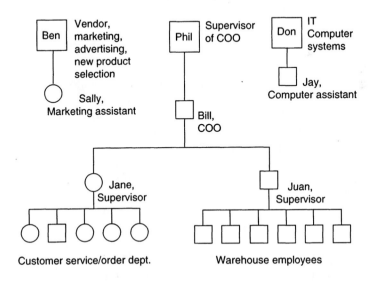

FIGURE 15.9. Second Modification of the Organization

of the partnership relationship system. Ben expressed feeling depressed not only that the business had not been sold (as he had spearheaded those negotiations), but also because he felt that Phil's "star was rising and his own star was falling." Although he believed Phil's contributions were valuable and that he was the right man to undertake these responsibilities, he still had to wrestle with his feelings that his youngest brother was somehow beginning to overshadow him. Both Phil and Don responded by expressing affirmation for Ben's contributions and reassurance that he was as important to the business as ever. As Phil put it, "Everyone's star is rising."

Problems and distress can occur at any stage in a business, no matter how well the leadership functions. It was a mark of how far the brothers had come that they dealt directly and swiftly with Ben's concerns. The business did not seem to lose a beat at this time.

The focus and gains during this phase of the consultation were on expanding the business by using resources that involved looking beyond kin. This is a process that often stymies family businesses, which tend to be clannish and distrustful of outsiders, with the result they often do not look beyond their own family resources.

It is important to note that the ownership of the business had been equalized, per prior agreement, and went into effect, smoothly, six months prior to the mutually agreed upon termination of the consultation with the Rothstein family business.

CONCLUSIONS

The author has drawn conclusions from this consultation in the following areas: (1) changes that took place over the course of the consultation; (2) triangles and detriangling; (3) modification of leadership in the family business: from hierarchical to a collection of individuals; and (4) modification of differentiation in the context of family business consultation.

Changes That Took Place Over the Course of the Consultation

The following are some of the more concrete changes that took place over the course of consulting with the Rothstein family business:

- Lowered anxiety among the sibling partners
- Recognition of personal problems on the part of each sibling partner and concrete efforts to modify them

- Less triangling among the sibling partners, among the partners and their employees, and among the employees themselves
- More capacity to take "I-Positions" on the part of the sibling partners·
- Regular and open contact among the sibling partners and their nuclear and extended families
- Allowance for more interpersonal space between the sibling partners
- More clarity in functioning positions and responsibilities and more formalized business structures

The sibling partners went through many changes that included delineating their own functions and responsibilities in the business. They not only better defined their functions as individuals, but were better able to give and receive feedback and consult with each other. They were able to share projects, add new employees (including a COO), delegate supervisory responsibility, and create an informal advisory board.

Triangles and Detriangling

The consultants used the concept of the *triangle* to help the brothers understand how their family business operated as a multigenerational emotional unit. The triangle is the automatic mechanism that expresses how undifferentiation is manifested in the face of family and/or business anxiety. Considerable effort went into teaching the sibling partners the concept of the triangle, among other aspects of Bowen theory, and using that concept to help them understand their family business more clearly and manage themselves less reactively and more effectively. This included having the clients read a section from de Waal's (1989) *Chimpanzee Politics.* Reading about and discussing the bullying, bluffing, coalitions, and triadic behavior in a nonhuman species generated a humorous understanding of their triangling behavior in the family business and outside of it.

For the most part the consultants worked effectively to stay detriangled from each and all of the sibling partners, and they themselves did not get divided or triangled, with one consultant and the sibling partners in a close relationship, and with the other consultant in the outside position. The consultants' capacity to stay neutral and avoid triangling contrasted with the type of relationship the siblings had had with their father. This chapter described the effort that went into coaching the sibling partners to avoid triangling and to develop one-to-one relationships with each other. By staying detriangled, the consultants were not drawn into the functioning position of the father, the position of dominant leader. This provides space for the brothers to define and maintain their own positions.

The consultants did not conceptualize this difference as being a corrective experience. It was conceptualized as having provided the sibling partners with an opportunity to deal in a more direct and functional manner with each other, without triangling with the consultants. The consultants sought to avoid being emotionally caught up in the clients' emotional system, providing summaries of the clients' best thinking, and not offering authoritative advice.

The Modification of Leadership in the Rothstein Family Business: From Hierarchical Leadership Toward Leadership by a Collection of Individuals

Historically there were a number of modifications in the Rothstein family business that led from a more hierarchical form of leadership to one characterized by less hierarchy and an increased level of differentiation on the part of the three sibling principals.

In the first stage of the Rothstein family business an owner-managed, entrepreneurial structure was in place. It was run by a dominant, controlling leader. Thus it is not surprising that the functioning of leadership in the transition to a sibling partnership of the Rothstein business was fraught with conflict between the brothers.

The Rothstein brothers had grown up with a loving but sometimes controlling, entrepreneurial father who dominated the leadership of the business. Although they were emotionally reactive to their father's authoritarian style of leadership, they were, at least in part, formed through their relationship with him. Although they wanted a more democratic leadership structure, in the face of anxiety, they would sometimes temporarily adopt their father's dominating style. Anxiety can be bound through a transformation from *being done in* to *doing in the other*. The brothers came to understand that their hierarchical struggles took place within their sibling triangles and that those interlocked with the triangles that included their father and various groupings of themselves. The siblings came to understand that their triangling was a natural spin-off of what they had experienced with their father as they grew up and worked with him in the business. The negative view of their father was tempered by their acknowledgment of his positive qualities. Their mother, though not as focused upon in the context of this study of the family business, was naturally a part of these interlocking triangles.

In the Rothsteins' business, both Don and Phil felt that they had to defend themselves aggressively because each experienced the other as being like their aggressive, dominating father. To escape from being trapped in the "one down" position, both sought to occupy the "one up" position. Both their positions were reciprocally determined. Both positions represented a functioning level of self that was compromised.

During the course of the consultation, the brothers moved from an anxious and fused level of functioning, carving out more emotional space in which they could work together. They could then make efforts to define themselves as a collection of individual voices while demonstrating responsible leadership in their partnership. The three sibling partners developed an agreement to work toward an equally shared ownership and developing a style of leadership in which the hierarchy at the top of the system is not linear, but is instead horizontal. This form of leadership involved an increased capacity for being team players while at the same time increasing their capacity for responsible leadership. Each brother at times took the lead and at other times took a follower position; at times each defined a distinctly individual position and at other times compromised with his brothers' alternative positions. Their effort to grow the business involved developing the capacity to work together, often in reciprocal ways, and at the same time defining the individual responsibilities of each partner.

Bowen (1978) described an individual's *functioning position* as the way individual behavior is codetermined by the reciprocal functioning between family members. This is an important characteristic of Bowen's basic tenet: *the family is an emotional unit.* The sibling partners' *functioning positons* within the context of the family business shifted over the course of the consultation. Initially, Ben's position as the oldest sibling dovetailed with his position as "first among equals." He was the de facto leader of the business. Likewise, the family system attempted to push Ben to accept the position of "first among equals." However, he used the consultation to become more flexible and to resist automatically taking on that position. Reciprocally, the younger brothers were able to take on more leadership responsibility. There was an evident overall decrease in overfunctioning and underfunctioning between various combinations of the sibling owners/managers.

As the consultation moved forward, Ben's position changed from "controlling leader" to one of occasionally asking for help and direction, as well as giving it. Phil's functioning position changed from that of youngest sibling, "rebel/distancer," and "angry conscience for the partnership" to a position of respect within the business. Don, the middle sibling, went from occupying the position of "it," the primary recipient of the negative projection process in the family, to a position of respected, creative contributor.

When their anxiety was low, the sibling partners reached consensus easily, shared decision making, exhibited fairly clear boundaries between their functioning positions, and demonstrated a moderately high degree of differentiated leadership functioning. Each had the capacity and willingness to take responsibility for certain work-related functions and developing new initiatives as needed. When anxiety was up, triangling increased, consensus decision making was impaired, individuality was suppressed, and boundaries between functioning positions became more porous. Productivity and emotional functioning on the part of the sibling partners and their employees suffered. At such times the sibling partners gained from having a limited, but more structured format for decision making to fall back on. For example, when they agreed that under certain circumstances only two out of three needed to agree to make a decision, they avoided getting bogged down in stalemates around having to reach a consensus or a forced togetherness. In addition, by rotating the executive or chairing role among the sibling partners, the emotional inertia that came with anxiety could be overcome to some degree.

Modification of Differentiation in the Context of Family Business Consultation

In addition to coaching the brothers in their efforts to understand the interlocking family and business systems, and to define their individual and group missions, goals, and operating principles, a goal of the consultation was to enhance the brothers' functional levels of *differentiation* as expressed in their individual functioning, in their collective management and leadership of the family business, and in their family relationships. Rather than attempt to make the sibling partners better team players, the consultants wanted to help each sibling maximize his capacity to be *an individual on a team;* lower their levels of emotional reactivity, and increase their abilities to manage themselves responsibly: neither overfunctioning nor underfunctioning in their positions in the business and in their relationships with each other.

It is this author's view that the siblings may have not only improved their functional levels of differentiation of self, but one or more of them may have made at least a minimal gain in his basic level of differentiation. The idea that the basic level of differentiation may have risen for one or more of the siblings is based on the fact that while the three brothers were not being coached to work directly with their parents (the father died not long after the consultation began and the mother was ill and later died), the consultation offered opportunities to work with the secondary triangles within the sibling relationships, which as they were modified may have impacted on the relationships each sibling had with his parents in the primary triangles. Though the father died one year into the consultation and the mother toward the end of the consultation, the modification could be seen as occurring through the interlocking relationship between secondary and primary triangles, and the idea of old triangles, new players (see Chapter 1, p. 21 for a description of these processes). This may have been the case in this situation in the context of a six-year-long consultation in which the focus was developing their own I-Positions and managing their emotional reactivity to bring forth their most objective thinking and goal-directed behavior in relation to each other, in the context of the business and outside of it. Issues related to their spouses or significant others and other family members in the family of origin and extended family received some focus in the consultation.

Of course the caveat is, as was described in an earlier section on Bowen theory concepts, that the assessment of basic level change in differentiation can only reliably be assessed by observing the functioning of the offspring of the three siblings. Only Ben, the oldest, has two biological children now in young adolescence. Don, the middle sibling, has a couple of older step children whom he did not raise from childhood. The youngest brother, Phil, has two young adult stepchildren that he only helped raise when they were teenagers. Therefore, the answer to the question of basic level of change in differentiation remains unconfirmed, and would be difficult to ascertain even in the context of a longitudinal, multigenerational study.

Leadership by a collection of individuals, in this case siblings in a family business, is only possible when the individuals involved have a relatively high level of differentiation, and the group is characterized by a calm, non-rigid hierarchy. This allows for individuality in the context of being a team member. As the consultation progressed, in the view of this author, the Rothstein sibling partnership operated, with predictable fluctuations in response to stressors from both within and outside the family and business emotional systems, with an increasingly effective and stable level of functioning in their relationships with each other, and other family members, both within and outside the family business.

SUMMARY

Bowen theory has many nonclinical applications. This author applied Bowen theory in the arena of consultation to a family business owned and managed by three siblings. The case describes the two-generational presence and process of triangles and interlocking triangles and their effect on the functioning of the business. The chapter is an illustration of coaching the sibling partners to sharpen their individual functioning in the context of being team members.

REFERENCES

Bowen, M. (1978). *Family therapy in clinical practice.* New York: Jason Aronson.

de Waal, F. (1989). *Chimpanzee politics.* Baltimore, MD: The Johns Hopkins University Press.

de Waal, F. and Embree, M. (1997). The triadic nature of primate social relationships. *Family Systems, 4,* 5-18.

Ferrera, S. J. (1996). Lessons from nature on leadership. In P. A. Comella, J. Bader, J. S. Ball, K. K. Wiseman, and R. R. Sagar (Eds.), *The emotional side of organizations: Applications of Bowen theory* (pp. 200-210). Washington, DC: Georgetown Family Center.

Gersick, K. E., Davis, J. A., McCollom-Hampton, M., and Lansberg, I. (1997). *Generation to generation: Life cycles of the family business.* Boston, MA: Harvard Business School Press.

Gilbert, R. (1992). *Extraordinary relationships.* Minneapolis, MN: Chronimed.

Kerr, M. E. (2006). "The Role of Chronic Anxiety in Symptom Development," morning presentation of "A Day with Michael E. Kerr, MD: The Origin, Impact, and Management of Family Anxiety," New England Seminar on Bowen Theory, Clark University, Worcester, Massachusetts. Excerpts reprinted by permission.

Kerr, M. E. and Bowen, M. (1988). *Family evaluation.* New York: W.W. Norton and Company.

Toman, W. (1961). *Family constellation: Its effects on personality and social behavior.* New York: Springer Publishing Company.

Chapter 16

The Business of Triangles

Leslie Ann Fox

INTRODUCTION

"This would be a great place to work if it weren't for all the office politics!" It would be nice to have a nickel for every time someone makes that statement in workplaces across the world. Not only can office politics drive individuals to resign positions they once were happy to obtain, they impact the quality of products and services produced, the safety and well-being of employees and customers, and the profitability and longevity of business enterprises, not-for-profit organizations, and governmental agencies. Bowen family systems theory (1978) offers a useful way to think about office politics. Using systems thinking to understand politics in the workplace enables individuals to challenge the status quo of ingrained patterns of behavior in an organization.

The concept of triangles is one of the clearest of the theory's concepts to apply to relationships in organizations. As in families, when tensions rise between two individuals, the emergence of a third individual to bind the anxiety of the pair appears to occur automatically. Triangles reveal patterns of functioning in an organization as they do in families. Observing triangles in the workplace increases one's awareness of emotional process in the organization. Learning to manage oneself differently in triangles is one way for employees, managers, leaders, and consultants to gain alternative perspectives on workplace challenges. A new perspective on a problem or issue at work can suggest more options for action. It fosters more creativity and flexibility in resolving issues that are having a negative affect on individual or organizational performance.

In this chapter, the author describes the use of Bowen family systems theory in a consulting and temporary services company ("company") in the healthcare industry. The CEO, who is a partner and co-founder of the company, began in 1990 to incorporate the concepts of Bowen family systems theory into the company's approach to working with clients, vendors, and employees. Executives, managers and consultants in the company are exposed to Bowen theory as part of their orientation to the company's philosophy of business. The concept of triangles surfaces frequently when dealing with customer service issues that arise with the company's temporary services' clients, and when addressing leadership challenges in client organizations during consulting or project management engagements. Employees are also encouraged to "think systems" in managing their relationships with their co-workers, supervisors, and executives at the company.

The author has two objectives for this chapter. The first is to describe the company as a case study in which the CEO uses Bowen theory to inform her thinking and decision making in the business. The second is to relate examples of issues that the CEO and others in the company have addressed using the knowledge of triangles to understand and formulate action. The author will show how probing for more information about the internal relationships in a client, partner, or vendor organization informs the thinking of the company's employees to determine their actions in challenging situations.

THE COMPANY

The CEO and two partners founded the company in 1976. One of the partners, the president, died in 1979. The two remaining partners continued to operate the business as 50-50 shareholders until 1984, at which time they sought an investor to help finance a new line of software. The investor was a longtime family friend of the CEO. He purchased one-third of the shares of the company, becoming equal partners with the other two shareholders, but not participating in day-to-day operations. This situation could have created an anxious triangle with the new partner in the outside position. However, the two original partners elected him to be chairman of the board, which was one way of making the new investor feel like more of an insider. Another potentially anxious triangle was one in which the CEO and the chairman, because of their longtime personal relationship, might push the other partner to the outside. However, the first time that the chairman called the CEO after talking with the other partner about an issue, the CEO made certain she told the chairman that he had to communicate with and relate to both of the partners equally. She asked the other partner to join the call and

· the three reached a resolution of the issue to the satisfaction of all three. Thereafter the chairman always related to the two partners equally on matters of business.

The two original partners continued working in the business until 1996, at which time one partner retired and became vice chairman of the board. The vice chairman continued to be a principal shareholder, still owning one-third of the shares. Thus, in 1996 the CEO became the only principal shareholder working in the business and took the title of president and CEO. Again, an anxious triangle might have developed with the CEO in the outside position. However, with all sides of the triangle accustomed to open and direct communications, the three principals maintained respectful relationships with each other throughout the years. They have successfully managed many transitions and business challenges, achieving a company that after twenty-eight years remains intact, profitable, and highly regarded in the industry.

Organizational Change During Challenging Times

The CEO began in 1998 to develop an executive leadership team, with the goal of continuing the tradition of collaborative leadership in the company. She hired a vice president of finance, a vice president of operations, and a vice president of sales and marketing between 1998 and 2001. The three vice presidents and the CEO comprise the executive team. The three executives work well with each other, and with the CEO. They manage their differences thoughtfully and respectfully. The executive team managed the company through a particularly challenging period following the terrorist attack on September 11, 2001, and during the ensuing economic downturn, which lasted well into 2004 for the health care industry. Though revenues and profits fell during that period of time, the company overcame multiple business challenges including reduced demand for temporary services, many new competitors, and the emergence of disruptive technology. Under the executive team's leadership, the company returned to stability and is growing once again.

Another significant milestone in 2004 was a restructuring of the executive team. The CEO promoted the vice president of operations to president. The CEO continues in her role as CEO and as a member of the executive team and board of directors. She focuses primarily on business strategy, new product development, and external industry relations. The new president carries out the strategic plan, provides day-to-day oversight of business operations, directs future organizational development, and collaborates with the

CEO and executive team on business strategy and product development. She is also very involved with external relationships.

The result of the restructuring is that the president and CEO are co-leading the organization with the other members of the executive team, repeating the successful leadership model that the two original working partners had developed over the years. Most important, the company has a clear succession plan and is preparing a new president to lead the company when the CEO retires. Once again, the company successfully managed a significant transition at the top of the organization while having a successful year as measured by such indicators as minimal turnover in staff and a 10 percent growth rate.

The Consulting and Staffing Business Model Is a Triangle!

The company's engagements are performed in hospitals throughout the United States. They meet a need for leadership, management, content expertise, or temporary staff in health information management (HIM) departments of health care organizations. Thus, clients bring "outsiders" into their organizations to advise, teach, or work alongside their HIM department staff, creating a prime breeding ground for anxious triangles. Anxiety is passed between the company and client organizations through triangles and interlocking triangles occurring among executives, managers, and employees of each client organization and the company. Opportunities abound for anxiety to be escalated through the maze of interlocking triangles, creating business challenges for the company that are more thoughtfully addressed when the company's employees use systems thinking while observing and discussing client-consultant situations.

Family Systems Thinking As a Core Competency

The CEO of the company has encouraged the administrative and consulting staff since the early 1990s to view the workplace as an emotional system, and to analyze triangles to more fully understand anxiety in organizations. Observing triangles helps the staff to be calmer by offering a more neutral way to think about internal and external business relationships. The CEO emphasizes to staff that analyzing triangles is valuable in understanding the company's role in client-consultant issues, as well as understanding how triangles that develop in response to anxiety in the company affect clients. By raising awareness of triangles, the company conducts business in a way that encourages individual staff members to manage their own anxiety and to make efforts to clearly define their positions in relationships with clients, business partners, and vendors.

Twenty-eight years with the same ownership and the same corporate identity may be considered a long-lived company in an era when many companies are created to be sold or merged within as short a time as possible. It is impossible to directly attribute the company's longevity to the use of Bowen family systems theory by the company's leadership, but it is fair to say that it has contributed to the company's reputation for quality and professionalism, attributes that attract high performing staff and clients.

SYSTEMS-BASED APPROACH TO MANAGING BUSINESS RELATIONSHIPS

The following scenarios are a composite of cases with the names changed to protect the privacy and confidentiality of staff and clients. They illustrate typical situations that the company encounters in which awareness of triangles, and knowing how to manage self in an anxious triangle, can reduce tensions and improve outcomes for the client and the company. The author annotates the scenarios describing how the company executives encourage employees and consultants to manage themselves in relationships within the company and with clients.

Scenario One: Temporary Worker Deployed to Eliminate Record Processing Backlog

General Hospital requests help with a backlog in the HIM department. The company flies Sally, a qualified HIM technician, to work at the client site. The assignment calls for the HIM technician to stay in a hotel and work at the hospital for approximately eight weeks. Sally is assigned to work in the record processing section with the client's three record processing technicians. The client's record-processing manager, Judith, supervises the area. The technicians in the area are cordial toward Sally, inviting her to join them for lunch and breaks.

After several days on the job, one of the client's employees, Helen, is disturbed about a disagreement she has with John, another employee in the record processing section. At lunch one day she confides to Sally that John is a favorite of the record processing manager and that one of the reasons they are behind in processing is because Judith lets John come in late, take long breaks, and leave early. Helen is very angry about the situation. She also tells Sally that when processing records, instead of taking the records from the shelf in date order, John rummages through the stacks of records to pick out the "easy" ones. Helen warns Sally that if the backlog is not eliminated in eight weeks, the manager will blame Sally for not performing up to standard. Helen says "I've seen her do it to other temporary workers!" Helen wants Sally to go with her to complain to the director of the department about John and Judith.

Can the Consultant Manage Her Own Anxiety?

This scenario is a particularly "dangerous" one for Sally. If Sally sides with her new friend, the conflict will likely intensify and anxiety in the system will rise. As the system gets more anxious, everyone's ability to get the work done will be compromised. Sally would be "fanning the flames." However, if Sally is able to listen calmly and remain neutral, the opportunity for Helen to vent with someone who is neutral may reduce her anxiety and decrease the intensity of the conflict in the Helen, John, and Judith triangle.

Just think how challenging such a situation can be to Sally. She is away from home and might be a little lonely. Helen may have escalated Sally's anxiety by suggesting that Sally and the company could be in jeopardy. Sally likes her new friend, and she likes having a companion to chat with during lunch. If Sally is unaware of triangles, or cannot be thoughtful about the situation, she might give in to an "anxious" automatic impulse to side with Helen. Sally needs to be aware that she may be drawn into an anxious triangle, and she must manage herself in a thoughtful way.

How Does the Company Guide the Consultant?

It is not easy to resist the attraction of bonding with a newfound friend or a longtime co-worker. The company's managers and staff are aware that anxiety is contagious, and *togetherness* is one way of soothing an anxious mind. The inclination to manage one's own anxiety by joining forces with one or more individuals, at the expense of others in the group, is common. However, the company stresses in its training that when an individual manages his or her own anxiety in a more mature way, everyone is more successful—the consultant, the client, and the company.

Here is how the company wants Sally to think about such situations. Sally should realize that she has several options as to how she might handle the situation. She may choose to be very neutral and calm with Helen and comment very little about what Helen tells her. She can be noncommittal, or just say "Oh," and leave it at that. Helen may or may not continue trying to pull Sally into the anxious triangle with Judith and John.

Another option for Sally is to engage in a conversation that probes for facts, rather than drawing out further expressions of Helen's feelings. For example, Sally might ask, "How many times in the last year has the department developed a backlog in record processing? Can you think of any other possible causes of the backlogs? Were there vacant positions in the record processing area? Was there a recent change in technology or procedures? Would normal workload fluctuations and tight staffing budgets have anything to do with the backlogs? Does the department have written policies on tardiness or leaving early? What are those policies? Is John the only person who comes in late or leaves early?" The point of those questions would be to help Helen broaden her perspective to see more sides to the issue.

Sally might decide to make an effort to get closer to each of the other parties in the triangle (i.e., alternate going to lunch with each person). Or, she may go a little further and encourage Helen to address her issues directly with John and Judith. Most important, the company's approach to working with Sally would be to coach her to state her own position, based on facts, not feelings, and to avoid having a relationship with one person at the expense of another.

Scenario Two: An Account Manager, an Unhappy Consultant, and an Unhappy Client

Alice, a temporary services account manager, assigns Mary to provide vacation coverage in the record processing area of a client hospital. After a few days at the client site, Mary calls Alice to report that the hospital's census has been low and she is not being assigned enough work to fill an eight-hour day. The services contract requires payment for a full eight-hour day, but Mr. Cross, the HIM department director, has told Mary that he does not feel he should pay for time she does not work. When Alice calls Mr. Cross to discuss the issue, she gets his voice mail. She leaves a detailed message explaining the need for them to discuss the payment of downtime as required in the contract.

Alice receives a voice mail message in return from Mr. Cross. He states that the temporary employee is making too many mistakes in processing records. He is unhappy with Mary, and he does not want her to be sent to the facility in the future. Alice is bewildered by this complaint because Mary has been employed by the firm for several years and consistently gets good evaluations from clients. In the meantime, Mary contacts Alice again and indicates that she is very unhappy with the assignment. She indicates that she does not want to return to this client in the future. This scenario illustrates how the staffing business model is very much the business of managing triangles.

Alice is in a tough position in this scenario. She does not have all of the facts at hand. She is in an office several hundred miles away managing the client and her employee from a distance. She is unable to observe Mary's work or the interactions she has with Mr. Cross. Most important, Alice has not had direct contact with Mr. Cross. Their only contact around the issue has been through Mary, and via voice mail messages.

Managing Relationships from a Distance and Modern Technology: Two Sources of Anxiety

Managing client and staff relationships from a geographical distance, and using voice mail are two modern-day realities of the business world that make successful workplace relationships challenging. E-mail is another technology that saves time and may calm people by making it efficient to exchange routine information, but can also escalate anxiety when it is used to discuss sensitive issues. For individuals who manage their anxiety by distancing, e-mail and voice mail are too convenient. The company cautions staff to be aware of the anxiety that can be generated with the new technologies, and to be thoughtful in their use of e-mail and voice mail.

The Company Encourages Account Managers to Use Systems Thinking to Detriangle

How the account manager "thinks" about the situation in the scenario determines her behavior as she interacts with the client and the consultant. If Alice is not managing her anxiety, and is not on the lookout for a potential triangle, she can be easily drawn into a triangle. She might be tempted to side with Mary and blame Mr. Cross for not reading and abiding by the contract. She might suspect Mr. Cross of inventing the complaint about poor performance; or blame Mary for not reporting that Mr. Cross was unhappy with her work; or wonder if Mary was not very tactful in her discussions with Mr. Cross about the downtime issue.

Alice's supervisor prompts her to think "systems." She must first recognize that she is in a triangle that is becoming increasingly anxious. To detriangle, she would be expected to be calm, reflect on the events, and determine the role she played in elevating anxiety in the triangle. For example, did communicating important information via voice mail increase Mr. Cross's anxiety? Or was there a breakdown in following the company's protocols? Company policy requires the sales person and the accounts manager to have a transition meeting with the client to make sure that everyone is clear about the requirements of the client's engagement and the terms of the contract. Did the transition meeting take place?

The company also encourages its employees to observe and understand the emotional process in client organizations. While developing relationships with clients, account managers are expected to seek more information about recent and current stresses or challenges affecting the client's organization, specifically the HIM department. When issues arise during an engagement, and it is difficult to make contact with the client, the company wants its account managers to keep trying to stay connected. It is important to continue giving the message that they are available to work on resolving the client's concerns.

The account managers must also maintain contact with the other side of the triangle, the employee. Being open and honest with employees about issues that arise at client sites is important if the account manager hopes to have a clear picture of events. Often the employee continues to work at the client site while the account manager addresses problems. During such times the company's employees are vulnerable to the anxiety of the situation. They need to have complete information and contact with their supervisor so that anxiety in the triangle does not escalate further.

In addition, the company's executives and managers recognize that anxiety within their own organization contributes to problems. Account managers need to consider what stressors in the company's organization may be affecting the company's staff. Identifying all sources of stress and taking responsibility for one's own contribution to problems are keys to managing successful relationships in the consulting and staffing business.

A SYSTEMS-BASED CONSULTING APPROACH

An operations review of HIM departments is a primary consulting service that the company offers. The purpose of the service is to provide an objective third-party review and analysis of a department's organizational structure, functions, leadership, and management capabilities, staffing resources, technology, and business processes. Consulting services such as an operations review present a different type of emotional challenge from the temporary staffing services illustrated in scenarios one and two.

For a consulting engagement to have a successful outcome, the company's HIM consultants must be content experts as well as change agents. Clients may hire the company for its HIM content expertise, but clients need content consultants who are also accomplished *process consultants*. A process consultant has the capacity to facilitate positive change in the client organization. They not only identify where a department's performance can or needs to be raised to a higher level, but process consultants also interact with clients in ways that result in successful change for the client. Consultants, who use Bowen theory to inform clients as they work with them, do not tell the client how to change, but rather they gently lead the client through a change process.

It is the role of the change agent that is most challenging for the consultants, in which they are prone to emotional reactivity, which is often played out in triangles. For example, when a department director is not functioning well as a leader, the director's boss may expect the consultant to play a surrogate leadership role to facilitate the changes that are needed. The consultant then has the challenge of managing self in a director-boss-consultant triangle. Consultants who are aware of triangles can plan how they will manage themselves and can work at relating to each side of the triangle in an open and honest manner.

Spotting the Land Mines

Consulting engagements require consultants to be aware of emotional process in the workplace, particularly the organization's level of anxiety and how it is played out in triangles. Triangles are like "land mines." If they are not recognized and avoided or diffused, they can "blow up" in the consultant's face. One has to be on the lookout for them from the very first contact with the client.

A request for an operations review usually comes from the director of the HIM department, or from the director's boss, a senior executive in the organization. Clients who engage the company to do an operations review have various reasons for requesting the service. For some clients, the organization may be anticipating a major change, such as an implementation of electronic health records, an expansion of the organization's services, or a merger with another hospital. The client wants expert help in reengineering business processes, or may be requesting an HIM expert to facilitate the department's strategic planning process. In such cases, the consultants are usually being hired for their content knowledge and broad experience in the field.

However, some engagements are requested because the executive, or others in the organization are concerned about the performance of the HIM department or specifically the director of the department. The senior executive may be questioning the competence of the director and/or his or her management team. If physicians, patients, other departments, or other members of the hospital's executive team have complaints about the department, the executive initiating the consultation may want the consultant to determine if the director should be retained. These are engagements in which the consultant must be especially cautious about being "triangled" into an anxious system.

Scenario Three: Chief Information Officer, HIM Director, and HIM Consultant

The company receives a call from Tim Doe, Chief Information Officer (CIO) requesting an operations review of his hospital's HIM department. The company's director of consulting services, Lauren, does an intake to learn more about the requirements of the engagement. She learns from Tim that the HIM department reports to him. He has been at the hospital for about a year, overseeing the information technology (IT) department and the HIM department. During that time the hospital merged with another hospital in a nearby community. Many people lost their jobs as the hospitals' departments were merged to achieve economic benefits from the restructuring. Citizens in the two communities where the hospitals are located did not support the merger and recently the merged organization has been receiving a lot of criticism in the local press.

Tim explained that merging the HIM departments has been a particularly difficult process. All employees were asked to resign and reapply for the positions allocated to the merged department. The total number of positions for the merged hospital is fewer than for two independent hospitals, so several HIM employees did not get jobs in the merged department. For positions that require only one person, such as the position of director, administration chose between the two individuals who held that position at each hospital. The person selected to be director of the merged HIM department, Cora, is having difficulty winning over the employees that previously worked for the other director.

Another issue is space. One department has been closed and all employees who were hired for positions in the merged department must work in the space that previously housed the department of one hospital. The merged department is crowded and some employees are being required to work evening or nightshifts. Employees who had previously worked at the other hospital site have to commute a longer distance to work, and they complain to Tim that they are treated like outsiders.

In the months since the merger, the HIM department has developed large backlogs in key processing areas. Tim and the hospital administrator receive a lot of complaints about poor service from the department. Physicians, clinic administrators, and other departments say that they cannot always get access to patient records when they need them. The business office manager is also struggling with the merger, and has hired a business office consultant to help with billing issues. The business office consultant blames the HIM department for not getting discharged patients' codes needed for billing to the business office in a timely manner.

Tim asks Lauren for a proposal for a consultation to assess the current operations in the HIM department, and to advise him on whether or not he should replace the HIM director.

Detriangling from the "Get-Go"

Lauren realizes that the CIO is anxious about the problem he perceives in the HIM department and that he is inclined to blame the HIM director. Lauren wants to avoid an engagement that begins as a triangle of the consulting company, the CIO, and the director. She decides to detriangle immediately and responds to Tim by taking a differentiated position in the triangle. She does this by defining the company's consulting process.

Lauren informs Tim that the company's approach to the engagement would not be to focus solely on the HIM director, but to take a broader view of the situation, and a participatory approach to improving the department's performance. The consultant would do this by reviewing the department's systems, processes, and resources; interviewing employees and users of the department's services; and then working with Cora and her management team to develop an action plan to address operational and relationship issues. Upon hearing this, Tim calms down. He tells Lauren that he is pleased to hear that the company would try to help Cora and the department to improve. After receiving a written proposal, he agrees to hire the company for the consulting engagement. The director of consulting has just sidestepped the first potential landmine.

Lauren assigns Karen, a senior HIM consultant, to spend a week at the hospital conducting the operations review. Prior to the visit, the consultant contacts Cora to introduce herself, and explain the company's consulting process. She also begins to collect facts. The consultant requests the director to send information about the department's workload volumes, procedures, staffing, budget, and productivity results prior to the visit. She also sends the director two surveys to be distributed. One is a physician satisfaction survey that is sent to all the members of the medical staff. The other one is an employee satisfaction survey to be completed by the HIM department employees.

Anxious Behaviors Abound, and the Consultant Needs a Plan

Karen receives the completed surveys prior to the visit and learns that both physicians and employees are very dissatisfied. They blame the department's poor performance on Cora. Also prior to the visit, the consultant receives a telephone call from the business office consultant. He tells Karen that he can hardly wait for her to get to the hospital, because he is so frustrated with the HIM director's failure to meet the needs of the business office for billing. He explains that the hospital is in serious financial difficulty because the HIM department is late in getting medical codes needed for billing hospital services. Thus, billing is late, resulting in poor cash flow for the hospital. He tells Karen that he is counting on her support to get Cora to speed up the coding process.

Karen views the blaming behavior and intense focus on the HIM department and its director as symptomatic of a highly anxious organization. Knowing some of the recent history, and learning about the anxious behaviors in the organization before the onsite visit, she is alert to the potential emotional challenges in the upcoming engagement. Having this information gives her an opportunity to prepare to work with such intensely anxious people. Karen knows she has to plan carefully to avoid absorbing the anxiety in the system, and to envision how she will manage herself in the inevitable triangles.

The main elements of Karen's plan are to manage expectations and focus on facts. She will manage expectations by continually defining her role with whomever she is meeting. For example, she starts by defining her role to the business office consultant who says he expects her to get Cora to speed up the coding process. His behavior suggests that he assumes the HIM director and the HIM department are at "fault." Karen responds to him by explaining that her job is to determine where the system is breaking down and guide the organization in addressing the problem.

Karen also describes her process to the business office consultant, telling him that she observes the flow of information from the nursing units and other sources, as well as the complex process of record completion, which must be done by clinicians before the HIM department can perform the coding function. She reviews the technology available to the HIM department, the staffing resources allocated in the budget to coding, and the efficiency of the procedures in the department. She examines all aspects of the perceived problem and works with the organization to address any issues identified. By describing the comprehensive and fact-based process she undertakes, Karen is communicating her neutral position with respect to the HIM director. She is taking the anxious focus off of the HIM director and her department. She describes her role to the business office consultant as an objective observer and facilitator. She manages the expectations of others by expressing no prior assumptions as to causation, and by not guaranteeing a solution to the problem. She responds to anxious behavior by demonstrating to people how she objectively approaches issues.

Navigating Through Anxious Minefields to a Successful Outcome

Karen's decision to be in *observation mode* when she goes onsite is a key strategy for her success. She wants to present as many real facts as possible to people she meets and works with at the hospital. She observes their reactions and probes for their thinking on new information she presents. Her goal is to get people to reflect on the facts and to see options. Planning in advance to be a neutral observer helps her keep her own anxiety in check, which in turn helps the client's staff to be calmer and more thoughtful.

The next part of Karen's plan is to facilitate creative thinking and problem solving. When meeting with the department employees, she gives them ample time to vent their feelings about their situation, and then she gently asks them to think about alternative solutions to problems based on the facts that she is presenting. She is respectful of the employees' experience, knowledge, and opinions, but firm in challenging them to meet their responsibilities to the organization.

Karen also presents facts to people external to the department. She asks physicians, nurses, and other department managers for their ideas on how they can help resolve the issues that cause problems. She wants people throughout the organization to begin seeing that others also have a role in the successful outcomes of the HIM department. Karen does not hesitate to take positions, but bases her positions on observable facts, or her professional expertise. She knows that her ability to function at a high level of differentiation in the face of all the anxiety is key to mitigating the anxiety in the organization. She also is careful to avoid triangles and to detriangle when she does find herself in an anxious triangle.

Finally, she facilitates an action-planning meeting with Cora, her management team, Tim, and the hospital's quality assurance manager. Karen reports on the problems she has observed and helps the team identify goals and action plans to improve the department. She has determined through the process of observation and interviews that Cora is not a strong leader. Cora has excellent technical knowledge that is valuable to the organization, and though the employees say they like her, she does not inspire or motivate people to perform well. She is reactive with staff and customers of the department, and she plays an amplifying role in several anxious triangles. Taking sides with some employees has lost her the respect of others.

By involving the CIO in the action-planning meeting, Karen allows him to observe for himself the strengths and weaknesses of the director and her staff. Through the action-planning discussion Tim becomes aware of the resources and support that the department needs to be more successful. Karen also invites Sandy, the quality assurance manager, to the meeting. Sandy is responsible for making sure the hospital is prepared for their upcoming accreditation survey. She must work with the HIM department and the clinicians to make sure medical record documentation meets the required standards. Karen understands that Sandy needs to know the status of the organization's compliance with standards, and that Sandy is responsible for supporting the department in making changes that impact the organization's accreditation status.

Karen meets with the management team once a month for about a year after the initial consulting engagement. Her role is to hold them accountable for completing their action plans, and to advise them on technical issues when necessary. Tim eventually reorganizes the department. He demotes the director and relieves her of all supervisory duties, but keeps her in the department in a technical role. With input from the consultant and the management team, he organizes the department into three teams and selects team leaders to implement the department's improvement plan. Nine months later the hospital passes the accreditation survey with no compliance issues found in the HIM department. Complaints from physicians, the business office, and other departments are greatly reduced. A new director is hired about a year after the initial consultation.

Karen's consistency in taking calm positions with Tim and the HIM staff helps her avoid or minimize the intensity of triangles, and enables her to provide the technical expertise that the organization needs. If she had not managed her own anxiety successfully, she would have likely escalated the anxiety in the system through triangles, leaving the organization less, not more functional.

CONCLUSIONS

Using Bowen family systems theory as a lens through which to view relationships in organizations and to guide one's interactions with business clients is an interesting challenge to business and technical consultants. Most consultants are not trained to address the emotional side of organizations. They are usually sought more for their content expertise than for true process consulting. Yet, the success of consultants can be enhanced by having an awareness of emotional process in organizations and by using the concepts of Bowen theory to consult in a calm, thoughtful manner. Calming an anxious organization so that its employees become less reactive and more thoughtful, collaborative, and creative may be the most valuable service a consultant can offer.

Using Bowen theory as a theory of leadership may be even more challenging to business people. It is one thing to manage one's anxiety in a consulting relationship where the consultant is not enmeshed in the organization's emotional process to as great a degree as one is in his or her own organization. It is another thing to have the capacity to manage anxiety in self in one's own organization. Business leaders who use Bowen theory are most successful if they make a commitment to work on increasing their level of differentiation in their families as well as in their businesses.

Working with a leadership coach who is trained in Bowen theory helps business executives understand their organizations and the role they play in increasing or decreasing anxiety. Seeing how patterns of behavior in their family of origin play out in the workplace may offer unique insights to motivated executives. Learning to observe their systems for triangles is like learning to see a completely different organization chart. Coaching provides leaders with insights about their role in triangles, and with a broader perspective on the behavior of individuals and groups within the organization. Learning to see the emotional landscape provides a richer context for decision making, and often brings to light more alternatives and solutions to business issues in which relationships play a central role.

REFERENCE

Bowen, M. (1978). *Family therapy in clinical practice.* New York: Jason Aronson.

Chapter 17

Triangles in the Academy

Ona Cohn Bregman

INTRODUCTION

Academies of higher learning provide many triggers for activating the triangles that are basic to the functioning of any emotional system. The established structure in the university system has been in place over generations, and individuals within the system generally accept and operate within this established structure, regulated by a complex set of traditions and rules that can lead to an intense emotional process. This emotional process in humans is closely aligned with heightened anxiety, and movement within and between triangles is one way to bind that anxiety in the attempt to maintain stability. In the attempt to relieve anxiety and insulate oneself from "threat," triangles come alive. The academic system is hierarchical, and those who are lower in the hierarchy are particularly vulnerable, but those people at the other end of the continuum are not immune to the process and make a strong contribution to maintaining it. Active triangles flourish in this setting.

The discussion of triangles that follows is based on the concept of triangles developed by Murray Bowen (1978): a dyad is unstable in the long term and the triangle is the basic building block of any emotional system. The way a person operates in triangles is consistent across various settings and continues the pattern developed in his or her family of origin. These triangles operate automatically and all persons have a modus operandi that becomes second nature. Triangles are always in operation but not always apparent. When a system is in a calm state, the natural triangles are less

Parts of this chapter were presented by the author at the 39th Symposium of the Bowen Center for the Study of the Family (2002).

likely to become active or noticed. As stress increases, however, the process becomes observable. When discomfort arises between a twosome, a third person is added. When the anxiety is too much for the triangle to contain, the persons involved reach toward others and create interlocking triangles. These interlocking triangles can reduce the pressure on the original triangle. Active triangles dilute emotional intensity for individuals, functioning as one mechanism for managing anxiety. As the triangles join with other triangles, the impact on the system as a whole may be to maintain or increase anxiety in selective locations.

This chapter grew out of the author's observation of attempts to manage herself within the myriad of interlocking triangles in the several university systems of which she has been a part. In each case, the department in which she was involved was overall a well-functioning system in which people had respect for differences, relatively low levels of anxiety, and functional relationships. Compared with many university departments, these functioned very well. This does not prevent the use of triangles to manage anxiety. The primary vehicle for understanding the triangles selected for discussion in this chapter are the author's observation of the triangles and how she functioned within them. In addition, her observations of others are reported. It is impossible to escape some subjectivity as neither self-observation nor observation of others can be entirely objective.

The content of all examples is composite situations with some details changed in order to maintain anonymity. The examples are illustrative with a focus on process. An honest attempt is made to not get caught in the triangles that are operating in these examples. The task of attempting objectivity and not jumping into the triangles, even on the printed page, presented a surprising degree of challenge.

THE SETTING

The university setting provides a particularly inviting venue for spawning triangles and interlocking triangles. It is not that these triangles are different from those in any other system. Rather, the organizational structure and emotional climate of a university appear to this author to provide an ideal atmosphere for fueling anxiety, which in turn can lead to emotionally reactive behavior and triangling activity. As the anxiety in students, support staff, faculty, and administration is elevated, the emotional process engages these individuals in a series of interlocking triangles. How intense these triangles become depends on the level of ongoing chronic anxiety present in the participants and in the system.

Promotion and tenure are both anxiety producing phenomena. Faculty enter the system, in most cases at the lowest level, as either lecturers or assistant professors. It takes seven years to achieve tenure, which has a demanding set of requirements with regard to performance in the areas of teaching, scholarship, and service. Promotion and tenure decisions are made by committees of peers, deans, and officers of the academy. Merit pay is decided by deans and directors. Evaluation is an ongoing process, as professors evaluate their students and are evaluated by these students as well. Student evaluations are used as contributing data to the decision-making process in promotion and tenure. Support staff may be privy to both process and content in these situations. They also have their own individual relationships with many of the people involved. All of these contexts set the stage for triangles to become active and multiply.

OPERATIONALIZING THE TRIANGLES

The Student-Faculty Relationship

Bowen theory describes the triangle as the basic building block of a stable system and a dyad as potentially unstable. An individual student-faculty relationship in a university is a dyad. Its stability will depend on many factors including the interlocking triangles in which each is involved. The interlocking triangles may include but are not limited to other instructors who teach the same section of a class, other instructors who are allies (with either student or instructor) and those who are not, students who are reactive to the professor, and others to whom the professor reacts. For example, when experiencing disapproval from a student, the professor may seek others on the faculty or in administration to join as allies, responding to selected students critically and defensively. Interlocking triangles continue to form. One of the times of highest anxiety for students is during examination and term paper time. When student numbers are down, anxiety goes up, and admission standards are stretched. Then there are more students who quickly absorb the anxiety in the system. Following are some student-faculty examples in which the author was the key participating faculty member. She will be identified as the professor.

Example 1

Student A did not agree with much of what was presented in a class on clinical applications of various family systems theories. There was frequent dialogue about these differences. The dialogue appeared to be open and respectful, while in fact the student was speaking to many of her favorite instructors and to selected classmates about the professor's ideas which she considered, at the very least, to be sexist. At the very same time, the professor was discussing this student with other like-minded colleagues. Although appearing to engage in open and respectful discussion with the student, the professor was actually assuming that the student just did not understand the material, particularly Bowen theory. Neither party allowed for the possibility of differing assumptions or foci. They were each looking for another person to validate their position as well as to have an ally if a serious controversy should erupt. The student was concerned that the grade would be affected by her views. The professor was concerned that the differences would influence the student's evaluation of her. There were certainly others around who had decided that Bowen theory and other family systems theories were sexist and not generally applicable "today." If a student can persuade others that the professor is not open to different ideas or is indulging in an "-ism," it will help her make a case if the grade is not satisfactory to her. If the professor can persuade colleagues that this student just does not get it, and can find others who agree, she will have more backup should a poor evaluation ensue. Finding people to accept invitations into a triangle is never difficult. As alliances developed and the triangles multiplied, the student and the professor were able to avoid facing one another with honesty and respect.

The degree of anxiety and level of differentiation in each person will contribute in a major way to the degree of triangling that occurs in this situation. The clearer the professor became over the years regarding her thoughts about issues of gender in Bowen theory and the other systems theories, and the more confidence she had in her ability to assess a student and to appreciate different ways of thinking, the more she was able to avoid triangles about students and the less she worried about a negative response on evaluations. Early in her teaching career, however, with little experience in this area, she was less skilled and less confident. She began to note that as her anxiety intensified, she not only locked horns more often with students but also involved others in those situations. It was difficult for her to hold a position and withstand the repercussions without participating in multiple triangles to relieve her sense of threat. As the years moved on, this area became less threatening to her. She was able to respond to the above type of criticism from the position of her own understanding of Bowen theory and gender issues. She could state her position clearly and at the same time appreciate the position of others. To the degree the professor was able to do this, students and she were able to have honest dialogue and on many occasions respectful disagreements. In the earlier example, however, student A and the professor never really worked anything through. It got back to the professor that the student continued to talk negatively about her after she left school and there is little question that one of the poor evaluations the professor got that year was from student A. It was several years before the professor realized that her own role in this had contributed to the process.

Example 2

Student B was a good student and complied with most of the requirements but was frequently late with assignments, often without having informed the professor in advance. He complained about the amount of reading assigned and the expectation that assignments would be completed on time, stating he had many outside commitments and believed allowances should be made. Some allowances would indeed have been possible if arrangements were made in advance and this was clearly stated in the syllabus. Student B had not completed requirements by the end of the course. He made arrangements for an incomplete and a deadline was selected when materials would be submitted, following which the incomplete would be changed to a letter grade. This deadline was not met. He did not request an extension and the professor did not volunteer one. He did nothing and the grade automatically converted to an F. In order to complete the program, the student was required to repeat the class. He appealed the decision but the rules were clear and the student was held accountable. He did retake the class. To the professor's surprise, during the semester that was repeated, he was prompt with all assignments and did A level work. As he began to take an interest in Bowen theory he eventually recognized his piece of responsibility in the earlier situation. At the end of the semester he thanked the professor for holding him accountable. There were lessons for both the professor and the student in this situation. By taking responsibility for her position without triangling and getting caught up in the emotional process, the professor gave the student the opportunity to take responsibility as well. When faculty tried to influence her evaluation of this student the second time round, she did not interact with them about him. She not only provided an opportunity for him to do it differently but also learned the importance of not prejudging him based on other opinions and her own emotional response.

Example 3

Student C was a fine student and a talented clinician. She maintained excellent grades, although she missed many classes and was late when she did come. She turned in assignments late and did not register in a timely fashion.

She forgot to come for advisement which created other technical problems. She always had some excuse for why papers were handwritten instead of typed. She almost did not graduate because she neglected to complete the last course required, which she was taking with the professor who then facilitated her completion of this course, an example of overfunctioning on the part of the professor. This happened when the professor got caught in a triangle with someone at the student's internship who persuaded the professor to "help her out." This of course maintained the status quo and student C almost did not graduate when she did not do the necessary administrative paper work on time, creating a tremendous amount of extra work for support staff. It was very frustrating to deal with this student, and the professor often talked about her with other faculty, fueling her own anxiety about dealing with this student. Shortly after graduation, this student requested a letter of recommendation. The professor indicated a willingness to do this with positive statements about her clinical ability and relationship skills but with the intent to include a paragraph about her inability to meet deadlines. The student slammed down the phone. Although the professor believed the position she took was responsible, she noted that she continued to triangle, telling others about this incident and commiserating with support staff about problems this student created for them. In retrospect, the professor realized that the triangling throughout had diluted her attempts to hold the student accountable during their time together and had put each of them and their relationship at a disadvantage, a contrast to Example 2.

Example 4

Students D, E, F, and G (followed by the entire class) asked the professor to provide instructions and reviews that would make it relatively easy for students to prepare for exams. Some instructors do this, almost providing questions and answers in advance and students like it. Of course this leads to classes which often have inflated grades. Students D, E, F, and G were in several such classes and wanted the professor to provide sample questions and review outlines, among other things. The anxiety level goes up for students whenever exams approach. Simultaneously, instructors can also absorb the system's anxiety, both wanting to avoid hassles with displeased students and wanting to be assured of positive evaluations. Instructors are ranked in relation to one another and are rated on their teaching based on these evaluations. Most instructors know that holding a poor or irresponsible student accountable often results in a poor evaluation by that student. When it is time for an instructor to issue a final grade, it is very likely that some students will be dissatisfied with the instructor's evaluation of their academic performance. There is frequently much negative reactivity toward an instructor who has issued a grade that is not satisfactory to the student. In such situations, initially, it is common for a student to be more uncomfortable than the faculty member. If the discomfort associated with this experience is substantial enough, students may handle this discomfort by aligning with other dissatisfied students, leaving the instructor in the outside position in these triangles and perhaps the object of a complaint.

While the previously mentioned situations are occurring there are often other sections of the same course in progress, each with a different instructor. Students will often compare instructors by sharing information with each other about the instructors, their assignments, and their examinations. The result of these student exchanges, particularly when sufficient anxiety is present amongst faculty and administration, is the formation of numerous interlocking triangles—most often leaving the instructor in the outside position. Students sometimes complain to administration. Instructors are well aware of the fact that they are evaluated in relation to peers teaching the very same course as well as all other faculty. Their salary and potential for promotion can be influenced by this. All of these factors can make it difficult to not invest in one's evaluations, especially relative to those of one's peers. It is a challenge to hold one's position about evaluating students fairly and not compromise on one's principles in order to avoid being on the outside of these triangles. The better the professor became at holding a position, the more likely she was to drop a few levels in the rankings. It takes only a few angry students to have an impact on one's score.

Triangles, of course, are always forming, and those professors who did not do the review for students would talk about those who did and would perpetually raise the issue of inflated grading. Many who pretended to be in agreement would in reality continue the same patterns and frequently talk about those of us who expected too much from students. With faculty located at two corners of a triangle, there were times when an administrator's anxiety about maintaining a head count would have that person taking the third corner of many triangles in a fluctuating position. Sometimes the administrator promoted high standards and at other times, supported those who tended to give in to students. This ambiguity added to anxiety in the system and the perpetuation of endless triangles, as students who became aware of such fluctuations would appeal to the administrator for special consideration. Meanwhile, faculty continued to gossip about the administrator and the students, keeping themselves in the outside position in these triangles. This on occasion could lead to a conflictual relationship between a faculty person and administrator.

Example 5

Student H was an above-average student in intelligence but tended to maintain a B average. He frequently arrived at class late and often fell asleep in class. He often forgot about assignments, which had been discussed in class the week before and were also in the syllabus. Sometimes he made up the assignment and got points taken off his grade for tardiness, and some-times he decided not to do the assignment at all and voluntarily took an F. His contributions in class, however, were outstanding. They stimulated exceptional discussions and his participation was always valuable. When he did an assignment it always earned a well-deserved A. This is how he maintained the required average, as he did enough assignments to bring the lower grades up. The professor had many clear and direct conversations with him about responsibility. He never tried to make excuses and she con-tinued to hold him accountable. Although it was tempting, the professor did not discuss this student with other faculty. After graduation student H asked for a letter of recommendation to another program. Once again, as in the ex-ample of student C, the professor indicated there was much she could say that was positive, but expressed the fact that she would have to include his tendency to be irresponsible in some areas. His response was that he consid-ered this fair and appreciated that she had always been direct and fair with him. This was an unusual response and raised the question for her about what was different here from the example of student C. Although there is no way in hindsight to answer that definitively, perhaps one difference was that they had dealt directly and honestly with one another all semester, with the student being able to own his lack of responsibility while the professor held him accountable without either of them getting anxious or involving other people.

Example 6

In this situation, the "student" example is an entire class. Students in this class came in as a unit from another community on a special grant. They were already in semiprofessional jobs and needed an advanced degree for promotion. They were united as a group in their desire to spend as little time as possible on reading and assignments, most of them believing they were in school primarily for the ticket to job advancement. Most of the students were basically competent in their positions but limited by little theoretical knowledge and an average command of common methodologies. They were to be with the professor for a two semester practice class that was built on family systems theory. There had been other such groups in the past but this one was distinct. Early on, the professor recognized that she had never fully engaged this group and felt some of their resentment about assignments from the start, but had no idea how strong the reactions were until evaluations came out at the end of the first semester. They were extremely negative, placing her very low in the ranking that semester for this particular class. This was most unusual for the professor and her anxiety skyrocketed, though she did not realize it at the time. She talked with many other faculty, all of whom agreed that this group of students was impossible, thereby diminishing the threat she felt. Nevertheless, it was important as well as a challenge to her to try to hold them accountable.

At the beginning of the second semester, she engaged the class in a dialogue about the evaluations. The professor indicated areas in which she thought she could provide something different based on comments in the evaluations and asked them what contribution they could make to a better second semester. They were not very responsive but it appeared to her that the second semester was going better. This was not so, however, and that became quite clear when evaluations came out after the second semester. They were as low as the first. At that time, she was puzzled by this and decided it must have been the class. When it was discussed at year-end review, the dean supported that view, as did many other faculty with an abundance of triangles being formed, usually leaving this group of students in the outside position. They were not in the outside in every triangle, however, as they also brought a significant amount of money into the program. A certain amount of appeasement was needed to satisfy their funders, so on other occasions the funders and administrators were aligned and faculty were on the outside, labeled as too demanding.

The movement in these triangles provided momentary relief for some members in the short term, but much confusion and angst in the longer term. As time went on the professor became a more seasoned instructor, became less anxious about evaluations, and continued to develop her grasp of Bowen theory. She came to understand the role that she had played and her contribution to the burst of triangles coming alive in this group. Her own anxiety throughout both semesters hampered her ability to think through basic principles of Bowen theory and apply them. She did nothing about attempting to establish one-on-one relationships with the students, a common practice of hers in other classes. Nor did she consult with the funding group at all. By triangling in the fashion she did and responding to the class as a unit, she supported their attempt to unite in opposition to her. It is possible that nothing would have engaged individual members of this class, but it is a guarantee that by not connecting to each part of the system, by being intimidated by the "group think" presented to her and by focusing more on commiserating with other faculty than on her role in this situation, the professor did nothing to ameliorate it and likely stoked the fires.

Faculty and Administrative Relationships

Universities have senates, composed of faculty members who have a responsibility to represent faculty that govern, but administrators retain much power and often have a final say (overtly or covertly) on critical decisions involving individual faculty. Due to the fact that in recent years money has become scarce, there is much competition for funds—both for programming and faculty reward. This can on occasion create another kind of triangle, as both faculty and programs compete for the funds. A program's success will be measured in large part by money brought in. An equally valuable program educationally, which is smaller and brings in less financially, is put in a very vulnerable position. The smaller program must develop strategies to ensure its own survival and that of its faculty. This may take the form of interlocking triangles, if the smaller program begins to take shots at the relevance of the larger program, critiquing and misrepresenting its success and seeking alliances with other smaller programs. Without doubt a university is a business that must maintain its financial viability, but that very process is often distorted and morphs into turf wars governed by active interlocking triangles. On occasion, an administrator's hidden or not so hidden agenda can change the course or very existence of a program. During these times of tight finances, funded research is highly valued, and those whose research interest involves less fundable areas have less support and fewer of the rewards that go with funded research. Bowen (1978) discusses the analogy "between regression in a family and regression in larger social groups and society" (p. 277). Anxiety is high in the academic system during a time of limited budgets and program cuts. The situations just described represent some repercussions. The following examples are a combination of situations in multiple institutions combined to protect anonymity.

Example 7

A committee was meeting with a critical decision on the table. Members of the committee will be described by letters and numbers in order to distinguish differing positions on the issue. Committee members A, B, C, and D were of one mind. The author is D. Committee members 1, 2, 3, and 4 were of another mind. There was a ninth person who was *chairperson* and was quite emotional about the whole issue. The chairperson broke the tie by voting with A, B, C, and D. The administrator of this area appropriately had not been a part of this committee process. After the vote, which ran counter to the administrator's view, was reported to the administrator, he or she lobbied A, B, C, and D to change their vote, focusing mostly on B (who was asking for a favor) and D (who had a good working relationship with the administrator). B's vote then changed and the decision was reversed. When D asked B about the reason for the change in vote, the reply was that one has to know where one's bread gets buttered. The triangle of B, D, and the administrator became active. Following this incident, D could watch the interlocking triangles begin to form. A, C, and D continued to support positions consistent with those represented on the earlier committee. B began to support positions representing the positions of 1, 2, 3, and 4, which were close to the position of the administrator. Several subcommittees formed involving 1, 2, 3, and 4. A, C, and D were not invited to participate. These subcommittees began to suggest changes consistent with the philosophy of the administrator and 1, 2, 3, and 4. B joined this effort.

Example 8

When the time came to frame the changes described in Example 7, a large representative committee was formed. The committee included A, B, C, D, 2, 3, 4 and chairperson 1 from Example 7. In addition there were five other people who will be represented by the small letters m, n, o, p, and q and a new chairperson was selected. This person will be called chairperson 2. Chairperson 2 had outstanding leadership skills and the ability to be objective. These last five people and chairperson 2 were open to collecting data and did not appear to have any vested interests. All persons presented material as the previous process and content were reviewed. Labored discussion took place in the meetings. Committee members 2, 3, and 4 did active lobbying in the form of triangling both outside and inside the meetings. Chairperson 1 tried to balance that by lobbying against 2, 3, and 4 also in the form of triangling, but the emotionality of these efforts only fueled the triangling. As months went on the triangling intensified. Committee members A, C, and D worked hard at not triangling in the larger system, though they used their reasonably stable triangle for constant debriefing and strategizing using Bowen theory. What were the principles driving the positions that A, C, and D represented? How could each one of them best define a position in the meetings while managing his or her own emotional reactivity? How could each one work at not being defensive? How would each one manage his or her reactivity to some of the subtle but offensive comments directed at the three of them? For example, 2, 3, and 4 suggested that many of the ideas supported by A, C, and D were outdated and not generally applicable. There were strong challenges to systems thinking. Members A, C, and D

continued to present positions along with objective data that had been collected. The data incorporated some suggestions from 2, 3, and 4 but did not
buy into the entire package. A, C, and D were each committed to staying with
the data and not reacting (to whatever degree possible at the time) to pejora-
tive comments and facial expressions during meetings. In the author's opinion, the culmination of this project provided a satisfactory result that clearly
offered improvements both to the students and to the program, though it required change and challenge for faculty (including the author). A majority
of the ideas introduced by A, C, and D were incorporated into the final plan.
A contributing factor to this outcome was the result of skilled and objective
leadership by chairperson 2 as well as the contributions of the five committee
members who were new to these matters and able to base their positions on
factual data. In addition, A, C, and D avoided provoking reactivity by using
their familiarity with systems theory and triangles to manage their own
reactivity and not fuel the process.

Example 9

There were many changes taking place in the larger system of the university and all had a direct impact on smaller units. These were times of high
anxiety in the system and on occasion the author found the anxiety extremely
contagious. As she began to tire easily and not look forward to going in to
work, she wondered what was happening and how she got so caught up in
the passions of the moment. Following the experience in Examples 7 and 8,
the author began to observe herself in the system. She noticed that the chairperson from Example 7 would invite her into many situations, as their positions were similar. After those invitations the author would find herself
jumping onto the band wagon with an overly enthusiastic affect and pro-
ceeding to join a variety of triangles as well as invite others in. As the author
became aware of this and began to decline the invitations, she became more
centered, clearer on her own position, and less tired and negative. This also
led to a less intense connection with the chairperson. Once this took effect,
it became apparent that whenever the chairperson from Example 7 had an
interest in an issue, the system as a whole and many individuals in it tended
to become more anxious. Though the author was allied with this person in
many triangles, at the time she lacked the neutrality to note this.

Support Staff and Triangles

Members of the support staff are not innocent bystanders in the emotional
process described. They are an integral part of every one of the above trian-

gles. In fact, they may be the persons most invited into triangles. Support staff often function as family away from home to students, and students frequently confide in them, not only about personal matters but also about issues the students are having with faculty. Faculty also unload to support staff and may pump them for information as well. Administrators depend on support staff for their own functioning and as a result the support staff has much information. In recent years, the support staff has less information about faculty with the introduction of voice mail and computers, but they still tend to know a lot about what is going on with faculty. Even if they do not have as much information as they used to, there are still strong responses to how they view themselves being treated by faculty. At times, they might complain to one faculty member about another. Other times, they might complain to administration. Usually the issues are not dealt with directly with the faculty person, and once again triangles are formed. Sometimes the messages carried to administration or faculty provide data that can be used for or against a person. In the process of observing relationships involving support staff, it became apparent that all were involved in every type of triangle noted earlier.

CONCLUSION

Administrator–"faculty–support staff"–student interlocking triangles are a fact of academic life. In addition to the examples already cited, these triangles may operate through committee selection and assignment of tasks. They can operate by use of data about an instructor in a particular fashion that has a negative impact, while ignoring data that would have the opposite result. As noted earlier, promotions and tenure are recommended by committees of peers to deans and officers of the academy. The place one holds in the triangles that involve members of the decision-making committees tends to be influential in the decision-making process. Merit pay is usually a limited package and its distribution is decided by deans and directors. Much energy is invested in developing standards. These standards, however, are not always applied uniformly. Triangles and the emotional process fueling them have an influence on this too. For example, all decisions about tenure are approved or disapproved at high levels of administration, outside of a particular department after recommendation at lower levels in the hierarchy have taken place. It is possible for favored faculty to have an influence on the final decisions in subtle ways by contributing to the triangling process over a period of years in a fashion that stacks the deck for or against a person. Without a doubt, if a person has measured up unquestionably in every area examined, it would be difficult to reject that person. Likewise, if a person has obviously been negligent in more than one area it would be difficult to approve a decision for tenure. However, for those residing in a gray area, perhaps excelling in research but not in teaching or vice versa, active triangles fueled by intense emotional process can exert a strong influence on the final decision.

Ideally, administrators want to lead a well-functioning organization that holds its members accountable, and faculty members want to present their thinking competently and hold their students accountable. Similarly in an ideal situation, students want to take responsibility for their own learning and want to be challenged. Currently, in the real world of academia, however, an intense emotional process is very present. Money is tight and full enrollments are necessary. Administrators want students to feel satisfied and have good grades that reflect well on the school. They hope that students will provide positive marketing for the program and recommend it to others, so they want to keep them happy. Administrators want faculty to reflect well on the school and to bring in lots of money in funded grants, so expectations that faculty will perform in a variety of roles increase in times of financial crunch. Faculty members want to have good evaluations and be appreciated by students, respected by peers, and recognized and rewarded by administrators. Students want to have good grades without having to work too hard. Frequently, it appears that emotional process rules and as a result triangles are active and multiplying in academia. Clear and responsible thinking and acting is difficult in these circumstances when people are inclined to look for a quick fix and neglect the longer-term implication of decisions. An understanding of Bowen theory and the functioning of triangles could contribute to a more mature level of functioning in academia, but would also present a tremendous challenge. It is not easy to operate on principle by responding to and offering functional facts, keeping anxiety low, managing reactivity within self, and maintaining a connection with all parts of the system. The issues that come up in a dyadic relationship can get played out through interlocking triangles operating in an emotional field. The work is first to define self as clearly as possible and to define one's ethical and operating principles. After becoming clear on these for oneself, it is important to be able to present them without defending them against criticism or attacking the other person's position. This incorporates defining self in all areas—with students, support staff, peers, and administrators, always owning one's part in tense or conflictual situations and always being sure to get the job done while staying connected to all parts of the system. This, of course, represents the ideal. Nevertheless, academia provides an excellent place to study triangles as well as to study oneself. The person who does this may continue the work of defining a self while he or she also makes a contribution to his or her department, school, college, or university. By taking clear positions, regulating one's reactivity, learning to hear and respect opinions that are different, and maintaining consistency and integrity, one is not only less likely to push others toward polarized positions, but is also more likely to contribute to a milieu where people are free to think.

REFERENCE

Bowen, M. (1978). *Family therapy in clinical practice*. New York: Jason Aronson, Inc.

PART V:
TRIANGLES AND EMOTIONAL
PROCESS IN SOCIETY

Chapter 18

Triangles in Societal Emotional Process with an Example from the Russian Revolution

Katharine Gratwick Baker

INTRODUCTION AND OVERVIEW

Human societies are vastly complex and multilayered entities. Examining their internal processes through the framework of a theory that originated in a study of the family is a challenging exercise. It may, however, provide a clarifying perspective to the confusing and almost random elements of the larger social systems that shape our functioning.

Bowen theory focuses on human behavior in the context of the intense relationships of the human family (Bowen, 1978). It was only in the later development of his theory that Bowen came to see the connections between patterns in the family and patterns in larger human social systems. In this process, he developed a final concept that expanded his theory to *society* and larger nonfamily social units. He first referred to this concept as *societal regression* in 1972 (see Bowen, 1978, p. 385) and then three years later in 1975 came to describe it as *emotional process in society* (see Bowen, 1978, p. 426), a broader term that encompassed the many fluctuations in functioning that are observable on the societal level.

This chapter explores that final concept and its interconnections with Bowen's concept of the *triangle*. It begins with an introduction and overview of issues to be addressed. The next section includes a definition of the concept of emotional process in society, briefly describing the way that the seven earlier concepts from Bowen theory operate in social units that are larger than the family.

The link between triangles and emotional process in society is then explored in detail. Bowen extended his theory from the level of the multigenerational human family to the societal level, using the concepts of triangles and interlocking triangles.

An example of interlocking triangles that powerfully impacted societal process in the Soviet Union in the 1920s is then presented. The Bolshevik leadership triangle—Lenin, Trotsky, and Stalin—is analyzed through a brief discussion of the families of origin of each of these men, examining how family factors played out in the triangle of their relationships with each other, and then the way this interpersonal leadership triangle interlocked with societal emotional process in the years following the Russian Revolution.

Conclusions include an exploration of the following summary ideas that are expanded in the chapter: (1) the concept of the triangle and interlocking triangles from Bowen theory can provide a useful model for understanding processes in large, complex, social systems; (2) the reciprocal flow of emotional process between individuals, families, and larger social units is an ongoing phenomenon; and (3) the functioning of individuals and families is affected by societal process and vice versa.

DEFINITIONS AND THEORETICAL CONSIDERATIONS

Bowen theory contains two central variables: "one is the degree of anxiety, and the other is the degree of integration of self" (Bowen, 1978, p. 361) in human functioning. The concept of *differentiation of self* in Bowen theory describes how anxiety and integration of self vary along a continuum. Bowen's concepts of *emotional cutoff, the projection process, nuclear family emotional system,* and *sibling position* describe emotional processes that vary along the *scale of differentiation.* The concept of the triangle describes a pathway for emotional process that can also vary along a continuum. The *multigenerational emotional transmission process* is a description of emotional process extending through interlocking triangles into the broader, multigenerational family. The eighth and last concept, emotional process in society, is the only concept in Bowen theory that defines an arena beyond the family in which the other seven concepts operate.

With emotional process in society, Bowen asserted that the same emotional patterns could be observed not only in the human nuclear family, but in all other forms of human organization. At first he had been hesitant to jump to this conclusion, because it seemed to him that his theory could only apply to social systems through analogies. Later he "identified a link between the family and society that was sufficiently trustworthy for [him] to extend the basic theory about the family into the larger societal arena" (Bowen, 1978, p. 386).

This link was the *interlocking triangle*, providing a bridge from the human nuclear family to other societal and organizational systems that was far more substantial than analogy. The interlocking triangle made it possible for him to understand the connections between patterns for managing anxiety in individuals, families, and larger nonkin groups. As an example, Bowen described the interlocking emotional processes between nuclear family triangles, school systems, and court systems in dealing with the anxiety generated by delinquent adolescents.

In summarizing his theory in 1976, Bowen wrote:

> [W]hen a family is subjected to chronic, sustained anxiety, the family begins to lose contact with its intellectually determined principles, and to resort more and more to emotionally determined decisions to allay the anxiety of the moment. The results of the process are symptoms and eventually regression to a lower level of functioning. The societal concept postulates that the same process is evolving in society; that we are in a period of increasing chronic societal anxiety; that society responds to this with emotionally determined decisions to allay the anxiety of the moment; that this results in symptoms of dysfunction ... which increase the problem; and that the cycle keeps repeating. . . . My current postulation considers the chronic [societal] anxiety as the product of the population explosion, decreasing supplies of food and raw materials necessary to maintain man's way of life on earth, and the pollution of the environment which is slowly threatening the balance of life necessary for human survival. (Bowen, 1978, p. 386)

From this statement it is clear that, for Bowen, the patterns he observed in anxious human families could also be observed in larger social systems where anxiety was a predominant emotional underpinning. As noted earlier, the concept of emotional process in society provided an arena for observing these parallel patterns.

TRIANGLES AND EMOTIONAL PROCESS IN SOCIETY

In Bowen theory, the interlocking triangle is a pathway that links emotional process within and between the nuclear family, the extended or multigenerational family, and larger social systems. Bowen began his explanation of interlocking triangles with a description of the way discomfort builds up between two individuals and automatically leads to the involvement of a third party:

> The two person relationship is unstable in that it has a low tolerance for anxiety and it is easily disturbed by emotional forces within the twosome and by relationship forces outside the twosome. . . . When the intensity reaches a certain level, the twosome predictably and automatically involves a vulnerable third person in the emotional issue. (Bowen, 1978, p. 400)

Involvement of a third person decreases the anxiety level between the original two individuals, as a triangle is inherently more stable and flexible than a twosome.

Bowen then explored what happened when anxiety increased beyond the ability of the simple three-person triangle to *handle* it or stabilize it:

> At this point, one of the [three members of the original triangle] usually involves yet another outsider. Now the emotional forces follow the same triangle patterns between two of the original people and the [new] outsider. The other member of the original triangle becomes emotionally inactive. If anxiety remains high, the emotional process may involve still another outsider, or it may shift back to the original triangle. If anxiety continues to increase, the triangular spread can go outside the family to involve neighbors, friends, and people in the schools, social agencies, and courts. (Bowen, 1978, pp. 400-401)

Bowen described this triangular process at work when families and then schools and courts became anxious and reacted emotionally to adolescent delinquency.

As anxiety spreads through larger social systems, "the configuration spreads in a series of interlocking triangles. When a large group or crowd is involved in an active emotional issue, multiple people append themselves to each corner of the triangle" (Bowen, 1978, p. 401). Societal polarization usually includes at least two social units that are intensely connected through their "agreement" about a social issue of great concern, and a third social unit also with numerous suballiances that has taken an opposing stance.

The larger units that append themselves to the three corners of an emotional triangle can be large societal entities, and even population groups and nation states that take on or magnify the anxiety initiated in the smaller units. Anxiety can also be initiated in larger units and flow downward into smaller units, such as families and individuals. For example, when there is high anxiety at the societal level about an impending decision to go to war, families and individuals can pick up and magnify this societal anxiety within their intimate relationship units. Societal anxiety can be transferred, modified, or expressed in family triangles through seemingly unrelated content that may originate in the broader emotional environment.

Large groups can also interlock with other large groups. Again the content generating the anxiety may be different, but, according to Bowen, the emotional process of triangles is the same at all levels. The reciprocal process of *triangling* can flow through interlocking triangles from individuals, to families, to large social units and back again. The emotional pattern of the triangle is the same.

All three corners of a triangle can be in good balance, as in a *three-person relationship* that has an open flow of emotional connection between the three corners and between each dyad. Another possibility would be that two corners of the triangle might be very close and ally against a third corner. A third possibility would be that two corners of the triangle might conflict with each other while the third corner maintains a more comfortable outside position. These positions can be rigidly fixed, or they may fluctuate, depending on the level of differentiation and the amount of intensity or anxiety in the system. All three positions have emotional *agency* and a capacity to respond or react to the other positions, also based on the amount of anxiety in the system.

The extent to which additional outsiders are involved and interlocking triangles are formed depends on the level of differentiation as well as the amount of intensity or chronic anxiety in the system. Bowen used this formulation in his discussion of adolescent delinquency, a phenomenon that affects both the nuclear family of the teenager and the wider social environment in which the family is embedded. He described the reciprocal flow of reactivity between family, neighborhood, school, and juvenile court as occurring through triangles.

A HISTORICAL EXAMPLE

The concepts of Bowen theory provide a lens for understanding the human species in all its forms throughout human history. There are countless examples of societal triangles in all cultures over time. I have chosen to focus on the three leaders of the Russian Revolution and their relationships with each other in the postrevolutionary period, because of personal interest in this period of history. I have also been searching for interlocking triangles that describe connections between individuals, their families, and the social systems they are part of. Lenin, Trotsky, and Stalin were not only embedded, as we all are, in their own families of origin and nuclear families, but through their relationships with each other, their political group, and their nation, they shaped the Russian Revolution and its aftermath. There are perils in a retrospective examination of the lives of historical figures, but I have tried to use a factual approach in describing their participation in family and societal triangles.

The Russian Revolution was more than fifty years in the making. By the time it occurred in 1917, Russian society, its agricultural economy, and its autocratic political system were deeply fractured. In addition, the country was in the throes of a devastating world war. Compared with its western European cocombatants, Russia was a backward, rural nation, ruled for hundreds of years by despotic czars, with a very small middle class and a vast population of impoverished peasants recently emancipated from serfdom.

Through the lens of Bowen theory, prerevolutionary Russia could be described as low on the *societal scale of differentiation* or extremely regressed, with the decision making of its leaders driven by societal anxiety. The country had not kept up with the industrialization of western Europe and therefore could not participate successfully in World War I. Its rural population was desperately poor and, without sufficient supplies, equipment, or effective leadership, the peasant foot soldiers began to desert the army. Its domestic police force ruthlessly served the czars and suppressed attempts to broaden political participation. The Russian Orthodox Church also served the czars through its strict hierarchy.

In the late nineteenth century when Lenin, Trotsky, and Stalin were born and grew up, many young people of their generation became politically radicalized and disaffected from Russia's traditional political system (Malia, 1994). They joined embryonic terrorist groups, took on revolutionary pseudonyms, were arrested at a young age, sent to prison or exile in Siberia, and eventually escaped into emigrant exile in western Europe where they formed close personal attachments with other young Russian radicals, and plotted together to overthrow the czarist regime.

In presenting biographic summaries on Lenin, Trotsky, and Stalin, I have used materials from the three biographies of these men written by Dmitri Volkogonov in the late 1980s and early 1990s.[1] Volkogonov was a professional soldier during the late Soviet period who became Director of the Institute of Military History in Moscow in the mid-1980s. After the col-

---

[1]Because Volkogonov wrote his biography of Stalin in 1988, he had less access to the archives than when writing the two later biographies. I have therefore supplemented his materials on Stalin with a later biography (1996) written by Russian author and playwright E. Radzinsky.

lapse of the Soviet Union in 1990, he obtained access to the Soviet archives and wrote the first substantial biographies of the three leading Bolshevik revolutionaries that were grounded in archival fact rather than propaganda. In an introduction to his biography of Trotsky, Volkogonov (1996)[2] wrote:

> I have come to see, in writing my studies of Lenin, Trotsky and Stalin, that each one complements the other historically. Lenin emerges in revolutionary history as the inspirer, Trotsky as the agitator, and Stalin as the executor, the one who carried out the idea. The swerves, the collisions and the tragedies of Soviet history can be observed in sharp relief when seen through the prism of these three personalities. In this respect, the biographical method is quite effective, for it allows one to analyze an entire historical layer of time through the personal fabric of a human existence. (p. 31)

Although Volkogonov did not use the language of family systems theory, he too was searching for the connections between individual, family, and societal processes in his biographies.

EMOTIONAL TRIANGLES IN THREE FAMILIES

Lenin

Lenin was born Vladimir Ilyich Ulyanov on April 23, 1870, in Simbirsk, "the small leafy capital of the province of the same name" (Volkogonov, 1994, p. 3).[3]

He was the third of six siblings (see Figure 18.1). His mother's side of the family included Jewish doctors and prosperous Germans and Swedes. Her family was well educated and well-off. His father's side of the family were

---

[2]Quotations from this text: Reprinted with the permission of The Free Press, a Division of Simon & Schuster Adult Publishing Group, from *Trotsky: The Eternal Revolutionary* by Dmitri Volkogonov, translated by Harold A. Shukman. Copyright 1996 by The Estate of Dmitri Volkogonov. Translation, copyright 1996 by The Estate of Dmitri Volkogonov. All rights reserved.

[3]Quotations from this text: Reprinted with the permission of The Free Press, a Division of Simon & Schuster Adult Publishing Group, from *Lenin: A New Biography* by Dmitri Volkogonov, translated by Harold A. Shukman. Copyright 1994 by The Estate of Dmitri Volkogonov. Translation, copyright 1994 by The Estate of Dmitri Volkogonov. All rights reserved.

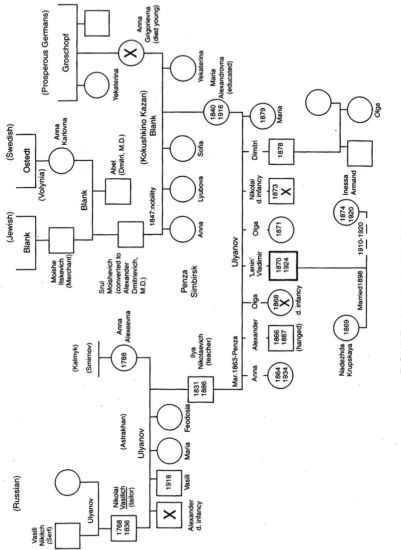

FIGURE 18.1. Lenin Family Diagram

Russians and Kalmyks, town-dwellers two generations removed from serf-dom. His father was a teacher of physics and mathematics who eventually became the director of schools in the Simbirsk district. According to Volkogonov (1994):

> The young Vladimir . . . was a gifted and capable child, qualities enhanced by the comfortable, supportive atmosphere of the home, thanks to his father's successful career. The family lived in a good house, the three eldest children each had a room of their own, there was a cook, a nanny, and servants to deal with the domestic chores. Lenin himself recalled that the family lacked for nothing. . . . The Ulyanovs' life was stable and secure—until, that is, Ilya Nikolaevich [Lenin's father] died in 1886, and, out of the blue, the eldest son, Alexander, was arrested and hanged in the following year. (p. 11)

In addition, Volkogonov (1994) describes the young Lenin as

> acquiring deep self-confidence and a sense of superiority over his peers. He was the family favourite, accustomed to being the centre of attention. Not that he was vain, but neither did he conceal his moral "right" to the primacy he believed was his, and even at that early stage he seems to have shown an intolerance of other people's views. (p. 11)

Volkogonov (1994) also speculates that "the harmony between husband and wife, their concern for the children, the equality between the siblings, the culture of hard work and diligence, all helped to form an extremely favourable soil for the seeds of free thinking, should they fall there" (p. 13). When Lenin's father died, his mother supported the family on her pension and the rent from a small country estate.

The death of Lenin's older brother Alexander in 1887, when Lenin was seventeen, became the catalyst for Lenin's early political radicalism. His brother had joined a university student group of conspirators who were plotting to assassinate Czar Alexander III. The whole group was discovered, arrested, and five of them, including Alexander Ulyanov, were swiftly hanged. When Lenin himself entered Kazan University in the same year, 1887, he was expelled for taking part in a student demonstration. He then "immersed himself in reading a wide range of western and Russian social-political literature" and eventually prepared himself to enter St. Petersburg University as an "external" student. "By the time he reached the age of twenty-two [in

1892], Lenin had acquired a first-class diploma from St. Petersburg and been accepted as a lawyer's assistant on the Samara circuit" (Volkogonov, 1994, p. 19).

Lenin was first arrested in 1895 "for being part of a Marxist propaganda circle—an almost routine event for men of Lenin's cast of mind at the time" (Volkogonov, 1994, p. 30). Later he was exiled to Siberia for three years, and then moved to western Europe in 1900, launching a revolutionary newspaper, *Iskra* (The Spark), and living in Switzerland, France, and England until the Revolution began in 1917. He married a fellow revolutionary, Nadezhda Krupskaya, in Siberia in 1898, and took on his revolutionary pseudonym (probably from the river Lena) while living there.

In describing Lenin's nuclear family, Volkogonov (1994) notes:

> [T]hroughout his life, Lenin's family circle consisted mostly of women: mother, sisters, wife and mother-in-law. In the absence of any children of his own, he himself was the constant object of their care and concern. He differed from his Party comrades in his puritanical restraint, steadiness and constancy, and would have been a model husband, had it not been for the ten-year relationship he began in 1910 with a lively [French] woman revolutionary called Inessa Armand. (pp. 29-30)

From this brief overview of Lenin's early life, one can only speculate about the emotional triangles of which he was part, as so little is known of the actual emotional process within the family. There was of course the primary triangle of himself and his parents, in which his father was the youngest of five and his mother was the fourth of five girls.[4] According to Volkogonov, he was the favorite of both parents and the dominant child, although he was the third in his own sibling group. However, he may have been closer to his mother who lived with him into his adult years. With the deaths of his father and older brother, Lenin's mother became intensely focused on Lenin, supporting him financially and encouraging his work throughout his life.

Another triangle was Lenin, his older brother, Alexander, and their father, in which Lenin may have been somewhat on the outside. According to

---

[4]Depending on the family's level of differentiation, parents, like Lenin's, who grow up as anxious youngsters may pass their anxiety on to a child who overfunctions in response to the parental leadership vacuum. Bowen describes this as the way "a particular child is chosen as the object of the family projection process" (Bowen, 1978, p. 385) through the primary triangle.

Volkogonov (1994), Lenin and Alexander were not particularly close before Alexander's untimely death:

> They were a close-knit family, but the children tended to pair off, and Vladimir was closest to his sister Olga, though he deferred to Alexander's intelligence. Anna, the eldest sister, recalled once talking with Alexander after their father had died, and asking him: "How do you like our Volodya?" Her brother replied: "He's obviously very gifted, but we don't really get on." (p. 15)

Lenin was always closer to his sisters than to his brother, and after Alexander was hanged, Lenin was the only survivor of the original nuclear family male triangle. With the inevitable anxiety accompanying these losses, he connected more strongly to his mother, his sisters, and his studies. One could speculate that an intellectual absorption with Marxism took up much of the emotional energy formerly attached to his father and brother. This shift toward Marxism and the fledgling socialist-revolutionary movement in Russia led to interlocking relationship triangles with other young revolutionaries and the formation of small illegal political movements.

Emotional attachment to ideas, and the individuals who generate those ideas, can become ways of managing anxiety, leading to interlocking triangles with collections of individuals and larger groups who share one's ideas. In prerevolutionary Russia, groups of like-minded individuals began to form political parties that competed with other similarly formed groups or parties with different sets of ideas. These embryonic political parties formed interlocking triangles with each other as they struggled to determine the most effective methods for promoting political, economic, and social change in czarist Russia.

Lenin assumed the dominant position he had taken in his family of origin triangles, and became an early leader among the young revolutionaries both in Russia and in exile in western Europe. He founded the Bolshevik party with a group of like-minded colleagues, and then struggled with other Bolsheviks to form alliances or to compete with other revolutionary parties such as the Mensheviks and Social Revolutionaries, in defining Russia's future. The shifting triangles among these small but intense political groups ultimately led to the Revolution of 1917.

Trotsky

Trotsky was born Lev Davidovich Bronshtein on November 7, 1879, in Yanovka, near Yelizavetgrad in Ukraine.

He was the third surviving child, and youngest son, of four surviving siblings, following the deaths of four older siblings in infancy (see Figure 18.2). Both sides of the family were Jewish. Trotsky's mother, Anna, "was a typical Jewish town dweller from Odessa, where she had received a modest education" (Volkogonov, 1996, p. 3). His father was an illiterate but "tough and enterprising farmer," who, "by dint of hard labour and close-fisted resourcefulness, and by the constant acquisition of more and more land, became a substantial landowner" (Volkogonov, 1996, p. 2).

Trotsky described his childhood as

> a bleak sufficiency, for the family "strained every muscle and directed every thought towards work and savings," and children were accorded little space in such an environment. "We were not deprived, except of life's generosity and tenderness. . . . It was the grey childhood of a petty bourgeois family, in the countryside, in the sticks, with wide-open spaces and narrow, mean interests and values." (Volkogonov, 1996, p. 3)

Trotsky's mother encouraged her children to read and write, and Trotsky became a top scholar at a good state school in Odessa ("no simple matter, as a quota operated, according to which Jewish children must not exceed 10 percent—in some cases 5 or 2 percent—of the pupils in a school" [Volkogonov, 1996, p. 4]).

There is no specific information available about the emotional dynamics in Trotsky's family of origin. Based on reports of his adult functioning, one may assume that Trotsky may have kept himself somewhat apart from the emotional vortex of his large family and busied himself with his studies and intellectual life.

Volkogonov (1996) describes Trotsky's personality as difficult:

> He had many admirers and as many detractors, for talent is rarely forgiven, and in time, moreover, the sense that he was exceptional generated in him marked egoistic and egocentric traits. This was underlined by the fact that, even when he was popular, he had no close friends, for friendship demands equality. From childhood on, Trotsky was unwilling to recognize his intellectual equal in anyone, except possibly in Lenin, and even then only after October 1917. . . . He would often say

that there were too many mediocrities in the world, and he did not suffer fools gladly. (p. 5)

After leaving high school at age seventeen, Trotsky joined the revolutionary movement, and received no further formal education, although he continued to read and write voraciously throughout his life. Like Lenin, he became intellectually involved with Marxist ideas and subsequently with individuals and political groups that developed around those ideas. Those individuals and groups became components of the interlocking triangles that led to his involvement in and impact on larger societal systems.

Volkogonov (1996) notes:

Trotsky's family could not of course have created the revolutionary in him, but it gave him an insight into petty bourgeois life, permitted him to obtain an education, and supported him financially right up to the revolution. In this respect, his position was greatly preferable to that of the majority of revolutionaries. Thanks to his versatility, moreover, he also had access to a variety of other sources of financial support; from lecturing, grants from charities and earnings from journalism. (p. 6)

Trotsky was arrested for the first time in January 1898, and spent time in Butyrka prison in Moscow, and then in exile in Siberia for two years, before escaping from exile, adopting the pseudonym of Trotsky, and illegally leaving the country in 1902. He met Lenin for the first time in London that year, although Trotsky was more involved with the Mensheviks and other more reformist political parties than with Lenin's Bolshevik party until just before the Revolution:

Up until 1917 Trotsky was in virtually permanent opposition to Lenin, at times conducting veritable war [with him]. . . . While essentially a leftist in outlook, Trotsky also harboured reformist ideas, which to a great extent can be explained by the company he kept when in exile in the West. In due course he would come to mix his radicalism with his reformism, and this dualism would last until the tumultuous events of 1917. (Volkogonov, 1996, p. 46)

While in prison, Trotsky married Alexandra Sokolovskaya, a fellow revolutionary. Less than three years later he abandoned her and their two small daughters in Siberia, and never again returned to his first family, although

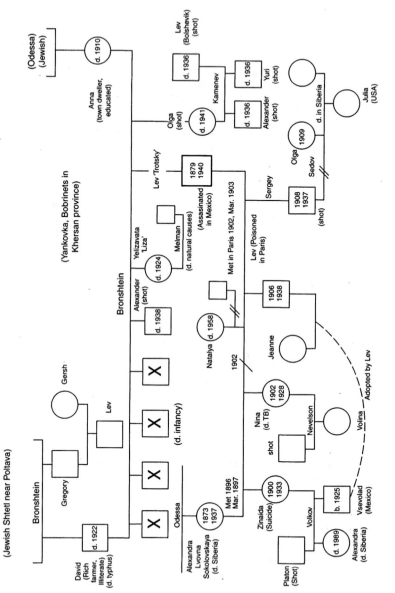

FIGURE 18.2. Trotsky Family Diagram

· he corresponded with them for the rest of his life. While in Paris, in 1903, he met his second wife, a free-thinking Russian art student named Natalya Sedova,[5] with whom he had two sons, Lev and Sergei.

Over the next fourteen years, Trotsky was active as a writer, a revolutionary (participating in the first Russian Revolution in 1905), and a war correspondent. He was arrested and exiled to Siberia in 1906, and again in 1916. He spent a third of his life, or more than twenty years, in exile.

Trotsky first met Stalin in 1907 at the Fifth Party Congress in London, and then again in 1913, when they began to work for common goals. Owing to Trotsky's conflict with Stalin in the 1920s, most of his relatives, including three of his four children and their spouses, two of his three siblings, a brother-in-law (Kamenev), and his two nephews were executed. His oldest daughter, Zinaida, committed suicide in 1933. Trotsky himself was assassinated by one of Stalin's men in 1940, while he was living in exile in Mexico.

In his primary nuclear family triangle, Trotsky was indulged and supported by both parents, although he may have been closer to his educated mother than to his illiterate father and therefore perhaps in the inside position with his mother. His mother supported his writing and intellectual development, and his father supported him financially. In his sibling group, and later with his wives, children, friends, and colleagues, Trotsky maintained a reactively distant or outside position in relationship triangles. This tendency toward taking a distant or outside position made it impossible for Trotsky to compete successfully with Stalin during their savage succession struggle after Lenin's death in 1924. Stalin apparently knew how to manipulate the power dimension of triangles and Trotsky did not.

Volkogonov (1996) notes:

> Trotsky was essentially different from Stalin in that from an early age he strove for intellectual greatness. Power and glory were not his passion, as they were Stalin's but the inevitable attributes of intellectual superiority. Intellectual recognition was for Trotsky immeasurably more important than official posts or political status. (p. 21)

Trotsky came late to Lenin's Bolshevik party and was in fact a Menshevik for many of the years leading up to the Revolution. When he did join the Bolsheviks, as the Revolution was breaking out, he came as somewhat of an

---

[5]Natalya Sedova was married at the time they met, but soon left her husband to live with Trotsky. Volkogonov (1996) notes that "it is not known when—or even if—he married Sedova. Their sons were always called Sedov, rather than Trotsky, and common-law marriages were normal among revolutionaries" (p. 33).

outsider whom Lenin accepted because of his intellectual and oratorical gifts. Trotsky's focus on intellectual power also distanced him from manipulating the relationship triangles that were crucial to gaining and maintaining power in the 1920s.

Stalin

Stalin was born Joseph Vissarionovich Dzhugashvili on December 21, 1879, in the village of Gori near Tiflis in Georgia, a small country in the Caucasus ruled at the time by Russia, and then later becoming part of the Soviet Union. Georgia was briefly independent after the Russian Revolution, but not fully independent again until after 1990.

Both sides of the Dzhugashvili family were Georgian peasants (see Figure 18.3). Stalin's mother was religious, somewhat literate, and loved music. His paternal great-grandfather, Zaza Dzhugashvili, apparently participated in a bloody peasant revolt in the mid-nineteenth century. Zaza was arrested, beaten, and jailed, but escaped, rejoined the rebellion, was rearrested, and again escaped. Stalin's semiliterate father, Vissarion, a brawler and drunkard, worked sporadically as a shoemaker. He is described as "a man consumed by anger. He was dark, of medium height, lean, low-browed, with mustache and beard" (Radzinsky, 1996, p. 19).

The first two Dzhugashvili children died in infancy. The third and only surviving child, Joseph, was "small and weedy" with a pockmarked face, the legacy of an illness at age six. He also had a deformed left hand. There was apparently considerable violence in the family, and Stalin's father disappeared from Gori in 1888 or 1889. Biographers report that his father later died "in a drunken brawl," although no date is given (Radzinsky, 1996, p. 31).

In 1888, Stalin entered the Gori Church School where he was a star student, fulfilling his mother's dream that he study for the priesthood. In 1894, he left the Church School with top marks and entered the first form of the Tiflis[6] seminary. In order to attend the seminary, Stalin moved out of his mother's home in Gori for the first time and lived with his fellow students in the seminary building in the capital city of Tiflis. He began to read revolutionary literature, and made his first contact with revolutionaries in the underground. During this period he took on the pseudonym Koba,[7] which

---

[6]Tiflis, now Tbilisi, was the capital of Georgia.

[7]Koba was the hero of Stalin's favorite book in his youth, *The Parricide,* by Kazbegi. Koba was a Georgian Robin Hood who robbed the rich and gave to the poor.

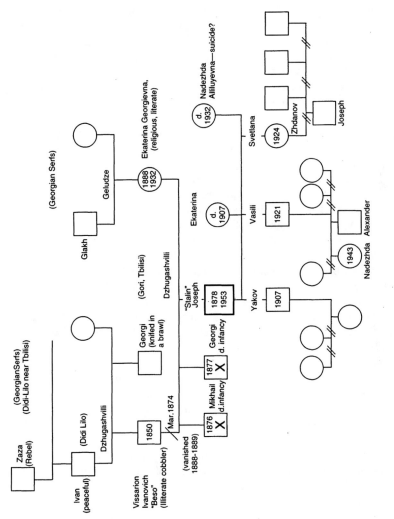

FIGURE 18.3. Stalin Family Diagram

437

became his revolutionary name for almost twenty years. Radzinsky (1996) describes the changes in Stalin:

> He no longer studies. He is not prepared to waste time on it. Yet, interestingly, he becomes one of the most important figures in the life of the seminary. The whole establishment divides into friends and enemies of Koba. Even his enemies fear his secretive, vengeful character, his subtle sarcasm, his rough outbursts of anger. And the vengeance of his friends. The strongest boys for some reason slavishly submit to this puny seminarist with the little eyes, which blaze with a menacing yellow light when he is furious. (p. 40)

He was frequently reported to the school authorities for reading forbidden books or speaking rudely to teachers, and in 1899 he was expelled from the seminary. He worked briefly for a local observatory and joined the Social Democratic Workers Party, participating in a number of demonstrations, reading works by Lenin that found their way to Tiflis, escaping arrest for several years, and living as an underground "illegal."

Stalin was first arrested on April 5, 1902, during a secret revolutionary meeting in Batum. In prison he befriended the criminals: "It was not difficult for this pauper son of a drunkard to find a common language with them, [and] he realized their potential, the contribution that criminals could make to revolution" (Radzinsky, 1996, p. 50). Stalin was eventually sent into exile in Siberia, though he escaped and returned to Tiflis where he again lived as an "illegal" from 1904 to 1908. During this period he became known throughout social revolutionary circles as an effective "fund-raiser" for the movement:

> Robbing banks or rich people's homes to raise funds for the revolution was called "expropriation." The militants and fighting squads who carried out these murders and expropriations were seen as so many romantic Robin Hoods. (Radzinsky, 1996, p. 57)

Stalin/Koba came to Lenin's attention during this period as someone who was effective at organizing assassinations and robberies. He spent time in the oil fields of Baku "doing revolutionary work":

> Together with his fighting squad he exacted protection money from the oil magnates by threatening to fire their wells. Sometimes the revolutionaries carried out the threat, and an angry red glow, together with clouds of smoke, hung over the oil fields for weeks on end. They

also organized strikes, though these were profitable rather than otherwise to the owners. They raised the price of oil and made an additional payment. Yet Koba himself lived more or less the life of a tramp. All the proceeds were sent in full and promptly to Lenin. (Radzinsky, 1996, p. 63)

Lenin played an important part in Stalin's involvement with Marxism. Lenin was "very attentive to revolutionaries from the national minority borderlands" and wrote to Stalin regularly, after some of Stalin's publications came to his attention (Volkogonov, 1988, p. 11).

In 1906 Stalin/Koba married Ekaterina Svanidze, the sister of a fellow revolutionary. Their son, Yakov, was born shortly before his mother's death in November 1907, and was raised by Ekaterina's sister, Maria Svanidze. Soon after, Stalin/Koba was arrested by the czarist police and sent into exile in Siberia. He escaped in June 1909, returned to Tiflis, was rearrested and sent again to Siberia. In 1912, he escaped again and this time made his way to St. Petersburg, and eventually to Krakow, Poland, where he met Lenin whom he followed to Austria.

Trotsky had first met Stalin in 1907, but did not remember him. In 1913, he too was in Austria and wrote this description of his first encounter with Stalin/Koba:

> Suddenly the door opened without a knock and . . . a strange figure appeared on the threshold: a very thin man, rather short, his face swarthy with a grayish tinge and clearly visible pockmarks. He looked anything but friendly. This stranger emitted a guttural sound, which might have been taken for a greeting, silently poured himself a glass of tea, and just as silently left the room. "That's the Caucasian, Dzhugashvili," Skobelev explained. "He's just got into the Bolshevik Central Committee and is obviously beginning to play an important part there." The impression he made was difficult to describe, but no ordinary one . . . the *a priori* hostility, the grim concentration. (quoted by Radzinsky, 1996, p. 74)

Stalin/Koba began to work with Lenin in 1913, and wrote an article, which he signed for the first time with his new revolutionary pseudonym, Stalin—or Man of Steel. In 1920 he married his much younger second wife, Nadezhda Alliluyeva, the sixteen-year-old daughter of a revolutionary comrade. He and Nadezhda had two children, Vasily born in 1921, and Svetlana born in 1924. Nadezhda may have committed suicide in 1932 following an argument with Stalin, although the exact cause of her death is not known (see Volkogonov, 1988, p. 154).

The primary triangle Stalin grew up in was intensely violent and burst apart when his father left the family in 1888 or 1889, never to return. His father was in the outside position in the family triangle, in conflict with both wife and son. Stalin and his mother formed a strong attachment in the inside positions. This was a relationship pattern that Stalin repeated many times in his adult life. He formed close alliances in which his political competitors were on the outside and eventually excluded from power. Like Lenin, Trotsky, and many others of his generation, Stalin also became involved with groups of revolutionary individuals through which he participated in interlocking triangles that led to a wider societal process. However, Stalin, early on, attached himself personally to Lenin as a dynamic leader, serving him through power and inside relationships rather than through contributing intellectual ideas to the political process.

TRIANGLES IN THE REALM OF IDEAS

Lenin believed that "devoid of proper theory, no effective revolutionary action could be mounted" (Harding, 1996, p. 77) in Russia. During the chaos of the early years of World War I, Lenin went to the Berne public library in Switzerland and studied the works of the German philosopher, Georg Wilhelm Friedrich Hegel (1770-1831), in order to try to understand what was happening and how to foster revolution in Russia. Hegel's principle contribution to philosophy was the idea of the "dialectic," a process of change in which an original idea (a thesis) can be transformed into its opposite (the antithesis), and the combination of the two are eventually resolved in a higher form of truth (the synthesis). Hegelian dialectics described the conflict of opposites leading to a resolution in which each of the original ideas was subsumed and enhanced. The new synthesis then "assumed the role of the old thesis and it would, in time, be confronted with a new antithesis, from which a synthesis on a higher plane would eventually emerge" (Harding, 1996, p. 227).

The dialectical process became the central intellectual underpinning to Lenin's revolutionary strategy, as he attempted to operationalize it. Bolshevism itself has been described as an intellectual and practical synthesis of two opposing revolutionary sets of ideas: populism and Marxism. According to Hosking (2000):

Like the Marxists, Bolshevism was internationalist in its outlook and put its faith in the working class as bearers of revolution, but like the populists it accepted the notion of leadership by a small group of intellectuals. It also . . . took the peasantry seriously as a revolutionary class, and, by mobilizing the peasantry, it aspired to overstep the "bourgeois" phase of economic development and proceed straight to socialism. (p. 362)

Lenin, the thinker and planner, took Hegel's abstract ideas and molded them into a plan of action based on the integration of populism and Marxism, as czarist Russia began to collapse during the war. Trotsky became the inspirational writer and charismatic "orator-in-chief" of the Revolution, the firebrand who could "strike a spark from a crowd, make the crowd believe in a slogan, or divert hundreds and thousands of people by a few passionate phrases and convince them to follow an idea" (Volkogonov, 1996, p. 83). Stalin, the practical one with perhaps a more intuitive sense of managing societal anxiety, manipulated the relationship triangles—not the dialectic—eventually accruing absolute power in the new Soviet Union.

SUCCESSION AND THE CONSOLIDATION OF POWER

This chapter cannot address the vastly complex history of the Russian Revolution of 1917, nor the subsequent Civil War that tore Russia apart between 1918 and 1920. Suffice it to say that the human costs of the Revolution and Civil War are impossible to estimate, including as they did combat fatalities, victims of epidemics and peasant uprisings, those who died from malnutrition, and those who died of the cold or committed suicide. Pipes (1994) estimates that 91 percent of the victims of the Civil War were civilians (see p. 139). He also notes that one and a half to two million people emigrated to western Europe or China at the end of the Civil War. The majority of these emigrants were bureaucrats, professional people, businessmen, intellectuals, and artists—in other words, the heart of the embryonic middle class that had just begun to develop in Russia before the war. These people left and did not come back, forming a Russian *diaspora* that continues into the fourth generation today. The society lost a large intellectual, cultural, and professional population group that affected its functioning throughout the rest of the twentieth century.

Following the end of the Civil War, the Bolshevik leadership settled into rebuilding the devastated country and consolidating its leadership, again an enormous topic far beyond the scope of this chapter. Instead the chapter focuses exclusively on triangles in the leadership succession process during the 1920s, culminating in Stalin's consolidation of power in 1929.

After the Revolution and the Civil War, the first task of the Bolshevik leadership was to develop a structure of government that would reflect their ideological beliefs and effectively address the vastly complex problems of running the country. Lenin believed in a "dictatorship of the proletariat" with the Party functioning as an elite group that decided what was in the best interests of the proletariat. In February 1917, the Party had 23,000 members with Lenin at its head, but this number grew rapidly during the months leading up to the Revolution, and by October 1917, it had 350,000 members. The Party was run by a Central Committee, initially a group of nineteen Bolshevik leaders that eventually expanded to over 300 members with a vast bureaucracy under it. In October 1917, Lenin formed a small Political Bureau or Politburo of seven members (including himself, Trotsky, and Stalin) to make immediate decisions about current issues, as he felt that "the entire Central Committee could not be readily assembled to debate everyday matters" (Volkogonov, 1994, p. 246). The Politburo began meeting regularly in April 1919:

> This small group of people, none of whom had any governmental experience, and dealing as they were with a vast range of issues—social, economic, political, Comintern [Communist International movement], Cheka [the secret police], military, diplomatic, financial, food production and cultural—many of which they could not understand, were determining the fate of millions and millions of people. (Volkogonov, 1994, p. 306)

Lenin was the leader of the Party, and Trotsky was his second in command during the Revolution and Civil War, as the People's Commissar for the Army and Navy, and Chairman of the Military Revolutionary Council. Stalin had not been active during the early days of the Revolution, but he was a member of the Central Committee, and Lenin soon appointed him the People's Commissar for Nationalities. In April 1922, Stalin became the General Secretary of the Central Committee, essentially running government operations.

In terms of the relationship triangle between these three men, Lenin, as founder of the Bolshevik Party, initiator, and implementer of the Revolution, was clearly the leader or "parental" figure not only for Trotsky and Stalin, but for the entire Party and the newly created Soviet Union. Trotsky and Stalin jockeyed for personal and political closeness with Lenin, and therefore legitimacy, until Lenin's premature death on January 21, 1924. After Lenin's death, attachment to pure "Leninist" thinking, a record of closeness to Lenin through photographs and letters, records of Lenin's presumed preferences, and other records of connection with the dead leader, became powerful artifacts in the succession struggle.

The leadership crisis began on May 22, 1922, when Lenin had his first stroke. Subsequent strokes occurred on December 16, 1922, and March 10, 1923. On December 23, 24, 25, 26, and 29, 1922, anticipating his impending death, Lenin dictated a "Letter to Congress," often referred to as his "Testament," in which he described his views of the Politburo members and their capacity for succeeding him in leadership. This Testament set the stage for a series of triangles through which the succession struggle played out.

Lenin's View of Trotsky and His Relationship with Him

In his final "Testament," Lenin described Trotsky as "the outstanding leader of the present Central Committee." He admired Trotsky's "superior intellect, but had also noted his weaknesses, his self-assurance and his inclination toward the 'administrative side of the cause'" (Volkogonov, 1994, p. 249). In the years before the Revolution, they had had many ups and downs in their relationship, often disagreeing in their ideas about revolutionary strategy, as Trotsky remained a member of the Menshevik party until 1917. By February 1917, when the Revolution was finally upon them, they finally fully agreed with each other:

> Lenin knew that in Trotsky he had found an outstanding organizer, able to function in any sphere of activity, who compensated for his own [Lenin's] reluctance to stir from "headquarters." It suited Lenin that Trotsky had almost at once accepted second place, that he was not a rival, even if at times his popularity exceeded Lenin's own. (Volkogonov, 1994, p. 251)

They worked well together during the early years of the Revolution and during the Civil War, when Trotsky was People's Commissar for Military and Naval Affairs, in effect the commander in chief of the Red Army. After the Civil War, Lenin had less confidence in Trotsky, and occasionally enlisted other members of the Central Committee to put pressure on Trotsky to change his views (see Volkogonov, 1994, p. 257). During Lenin's final illness, Trotsky did not visit Lenin at home and kept his distance, in contrast to Stalin who was frequently at Lenin's bedside. In the end, Trotsky did not attend Lenin's funeral probably because Stalin apparently misinformed him about when and where it was to take place, but Trotsky also did not make the effort to get accurate information about it. This pattern fits with an earlier observation that Trotsky had tended to take the outside position in nuclear family triangles as he was growing up.

Lenin's View of Stalin and His Relationship with Him

Stalin was a "diligent executor" of Lenin's orders before, during, and after the Revolution, and his relationship with Lenin was extremely close. Volkogonov (1994) writes:

> Lenin and Stalin were alike in their self-confidence, their belief in their infallibility, their absolute faith in the universality of the dictatorship of the proletariat, their ability in handling the masses, their caution and craftiness, their ruthlessness. (Volkogonov, 1994, p. 271)

During Lenin's final illness Stalin visited him constantly, more than any other member of the Central Committee, keeping him informed about the leadership and its decisions. However, in his final Testament Lenin described Stalin as

> crude, [stating that] this failing, which is tolerable in our milieu and in dealings between us Communists, becomes intolerable in a General Secretary. I therefore suggest that the comrades think of a way of moving Stalin from this post and replacing him with someone who in every other way differs from Comrade Stalin in his superiority, that is, is more patient, more loyal, more respectful and more attentive to his comrades, less capricious and so on. (Volkogonov, 1994, p. 273)

The Triangle

Clearly Lenin had mixed feelings about both Trotsky and Stalin and was concerned that neither of them could effectively take on the leadership of the Party and the nation after his death. According to Volkogonov (1994):

> Lenin was well aware of the hostility between Trotsky and Stalin and tried repeatedly to normalize their relations. Although he occasionally took one side or the other, on the whole he tried to remain above the fray, and at times he criticized them both publicly. (p. 256)

Lenin's effort at detriangling was reasonably effective as long as he was alive, as both men wanted to please him by doing their best work for the Party. Trotsky, however, put more time into his writing and tended to avoid committee meetings which he found boring. Stalin, in contrast, spent his time putting his own loyal supporters in significant positions and consolidating his personal power. Volkogonov (1994) notes that "Trotsky's lack of concern and his vanity let him down at the crucial moments, when Lenin retired from active work and when he died" (p. 253). Stalin by then had solidified his power, and Trotsky, although closer to Lenin in the realm of ideas, was firmly on the outside in the Bolshevik relationship system.

Triangles After Lenin's Death

After Lenin's first stroke and during the period leading up to his death, Stalin began to form alliances with other members of the Politburo, most notably Zinoviev and Kamenev, that further pushed Trotsky to the outside. Kamenev was head of the Moscow Party organization and was also married to Trotsky's sister, Olga.[8]

Zinoviev was chief of the Petrograd[9] Party organization as well as the Comintern. They were close friends and together with Stalin formed a "troika,"[10] a very Russian triangle, that increasingly dominated the Politburo and the government:

> By virtue of their collaboration in a Politburo that at the time had only seven members (in addition to them and the absent Lenin, Trotsky, Tomskii, and Bukharin), the troika could have its way on all issues and isolate Trotsky, who had not a single supporter in that body. (Pipes, 1994, p. 466)

Stalin manipulated these relationships so successfully that no one seemed to be aware of the way he was consolidating power:

> He always claimed to have the good of the party uppermost in mind. He seemed devoid of personal ambitions and vanity, quite content to let Trotsky, Kamenev and Zinoviev bask in the public limelight. He did this so skillfully that in 1923 it was widely thought that the battle for Lenin's succession pitted Trotsky against Zinoviev. . . . In dispute

---

[8]Although Trotsky had been close to his sister Olga when they were growing up and she had met her husband through him, Russian revolutionaries generally considered personal relationships less important than accomplishing political goals. Stalin undoubtedly had little difficulty allying with Kamenev against his brother-in-law, if he defined the alliance as being for the good of the Party.

[9]Postrevolutionary name for the city of St. Petersburg, later renamed Leningrad.

[10]A small Russian carriage pulled by three horses abreast.

> [Stalin's] was always the voice of reason, striving to reconcile lofty standards with expediency, a model of moderation and a threat to no one. (Pipes, 1994, p. 466)

The troika of Stalin, Zinoviev, and Kamenev interlocked through Stalin with the original Lenin-Trotsky-Stalin triangle. With Lenin effectively out of the picture, the troika provided support to Stalin in his struggle with Trotsky. It suppressed the publication of Lenin's Testament, probably because the three members of the troika believed the Testament would support Trotsky's chances of taking power and spoiling their own. Trotsky still retained a significant following in the wider Party membership and was generally regarded as a hero of the Revolution almost on the same level as Lenin. He took on the struggle against Stalin in a series of letters and statements to the Politburo and the Central Committee, but spoke always from an isolated position and did not build alliances that might have supported him. He tended to attack the whole Party machine, thus rallying the bureaucracy defensively behind Stalin. He came under fierce attack from his former colleagues and the press, and became physically ill, eventually being unable to put up significant resistance or to defend himself.

In January 1925, Stalin as General Secretary of the Party relieved Trotsky of his posts as People's Commissar for Military Affairs and Chairman of the Revolutionary Military Council of the Republic. Stalin took Trotsky's place in both these positions, and Trotsky was given three lower level positions that "shifted him to the political sidelines and loaded him down with bureaucratic affairs" (Volkogonov, 1996, p. 269). At this time Zinoviev and Kamenev, the Bolshevik "twins," had become disillusioned with Stalin's powerful consolidation of the Party bureaucracy, and they moved to support Trotsky in the Politburo. In response to this, Stalin, through his control of the secret police, removed Trotsky and Zinoviev from the Politburo in October 1926, and from the Central Committee the following year. In November 1927, Trotsky was evicted from his apartment in the Kremlin and expelled from the Party. He was first banished to Alma Ata in Central Asia, and a year later he was expelled to Turkey.

Stalin had continued to use the triangle with Lenin in his struggle with Trotsky:

> Stalin had understood the importance of appearing as the defender of Lenin and his heritage. All of his speeches against Trotsky and the opposition were laced with quotations from Lenin and references to the dead leader. (Volkogonov, 1996, p. 274)

During 1925, relations between Zinoviev, Kamenev, and Stalin deteriorated, with Zinoviev and Kamenev asking for freer discussion within the Party. As they criticized Stalin's power, Stalin rallied the bureaucracy in his defense thus creating additional interlocking triangles. Zinoviev and Kamenev were defeated at the Fourteenth Congress of the Soviet Communist Party, and their leadership over the Party organizations in Moscow and Leningrad was effectively destroyed.

In 1925, Stalin had briefly allied himself with another old Bolshevik, Nikolai Bukharin, editor of *Pravda* and a leading theoretician, in order to mount an attack against Zinoviev and Kamenev. Bukharin had initially allied himself with Trotsky, but fear of Trotsky eventually turned him toward Stalin. He wrote a number of articles in *Pravda,* the Party newspaper, addressing economic issues that disturbed Zinoviev and Kamenev. As Radzinsky (1996) notes:

> They decided it was time to call Bukharin to order. By destroying Bukharin they would give Stalin a bit of a scare. He had lured this foolish pair out into the open: they now spent all their time sniping at Bukharin, while Stalin remained silent. Waiting. . . . [Then] Stalin passionately defended Bukharin: "You want Bukharin's blood? We shall not let you have his blood." Bukharin would recall these words as he went to his death [purged by Stalin] thirteen years later. (pp. 219-220)[11]

By December 1929, Stalin had effectively become the dictator of the Soviet Union. He organized a fiftieth birthday party for himself in which the whole country celebrated his leadership. At the Sixteenth Party Congress in July 1930, he summarized the relationship triangles he had manipulated through the 1920s:

> What would have happened if we had listened to the right-wing opportunists of the Bukharin group? . . . What if we had listened to the left-wing opportunists grouped around Trotsky and Zinoviev? (Radzinsky, 1996, p. 252)

While the others were focused on theoretical and ideological issues, Stalin focused only on a series of relationships that led him to full control of the political process. Through a series of interlocking triangles, he emerged as the political successor to Lenin. Earlier emotional triangles established in the family of origin played out in relationships among the three leading

---

[11]Zinoviev and Kamenev were also put to death by Stalin in the 1930s.

Bolsheviks that led to the shifting and interlocking triangles of power during the 1920s, and the ultimate political direction of the country for the remainder of its existence.

CONCLUSION

The primary conclusion of this chapter is that the concept of triangles from Bowen theory can provide a useful model for understanding processes in large, complex, social, and historical systems. The chapter begins by explaining how the emotional triangle provides a connection between individual and family functioning and the processes of a larger social system.

Through an examination of the nuclear family systems of Lenin, Trotsky, and Stalin, patterns were observed in the functioning of these three men that played out as they became central figures in the drama of the Russian Revolution and its aftermath. All three men were dynamic, self-promoting individuals with close emotional ties to literate mothers who encouraged their intellectual development. In their search for interlocking triangles outside the family of origin, all three men attached themselves to groups of revolutionaries involved in the radical political movement that attracted so many of the disaffected young intellectuals of their generation in czarist Russia. All three of them had a capacity for brutality and ruthlessness in pursuit of political goals. For Stalin, this probably emerged from his early experiences of violence in his nuclear family, and for Lenin and Trotsky from the fanatical intensity of relationships within a political movement in which the end always justified the means. One reason for Stalin's ultimate political success may have been that he had more direct experience with brutality than the other two.

The triangles in Lenin's family of origin supported his assuming a leadership position as an adult and his ability to connect with others in pursuing common goals. He also seems to have acquired the ability to balance numerous intense relationships, while always keeping his eye on long-term political goals.

The primary triangle in Trotsky's nuclear family supported his autonomy, intellectual brilliance, and personal arrogance. His parents gave him opportunities as a youngest son that his siblings did not receive, and supported him financially throughout his life. He was an emotional outsider early on, both in the family and in the wider culture, as a Jew in an anti-Semitic society. The outside position is a desirable one for many individuals who experience the inside of the triangle as conflictual or painful. Trotsky seems to have sought the outside during the years before the Revolution when he often took political positions in opposition to Lenin, and during the 1920s, when he never really took on Stalin effectively in their insider struggle for power.

Stalin was caught in a violent primary triangle from earliest childhood. The struggle between his parents led to a lifelong cutoff from his father, who abandoned the family when Stalin was eight. He remained with his impoverished but doting mother who did everything she could to promote his becoming educated for the priesthood. His subsequent intense attachment to his hero, Lenin, could be seen as an interlock with this primary triangle, when the father was no longer available to his son. In the succession struggle after Lenin's death, Stalin knew exactly how to form inside alliances, extruding the outsider, and then moving on to a new interlocking triangle from which he always emerged as the leading figure. He allied closely with Lenin against Trotsky, during Lenin's final illness; then he allied with Zinoviev and Kamenev also against Trotsky, ultimately extruding Trotsky; then he allied with Bukharin against Zinoviev, ultimately extruding Zinoviev. He repeated this pattern throughout the rest of his rule, eventually, through the purges of the 1930s, eliminating all of the original Bolshevik revolutionaries and World War I military heroes who might have threatened his absolute power.

The reciprocal flow of emotional process through interlocking triangles, from individuals to their families to larger societal units, is an ongoing phenomenon. With the study of Lenin, Trotsky, and Stalin it is particularly interesting to observe the reciprocity between these individuals and the wider societal movement at the time they lived. Russia as a nation was in a period of societal regression when these men were growing to manhood and seizing leadership. Their leadership did not emerge from a democratic process, and it reflects to some extent the society's regressed position on a functional continuum. All three men were probably not very high on the scale of differentiation (considering the amount of cutoff from their families of origin, their attachment to brutal methods for achieving their societal goals, and the functioning of their offspring in Trotsky and Stalin's cases). Their type of leadership at a time of societal collapse had aspects of inevitability, as there is usually a congruence between leadership functioning and societal functioning.

The study of the primary triangles of societal leaders and their relationship to the social systems they lead could be expanded to the study of leaders in any human society in any period of human history where the family information is available. Looking at the triangular emotional process from individuals to their families to the wider society which they are part of, provides a different lens for understanding the unfolding of historical process.

Lenin, Trotsky, and Stalin were chosen for this chapter because they represent a particular area of interest for the author and also because of the historical materials now available for the first time with the opening up of the Soviet archives. However, applying the perspective of Bowen theory to studies of other leaders in other cultures could lead to a broader understanding of the relationship between leadership and societal process more generally.

REFERENCES

Bowen, M. (1978). *Family therapy in clinical practice*. New York: Jason Aronson.

Harding, M. (1996). *Leninism*. Durham, NC: Duke University Press.

Hosking, G. (2000). *Russia and the Russians*. Cambridge, MA: Harvard University Press.

Malia, M. (1994). *The Soviet tragedy: A history of socialism in Russia, 1917-1991*. New York: Maxwell Macmillan International.

Pipes, R. (1994). *Russia under the Bolshevik regime*. New York: Alfred A. Knopf.

Radzinsky, E. (1996). *Stalin*. New York: Doubleday, a division of Random House, Inc. Excerpts reprinted by permission.

Volkogonov, D. (1988). *Stalin: Triumph and tragedy*. New York: Grove Weidenfeld.

Volkogonov, D. (1994). *Lenin*. New York: The Free Press.

Volkogonov, D. (1996). *Trotsky: The eternal revolutionary*. New York: The Free Press.

Chapter 19

The Triangle
As the Cornerstone of the Government
of the United States of America

Edward W. Beal

INTRODUCTION

Bowen family systems theory (BFST) suggests that emotional triangles and interlocking ones are ubiquitous in human functioning and useful in describing and explaining human behavior. They are the basic building blocks of any emotional system, be it family or any other group (see Bowen, 1978, p. 373). This chapter uses two distinctive structural triangles: (1) the separation of powers triangle; and (2) the three-fifths compromise triangle and the underlying emotional process to demonstrate how political attitudes and behavior persist in the functioning of the U.S. Constitution over generations.

Bowen family systems theory traditionally describes triangles as emotional relationships existing between three people. This chapter extends that understanding to emotional processes that exist between societal organizations mediated by the individuals within those institutions. Triangles are living structures that exist within families (mother, father, and child) and are mediated significantly by the various emotional triangles between its members determined by level of differentiation and degree of anxiety. Similarly, structural triangles exist within societal organizations such as the federal government's executive, legislative, and judicial branches. These structural triangles, in the presence of high anxiety and a range of interpersonal immaturity, are significantly mediated by the various emotional triangles among its members.

James Madison spoke of the need for checks and balances on the corrupt nature of human behavior. These checks and balances manifested as triangular structures in the U.S. Constitution by Madison's design, after the tradition described by Montesquieu. The checks and balances of the separation of powers triangle were established to contain the emotional triangle represented by concerns about tyranny (executive branch), mob rule (legislative branch), and individual rights (judicial branch).

Furthermore, in the process of establishing the U.S. Constitution a previously existing emotional triangle emerged between the North and South over the use and definition of black slaves. This emotional process led among other things to contrived agreements such as the three-fifths compromise, the Fugitive Slave Act, the gag rule, and the importation restrictions on slaves after 1808. In this chapter, the term three-fifths compromise triangle will be used as a structural example of an emotionally based anxiety binding mechanism which was a manifestation of the underlying emotional triangle. The term three-fifths compromise triangle was an ongoing process primarily in Congress between the North and South over the role of slaves in society, which reflected the effects of an underlying triangular emotional process.

An example of the emotionally driven nature of the three-fifths compromise triangle occurred in Congress in March 1855. Charles Sumner, Republican senator from the North, gave a speech excoriating other senators for their "complicity in slavery." Two days later Preston Brooks, a Democratic congressman from the South, struck Sumner over the head multiple times while the latter sat at his Senate desk. Three years passed before Sumner could return to the Senate (see Boyer et al., 1993, p. 460).

The U.S. Constitution serves as a beacon of enlightenment for all peoples and countries interested in establishing governments based on self-determination and individual rights and freedom. The origin, development, implementation, and function of the U.S. Constitution is a history of trial and error, conflict and compromise. The structural triangles resulting from conflict and compromise, which are an integral part of the foundation of the U.S. Constitution, have not been equally efficient.

Structural triangles based on principle are enduring foundations of societal structure. Their stability and survival are a function of counterbalancing processes and inherent flexibility. Structural triangles based on compromises over irreconcilable differences and inflexibility, however, almost always collapse. Their survival and stability require calmness between the conflicting parties.

This chapter uses the lens of the BFST to compare and contrast the functioning of two structural triangles in the U.S. Constitution: (1) the separation of powers forms the executive, legislative, and judiciary triangle, and

(2) the three-fifths clause creates a triangle resulting from the compromise of the conflict between Northern and Southern colonies over federal representation. Both structural triangles resolved the problems of that period but the latter had inevitable long-term negative consequences.

Bowen family systems theory acknowledges that two-party relationships are essentially unstable and tend to stabilize by drawing in a third person or issue (see Kerr and Bowen, 1988, p. 136). Triangular relationships are emotional in nature in that they function to reduce anxiety levels in individuals and/or the relationships in which individuals operate. The triangle, the smallest unit of an emotional system, describes the predictable patterns of emotional influencing among any three people or institutions. The process "begins with emotional tension in a bipolar situation and spreads" by emotionally involving others, and is fed by accusation, denial, and generalized emotional reactivity (Bowen, 1978, p. 439). The triangular emotional system is most evident when anxiety is intense and less visible when the participants are calmer (see Bowen, 1978, p. 439).

During courtship, both individuals are almost always eager to unite and anxious about intimacy. Sometimes the romance is sufficiently intense to avoid a realistic discussion of the purpose of the marriage—peer relationship, production of children, and a necessary division of labor. However, a mutual agreement to engage in all three in an egalitarian manner has a better prognosis than one in which there is no premarital understanding about the production of children, their religious education, and whether one or both parents will be breadwinners or homemakers.

Two individuals, anxious about forming a marital union, can have triangles with the past (their respective family systems), their future (will we have children and who will raise them?), or a mutual religion. Similarly, members of the Continental Congress experienced triangular relationships, not unlike the BFST description of triangles, about their past (should we separate from England and how?), their future (what is the nature of our shared sovereignty?), and whether they should separate church and state in the Constitution.

Family members reproduce the same emotional patterns in society as in their own respective families (see Bowen, 1978, p. 438). BFST's concept of "emotional process in society describes the ideas" and "extension of family emotional process into larger social systems and to the totality of society" (Bowen, 1978, p. 426). "The family projection process (or societal projection process) is a triangular emotional process through which two powerful people (parents, colonies) in a triangle reduce their own anxiety and insecurity" by focusing on a third person or group (Bowen, 1978, p. 434).

The essentials of the societal emotional process are three people/institutions and anxiety. "The family projection process is as vigorous in society as in the family" (Bowen, 1978, p. 443). "Two individuals (institutions) get together and enhance their functioning at the expense of a third" (Bowen, 1978, p. 443). Bowen asserts, "a universal target of the projection process is the scapegoating of vulnerable minority groups" who "fit the best criteria for the long-term anxiety reducing projection" (Bowen, 1978, p. 445).

The question of this chapter, then, is: How does the BFST concept of emotional triangles contribute toward understanding our Constitution's origins and ongoing implementation? This chapter describes the history and associated anxiety about the formation of the union: the Constitution, or the shared sovereignty of the states, as resolved through two specific structural triangles. Furthermore, this chapter examines the evolution and functioning of these two triangles in the Constitution—the separation of powers triangle with its functional checks and balances and the three-fifths compromise triangle, with its failure to resolve irreconcilable differences, thus becoming a major factor leading to the Civil War.

The author suggests that emotional triangles are an inevitable component of unions and that the two structural triangles mentioned above were established in the context of the Founding Fathers' anxiety about shared sovereignty. Both may have been necessary for the formation of the union, but one was eliminated so that the union could continue. Knowledge about the functioning of emotional triangles in government, just as knowledge about the functioning of emotional triangles in families, is useful. The understanding of the triangular relationship between political positions—just as the triangular relationship between people—opens windows that a dyadic perspective does not.

BACKGROUND

The Magna Carta, the cornerstone of the unwritten British Common Law Tradition established in Britain in 1215, was an early self-government model for the colonies. The notion of a triangle may be a strong, although unnamed structural component of the Magna Carta—the result of the conflict between King John and his noblemen. The colonial fathers understood that the origin of their current effort lay in their ancestors' struggle over the establishment of the Magna Carta. That major conflict was represented by the English Kings' perceived arbitrary right to tax, to seize property without consent, and to allow unlawful arrest. These early strands of self-government were exported to the North and the South of the New World with different points of view about their multigenerational origin in the conflict among the nobles against the king.

New England

The Mayflower Compact, formed in 1620 by Pilgrim leaders, who were anxious about self-government in New England, was one of the first documents in history in which a small number of people with little formal education resolved "to covenant and combine ourselves together with a civil body politick" (Smith, 1980, p. 24). This document, combined with John Winthrop's Modell of Christian Charity in 1630, provided the philosophical underpinnings of a new consciousness about self-government emerging in the Massachusetts Bay Colony. John Adams developed these ideas by writing in the Massachusetts State Constitution that the government was obligated to educate all its citizens (McCullough, 2001).

Virginia

In contrast, the Jamestown Colony, founded in 1607 in what eventually became Virginia, was a basically commercial undertaking designed to make money for London merchants. Jamestown was run like a business with no hint of self-governance for its inhabitants.

Despite the attitudinal differences between these colonial areas, the settlers came to a mutual belief that their rights were contained in a higher law of various documents, statutes, and agreements called the British Common Law Tradition. Although multigenerational differences about the nature of self-government existed, they agreed the right of self-government lay in the natural order of things (see Smith, 1980, pp. 43-47, and Wilkins, 2002, pp. 29-33).

THE DEBATE OVER THE WAR FOR INDEPENDENCE

Each geographic section understood its desire for self-government and self-determination differently. No matter how the colonies started and what their documents stated, different attitudes about self-government evolved. The South developed a rather paternalistic, quasi-feudal agrarian culture, whereas New England comprised more democratic communities (see Smith, 1980, p. 37). This difference would eventually creep into their view of shared sovereignty.

Anxious to end colonial dependence on the English crown, John Hancock and fifty-five others signed the Declaration of Independence on July 4, 1776. Jefferson, with the help of some others, was primarily responsible for drafting this document. These men were united in their opposition to the injustices of the king, and they wanted a literal divorce from their political forebears.

United in opposition to the injustices of the English king and unanimous in declaring war, they nevertheless disagreed for months over the purpose of the war. New England and Virginia, with their focus on self-government, wanted a war for independence. The remaining colonies, mostly the mid-Atlantic ones, called Reconciliationists, preferred a negotiated economic settlement with England in the midst of the war before fighting for independence. John Adams, the leader of the delegates for independence, thought the Reconciliationists' position was a "naïve delusion." Thomas Clifford, a Philadelphia merchant, said independence "would 'assuredly prove unprofitable'" (Ferling, 2004, p. 99). These factions formed a contentious triangle with New England and Virginia opposing the remaining colonies about the purpose of the war with England.

United in divorce from the king, but disagreeing about the reasons, the colonies looked not unlike many divorcing spouses. The tension dividing the colonies centered on whether the war was for self-government or for preserving an economic system with independence and, second, this tension would resurface eleven years later in the constitutional convention. Eleven years after winning their freedom, these issues of self-government versus attempts to preserve an economic system became the cornerstones in both the separation of powers triangle and the three-fifths compromise triangle.

Although Virginia would change its position in the triangles, the attitudes and behavior persisted. The Constitution would be based on a compromise similar to the "naïve delusion" observed by Adams, which was to establish and organize freedom while preserving an economic system that enslaved many of its inhabitants. The colonies retained a not yet clearly defined view of their future together. They agreed, however, that they had to fight the British and that George Washington would be their leader.

Washington knew how to define leadership by holding the country together. He literally invented military and presidential leadership in the United States. He formed alliances well and could find common ground beneath controversy. His ability to avoid unnecessary conflict was mythical (see Wilkins, 2002, pp. 42-44, 58). The nature of Washington's leadership and the mutual enthusiasm of disparate groups throughout the country concealed many differences and contradictions. Although the colonies shared the utility of a common enemy, at this point the "only thing holding the country together was the regard for Washington" (McCullough, 2001). His well-defined leadership persisted throughout the war, his presidency, and even in his retirement, when he made clear that his willingness to relinquish power was important to the future of democracy.

WHO WOULD BE GOVERNED?

The strikingly bold clause, "We hold these truths to be self evident that all men are created equal" was the cornerstone of the delegates' mutual pledge in the Declaration of Independence. As primary author, Jefferson relied on the Virginia Declaration of Rights drafted earlier in 1776 by George Mason, who had asserted, "That all men are free and independent, and have certain inherent rights" (Wilkins, 2002, p. 30).

Modern-day readers can be excused for thinking that the belief, all men are created equal, referred to all people. Roger Wilkins suggests that the men of Virginia were looking only at those who exercised power over them and owned property and not at those over whom they exercised power (see Wilkins, 2002, p. 32). As blacks were first sold at Jamestown in 1619, the question of whether blacks possessed human qualities had been debated in Virginia for over 150 years. Virginia resolved this question in 1776, by concluding in an amendment to the Mason proposal that "the equality guaranteed by natural law did not adhere to all men who were born and breathed but only to those who 'had entered into a state of society'" (Wilkins, 2002, p. 88). Thus, Virginia amended its Declaration of Rights to exclude blacks (see Wilkins, 2002, p. 88). Mason remained silent during the amending debate. Whether blacks had the same rights as whites was not specifically debated in the Second Continental Congress writing of the Declaration of Independence. Nevertheless, everyone from Virginia understood that blacks did not have the same rights and that in 1776, "all men are created equal" did not include blacks. It would be four score and seven years before this principle would be fulfilled.

Not having entered into "a state of society," blacks were not included. If everyone was not clear on that point in 1776, they were in 1787. To say, eleven years later, however, when the U.S. Constitution was written, that blacks were not part of the society that framed the events surrounding the Revolutionary War requires a level of moral fiction. Or, at least, it requires a kind of denial reinforced by the anxiety of the times (see Wilkins, 2002, pp. 60-64).

During the Revolution, blacks comprised 40 percent of the inhabitants of Virginia and by the end of the war they were 20 percent of Washington's

Army (see Wilkins, 2002, pp. 44-45, 51). Crispus Attucks, a black man, was the first American killed in the Revolution. Blacks formed part of the army at Lexington and Concord and Bunker Hill (see Wilkins, 2002, p. 107). This legal reinforcement of a moral fiction continued even through the Dred Scott decision by the Supreme Court in 1857 and the legal viewpoint argued by Douglas in the Lincoln-Douglas debates in 1858.

White men recognized that rights were no longer given by the king but were in the natural order of things. They described themselves as having been enslaved by the monarchy. To hold this position and think that blacks were not part of the natural order but had to be given rights or freedom by whites required that "whites had to convince themselves that black subordination was in the natural order of things"; Wilkins suggests that a "good part of white self-esteem flowed simply from *not being black*" (Wilkins, 2002, p. 109). Therefore, blacks had to be property and without rights. This concept, then, was considered the natural order of things (see Wilkins, 2002, p. 109).

In spite of these differences, the Founding Fathers were clear for whom the government was going to be run but not how it was going to be constructed. By the end of the Second Continental Congress in 1776, Americans had decided who was going to govern but not how.

HOW THE GOVERNMENT WOULD RUN

A draft of the Articles of Confederation was ready for consideration just after the printing of the Declaration of Independence on July 4, 1776. United in opposition to the king but anxious about the future, the colonies' primary loyalties were to their state or region and not to the union. The Virginians in particular were loyal to their own colony, a sentiment that would persist even after Robert E. Lee declared his loyalty to Virginia on April 20, 1861. The commitment to oppose the king was stronger than their commitment to live with one another as united colonies. The Articles of Confederation reflected this tenuous and uncertain commitment. The colonies delayed ratifying the document for five years until March 1781, a few months before victory at Yorktown. Nevertheless, the colonies demonstrated their ability to fight a long and demanding war before adopting this legal agreement. Readers may recognize the familiar family triangle of two young people, united in perennial courtship, who run away from their respective parents but remain uncertain about committing to marriage.

In March 1781, the Articles of Confederation reflected a compromise formed from many anxieties and thus was a poorly differentiated form of government. This loose confederation of colonies organized a government in which the population comprised citizens of the states first and the federation second. The power in the Federal legislature was shared not by population distribution but equally by each colony. There was no mechanism to change the representation consistent with changes in population distribution. Large populous colonies were allegedly bitter because of their under-representation. Amendments to this agreement required a three-fourths majority. The South, which was represented by five of the thirteen colonies, had a de facto veto power over changes in the Articles. This functional veto power would resurface in the Constitution under the three-fifths clause (see Wills, 2003, p. 54).

With their concern about tyranny, the legislature created a Congress that had no effective executive function. This legislative body could pass everything and enforce nothing. Moreover it had the power to levy taxes but no power to collect them. The states were, in effect, living together without a real commitment to shared sovereignty—cohabitation with no way to enforce a professed commitment to the relationship. The absence of a well-defined government structure, based on a separation of powers, precluded both effective legislation and effective enforcement of the legislation. Furthermore, any anxiety about the legislation and its effect on the future of shared sovereignty could not be debated and properly processed in a poorly differentiated government.

The functions of government at that time were not sufficiently differentiated into structures of government. These ineffective triangles were based on anxious compromises over issues that were not fully established as principles. Seven more years of anxious cohabitation ensued before they separated the functions of government into executive, legislative, and judicial arenas, creating the separation of powers triangle.

PERIOD OF ANXIETY

Without changing government structures, the Confederation's survival remained in question in the years following the victory at Yorktown, October 19, 1781. In effect, no sufficiently differentiated relationship existed between the national and state governments. Fiske, a nineteenth century historian, said the five years following the peace at Yorktown were "the most critical moment in all the history of the American people" (Smith, 1980, p. 82). They were no longer united by their mutual emotional antipathy toward the defeated English Crown. Josiah Tucker, a British friend of America, reported on this moment in time:

> [T]he mutual antipathies and clashing interest of the Americans, their difference of government, habitudes, and manners, indicate that they will have no centre of union and no common interest. They never can be united into one compact empire under any species of government whatever; a disunited people till the end of time, suspicious and distrustful of each other, they will be divided and subdivided into little commonwealths, or principalities. (Smith, 1980, p. 82)

Not only Englishmen but Americans also shared this view. George Washington himself wrote to Madison in 1787 stating, "We are fast verging to anarchy and confusion" (Smith, 1980, p. 83). In 1786, Daniel Shays, a veteran of the Revolution, led an uprising of Massachusetts's farmers protesting taxation. John Jay wrote to Washington saying, "I am uneasy and apprehensive; more so than during the war . . . we are going and doing wrong, and therefore I look forward to evils and calamities" (Smith, 1980, p. 84). Jay was concerned that the population upset "'by the insecurity of property,' might consider 'the charms of liberty as imaginary and delusive,' and turn to a dictator or King" (Smith, 1980, p. 84). Washington responded in part, "What a triumph for advocates of despotism to find that we are incapable of governing ourselves" (Smith, 1980, p. 84). Under Washington's leadership the colonies knew how to win freedom from a common enemy. However, in the process of organizing that freedom, they had neither collectively envisioned a society without slavery, nor a republic in which the states would create a power superior to their own to which they would defer in specific ways.

DEVELOPMENT OF THE CONSTITUTION

James Madison, the mastermind of the Constitution, had a plan for the government that went a long way toward containing the infectious societal anxiety. Aware of this anxiety as well as the deficiencies of the Articles of Confederation, Madison had been reading the known literature about Republican governments. Madison's new friend, Thomas Jefferson, who was the American minister to France, sent him all the appropriate books he could find in Paris. Madison's plan would ultimately be the initial working document at the Constitutional Convention (see Wilkins, 2002, p. 54).

Management of Preconvention Anxiety

Madison used a jurisdictional dispute between Maryland and Virginia to arrange for a wide-ranging meeting in Annapolis to resolve this issue and bring some general order to foreign trade. Although there were conflicting interests, the Annapolis Convention was a step forward. Well-educated professionals, merchants, and landowners were willing to meet and discuss trade, taxation, regulation of law, and the relationships between states. The remaining 90 percent of the population were subsistence farmers anxious about providing food for their families. An agreement arose that each colony would send representatives to a convention in Philadelphia the following May 25, 1787.

Madison recruited a stellar group of Virginians to represent their state, including a reluctant George Washington. Washington's rather silent leadership but extensive relationship skills were critical to containing the anxiety throughout the convention. Although silent during the meetings, Washington dined with different delegations each night. Many of the delegates were unaware that they would be asked to engage in a process that was without modern precedent. As members of state delegations, they would create a power superior to their own and then defer to the federal government in carefully delineated ways. Sovereignty would be shared (see Smith, 1980, p. 88).

The Work of the Convention

Despite their anxiety about sailing in uncharted governmental waters, their common set of experiences during and after the Revolution had unintentionally created a moral and psychological compass (see Smith, 1980, p. 88). Behind the scenes Madison held the blueprint and arranged the players. Sitting in front of the convention, he charted a daily log of all that transpired.

Washington presided silently for the most part but lent a dignified and calming presence. Jefferson was in France and Adams in England, both as ambassadors. Franklin initially was at home and sick. Edmund Randolph delivered the Virginia Plan, the product of months of Madison's reading, deliberation, and extensive networking with other delegates. In a bold stroke, the document outlined a broad concept to move the government from a loose confederation of states to a sovereign union with a constitution. Ingeniously the plan incorporated most of the constitutional principles advanced earlier by the absent John Adams. Therefore, in concept if not in detail, the plan bridged the multigenerational self-government differences that previously existed between the North and the South.

The most controversial section proposed that voting in Congress be proportional to taxation, or number of free inhabitants. This issue—that states would vote proportionally and not equally—nearly defeated the work of the convention. Yet with this bold proposal, Madison gained significant tactical advantage at the convention. The plan forced the delegates' anxieties about shared sovereignty to surface in the ensuing coalitions, the contents of which were held secret from the public.

Separation of Powers Triangle

The one anxiety shared by all delegates was how to ensure the survival of a republican form of government. Two hundred years later, author David McCullough wrote that their anxiety was especially high because no colony had ever accomplished what they were about to do—establish a republican form of government after successfully rebelling against an empire (McCullough, 2001).

History suggested two likely scenarios. Republics either (1) became dominated by dictators or one-issue minorities, or (2) descended into anarchy dictated by mob rule. Madison's studies and Montesquieu's *Spirit of the Laws,* which was read by most of the delegates, suggested that in fact British Common Law had been operating in the counterbalancing structures of a separation of powers government. The convention, with Montesquieu's ideas and Madison's assistance, built checks and balances into separate structures of government to deal with the anxieties manifested by the delegates.

Madison redefined one of the first conflicts in the convention—large states versus small states—as a conflict between the Northern region of interest and the Southern region of interest. The question of equal versus proportional representation incorporated within the idea of a bicameral legislature was fostered by Franklin (Isaacson, 2004, p. 452). The Senate would have equal representation among states, and the House of Representatives would have proportional representation based on population distribution.

By assigning specific tasks for each branch of the legislature, Madison provided that "an extended republic comprising many contending voices would serve as a balance wheel" (Wilkins, 2002, p. 60). A strong central executive branch, the presidency, corrected some weaknesses of the Articles of Confederation. Had Washington, the obvious choice, not been there to literally define the office of the presidency, anxiety about dictatorship would have been higher. The creation of a federal judiciary and the Supreme Court protected individual rights by counterbalancing the strong executive branch. The genius of the separation of powers triangle was that none of the three branches could dominate the other two.

For each issue, Madison structured his responses so that each was based on discussions with the delegates, resulting compromises, and the historical understanding that created the separation of powers triangle. This structural triangle had sufficient flexibility with its checks and balances to accommodate future irrational and irresponsible behavior by members of each branch and still remain intact. Should individuals not behaving responsibly overcome the responsible functioning of this triangle, a procedure to reform or amend it could be instituted by the people and the states and not by the federal government itself. Furthermore, the Congress could impeach the president and justices, legislators could be voted out of office, and the president could veto legislation, which Congress could override while the Supreme Court could rule on its conformity to the Constitution. The triangle, the tripartite structure of government, based on carefully defined principles, would be the bedrock of the U.S. Constitution. Moreover, the triangle accommodates for the undifferentiation or immaturity of its participants.

Before *Marbury v. Madison* in 1803, the Supreme Court had not exercised as much influence in the separation of powers triangle as the other two components. Nevertheless, justices were to be appointed for their talent and virtue and not by virtue of their politics. Recognizing the potential importance of the Supreme Court and the judiciary in general in the functioning of the government, members of the executive and legislative branches attempted to politicize their judicial appointments. They wanted judicial decisions made in their favor. All that changed with John Marshall's decision in *Marbury v. Madison*. He ruled that the executive branch and Congress had passed laws giving them powers not explicitly granted by the Constitution and therefore their behavior was unconstitutional (see Boyer et al., 1993, pp. 247-248). The emotionally based togetherness between the executive and legislative components in attempting to politicize the Supreme Court was trumped by Marshall's well-defined, clearly articulated opinion. A precedent was established.

Shortly thereafter, the direction of this emotional process was reversed. Instead of trying to politicize their judicial appointments, Congress and the executive accused Supreme Court Justice Samuel Chase of being too political. The House of Representatives with Jefferson's support impeached Chase for his notoriously partisan judicial behavior. If one cannot appoint politically favorable judges at least one could get rid of those who were oppositional. Fortunately, the Senate, in a more reflective posture, doubted "whether impeachment was a solution to the issue of political partisanship" (Boyer et al., 1993, p. 247). More recently, in *Bush v. Gore* most observers believe the Supreme Court acted too anxiously in imposing itself in Presidential politics at the state level. Nonetheless, the American people agreed to abide by the judicial decision and the functioning of the separation of powers triangle. In spite of the court's political support of the president, the Court subsequently ruled against the executive and legislative components when they exceeded their authority under the Patriot Act.

A more current example of this emotional process is cited by Justice Sandra Day O'Connor in the *New York Times* when she recently stated "the relationship between Congress and the federal courts was 'more tense than at any time in my lifetime'" (Greenhouse, 2005, p. 1). She was referring to the Reaffirmation of American Independence Resolution by the House of Representatives that stated "inappropriate judicial reliance on foreign judgments, laws or pronouncements threatens the sovereignty of the United States, the separation of powers and the president's and Senate's treaty making authority." One of its sponsors believes that judges who make decisions based on foreign precedents risk impeachment. Chief Justice Rehnquist believes historical precedent dictates that "a judge's judicial acts may not serve as a basis for impeachment." He cites the politically driven case of Justice Samuel Chase's impeachment in which the Senate decided not to convict him. Rehnquist believes this decision "represented a judgment that impeaching should not be used to remove a judge for conduct in the exercise of his judicial duties" (Greenhouse, 2005, p. 1). This example illustrates how the separation of powers triangle accommodates for the undifferentiation or immaturity of its participants in the underlying emotional triangle.

By contrast, the three-fifths compromise triangle—an agreement demanded by the South, acceded to by the North under duress, and based on a legal and moral fiction regarding slaves—would become a structural triangle that fostered polarization in the electorate rather than counterbalancing forces. Its structural inflexibility was a function of the emotional forces during its conception and ongoing implementation. The three-fifths clause compromise became a political and emotional regulator of the ongoing tension between the North and South and their mutually differing view of black people as slaves or free.

Three-Fifths Compromise Triangle

Just as the separation of powers triangle had its origin in the weakness of the Articles of Confederation, so did the three-fifths compromise triangle. The former triangle was designed to grant counterbalancing power throughout the entire government by containing, dissipating, and managing the anxiety associated with power and political issues. Through checks and balances its flexibility would accommodate future emotional and irrational behavior by its members. The three-fifths compromise triangle was a mechanism for exercising power and influence in the lower house by fostering the polarizing effects of anxiety toward the maintenance of the political power of the South. Its inflexibility would eventually not be able to contain the rising emotional forces surrounding the issue of how the United States would include blacks in society.

The origin of the latter triangle lay in the conflict between the North and South over federal representation and the role of blacks in society. White colonists consulted one another about defining and excluding blacks (see Wilkins, 2002, pp. 88-89). The differing idea of how to treat blacks would function as the third corner in the North-South conflict over representation.

The delegates understood that the power to influence and pass legislation and protect their self-interest lay in representation. Although they agreed that representation in the House of Representatives would be proportional, they had not agreed what the proportions would be.

Ultimately, the North and the South would reduce their anxiety about joining the union by creating a legal fiction based on a moral fiction—that blacks would count as three-fifths of a person for calculating each state's federal representation in Congress and the Electoral College. Slaves would function as the third point in the North-South conflict over representation, changing the triangle from one of conflict to compromise. Compromising the conflict in this manner would enable the South to count slaves in their voting, thus disproportionately influencing federal legislation over the next seventy years (see Wills, 2003, pp. 1-13). It is accurate to point out that white colonists did what they always did when dealing with the status and definition of black people, they consulted one another and excluded blacks (see Wilkins, 2002, pp. 88-89). Constructing the triangle in this manner accentuates the undifferentiation or immaturity of its participants.

Edmund Randolph, the governor of Virginia, introduced Madison's initial proposal about proportional representation. It attracted so much of the generalized anxiety about survival and union that Madison moved immediately to modify it. He surmised that the phrase "'proportioned . . . to the number of free inhabitants'. . . would divert the Committee from the general question as to whether the principle of representation should be changed" (Smith, 1980, p. 102).

Madison, ingeniously or inadvertently, kept the issue of representation of blacks out of the discussion. The delegates were anxious enough about living together to not have to debate whether blacks should live equally with them. Before a vote on Madison's proposal (changing the equal representation in the Articles of Confederation to a more equitable ratio) could be taken, the whole question of representation was postponed and did not resurface for weeks. Had it not been postponed, Delaware would have considered seceding from the convention (see Smith, 1980, pp. 102-103). In retrospect, it seems clear that, while fighting for freedom in the revolution, blacks were included. Yet, while organizing the freedom in the U.S. Constitution, blacks were not yet welcomed.

For seven weeks, while the separation of powers triangle was debated, anxious conversation about representation increasingly surfaced. Not until the equal representation in the Senate and proportional representation in the House were agreed upon could this discussion progress. As it surfaced, some Northern delegates opposed counting slaves and some Southerners wanted all of them counted (see Wills, 2003, p. 54).

Seeking compromise, James Wilson introduced the three-fifths ratio derived from a debate in the Articles of Confederation about taxation and not about representation (see Wills, 2003, p. 54). The "South deftly switched its emphasis from taxation and productivity arguments . . . [which had been] used in the Articles debate, to a new concern—a balance of representation between North and South" (Wills, 2003, p. 54).

In changing the debate between large and small states to one of Northern versus Southern interests, Madison noted the division of geography and climate as well as the effects of having or not having slaves. He suggested that any proportional representation should account for these differing interests. The South, fearful that uniting with the North would eliminate its way of life with slaves, was looking for ways to maintain the power it held under the Articles. Under the equal representation of the Articles, the Southern states were outnumbered eight to five. However, a majority of nine was required to make any significant change. Thus, under the Articles, the South retained veto power in matters of its vital interest such as slavery. The South looked for the power to maintain its way of life under the new Constitution. Ingeniously and ironically, the South seized upon "slave power" to assist itself against the fact that there were more free whites in the North than in the South (see Wills, 2003, pp. 54-55).

If slaves counted equally with free inhabitants for proportional representation in the new Constitution, the South would retain equal power with the North in the House of Representatives. "Counting them at three-fifths would give the South, which had only 41 percent of the white population, 47 percent of the delegates" (Wills, 2003, pp. 54-55). This discussion of representation was never about who had the right to vote but rather about how the states would be represented in the new federal congress.

The South said slaves were not free and therefore could not vote. The North said that if the slaves could not vote they should not be represented. The South declared that without this concession, ultimately the greatest one made at the convention, there would be no union. Even Alexander Hamilton considered it essential for ratification. In the end, the North voted with the South to consider slaves in representation. If there was to be a union, the North had no choice.

The concession the North obtained was a guarantee that the slave trade would continue only for the next twenty years. One wonders in hindsight why the North would agree to such a compromise. Franklin mused that the world was watching their work, and if they could not accomplish this, it was failure on a grand scale. The genius of this compromise was that it enabled the union to emerge, but its weakness gave overbalancing power to the South.

Origin of the Three-Fifths Ratio

How did these well-educated men agree to settle their differences by counting each slave as the equivalent of three-fifths of one white male? While operating under the Articles of Confederation, taxes were levied on the number of inhabitants in each colony. The South argued against counting blacks for taxation because they were not represented and that amounted to taxation without representation. In the spirit of compromise, Virginia conceded a partial representation stating that blacks did not work as hard as free men did and so they should be counted at one-half the rate for the purposes of taxation. John Adams, among other Northerners, argued that they should be counted at 100 percent just as free inhabitants were counted.

Lacking any scientific objectivity, debates about slave productivity ranged from one-half to three-quarters that of a white man. The discussion culminated in a proposal to count slaves as two-thirds as productive. This ratio was defeated. Madison offered a compromise of three-fifths, which was between the three-fourths choice of the North and the one-half choice endorsed by the South. This three-fifths ratio established for taxation was never adopted under the Articles. It remained in the minds of the delegates to resurface later as a compromise measure to deal with their anxiety about representation under the Constitution (see Wills, 2003, p. 53). These debates between white delegates were always about the use of blacks in the distribution of power and representation. They were never, in fact, about blacks being represented or about blacks voting. "The three-fifths rule was adopted not because of any estimate of the blacks' productivity, or even of a tradeoff between representation and taxation. It was because the South felt it needed a greater share in the representation" (Wills, 2003, p. 56).

THE RELATIONSHIP BETWEEN
THE SEPARATION OF POWERS TRIANGLE
AND THE THREE-FIFTHS TRIANGLE

The functioning of the three-fifths triangle would be a factor in many of the major political decisions until the Civil War. In essence, it meant that white Southerners could count three-fifths of their black slaves to enhance Southern representation in the federal congress. If there were ever an equal number of free white males in both the South and the North, the South could exercise power over the North by counting nonfree blacks for purposes of federal representation.

Madison understood this triangle even before the convention considered it and wrote to Jefferson, Washington, and Patrick Henry about it before the convention. He predicted that representation by population would appeal to the North because of its current superiority in numbers of free white males and to the South because of its expected superiority in the number of anticipated slaves (see Wills, 2003, p. 58). Everyone agreed that the United States would be expanding to the South and West. It is doubtful that Madison fully understood or could have predicted how the South would use this triangle, and many other clauses in the Constitution, to protect its way of life as well as the continuation of slavery. In addition, no one anticipated the impact of Eli Whitney's cotton gin and the dramatic spread of slavery.

The three-fifths compromise triangle had nothing to do with the approval of slavery but everything to do with the power to continue it. It granted the South the representational power to politically protect the Southern economy. The anxiety surrounding the triangle and its use would influence presidential politics, the management of the federal government, the expansion of the United States, the secession of the states from the union, and the Civil War. Were it not for the separation of powers triangle in managing the imbalances of the three-fifths compromise triangle, the United States would probably have dissolved.

Presidential Politics

The most direct effect of the three-fifths compromise triangle on presidential elections occurred in Jefferson's election in 1800. The Electoral College was based on the House and Senate numbers for each state in Congress, which included a representational allowance for the three-fifths compromise. If they counted only the votes of free white males, John Adams would have been reelected. Jefferson won the Electoral College vote over Adams by eight votes. Twelve of Jefferson's electoral votes were based on representation of black slaves owned by Southern whites. Although Jefferson's election is the only presidential one directly affected by the slave representation vote, it prompted sufficient anxiety to elicit discussion of secession by the North (see Wills, 2003, p. 6). Furthermore, during fifty of the first sixty-two years of the United States, other presidents like Jefferson were slave owners, making almost one-quarter of U.S. presidents slave owners (see Wills, 2003, pp. 6-7, and Richards, 2000, p. 9).

Management of the Federal Government

Direct effects of the three-fifths clause allowed the South to disproportionately control Congress. "The North had almost twice the free population of the South" (Burch, 1981, pp. 236-237). Yet "The slave states always had one-third more seats in Congress than their free population warranted" (Richards, 2000, pp. 56-57). By 1824, the Speaker of the House would be a Southerner 79 percent of the time, and the chairperson of the Ways and Means Committee was a Southerner 92 percent of the time (see Richards, 2000, p. 9). Without this political influence, slavery would have been banned from Missouri and the territory won in the War with Mexico in 1846. This combination of presidential and congressional power appointed eighteen slaveholders out of the first thirty-one Supreme Court justices. The majority of those justices who made the Dred Scott decision in 1857 were slaveholders (see Richards, 2000, p. 9).

Southern politicians used other clauses within the Constitution in conjunction with the three-fifths clause to manage the government. They used the states rights clause to suggest that slavery was no one else's business. They imposed a ban on taxing exports, which favored products of slave labor. They used the domestic insurrection law to get federal assistance should slaves riot. "The 'full faith and credit clause' made other states recognize all the South's legal provisions for slavery." (Wills, 2003, p. 11). Moreover, Southern politicians developed coalitions with Northern politicians to be silent on slavery in order to pass laws favorable to the North. Immigrants in the North favored these policies because they did not want to compete with freed blacks (see Wills, 2003, p. 11). In spite of these imbalances, no part of the separation of powers triangle dominated the government.

Expansion of the United States

Jefferson proposed to purchase the Louisiana Territory, which would provide for the single greatest expansion of the United States. This reignited the anxiety about the three-fifths compromise triangle. The North denounced this proposal as a plan to expand slavery from the South to the West. Northerners also said the proposal enhanced the Southern power in the Federal government and allowed them to sell more slaves whose value was enhanced with the coming cessation of slave importation. The gradual decline in slavery in the North and its increase and expansion in the South and West were shifting the balance of political power and significantly increasing the anxiety of Northern citizens. The Massachusetts Legislature authorized an amendment to the U.S. Constitution removing the three-fifths clause, saying it was neither a matter of legal equity nor moral right (see Wills, 2003, pp. 122-123). Others argued that the three-fifths clause might have been appropriate to the balance of power in 1787, but that it should be repealed because it was now inappropriate. The three-fifths compromise triangle generated anxiety, but the Constitution remained unchanged.

By 1800 almost all blacks in the North were free and almost all blacks in the South were slaves. Further expansion of the borders of the United States continued the argument about the spread of slavery; the evils of slavery, however, were not initially part of these discussions.

Slavery was guaranteed by the Constitution, but the struggle concerned the question of whether the South could maintain the power to preserve slavery, which, in turn, preserved the power of the three-fifths compromise triangle.

Two laws, the Fugitive Slave Act of 1793, and the Northwest Ordinance of 1787, constrained the South's ability to maintain slavery on both an individual and societal level. The former required Northerners to provide access and cooperation to Southerners seeking individual runaways who were additionally deprived of any civil rights. Eventually this act required the cooperation of the North to continue slavery and made the latter a national rather than a regional problem. The Northwest Ordinance allowed Congress to ban slavery from new territories especially in the Louisiana Purchase. These two constraints and their permutations comprised the major political issues from 1820 until Lincoln's election in 1860. The South needed to continue to pass legislation in Congress to enable it to preserve its power. As new states entered the Union, at least half of them needed to be slave states in order for the South to retain its power.

In 1819 there were eleven slave states and eleven free states. Congress was considering admitting Missouri as a slave state. The North believed the South was trying to extend slavery. The South worried the North was trying to destroy the union and end slavery. A compromise allowed a paired admission of Missouri as a slave state and Maine as free with an agreement to prohibit slavery in the Northern part of the Louisiana Purchase. This compromise reaffirmed the Congressional power of the Northwest Ordinance to prohibit slavery in new territories (see Boyer et al., 1993, pp. 270-271), and also continued the legal approach to the moral fiction.

Thirty years later there were fifteen slave states and fifteen free states. The compromise of 1850 solved many issues but not the major differences between the North and the South. Could Congress prohibit slavery in the territories outside those acquired in the war with Mexico or, as the South argued, should states have the right to bar or permit slavery? This compromise, passed in five different sections, reflected no clear majority consensus on the continuation of the preservation of the power of the three-fifths clause. Popular sovereignty was used as a means to decide slavery in the new territories but the "free soilers" position (that Congress rather than the states should make the decision) remained possible. The ability of the South to maintain its power through the three-fifths clause was deteriorating, and anxiety was increasing on both sides. The presidential leadership in the decade before Lincoln's election was ineffective in reducing this anxiety.

Secession of the South

Stephen Douglas, the Senate leader on the Kansas Nebraska Act of 1854, misidentified the driving force behind these issues. He assumed others were concerned, as he was, about the expansion to the West Coast, rather than about extending slavery and the right to enforce it through the three-fifths triangle. His misunderstanding of the driving issue—would Congress or the states have the right to decide slavery in the new states—inflamed the argument and incited the citizenry (see Boyer et al., 1993, pp. 464-465). All these compromises were variations on how the South could preserve its power, slavery, and its way of life.

The Whigs, a national party in both the North and South, was unable to resolve its position on the morality of slavery and disintegrated over its anxiety. The "free soilers" similarly could not resolve the moral issue of slavery but united around their certainty of its economic devastation to white citizens. The anxiety, emotional reactivity, and personal passion exhibited by Congressmen shifted the debate from one of preservation of the power of the South to one of honor and sectional pride (see Boyer et al., 1993, pp. 468-474). Some Southerners argued that the North was trying to enslave the South. As abstract issues became personalized, people attacked each other and their opinions.

Douglas's skillful legislative efforts favored the legal maintenance of the moral fiction exhibited in the three-fifths clause. Douglas personally wanted to remove slavery as a political impediment to white Northern expansion, and he thought popular sovereignty was the least disruptive way to accomplish this objective. To make matters more complicated, the Dred Scott decision in 1857 ruled that blacks were property and could not be citizens. In addition, the majority of slave holding Supreme Court judges, under the guidance of Chief Justice Roger B. Taney, rejected the idea that Congress could prohibit slavery in the territories. This decision was a clear victory for states' rights, slave power, and the three-fifths clause.

The societal reaction to this decision made it clear that there was no legal nonpartisan solution to the problems of the three-fifths compromise triangle (see Boyer et al., 1993, p. 462). Slavery, much like the abortion issue one hundred years later, was a moral issue, not a legal one, and therefore any legal resolution would just further polarize the electorate. A legal decision or legislation would further polarize the debate just as *Roe v. Wade* did years later. The separation of powers triangle, under the influence of the Supreme Court or the Congress, could not reduce the anxiety engendered by the three-fifths triangle.

Civil War

Legal means could no longer contain the anxiety and discord surrounding the moral fiction represented by free whites working alongside enslaved blacks in a democracy. Lincoln's "A House Divided" speech in 1858 presaged a beginning of understanding that the urgency of the current situation required a paradigm shift, from the legal to the moral level. This shift accelerated in the Lincoln-Douglas debates and reached its pinnacle in the Gettysburg Address and Lincoln's second inaugural address.

By the time Lincoln was elected president in 1860, the South understood that the power of the three-fifths clause was over as long as the South remained a part of the Union and the separation of powers triangle. Lincoln at first insisted that the South had the constitutional right to retain slavery. Yet, his election and the Southern response changed the triangle from a conflict focused on extension of slavery, or on the power of the three-fifths triangle, to one over secession.

Lincoln asserted that the imperfections of the three-fifths triangle and the declining power of the South should not be permitted to destroy the counterbalancing forces of the separation of powers triangle. To capitulate to the South would undermine the principal of majority rule—"a government of the people, by the people and for the people." The Union begun in 1787, the imbalances of the three-fifths compromise clause, and the Northern capitulation to the South could not be permitted to continue under the same terms. The Civil War began.

With the war and the Gettysburg Address (1863), Lincoln redefined the terms under which the separation of powers triangle would endure. By the use of the phrase, "four score and seven years ago" he bypassed the U.S. Constitution (1789), returned to the Declaration of Independence (1776), and redefined what our government meant by "All men were created equal" (see Wills, 1992, pp. 90-120). Lincoln made clear that this principle did include blacks. His words in the second inaugural address fulfilled the prediction of George Mason, "that all men are free and independent, and have certain inherent rights" (Wilkins, 2002, p. 30). Over the years the government has become increasingly democratic. How democracy and equality would be accomplished personally and politically has remained an enigma for over a hundred years and remains embedded in the minds and hearts of all citizens.

CONCLUSION

Bowen family systems theory provides a unique window into the functioning of human families over several generations. This chapter, with its emphasis on BFST, provides a similar view of how individuals unite to form self-governing institutions.

"The essence of a liberal" democracy is the "construction of a rich complex social order" (Zakaria, 2003, p. 26). The fall of communism and the end of the "cold war" leaves liberal democracy as the model and building block for governments throughout the world. The advent of militant Islamic extremism is the major external threat to this form of government. This threat requires "a new set of strong federal and multilateral self-governing institutions throughout the world to defeat this" enemy (Brooks, 2004, p. 37).

The obvious model is the work of the American Founding Fathers in establishing the U.S. Constitution. Ironically,

> Americans in particular have trouble seeing any tension between democracy and liberty because it is not a dominant theme in our own history—with one huge exception. Slavery and segregation were entrenched in the American South through the democratic system. (Zakaria, 2003, p. 21)

With the Founding Fathers' anxiety to form a sovereign union, the American experiment was in part built on the backs of slaves—politically, economically, and morally. Through the leadership of Lincoln, Americans revised and preserved their union as the last best hope for mankind.

In this age of globalism, Americans and their government have the opportunity to significantly influence the nature of self-government in the world. Multiple opportunities in Eastern Europe, the Middle East, and Asia, as well as world government, may emerge. Our own experiment will obviously influence these efforts.

All societies with self-governing institutions experience tension between equality and democracy. This chapter illustrates specific functional and dysfunctional structural triangles established in attempting to resolve that tension. Slavery as a legal part of the U.S. Constitution may be a rather unique dysfunctional structural triangle in the resolution of tension in self-government.

Bowen family systems theory, with its focus on the triangular nature of human emotional relationships, highlights the short- and long-term consequences of specific compromises and can provide a vehicle for understanding the function of the separation of powers triangle and the three-fifths compromise triangle. The nature of the triangles, the compromises made, and their implications may serve as a guideline for future self-governing bodies. America and its citizens would do well to understand how their past decisions have influenced subsequent behavior and, perhaps more importantly, how these decisions influence current world conflict and attempts at resolution.

Compromises made by our forefathers have had wide-ranging implications for our fellow citizens. This chapter illustrates that principled versus unprincipled compromises do make a difference. Each of us should be aware of the compromises we make in our own personal and political behavior.

REFERENCES

Bowen, M. (1978). *Family therapy in clinical practice*. New York: Jason Aronson, Inc.

Boyer, P., Clark, C., Kett, J., Salisbury, N., Sitkoff, H. and Woloch, N. (1993). *The enduring vision: A history of the American people*. Lexington, MA: D.C. Heath and Company.

Brooks, D. (2004). How to reinvent the G. O. P. *The New York Times Magazine,* August 29.

Burch, P., Jr. (1981). *Elites in American history, Vol 1: The federalist years to the civil war*. New York: Holmes and Meier Publishers, Inc.

Greenhouse, L. (2005). Rehnquist resumes his call for judicial independence. *The New York Times.*

Isaacson, W. (2004). *Benjamin Franklin: An American life*. New York: Simon & Schuster.

Richards, L. (2000). *The slave power: The free north and southern domination*. Baton Rouge, LA: Louisiana State University Press, pp. 1780-1860.

Smith, P. (1980). *The constitution: A documentary and narrative history.* New York: Morrow Quill Paperbacks.

Wilkins, R. (2002). *Jefferson's pillow: The founding fathers and the dilemma of black patriotism.* Boston, MA: Beacon Press.

Wilkins, R. (2004). *Politically speaking.* Washington, DC: National Public Radio, June 10.

Wills, G. (1992). *Lincoln at Gettysburg: The words that remade America.* New York: Simon & Schuster.

Wills, G. (2003). *The Negro president: Jefferson and the slave power.* New York: Houghton Mifflin Company.

Zakaria, F. (2003). *The future of democracy.* New York: W. W. Norton & Company.

Chapter 20

Triangles, Leadership, and the United States Supreme Court

Ann V. Nicholson

INTRODUCTION

The U.S. Constitution is a guide that has offered generations of Supreme Court justices the opportunity to interpret principle in relation to the challenges of the times. The interpretation of this document reveals how differently justices *think* and hence interpret the meaning of the Constitution. Some justices defend their positions based on what our forefathers would have done, others try to interpret what our forefathers meant when they wrote it, and others seem to have more flexibility in adjusting the Constitution to the needs of the day or, as they put it, *the felt necessities of the times.*[1] There are a limited number who come to the Court with a vision of what might be and lead the court to utilize the principles of the document, rather than focusing on the content at hand.

The justices' ability to distinguish the difference between thinking and feeling, fact and subjectivity, is reflected in Court decisions and the emotional environment in which these decisions were made. It is the premise of this chapter that emotional process has a powerful impact on Court decisions, and these decisions reflect the ability of the justices to *think* rather than *react.*

---

[1]In his published lectures, *The Common Law* (1881), Justice Oliver Wendall Holmes states, "The life of the law has not been logic, it has been experience." In his description of experience and how justices determine the law, he includes "the felt necessities of the times, the prevalent moral and political theories" (Schwartz, 1993, p. 191).

Liberalism and conservatism, judicial restraint, and judicial activism do not fully explain the underlying processes that influence the functioning of the Court. Justices shift position in response to emotional pressure and emotional alignments. It is often difficult to assess what opinions and dissents are determined by the intellect versus the emotional process given how the most reasoned argument can be driven by the emotional system. The ability to separate thinking from feeling appears to present the same challenge for Supreme Court justices as it does for most humans.

This chapter includes an overview of the relationship system on various courts with a particular focus on (1) the emotional process as it is played out through the triangle; (2) the role of leadership and how individual chief justices influenced and were influenced by the emotional environment on their respective courts; (3) the utilization of Bowen theory providing a unique view of leadership, Court decisions, and the overall functioning of individual courts.

There have been seventeen chief justices to date, covering a span of 216 years. The chief is "first among equals," meaning the vote of all justices is equal. The authority of the chief is administrative only. A chief's ability is often evaluated by the way he leads the conference where cases are discussed and opinions decided. Some view the assignment of opinions as the chief's greatest power, but even that can be changed by a majority vote of the *brethren* (see Cray, 1997, p. 268). When the chief justice is in the minority, the assignment of the opinion goes to the most senior justice in the majority.

The following basic assumptions establish a framework for understanding leadership in the Court:

1. All levels of differentiation can be found among the justices.
2. Leadership is different at different levels of differentiation. The ability of the chief to uphold a vision and maintain a principled course reflects his level of differentiation and will influence the functioning of the Court.
3. Principles are defined and interpreted differently at different levels of differentiation.
4. Any issue not resolved by the original parties of the Constitution and subsequent Courts is bound to be a source of conflict in the future.
5. The family relationship system of the chief justice has an important influence on his functioning, his capacity for leadership and his overall performance on the Court.
6. The emotional process on the Court, as in other living systems, is played out through the triangle.

7. The emotional process and the way it plays out in the relationship system (on and off the Court) has an impact on the law and how it is interpreted.

8. The opinions and dissents reflect the emotional process and overall level of functioning on the Court. There is clear evidence of both emotional and intellectual processes influencing opinions and dissents.

9. Progression and regression are as evident on the Court as in other human groups.

10. Progression and regression on the Court must be seen in the context of progression and regression in society.

BOWEN THEORY, THE EMOTIONAL PROCESS, AND THE TRIANGLE

Bowen theory is a unique guide to a more objective and factual view of human behavior. When we come to understand the emotional process as a basic force driving human behavior, we are able to get beyond polarizations, debates, and justifications.

The emotional process includes all the automatic behaviors/responses that occur within an individual and between members of a group. It is the part of man that he shares with other life forms, the automatic processes that govern all life, similar to instinct. What makes man different is his highly developed cerebral cortex that allows him, in varying degrees, to observe and regulate these automatic/instinctive processes within self while observing and influencing them in others.

The ability to separate thinking from feeling, fact from subjectivity, is what allows people to think clearly in an anxious environment. To the degree the feeling world cannot be separated (and this is relative), the ability to regulate self is diminished or lost. Feelings override the intellect when anxiety reaches levels that are no longer manageable for the organism. Differentiation measures a person's ability to separate thinking from feeling, to choose to act on one's own behalf (based on principle) or act for the group (based on principle), rather than respond to the immediate need/demand of the moment. Differentiation allows people to be close to each other yet pull out of the *togetherness* or closeness to choose a more self-determined course. It gives people a greater tolerance for discomfort and that increases their flexibility and options as anxiety increases. This is, of course, a matter of degree and develops as one goes up the scale of differentiation. Abilities found at higher levels of differentiation are reduced or eliminated as one goes toward lower levels of differentiation. Differentiation explains how some people acquire more individuality than others, and it accounts for the differences between people. It explains the differences between siblings, between leaders, and between generations.

There are two levels of differentiation that operate in everyone, a basic level and a functional level. Basic level refers to the part of self that cannot be changed except from within self. It is based on principles and beliefs that are developed by careful *thinking,* while utilizing available (factual) knowledge and incorporating that into one's own thinking system. Thinking can be changed over time, but it is based on new information and knowledge rather than a response to emotional pressure. Basic level of differentiation is pretty well established before one leaves the parental home (perhaps much earlier than that) and is greatly influenced by one's emotional history in one's family of origin and one's functioning in the parental triangle. The basic level of differentiation of one's parents, grandparents, and past generations also influences it.

Functional level of differentiation is determined by the relationship process and an individual's or group's functioning position in the relationship system, the family of origin, nuclear family, and extended family. It is influenced by the degree of interdependency between people and how people handle this. In any relationship system there are members who are more vulnerable to giving up or losing self to others. This is a reciprocal process whereby one may lose self and the other gains self, but each is equally dependent on the other. Functioning that is dependent on the emotional process via the relationship system can fluctuate significantly depending on the level of anxiety in the system over time and the presence or absence of favorable conditions. From a Bowen theory perspective, the emotional process is neither right nor wrong, good or bad; it simply *is.*

The emotional process is played out through the triangle. The triangle serves a function; it serves to enhance the functioning of some at the expense of others in an anxious field. It allows for some to maintain closeness and comfort while others are pushed into a more negative or uncomfortable outside position (until they find someone to join them in a *togetherness* at the expense of a third or work toward more differentiated functioning). If this is part of the natural wiring of humans and other species, why should we be so surprised by our own behavior and that of others?

Anxiety is the driving force behind the triangle. Anxiety influences the overall level of arousal or responsiveness of the organism. Acute anxiety is a response to what is, a real threat and is generally time limited. Chronic anxiety is a response to what might be, an imagined threat that resides within the organism for long periods of time and is passed on to subsequent generations in varying degrees (see Kerr and Bowen, 1988, p. 113). Humans seem to be fairly adaptive to acute anxiety, but the level of chronic anxiety within the system influences this as well. Chronic anxiety is an outgrowth of the family relationship system over generations. Individuals, families, organizations, and societies live with varying levels of chronic anxiety that influences adaptability. As the level of differentiation goes down, the level of chronic anxiety increases, and this influences an individual's or group's adaptability to changing conditions. In higher functioning or differentiated groups, the adaptability to anxiety is greater. Hence, it would require a higher level of anxiety for symptoms to occur, and the symptoms would be less apt to be chronic. (The presence of symptoms is one indicator of a regression.) Once the anxiety is reduced, more highly differentiated people return to their previous level of solid functioning. Groups at a lower level of differentiation live with more chronic anxiety and hence are more intensely reactive to changing conditions or added stressors. There is less ability to separate thinking from feeling; the automatic instinctive processes take over, and the life course is influenced far more by *feeling* than *thinking*. The impact of differentiation on functioning cannot be overlooked. It will take more anxiety to fuel a regression in a more highly differentiated group than in a less differentiated group. It is the emotional system that fuels a regression.

Regression is the movement toward a lower level of functioning driven by the level of chronic anxiety within individuals, families, organizations, and society. Once the regression has been established, Bowen (1978) notes that the norm in all organizations gradually falls to fit the regression or new level of functioning (see p. 280). Therefore, one would expect that the Court would also reflect the overall level of functioning in society at any given time, as a regression will impact the functioning of individuals in all professions. In a regression, "The vocal segment of society begins pressuring public officials to conform" and eventually "Some of these issues reach the Supreme Court for reinterpretations of the law that more nearly fit the new level of regression" (Bowen, 1978, p. 280). To the degree the Court is responsive to emotional pressure, the majority of the Court will interpret the Constitution according to the present level of regression. This is why the dissents are so important. At times of regression, they may well speak to a more differentiated understanding of the law.

Principles are negotiable in a regression, even more so as the group moves toward lower levels of differentiation. Bowen (1978) states: "In a regression, time honored principles that have been cornerstones of our democratic society are also misused to promote the regression [such as principle of rights, freedom of speech, freedom of the press]" (p. 281). Bowen continues: "A regression stops when anxiety subsides or when the complications of the regression are greater than the anxiety that feeds the regression" (p. 281).

It is the premise of this chapter that the emotional process has an important impact on the interpretation of the law and that it reflects the overall level of societal functioning at any given time, be it movement toward progression or regression. The ability to move from regression to progression is dependent on: a reduction in anxiety; the ability to *think* versus *react,* the ability to override the emotional system with one's intellect, the ability to be an individual in a group, and the ability to maintain *self* in the presence of emotional pressure. Bowen (1978) states:

> In a small or large social system, the move toward individuality is initiated by a single, strong leader with the courage of his conviction who can assemble a team, and who has clearly defined principles on which he can base his decisions when the emotional opposition becomes intense. (p. 279)

To clarify, the greater the level of individuality, the more principled or differentiated the course; the lower the level of individuality, the more reactive and group determined (less differentiated) the course. This speaks to the difference between progression and regression.

Bowen made a distinction between a group and a collection of individuals:

> In a group, emotional process is always operating to a greater or lesser degree. Groups are vulnerable to disruption or disintegration because emotional process will always do somebody in, or if it gets intense enough, will do in the whole operation. (Ferrera, 1995, p. 207)

This process plays out through the triangle by enhancing the functioning of some at the expense of others. In contrast, "a collection of individuals is relatively free of emotional process, and interaction works to support individual functioning to spur each person to go further than he or she could go alone" (Ferrera, 1995, p. 207). This reflects the difference between lower and higher levels of differentiation. There is less *need* to triangle others when people are more emotionally contained entities, as seen at higher levels of differentiation.

One can see a wide variation in functioning on the Court, and the next section addresses this as it cites examples of the emotional process on the Court.

THE EMOTIONAL PROCESS ON THE COURT, TRIANGLES IN ACTION, AND THE IMPACT OF LEADERSHIP

Anyone who takes on the job of defining a self, by assuming positions that are in conflict with the accepted way of thinking, and acting more independent of the emotional system, will evoke a negative reaction from the group. One has to expect this as a predictable and knowable response. Knowing the triangles and interlocking triangles in the system gives one a broader view of the emotional forces and what one is up against. The great leaders seem to know this and avoid getting bogged down in reacting to the forces that seek to undermine them. Others become more a part of the emotional system and then the Court's future is more determined by *feeling* than *thinking*.

In writing the Constitution, our forefathers were well aware of forces that would potentially undermine the new government they were creating. Much of this came from their knowledge of history, their experience with Great Britain, and the Revolutionary War and its aftermath.

The Constitution was their attempt to establish laws that would serve to regulate *power* or *control,* so the functioning of some members of this new government (including the populace) would not undermine others. They chose to divide the power/control amongst three separate branches of government with different responsibilities. Their goal was to implement a system of *checks and balances* on the degree of control experienced by any one branch at any given time.

A study of the Supreme Court and its emotional process shows us that one cannot regulate emotional process by law or, to put it another way, regulate control or dominance by law. The emotional process runs much deeper. It is part of the natural wiring within us on the level of biology. Therefore, how could man-made laws regulate this deeper process?

Our forefathers did not have knowledge of triangles, but they had an unusual capacity to know and understand human behavior and how man is likely to act under a wide variety of conditions. They were well aware of the innate struggle between self-interest and the interest of the group. They were intent on establishing a government that would be able to create and maintain order in a developing country that would continue to grow and change over time.

In the following section, the influence of various chief justices is described as they tackled the emotionally charged and challenging issues of their day. The emotional process is described utilizing Bowen theory as a guide.

CHIEF JUSTICES OF THE U.S. SUPREME COURT

John Marshall, 1801-1836

In the first three courts led by John Jay (1790-1795), John Rutledge (1795), and Oliver Ellsworth (1796-1800), the Supreme Court was considered the most insignificant branch of government. There were those who wondered if it should exist at all. There had been little public interest in the Court. All that changed when John Marshall came to the bench as the fourth chief justice in1801. Marshall set out to make the Court the "final authority on the law" (Severn, 1969, p. 134).

He set precedent in his opinions and in his actions as the leader of the Court. He wrote the majority of opinions, always presenting the broadest viewpoint before addressing the content of the case before him. In his decisions, he emphasized the limits of power for each branch of government and for the citizens as a whole. He was committed to a strong national government.

The Court's opinion in *McCullough v. Maryland* (1819) placed the federal government over the states when their laws were in conflict (see Severn, 1969, p. 200). States could no longer enforce legislation that would interfere with federal legislative policy (see Severn, 1969, p. 200). A unanimous vote on the Court, it brought outrage, hate, and disgust initially but order followed. If each state were free to pursue its own interests, chaos would ensue. There had been much competition between the federal and state governments for control. With the *McCullough v. Maryland* decision, there was no question that the federal government would rule over state governments when their laws conflicted. The Constitution had new meaning.

Before Marshall, the Court[2] had been in the outside position in the triangle comprised of the three branches of government and its members. The Court had no direction independent of the other branches, and the members of the executive and legislative branches were functioning at a better level than the members of the Court. The Marshall Court changed that. It was not only defining the judiciary, but the relationship between the federal and state governments, and later it would clarify the duties of all three branches of government. The Court continued to be in the outside position as it took clear positions on the law and how the Constitution was to be interpreted. The Court not only spoke as the "final authority on the law" but also acted accordingly by interpreting the Constitution in a way that gave it new meaning

---

[2]The Court in most instances in this chapter is referring to the group of individual justices, the brethren.

and a new direction for all to follow. Marshall and his brethren functioned differently than those before them and used the outside position to define a more autonomous position for the Court in relation to the other branches of government. This gave new life to the Court, and now people everywhere paid attention to what the Court was doing. It had become a significant branch of government.

Marshall came to the Court at the onset of the Jefferson presidency. President Adams appointed him just as he was leaving office, hence denying Jefferson the opportunity to appoint a new Chief Justice when he took office. The timing of a chief justice's resignation (e.g., between administrations) can fuel emotional reactivity when the environment is right for this.

Thomas Jefferson and John Marshall were cousins. The relationship between both families was distant and negative. Their mothers were both from the Randolph family. There was tension between the two families dating back at least two generations when Marshall's grandmother was disowned by the Randolph family, while Jefferson's ancestors maintained a more positive position in the clan (see Robarge, 2000, p. 160). Later Marshall married Mary Polly Ambler, daughter of Rebecca Burwell and Jacquelin Ambler. Rebecca had spurned Jefferson's efforts to court her, preferring to wed Mr. Ambler (see Robarge, 2000, p. 160). So from Marshall's own family history and that of his wife, the stage was set for conflict and tension between Marshall and Jefferson.

People bring their own unresolved issues from their family of origin into their adult relationships. Many of these issues are out of awareness but are demonstrated by the sensitivities of individuals to each other, as seen between Marshall and Jefferson. The problem may have had more to do with their family programming than differences of opinion on law and government. At the very least, the differences of opinion might have been more workable and heard differently without the family emotional programming playing such an active part.

They each had a different vision for the government, at least during this period of history when Marshall was on the Court and Jefferson in the White House. Marshall sought a strong national government bringing order and stability to the states and populace. Jefferson sought to emphasize the rights of the states and questioned the power of the Court. He thought the President and Congress should be able to make some decisions independent of the rulings of the Court. The decisions of the Marshall Court only intensified the negative and distant relationship between these two men.

In *Marbury v. Madison* (1803) the Marshall Court faced a huge challenge because aligning with either side (Marbury or Madison) would compromise the position of the Court then and in the future. The Judiciary Act of 1801 was passed by the legislature in the final days of the Adams presidency. That law provided for the appointment of several new federal judges. Adams promptly appointed fifty new judges, all confirmed by the Senate. John Marshall, as outgoing Secretary of State, was to deliver the commissions. This task was not completed, and Jefferson as the new president, and his Secretary of State James Madison, refused to deliver the remaining commissions. Adams had appointed judges who were aligned with his way of thinking, and Jefferson wanted that opportunity for himself. Hence, he advised his secretary of state to hold the commissions. One of those appointed justices was William Marbury who awaited his commission as a justice of the peace for the District of Columbia. "Marbury brought action for *mandamus*[3] against Madison and asked the Court to order Madison to deliver his commission," under Section XIII of the Judiciary Act of 1789, "which gave the Court original jurisdiction in mandamus cases against federal officials" (Schwartz, 1993, p. 40). In this case, the judicial order was directed at Madison (see Simon, 2002, p. 178). The question was whether the Court could issue a judicial order against the secretary of state, in keeping with standards set by the Constitution.

The case came before the Supreme Court in 1803. What was Marshall to do? If he aligned with Marbury, and ordered Madison to deliver the commission, the executive branch would likely refuse and the position of the Court would be weakened once again. The judicial branch does not have the power to enforce the law. That is the job of the executive branch. If the Court determined that the judicial branch had no authority over the executive branch, the Court would undermine its own position. In the Court's opinion, Marshall said the Court did not have the jurisdiction to do what Marbury asked them to do. Although Congress had given the Court this jurisdiction in Section XIII of the Judiciary Act of 1789, the Constitution did not give the Court this jurisdiction in this case. So the Court ruled that Section XIII of the Judiciary Act of 1789 was unconstitutional. Marshall said: "the Court owed allegiance to a higher authority, the Constitution" (Simon, 2002, p. 185). If the Constitution did not give them jurisdiction, the Court did not have it. The Marshall Court, for the first time, had declared an act of Congress unconstitutional. Here Marshall defined the role of the Court, the power to review acts of Congress and determine their constitutionality. He aligned neither with Marbury or Madison/Jefferson, thus maintaining a neutral position in the triangle. He focused on the broader issue of judicial review. Some report that Jefferson was furious, recognizing the direction the

---

[3]"A writ of *mandamus* is a judicial order to a government official directing him to do his legal duty" (Simon, 2002, p. 178).

Court took but there was little he could do. After all, the Court had not opposed him. Marshall had defined the review power of the Court and that "has never since been legally doubted" (Schwartz, 1993, p. 42). "Judicial review, as declared in *Marbury v. Madison,* has become the *sine quo non* of the American constitutional machinery: draw out this particular bolt, and the machinery falls to pieces" (Schwartz, 1993, p. 43).

The hostile reactions by the Congress and the executive branch to the positions of the Court continued. Clear evidence of this came with the impeachment proceedings of Associate Justice Samuel Chase in 1805. Marshall and others saw this action as politically driven rather than based on the presence of high crimes and misdemeanors as required by the Constitution. Marshall feared he would be the next to be impeached. He was called to testify. John Quincy Adams wrote to his father: "The assault upon Judge Chase was unquestionably intended to pave the way for another prosecution, which would have swept the Supreme Judicial Bench clean at a stroke" (Schwartz, 1993, p. 57). The trial ended with an acquittal. In Marshall's testimony before the Senate he did not attack the Congress or align himself with Chase, fully recognizing how the political activities of Samuel Chase (who had been deeply involved in the recent presidential campaign for John Adams and was a most polarizing figure in political debates) had invited this focus. Had the Court been functioning in accordance with the emotional demands of the Congress and president, the impeachment case most likely would not have occurred. This was the price for being a self, and Marshall led his Court in the effort to define what the Court was and what it would become. He did not battle with the opposition or participate in the emotional reactivity surrounding him. He remained focused on his goal to establish a strong national government and his Court followed. Marshall maintained a neutral position in this triangle (Congress, Chase, and Marshall) by aligning with neither the Congress nor his fellow associate on the bench, Samuel Chase. An emotionally neutral position appreciates what both sides are up against and yet avoids taking sides. An emotional or reactive response to this case would have put Marshall and the Court in a positive relationship with one side (those opposed to impeachment) and a conflictual relationship with the other side (those in favor of impeachment). When caught in the triangle, one perpetuates the problem. Marshall stayed focused on himself and the work of his Court.

Again at the Aaron Burr trial in 1807, Marshall faced another emotional storm. Aaron Burr had been vice president during Jefferson's first term in office. He was replaced by George Clinton when Jefferson was elected for a second term. Historically, the relationship between Jefferson and Burr had been negative and distant. Burr was indicted for treason along with other misdemeanors. The case was heard in Richmond, Virginia, where Marshall was the presiding justice (as part of his Circuit Court duties). Marshall made it clear that in order to establish a guilty verdict, "one had to prove an overt act of war against the United States and then prove the individual's part in it" (Severn, 1969, p. 169). Marshall stated: "Conspiring or plotting treason is not treason in itself" (Severn, 1969, p. 169). He reminded the jury of this concept throughout the trial. The government attorneys pressured Marshall to align with them by hinting, "he might yet be impeached, or that Congress might amend the Constitution to deprive the Court of some of its independence" (Severn, 1969, p. 169). In his opinion, Marshall responded to these threats: "That this Court dares not usurp power is most true, but that this Court dares not shrink from its duty is not less true" (Severn, 1969, p. 169). Burr was acquitted. Marshall's ability to define where he stood in relation to the law without being swayed by threats and emotional pressure from both sides is evidence of taking a well differentiated I-Position in the triangle. This is the essence of leadership.

It is said: "Jefferson believed Marshall had conspired to prevent the real evidence against Burr from being presented to the public" (Severn, 1969, p. 170). Jefferson asked Congress for an investigation. Public demonstrations followed. Marshall and Burr were hung in effigy in Baltimore. Marshall's wife, who had been symptomatic early in their marriage, was so upset by the reaction to her husband that she suffered a severe emotional breakdown (see Severn, 1969, p. 167).

Again, Marshall demonstrated his ability to withstand the pressure of the group and define where he and the Court stood on the important issues of the day. After the tumultuous response, a new level of order and calm followed. One can easily identify many of Marshall's decisions as thoughtful (as opposed to feeling generated decisions), given the long-term positive impact they had on the Court, the government, and this country. One could also say that his wife's symptomatic state indicates that she absorbed a greater amount of the anxiety for the family system, a factor that would predictably allow Marshall to function at a higher *functional* level of differentiation. To the degree that one or more members of the group are undermined (as evidenced by their symptomatic state) others are freer to function at a higher functional level and with less anxiety. This is a reciprocal process that operates within the relationship system. It appears Marshall's wife functioned more for the group (family) than for self.

In all of these examples, one sees Marshall and his Court in the outside position of the triangle and using it to define standards and principles for the Court and others to follow. One can clearly see the pressure the Court was under to join the *togetherness* forces or the accepted thinking of the time.

The executive and legislative branches, or two or more members of the same branch, banded together to exert pressure on the Court to do what they expected. It is automatic for the human to react to emotional pressure, and, predictably, he or she will become angry with the opposition, do the opposite of what the other wants, or yield. The automatic response serves to keep the triangle alive and either intensifies the conflict and/or shifts the conflict. It does not resolve conflict. In contrast, by using the outside position to relate to the togetherness without becoming a part of it and reacting to it, one can define a new direction for self and the group that is not determined by emotional forces but by objective thinking. This in turn benefits the entire group. This is evidence of more differentiated leadership that is not dependent on the relationship system but the individual acting autonomously.

Roger Brooke Taney, 1837-1864

In spite of the conflict and polarizations on the Taney Court, the overall accomplishments were significant for the first twenty years. The Court was respected as a solid branch of government and Taney and his brethren were well regarded for their efforts in bringing the powers of the state into a more workable equilibrium with the federal government. Taney was known for his commitment to judicial self-restraint[4] and his overall effort to keep the Court out of the politics of the day. In keeping with this standard, he had consistently avoided pressure to take on slavery cases as a Constitutional issue. Instead, most slavery cases were decided according to the law of the particular state involved.

The emotional environment on the Court became increasingly intense during the mid-1840s and particularly the 1850s as it did throughout the country. As the United States gained control of more territory through negotiation or war, the debate on "slave or free" states intensified. It became increasingly apparent that if the new territories were free of slavery, the balance of power/control would shift markedly leaving the Southern slave states with little representation or control. As both sides (those opposing slavery and those supporting slavery) polarized around this issue, there was more pressure placed on the Court to decide, once and for all, the slavery issue.

When *Dred Scott v. Sanford* (1855) came before the Court initially, Taney joined the majority in conference to dismiss the case without a hearing. Their decision was based on the fact that Dred Scott was a slave, not a citizen.

---

[4]Judicial self-restraint: "The judge, in applying constitutional limitations must restrain himself and leave the maximum of freedom to those agencies of government whose actions he is called upon to weigh" (Schwartz, 1993, p. 94).

Therefore, he did not have the right of citizens and could not bring a suit in federal court. The Court was asked to answer the following questions: Did Dred Scott become a free man when he left his slave state with his master and moved to a free state? Did he hence return to his slave state as a free man or slave? This case raised other issues as well. Did Congress have the right to determine the slave status of new territories, or was this to be a judicial issue? Then, there was the question of whether a slave, even if free, could become a citizen of these United States. However, the Court was not required to address these last two issues in this case.

Congress had long struggled with slavery issues and in the process become increasingly divided. In 1820, Congress passed the Missouri Compromise that "prohibited slavery in the remainder of the territory included in the Louisiana Purchase north of a prescribed line, 36 degrees 30' of north latitude" (Schwartz, 1993, p. 106). Later there were those who wanted this line extended in order to maintain a balance between slave and free states, but all attempts to expand this were voted down in Congress (Schwartz, 1993, cf. p. 108). The Kansas-Nebraska Act of 1854 "indicated congressional intent not to deal with slavery in the territory and authorized liberalized appeals to the Supreme Court in slavery cases" (Schwartz, 1993, p. 111). It seems that Congress had reached an impasse and looked to the Court to decide the slavery question. As tension mounted between factions within Congress, they pressured the Court to join one or the other side of the triangle. The newly elected president, William Buchanan, looked to the Court to bring peace to this increasingly divided country by resolving the slavery issue. Even Lincoln sought resolution through the Court in 1856, and the public too clamored for the Court to decide. The pressure on the Courts to move differently than they had before was enormous.

On the Court, Taney was pressured by Justice Wayne and other justices from the Southern states to take on all aspects of the slavery issue (pressure to move away from his commitment to judicial self-restraint) with the expectation that it would bring resolution and harmony. It is said that Taney thought a judicial opinion on the slavery issue would have the opposite effect and further inflame the country. Associate Justice John McClain, a staunch abolitionist with unrestrained presidential ambitions, also harbored much hostility toward Taney. Taney was clearly sensitive and reactive to the emotional environment on the Court throughout his tenure but more so in December 1855 when this case came before the Court for hearing. Taney was more personally vulnerable after the deaths of his wife, daughter, and son-in-law in 1855, just months before *Dred Scott v. Sanford* was heard. The case was decided seven to two and Chief Justice Taney, representing the majority, read the opinion (March 1857). It stated that Negroes, free or slave, could not become citizens. Congress did not have the power to decide slaveholding in the territories, as the Missouri Compromise implied (see Schwartz, 1993, p. 115). Dred Scott was not freed by taking up residence with his master in Illinois, a free state. "The Missouri Compromise prohibition against the holding of property in slaves is unconstitutional" (Schwartz, 1993, p. 116). Scott had to adhere to the laws of Missouri once he returned to his home state, and that state court had decided Scott would remain a slave (see Schwartz, 1993, p. 115). Each justice wrote a separate opinion emphasizing the divisiveness on the Court. It is said Taney's detailed opinion in *Dred Scott v. Sanford,* that included a fierce attack on abolitionists, evoked more of a reaction than the vote itself. In fact, most of the country paid little attention to this case until the Lincoln-Douglas debates one year later that served to further polarize the slavery issue.

Here one sees the emotional process played out through the triangle very clearly. When Congress reached an impasse on slavery, its members shifted the anxious focus to the Court. Now the Court sat with more of the anxiety, and the tension between the warring factions (in Congress) eased somewhat. Each side wanted the Court to agree with their respective position. The Court was invited to align with one or the other side of the conflict (for or against slavery).

All people are vulnerable to changing levels of anxiety particularly within their own family, and anxiety (at varying levels) clearly influences one's ability to think. Three significant deaths in 1855 left Taney devastated and hence more vulnerable to emotional pressure at that time. Taney had withstood the pressure to take on slavery as a constitutional issue and consistently adhered to the standard of judicial self-restraint up to that point. He yielded to the emotional forces on and off the Court at a time of peak anxiety within his family, the Court, and the country. When one reacts to emotional pressure, it serves to intensify the emotional responsiveness in the system as is seen in the Court decision regarding Dred Scott. Taney, in his opinion, attacked the opposition, thus communicating that he was *caught* in the emotional process. Emotional reactivity indicates that one is caught in the triangle and the inevitable polarizations influenced by the feeling world. This further intensifies the problem as is seen in this case.

At times of peak levels of anxiety, one's primary goal is to decrease the anxiety within self and then relate more calmly to one's environment. When Taney shifted his position from judicial self-restraint and took on the constitutional issue of slavery, it intensified the reactivity on the Court and pushed the country toward increased levels of reactivity as well. To stay with his previous position of judicial self-restraint would not have resolved the slavery issue, but it would not have intensified (to the same degree) an already exploding situation.

The impasse and polarizations within the Congress were played out on the Court. The country, along with the three branches of government, was in a regression and nearing the end of its adaptability. The country went on to polarize not only around the issue of slavery, but also the issue of secession, as well as the existence of the Court itself. The country came to praise Lincoln while Taney was denigrated for generations to come.

Historians think the Court was weakened by the *Dred Scott v. Sanford* opinion. However, it is the emotional process and the justices' functioning in the triangle that weakened the Court. One does not get into a position of weakness all by oneself. The emotional forces worked to keep the Court in this position as the Congress and particularly the executive branch gained strength in the war effort to keep the states *united.* During the Civil War, the Court was in the outside position in the triangle with the other two branches of government residing in the inside positions. The executive branch became stronger as the Court weakened. This is a reciprocal process.

One can also see how the unresolved issues of the past continue to plague future generations. The issue of slavery was avoided in the writing of the Constitution. It seemed to the members of the Constitutional Convention (1787) that if they pushed the slavery issue, there would be no Constitution. The problem was left to future generations and became the focus of the regression. It was not the cause. Bowen theory gives one a broader view of war, which is a symptom of regression.

Charles Evans Hughes, 1930-1941

The tenure of Chief Justice Charles Evans Hughes clearly demonstrates the significant triangle involving the Court and members of the executive and legislative branches. In the 1931-1937 terms, the Court majority opposed most of the New Deal legislation that had been enacted to assist the country as it dealt with the Great Depression, an unparalleled economic disaster in U.S. history. This legislation sought to increase the regulatory powers of the federal government significantly and involved such factors as farm debtors' relief, bankruptcy relief, minimum wage, and regulation of the bituminous coal industry (see Schwartz, 1993, p. 232). The basic issue had to do with the Court's interpretation of the Constitution. Was it to be interpreted as written (more content focused and more by the written word of the framers who could not have predicted the environmental conditions of a future time)? Or, was it to be adjusted to the issues of the day or *the felt necessities of the times?* How much can one *adjust* the Constitution before losing sight of the principles on which it is based? How much can one *restrict or expand* the Constitution before losing sight of the principles on which it is based? This seems to be a dilemma for all times. With few exceptions, the Hughes Court had adhered to a laissez-faire jurisprudence opting to maintain a more restrictive (content focused) view of the Constitution. This had been the pattern followed by earlier Courts, but now the country was in a different place challenged by a crushed economy. The Congress enacted several pieces of legislation in keeping with the policies of Franklin Roosevelt's New Deal administration. The efforts of both executive and legislative branches of government went toward energizing the economy by increasing governmental intervention (see Schwartz, 1993, p. 232). Congress, in close alignment with the president, produced legislation that challenged the current laissez-faire jurisprudence on the Court. Congress and the president were asking for far more control than ever before, and the Court resisted (mainly with the swing vote of Associate Justice Owen Roberts who was often joined by the chief justice).[5] Tension mounted in 1934 through 1936 as the Court invalidated twelve congressional laws partially or completely (see Schwartz, 1993, p. 234). For example, the Court struck down the Agricultural Adjustment Act of 1936 stating: "Agriculture, like manufacturing, is not commerce and hence is immune from federal control" (Schwartz, 1993, p. 232). This clearly stopped legislation that was geared to increase governmental assistance to the agriculture industry and enhance the general welfare at a time of great need. The question became whether Congress had the power to tax and spend to enhance the general welfare within the limits of the Constitution (see Schwartz, 1993, p. 233). President Roosevelt saw the balance of power shifting with the Court's restricted theory of governmental functioning and saw the Court as a clear threat to New Deal legislation and progress for the country (Schwartz, 1993, p. 233). The Court was in the outside negative position in the triangle with most of the conflict/tension expressed between it and the executive branch. The legislature was in close alignment with the executive branch. President Roosevelt came forward with his Court packing plan on February 5, 1937. This plan would remake the Court by allowing the president "to appoint another judge for every federal judge who was over seventy years of age and had not retired" (Schwartz, 1993, p. 233). This would have given Roosevelt the opportunity to appoint six new Supreme Court Justices (see Schwartz, 1993, p. 233), whose thinking would be more aligned with his own (and provide for the development of several new

---

[5]When the votes on the Court are an even split, or close to being split, the justice who holds the swing vote is in a most important position. He is viewed as the one with the control.

interlocking triangles). This was an emotional response focused on finding a solution to the immediate problem without thoughtful recognition of the long-term impact of that decision. Anxiety drives one to find answers for today (to relieve the tension of the moment) without recognizing the long-term complications for self and others. In fact, Roosevelt's Court packing plan would have threatened the future effectiveness of the Court and possibly erased it altogether. Likewise, the justices had failed to recognize how their actions (continued resistance to change, voting against acts that would allow for more governmental input and control during the Depression) and fueled reactivity from the other side. Had Hughes bought into the emotional process, the Court would have been undermined. Had he caved in or attacked, he would have intensified the emotional process and the Court, government, and country would have lost.

Any leader can get caught in the emotional process. This is part of the human phenomenon. How one manages self in the emotional arena is key. Hughes sent a surprise letter to Senator Burton Wheeler, leader of the opposition to the Court plan, who in turn presented it to the Senate Judiciary Committee as it evaluated Roosevelt's Court packing plan. In this letter, Hughes focused on the facts of functioning of the Court. He noted:

> An increase in the number of Justices . . . would not promote the efficiency of the Court. . . . In fact, it would impair that efficiency so long as the Court acts as a unit. There would be more judges to hear . . . confer . . . discuss . . . convince . . . and decide. (Hendel, 1968, p. 251)

Hughes emphasized that the "Constitution vested judicial power in only one Supreme Court, not two or more as some suggested" (Hendel, 1968, p. 251). One week later, on March 29, 1937, the chief justice changed his position on the New Deal legislation and completely overruled earlier decisions, shifting the balance on the Court. The Court now upheld a minimum wage law for women, provided for mediation and collective bargaining in railroad labor disputes, provided relief for farm mortgagers (previously held unconstitutional), and allowed for unemployment and old age features to Social Security (see Hendel, 1968, cf. p. 252). Congress was now allowed to spend to aid in the welfare of the citizenry. As the Judiciary Committee debated the president's plan, the Court changed. Some believe, including the chief justice, that the change began even before the Court packing plan was announced. The chief justice had the courage to move differently than he had before and led the swing vote followed by Associate Justice Owen Roberts. This changed the future course of the Court. Many people even today see Hughes as retreating in response to a threat. Hughes and the Court were in the outside position of the triangle, but he was no longer caught in the emotional process. He led the Court by clearly defining a differentiated position for self. He did not react to the emotional forces that sought to undermine him or the Court, but stayed focused on the work of the Court and his part in it.

Every great leader has the capacity to change his thinking and direction based on the acquisition of new information. Hughes led the Court to move differently than it had before by redefining his own position. The Court and the country benefited. The crisis ended and what is considered a "Constitutional Revolution" began. The three branches of government were intact. It is said: "No other justice excepting John Marshall, played as vital a part and one so fraught with historic consequences in our constitutional history" (Hendel, 1968, p. 280).

THE STONE AND VINSON COURTS, 1941-1953

Fast forward to the Stone and Vinson terms. The country was either at war or in a pre/postwar period during their terms. Again the strength in the executive branch followed by the legislature is apparent. There is no question that underfunctioning or weakness on the Court strengthens the functioning of the other two branches. In war, the executive branch takes the lead, the legislature complies, and the Court rarely speaks. Historically, the Court votes with the necessities of war (however they may be viewed at the time) over individual rights. It is interesting to see how heightened anxiety during wartime influences the interpretation of the law. Individual rights are increasingly restricted when in conflict with what is perceived as military necessity. The executive branch not only takes the lead in war but has at times usurped power/control beyond its established limits as defined by law.[6]

The underfunctioning (weakness) on the Court enhances the functioning (strength) of the others. Overfunctioning by the executive branch in alignment with the legislature serves to undermine the functioning of the Court. This is a reciprocal process. One can say the justices absorb a greater amount of anxiety, freeing others in the executive and legislative branches to gain functioning. One can also see how one branch impinges on the functioning

---

[6]For example, in the Merryman case (*Ex Parte Merryman,* May 1861), Chief Justice Taney on the Circuit Court in Baltimore held actions of the president as illegal when he and the military suspended habeas corpus and arrested a civilian without a warrant and hearing (see Schwartz, 1993, p. 128). Taney defined the law in this case but did not hold the power to enforce it.

of the other in order to enhance its own position. This is an automatic (in-stinctive) process and for the most part is out of awareness.

When the problem is projected onto the other, the other reacts in a way that gives further evidence that the problem is in him or her and that individual or group will in time manifest that anxiety in the form of symptoms.

Harlan Stone, 1941-1946

Harlan Stone was appointed to the Court as an associate justice in 1925 and was regarded as a superior justice. As chief justice, Stone was swept into the emotional reactivity of the Court and behaved in ways that clearly perpetuated it. He demonstrated little control of the Court conference; case discussions were endless, debates lengthy (always joined by the chief justice), often leading to intense conflict and unresolved differences. There seemed to be little ability to regulate intense emotion within the group and the endless debates only served to intensify feelings. Stone's Court was comprised of a group of talented individuals who for the most part were of similar views (seven Roosevelt appointees), and yet the Court was divisive and fewer than half its decisions were unanimous (see Renstrom, 2001, p. 89). The number of split decisions reached unprecedented levels (see Renstrom, 2001, p. 181).

There was tremendous personal animosity between two of the associate justices, Jackson and Black. The conflict between two or more members of the group is seen as the negative side of the triangle and a symptom of a larger problem, rather than the problem in and of itself. The leader plays a part in this, either overtly or covertly, by the way he manages himself and actively participates in the conflict or avoids it altogether.

This triangle included Chief Justice Stone in the outside position, with Associate Justices Jackson and Black assuming the inside positions and absorbing more of the anxiety and tension in their relationship. Other justices could join one or the other side of the triangle at any time. A symptom (in this case, intractable conflict) is evidence of the *fixed* nature of the triangle. As tension mounted on the Court, the conflict between Jackson and Black would automatically intensify. The triangle is a good barometer for assessing the emotional climate of the system. The conflict between Jackson and Black absorbed more of the anxiety, allowing others to function outside of it to varying degrees. It is in the best interest of those outside the conflict, in terms of comfort for self, to maintain and contain the conflict in the original triangle.

History gives one a broader perspective on this triangle. Justices Frankfurter and Black had maintained what is described as an "intellectual feud" during their years on the Court. Justice Frankfurter upheld a more conservative view and a more restricted interpretation of the Constitution. In contrast, Justice Black represented a more liberal view intent on interpreting the Constitution to meet the needs of changing times (according to his view of current needs). People saw their different viewpoints as the *cause* of their conflict.

When Jackson came on the Court, he was quickly swept into the emotional process by emotionally aligning with Frankfurter, leaving Black in the outside negative position in this interlocking triangle. Jackson's behavior is good evidence that he picked up the tension between Frankfurter and Black and took it on as his own. He was playing out a conflict that originally belonged between Frankfurter and Black. For the most part, this process occurs outside of the awareness of the individuals involved. Jackson frequently voted with Frankfurter and Stone with Black and other justices dissenting. This begs the question: how much is one's vote influenced by the emotional process? The more one emotionally aligns with one viewpoint, the more they automatically invite the opposing viewpoint.

This example speaks to the regulatory function of the triangle. As long as Jackson absorbed the anxiety and contained it in his relationship with Black, the tension between Black and Frankfurter diminished to the level of *intellectual differences.* The tension between Black and Jackson also prevented the tension being directed at the chief justice. Stone was able to maintain a more comfortable position for himself as long as others were feuding.

The emotional process is what undermined the functioning of the Stone Court as well as individuals on the Court. More life energy was invested in the relationships than in the work of the Court, and that prevented this Court from becoming a more effective team. Had the level of differentiation been higher, the conflict would not have been so fixed and unregulated. With increasing levels of differentiation, one finds greater tolerance for differences as well as a greater ability to evaluate objectively new and differing ideas. Had the anxiety level been lower, the symptom would have been less severe and more manageable. A very low level of anxiety can allow people of varying levels of differentiation to tolerate differences better, but it is difficult to maintain a very low level of anxiety in any system over time.

Anxiety that is played out on the Court, or absorbed within the Court relationships, is not necessarily limited to the Court. It is also influenced by anxiety in the larger governmental system and society as a whole. The unregulated tension on the Stone Court may also reflect the tension in the interlocking triangles between the three branches of government and their respective leaders as well as the tension in the country and society. Do not forget that the country was at war or moving in that direction.

It is important to remember that one's ability to lead effectively is undermined when one is reactive to the emotional process of which one is a part. Justice Jackson said: "The difficulty with Stone was that he dreaded conflict and his dread was so strong that it seemed that he feared taking action which would bring it about" (Renstrom, 2001, p. 35). This speaks to the emotional process.

Frederick Vinson, 1946-1953

Frederick Vinson was appointed by President Truman in 1946, and is regarded as the least effective head of the Court. President Truman was caught in the conflicts on the Court as seen during the appointment process of the new chief justice. It was reported that Truman wanted to appoint Justice Jackson but was told that if he did Justice Black would resign. Likewise, if he appointed Justice Black, Justice Jackson would resign (Schwartz, 1993, see p. 254). The conflict between Justices Black and Jackson was intense and intractable. Hence, Truman appointed Vinson with the expectation that he would ease the conflict and bring peace to the Court. As often happens the overinvestment in peace produces the opposite. Vinson may have been undermined by the focus on peace and his pattern of getting along with others. The tension on the Court quickly focused on the new chief justice and his perceived weakness. This action inevitably pushed Vinson closer to Truman, who had an established relationship with him given Vinson's former position as secretary of the treasury. One can assume that neither Truman nor Vinson would have perceived how each of them was participating in the problem by the way they responded to it. The tension on the Court had shifted to Vinson and his divisive brethren, with Vinson in the outside position in the central triangle, while maintaining an inside position in an interlocking triangle with President Truman, with the brethren in the outside position. The togetherness with Truman made functioning independently more difficult. Vinson was unable to deal with the conflicts on the Court and the tension directed at him without moving away from the group and aligning with his president, who also stayed caught in the tension on the Court.

The functioning of the Court was undermined by the relationship process, not necessarily by the abilities of the individuals. It is difficult to know how Chief Justice Vinson would have functioned had he not been caught in the emotional process which directed his energies toward relationships and away from the work of the Court. In Vinson's last term, "only nineteen percent of the cases were decided unanimously, a record low" (Schwartz, 1993, p. 254).

In both the Stone and Vinson Courts one sees how the emotional process undermined some individuals on the Court, as well as the effectiveness of these Courts. If the anxiety escalated further, it would undermine the entire court.

Earl Warren, 1953-1968

Following the death of Chief Justice Vinson, Earl Warren was appointed by President Eisenhower to take over the leadership on the Court and he did just that. Justice Frankfurter noted the new chief's qualities: an ability to "focus on the work of the Court, willingness to work hard, an ability to grow in the job, to learn, and a capacity to truly listen to others" (Cray, 1997, p. 272).

Brown v. Board of Education of Topeka had been held over from the Vinson Court and was scheduled for reargument in December 1953. In this case, "Reverend Brown, a black man, sought to send his daughter to a school closer to home, a school designated by the board for whites only" (Cray, 1997, p. 277). The chief justice opened the Court conference with a clear view of the basic issue in this case: "Segregation could be justified only by belief in the inherent inferiority of blacks" (Schwartz, 1993, p. 267). If the Court were to follow *Plessy v. Fergusson,*[7] it had to be based on this factor, "the inferiority of blacks" (Schwartz, 1993, p. 267). Warren delayed the vote (a most unusual procedure), creating the opportunity for justices to discuss their viewpoints in conference and individually with the chief justice and others. Warren saw a unanimous vote as essential, something that would have been impossible on the Vinson Court a few months earlier. Warren thought the fact that the justices did not polarize in the beginning helped them to come out unanimously in this case (see Cray, 1997, p. 283).

The only change in the membership on the Court at this time was the leadership. The Brown decision ruling that school segregation was unconstitutional was unanimous. In May 1954, one year later, in the Court's second Brown decision (known as Brown II, May 1955), the Court spoke of the implementation of desegregation leaving the responsibility to the district courts "to take such action as was necessary and proper to ensure the non-discriminatory admission of plaintiffs to schools with all deliberate speed" (Schwartz, 1993, p. 277). These decisions led to massive resistance. Nineteen senators and eighty-two representatives issued the Southern Manifesto condemning the Court and the Brown decision (see Cray, 1997, p. 320). As they saw it, the Court was ignoring 100 years of precedent (see Cray, 1997, p. 320). President Eisenhower did not speak publicly in support of desegre-

---

[7]*Plessy v. Ferguson* (1896) upheld a Louisiana law providing for "equal but separate [railroad] accommodations for the white and colored races" (Schwartz, 1993, p. 188).

gation. Warren thought this fueled resistance in the country. Clearly there was emotional pressure from the chief executive for Warren and the Court to go slowly or perhaps not go at all. In the end, Eisenhower sent troops to Little Rock to enforce the law, as he was required to do to uphold his oath of office. Resistance continued in the 1960s including threats to close down the school system rather than integrate (*Griffin v. County Board of Prince Edward County*, 1964). Freedom of choice plans geared to maintain segregation in schools were also voted down by the Court in 1968. The Court required school boards "to come forward with a desegregation plan that promises realistically to work now" (Schwartz, 1993, p. 277). The Court recognized the avoidance tactics inherent in these plans (*Green v. County School Board*, 1968).

Following the Court's decision (*Engel v. Vitale*, 1962) that holding school prayer in public schools was unconstitutional, billboards all over the country clamored for Warren's impeachment (see Cray, 1997, pp. 387-392). Laws protecting the rights of persons accused of crimes followed, such as the Miranda rights (*Miranda v. Arizona*, 1966), the right to an attorney (court appointed, if needed), and the right to remain silent. How investigations were to be carried out by police were changed to protect the individual rights of those accused of crimes. Nonwhites now had the same rights to vote as whites[8] and to be equally represented in state and federal government via the reapportionment decisions (*Baker v. Carr*, 1962; *Reynolds v. Sims*, 1964).

In all these examples, the interpretation of the principle of equal rights under the law was changing, and people reacted. Warren had an appreciation of the reactions to the Court and did not become defensive or react to the onslaught of criticism projected onto him or the Court. Had he done so, he would have been *caught* in the emotional process and lost his focus on goals and principles. The challenge is to keep oneself outside of the emotional process as much as possible while relating to both sides (in this case, those for and against change) and aligning with neither. Warren led his Court to stay with a principled position in spite of enormous emotional pressure to change back. The benefits of this effort were far-reaching and beneficial to all in the long term.

Even Warren's resignation as chief justice at the end of the term in June 1968 was fraught with accusations and criticism. He was accused of being disloyal to his party by not waiting for a possible Republican president to appoint the next chief justice. When President Lyndon Johnson nominated Associate Justice Abe Fortas to replace Warren, the Congress exploded with

---

[8]In 1966, the Court upheld the constitutionality of the Voting Rights Act of 1965 (see Cray, 1997, p. 469).

emotion. The polarization was intense and many saw Congress as reacting as much to the Warren Court as to Abe Fortas. On the heels of a filibuster, Abe Fortas withdrew his nomination. The close association of Abe Fortas with Lyndon Johnson and his administration, even while on the Court, also fueled emotional reactivity within Congress. In this triangle, Abe Fortas and Lyndon Johnson were in the inside position and Congress was in the negative outside position.

Richard Nixon, the Republican presidential candidate of 1968, used the Court and its actions as a campaign issue, indicating his alignment with those opposing the Warren Court decisions and placing the Court in the outside negative position in this triangle.

The degree of emotional pressure on all leaders is greater than most appreciate. It appears there are few leaders who can define self and act accordingly when the whole nation or world opposes. There is little doubt that Chief Justice Earl Warren was able to do this and over time led his Court and his country to a new level of functioning, one that clearly reflected his sense of fairness to all people.

CONCLUSION

This chapter has been an attempt to research evidence of the emotional process as it is played out through the triangle on the U.S. Supreme Court. Bowen theory provides a more objective view of the emotional process that drives behavior in all human groups. The ability of the Court to function more autonomously and independent of the emotional process has varied throughout its history, as one would expect. The ability of the leader to define a clear position for self has a calming impact on the group (over time) and allows the Court to move from a *group* to a *collection of individuals,* from regression to progression.

Bowen theory provides a high-powered lens to view the emotional system, how it works, and how it influences the functioning of the justices at any given time. When the emotional process is the *focus,* as opposed to Court decisions, one can begin to see the multiple forces influencing the justices' ability to *think* versus *react.* Each Court decision can then be viewed in a broader context eliminating the polarities of good and bad, right and wrong, liberal and conservative. A focus on understanding the emotional process via the lens of Bowen theory enhances objectivity and ultimately can provide more options to respond to the issues of the day.

REFERENCES

Bowen, M. (1978). *Family therapy in clinical practice*. New Jersey: Jason Aronson.

Cray, Ed. (1997). *Chief justice: A biography of Earl Warren*. New York: Simon & Schuster.

Ferrera, S. J. (1995). Lessons from nature on leadership. In P. Comella et al. (Eds.), *The emotional side of organizations: Applications of Bowen theory* (pp. 200-210). Washington, DC: Georgetown Family Center.

Hendel, S. (1951, 1968). *Charles Evans Hughes and the Supreme Court*. New York: Russell and Russell.

Kerr, M. and Bowen, M. (1988). *Family evaluation*. New York: W.W. Norton and Co.

Renstrom, P. G. (2001). *The Stone Court: Justices, rulings, and legacy*. Santa Barbara, CA: ABC-CLIO.

Robarge, D. (2000). *A chief justice's progress: John Marshall from revolutionary Virginia to the Supreme Court*. Westport, CT, and London: Greenwood Press.

Schwartz, B. (1993). *A history of the Supreme Court*. New York: Oxford University Press.

Severn, B. (1969). *John Marshall: The man who made the court supreme*. New York: David McKay Company, Inc.

Simon, J. F. (2002). *What kind of nation?* New York: Simon & Shuster.

Chapter 21

9/11: Societal Emotional Process and Interlocking Triangles

Carol Moran

You can look at all the parts of a terrible thing until you see that they're assemblies of smaller parts, all of which you can name, and some of which you can heal or alter, and finally the terror that seemed unbearable becomes manageable.

Barbara Kingsolver (2002)

On September 11, 2001, nineteen suicide terrorists took their own lives and the lives of 2,996 U.S. residents in four fiery airplane crashes. Symbolically targeting the World Trade Center and the Pentagon, this small cadre of men, fifteen of them citizens of Saudi Arabia, struck terror in the heart of the largest economic and military power in the world. Stunned by such awesome intentional evil, watching heroes rescue the dying and injured, and weeping with my fellow citizens, I searched for comprehension and a way to safety. Inspired by Barbara Kingsolver, I began to look at the "assemblies of smaller parts" to see if I could name them. I used the concepts of Bowen theory as my theoretical guide. For facts—past as well as ongoing—I scoured historical texts, government documents, foreign affairs journals, first person insider accounts of recent events, and breaking news in the *New York Times* and the *Wall Street Journal*.

Today, four years later, it is evident that the attacks of 9/11 are simply parts—tragic steps—of escalating societal anxiety. The trigger to this anxiety has been, and continues to be, the ongoing depletion of a natural resource intrinsic to the extraordinary emergence of the United States as the economic and military unipolar power in the world. Building over time in its intensity and negativity, this societal anxiety can be tracked, in retrospect, through interlocking national and international relationship triangles, from its relatively benign beginning in the past century, to its 9/11 explosions at the beginning of this century. This socioemotional reality becomes manifest when historical facts are investigated through the lens of two concepts from Bowen theory: *societal emotional process* and *interlocking triangles.*

Increasing societal anxiety poses a danger to every citizen of the world because it leads to a decline in healthy functioning that spreads through the entire relationship network of the vast international community. Mounting societal anxiety particularly poses an exacting strategic challenge to the citizens of the United States, due to the enormous economic and military influence this democratic nation wields. As international war and suicide terrorism refuel each other unabated, and as death tolls rise daily, is citizen fear and stunned vulnerability inevitable? Is it permanent, or can it be informed and transformed? Can the individual citizen behave in a way that calms the frightened nation, contributes strategically to national integrity, and removes the underlying trigger to international violence? Can Bowen theory's concept of *differentiation of self* provide any guidelines to the individual for defining the *citizen self* during confusing and dangerous times?

The answer to this last question is easier than predicting future answers to the previous ones. The answer to the last question is yes. However, before a citizen can participate intentionally and strategically in national and international communities, it is necessary to understand where one is situated—in place, in time, and in society's emotional process.

SOCIETAL EMOTIONAL PROCESS

Evidence of Societal Regression

Bowen theory posits that a well-balanced society provides for optimum functioning of the individual citizen within the society, and of the nation within the broader international community, by making decisions based upon principle. Societal regression occurs in response to chronic anxiety when society repeatedly makes important decisions to allay the anxiety of the moment instead of acting to resolve the underlying problems that are fueling the chronic anxiety. This decline in societal functioning is marked by an increase in four observable behavioral patterns in the society as a whole. Examples of these markers have been in evidence in the wake of the 9/11 attack.

Focus on a Previously Ignored Symptom

As will be described later in this chapter, suicide terrorist attacks against the United States had been occurring far away overseas since 1995 (Pape, 2005). However, the 9/11 suicide attacks occurred on American soil. The ensuing effort to rescue, identify, eulogize, and honorably bury the remains of thousands of dead, as well as to comfort and support their families, was extraordinary. Even as the rubble of the World Trade Center and the Pentagon smoldered, the massive cleanup began. Via television the entire nation was witness and mourner. The federal government reorganized twenty-two agencies, 180,000 people, into the Department for Homeland Security with a single mission, to defend the United States against terrorists (Homeland Security Act, 2002). The nation went to war in Afghanistan.

Simplistic Cause-and-Effect Thinking

The president of the United States identified Osama bin Laden as the "evil one," blamed him alone as the cause of the 9/11 tragedy, and announced that bin Laden's capture "dead or alive" would make the nation safe again (see Woodward, 2002, p. 97).

A Push for Togetherness in Feelings and Thought

The Pew Research Center for the People and the Press reported that public approval for the president rose a sudden 39 percent in a little over a week, from 51 percent on September 5 to 80 percent on September 13, 2001 (Pew Center, 2001). The Project for Excellence in Journalism found that in the three months following 9/11 there was a 12 percent reduction in straight factual reporting, fewer sources of information were consulted in preparing news reports, and less than 10 percent of coverage evaluating national policy offered significant dissent (Kovach and Rosenstiel, 2002).

A Focusing on Rights for Self and Violating the Rights of Others

The USA Patriot Act (2001) changed U.S. law in significant ways. It allowed detainees, including American citizens, to be held indefinitely, unidentified, and without counsel; allowed prisoners of war to be held without the protection of the Geneva Conventions; and allowed government agents to eavesdrop on attorney-client conversations. Under this law military tribunals were set up which, unlike the Uniform Code of Military Justice, did not require a public trial, evidence against the accused, proof beyond a reasonable doubt, the right of the accused to choose counsel, unanimity in death sentencing, or appellate review by civilians confirmed by the Senate.

Disharmony Between the Human and Nature

Bowen theory moves beyond behavioral markers to discern the broader underlying context in which observable social symptoms are embedded. The theory posits that what triggers the sustained anxiety driving societal regression is the society's repeated efforts to "allay the anxiety of the moment" (Bowen, 1978, p. 277) rather than deal realistically with a disharmony that exists between the human and nature. As time goes by, the building chronic anxiety and ongoing disharmony increasingly threaten the survival of the society. From the perspective of Bowen theory, it appears that the extraordinary attacks of 9/11, combined with the dramatic behavioral shifts in the United States subsequent to the attacks, suggest that an enormous issue has been ignored, untended, and unresolved. The quickened pulse rate and airport wariness of the citizenry are now ample evidence of active continuing sustained anxiety.

Eventually, either a society will make the changes that nature requires or the society will not survive. If the society can shift its focus from the symptoms of a regression, and direct its attention and ingenuity toward rebalancing its relationship with nature, then there is the infinitely better possibility that the society will survive.

Bowen theory suggests that one kind of significant imbalance that can occur between the human and nature is "the approaching depletion of raw materials necessary to sustain life" (Bowen 1978, p. 272). A clue as to which raw material might be related to the 9/11 attacks can be found in the relationship between two nations: the nation from which the attackers came, and the nation that they attacked. That raw natural resource is oil. Petroleum export is the major source of income in the Saudi Arabian economy, and the United States is its largest customer. Petroleum import is a major raw resource fueling the U.S. economy, and Saudi Arabia continues to be the United States' most reliable supplier.

A Depleting Natural Resource

Oil is a natural resource that has been essential to the rise of the United States as the largest economic and military power in the world, and oil— cheap, accessible, and in huge amounts—continues to be an energy source that is inextricably woven into the structure and fabric of the nation's daily life (Brooks and Wohlforth, 2002; Mandelbaum, 2002; Yergin, 1991). Cur-

rently in the United States, approximately two-thirds of the nation's oil supply fuels cars, trucks, and airplanes (Appenzeller, 2004). Food, the fertilizers,
herbicides, and pesticides we use to grow plants, synthetic fabrics in our
wardrobes, the plastics in almost everything we touch, and the pharmaceu-
ticals that we use to medicate ourselves, all have, or utilize in their manufac-
ture, raw materials that come ultimately from fossil fuel (Manning, 2004).

The United States was the first country in the modern world to develop a
large-scale petroleum industry (Klare, 2004). From 1860 through World War
II, when the United States was able to extract enough oil from domestic
fields to satisfy the enormous requirements of its own and allied forces, the
United States was the world's leading oil producer. Actually, until the 1940s,
oil availability was primarily a domestic policy matter, as the United States
possessed adequate untapped supplies to meet the country's basic needs.

However, near the end of World War II, it was apparent that the United
States would eventually begin to exhaust its own petroleum reserves, and
would become dependent upon large amounts of imported oil both to com-
pensate for the decline in domestic output, and to satisfy the new demands
of a booming economy. U.S. Department of Energy documents indicate
that in 1972, U.S. oil production "began an irreversible decline," and in
1998, American dependence on imported petroleum "crossed the 50 percent mark" (Klare, 2004, pp. 10, 13). Thus, oil became a foreign policy
issue, with the federal government assuming a direct role in the pursuit of
imported oil, as well as in that foreign oil's protected transit to American
shores.

The U.S. Department of Energy predicts that in twenty years the United
States will be importing nearly 70 percent of the oil it uses (Klare, 2004).
From where can this oil come? As of 2002, 64 percent of the world's remaining proven oil reserves were located in the Persian Gulf countries: Saudi
Arabia, 25 percent; Iraq, 10.7 percent; the United Arab Emirates, 9.3 percent; Kuwait, 9.2 percent; Iran, 8.6 percent; and Qatar, 1.5 percent. Herein
lies a challenge. Some years ago, when examining the availability of natural
resources such as water, minerals, timber, and oil, Klare (2002) coined the
term "resource wars" to describe conflicts which arise during a nation's
pursuit or possession of critical natural resources. He warned that:

> However divided two states . . . may be over matters of politics or reli-
> gion, the likelihood of their engaging in mutual combat becomes con-
> siderably greater when one side believes that its essential supply of
> water, food, or energy is threatened by the other. (p. 25)

In summary, Bowen theory identifies four types of social behavior that indicate increasing chronic societal anxiety when a society repeatedly makes important decisions aimed at temporary anxiety relief, rather that principled problem resolution. Those distinguishing characteristics, vividly obvious in the United States following the 9/11 terrorist attacks, are focused on a previously ignored symptom; simplistic, cause-and-effect thinking; a push for togetherness in feelings and thought; and focusing on rights for self while violating the rights of others. These behavioral markers intensify over time when there is an ongoing and significant imbalance between the human and nature. The looming and continuing depletion of earth's oil, a resource essential to America's economy, technological growth, and military might, has been for decades a problem foreseen, but unsolved.

With Klare's warning about resource wars echoing in our minds, let us move to another concept of Bowen theory, namely, *interlocking triangles*.

INTERLOCKING TRIANGLES

Description of Triangles and Interlocking Triangles

Bowen theory (1978) defines the triangle as a three-person configuration that is the basic building block of any human relationship system, whether that system is a family, a group, or a society. In larger human systems, many individuals, or groups of individuals, may aggregate at one or more of the three points of the triangle. A two person—or two group, or two society— relationship will remain a stable twosome until a threat, or perceived threat, to one or both members triggers an increase in anxiety that overtaxes the coping skills of the twosome to manage anxiety within the twosome. At that point, the twosome will involve another person, group, or society that is vulnerable to the draw of the twosome, and thus a triangle is established. The triangle stabilizes the original two-person system by opening an additional channel into which anxiety can be shifted. Tension can then move among the three members of the triangle. The original twosome, now carrying a lighter load of anxiety, will stabilize and experience less urgency to resolve the issue that originally triggered their anxiety.

As the original threat remains unsolved and additional anxiety builds in the triangle, one of the involved twosomes will triangle in a fourth member. Thus, a series of interlocking triangles is initiated that will siphon the anxiety farther away from the twosome where the original anxiety-provoking challenge began. Emotional tension will continue to build in the network as the anxiety triggering issue in the original twosome continues unresolved.

This tension will move from one active triangle to another and another, circuiting through the larger system until it settles into the most vulnerable point in the network of interlocking triangles in the relationship system. The member of the emotional system at this point, unable to solve a problem that is in the domain of the original twosome, will absorb the heaviest brunt of the anxiety and will be damaged or destroyed. All of these emotion driven relationship dynamics—triangles and interlocking triangles—occur automatically, and for the most part, outside of the awareness of the members of the relationship system.

Viewing the 9/11 attacks through the lens of Bowen theory, we have identified societal behaviors indicating that a societal regression is occurring in the United States. Also, it appears that there is a critical imbalance between current human behavior and the approaching depletion of an energy source, oil, which is essential to the economies of both Saudi Arabia and the United States. If this is accurate, then the next emotional dynamic that should be detectable in the presence of mounting anxiety over this unresolved imbalance is the presence of triangles and interlocking triangles.

Triangle Number One

The first triangle that is identifiable started as a twosome within the United States. At one point in this twosome is the American population that elects its political leaders, and purchases petroleum-based products. At the other point of this twosome are two groups: the government, which ensures the availability and safety of the oil that is supplied to the population; and the petroleum industry, which supplies oil to the population. Let us examine briefly how the population at one point in this twosome interacts with the government and with the oil industry, both of which are at the other point.

The Population–Government Relationship

In the United States, a democracy, the citizens choose each administration with votes, pay for government activities with taxes, and fill the armed services with its young men and women. In return, during its term in office, each elected administration is responsible for promoting the general welfare and providing for the common defense. If the population does not approve of the direction a particular administration is taking, the citizens vote it out of office. As a form of leader selection, the purpose of a democracy is to guarantee that the leadership of the country reflects and acts upon the choices of the citizens. Voters and nonvoters, smart voters and not-so-smart voters, reasonable voters and hysterical voters—all participate in the choice. As such, the conduct of the elected leadership in a democracy is both a consequence and a measure of the functioning of the nation as a whole.

In relation to oil, national security policy in the United States has been defined repeatedly as ensuring U.S. access to large amounts of cheap oil safely delivered to American shores, in order to keep the American economy booming and the armed forces able to enforce American national interests anywhere in the world (Klare, 2004; Yergin, 1991).

The Population–Oil Industry Relationship

The population supports the oil industry by purchasing fuel and petroleum-based products, and by investing as stockholders in the many companies connected to the petroleum industry. In return, the oil industry searches for, invests in, extracts, conveys, refines, researches, manufactures, markets, distributes, and delivers oil and its thousands of products to the American population. Capitalism, the economic system in the United States, insures a close and reciprocal relationship between the American oil industry on one hand, and the industry's stock and product purchasers on the other hand. In this regard, the activities of a capitalistic economy reflect the choices of the community it serves, and are both a consequence and a measure of the functioning of that community.

The Government–Oil Industry Triangles
in the Saudi Arabian Monarchy

As we saw earlier, there came a time when the U.S. government and the American oil industry were unable to supply their nation's energy demands with available American oil. At this point, the national oil supply process shifted from being a domestic policy issue to being a foreign policy issue. In 1945, the United States needed additional oil facilities to adequately supply forces fighting in World War II. At the same time, security was a serious concern of the king of Saudi Arabia. President Franklin Roosevelt invited King Abd al-Aziz to meet him aboard the USS *Quincy,* docked in the Suez Canal where the two leaders made a secret oil-for-security pact. The king promised the president that the U.S. oil industry would have continuing access to Saudi oil. In exchange, the U.S. president agreed to provide military assistance and training to Saudi Arabia and to build the Dhahran military base in Saudi Arabia (Klare, 2004; Yergin, 1991). Figure 21.1 illustrates the U.S. government oil industry implementation of a secret pact with the Saudi Arabian monarchy.

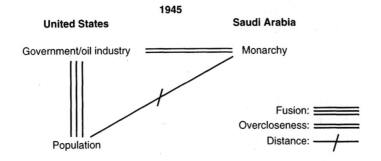

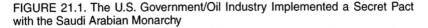

FIGURE 21.1. The U.S. Government/Oil Industry Implemented a Secret Pact with the Saudi Arabian Monarchy

Thus, when the original twosome, the population and the government/oil industry, was unable to manage the growing discrepancy between the nation's rising demand for cheap energy and the available reserves of American oil, the U.S. government/oil industry involved a third entity, the Saudi Arabian monarchy, in a triangle. A previous economic exchange, cash-for-oil, influenced by the urgency of World War II, became a military exchange, arms-for-oil. The new supply of oil was insured at a price that would eventually imperil all three members of the triangle: the U.S. population, the U.S. government/oil industry, and the Saudi Arabian monarchy.

Since 1945, relationships between Saudi leaders and American leaders in government and commerce have become numerous, multifaceted, complex and, often, secret. During the years since that secret precedent-setting meeting on the USS *Quincy,* all six Saudi kings have negotiated with the United States. Every American administration since then, whether Republican or Democratic, has done whatever was necessary to ensure that there was enough foreign oil to satisfy American economic and military agendas. The U.S. government has repeatedly proclaimed access to Saudi Arabian oil to be a national security issue; has sent ever-increasing numbers of the newest and most sophisticated weapons, accompanied by military advisors and technicians, to Saudi Arabia; has constructed the headquarters of the Saudi National Guard, the official protectors of the monarchy itself; and has provided training and equipment for the Saudi National Guard, the Saudi Army, the Saudi Navy, and the Saudi Air Force (Klare, 2004). Simultaneously, U.S. companies have pumped and purchased hundreds of billions of dollars of Saudi oil at low prices; members of the Saudi royal family have invested hundreds of billions of petrodollars in U.S. equities; and a complex and enormously influential network of investment banking, arms, construction and oil companies, political, governmental and personal relationships have been woven together among leaders in both countries (Phillips, 2004; Unger, 2004).

Eventually, though, as American oil dependence increased, conflict erupted and the United States used the threat of invasion to coerce the Saudi monarchy to supply oil (Yergin, 1992; Klare, 2004). In the early 1970s, in the face of rapidly rising national and international demands for oil, as oil extraction from American fields began its irreversible decline and the phrase "energy crisis" entered American political discourse, the Organization of Petroleum Exporting Countries (OPEC) demanded higher prices for the oil being extracted from the Persian Gulf. Oil price negotiations were stalemated. Then the 1973 Arab-Israeli War broke out. When the United States sent supplies to Israel, OPEC used its "oil weapon." It embargoed oil to the United States. With available supplies for the Vietnam War declining, the Nixon Administration threatened the Saudi monarch that the United States would send American forces to Saudi Arabia to ensure that Saudi oil supplies to the United States would not be interrupted. Saudi Arabia secretly sent oil to the U.S. Navy until the OPEC embargo ended in 1974. Thus, as American anxiety increased concerning declining domestic oil reserves, the alliance between the U.S. government/oil industry and the Saudi monarchy became more intense, negative, and coercive. Figure 21.2 illustrates the relationship between the U.S. government and the U.S. oil industry in the inside position of the triangle and the Saudi Arabian monarchy in the outside position.

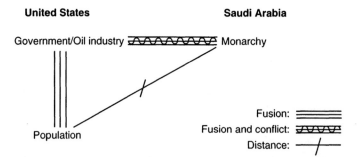

FIGURE 21.2. The Relationship Between the U.S. Government/Oil Industry and the Saudi Arabian Monarchy Became Coercive

Over sixty years ago, the U.S. government/oil industry coalition chose to fill the energy demands of the American people by establishing a quid pro quo arrangement with the Saudi monarchy—first, cash-for-oil, then guns-for-oil. The dependency of the United States upon Persian Gulf countries intensified and the relationship became conflictual during the 1970s. The U.S. domestic oil extraction began its inevitable decline, OPEC raised the price of oil and embargoed oil to the United States, and the U.S. government coerced the Saudi monarchy to provide oil secretly. Thus the first triangle stabilized.

Triangle Number Two

The second triangle that can be identified started as a twosome in Saudi Arabia. At one point of this twosome is the House of Saud, the king and princes of the Saudi Arabian monarchy. At the other point is the population, the subjects of the kingdom. Let us examine briefly the relationship between the monarchy and the population.

The Monarchy-Population Relationship

In 1922, after over two centuries of tribal power struggles, the House of Saud consolidated Arab lands under its rule. In 1926, the head of the Saudi dynasty was proclaimed king and keeper of the Muslim holy places in the cities of Mecca and Medina, and in 1932, the name of the country was changed from the "Kingdom of the Hejaz and Nejd and Its Dependencies" to Saudi Arabia (Yergin, 1991, p. 286). The discovery of oil in Saudi Arabia in 1938 made possible two socioeconomic processes (see Figure 21.3). First, extraction of large quantities of oil to meet the voracious energy needs of the world allowed the Saudi monarchy to guarantee a job and income to every Saudi citizen. This abundance kept the population from seeking a more representative government, even as the economic gulf between the royal family and the average family widened exponentially. Second, since the seventeenth century, the House of Saud had espoused a strict form of Sunni Islam called Wahabism. Oil fortunes provided the monarchy with the means to contribute richly to charities and schools run by the Wahabis (Friedman, 2002a).

Eventually, though, tension between the Saudi monarchy and the Saudi population developed. Beginning in 1980, Saudi Arabia's population exploded from 7 million to 19 million; simultaneously, the per-capita oil income fell from $19,000 in 1981 to about $7,300 in 2002 (Friedman, 2002b). At the same time, citizens, schooled in the Wahabi tradition to be anti-modern and anti-Western, objected to the expanding presence of American troops,

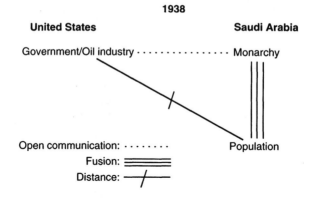

FIGURE 21.3. The U.S. Government/Oil Industry Had a Cash-for-Oil Relationship with the Saudi Arabian Monarchy

military installations, and cultural influence in the Saudi homeland, a result of the decades old guns-for-oil pact entered into by the House of Saud. Dissatisfaction with the monarchy and its partners, the Western occupiers, escalated to fury as the rapidly increasing number of young, jobless males, trained in strict Wahabi values, entered adulthood (Huntington, 1997).

Some of these young men saw religious legitimacy in suicide terrorist attacks. They wanted to overthrow the "apostate regime" of the Saudi monarchy and return Muslims to a radically conservative version of seventh-century Islam (Danner, 2005). However, beyond the monarchy, the "near enemy," these men also saw the "far enemy" (Danner, 2005, p. 48), the American superpower that supported the Saudi monarchy both financially and militarily. The imbalance of power between the radical Saudis and the superpower United States led to the reemergence of a centuries old tactic of the less powerful combatant, the suicide terrorist attack, a highly lethal technique in which the attackers expect to use their own deaths to kill a maximum number of people (Pape, 2005). By piercing the protective security of a more powerful enemy, the suicide terrorist aims to attract more comrades from the homeland to the radical cause by dramatically demonstrating the vulnerability of a previously invincible enemy. Since the 1980s, the strategic goal of modern suicide terrorism has been "to compel modern democracies to withdraw military forces from territory that the terrorists consider to be their homeland" (Pape, 2005, p. 4).

The Monarchy-Terrorists Relationship Triangles in the U.S. Government/Oil Industry

In 1990, when Iraq invaded Kuwait and threatened to invade Saudi Arabia, the Saudi king and the U.S. government agreed that the United States would defend Saudi Arabia. American troops, 500,000, were sent to Saudi Arabia and nearby countries to stop Iraq. However, following the Gulf War defeat of Iraq, and contrary to the U.S. government promise made prior to the war, the U.S. military remained on Saudi soil. Muslim clerics, reform-minded Saudi citizens, and citizens seeking abolition of the monarchy were angered that the Saudi monarchy tolerated the presence of so many American infidel soldiers occupying their country (Klare, 2004; Yergin, 1991).

A series of suicide terrorist attacks began against the United States: in 1995, at the Saudi National Guard Training Center in Riyadh, Saudi Arabia; in 1996, at a U.S. military base in Dhahran, Saudi Arabia; in 1998, at the American embassies in Nairobi, Kenya, and in Dar es Salaam, Tanzania; in 2000, at the USS *Cole* berthed in Aden, Yemen. Nevertheless, a large contingent of U.S. soldiers remained in Saudi Arabia. Thus, the second triangle stabilized: the U.S. government/oil industry and the House of Saud were deeply allied through complex financial and military relationships, while suicide terrorists from the Saudi population were defying the monarchy and attacking the U.S. government/oil industry. Figure 21.4 illustrates the U.S. government–Saudi Arabia–terrorist triangle.

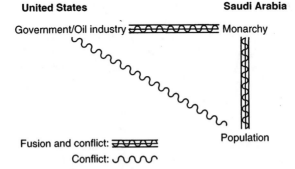

FIGURE 21.4. Some Saudi Arabian Citizens, Conflicting with the Saudi Arabian Monarchy, Attacked the Partner of the Monarchy

In summary, during the early half of the twentieth century, the discovery of oil in Saudi Arabia helped the House of Saud solidify its position as the ruling tribe in the unified Arab lands under its rule. Then, during the last two decades of the twentieth century, important shifts occurred. The Saudi Arabian population expanded rapidly while per-capita income dropped proportionately; the U.S. military increased and lengthened its presence on Saudi soil; and, politically and religiously radical Saudi citizens sought to overthrow the monarchy and expel the United States from their homeland. The complex of interdependent relationships between the House of Saud and the U.S. government/oil industry held tight as the anger of the suicide terrorists escalated into deadly attacks against the monarchy's superpower partner, the U.S. government/oil industry, both in Saudi Arabia and beyond Saudi borders.

Triangle Number Three

In fiery balls of sudden smoke and vivid collapse, the third triangle flew into the heart of a naïve and unprepared American population (Posner, 2003). After a half century of mounting chronic anxiety circuiting through newly forming interlocking triangles, this last triangle boomeranged back to the United States, striking the population as well as the government/oil industry complex.

The Terrorists Triangle in the Population of the United States

As mentioned previously, throughout the last decade of the twentieth century, the governance of the House of Saud, particularly its distribution of the immense wealth being extracted from Saudi soil, its position on civil and religious rights, and its national security decisions, fostered smoldering antagonism in some Saudi citizens against the ruling house and its powerful American ally (Birdsall and Subramanian, 2004; Doran, 1990, 2002; Lewis, 2002). Simultaneously, anti-American sentiment developed in other Persian Gulf countries where citizens were angered by U.S. support of despotic regimes (Ajami, 2001; Klare, 2004; Pape, 2005). Osama bin Laden, a citizen of Saudi Arabia until he was branded a terrorist and his citizenship was revoked by the Saudi monarchy in 1994 (9/11 Commission Report), was the leader of a terrorist group called Al Qaeda. Evoking seventh-century Crusader-Muslim wars, bin Laden exhorted suicide terrorists to become soldiers in a new holy war against Western, Judeo-Christian infidel occupiers of sacred Islamic lands, especially in Saudi Arabia (Gerecht, 2002). As Osama bin Laden's terrorists moved their attacks against the United States in Saudi Arabia, to American outposts in other parts of the world, and eventually to the United States itself, others joined his call to Jihad. Thus, the United States—government, oil industry and citizens—was triangled into the turmoil brewing in Saudi Arabia in a new way.

On September 11, 2001, suicide terrorists moved onto American soil, destroying the World Trade Center in New York, breaching the outer ring of the Pentagon in Washington, and crashing a plane into a field in Pennsylvania. In addition to the suicide terrorists themselves, 3,262 people died in the six attacks between 1995 and 2001 (Pape, 2005). The American population became aware that it was involved in a terribly dangerous situation. Thus the third triangle stabilized: the U.S. government/oil industry, the suicide terrorists, and the U.S. population. Figure 21.5 illustrates this triangle.

In the original twosome cited in this chapter, the U.S. population was at one point, and the U.S. government/oil industry was at the opposite point. How the population negotiated with the government/oil industry regarding management of energy requirements, sources, and supplies directly affected how the government/oil industry in the United States related to the monarchy in Saudi Arabia. This occurred as part of the normal shifting of anxiety among the three points of the triangle: the U.S. population, the U.S. government/oil industry, and the Saudi monarchy. Then, through its close military and economic alliance with the Saudi monarchy, the U.S. government/oil industry, the "far enemy," became a target of terrorists rebelling against the military, economic, and religious decisions of the Saudi Arabian monarchy, the terrorists' "near enemy." This endangerment was also due to the predictable shifts of anxiety among the members of a triangle, in this case the second

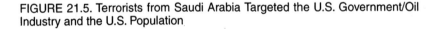

9/11/2001

United States   **Saudi Arabia**

Government/Oil industry

Fusion: ═══

Conflict: ∿∿∿

Population ∿∿∿∿∿∿∿∿∿ Population

FIGURE 21.5. Terrorists from Saudi Arabia Targeted the U.S. Government/Oil Industry and the U.S. Population

triangle described in this chapter: the Saudi monarchy, the Saudi terrorists, and the U.S. government/oil industry. As the suicide terrorists moved their attack from Saudi Arabian land, to offshore territories and installations of the United States, the alliance between the U.S. government/oil industry and the House of Saud remained tight. It was then that the suicide terrorists expanded their focus toward the continental United States and its population. Thus the third interlocking triangle was formed: the suicide terrorists, the U.S. government/oil industry, and the U.S. population. Figure 21.6 illustrates this interlocking process.

THE CITIZEN SELF

Klare (2004) identifies the bind the United States is in, due to our inability to balance independently our energy demands and our access to energy, when he writes, "Oil makes this country strong; dependency makes us weak" (p. 11). He points to the United States' vulnerability to oil supply disruptions abroad; the massive shift of economic resources and weaponry from the United States to our foreign suppliers, whether we like their policies or not; the violent hostility of political and religious factions that resent the U.S. military occupation of their homeland; and, our entanglement in overseas oil wars.

Bowen predicted that a regression will end when the chronic anxiety caused by the symptoms of disharmony is worse than the anxiety associated with making the necessary changes required to live in harmony with nature,

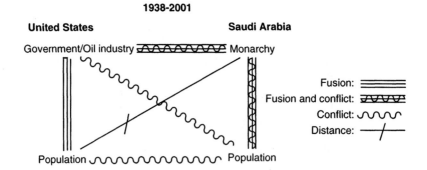

FIGURE 21.6. Increasing Anxiety Circuited Through Interlocking Societal Triangles

when it becomes harder to ignore a problem than solve it. He wrote (Bowen, 1978) that the human can "modify his future course if he can gain some control over his reaction to anxiety and his 'instinctual' emotional reactiveness, and begin taking constructive action based on his fund of knowledge and on logical thinking" (p. 281).

To pull back from the brink of the mutual destruction that America is involved in with countries rich in oil, Klare (2004) calls for a return to national autonomy and integrity. He defines autonomy as "the self-reliance and freedom of action to extricate ourselves from the pernicious effects of petroleum dependency" (p. 186). He describes integrity as making personal and national decisions on energy policy that stop our collusion in despotism and denial of human rights, and do not leave an unconscionable burden on the shoulders of our grandchildren. He believes that a national energy strategy of autonomy and integrity would require three steps:

- Divorce energy purchases from overseas security commitments.
- Reduce reliance on imported oil.
- Prepare now for the inevitable transition to a postpetroleum economy.

So how does one define one's self as a citizen in relation to problems on a scale as large as the one we have been looking at in this chapter? I think we just take a deep breath, relax, and once again ask ourselves these familiar questions:

- How does the emotional system operate?
- Where am I in the emotional system?
- What do I do that keeps the system operating as it does?
- What is my vision for how the emotional system could become healthier?
- How might I change myself so that my part of the emotional system will become healthier?

We started with a quote from Barbara Kingsolver (2002), and we will end with one from the same source.

> We've been delivered huge blows but also huge opportunities . . . depending on where we look for honor and how we name our enemies. The easiest thing is to think of returning the blows. But there are other things we must think about as well, other dangers we face. A careless way of sauntering across the earth and breaking open its treasuries, a

terrible dependency on sucking out the world's best juices for our-selves—these may also be our enemies. The changes we dread most may contain our salvation.

REFERENCES

Ajami, F. (2001). The sentry's solitude. *Foreign Affairs, 80*(6), 2-16.

Appenzeller, T. (2004). The end of cheap oil. *National Geographic,* June, 81-109.

Birdsall, N. and Subramanian, A. (2004). Saving Iraq from its oil. *Foreign Affairs, 83*(4), 77-89.

Bowen, M. (1978). *Family therapy in clinical practice.* New York: Jason Aronson, Inc.

Brooks, S. and Wohlforth, W. (2002). American primacy in perspective. *Foreign Affairs, 81*(4), 20-33.

Danner, M. (2005). Taking stock of the forever war. *The New York Times Magazine,* September 11, 44-87.

Doran, M. (1990). The roots of Muslim Rage. Available at: theatlantic.com/issues/90sep/rage.htm.

Doran, M. (2002). Somebody else's civil war. *Foreign Affairs, 81*(1), 22-42.

Friedman, T. (2002a). Drowning in oil. *The New York Times,* Op-Ed, August 25.

Friedman, T. (2002b). The Saudi challenge. In *Longitudes and attitudes: Exploring the world after September 11.* New York: Farrar, Straus and Giroux.

Gerecht, R. (2002). The gospel according to Osama bin Laden. *The Atlantic Monthly,* January, 46-48.

Homeland Security Act of 2002. Available at: www.dhs.gov.

Huntington, S. (1997). *The clash of civilizations: Remaking of world order.* New York: Simon and Schuster.

Kingsolver, B. (2002). *Small wonder.* New York: Harper Collins Publishers.

Klare, M. (2002). *Resource wars: The new landscape of global conflict.* New York: Henry Holt and Company.

Klare, M. (2004). *Blood and oil: The dangers and consequences of America's grow-ing dependency on imported petroleum.* New York: Henry Holt and Company.

Kovach, B. and Rosenstiel, T. (2002). In wartime, the people want the facts. *New York Times,* January 29.

Lewis, B. (2002). What went wrong? *The Atlantic Monthly,* January, 43-45.

Mandelbaum, M. (2002). The inadequacy of American power. *Foreign Affairs, 81*(5), 61-73.

Manning, R. (2004). The oil we eat. *Harper's Magazine,* February, 37-45.

Pape, R. (2005). *Dying to win: Strategic logic of suicide terrorism.* New York: Random House.

Pew Research Center for the People and the Press. (2001). "Do you approve or disapprove of the way George W. Bush is handling his job as president?" September 5 to September 13. Available at: www.pollingreport.com.

Phillips, K. (2004). *American dynasty: Aristocracy, fortune, and the politics of deceit in the house of Bush.* New York: Viking Penguin Group.

Posner, G. (2003). *Why America slept: The failure to prevent 9/11.* New York: Random House.

Unger, C. (2004). *House of Bush, House of Saud: The secret relationship between the world's two most powerful dynasties.* New York: Scribner.

USA Patriot Act of 2001. Available at: www.gpoaccess.gov.

Woodward, B. (2002). *Bush at war.* New York: Simon and Schuster.

Yergin, D. (1991). *The prize: The epic quest for oil, money and power.* New York: Free Press.

Appendix

A Key for the Family Diagram and Emotional Process Symbols

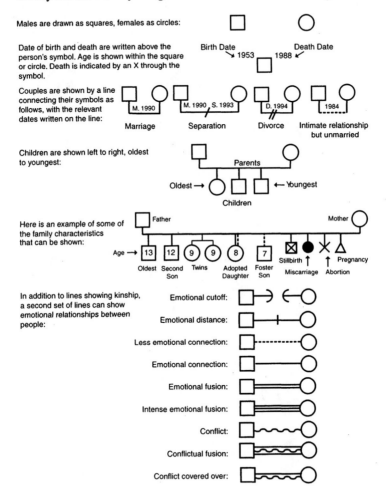

Males are drawn as squares, females as circles:

Date of birth and death are written above the person's symbol. Age is shown within the square or circle. Death is indicated by an X through the symbol.

Birth Date ↘ 1953   Death Date 1988 ↙

Couples are shown by a line connecting their symbols as follows, with the relevant dates written on the line:

M. 1990 — Marriage

M. 1990 / S. 1993 — Separation

D. 1994 — Divorce

1984 — Intimate relationship but unmarried

Children are shown left to right, oldest to youngest:

Parents

Oldest → ← Youngest

Children

Here is an example of some of the family characteristics that can be shown:

Father   Mother

Age → 13 12 9 9 8 7 Stillbirth ↑ ● Miscarriage ↑ X Abortion ↑ △ Pregnancy

Oldest Second Son Twins Adopted Daughter Foster Son

In addition to lines showing kinship, a second set of lines can show emotional relationships between people:

Emotional cutoff:

Emotional distance:

Less emotional connection:

Emotional connection:

Emotional fusion:

Intense emotional fusion:

Conflict:

Conflictual fusion:

Conflict covered over:

523

Index

Page numbers followed by the letter "f" indicate figures.

Abortion issue, 472
Absorber, 29
Academy triangles
  faculty and administrative
    relationships, 412-414
  anxiety in the system, 414
  committee decision, 412-413
  competition for funds, 412
  representative committee
    formation, 413-414
  merit pay, 405, 415
  overview, 403-404, 415-417
  promotions, 405
  senate, 412
  setting, 404-405
  student-faculty relationship, 405-412
  accountability for assignments,
    407-408, 410
  agreement on issues, 405-407
  instructor evaluations, 408-409,
    410-412
  support staff, 414-415
  tenure, 405
Acepromazine, 231
Acute anxiety
  adaptability, 480-481
  defined, 21, 361, 480
Adams, John
  education issues, 455
  federal judge appointments, 486
  presidential politics, 468, 487
  Supreme Court appointment of
    Marshall, 485
  three-fifths compromise, 467

Adams *(continued)*
  U.S. Constitution development, 461
  war for independence, 456
Adams, John Quincy, 487
Adaptive mechanisms of emotional
  triangles, 130
Affair. *See* Extramarital affair
Afghanistan, war in, 505
Agricultural Adjustment Act of 1936,
  493
Alcohol
  abuse, 315. *See also* Substance
    abuse
  in Smith family history, 133, 134-135
  as third person in a triangle, 24, 315
Alliluyeva, Nadezhda, 439-440
Alpha
  in canine hierarchy, 227-229, 234,
    237
  chimpanzee males, 334-335
  family business leadership
    evolution, 359
Ambler, Jacquelin, 485
Ambler, Mary Polly, 485
Amitriptyline, 226-227, 231, 232
Amoebae, 68-69
Amplifier, anxiety, 29, 232
Anger, coordinated anxiety or anger, 70
Animals
  amoebae, 68-69
  bird polygynous behavior, 335
  canines, 221
  cat, in LaForte family triangle, 208,
    208f

Animals *(continued)*
    chickens, 235
    chimpanzee. *See* Chimpanzee
    dogs, 221
    dolphins, 68
    klipspringer, 245
    pack behavior. *See* Pack behavior
    polygamy, 245
    primates, 18, 363
    reproductive units, 69-70
    rhesus monkey, 100
    squirrel monkey, 235
    triangles in other species, 66-69
    vervets. *See* Vervet monkey
    wolves, 221
Anonymous Paper, 85-88
Anxiety
    acute. *See* Acute anxiety
    amplifier, 29, 232
    calming, in pack behavior,
        237-238
    in child-focused families,
        265-266
    chronic. *See* Chronic anxiety
    coordinated anxiety or anger, 70
    dampener, 29, 232
    differentiation of self and, 34-36
    Family Anxiety Scale, 191-192,
        192f
    generator, 29, 232
    LaForte family, 198, 199
    reduction of, 29-30
    separation anxiety, 226
    shifting to third person, 74
    stress reactivity, 74-75
    triggers, 75
Aronson, Gerald, 4
Arthur Marshall Distinguished
        Alumnus Award, 6
Articles of Confederation, 458-459,
        467
Attachment
    unresolved, and marital triangles,
        248-251
    unresolved emotional attachment,
        333, 346, 349
Attitude of neutrality and detriangling,
        42-43
Attucks, Crispus, 458

Back-door triangle, 54
Bacteria
    Escherichia coli, 69
    function in multicellular units,
        69-70
Baker, Katharine Gratwick, 421
Baker v. Carr, 500
Basic self, defined, 35
Basmania, Betty, 9
Beal, Edward W., 451
Berenson, 32
Beta, in canine hierarchy, 228, 237
bin Laden, Osama, 505
Biology
    differentiation, 66-67
    evolution of, 34
    evolutionary foundation, 18-19
    natural systems theory, 11
Bird polygynous behavior, 335
Birth of children and couple's
        togetherness, 178
Blacks in U.S. history
    desegregation, 499-501
    governing of, 457-458, 465-467
    three-fifths compromise. *See* Three-
        fifths compromise
Bolsheviks
    background, 440-441
    Central Committee, 442
    consolidation of power, 441-442
    founding of, 431
    government structure, 442
    joining of Trotsky, 435-436
    leadership triangle, 422
    the Party, 442
    Politburo, 442, 443, 445
    Political Bureau, 442
    revolution. *See* Russian Revolution
Bowen family
    background of study, 109-110
    business. *See* Luff-Bowen, Inc.
    business reorganization, triangle
        two, 114-115, 115f
    death of family member, triangle
        four, 116-117, 117f
    detriangling during 1954-1966,
        119-120
    detriangling during 1966-1967,
        120-128

Bowen family *(continued)*
  family distancing, triangle six,
    118-119, 119f
  health issues, triangle three,
    115-116, 116f
  history of triangles, 110-111, 111f
  interlocking triangles, triangle five,
    117-118, 118f
  low stress, triangle one, 112-114,
    112f-114f
  overview, 109-110, 128
Brain, prefrontal cortex for self-
    regulation, 130
Bregman, Ona Cohn, 403
British Common Law Tradition, 455
Bronshtein, Lev Davidovich, 432. *See
    also* Trotsky
Brooks, Preston, 452
*Brown v. Board of Education of
    Topeka,* 499
Bryan, D. C., 235
Bukharin, Nikolai, 447
Burke, T., 335
Burr, Aaron, 487-488
Burwell, Rebecca, 485
Bush v. Gore, 463
Business. *See* Family business

cAMP (cyclic adenosine
    monophosphate), 68-69
Candleland, D. K., 235
Canines, 221. *See also* Pack behavior
Case examples
  children after divorce and
    remarriage, 304-307, 305f
  chronic illness. *See* Illness, triangles
    at time of
  contact after divorce, 307-308, 307f
  death. *See* Death, triangles at time of
  death of leader, 304-307, 305f
  differentiation of self, 80-85, 82f
  extramarital affairs, 339-353, 341f,
    344f, 348f, 351f
  interdependency, 343-346, 344f
  marital triangles, 259-263, 260f
  stepfamily interlocking triangles,
    300-302, 301f

Case examples *(continued)*
  stepfamily triangles after death,
    302-304, 302f
  swimming incident, 80-85, 82f
  teenage rebel, 316-320, 317f-319f
  unresolved emotional fusion,
    339-343, 341f, 349-352, 351f
Cat, in LaForte family triangle, 208, 208f
Cauley, Kathleen Cotter, 291
Cauley family diagram, 293f
Cause and effect
  human behavior research, 335
  results of relationships, 337
  September 11, 2001, terrorist
    attacks, 505
Cellular slime mold, 68-69
Change-back messages
  differentiation of self, 78
  hidden triangle threats, 65
  triangle hypothesis and, 77
Chase, Samuel, 463, 464, 487
Chickens, social relationships, 235
Child focus
  beginning of problems, 266-268
  consultation with Bowen theory,
    268-269
    distance in the marriage clinical
      report, 282-289, 283f-289f
    divided loyalties clinical report,
      273-275, 274f, 276f
    fatherless child clinical report,
      280-282, 282f
  decreasing tension, 274, 274f
  described, 265
  distance in the marriage clinical
    report, 282-289, 283f-289f
  divided loyalties clinical report,
    269-275, 270f-274f, 276f
  fatherless child clinical report,
    276-282, 277f-280f, 282f
  overview, 265-268, 289
  process diagram key, 269f
  projection on the child, 314, 315f
Children
  after divorce and remarriage,
    304-307, 305f
  birth of children and couple's
    togetherness, 178
  child focus. *See* Child focus

Children *(continued)*
dysfunctions, 245-246
man of the house after father's
death, 176-177, 179-180
marital triangles, 251-253
Chimpanzee
biological foundation of emotional
systems, 18
Chimpanzee Politics, 381
mating rights, 334-335
triangular emotional process, 363
Chimpanzee Politics, 381
Chronic anxiety
adaptability, 481
as cause of extramarital affair,
342-343, 346, 352
defined, 21, 35, 342, 361, 480
differentiation of self and, 266
manifestation of, 195-196
regression and, 481-482
from unresolved emotional
attachment, 333
Chronic illness. *See* Illness, triangles at
time of
Civil War, 472-473
Clifford, Thomas, 456
Clinical reports
consultation with Bowen theory
distance in the marriage clinical
report, 282-289, 283f-289f
divided loyalties clinical report,
273-275, 274f, 276f
fatherless child clinical report,
280-282, 282f
distance in the marriage, 282-289,
283f-289f
divided loyalties, 269-275, 276f,
277f-280f
fatherless child, 276-282, 277f-280f,
282f
overview, 289
Clinton, George, 487
Closed emotional system
characteristics, 32
open system vs., 33
triangles and communication, 169
Coach
attitude of neutrality, 43
defined, 44

Coach *(continued)*
defining an I-Position, 47
detriangling, 44, 46-48
detriangling of marital triangles,
56-58
differentiation of self case example,
80-85, 82f
functions of, 44-45, 46-47
role in coping with extramarital
affairs, 353
teaching how family systems
operate, 47
Coercive triangle, 64, 76
Collection of individuals vs. group, 482
Community and marital triangles,
254-255
Company triangles
account manager, 393-395
backlog in record processing,
391-393
CIO, HIM director and HIM
consultant, 397-401
company background, 388-389
consulting and staffing business
model, 390
detriangling, 394-395, 398
distance managing, 394
executive team restructuring,
389-390
land mines, 396-397, 400-401
office politics, 387
organizational change, 389-390
overview, 387-388, 401-402
process consultants, 395-396
systems thinking, 390-391, 394
systems-based consulting, 395-401
systems-based relationship
management, 391-395
temporary workers, 391-393
unhappy consultant and client,
393-395
Complementarity, sibling position
functioning, 39
Concept of triangles
misunderstandings, 18-19
relationship to other Bowen
concepts, 33-41
Confrontation, error of, 86-87
Congress, 459, 462, 463

Constitution. *See* U.S. Constitution
Consultants. *See* Company triangles
Coordinated anxiety or anger, 70
Core competency, 390-391
Cost-benefit analysis of vervet
    monkeys, 95, 99
Countertransference, 4, 42
Court cases
    Baker v. Carr, 500
    Brown v. Board of Education of
        Topeka, 499
    Bush v. Gore, 463
    Dred Scott v. Sanford, 458, 469,
        472, 489-492
    Engel v. Vitale, 500
    Green v. County School Board, 500
    Griffin v. County Board of Prince
        Edward County, 500
    Marbury v. Madison, 463, 485,
        486-487
    McCullough v. Maryland, 484
    Miranda v. Arizona, 500
    Plessy v. Fergusson, 499
    Reynolds v. Sims, 500
    Roe v. Wade, 472
Cutoff. *See* Emotional cutoff
cyclic adenosine monophosphate
    (cAMP), 68-69

Dampener, anxiety, 29, 232
Darwin, 66, 332
de Waal, F., 18, 363, 381
de Waal, Frans, 334
Death, triangles at time of
    communication and action, 167-169,
        171
    conflict about religious matters,
        166-167
    detriangling principles, 163-169
    impact on children, 162-163, 167
    LaForte mother's death, 208-210
    marital relationship and, 167
    outcomes, 169-171
    overview, 157-158, 171-172
    patient's responsibility for self,
        164-165
    person behind the symptom, 164

Death, triangles at time of *(continued)*
    spousal connection to patient's
        family, 165-166
    in stepfamilies, 302-304, 302f
    triangle issues, 157-158
Deceased people
    detriangling, 56
    as third person in a triangle, 24-25
Declaration of Independence, 456, 473
Definition of triangle, 13, 63-64, 363
Delinquency, societal emotional
    process, 40-41, 424
Description of triangles, 297, 508-509
Desegregation of blacks, 499-501
Destabilization
    children, and marital destabilization,
        252
    of marital triangles, 244-245
    third person for destabilization of
        dyad, 31-32
Detriangling
    with absent members, 52-56
    attitude of neutrality, 42-43
    Bowen family, 119-128
    chronic illness and death, 163-169
    clinical issues, 52-59
    communication and action, 167-169,
        171
    company triangles, 394-395, 398
    conflict about religious matters,
        166-167
    deceased persons, 56
    defining an I-Position, 47, 127
    differentiation of self, 47-52
    divorced families, 52-54
    emotional reactivity, 48
    evolution of clinical approaches,
        43-45
    extramarital affairs, 54-56, 57-58
    family business, 371-372, 381-382
    LaForte family, 204-206, 216-218,
        218f
    in marital triangles, 56-58, 167
    multigenerational triangles, 58-59
    neutrality and, 42-43, 371-372
    partial mental construct triangle,
        51-52
    patient's responsibility for self,
        164-165

Detriangling *(continued)*
  person behind the symptom, 164
  process of differentiation of self,
    45-47
  in remarried families, 54
  research attitude, 50
  schizophrenic patients, 42, 44
  secondary triangles, 58-59
  spousal relationship, 46-47, 165-166
  systems questions, 50-51
  systems thinking and, 394-395
  teaching how family systems
    operate, 47
  use of humor, 50, 125
  use of reversal, 49
  use of seriousness, 50
  voluntary process of, 29
Development of triangle, 19-23, 20f
Dialectic, 440-441
Differentiation
  after divorce, 308
  basic level, 362-363, 480
  defined, 66, 361
  family business leadership, 360,
    384-385
  functional level, 362-363, 480
  in marital triangles, 243-244
  of self. *See* Differentiation of self
  in stepfamilies, 298-300
  in the Supreme Court, 479-480
Differentiation of self
  Bowen family. *See* Bowen family
  chronic anxiety and, 266
  clinical example, 80-85, 82f
  defined, 35, 67, 311, 422
  defining an I-Position, 47, 127
  detriangling, 45-52
  documentation, 79-80
  emotional system, triangles and,
    76-77
  in family business, 361-362
  family projection process, 336
  genetic-like transmission, 75-76
  increasing of, 77-80
  LaForte family, 203
  as lifetime process, 154-155
  overview, 14
  of past generations, 131-132
  process of, 45-47

Differentiation of self *(continued)*
  relationship to triangles, 33-36
  sibling position functioning, 39-40
  spousal relationship, 46-47
  steps in triangle utilization, 79
  teaching how family systems
    operate, 47
  use of triangles, 86-88
Disabilities, 39
Displacement stories, 372
Distancer
  functioning position, 29
  mother and son, 190-191
Distancing
  for emotional pain management, 295
  marital distance, 246-247, 254
  in the marriage, clinical report,
    282-289, 283f-289f
Divided loyalties clinical report,
    269-275, 270f-274f, 276f
Divorce
  back-door triangle, 54
  caused by extramarital affair, 338
  children after divorce and
    remarriage, 304-307, 305f
  contact after divorce, 307-308, 307f
  detriangling, 52-54
  emotional, 9, 186
  legal divorce, 186
  remarriage. *See* Remarriage;
    Stepfamilies
  stepfamilies. *See* Stepfamilies
  substance abuse and, 320-325, 321f,
    323f, 325f
Dogs, 221. *See also* Pack behavior
Dolphins, 68
Domestic violence and substance abuse,
    320-325, 321f, 323f, 325f
Dominance hierarchy, 334-335
Douglas, 458, 472
Douglas, Stephen, 471-472
Dred Scott v. Sanford, 458, 469, 472,
    489-492
Drug abuse. *See* Substance abuse
Dyad relationship
  destabilization of, 31-32
  instability of, 403-404, 405
  stabilization of, 31-32
  student-faculty relationship, 405

Dysfunction. *See* Functional dysfunction
Dysinger, Robert, 9
Dzhugashvili, Joseph Vissarionofich, 436. *See also* Stalin

Eisenhower, Dwight, 499-500
Electoral College, 468
Ellsworth, Oliver, 484
Embree, M., 18, 363
Emlen, Stephen, 335
Emotional
    agency, 425
    cutoff. *See* Emotional cutoff
    defined, 18, 129
    divorce. *See* Emotional divorce
    emotionality management, 256-257
    fusion, 342. *See also* Undifferentiation or fusion
    pressure. *See* Emotional pressure
    process. *See* Emotional process
    reactivity. *See* Emotional reactivity
    regression, in schizophrenic patients, 4
    shock wave, 208-209
    space, 21
    symbiosis. *See* Emotional symbiosis
    system. *See* Emotional system
    triangle. *See* Emotional triangle
Emotional cutoff
    in child-focused family, 275
    defined, 38, 422
    fatherless child clinical report, 278, 279f
    LaForte family, 192f, 204, 215, 215f
    LaForte family, bridging of, 216-218, 218f
    Maloni family, 177, 179
    relationship to triangles, 33-34, 38-39
    Smith family, 137-138, 149-150
Emotional divorce
    impact on later generations, 186
    parents of schizophrenics, 9
Emotional pressure
    control of individuals, 78
    sensitivity of individuals, 70-71
    threats of, 74-75
    two-or-more-against-one triangle, 64-65

Emotional process
    in society (societal regression), 40-41, 421. *See also* Societal emotional process
    in the Supreme Court, 479-482
    symbols, 523
Emotional reactivity
    after nodal events, 210-212
    in detriangling, 48
    in marital triangles, 243
    in substance abusing families, 319, 319f
    two-against-one triangle, 68, 73, 80
Emotional symbiosis. *See also* Symbiosis
    in child-focused families, 268
    defined, 268
Emotional system
    defined, 34, 66, 67, 129
    differentiation-of-self, triangles and, 76-77
    family business, 360
    functioning as a unit, 75
    guidance system, 76
    purpose of, 67-68
    use of partial mental construct triangles, 51-52
    vervet monkey, 95
Emotional triangle
    configurations, 24-28, 26f
    deceased persons, 24-25
    defined, 130
    degree of intimacy, 196
    evolution of, 18
    interlocking, 130
    Oedipal triad vs., 16-17
    of past generations. *See* Emotional triangles of past generations
    theory development, 16-17
    third person, 24
Emotional triangles of past generations
    alcohol issues, 133, 134-135
    father's family of origin, 132-139, 133f
    maternal grandfather's family of origin, 141-142
    maternal grandmother's family of origin, 142-144
    mother's family of origin, 139-144, 140f

Emotional triangles of past generations
   (continued)
   overview, 129-132, 153-155
   paternal grandfather's family of
      origin, 135-138
   paternal grandmother's family of
      origin, 138-139
   slavery issues, 136
   Smith's family of origin, 144-153
Emotionality, management of,
   256-257
Energy, national strategy, 519. *See also*
   Oil
Engel v. Vitale, 500
Escherichia coli, 69
Evolution
   biological foundation of emotional
      systems, 18-19, 34
   proximate vs. ultimate explanations,
      95-97
   vervet monkey, 95-97
Examples. *See* Case examples
Executive branch of government,
   26-28, 27f
Extramarital affair
   after nodal events, 212
   as cause of divorce, 338
   causes of, 253-254, 337-338
   characteristics, 337
   chimpanzee behavior, 334
   coach, roles of, 353
   detriangling, 54-56, 57-58
   factors for vulnerability, 254
   family emotional process, 335-336,
      352
   function of, 333, 336
   interdependency, case study,
      343-346, 344f
   marital destabilization with addition
      of children, 252
   marital stabilization with addition of
      children, 253
   marital triangles, 247, 249
   nature of triangles, 331-332
   in nonhumans, 334-335
   nuclear family emotional system, 37
   overview, 331, 353-354
   partial mental construct triangle, 55
   possessive behavior of males, 334

Extramarital affair *(continued)*
   principles or standards in marriage,
      247
   self-management, 334
   triangle operation in families,
      332-333
   unresolved emotional fusion, case
      study, 339-343, 341f,
      349-352, 351f

Faculty
   faculty and administrative
      relationships, 412-414
   anxiety in the system, 414
   committee decision, 412-413
   competition for funds, 412
   representative committee
      formation, 413-414
   promotion and tenure, 405
   student-faculty relationship,
      405-412
   accountability for assignments,
      407-408, 410
   agreement on issues, 405-407
   instructor evaluations, 408-409,
      410-412
Fairbanks, 31
Fairbanks, Lynn A., 91
Family
   Bowen family. *See* Bowen family
   business. *See* Family business
   defined, 129
   detriangling in divorced families,
      52-54
   detriangling in remarried families, 54
   development of interlocking
      triangles concept, 14-15
   diagram symbols, 523
   Family Anxiety Scale, 191-192,
      192f
   marital triangles, 245-246
   marital triangles and family of
      origin, 248-251
   nuclear family emotional system,
      422
   past generations. *See* Emotional
      triangles of past generations

Family *(continued)*
projection. *See* Family projection process
schizophrenia and, 9. *See also* Schizophrenia
systems thinking, 390-391
teaching how family systems operate, 47
tension, handling of, 312-314, 312f-315f
triangle concept and changes to families, 329-330
undifferentiated family ego mass, 44
Family Anxiety Scale (FAS), 191-192, 192f
Family business
acute anxiety, 361
application of Bowen theory, 360-364
chronic anxiety, 361
differentiation, 361-363
forms of leadership, 357-358
functioning position, 359-360
leadership development, 358-359
overview of business, 357
Rothstein Books
changes during consultation, 380-381
consultant format, 370-371
consultant functions, 371-373
consultant neutrality and detriangling, 371-372
detriangling, 381-382
development of structures and procedures, 372-373
differentiation, 360, 384-385
emotional space, 374-376
expanding the business, 378-380, 379f
history of, 365-369, 366f-370f
history of triangles, 367-369, 367f-370f
individuality development, 376-378, 377f
interlocking triangles, 369, 369f
leadership modification, 382-384
lowering anxiety, 373-374
nodal events, 366-367

Family business *(continued)*
organization of, 364-365, 365f, 377, 377f, 379, 379f
relationship processes, 371
teaching system operation, 372
Family diagram symbols, 523
Family Evaluation, 334
Family projection process
child focus, 265
defined, 265, 453
differentiation of self, 336
extramarital behavior, 335-336
LaForte family, 203, 203f
overview, 14
relationship to triangles, 33-34, 37
Family systems thinking, 390-391
FAS (Family Anxiety Scale), 191-192, 192f
Fathers
fatherless child clinical report, 276-282, 277f-280f, 282f
of schizophrenic patients, 9
Fay, L. F., 24
Ferrera, S. J., 358
Fidelity. *See* Extramarital affair
Fiske, 459
Five-person system, 22
Fleming, Linda M., 221
Flirting, 254
Fogarty, T., 19, 24
Fogarty, T. F., 24
Fortas, Abe, 500-501
Four-person system, 22
Fox, Leslie Ann, 387
Franklin, 461, 462
Free soilers position, 471
Freud
Little Hans, 17
Oedipal triad, 10, 16-17
Fromm-Reichman, Frieda, 5
Fugitive Slave Act, 452, 470, 471
Function of triangles
for anxiety reduction, 29-30, 364, 480
equilibrium regulation, 30-31
evolution of, 18
regulatory function, 76
Functional dysfunction
defined, 131
physical health, 152
Smith family, 135, 140-141, 150, 152

Functional oldest family position,
    LaForte family, 194, 196-197
Functional self, defined, 35
Functioning position, family business
    leadership, 359-360, 383
Fusion. *See* Undifferentiation or fusion

Gag rule, 452
Generator, anxiety, 29, 232
Genetic-like differentiation-of-self
    transmission, 75-76
Georgetown University Medical
    Center, 12-14
Gettysburg Address, 472, 473
Gilbert, R., 358
Goodall, Jane, 334-335
Gossip, 5-6
Gottlieb, Eileen B., 331
Government, United States
    Articles of Confederation, 458-459,
        467
    background, 454-455
    checks and balances, 452-453, 483
    Congress, 459, 462, 463
    Electoral College, 468
    globalism, 473-474
    House of Representatives, 462, 466
    Magna Carta, 454-455
    New England, 455, 456
    period of anxiety, 459-460
    Revolutionary War, 457-458
    Senate, 462, 466
    slavery issues, 452, 466-467. *See
        also* Three-fifths compromise
    Supreme Court. *See* Supreme Court
    three-fifths compromise. *See* Three-
        fifths compromise
    U.S. Constitution. *See* U.S.
        Constitution
    Virginia. *See* Virginia
    war for independence, 455-457
    who would be governed, 457-458
Government structure
    globalism, 473-474
    mental construct triangle, 26-28, 27f
    treaties, 27
    United States. *See* Government,
        United States

Grandmother
    detriangling mother-daughter
        relationship, 59
    vervet monkey, 100-102, 102f
Great Depression, 492, 494
Green v. County School Board, 500
*Griffin v. County Board of Prince
    Edward County,* 500
Group
    collection of individuals vs., 482
    defined, 67
    group think, 411
Gryphon, the white terrier, 223-224
Guerin, P., 24

Hamilton, Alexander, 467
Hancock, John, 456
Healthcare industry. *See* Company
    triangles
Heart rate and social rank, 235
Hegel, Georg Wilhelm Friedrich,
    440-441
Hierarchy
    dominance, 334-335
    in family business leadership,
        357-358
    pack behavior, 227-229
    rituals for reinforcement, 233
    social hierarchy, 358
Hosking, G., 440-441
House of Representatives, 462, 466
How question, 28
Huether, Gerald, 335
Hughes, Charles Evans, 492-495
Human-canine pack. *See* Pack behavior
Humor, use in detriangling, 50, 125

Illness, triangles at time of
    communication and action, 167-169,
        171
    conflict about religious matters,
        166-167
    detriangling principles, 163-169
    family data, 158, 159f, 160
    fix-it orientation, 161
    illness at triangle point, 160

Illness, triangles at time of *(continued)*
impact on children, 162-163, 167
marital relationship and, 167
outcomes, 169-171
overview, 157-158, 171-172
patient, illness and medical
establishment, 161
patient, spouse and children,
162-163
patient's family of origin, 161-162
patient's responsibility for self,
164-165
person behind the symptom, 164
spousal connection to patient's
family, 165-166
spouse's family of origin, 162
triangle issues, 157-158
Imodium, 231
Impeachment, 463, 464, 487
Individuality
biological roots, 34
family business, 360
in family business, 376-378, 377f
Infidelity. *See* Extramarital affair
In-laws
marital triangles, 250-251
triangle, in child-focused family,
270, 271f
Inside position
creation of, 314
defined, 72
as preferred position, 21
shifting of position, 72-73
taking sides, 73-74
Instinctual inheritance, 245
Instinctual system, 66, 129
Interdependency
as cause of extramarital affair, 343,
346
interdependent triad, 4, 10, 12
Interlocking triangles
in Bowen family, 110, 111,
117-118, 118f, 120-128
concept development, 13, 14-15
creation from stress, 404
defined, 13, 423-424, 508-509
delinquent adolescents and parents,
40-41
development of, 21-23, 22f

Interlocking triangles *(continued)*
emotional triangles, 130
for equilibrium regulation, 30-31
evolution of, 18
LaForte family triangles, 201-204,
203f, 215, 215f
in large groups, 423-425
pack behavior, 233-235, 236-237,
238f
process, 21-22
Rothstein Books family business,
369, 369f
September 11, 2001, terrorist attacks
description of triangles, 508-509
government-oil-Saudi triangle,
510-513, 511f, 512f
population-government
relationship, 509-510
population-oil industry
relationship, 510
Saudi Arabian monarchy-
population relationship,
513-514, 514f
Saudi Arabian monarchy-
terrorists-U.S. oil triangle,
515-516, 515f
terrorists and U.S. population,
516-518, 517f, 518f
of stepfamilies, 300-302, 301f
student-faculty relationship, 405
teenage rebel case, 318, 318f
Internet flirting, 254
Intrapsychic phantasy, 17
Invitations
intensity of cues, 74-75
to join emotional process, 65
Involuntary response, 130
I-Position
in Bowen family detriangling, 127
defining of, 47
for detriangling, 48
teaching system operation, 372
Iskra, 430
Italy. *See* Maloni family

Jamestown Colony, 455
Jay, John, 460, 484

Jefferson, Thomas
  drafting Declaration of
    Independence, 456, 457
  drafting the Constitution, 460, 461
  Marshall, John, and, 485
  presidential politics, 468-469
  Supreme Court appointments,
    487-488
Johnson, Lyndon, 500-501
Judicial self-restraint, 489
Judiciary Act of 1789, 486
Judiciary Act of 1801, 485-486
Judiciary branch of government, 26-28,
  27f

Kamenev, 445-447
Kansas Nebraska Act of 1854, 471
Kauto, J. G., 24
Kerr, M.
  anxiety concept, 21
  detriangling, 41
  extramarital relationships, 334, 337,
    338
  triangle concept, 24-25, 29
Kerr, M. E.
  emotional reactivity, 361
  human-canine triangles, 227, 232
  triangle concept, 27, 31
Kerr, Michael, 86
Kerr, Michael E., 297
Key for family diagram and emotional
    process symbols, 523
Kingsolver, Barbara, 503, 519-520
Klare, M., 507, 518, 519
Klever, Phillip, 243
Klipspringer, 245
Koba, 436, 438-439
Kopf, K. J., 235
Krupskaya, Nadezhda, 430

LaForte, Jack, 189
LaForte family triangles
  author's position in primary
    triangle, 196-197
  calm state of family triangle,
    206-208, 206f

LaForte family triangles *(continued)*
  cat included in the triangle, 208,
    208f
  Dance Club project, 213-214
  detriangling, 204-206, 216-218,
    218f
  emotional cutoff, 192f, 204, 215,
    215f
  emotional cutoff, bridging of,
    216-218, 218f
  Family Anxiety Scale, 191-192,
    192f
  father's position in primary triangle,
    193-196, 193f, 195f
  husband, wife and child triangle,
    198-201, 200f, 201f
  interlocking triangles, 201-204,
    203f
  mother, father, son triangle,
    190-198, 192f
  mother, son and new wife, 214-215
  mother's anxiety, 198
  mother's death, 208-210
  new triangle development, 212-214
  nuclear family triangle, 200-201,
    200f
  overview, 189-190, 218-219
  remarriage, 215-216
  sister's position in the family,
    197-198
  wife's family of origin and family of
    procreation, 201, 201f
Land mines, 396-397, 400-401
Lassiter, Laurie L., 63
Leadership
  collection of individuals, 357-358,
    382-384
  family business. *See* Family
    business
  stages of development, 358-359
Lee, Robert E., 458
Legislation
  Agricultural Adjustment Act of
    1936, 493
  Fugitive Slave Act, 452, 470, 471
  Judiciary Act of 1789, 486
  Judiciary Act of 1801, 485-486
  Kansas Nebraska Act of 1854, 471
  New Deal, 492, 493, 494

Legislation *(continued)*
 Northwest Ordinance of 1787,
  470-471
 USA Patriot Act, 505-506
Legislative branch of government,
 26-28, 27f
Lenin
 biography, 427-431
 Bolshevik leadership, 422, 442-443
 dialectic, 440-441
 family diagram, 428f
 history of, 425-427, 448-450
 Stalin and, 438-439, 440, 444-445
 triangles after death, 445-448
 Trotsky and, 435-436, 443-445
Lincoln, Abraham, 472-473
Lincoln-Douglas debate, 458, 472
Little Hans, 17
Louisiana Purchase, 469-470
Loyalties, divided, clinical report,
 269-275, 270f-274f, 276f
Luff-Bowen, Inc.
 background of business, 110, 111f
 background of study, 109-110
 business reorganization, triangle
  two, 114-115, 115f
 death of family member, triangle
  four, 116-117, 117f
 detriangling during 1954-1966,
  119-120
 detriangling during 1966-1967,
  120-128
 family distancing, triangle six,
  118-119, 119f
 health issues, triangle three,
  115-116, 116f
 history of triangles, 110-111, 111f
 interlocking triangles, triangle five,
  117-118, 118f
 low stress, triangle one, 112-114,
  112f-114f
 overview, 109-110, 128

Madison, James
 drafting the Constitution, 452, 460,
  461, 462-463
 three-fifths compromise, 465-466,
  467, 468

Magna Carta, 454-455
Maine as free state, 470
Maloni, James C., 173
Maloni family
 background, 174-179
 early years in Italy, 177-179
 early years in the United States,
  175-177
 functioning levels, 182-184
 Italian background, 173-174
 from Italian to American triangles,
  180-181, 181f
 multigenerational emotional
  process, 184-186, 185f
 overview, 173-174
 paternal family diagram, 174f
 relationship to Pistilli family,
  179-180
 study impact on Maloni's work,
  186-187
Man of the house after father's death,
 176-177, 179-180
Mandamus, 486
Many-against-one triangle, 64
Marbury, William, 486
Marbury v. Madison, 463, 485, 486-
 487
Marital triangles
 affairs, causes of, 253-254, 337-338.
  See also Extramarital affair
 assessment of, 255-256
 bad parents and stuck together
  couple, 249
 children and, 251-253
 clinical example, 259-263, 260f
 clinical management of, 257-258
 clinical work with, 255-259
 clinician's fusion, 258-259
 with the community, 254-255
 conclusion, 263
 contributing factors, 245-248
 during courtship, 453
 destabilizing, 244-245, 252
 detriangling, 56-58, 167
 differentiation and, 243-244
 emotionality management, 256-257
 family of origin, 248-249
 good parents and distant, tense
  marriage, 249-250

Marital triangles *(continued)*
  immaturity within marriage, 243
  in-laws, 250-251, 270, 271f
  instinctual inheritance, 245
  marital distance, 246-247, 254
  multigenerational family, 245-246
  principles or standards for outside
    relationships, 247
  reactivity, 243
  regulation, 246
  spouse focus, 247
  spouses, differentiation of self,
    46-47
  stabilizing, 244, 252-253
  stress, 248
  third parties, relating to, 257
  triangling as emotional process, 256
  wife, child and husband, 253
Marshall, John, 463, 484-489
Marxism
  Bolshevism and, 440-441
  Lenin and, 431
  Stalin and, 439
  Trotsky and, 433
Mason, George, 457, 473
Massachusetts Bay Colony, 455
Mathematical triangles, 19
Mayflower Compact, 455
McClain, John, 490
McCullough, David, 462
McCullough v. Maryland, 484
McKnight, Anne S., 311
Mechanism, defined, 68
Medications
  abuse. *See* Substance abuse
  acepromazine, 231
  Amitriptyline, 226-227, 231, 232
  Imodium, 231
  Xanax, 231, 232
Menninger, Karl, 4, 7
Menninger, William, 4, 5
Menninger Foundation, 4-7
Mensheviks, 433, 435
Mental construct triangle
  configurations, 25-26, 26f
  government structure, 26-28, 27f
  nonliving entities, 25-26, 26f
  partial mental construct triangle, 26,
    26f

Merit pay, 405, 415
Miranda v. Arizona, 500
Missouri as slave state, 470
Missouri Compromise, 491
Modell of Christian Charity, 455
Monkey
  rhesus monkey, 100
  squirrel monkey, 235
  vervets. *See* Vervet monkey
Montesquieu, 462
Moore family clinical example,
    259-263, 260f
Moran, Carol, 503
Moscow party, 445
Mother-daughter relationship,
    detriangling, 58-59
Multigenerational family
  behavior of family members, 336
  deceased persons, 25
  detriangling, 58-59
  emotional transmission, 422
  emotional triangles. *See* Emotional
    triangles of past generations
  extramarital affairs and, 337, 342,
    349
  genetic-like differentiation-of-self
    transmission, 75-76
  Maloni family, 184-186, 185f
  marital triangles, 245-246
  process of patterns, 342-343
  study impact on clinical work, 187
  substance abusing teenager case, .
    325-329, 326f, 328f
  tension, handling of, 312-314,
    312f-315f
  transmission process, 14, 37-38
  triangle concept in, 17
  vervet monkey, 100-102, 102f
Multiple sclerosis, 160

Naïve delusion, 456
National Institute of Mental Health
    (NIMH)
  attitude of neutrality, 42
  overview of triangle theory, 7-12
  two-against-one triangle, 64
Natural resource depletion, 506-508

Natural selection
  danger detection system, 96
  defined, 331-332
Natural systems
  disharmony between human and
    nature, 506
  evolutionary biology, 34
  schizophrenia, 10-11
  triangle concept, 18-19
Nature of triangles in the living world,
  331-332
Nazar, B. L., 235
Neutrality and detriangling, 42-43,
  371-372
New Deal, 492, 493, 494
New England, 455, 456
New players, old triangles. *See* Old
  triangles, new players
Nicholson, Ann V., 477
NIMH. *See* National Institute of Mental
  Health (NIMH)
Nixon, Richard, 501, 512
Nodal events
  birth of granddaughter, 215
  emotional shock wave, 208-210
  family business leadership, 359
  family system impact, 219
  LaForte mother's death, 208-210
  Rothstein Books, 366-367
  symptomatic family members,
    210-212
Nonliving entity. *See also* Partial
  mental construct triangle
  deceased persons as third persons in
    triangle, 24-25
  extramarital affairs, 55-56
  in mental construct triangles, 25-26,
    26f
Northwest Ordinance of 1787, 470-471
Nuclear family emotional system
  defined, 422
  overview, 14
  relationship to triangles, 33-34,
    36-37

O'Connor, Sandra Day, 464
Oedipal triad, 10, 16-17
Office politics, 387

Oil
  depletion of, 506-508
  national energy strategy, 519
  OPEC, 512-513
  population-oil industry relationship,
    510
  Saudi Arabian oil-for-security pact,
    510-513, 511f, 512f
*Old Loyalties, New Ties: Therapeutic
  Strategies with Stepfamilies,*
  292
Old triangles, new players
  deceased persons, 25, 56
  described, 21
Omega, in canine hierarchy, 227-228,
  234, 235
One-to-one relationship, 65-66
OPEC (Organization of Petroleum
  Exporting Countries),
  512-513
Open emotional system, 32, 33
Organization of Petroleum Exporting
  Countries (OPEC), 512-513
Outside position
  creation of, 314
  defined, 72
  as preferred position, 21
  shifting of position, 72-73, 77-78
  taking sides, 73
Over/underfunctioning reciprocity,
  9-10, 37, 212
Overview of triangle theory
  Bowen's family, 14-16
  Bowen's family systems triangle,
    16-17
  detriangling, 41-60
  evolutionary biological foundation
    of emotional systems, 18
  Freud's psychoanalytic Oedipal
    triad, 16-17
  generally, 4, 14
  Georgetown University Medical
    Center, 12-14
  interlocking triangles, 19-23
  Menninger Foundation, 4-7
  National Institute of Mental Health,
    7-12
  natural systems theory,
    misunderstandings, 18-19

Overview of triangle theory *(continued)*
  primary triangles, 23
  relationship of triangles and other
      concepts, 33-41
  secondary triangles, 23
  triangle characteristics, 23-33
  triangles, 19-23

Pack behavior
  alpha, 227-229, 234, 237
  beta, 228, 237
  calming of anxiety, 237-238
  Gryphon, the white terrier, 223-224
  hierarchy, 227-229
  identifying the triangle, 231-233
  interlocking triangles, 233-235,
      236-237, 238f
  Jim as fourth pack member, 234-235
  leadership, 227-228, 228f
  Linda's background, 222, 222f
  omega, 227-228, 234, 235
  overview, 221, 239
  pack establishment, 226-231, 228f,
      229f
  Shayne, the dog, 224-226
  social status change and symptom
      formation, 235-236
  stabilization, 236-239, 238f
Papero, D., 41
Parables, 372
Parents, detriangling in divorced
      families, 52-54
Partial guidance system, 76
Partial mental construct triangle
  defined, 25
  for detriangling, 51-52
  extramarital affairs, 55
  illustrated, 26f
Past generations. *See* Emotional
      triangles of past generations
Patriot Act, 464
Peace and agree approach, 207, 211
Pentagon, 503, 505, 517. *See also*
      September 11, 2001, terrorist
      attacks
Person-to-person relationship, 65-66
Petrograd Party, 445

Pew Research Center for the People
      and the Press, 505
Pheromone, 68-69
Pipes, R., 441
Pistilli, 179-180. *See also* Maloni
      family
Plants, reproductive units, 69-70
Plessy v. Fergusson, 499
Point of view, 73
Polarization, 43, 424
Politburo, 442, 443, 445
Polygamous animal triangles, 245
Polygyny, 335
Populism, 440-441
Possessive behavior of males, 334
Prefrontal cortex, 130
Primary triangle
  child-focused family, 270f
  defined, 23
  detriangling by accessing secondary
      triangles, 58-59
  LaForte family, 190-198, 192f,
      193f, 195f
  between parents and child, 329
Primates
  biological foundation of emotional
      systems, 18
  triangular emotional process, 363
Process in the triangle, 28-29
Project for Excellence in Journalism,
      505
Projection
  defined, 422
  described, 9
  family business leadership, 360
  family projection. *See* Family
      projection process
  LaForte family, 189
  problem child focus, 314, 315f
  in relationship systems, 332
  in schizophrenics, 9-10
  societal projection process. *See*
      Societal emotional process
Projector, 29
Promotion of academic faculty, 405
Proximate explanation
  ultimate explanation vs., 31,
      95-97
  vervet monkey, 95-97, 102

Psychoanalysis
  Bowen's background, 11-12
  Oedipal triad, 10, 16-17
  Pursuer, 190-191

Quasi-triangles, 26

Radzinsky, E., 438-439, 447
Randolph, Edmund, 461, 465
Rauseo, Eva Louise, 265
Reactivity. *See* Emotional reactivity
Reciprocity
  family business leadership, 358
  functioning, Maloni family, 182-183
  functioning positions, 131
  loss of family members and,
    295-296
  nuclear family emotional system, 37
  over/underfunctioning, 9-10, 37,
    212
  societal emotional process, 425
Reconciliationists, 456
Regression
  chronic anxiety and, 481-482
  in schizophrenic patients, 4
  societal. *See* Societal emotional
    process
Regulatory function
  Anonymous Paper, 85-88
  of cellular slime mold, 68-69
  clinical example, 80-85, 82f
  control function of triangles, 64
  differentiation-of-self, increasing,
    77-80
  emotional pressure, 64-65
  evidence for hypothesis, 65
  exploitation, 71-77
  hypothesis, 63, 64
  many-against-one triangle, 64
  in marriage, 246
  overview, 63-66, 88-89
  point of view, 73
  triangle as coercive, 64, 76
  triangle concept, 63-64
  triangle functions, 76
  triangle in other species, 66-69

Regulatory function *(continued)*
  of triangles, 30-31
  the undifferentiated, 69-71
Rehnquist, 464
Relationship system
  defined, 34, 129
  family business, 360
  function of triangles, 332
Religion, during chronic illness,
    166-167
Remarriage
  children after divorce and
    remarriage, 304-307, 305f
  detriangling, 54
  LaForte family triangles, 215-216
Reproductive unit, 67
Research attitude, use in detriangling,
    50
Resource wars, 507
Reversal
  in Bowen family detriangling, 122,
    125
  use in detriangling, 49
Revolutionary War, 457-458
Reynolds v. Sims, 500
Rhesus monkey, 100
Rigid triangle, fatherless child clinical
    report, 279, 280f
Rituals, for reinforcement of hierarchy,
    233
Roberts, Owen, 493, 494
Roe v. Wade, 472
Roosevelt, Franklin, 493-494, 510
Rothstein Books
  changes during consultation,
    380-381
  consultant format, 370-371
  consultant functions, 371-373
  consultant neutrality and
    detriangling, 371-372
  detriangling, 381-382
  development of structures and
    procedures, 372-373
  differentiation, 360, 384-385
  emotional space, 374-376
  expanding the business, 378-380, 379f
  history of, 365-369, 366f-370f
  history of triangles, 367-369,
    367f-370f

Rothstein Books *(continued)*
  individuality development, 376-378, 377f
  interlocking triangles, 369, 369f
  leadership modification, 382-384
  lowering anxiety, 373-374
  nodal events, 366-367
  organization of, 364-365, 365f, 377, 377f, 379, 379f
  relationship processes, 371
  teaching system operation, 372
Russian Revolution
  background, 425-427
  beginning of, 441
  human costs, 441
  leadership, 441-443
  Lenin and Trotsky's leadership, 443-444
  overview, 448-450
  Russian diaspora, 441
  triangles after Lenin's death, 445-448
Rutledge, John, 484

Saudi Arabia
  government-oil-Saudi triangle, 510-513, 511f, 512f
  monarchy-population relationship, 513-514, 514f
Schizophrenia
  detriangling, 42, 44
  emotional divorce, 9
  emotional regression, 4
  family relationships, 9
  natural systems theory, 10-11
  schizophrenogenic mother, 5
  symbiosis, 7-8
  triads, 8-9
Scott, Dred. *See Dred Scott v. Sanford*
Secondary triangle
  configurations, 23
  defined, 23
  detriangling, 58-59
Sedova, Natalya, 435
Seduction hypothesis, 17

Self
  basic self, 35
  differentiation. *See* Differentiation of self
  functional self, 35
  self-management, 44-45, 334
  self-regulation in marriage, 246
  we-self phenomenon, 144, 148, 149
Senate, 462, 466
Sendor, M., 235
Separation anxiety of animals, 226
Separation of powers triangle, 462-464. *See also* Three-fifths compromise
September 11, 2001, terrorist attacks
  business impacts of, 389
  citizen self, 518-520
  interlocking triangles
    described, 508-509
    government-oil-Saudi triangle, 510-513, 511f, 512f
    population-government relationship, 509-510
    population-oil industry relationship, 510
    Saudi Arabian monarchy-population relationship, 513-514, 514f
    Saudi Arabian monarchy-terrorists-U.S. oil triangle, 515-516, 515f
    terrorists and U.S. population, 516-518, 517f, 518f
  national energy strategy, 519
  oil depletion, 506-508
  societal anxiety, 503-504
  societal emotional process, 504-508
    cause-and-effect thinking, 505
    disharmony between human and nature, 506
    evidence of societal regression, 504-506
    natural resource depletion, 506-508
    previously ignored symptom, 505
    togetherness, 505
    USA Patriot Act, 505-506
Seriousness, use in detriangling, 50

Shayne, the dog, 224-226
Shays, Daniel, 460
Shifting triangles
    after death of leader, 306-307
    outside position, 72-73, 77-78
    for release of family tension,
        312-314, 312f-315f
    return to original triangles, 295,
        296
    substance abusing teenager case,
        325, 325f
Shock wave, 208-209
Sibling position
    defined, 422
    family business leadership, 359. *See
        also* Rothstein Books
    of only children, 135-136
    overview, 14
    relationship to triangles, 33-34,
        39-40
    in Smith family, 135-136
Simon, R., 5
Single parent family, 314
Slavery
    Dred Scott v. Sanford, 458, 469,
        472, 489-492
    Fugitive Slave Act, 452, 470, 471
    Northwest Ordinance of 1787,
        470-471
    as social issue, 136
    three-fifths compromise. *See* Three-
        fifths compromise
Slime mold, 68-69
Smith, James B., 129
Smith, James William, 136
Smith, W., 25
Smith family
    alcohol issues, 133, 134-135
    father's family of origin, 132-139,
        133f
    maternal grandfather's family of
        origin, 141-142
    maternal grandmother's family of
        origin, 142-144
    mother's family of origin, 139-144,
        140f
    overview, 129-132, 153-155
    paternal grandfather's family of
        origin, 135-138

Smith family *(continued)*
    paternal grandmother's family of
        origin, 138-139
    slavery issues, 136
    Smith's family of origin, 144-153
Social hierarchy, 358
Social rank and heart rate, 235
Social status change and symptom
        formation in pack behavior,
        235-236
Social system, defined, 67
Societal emotional process
    composition of, 454
    defined, 453
    definitions, 422-423
    large groups, 424-425
    Lenin. *See* Lenin
    overview, 14, 421-422, 448-450
    polarization, 43, 424
    relationship to triangles, 33-34,
        40-41
    Russian Revolution. *See* Russian
        Revolution
    of September 11, 2001, attacks,
        504-508
        cause-and-effect thinking, 505
        disharmony between human and
            nature, 506
        evidence of societal regression,
            504-506
        natural resource depletion,
            506-508
        previously ignored symptom,
            505
        togetherness, 505
        USA Patriot Act, 505-506
    Stalin. *See* Stalin
    theoretical considerations, 422-423
    triangles and, 423-425
    Trotsky. *See* Trotsky
Societal regression. *See* Societal
        emotional process
Sokolovskaya, Alexandra, 433
Southern Manifesto, 499-501
Soviet Union. *See* Russian Revolution
Spirit of the Laws, 462
Spouses, differentiation of self, 46-47
Squirrel monkeys, social relationships,
        235

Stalin
    biography, 436-440
    Bolshevik leadership, 422, 442-443
    family diagram, 437f
    history of, 425-427, 448-450
    Lenin and, 438-439, 440, 444-445
    Russian Revolution, 441
    triangles after Lenin's death,
        445-448
    Trotsky and, 435, 439
Stepfamilies
    Cauley family diagram, 293f
    children after divorce and
        remarriage case example,
        304-307, 305f
    contact after divorce, 307-308, 307f
    death of leader, case example,
        304-307, 305f
    interlocking triangles case example,
        300-302, 301f
    Old Loyalties, New Ties:
        Therapeutic Strategies with
        Stepfamilies, 292
    original triangles, 295-297
    overview, 291-292, 309
    stepdaughter perspective, 292-299,
        293f
    stepmother perspective, 292-299,
        293f
    triangles after death, 302-304, 302f
Stone, Harlan, 496-498
Stress
    as cause of extramarital affair, 254
    creation of interlocking triangles,
        404
    management of, with triangles, 312
    marital triangles, 248
    reactivity, 74-75
    transfer of, 77
Structure in the triangle, 28-29
Student-faculty relationship, 405-412
Substance abuse
    child of divorce and domestic
        violence, case study, 320-325,
        321f, 323f, 325f
    as coping mechanism, 315
    interlocking triangles, 318, 318f
    overview, 311, 330
    role in family triangling, 330

Substance abuse *(continued)*
    teenage rebel case, 316-320,
        317f-319f
    in teenagers, 315-316
    three-generation triangle, 325-329,
        326f, 328f
Sumner, Charles, 452
Support staff, academy, 414-415
Supreme Court
    Bowen theory and, 501
    chief justice
        described, 478
        Hughes, Charles Evans, 492-495
        Marshall, John, 463, 484-489
        Stone, Harlan, 496-498
        Taney, Roger Brooke, 472,
            489-492
        Vinson, Frederick, 498-499
        Warren, Earl, 499-501
    emotional process, 479-482, 483
    influences on, 478
    judicial self-restraint, 489
    leadership assumptions, 478-479
    separation of powers, 463-464
    think or react in decisions, 477
Svanidze, Ekaterina, 439
Swimming incident case example,
    80-85, 82f
Symbiosis
    in child-focused families, 268
    emotional fusion, 268, 342
    emotional symbiosis, 268
    in the living world, 331-332
    in schizophrenia, 7-8
    unresolved emotional attachment,
        349
System
    business relationship management,
        391-395
    closed emotional system, 32, 33, 169
    defined, 67, 129
    emotional. *See* Emotional system
    family systems thinking, 390-391
    five-person system, 22
    four-person system, 22
    instinctual, 66, 129
    natural. *See* Natural systems
    nuclear family. *See* Nuclear family
        emotional system

System *(continued)*
open emotional system, 32, 33
partial guidance system, 76
relationship. *See* Relationship system
social system, defined, 67
systems questions, use in detriangling, 50-51
systems thinking, 390-391, 394
systems-based consulting, 395-401
three-person system, 22

Taking sides
in child-focused family, 271
inside position, 73-74
in marital triangles, 258-259
outside position, 73
Taney, Roger B., 472, 489-492
Teenagers and substance abuse. *See also* Substance abuse
reasons for, 315-316
teenage rebel case, 316-320, 317f-319f
Tempest in a teapot, 121, 122, 124
Tension, shifting of position, 312-314, 312f-315f
Tenure of academic faculty, 405
Terrorism
purpose of, 514
September 11 attacks. *See* September 11, 2001, terrorist attacks
suicide attacks, 515
Therapist. *See* Coach
Third person in a triangle
alcohol as, 24, 315
deceased persons, 24-25
destabilization of dyad, 31-32
Thomas, E. M., 227
Threats
emotional pressure, 74-75
perceived threat, 77
of rejection, as control, 80
Three-fifths compromise
background, 452, 453
Civil War, 472-473

Three-fifths compromise *(continued)*
expansion of the United States, 469-471
federal government management, 469
impact of, 464
origin of ratio, 467
presidential politics, 468-469
purpose of, 464-465
secession of the South, 471-472
veto power, 459
Three-person system, 22
Titelman, Peter
detriangling, 41, 46, 109
family business leadership, 357
sibling triangles, 357
triangle concept, 3
Togetherness position
after September 11, 2001, terrorist attacks, 505
biological roots, 34
in company business, 392
family business, 360
as preferred position, 21
Toman, Walter, 39
Transference, 4
Transmission, 14, 37-38
Treaties of governments, 26-27
Triadic relationships
interdependent triad, 4, 10, 12
Oedipal triad, 10, 16-17
in schizophrenics, 8-9
in vervets. *See* Vervet monkey
Triangle, interlocking. *See* Interlocking triangles
Troika, 445-446
Trotsky
biography, 432-436
Bolshevik leadership, 422, 442-443
family diagram, 434f
history of, 425-427, 448-450
Lenin and, 435-436, 443-445
Russian Revolution, 441
Stalin and, 435, 439
triangles after Lenin's death, 445-448
Truman, Harry, 498
Tucker, Josiah, 459-460
Two-against-one position, 68, 73, 80

Ultimate explanation
 proximate explanation vs., 31,
  95-97
 vervet monkey, 95-97
Ulyanov, Vladimir Ilyich, 427. *See also*
  Lenin
Undifferentiation or fusion
 as cause of extramarital affair, 254
 causing marital distance, 246-247
 concept of triangles, 35. *See also*
  Differentiation of self
 defined, 67
 extramarital affair case study,
  339-343, 341f, 344f, 348f,
  349-352, 351f
 family ego mass, 44
 family projection process, 37
 functioning and, 70-71
 of humans, 70
 mother and son, 195, 196
 regulatory function, 69-71
Unfaithfulness. *See* Extramarital affair
Unit
 defined, 67
 emotional system as, 75
University. *See* Academy triangles
U.S. Constitution
 branches of government, 462-464
 checks and balances, 452-453, 483
 Constitutional Revolution, 495
 convention, 461-462
 development, 460-467
 House of Representatives, 462
 naïve delusion, 456
 preconvention anxiety, 461
 purpose of, 483
 Senate, 462
 separation of powers, 462-464
USA Patriot Act, 505-506
Use of triangle term, 12-13

Vervet monkey
 adult males group integration, 97
 babysitters, 92-95, 94f, 96-97
 background, 91-92

Vervet monkey *(continued)*
 cost-benefit analysis, 95, 99
 fertility and reproduction, 94-95
 grandmothers, 100-102, 102f
 infant males, 97-98
 infant restraint, with new resident
  males, 98, 99f
 mother's rejection of infant, 99-100,
  100f
 overview, 103
 proximate fitness model, 95-97
 social status of mothers, 92-93
 ultimate fitness model, 95-97
Vinson, Frederick, 498-499
Violence. *See* Domestic violence
Virginia
 black population, 457-458
 colony loyalty, 458
 history of, 455
 three-fifths ratio, 467
 Virginia Plan, 461
 war for independence, 456
Visher, Emily B., 292
Visher, John S., 292
Volkogonov, D., 429-433, 435, 444,
  445
Volkogonov, Dmitri, 426-427
Voluntary process, 29
Voluntary response, 130
Von Bertalanfy, L. V., 19

Warren, Earl, 499-501
Washington, George, 456-457, 460,
  461, 462
We-self phenomenon, 144, 148, 149
What question, 28
Wheeler, Burton, 494
When question, 28
Where question, 28
Whigs, 471
Whitney, Eli, 468
Who question, 28
Wilgus, Anthony J., 157
Wilkins, Roger, 457, 458
Wilson, James, 466
Winthrop, John, 455

Wolves, 221. *See also* Pack behavior
World Trade Center, 503, 505, 517. *See
    also* September 11, 2001,
    terrorist attacks

Xanax, 231, 232

Zinoviev, 445-447